# HOPKINS

# Hopkins

*A Literary Biography*

‿ɔ

NORMAN WHITE

CLARENDON PRESS · OXFORD

Oxford University Press, Walton Street, Oxford OX2 6DP

Oxford New York
Athens Auckland Bangkok Bombay
Calcutta Cape Town Dar es Salaam Delhi
Florence Hong Kong Istanbul Karachi
Kuala Lumpur Madras Madrid Melbourne
Mexico City Nairobi Paris Singapore
Taipei Tokyo Toronto
and associated companies in
Berlin Ibadan

Oxford is a trade mark of Oxford University Press

Published in the United States
by Oxford University Press Inc., New York

© Norman White 1992

First published 1992
Reprinted (with corrections) 1992
First published in Clarendon paperback 1995

British Library Cataloguing in Publication Data
Data available

Library of Congress Cataloging in Publication Data
White, Norman, 1937–
Hopkins : a literary biography / Norman White.
Includes bibliographical references and index.
1. Hopkins, Gerard Manley, 1844–1889.  I. Title.
PR4803.H44Z924    1992
821'.8—dc20
[B]    91–4935
ISBN 0–19–812099–0
ISBN 0–19–818350–X(Pbk)

Printed in Great Britain
on acid-free paper by
Bookcraft Ltd
Midsomer Norton, Bath

*To Kate Holloway*

# PREFACE

The central achievement and interest of Gerard Hopkins's life is his body of literary writings; but for them his public memory would not be worth preserving. Besides being some of the most remarkable works of art ever produced, his poems and journals are subtle autobiographical documents, and central to this literary biography. But an overall and coherent pattern cannot be imposed on the works as a whole, nor on the life.

The sudden and meaningless end to Hopkins's life emphasizes its lack of shape. It was an unpatterned succession of turmoils, sometimes with an apparently successful climax which did not fulfil its promise or which led to a contradictory outcome. His undergraduate days at Oxford proceeded to one kind of climax, in his intellectual and cultural training, but also contained a terrible crisis of identity and lost confidence. In a similar way, the writing of 'The Wreck of the Deutschland', his first great artistic achievement, was immediately followed by its official rejection, a fatal prediction that artistic and professional fulfilment would not coincide in his mature life. His 'salad days' in Wales ended with the failure of his theology examination. The subsequent unsettled period as 'Fortune's football' was at last relieved by a permanent posting, but this proved the one from which he most needed change. His time in Dublin of near madness and despair was calmed only by his death.

Hopkins's powerful and original temperament, a strange mixture of innocence and expertise, of old prejudices and clear-sighted observations, worked against his achieving happiness and success. It constantly expressed itself in enthusiasms and antipathies rather than calm appraisals. He adored or hated his environments; his reactions to place and to the lack of a settled home are centrally important to Hopkins and his poetry. He sometimes despaired at his apparent inability to control himself and his destiny. His solutions were typically impractical and extreme. He attempted to simplify his problems and evade his demons by complete submission to ancient comprehensive ideological systems; he became a Roman Catholic and then a Jesuit. His university and personal education had taken him into a subtle and confused modern English world more suited to experiment and individual response than to the judgements of an imposed doctrinal framework. Within the religious discipline his problems were sometimes crushed but never worked out, and they continued to surface to the end of his life. In poems Hopkins wrote in Wales richly vigorous personal responses to experience were squeezed into a moral grid, the results attempting to be conclusions of universal value. After his leaving Wales the possibility of an audience diminished; the mood of the poetry darkened as the opportunity for unified self-exploration increased. Sometimes he sought a land of Lost Content in Victorian poems whose sentiments are difficult for modern readers. Finally in Ireland a new power and kind of originality were forced into his poems of self-examination by his diminished loyalties and many dimensions of isolation.

The poetic texts are prominent in the book as they are the most vital features of Hopkins's life; but I have sometimes aimed at defamiliarising well-known poems by adopting early versions.

It was originally proposed that this *Life* would be co-written by Tom Dunne and myself. Dr Dunne withdrew, but has been a constant source of encouragement. I am particularly grateful to Barbara Hardy for her detailed, patient and helpful criticisms at all stages. R. K. R. Thornton read and commented on the first draft with careful judgement and thoughtful sympathy. The friendship of Ann Stephens has been invaluable, and the book owes much to her. Other considerable debts are inadequately acknowledged here to Richard Giles, Alison Sulloway, Joseph J. Feeney SJ, Mary Jo Calarco, Elizabeth Sheehan, Geoffrey Pargeter, Vernon E. Brooks, and Susan Kwiatkowski. No chapter was written without the help of other people, and I hope I have given some recognition to all the many kindnesses of people not mentioned above in the appropriate place in the end-notes.

The family of the late Humphry House generously loaned me and granted permission to quote from his Hopkins files and papers, and I am most grateful to Dr John House. I owe much to Hopkins's great-nephew, Leo Handley-Derry. Lord Bridges kindly allowed me to photograph and reproduce the painting of Hopkins by Wooldridge. The Trustees for Roman Catholic Purposes Registered gave permission to quote Hopkins works in copyright. Extracts from Dennis Meadows, *Obedient Men* (1955) are reprinted by permission of Longman Group UK Ltd.

This book has been aided by a Royal Irish Academy/British Academy Exchange Fellowship, a Research Fellowship of the Institute for Advanced Studies in the Humanities at the University of Edinburgh, and travel grants from University College, Dublin. For permission to consult and publish materials I am grateful to: the Bodleian Library; the British Library; the library of Trinity College, Dublin; the Humanities Research Center at Austin, Texas; the Master and Fellows of Balliol College, Oxford; Campion Hall, Oxford; the libraries of the Society of Jesus at Mount Street, London, St Beuno's, Wales, and at Lower Leeson Street and Milltown Park, Dublin.

*Dublin* N.W.

# CONTENTS

ᐁᏉ

## PART IV. THE POET, 1874–1877

## PART V. FORTUNE'S FOOTBALL, 1877–1884

## PART VI. THE STRANGER, 1884–1889

# LIST OF ILLUSTRATIONS

*Between pages 270 and 271*

The author and publishers are grateful to the following for permission to reproduce the above:

Lord Bridges: 1, 18; The Master and Fellows of Balliol College, Oxford: 2, 3, 4, 5, 6, 7; The National Portrait Gallery, London: 8, 9, 19, 20; Dr Lindsay Boynton: 10; Leo Handley-Derry Esq.: 11, 14, 15; The Society of Jesus: 6, 12; The Ashmolean Museum, Oxford: 13; D. Waterhouse Esq.: 18; Trustees of the late Barbara Hannah: 21; The Trustees of the British Library: 23; Mount St Mary's College, Fr F. Keegan SJ, and R. K. R. Thornton: 24; Trustees of the late Katharine Tynan and Dr Peter van de Kamp: 27.

Grateful thanks also to R. K. R. Thornton, Richard Giles, and the Audio-Visual Department of University College, Dublin.

# CHRONOLOGICAL TABLE I: LIFE

৩১

1818    Manley Hopkins born at Dulwich, to Martin Edward and Ann (née Manley) Hopkins.

1821    Kate Smith born at Trinity Square, London, to Dr John Simm and Maria (née Hodges) Smith.

1843    Manley Hopkins married to Kate Smith, and they settle at The Grove, Stratford, Essex.

1844    Gerard Manley Hopkins born at Stratford, 28 July.

1852    Hopkins family move to Oak Hill, Hampstead.

1854    Gerard attends Highgate School (for 9 years).

1863    April. Enters Balliol College, Oxford as Exhibitioner.

1864    First Class in 'Moderations'.

1865    Meets Digby Dolben.

1866    Received by Newman into Roman Catholic Church, 21 October.

1867    Graduates as BA, with First Class in 'Greats', June; teaches at Oratory School, Birmingham (2 terms).

1868    May, decides to become priest and (later) a Jesuit; burns poems. July–August, walking holiday in Switzerland. September, enters Jesuit Novitiate at Roehampton, near London (2 years).

1870    Jesuit Philosophate, St Mary's Hall, Stonyhurst, Lancashire (3 years).

1873    Teacher of Rhetoric at Roehampton (1 year).

1874    Theologate, St Beuno's, North Wales (intended for 4 years, but fails examination at end of 3rd year).

1875    Writing poetry; the *Deutschland* is wrecked (December).

1877    September, ordained priest. October, teacher at Mount St Mary's College, near Sheffield (7 months).

1878    April, teaching senior students at Stonyhurst College (3 months). July–November, curate at Farm Street church, central London. December, curate at St Aloysius' church, Oxford (10 months).

1879    October, curate at St Joseph's church, Bedford Leigh, Lancashire (3 months).

1880    January, curate at St Francis Xavier's church, Liverpool (1 year and 7 months).

1881    August, temporary curate at St Joseph's church, Glasgow (2 months). October, Tertianship at Roehampton (1 year).

1882    September, teacher at Stonyhurst College (1 year and 4 months).

1884    February, appointed Professor of Greek at University College, Dublin, and Fellow in Classics of the Royal University of Ireland.

1889    Dublin, 8 June, dies of typhoid.

1897    Death of Manley Hopkins.

1918    December, first edition of *Poems of Gerard Manley Hopkins*, edited by Robert Bridges.

1920    Death of Kate Hopkins.

# CHRONOLOGICAL TABLE II:
## MAJOR POEMS

෴

| | |
|---|---|
| 1860 | 'The Escorial' |
| 1862 | 'Il Mystico', 'A Vision of the Mermaids' |
| 1863 | 'Winter with the Gulf Stream' |
| 1864 | 'Heaven-Haven', 'Floris in Italy', 'A Voice from the World', 'Richard', and many others |
| 1865 | 'Easter Communion', 'The Half-way House', 'Where art thou friend', 'To Oxford', 'The Beginning of the End', 'The Alchemist in the City', and many others |
| 1866 | 'The Nightingale', 'The Habit of Perfection', and others |
| early 1870s | 'Ad Mariam' |
| 1875–6 | 'The Wreck of the Deutschland' |
| 1876 | 'The Silver Jubilee', 'Cywydd', 'Moonrise', 'The Woodlark' |
| 1877 | 'God's Grandeur', 'The Starlight Night', 'As kingfishers catch fire', 'Spring', 'The Sea and the Skylark', 'In the Valley of the Elwy', 'The Windhover', 'Pied Beauty', 'The Caged Skylark', 'The Lantern out of Doors', 'Hurrahing in Harvest' |
| 1878 | 'The Loss of the Eurydice', 'The May Magnificat' |
| 1879 | 'Duns Scotus's Oxford', 'Binsey Poplars', 'Henry Purcell', 'The Candle Indoors', 'The Handsome Heart', 'The Bugler's First Communion', 'Andromeda', 'At the Wedding March', and others |
| 1880 | 'Felix Randal', 'Brothers', 'Spring and Fall' |
| 1881 | 'Inversnaid' |
| 1882 | 'The Leaden Echo and the Golden Echo' |
| 1883 | 'Ribblesdale', 'The Blessed Virgin compared to the Air we Breathe' |
| 1884 | (most of) 'St. Winefred's Well', 'Spelt from Sibyl's Leaves' (finished in 1886) |
| 1885 | probably the 'Sonnets of Desolation', viz.: 'To seem the stranger', 'I wake and feel', 'No worst', 'Not, I'll not, carrion comfort', 'My own heart', 'Patience, hard thing!'; also 'To what serves Mortal Beauty?', (The Soldier) |
| 1886 | 'On the Portrait of Two Beautiful Young People' |

# PART I

# The Boy, 1844–1863

I do remember that I was a very conceited boy.
*(Hopkins to Dixon, 5 October 1878)*

# Kate Smith and Manley Hopkins

Haslemere, Surrey: December 1918. Into the hands of a bedridden lady of nearly ninety-eight, twenty years a widow, was placed one of the first copies of a small edition of poems written by her eldest son, who had been dead for twenty-nine years. The book was delicately produced, considering the austerity of the war years: the white wove leaves unevenly trimmed, and bound in light-blue paper boards, with a cream label on its spine. One of the poems in the book, elegantly penned and illuminated on parchment, had hung in the house since she had first lived there over thirty years before. On the book's dedication page was printed

CATHARINAE

HUNC LIBRUM

QUI FILII EIUS CARISSIMI

POETAE DEBITAM INGENIO LAUDEM EXPECTANTIS

SERUM TAMEN MONUMENTUM ESSET

ANNUM AETATIS XCVIII AGENTI

VETERIS AMICITIAE PIGNUS

D D D

R B

[This book is dedicated to Catharine, in her ninety-eighth year, as a pledge of long-standing friendship, to be a memorial, though late, of her beloved son, a poet awaiting the praise due to his genius. RB]

The book was the first edition of the poems of Gerard Manley Hopkins; its editor was the Poet Laureate, Robert Bridges, and the dedication (composed by A. E. Housman) was to the poet's mother, Kate Hopkins, née Smith.

℅

Kate Smith was the eldest of the seven children of Dr John Simm Smith and Mrs Maria Smith, née Hodges. In the years just before Princess Victoria came to the throne, the Smiths, with their five or six servants, lived at 17 Trinity Square, Tower Hill, at the south-east corner of the City of London, almost on the north bank of the Thames. Kate's daily wanderings within the walls of the Tower gave her a strong sense of the bloody reality of English history; thirty yards from her front door was the site of the scaffold.[1]

There was a lively social life in Trinity Square, with medical parties, musical evenings, and Christmas gatherings. The Smiths spent summers on the borders of the Hainault Forest, at Grange Cottage, Chigwell, built by Dr Simm Smith when the cholera epidemic threatened England in 1832, and they visited the nearby Fairlop Fair each July. The lively and carefree Smith children were ignorant of other classes. Of the two Doctors Smith in Trinity Square, it was Southwood Smith, a friend of Dickens, who was concerned with questions of public health and responsibility. Simm Smith visited people and accumulated wealth. In a Court of Probate case in 1867 it was revealed that a patient of his, whom he had attended since she had a 'nervous fever' in 1832, a wealthy widow, Mrs Thwaytes, had been paying him an annuity of £2,000 for thirty years, and he had also received from her gifts of almost £50,000.[2] He would have received an additional £180,000 from her will, but the court declared it invalid.

Kate's upbringing had as little religion in it as would be compatible with conventional social behaviour. In accounts of their childhood written by her and her brother and sisters, only Edward, the youngest, mentioned going to church—he remembered the monument opposite their pew in All Hallows, Barking. The Smith girls were greedy for Dickens, tricking the postman into giving them the weekly parts meant for the adults, but they read few books. None of them liked school, nor had much formal learning. Kate attended Brunswick House, a modest private school, from eight to fifteen or sixteen, and won a few second and third prizes in very small classes. After she left school she studied Italian during summers at Chigwell, and had a few German lessons one winter, but never became proficient in it, though she stayed for a time with a family in Hamburg. Once she was married she either had little time for reading or lacked the inclination, and after her death her children did not speak of her reading, but stressed her love of history and anecdote.

℘

Round the corner from 17 Trinity Square was Savage Gardens, and in the early 1830s an indigo merchant, Martin Edward Hopkins, moved into No. 4, with his wife and five children. After a promising start, when at twenty-three he had been made a Freeman of the City of London, Martin Hopkins had a business address near the Bank of England, and in 1819 or 1820 had taken a house with nearly half an acre of garden at The Grove, Stratford. But he speculated unsuccessfully in various commodities,[3] and when he died in 1836 left an estate of only £200.

Martin's eldest son, Manley, three years older than Kate, had left school when he was fourteen and gone to work in the City, probably because the family could not afford to send him to a university. Manley Hopkins knew from the example of his father the results of failure, and applied his efforts to one narrow line, putting aside any disappointment at not going to a university. After a period in an insurance-broker's office, he moved to the firm of William Richards, possibly the first to call themselves Average Adjusters, 'average' in the sense of marine law; they made the statement of liabilities incurred after a ship's wreck or damage, and divided expenses and losses among the underwriters.[4] Manley became a leading member of the firm and started his own business, which prospered until it had branches in all the principal English ports. 'What fun', Manley's eldest son remarked to his friend Robert Bridges one day, 'if you were a classic!'[5] By that time Gerard's father was a classic in his line, having published in 1857 *A Handbook of Average*, which became a standard reference-book, and ten years later *A Manual of Marine Insurance*. He helped to bring into existence the Association of Average Adjusters, which administered professional examinations. Gerard Hopkins never mentioned his father's job in letters, and showed no awareness that his comfortable home and education were dependent on his father's hard-won income and social position.

Manley cultivated his talents also in other areas, but in the domestic realm admired qualities which had made him successful in business. Freedom of expression, extravagance, and individuality had no part in Manley's poems; his poetry and other non-professional publications had a part to play in forming a refined bourgeois household. He possessed certain qualities which it is possible also to see in Gerard, the most obvious being voracity of mind. Manley's interests were very varied; besides books on average adjustment, marine insurance, and maritime procedure, he produced two books of poetry, a drawing-room play, *The New School of Design*, a historical account of Hawaii, and, with his brother Marsland, a book of religious poems, different from his other poetry. He wrote book criticism for *The Times*, including a review of *In Memoriam*, articles for *The Cornhill* and *Once a Week*, dramatic monologues, hymns, letters, and poems to newspapers. He had a regular column in the official Hawaiian newspaper, commenting on political and social events in London, and two other works—an essay on Longfellow and a novel—were rejected by publishers. Some of his poems were printed in anthologies such as *Lyra Eucharistica* and *Lyra Mystica*, alongside poems by Christina Rossetti.[6] He was an assiduous sketcher and writer of songs. His library included works on the orders of chivalry, rose-growing, astronomy, and piquet.

In one book father and son combined, and it is difficult to say with certainty where Manley's contributions ended and Gerard's began. This was *The Cardinal Numbers* by Manley Hopkins, published in 1887. On page v the author expresses his thanks 'for valuable aid and useful criticism afforded me by my friend the Rev. Sherrard B. Burnaby ... and in like manner to my near relative the Rev. G. M. Hopkins, of University College, Dublin'. I have not been able to trace 'the Rev. Sherrard B. Burnaby', and the name possibly masks other contributions made by Gerard. The prose is mostly direct and lucid. Sometimes there is a minor essay on a word, as often in Gerard's early journals:

['Cardinal'] is also used in respect of other things. In the crypt of a cathedral, the principal pier is sometimes spoken of as the cardinal column. In the Roman Church the most exalted of the Clergy are by preëminence Cardinals—though other derivatives have been claimed for this title. In the same sense of superiority there are cardinal virtues, cardinal colours, the cardinal points in the mariner's compass, & C.

Manley cannot resist elaborating on inferences, tendencies, and connections. One form that this takes is extended mathematical calculation. (Gerard wrote a neurotically elaborate sum of Roman sesterces in a Dublin notebook.[7]) Facts become isolated from the argument in which they arise and, like the encyclopaedic facts in Gerard's diaries,[8] are marvelled at in their own right. Within two pages of the book Manley uses examples of parallel numerals from the Indian, Arabic, Phoenician, Hebrew, Greek, Egyptian, and Roman, with a careless and spurious fluency, and his son also loved parallels in an unexpected language.

The contributions acknowledged as Gerard's are connected with Welsh methods of reckoning and with 'spectral numbers', or 'the mental visibility of numbers'; neither father nor son appears to see anything extraordinary about the following passage, though the *Saturday Review* made fun of it:

From No. 1, which is scarcely seen, to 12, the numbers rise either uprightly, or leaning a little to the right, rising a little, and are in a cheerful day-light. From 20 to 100, the numbers are as if far away to my right, and seem as in another 'reach'—distant and indefinite. They appear to be returning to the left. A million is in a clear light, far off, on the left. Still farther, and behind, scattered over a sort of vague landscape, are billions, trillions, and the rest—all to the left; in blocks, not in lines. On the left of number *one* are a few minus numbers, and below it, swarms of fractions. The place where they appear is gloomy grass. Backgrounds of rooms and remembered open-air scenes appear in different parts of this picture or world.[9]

The relationship between the minds of father and son is plain in *The Cardinal Numbers*. Several other parts of the book could be examples of something Gerard had noted. The possible derivation of 'Mind your Ps and Qs' from a landlord's chalking up his debts in pints and quarts, for example, or a rural numerical jingle, used for scoring sheep or counting stitches: 'Iny, tiny, tethery, fethery, phips, ither, lather, cother, quather, dix, iny-dix, tiny-dix . . .'.

Parts of Manley's second chapter, on 'One', bear a relationship to Hopkins's ideas of *one* and *selfhood*:

Visible, conceivable and central is the Oneness of Self. Number *one*, as applied to our own individuality, is to each the central point about and around which all things stand or revolve. In our mental optics the whole perspective converges in Self . . . . Education and implanted influences may produce in us a generous altruism, but this alterity—this *otherness*, not ourself,—however far it may go in determining us to see with others' eyes, cannot altogether overcome the laws of being.[10]

Compare Hopkins's:

I consider my selfbeing, my consciousness and feeling of myself, that taste of myself, of *I* and *me* above and in all things, which is more distinctive than the taste of ale or alum . . . and is incommunicable by any means to another man . . . . Nothing else in nature comes near this unspeakable stress of pitch, distinctiveness and selving, this selfbeing of my own. . . . And even those things with which I in some sort identify myself, as my country or family, and those things which I own and call mine, as my clothes and so on, all presupposes the stricter sense of *self* and *me* and *mine* and are from that derivative.[11]

Even some of the rhythms of the two passages are similar. Like Hopkins's is the consciousness shown of the part numerical symbols play in religion: 'She was first of a five . . . . Five! the finding and sake/ And cipher of suffering Christ'.[12]

Religion was present in all Manley's writings except those directly concerned with his profession. At his death there were books in the family library which show his continual—not extensive—reading in religion. Among his earliest books were the works of Paley and Jeremy Taylor's *Holy Living*. There were the *Pilgrim's Progress*, volumes of Church history, Biblical comment, and late Victorian questions of belief, a book of hymns, the *Book of Common Prayer*, and at least two bibles; he had given his wife as a thirty-fourth birthday present a book of meditations and prayers on the Holy Eucharist.

In 1849, with his brother Marsland, who had just been ordained, Manley published *Pietas Metrica; or, Nature Suggestive of God and Godliness. By the Brothers Theophilus and Theophylact*. The dedication read: 'To the Church, This Little Volume is dutifully offered, by two of her sons'. Its aim was 'to blend together two of Man's best things, Religion and Poetry', and to that end 'the books of Nature and Revelation have been laid side by side and read together'. The fifty-eight poems have little force:

> What buds are to the flowers,
> Like the first vernal showers,
> And the clear morning hours,—
> Such children are.

But in the carefully designed title-page, with red gothic type creating a Puginesque effect, the spacious and neat printing, and the way the title of every poem is thoughtfully connected to the body by a biblical text, the solemnity and sincerity of the book are impressive. Their religion was an everyday, real presence to the brothers:

> O Omnipresent Eye, how dread, how sweet,
> Is Thy companionship! About our bed,
> Our path, our converse, ever standing near.

Religion was not a background to life, but the central activity:

> The weapons of *their* warfare, lo! are thine,
> Gird up thy loins, *and be thyself a saint.*

இ

By the early 1840s Manley knew the Smith family well. He lived nearby, and may have been connected with them by Grandfather Hodges's insurance dealings. Moreover, Kate Smith's father was a cousin of Sydney Smith, the wit and political journalist, who for a time had been vicar of Halberton parish in Devon, where the Manley family originated.[13] Manley's aunt Elizabeth married one of Smith's curates, the Reverend John Eagles, scholar, painter, and poet. Manley and Kate became engaged. Manley wrote an 'Impromptu on a Friend's Name— "Smith" ',[14] and gave Kate for Christmas 1842 a copy of Scott's *Marmion*; on a flyleaf he drew *K* and *M* intertwined. Before the marriage he wrote an impatient poem, 'Non Satis'. Tension and desire come through the banal language. The start is oblique, conveying the distance expected of early Victorian lovers: ' 'Tis not enough to meet thee, as by chance,/ In lighted rooms, and feign a cold repose'. The last stanza, with its frustrated italics and capitals, is the strongest expression of passion in Manley Hopkins's poems:

> Because I want thee ALL; and nothing less
>   Than thy *whole being* will my heart suffice,
> Thee and thy love entire must I possess;
> No jot withheld,—no atom of thy love.[15]

(Lines 5 and 10 of Keats's plea to Fanny Brawne, 'I cry your mercy, pity, love', are: 'Oh, let me have thee whole—all, all, be mine', and 'Withhold no atom's atom or I die'.)

On 8 August 1843, at the village church at Chigwell, Manley, aged twenty-five and described as 'A gentleman from Stratford', was married to Kate; Dr Simm Smith and Manley's second brother Charles were witnesses. As she came out of the church her ten-year-old brother Edward, in front of a crowd of villagers, shyly presented Kate with a ring which his mother had given him for the purpose. He was terrified of such a public act, but Kate 'stooped down and kissed [him] and took off the edge of the pain'. Two of Kate's sisters, Maria and Tillie, were bridesmaids, and were criticized for choosing unsuitable brown and buff striped silk dresses, on some whim.

## 2

# *Stratford*

Shortly before the marriage Manley had taken possession of 87 The Grove, Stratford, the village just outside London's eastern boundary. Almost opposite his father's old house, it was the left-hand tenement of a pair which had been one mansion; Manley leased it from Mrs Ann Rawes. With three stories and a basement it was a solid, ugly, eighteenth-century brick house, its large front windows emphasized by surrounds of darker bricks. In going back to Stratford and The Grove, ten years after the family had given up living there, Manley was announcing a new start. To emphasize the continuity, his mother, his sister Ann, and his brother Charles came to live with Manley and his wife. Of the other two brothers, Edward was abroad with the Hudson's Bay Company, and Marsland, aged nineteen, had started as a pensioner at Peterhouse, Cambridge. It may be surprising that Manley could afford to send his younger brother to college and set up a new home before he became self-employed, but the Smith alliance was probably proving useful.

A month before Kate and Manley's first child was due, a brass plate was fixed to the door of No. 69 Cornhill, stating that Manley Hopkins (aged twenty-six) had set up as Adjuster of Averages. On 28 July 1844, at quarter past four in the morning, a son was born. On 24 August he was baptized Gerard Manley at the Gothic Revival parish church of St John the Evangelist, Stratford, on the edge of the village green; it had been Martin Hopkins's family church twenty years before. It was said that Gerard's parents 'came across a mention of "the monk Gerard" ' in some medieval document, and liked the name. The suffix *-ard*, related to *hard* and *hardy*, had vigorous connotations, and with *Manley* formed a strong-sounding name (two of the five subsequent boys were also christened with an *-ard* suffix). On Christmas Eve Manley composed 'To my child, Gerard Manley':

Hail! little worshipper of Light!
Most sunny is thy sunny face at noon:—
Why dost thou fix so earnestly thy gaze
Upon the wandering moon,—
And thy young eyes upraise
Adoringly to her that melts the night?—
Why do thine impotent hands
Seek—seek for ever
To clasp the lamp-flame bright
And everything that flings thee lucent rays?[1]

Cyril was born on 18 March 1846, Arthur on 30 December 1847, and on 17 October 1849 Milicent, who in infancy could not pronounce her name and became for a time Missie. Charles sailed for the Sandwich Isles, and Marsland became an Anglican priest within the London diocese, and was engaged to Katherine Beechey, the eldest daughter of Rear-Admiral F. W. Beechey, a geographer. The household at Stratford consisted of Manley and Kate, Manley's mother, Ann (thirty-five and unmarried), the four children, and cook, nurse, housemaid, and nursemaid.[2]

There is a photograph of Kate taken probably in the early 1850s. She is not pretty, and her party-dress, just off the shoulders, reveals a heaviness and stolidity, heightened by a gloomy pose. Her eyes appear dull but determined; her arms and hands are not delicate. Her hair, which in a sketch by Maria when she was seventeen was in two fashionable bunches of ringlets, is still long but has a harsh white parting, from which it is severely brushed down the sides of her face, in the current fashion. A crude cross hangs from a dark ribbon around her neck, and pinning a fringed modesty-shawl is a ponderous cameo brooch, the portrait of a child much like Aunt Annie's sentimental impression of Gerard in the National Portrait Gallery. She wears rings on the wedding and middle fingers of her left hand, and plait-work bracelets on her wrists.

The first surviving letter of Gerard's, probably dating from February 1852, was kept by the family partly because it refers to a happy event which would turn to tragedy, the birth of the fourth son, Felix Edward, on 21 February 1852. The letter was probably written by Aunt Annie on Gerard's behalf in reply to Kate, who had gone to her parents' home to have the baby:

My dear Mamma—
I hope dear Granmamma is better, my love to her. I am better, my cough nearly gone, but Uncle Marsland says if I don't eat more meat Cyril will come

home bigger than *i*—He says suppose, Cyril were to come home a little man
with whiskers and turned up collars! Thank you for your nice letter, My love to
Grandpapa and grandmamma and Aunties and Missie and Cyril and darling
baby and Papa and you

> Aunt Ann's love
> Your little Pet
> Gerard M. Hopkins[3]

Annie became Gerard's governess, and he probably did not go to school
until 1852.

☙

Most of Manley's poems show him in a family role. Poems about
holidays record the family's experiences in the valley of the Issbach, at
Rye and Winchelsea, Tintern Abbey, Morecambe Bay, and on the Wye
at Penalth. An impression of the group in the parlour is given by
musical poems like the glee or round 'Twelve', approximating words to
fit each church bell's individual sound. There are pastiche Elizabethan
songs, musical poems written for church or Sunday school activities,
and many 'songs for music', such as 'A moorland stream', 'To the
cuckoo', and 'The Message', some of which have an accompaniment by
solo instrument as well as piano: there is a flute obbligato to 'If I could
like a robin sing', where each stanza imitates a different bird. There are
poems of bereavement, love, and some propagating domestic virtues
('Once you loved me; then you wronged me,/ And you left me. Now I
die'). At least one was written jointly with another member of the
family. Several show the family liking for humour and satire. He wrote
nursery ballads which infants would find funny, such as a version of the
tale of Cophetua, in which Lewis Carroll is mingled with Thomas
Hood:

> 'O maiden,' he cried, 'just say that you'll wed
>   'That word of affirmative, utter.
> 'Are you feared of my mantle of ermine and red?
>   'It shall slip off my shoulders, like butter.
> 'Or is it my crown? It shall fall from my head,
>   'And I'll kick it along the gutter!'[4]

His epigrams sometimes struggle to fit the line, like Gerard's, but
others are more successful than any of his son's:

> I asked my neighbour, so demure,
>   At dinner, if she'd take liqueur. . . .

'Elixir, Cognac, and Noyau.'
To each she softly answered 'No.'
Then blushing, 'If my glass you'll pour,
'I'd try, with you, *Parfaite Amour.*'

Most of the funny poems are laboured: 'Queen Dido died! O Dodo, do you do/ The deed she did, and die as dead as she!' Several poems show knowledge of the classics and modern poetry—Wordsworth, Gray, Coleridge, Scott, Tennyson, Shakespeare, Keats, Pope, Chateaubriand, and St Francis de Sales—poets represented in the Hopkins library. Other poems express ideal sentiments, like 'Fair Drinking', which advocates popular education. 'The Beggar and the King' is democratic in a drawing-room sort of way, although Manley can be conservative, attacking John Bright and other 'Demagogues', and expressing revulsion (in a letter of 1874) against Gladstone and liberalism (his son once said that Gladstone 'ought to be beheaded on Tower Hill').[5]

The pose in a photograph by George Giberne (who had married Maria Smith) of Manley in middle age defies interpretation. The fingering of his watch is purposeless, the fist on the hip awkward and falsely assertive, while the diffident and melancholy head and eyes belie the bravado of the pose. The impression of remoteness or offhandedness, and the long nose with low septum, remind us of his son.

၁၀

As Manley's business became successful, it was obvious that the Hopkins household would have to move. The village of Stratford was changing fast. The metropolitan area was being protected from some of the worst effects of industrialization, but Stratford was just outside London's eastern boundary of the river Lea, and received refugees and rejects from the city.[6] The Metropolitan Buildings Act in the year of Gerard's birth restricted offensive trades in London, so soap-works, bone-boilers, varnish-makers, vitriol-manufacturers, and chemical manure works set up in the Stratford area; chemical works had already been established either side of the High Street. Within a hundred yards of 87 The Grove was a vast network of railway sidings. In 1852, the year the Hopkinses moved to Hampstead, the Metropolitan Water Act compelled London water companies to filter all river-derived water for domestic use, but again Stratford was outside this area. Cholera was raging in the neighbourhood. Stratford had turned into a Victorian industrial town.

# Hampstead

In 1852 the Hopkinses moved from the eastern marshlands of Stratford to the northern height of Hampstead.[1] From the highest point of Hampstead, Whitestone Pond, you could see St Paul's and the City, framed by the oaks and beeches of the Heath, and the southern rim of the London basin, from Blackheath to the Surrey hills. It would not legally become part of London until the end of the century, but Hampstead was never a typical village.

The few hundred acres of the Heath, left over from the ancient forest of Middlesex, protected Hampstead. On the higher, sandy ground were beech and oak woods; below them grasslands with ash, yew, elm, chestnut, and lime, wetlands and marshy lowlands with willow, alder, and poplar, and heathlands with silver birch. There were streams and the chains of artificial ponds, from which London took its water supplies, and where the Hopkinses bathed. Hampstead's micro-climate was healthy, its slopes free from the thick yellow fogs of the city, and it was once planned to pipe its fresh air into the city centre. The Gunpowder Plot conspirators gathered on the Heath to watch Parliament explode, and in 1736 and 1881, when Whiston and Mother Shipton had prophesied the end of the world, crowds gathered on the Heath to look down on it. Hopkins's poem 'Spelt from Sibyl's Leaves' pictures doomsday from the point of view of someone immersed in the drama of dusk, in a panorama of sky and horizon with a close-up of trees, a Hampstead scene.

In 1852 sheep grazed on the Heath, the landscaped areas of Ken (or Caen) Wood and South and North Woods were privately owned, there were avenues of elms between the ponds and Highgate village, and on fine days the Heath was white with linen spread to dry on the gorse and broom bushes by the most numerous profession in Hampstead, the laundresses. The village population had increased threefold since the beginning of the century. Estates of white stuccoed houses were replacing the old mansions and country houses. Trains were a new amusement, though there was a fear they would leave the line and career about Haverstock Hill. The village was surrounded by open fields.

By 1852 Hampstead had established a reputation as a place for artists. The Bull and Bush, near Keats's house, had been the country mansion of Hogarth, who laid out gardens where Gainsborough, Reynolds, Romney, and Constable walked. Constable rented 40 Well Walk, and his grave in the yard of St John's, the parish church of Hampstead, was only fifteen years old when the Hopkins family first worshipped there. When the Hopkinses set up house at Oak Hill, Hampstead's artist in residence was Ford Madox Brown. Brown's 'An English Autumn Afternoon', painted from a back window of his lodgings looking out over the Heath, gives a good idea of Hampstead as it was when Hopkins first lived there, neither rural, as Keats had known it, nor urban, as it is today. In Holly Mount, off Heath Street, there were excavations, probably connected with the village's appalling sanitation. Brown was impressed by the navvies, sweating in 'manly and picturesque costume', and sketched the scene, exciting 'the admiration and astonishment of idle passers-by'.[2] Thirteen years later, when Brown's 'Work' was on show at 191 Piccadilly, Hopkins, an Oxford undergraduate, went to the exhibition and copied down in his commonplace-book the sonnet Brown had written to accompany the painting.[3] Twenty-two years after, he used this poem to formulate ideas for his own sonnet on the same theme, 'Tom's Garland'.

Gerard's Hampstead surroundings and upbringing were secluded. Between Oak Hill and the High Street lay the notorious Crockett's Court, and the slightly less repulsive Bradley's Buildings and Perrin's Court, overcrowded, filthy, ill-ventilated, and foul with cesspools. To reach the High Street from Oak Hill for shopping, or to board the four-horse omnibus to London from the Bird in Hand yard, Mrs Hopkins would have walked down Frognal, turned off past St John's into the once fashionable Church Row, and then, to avoid the slum courts, would have turned right, in front of the Oriel House. Church Row was the western boundary to the slums. Westward beyond the churchyard of St John's was the narrow lane of Frognal, guarded by toll-house and gate. The road called Oak Hill Park (its name in all the returns, although the Hopkinses always called it Oak Hill) rose steeply on the left out of Frognal. On one of Hampstead's prominent heights, it was a new development, chiefly stuccoed houses of three stories and a basement, which won a design award for gentlemen's dwellings in the Great Exhibition of 1851.

The Hopkins house (destroyed in 1961 to make way for development, like all except two of the original houses) was one of a semi-detached pair, large, comfortable, and unpretentious. The oaks which had covered the hill had been cut down in 1470, except for fifty which the monks insisted be left. Those remaining were known for their beautiful symmetrical growth. Immediately behind the houses were Oak Hill Fields, rich grazing, bordered by old hedgerows and oaks. A popular walk for the villagers was the path by the fields, where hawthorn, elder, wild rose, and woodbine grew. Several of the Hopkins family took to sketching in the nearby fields. During their thirty years at Oak Hill their neighbours were professional men, rich merchants, and retired or leisured people. For ten years from 1863 George Smith, the publisher (of Smith, Elder & Co.) and founder of the *Cornhill*, the *Pall Mall Gazette*, and the *Dictionary of National Biography* (which still has no entry for Gerard Hopkins), lived at Oak Hill Lodge, near Frognal at the bottom of the Park. The Hopkinses used to watch arrivals for the weekly reception on Fridays—Thackeray, Millais, Leech, Trollope, Wilkie Collins, Browning, Meredith, Frederick Leighton, Turgenev, Mrs Gaskell, and the painter Frederick Walker. Florence Nightingale stayed at Oak Hill Park for the sake of her health some time after she returned from the Crimea, and Manley Hopkins once sought her help over a Hawaiian problem.

The number of living-in servants for Oak Hill Park households ranged from three to eight. The George Smiths and the Sheffield Neaves had eight; the Hopkinses made do with a nurse, a cook, and a housemaid, until the children were old enough for the nurse to be replaced by another maid. For a time in the early 1860s they employed a boy, Edward Green, as a 'page'. Their servants often stayed for more than a decade—the housemaid Mary Leach for at least twenty years, a cook, Mary Mitchell, a Nottinghamshire country girl, and the nurse from Hampshire, Elizabeth, for over ten years.[4]

The family did not keep a carriage. Opposite the house were the Oak Hill Park stables, where Manley Hopkins sometimes hired a horse to ride into the City, and where the children were taught to ride. The four-horse bus, licensed to carry twelve cramped passengers inside among the lane of knees and the evil-smelling straw, unless one risked the knifeboard seats on the open top, ran every twelve minutes from the High Street down Haverstock Hill to Tottenham Court Road, then Holborn, finishing up in Cheapside, by St Paul's. The full fare was sixpence. Other buses went to the new railway station at Charing Cross, or down Baker Street to Marble Arch and the West End. A hansom from Hampstead High Street to the Pimlico Station, later known as Victoria, cost about three shillings.

Hopkins had the advantages of the countryside and the largest city in the world. He could go to the galleries, special exhibitions, museums, churches, meetings, open-air spectacles, the London parks, and theatres. As a country boy he became accustomed to trees and open skies, although he could never name trees and plants swiftly and accurately. A younger brother remembered how, as a schoolboy, Gerard used to climb dangerously high up an elm in their Oak Hill garden;[5] even after he became a Jesuit he retained his love of climbing.

In the year the Hopkins family moved to Oak Hill, Christ Church was built on the east side of Hampstead, to relieve the pressure on St John's. Although Mr and Mrs Hopkins came to be on social terms with the Vicar of Christ Church, their children were told that he was 'very low', and suspected him of dark crimes.[6] After their marriage Kate joined her husband in his moderately High Anglicanism; they believed in the Catholic validity of Anglican orders. Their church was national and local: the colours of the Loyal Hampstead Association, a corps of gentlemen volunteers who had once drilled on the Heath in uniform and with muskets, but had been disbanded in 1813, hung in St John's. Manley and Kate were strongly religious, yet without the precision and rigidity which caused unhappiness among many nineteenth-century Christians. When Milicent joined the sisterhood of All Saints', Margaret Street, the Puseyite tendency was considered extreme, but the change was accepted, and the family affection remained. Despite the agonies caused by Gerard's conversion, their belief allowed natural affection to win. Surprisingly quickly, thought Gerard, they came to accept the change, even after he became a Jesuit. (Gerard was not so tolerant.) Grace and Kate remained devout Anglicans all their lives, although none of the boys retained more than a vestige of their childhood religion.

Although Protestant was not a word they would have used, Mr and Mrs Hopkins were mainstream Anglican and Protestant in their repudiation of Roman practices such as private confession, spiritual direction, and Mariolatry, and would not have acknowledged a priest's status in the same way. As a student Gerard made fun of one of the St John's curates, Mr Herclots, but later, in Dublin, he was indignant at the lack of respect his students showed him as a priest.[7] The Hopkinses believed in infant baptism—it was recorded for posterity in February 1848, when Arthur was baptized in water from the River Jordan. Holy Communion was the climax of their devotional practice. The children were taught to read the Bible and pray, and there were family prayers and a Bible-reading in the house every morning before breakfast, with all the servants present. Manley said prayers and read the lessons.

There were also family prayers at night. Manley had a copy of the Revd Alexander Watson's *The Devout Churchman*, an anthology of daily meditations.[8] The family religion was neither extravagant nor self-sacrificial, but conventional and domestic.

They attended St John's, an airy classical building of 1745 which resembled St Martin-in-the-Fields in its Roman windows, low balcony, prominent coat-of-arms, and lack of dim religious light. It was anathema to Gerard Hopkins's gothic prejudices; 'the church is dreary', he wrote.[9] Manley Hopkins was a churchwarden. He did not take a prominent part in local politics: his name does not appear often in the minutes of the Hampstead vestry. He attended a few important meetings only as one of a large number of parishioners, although in 1866 he was elected a trustee under the Church Act.[10] He took an interest in the Hampstead Public Library, and was elected to the committee in April 1857; but the annual report at the same meeting showed that the library was little used, an average of fewer than four books per session. His name appears again on the 1877 committee; to judge from the fourteen titles ordered that year, undemanding children's favourites, the library was unambitious and run on a shoestring.

Manley Hopkins gave most of his time beyond his duties as average adjuster to an unusual activity. In February 1856 he was appointed the consul-general in London for Hawaii, on the recommendation of his brother Edward, now in the Hudson's Bay Company: 'I can answer for Mr M. Hopkins' high respectability and position. . . . I may, moreover, mention that he is personally acquainted with his present Majesty and that he is the brother of Mr Charles Hopkins who has for several years past filled confidential situations under the Hawaiian Government.' In 1845 Charles had taken up the position of court stenographer in Honolulu, and by the end of 1848 he had been 'Judge of Foreign Causes' (known as 'Judge Hopekini'), clerk of the Supreme Court, secretary of the Privy Council, director of the Government Press, and editor of *The Polynesian*. Two years later he was practically a member of the royal household, had acquired a cattle ranch of twelve thousand acres, and had adopted 'accepted features' of the native Hawaiian lifestyle, which included *punalua*, or 'spouses sharing a spouse'. In 1853 a son, Charles L. Hopkins, was born to a Hawaiian woman, Kahanu. American missionaries were worried about 'Hopkins's low moral tone'.[11]

Manley was to hold his Hawaiian appointment for thirty years. He was not a typical Victorian colonialist, yet his appointment was made partly in order to 'counterbalance the influence of the U. States here';

and he helped in the English–French–American subordination of a friendly people. He became the force behind the establishment of an Episcopal church in Honolulu, attached to the Anglican communion, and *Hawaii: The Past, Present, and Future of Its Island-Kingdom* (1862) revealed the failure of American Protestant and French Catholic missions, and the need for an English one. *The Saturday Review* praised it, observing that its author 'speaks rather obscurely of the present habits and morals and culture of the Hawaiians'.[12] (Manley never set foot on Hawaii, and the book was probably ghosted in large part by Charles.)

In 1876 Manley Hopkins received an embarrassing letter stating that 'King Kalakua would be obliged if CGH would resign his seat in the House of Nobles'. Charles Hopkins had sailed from Hawaii in October 1867, never to return, although Manley, later assisted by his son Cyril as vice-consul, continued to serve after Hawaii became a republic, and was reinstated after an ignominious dismissal in 1886.[13]

When he was six Gerard had met two Hawaiian princes, who had stayed with the family at Stratford. As an adult his silence on the Hawaiian connection is remarkable. The exploits of Charles Hopkins must have been the subject of remarks at home, and the grandeur represented by his father's sword and cocked hat gave him opportunities for his powers of mimicry.[14]

&

In October 1854 Manley wrote in an exercise-book bound in green leather 'A Story of a Doll', perhaps a male version of one of the Smith girls' stories from twenty years before.[15] On the first page was pasted an ink drawing by Thomas Hood of a boy in a medieval or faery costume gazing at a doll in a shop-window. It is a tale of a mistreated ten-year-old orphan, put to work in a tobacco warehouse, who becomes aware of beauty through seeing a 'clean and happy' doll in a toyshop. The doll becomes a comforter, disappears, and Hugh succumbs to the fogs and damps. Converted by suffering and pious advice, he dies asking if dolls can be immortal. Hugh's age is said to be the reader's, which makes Gerard the likely recipient. It was a misjudgement of a ten-year-old's tastes, especially those of Gerard.

Gerard was precocious and original, and his aesthetic preferences were decided. When he and Cyril had some childish illness his mother found him crying, 'because Cyril has become so ugly!'[16] From an early age he showed a combination of inventiveness and didacticism, which was to become a characteristic of his poetry. One spring, when he was at Blunt House, Laura wrote to Kate: 'Gerard has been ecstatically happy all this afternoon in the company of Teddy Phillips who came to dine & play with him. They got on famously together—*out-romancing* one another. Gerard being beyond measure patronising [sic] and instructing.'[17] As egoism grew, he became aware of the gap between the self and other existences, asking himself, 'What must it be to be someone else?'[18]

A sense of the particularity of objects was stimulated by his study of art. The fashionable aim in drawing was the reproduction of objects by copying; suggestion was lazy and incorrect. The observer had to visualize the object as a collection of details before transferring it to paper. This habit of close observation and reconstruction was well established in nineteenth-century art before Ruskin and the Pre-Raphaelite painters formalized and sanctified it. Gerard's earliest drawing teacher is said to have been his Aunt Annie, whose surviving pictures are marred by a mawkish sentimentality. House wrote of her portrait of the ten-year-old Gerard: 'the expression of soft sanctimoniousness is one which many of his admirers would gladly believe he had never been asked or forced to assume.'[19] His Aunt Maria provided more practical encouragement. She used to take him sketching in the garden of Blunt House, Croydon, a huge eighteenth-century red-brick mansion. Several drawings he did there exist: a detailed one of a plane tree, and another of the flat landscape, with woods, farm buildings, hedges and fields. There were excursions in the countryside around Epsom, where they sat side by side with their sketch-books, making faithful outlines, then filling in minutiae. Many of his early sketches were done in the Hampstead garden, where there was a tall and luxuriant mass of trees, and from the end of which he could sketch open countryside.[20] It was by getting to know trees by sketching that Hopkins became so absorbed by them that his poems, journals, and drawings would be filled with their presences.

A restrictive habit was also fostered by contemporary methods. The building up of a total picture by a long, laborious, eye-tiring process meant that the artist had to develop patience and self-abnegation. It also meant that he had to keep a sense of proportion. Hopkins's extant sketches show less control over his impatience than do those of Arthur. He sometimes isolated a narrowly focused detail without a sense of context. Sketches of natural features (clouds, trees, foliage, water) and architectural detail (sometimes helped by the photographs of his uncle George Giberne, Maria's husband) became ends in themselves. Hopkins never fulfilled his early promise as a visual artist; when he was ten he drew a fat rabbit and a parrot, and the head and wings, expression of the eye, and the angle of the body are excellent,[21] but his Oxford drawings are not extraordinary.

Another interest he developed at home, and which encouraged him to focus his eyes and mind on detail, was architecture. When he was thirteen he was given Parker's *Introduction to the Study of Gothic Architecture*, a manifesto of the Oxford Society for Promoting the Study of Gothic Architecture, which played a defining role in the Gothic Revival.[22] With the more scholarly, two-volume Parker's *Glossary*, it became perhaps the most lastingly influential book in his early education, responsible for forming tastes which went well beyond architecture. It was out to make converts, and Hopkins became dictatorial and priggish in advocating its values.

'Gothic' had often been loosely used to describe the early Christian styles of Roman, Saxon, and Norman. According to Parker, 'Saxon' was to indicate 'rude' or uncertain style ('supposed to be Saxon'); 'Romanesque' was 'debased Roman', and Roman itself was characterized by the lifeless terms 'massiveness', 'circularity', 'squareness', and 'rectangularity'. Even the integrity of a Greek style was untrustworthy: 'the Anglo-Italian Style of the last century, commonly called Grecian'. All styles except Gothic were frequently described in crypto-moral words, such as 'debased', 'rude', and 'crude'. Gothic is distinguished not just by the pointed arch, but by qualities which could be considered aesthetically superior, such as variegation, clustering, slenderness and delicacy, flexibility, and ramification. Gothic architecture (says the *Glossary*) implies graceful movement and life: lines 'shoot upwards', the piers 'send up vaulting shafts'. The capital has no longer the Norman 'thick square abacus', but is a 'graceful bell, with foliage tending upwards, and curling in an extremely free and elegant manner'. Skill, taste, and morality come to life in Gothic architecture.

From looking at and describing architecture, Hopkins picked up some of his distinctive methods of writing about nature. Describing it in exaggerated terms of shape and movement ('weeds in wheels shoot'[23]), his words recreate nature's hidden and charged character. His compulsions are to convey perceptions rather than mere sights, and to focus on detail, urges of the Gothic Revivalists. Much of a vocabulary which looks extraordinary in a nature poem originates in the *Glossary*, for instance, bay, boss, canopy, cluster, crest, cusp, fan, flush, fret, hearse, hip, hood, image, jut, moulding, pitch, principal, quoin, rib, and vault. On one page of his 1865 notebook he recorded 'water ribs', 'ash clusters', 'bossy water', 'glazed water vaulted o'er a drowsy stone', and 'a remarkable fan of clouds traced in fine horizontals'.[24] Hopkins adapted architectural vocabulary because it could represent, not merely describe, visual reality. It is ironic that this technical vocabulary has so often been judged ambiguous or obscure.

Hopkins was always a close observer of nature. A Jesuit brother remembered him in 1882: 'Ay, a strange yoong man, crouching down that gate to stare at some wet sand. A fair natural 'e seemed to us, that Mr 'opkins.'[25] Gerard's cousin Isabel remembered that, as a boy in the Epsom garden, he would arrange stones and twigs in patterns.[26] Architecture's basic contrast-pattern was of course that of substance and space: Hopkins came to see deep significance in stark natural contrasts, whether pleasurable, as in 'Pied Beauty', or painfully extreme, as the black and white in 'Spelt from Sibyl's Leaves'.

He may also have gained from these books his first knowledge that there was an Oxford way of looking at things, because the authors made lavish use of engravings of Oxford college and church architecture. The books also made him familiar with medieval monasticism and religion, out of which Gothic architecture had been formed. Many of his early books were medievalist or antiquarian. The family had a twelve-volume set of the Waverley novels, the most heavily thumbed of which was *Ivanhoe*. Although as an adult he judged Scott's novels as 'scarcely to be called works of art', he must have responded to the stories and their illustrations—'little vignettes of mossy and ivy-grown ruins, pieces of armour and ancient weapons, tombs, traceried windows, ecclesiastical objects and vestments, gauntlets, banners, heraldic shields'.

In one way Hopkins missed the opportunities presented to him in childhood. He had a clear, sweet voice as a child but could not read music, and in spite of the family interest in music never learned to play an instrument properly. (It is possible that he felt stifled by the family's musical confidence.) Before he went to Dublin in his forties he had not even learnt the principles of harmony, and in Dublin, when he tried to play and compose, he had to teach himself out of a textbook by trial and error; then he had to get help from the family expert, Grace. He ruefully reported to Baillie: 'I am now very keen [on music] and in the face of difficulties never yet known in the whole history of the art— upon my word this is true, for however humble may have been the station from which musicians have risen to eminence, at least they *cd.* *read music* and *play some instrument* before they attempted composition; whereas I . . .'.[27] His most interesting tune, the setting of Dixon's poem 'Fallen Rain', he could trust no one to provide the harmony for, and left it until he himself could do it, but he never did.

One of his sisters said that the family liked sixteenth- and seventeenth-century songs: they possessed an old song-book of the early eighteenth century, a miscellaneous collection stretching back over two centuries, including love songs, drinking songs, ballads, and airs by Handel and Purcell, the composers most admired by Hopkins.[28] In childhood, too, he acquired a liking for popular Elizabethan songs such as 'Watkin's Ale', which had lost sexual exuberance as its title became discreetly altered to 'Mother Watkins' Ale'.[29] The book also contained a song by John Gay which Hopkins quoted in his rhetoric lectures and in a letter to Bridges in 1881:

> 'Twas when the seas were roaring
> With hollow blasts of wind;
> A damsel lay deploring
> All on a rock reclined.[30]

When a pianist in the 1880s said to him, 'Your music dates from a time before the piano was invented',[31] it meant that Hopkins remembered this childhood book. When he lectured on the structure of verse he returned even further into his past and recalled 'Ding dong bell', 'One, two, buckle my shoe', and 'March dust and April showers', rhymes sung by him in the nursery at Stratford.[32]

# Highgate

For two years Hopkins went to a small private school in Hampstead, and then in September 1854 started at Sir Roger Cholmeley's School at Highgate.[1] At ten years old he was small for his age and delicate-looking, his head large in proportion to his trunk and shoulders. Photographs of him in the junior school show his mouth hanging open, eyes hooded, with the top lids heavy and half-closed. He had a long cleft chin, a long and low nose, and a well-shaped upper lip. His hair was dark brown to ginger, with golden lights and streaks, and tinges of red; it tended to fall wild and long on either side. His eyebrows were already permanently raised, with an appearance of sardonic superiority. Victorian photographic conditions produced solemn portraits, and unfortunately none survives which suggests Hopkins's humour or levity.

Highgate was built on a hill a few miles north of London. Controlled by professional men and a wealthy élite, it was not a typical village, though still a staging post for sheep and cattle. Schoolboys with red and blue ribbons round their felt hats in winter, and straw hats in summer, used to watch the buses, carriages and cabs toiling up Highgate Hill. Sir Roger Cholmeley founded his Grammar School in 1565 to provide a free education for poor boys. Like most schools which started with charitable intentions, it became one to which only the privileged could afford to send their sons, the name 'public school' becoming ironic. The Lord Chancellor, Lord Eldon, gave a judgement in 1829 which, while keeping within the strict terms of the foundation, allowed the headmaster to attract fee-paying pupils from upper-class families.

In 1854 the Reverend John Bradley Dyne had been headmaster for sixteen years, and remained for another thirteen after Hopkins left in 1863. When he took over there were only nineteen foundation pupils, and there were about 130 when Hopkins left. Dyne's policy was to exclude tradesmen's sons and encourage those of the professions and from further afield than London and Middlesex. (In 1833 the Highgate

National School had been built for the excluded children of the poor.) In the original charter the free education of the forty foundationers was only in Greek and Latin and in the religion of the Church of England. So Dyne charged £8 per annum for mathematics and £3 for a modern language, and made both subjects compulsory. There were also obligatory charges for the library and buildings, so the forty so-called Free Scholars had to pay £15 a year. As a result, nearly all Hopkins's contemporaries were the sons of clergymen, bankers, merchants, and army officers.

Dyne's academic policy was to prepare boys for Oxford, Cambridge, and the learned professions, while a few entered the Indian Civil Service or a military academy. Among his pupils had been W. W. Skeat, the etymologist, and the classical translator Philip Worsley, who had won all the school prizes a few years before Hopkins, and the Newdigate at Oxford. In 1865 the Commissioner on Endowed Schools reported that the standard of education was 'higher here than at any other school in this District except at the City of London School, and among the Grecians at Christ's Hospital'. He stressed that the school was 'doing very good work for the upper middle classes'.

The syllabus was old-fashioned. It was recommended by the educational Commissioners that between one-eighth and a quarter of the teaching hours should be devoted to Natural Science, and many of the great public schools, such as Rugby, Cheltenham, and Marlborough, had set up Modern Departments. But Dyne was 'a type of the old-fashioned pedantic school which ... thought the study of Latin and Greek as the primary object of our creation'. Natural Science was not taught at Highgate, whereas Classics, with History and Divinity, was allocated sixteen and a half hours a week, a larger proportion than the ideal of the time. Of the nine masters at the school five, including the Head, taught Classics, or one to every twenty-four boys, a high ratio (at Eton it was one to forty).

Dr Dyne not only achieved results in university scholarships but must also have been gifted as a teacher of the Classics. Philip Worsley dedicated to Dyne his famous translation of the *Odyssey* into Spenserian stanzas, and Hopkins seems to have found his classical grounding a fine training in the elements of language, and in the expressive and rhythmical powers of poetry. The scrupulous narrownesses of the old system were as useful to Hopkins as the comparatively expansive Oxford methods. Competition was intense. At Easter each year the school was examined in classics by an external examiner from Oxford, and the results determined progress up the school, form prizes, and sixth-form awards such as the Governors' Gold Medal for Latin Verse, and the Exhibition tenable for four years at Oxford or Cambridge. Charles Luxmoore describes another form of competition, a verse race between himself and Hopkins:

I remember very well my first introduction to [Hopkins], coming down the narrow staircase from Dyne's room with the IVth form, when as a new boy I had been put thro my paces, not without credit. I suppose I had seen him the evening before, but among so many new faces I did not identify him, until he and Karslake came and took charge of me with congratulations on getting into their form. That evening we had elegiacs to do, for which Gerard had a very great name, and much excitement was caused by 'the new fellow' being also a dab at them, and the two racing them off so that in as many minutes the 24 verses were done, and honors were claimed by our relative backers to be equally divided between us.[2]

Almost all the history taught was of ancient Greece, Rome, or Israel. An exercise book of Hopkins's shows that the subject was taught with care and thoroughness. It contains notes on Thucydides, illustrated by well-executed plans of the battle of Naupactus.[3] As House comments, 'the amount of patience and attention given to the making of these lovely plans shows a solid practical side of Hopkins's character which was always there and always linked with a sort of sensual satisfaction in getting details beautifully right'.[4] Textbooks Hopkins used in the senior forms included *Dr Smith's History of Greece* and *The Student's Rome*, both imaginatively illustrated with pictures of archaeological objects and famous ruins. In his freshman year at Oxford he produced a parody of the sceptical style of *The Student's Rome* in 'The Rape of the Scout'.[5]

Dyne 'despised modern languages and foreign countries', so the subjects were given only three hours a week, those mainly because of the demands of the Indian Civil Service and Woolwich Academy. A boy could learn French or German. Hopkins was taught French indifferently by M. Prosper Puyo, and never became well-read in French literature. English literature was a poor relation at English public schools, and in Hopkins's day had no space in the curriculum. It was for private reading rather than a subject for study, although some came into classical studies in passages for translation—Milton, Addison, Gibbon, Johnson, and Burke.

ॐ

The school's religious teaching was regular and thorough. In the first form, boys studied the collect and gospel for the week, and there were 'Doctor's Lessons', described as 'a formidable catechism in The Awful

Presence' (of Dyne, not God). Once during the weekly catechism class Dyne asked a new boy 'Who is your neighbour?' The boy answered 'Smithers', the owner of the house next door, and out came the birch. In the sixth form there was still the catechism, the thirty-nine articles in Latin and English, and Whateley's *Christian Evidences*, together with historical and doctrinal teaching of the Bible. The upper forms studied the Greek Testament every Saturday. The school's Protestantism must have been above reproach, as two Venn boys, from a famous Clapham Sect family, were boarders in 1846.

There was no school chapel when Hopkins was there; daily prayers were said in the main schoolroom. The new church of St Michael's was used on Sundays, saints' days, and special occasions. When Hopkins was at school, the incumbent of St Michael's (who always had to have a good public relationship with Dyne) was the Revd C. B. Dalton. He sent his sons to Sir Roger's, although his church was in the Puseyite tradition, while Dyne was strongly anti-Tractarian. Holy Communion was regularly sung on Sundays, and major festivals like the Circumcision celebrated. A series of sermons in Lent 1863 dealt with symbolic uses of the Old Testament in the Puseyite tradition, and there were visiting Tractarian preachers. St Michael's gave Hopkins his first impressions of an Anglican tradition different from that of his school and St John's. His interest in ecclesiastical architecture had little to do with his boyhood worship: St Michael's had been built in 1832 in Commissioners' Gothic, a stark sham compared with the gothic of Parker's architectural books. Parker awoke his passionate interest in the Revivalist work of Butterfield and Street.

૭

The entrance to the school was a weather-beaten oak door in the four-foot-high North Road wall. Above it was a triangular canopy with a bell dating from 1768, and on the right a barkless yew, shiny from generations of leaning boys. The school buildings were entered through a small outbuilding, paved with flagstones bordered by yellow bricks, where boys hung their outdoor clothes on the rows of pegs, and the small ones spun tops. The rooms were overcrowded and badly ventilated, the sanitary arrangements unsatisfactory, and the scattered nature of the buildings made discipline difficult.

In the school yard were sold tarts, oranges, and a unique sweetmeat called Cushions. To the north of the playground were shops let to tradesmen, to the south a yard for hockey, bounded by the surviving wall of the old Cholmeley chapel, in the burial-ground of which was the tomb of Samuel Taylor Coleridge. Boys used to climb over the thickly ivied wall searching for fives balls; the continuation of the wall, divided by buttresses, formed an unsatisfactory sloping fives court. Rugby football was not started until the year before Hopkins left. There were organized games, but they were not compulsory; the school was comparatively free from athletic hero-worship. Luxmoore said that Hopkins took some part in games but did not put them first, more likely going on the permitted walks. In summer there was cricket; it was possible to slip away unseen from the field, and ramble around Ken Wood.

The school prided itself on its rural situation. Paper-chases were held on Shrove Tuesday and at Michaelmas around the local villages, finishing with refreshments at Barnet. There were summer strolls through the woods to Finchley, or on the Heath near the Spaniards Inn. The boys were allowed by Lord Mansfield to bathe in a deep meadow pond near a wooded part of Ken Wood. There were organized swimming and diving lessons under Beckwith, the champion of the Thames.[6]

For most of his time at Highgate Hopkins boarded at Elgin House, 2 High Street, on Highgate Hill; from the back there was a marvellous view over the Lea Valley to Epping and Hainault Forests. For the latter part of his time at Elgin House it was under the charge of a master, J. C. Nesfield, who had been a boy at the school before going as Postmaster to Merton, and a matron, Mrs Chappell, whom Hopkins liked enough to make a note of her new address after she retired. The day-boys were considered uninteresting, but there was rivalry between the two boarding-houses, Grove Bank and Elgin House. When Cyril came to the school two years after Gerard, he was in Elgin House, and became Hopkins Secundus.

They made their own way from the boarding-house to school every morning, sometimes passing the crocodile of a young ladies' school 'with a rearguard of elder pupils and assistant governesses'. Sometimes they met a Punch and Judy man, a group of strolling acrobats, or an old man 'with a perambulating menagerie of small animals possessed of antagonistic natures, such as cats, mice, and birds huddled together in a cage, and designated by a dirty label as "The Happy Family"'. One Derby Day Cyril and a friend met three musicians, a harpist, a fiddler, and a woman singer, who to recoup their losses played and sang for them a ballad 'Who shall be fairest?'. Occasionally there were miniature versions of town-and-gown fights with local youths.

Elgin House contained a meagre library which the boys used on

Sunday afternoons and wet half-holidays. The books were 'neither stimulating nor refreshing', mainly of the type of *Nicholl's Help to Reading the Bible*. Both Cyril and Gerard read nautical stories. There were hobbies such as keeping silkworms, collecting stamps and butterflies, and skating. Sometimes the younger boys were required to fag for the sixth-formers, although the system was not as fully developed as at some schools. As in most schools, seniors sometimes abused their privileges: while Hopkins was there there was a junior 'whose rich and rare plumcake' was 'incontinently devoured by a large creature with red whiskers, a ring, and a reputation for smoking and intrigue, who calls himself "Cock of the School"'. At the end of term there was a breaking-up supper at each assistant master's house, at which all who could sing were expected to do so. One boy sang a ballad enumerating the virtues of the British yeoman, each verse ending with the line 'And *I* manage to exist and be content, John Brown', while Marcus Clarke[7] gave 'Bryan O'Lynn' and 'Having tea in the arbour', both comic ditties.

Cyril and Gerard had met Marcus Clarke in 1854, on a summer holiday at Seaview on the Isle of Wight. Although he was nearer Cyril's age he had a large influence on Gerard's early development. Like Hopkins he was slightly built, his left arm at least two inches shorter than his right; he had a stutter, sometimes exaggerated for dramatic purposes. Hopkins was attracted by his powers of raillery, but mostly by his literary and artistic gifts. He tried to compensate for his delicacy by physical risks, becoming an expert diver in the Ken Wood pond, collecting many bruises and cuts in school-yard hockey, and climbing fearlessly, like Hopkins; and he was fond of all sorts of extravagant behaviour. Hopkins described him as a 'kaleidoscopic, parti-coloured, harlequinesque, thaumatropic Being'.[8] He liked telling tales about the 'promiscuous society' forced on him by his father—tales which the strait-laced Cyril thought shocking. He was always 'avid for recondite knowledge', said Cyril, who considered his reading 'promiscuous'. Clarke had a gift for rapidly assimilating what he was reading: he was interested in the occult, the Ingoldsby Legends, Edgar Allan Poe—as a parting gift he gave Hopkins a volume of Poe's poetry, which Gerard passed on to Cyril when he joined the Jesuits. He laughed a great deal, sang Italian operatic arias, and at one period prefaced his remarks with 'A vous parler franchement'. He was capricious and liable to irritability, which Cyril put down to his artistic temperament. Clarke was a strong art-lover, on good terms with Mr Harley, the drawing-master. He drew, and in adult life wrote essays on artists, including one on Gustave Doré. It was under Clarke's influence that Hopkins developed his liking for Millais and Frederick Walker. To the end of his life Clarke treasured a fine engraving of Millais's 'The Huguenot', a painting which Hopkins was still using as a critical illustration in an 1881 argument with Bridges.[9]

Cyril, Gerard, and Marcus Clarke jointly subscribed to *Once a Week*, famous for its combination of text and pictorial art; they looked eagerly for each issue, and devoured its stories, such as 'The Pythagorean'. Like Hopkins, Clarke disliked Scott and George Eliot. He experimented in prose and verse. He and Hopkins exchanged ideas and images, and practised descriptions and diagrams of sunsets; on his way to Australia when he was seventeen he sent this to the Hopkins family:

Last night there was an exquisite sunset. The whole sky one large fleecy cloud, save in the extreme East where it suddenly stopped like a curtain, leaving the rest of the Heavens a pure applegreen. As the sun sank, the fleece became pink, rosy-red, and finally like blood-red wool, torn with a reaping-hook in pillows or haycocks; while the applegreen became violet and then saffron. The sun slowly dipped, a bloody disk, into the creaming waves, and, as he did so, one long, milky cloud like a milky, opaque opal shadowed out (for I can use no other term) from the mass of delicate, crimson foam and completely obscured it so that the horizon and a small space above it was in this form. [diagram]

This has much in common with the undisciplined description in Hopkins's 'A Vision of the Mermaids', written when he too was seventeen.[10]

Clarke was a lonely child, motherless in a household of men. He had a gift for telling stories, some of which he used to write down and get Hopkins to illustrate. Hopkins was well-known at school for his comic and grotesque drawings, and often illustrated his letter-headings. One of Clarke's best stories was a 'weird and powerful' tale in verse, 'The Lady of Lynn', about a medical student called Edward Moreton, who develops an interest in the occult, which leads to murder:

> A taper burnt on the pulpit rail
> And flickered over his features pale
> As he picked his teeth with his horny nail
> And twitched up his mouth to the roots of his hair
> His eyes had a deadly phosp[h]oric stare
> His teeth gleamed white with a ghastly glare.

Hopkins's frontispiece drawing to 'The Lady of Lynn' was of Moreton entering a moonlit attic on a stormy night, horror-struck at what he sees. A misshapen man leans over an open chest, in which is a body with a dagger protruding. The room is filled with objects: a skull, books, a pestle and mortar, surgical instruments, a phrenologist's bust, anatomical drawings and models. Hopkins produced his poetic variations on the theme of arcane knowledge in 'The Alchemist in the City'.

When his father died, Clarke was sent to Australia, where he had a successful career as a literary journalist and story-writer. His writings often recalled his Highgate schooldays, and included characters called Hopkins, Cyril, Gerard, and Gerrard. After Clarke had left, Hopkins's methods of self-expression in his remaining years at school took their tone of enthusiastic eclecticism from Clarke: 'I have been writing', he told his old school-friend 'Poet' Coleridge, now at Sherborne, 'numbers of descriptions of sunrises, sunsets, sunlight in the trees, flowers, windy skies etc etc. I have begun the story of the Corinthian capital. . . . I have done two thirds of "Linnington Water, an Idyll", and am planning "Fause Joan" a ballad in the old style. All these things are done in scraps of time.'[11]

A letter[12] Hopkins wrote to the German teacher may have originated in a joke contrived by him and Clarke. Professor Müncke had received a French lance-wound at the Battle of Waterloo, where he had been in Blücher's army, and was 'a tall, round-shouldered but rather fine-looking man, past middle life, who wore gold-rimmed spectacles and was consumed with self-importance'. Like Hopkins exiled in his Dublin classroom thirty years later, he was bad at estimating what to tell his class about himself. He told them that, should they ever visit Egypt, they would find his name inscribed on the Pyramids, and left them speculating whether it would be 'scratched in chalk or notched with a pocketknife'. Clarke was amused by Cyril's accounts of Müncke's staccato speech and sayings, particularly his assertion that 'the use of the personal pronoun "I", written with a capital, was a striking proof of the intense egotism of the British nation'. Clarke thought him 'a worthy disciple of Baron Münchausen'.

In spite of its pompousness, the letter to Müncke reveals Hopkins's confident schoolboy learning, and his distaste for pretentiousness. It mimics Müncke's pompous formality: 'I take a great and unwarrantable liberty in thus addressing you, and one which I should be very unwilling to take, were it not that my brother Cyril enjoys the honour of your acquaintance and instruction'. The writer attempts, like many others, to rewrite the contract between Faust and Mephistopheles, and it is hard to separate Hopkins's bravado from his attempt at imitation:

It is not to be expected that without having read the very words of the great Poet and without having deeply considered the design of the Play I should be able to solve Metaphysical difficulties out of my own internal consciousness, but should have sought an explanation from one skilled in the literature of both Deutchland [*sic*] and my own nation. Under the hope that you will not resent this liberty, which arises from a sincere wish to comprehend the great ideas of Göthe, permit me to conclude, Sir, and to subscribe myself.

Yours very respectfully<br>
Gerard M. Hopkins

'I do remember', said Hopkins in later life, 'that I was a very conceited boy'.[13]

At the end of his first year at school, in 1855, Hopkins was fourth in the second form, and from there went up the school at short intervals; at the beginning of the school year in September 1859, when he was just fifteen, he entered the sixth form. A young master, R. W. Dixon, who eventually became an admiring if rather uncritical friend, recalled him as 'a pale young boy, very light and active, with a very meditative and intellectual face'.[14] The solemnity of this—written in response to Hopkins's letter renewing their acquaintance nearly twenty years later—does not acknowledge Hopkins's sense of fun, which sometimes showed a satiric or vicious side. Luxmoore's memory of him after his death is also falsified by piety: 'his face always *set* to do what was right'.[15] Hopkins was too fond of experiment to be pietistic. He liked to try things out, to find out what *would* happen *if*. (His obituary in *The Cholmeleian* mentions neither religion nor moral earnestness.) This is not to say that he was unprincipled. Luxmoore's letter continued:

When he moved into our bedroom he was the only boy who regularly read to himself a small portion of the New Testament, in accordance I think with a promise given to his mother. At first it provoked a little ridicule, in which [he] must have got the best of us, tho' we didn't then think so, and I remember that my set decided that the promise was quite a sufficient reason, and we all agreed that Skin was not to be hindered in any way.

Luxmoore recalled one of Hopkins's 'Homeric struggles' with Dr Dyne:

Such a conflict was aroused by [his] abstinence from all drink for three weeks, the pretext being a bet of 10/ to 6d, the real reason a conversation on seamen's sufferings and human powers of endurance. I was only the other day chatting it over with the Wilsons in Sussex, and one, then a big fellow, said he remembered Gerard showing him his tongue just before the end and it was black.[16]

His class was being drilled by Sergeant-Major Ruston when Hopkins collapsed, and had to go back to Elgin House. A boy told Ruston what had happened, but he refused to believe it, and the boy retorted: 'A lie indeed! *He* tell a lie. Why, he would rather die.' 'If only I'd have known it', said the astonished Ruston, 'I would have put his head under that pump.' On the twenty-second day, just after Hopkins had won his bet, Dyne swooped, 'blustered and threatened', and

finally to punish both 'betters' compelled Gerard to return the 10/, and bound both by solemn promises and unlimited threats not to pay or receive the bet. In vain [Hopkins] pointed out that such a decision really rewarded the other boy, and only punished him, who had endured the suffering and exhaustion of the effort. Dyne was obdurate and Gerard ... only heaped up to himself further punishment, but of course Dyne was absolutely and altogether in the wrong.

Hopkins's experiences of Dyne as a boy-bircher are supported by reminiscences of other Old Cholmeleians. Edmund Yates said that Dyne 'believed thoroughly in the virtues of corporal punishment', and was a 'desperate swisher', 'not over-burdened with tact, judgement, or impartiality.' Luxmoore, afterwards a master at Harrow, wrote of Dyne as 'heavy-handed': 'blustering Dyne's argument was always "hold your tongue Sir", his firm conviction that a boy must be always wrong, and his appeal never to reason, always to force'. Hopkins insisted, said Luxmoore, on 'arguing his case with a man whose logic was comprised in the birch, to whom an answer however respectful was at least mutiny, if not rank blasphemy'.[17]

There were other forms of punishment: fines, degradation, threats of expulsion, early bedtime, restriction of privileges, and lines. Birching was the commonest penalty, even when boys were caught in school hours returning from Christopher's shop in 'town'. When Dyne retired so did the birch, which was replaced by the cane; in the school magazine appeared a lament in Latin elegiacs from a redundant birch. Dyne's portrait hanging in the present-day school has been described:

A firm mouth with lips which are just too thin, sharp eyes small enough to appear cold and piercing as they gleam above a narrow and bony nose, side-whiskers framing a choleric complexion, and a triangular face accentuated by the double rectangle of clerical bands, a face which is alert and intelligent and full of energy, but also a little shy and reserved.

Eight years after Hopkins left Highgate Dyne became president of the Headmasters' Conference, and in 1876, when Highgate competed for the first time in examinations with other public schools, it headed the list of successes.

Cyril Hopkins left school after five years when he was only fifteen, to go into his father's office, and so absolved Gerard from any feelings of responsibility towards the family firm. Cyril was not academically promising, except in arithmetic. Even as an adult his spelling was poor, and his writing style ponderous. His memoir of Marcus Clarke is unpublishable, his judgements on Clarke's works sentimental and injudicious (he compares Clarke to Emily Brontë). Cyril started shaving before he had any facial hair, smoked furiously, and, according to his brother, was 'mad about the army', though 'utterly unpatriotic'.[18] The three younger Hopkins boys, Arthur, Lionel, and Everard, were sent to school at Lancing, Winchester, and Charterhouse, respectively. The gradual improvement of their father's social position is reflected in the status of these schools.

While Cyril Hopkins cultivated manliness in the City office, Gerard developed several friendships in his last years at Sir Roger's. Some he kept up by post with former pupils like Luxmoore and E. H. Coleridge,[19] with whom he exchanged poetry. Some were more intense, like his intimacy with Alexander Strachey. Strachey had cut Hopkins and would not go on walks with him, so Hopkins asked a mutual friend, Clarke, to discover the reason, but did not get a straightforward answer. He asked Strachey to come to his bedroom after prayers, and taxed him with his ingratitude:

that he had not spoken except on the most trivial subjects and on some days not even that, that he had taken no notice of me, and that I had been wretched every time I saw or thought of it, was only what I had bargained for, I sowed what I now reaped; but after this sacrifice to be told he did not walk with me because I never asked him was too much. I put a parallel case to him; I told him he might find many friends more liberal than I had been but few indeed who would make the same sacrifice I had; but I could not get him to see it: after I had said all, the others came up to bed. I asked him if he had anything to say. He objected that the others had come up to interrupt it. 'But should you have had anything if they had not?' I asked. 'No, I don't think so' he said with a cool smile, and I left him.[20]

'Perhaps', added Hopkins, 'in my next friendship I may be wiser.' There is an overwrought quality—as well as an innocence—about this exchange, recorded in such detail and sent to Coleridge. Hopkins and Strachey never made it up; Hopkins commented to Coleridge: 'Yet it is still my misfortune to be fond of and yet despised by him.'

Hopkins made a habit of being unpunctual at his duties on Sunday mornings, taking the day of rest, as he said, too literally. The fifth time he was late Dyne punished him by sending him to bed at nine, and for the third time that term he was threatened with expulsion, and with deprivation of the testimonial he needed to enter for the Governors' Exhibition.[21]

In April 1862 Hopkins was awarded the Exhibition. Five names were mentioned to the external examiner, Albert Watson of Brasenose, Oxford, and he chose Hopkins over his close rival Edward Beaumont, who eventually won an Exhibition at St John's, Cambridge. But the prize was not easily won. By that time Hopkins had been taken away from Elgin House and was a day-boy, walking across the Heath from Oak Hill. He felt at a severe disadvantage compared with his rivals. He had no separate study, and had to work to keep the noisy younger boys in order. Dyne had granted him a room with a fire, but for 'the most trifling ludicrous little thing' (something to do with accusing another boy of gambling) he was turned out of it, nearly expelled, and degraded to the bottom of the list of prefects. 'Dyne and I had a terrific altercation. I was driven out of patience and cheeked him wildly, and he blazed into me with his riding-whip.' The matter was cleared up and his room restored, but one Sunday night, after the candles had been collected at 'Lights Out', Hopkins took one back to go on working, and his room was taken away for another week.

Then came a worse row:

Clarke, my co-victim, was flogged, struck off the confirmation list and fined £1; I was deprived of my room for ever, sent to bed at half-past nine till further orders, and ordered to work *only* in the school room, not even in the school library and might not sit on a window sill on the staircase to read. Dyne had repeatedly said he hoped I might not be at the top of the school after the exam., so you may suppose, when he took these last measures, I drew my own conclusions.[22]

Although always near the top, Hopkins had not often been first in his class until he reached the sixth form. But in the spring term of 1862 he was placed first of the fifteen boys, and won the Governors' Gold Medal for Latin verse as well as the Exhibition. As early as November 1859 Manley Hopkins applied for his son's name to be put on the short list of possible admissions to Balliol for the Michaelmas term of 1862.[23] The choice of college was due to its reputation and to the advice of the Revd Edwin Palmer, a Tutor and Fellow of Balliol who had connections with Hopkins's school, and lived within walking distance of Oak Hill. On a dull day in the first week of October 1862 Hopkins, with his parents, took the train to Oxford to sit the scholarship examination for Balliol.

# PART II

# The Student, 1863–1868

Not to love my University would be to undo the very buttons of my being.

*(Hopkins to Baillie, 22 May 1880)*

# Balliol College

I believe the Balliol set is truly wise
(Arthur Hugh Clough)

There were two scholarships on offer, the blue ribbon of Oxford awards. Over twenty candidates, 'all the flower of England's youth, from Rugby, Harrow, Eton, Marlborough, and I know not whence',[1] sat the examination, one of the stiffest in the university. They were put up for their three days' stay in the students' rooms, with two beds in a set of rooms instead of the usual one. The examinations, in Greek and Latin translation, Greek and Latin verse composition, and an English essay, were written on blue foolscap paper. Hopkins was fascinated by the looks of another candidate, a 'dreadful and ghastly man', possessed of a 'haggard hideousness'. He had 'grey goggle eyes', he later told his mother, a 'scared suspicious look as though someone were about to hit him from behind', a 'shuddering gait or shuffle', and a 'pinched face'.[2] There was a *viva voce*, at which all the dozen or so Fellows of Balliol sat in a horseshoe, 'all intent, all silent' (according to another candidate), 'except when the illustrious but suspected Jowett puts a question in his silvery, comfortable, but withal searching tones, and I respond . . . not as I would, but as I can.'[3]

A contemporary of Hopkins who sat the same examination described how he learned the results at 9 p.m. on the third day:

I rushed, in a state of suspense I have never before or since experienced, to the door of Balliol College. There stood the burly porter answering inquiries. Two men came up—I knew not in the dark whether they were competitors or not—and put the question in my hearing, saving me the trouble, which was well; for my heart was behaving in so violent and obstreporous [*sic*] a manner that I do not think I could have found words to ask it.

'Do you know who has got the scholarships? Are they out?'
'Yes, sir. Mr Barratt of Rugby and Mr Geldart of Manchester.'
'Dash it!' was the comment, and the forms disappeared in the darkness.[4]

Hopkins had failed. Instead of going out into a new world, he had to return ignominiously to Highgate, to try again in three months' time. He must have spent the waiting period mainly in reading, but that Christmas he wrote a poem of 143 lines, 'A Vision of the Mermaids'.[5]

&

Headed by a circular ink drawing, six inches in diameter, the one manuscript copy of the poem is neatly written in double columns, as though intended for an illustrated journal. The drawing is of a sunset, theatrically presented on a stage formed by the line of the sea-shore. Between the audience of groups of mermaids and the performance is an expanse of sea, setting the onlookers at a distance from the sunset. Its amateurish draughtsmanship exposes the differences between Hopkins's abilities in his two media. The drawing differs from the poem in subject as well as quality. In the poem the narrator rows away from the sea-shore, rejecting civilization. Having reached a rock-island, he becomes voyeur of a complex vision of fleeting and violent sensuousness. Seascape is transformed into aesthetic drama: 'Plum-purple was the west; but spikes of light/ Spear'd open lustrous gashes, crimson-white.' The descriptions of water, sky, and mermaids involve frequent and lengthy parallel and counter images, the bewildering structure of which recalls Shelley's *Prometheus Unbound*, recently read by Hopkins:

> Soon—as when Summer of his sister Spring
> Crushes and tears the rare enjewelling,
> And boasting 'I have fairer things then these'
> Plashes amidst the billowy apple-trees
> His lusty hands, in gusts of scented wind
> Swirling out bloom till all the air is blind
> With rosy foam and pelting blossom and mists
> Of driving vermeil-rain; and, as he lists,
> The dainty onyx-coronals deflowers,
> A glorious wanton.

The colour vanishes from the west, diminished to monochrome, and elegiac sadness replaces wonder, anticipating the desolation and dissolution of a later sunset poem, 'Spelt from Sibyl's Leaves'. Hopkins's indulgence is not, like Tennyson's in 'The Mermaid' and 'The Merman', in furtive expression of forbidden desires, but in sensuous feelings for words. Words for him are things, rather than signs for things.

&

He sat the Balliol examinations again in January. It was his last chance, as he would be over the maximum age by the next October. This time he was successful, gaining one of the college Exhibitions, worth £60 a year. The elections were not made until February, when the Hilary, or Lent, term at Oxford had already started, so he had to wait until the Easter term to go up to Balliol. Still attending school, he was bitterly resentful of Dr Dyne's authoritarian manner: 'The Patriarch of the Old Dispensation at Highgate has the insolence to force me to go in for the Easter exam, in which I have of course nothing whatever to gain, but my *prestige* to lose.'[6] To make matters worse, one of the Highgate examiners was the Revd Edwin Palmer, so that if Hopkins did not do well he would make a bad impression on one of his future tutors.

He consoled himself by learning Oxford jargon and abbreviations, and showing them off in letters. 'I go up to reside on the 10th April I think', he wrote to Ernest Coleridge (whom he now addressed as 'my dear fellow'): 'I wish you would come up as soon as possible—to C.C.C. or Ch.Ch. or Balliol—Balliol of course I should like best. The probability is I shall not see you for an age, unless we can manage to meet in the Long.' Coleridge was two years younger than Hopkins; there was a long Balliol tradition in the Coleridge family, and Ernest went up in the Michaelmas term of 1866.

Hopkins was anticipating other Oxford pleasures. In the long vacation he would be free from family holidays, particularly from 'Cyril and other pomps and vanities of this wicked world'.[7] In the middle of February he had another success: his poem 'Winter with the Gulf Stream' was published in *Once a Week*.[8] It was put in as a space-filler at the end of an article, but on the opposite page was the start of 'an historiette', *The Hampdens*, by Harriet Martineau, together with an engraving by Hopkins's favourite artist, Millais. He was in distinguished company.

Millais's picture of a pair of lovers in Jacobean dress on a rock watching the sun set over the sea is remarkably similar to Hopkins's mermaid illustration; but 'Winter with the Gulf Stream' owes more than his previous poem to close observation of nature: 'Frost-fringed our ivies are, and rough/ With spikèd rime the brambles show'. The poem is mostly made up of material collected for 'A Vision of the Mermaids', and is little more than a list of discrete images, though there are one or two lively experiments in particularity and sound-pattern, such as

> But thro' black branches—rarely drest
> In streaming scarfs that smoothly shine,

Shot o'er with lights—the emblazon'd west,
Where yonder crimson fire-ball sets,
Trails forth a purfled-silken vest.

Hopkins's school days were not the happiest ones of his life, and he was not sad at leaving. He had been preparing for fulfilment elsewhere. He left with a psychological need to do some catching up in rank and status, and kept in touch with only a few Highgate boys afterwards, apart from those who went up to Oxford. His first letters home emphasize his sense of a rise. His school had failed to give him a secure basis for self-esteem, and if for some Etonians university would be an anti-climax, for him the rapture of youth would be discovered at Oxford.

გა

On Friday 17 April 1863, Hopkins travelled up to Oxford with his father. Though the railway offered the least imposing approach to the city, there was the view across Christ Church meadow, and Tom Tower rising above the dingy streets of St Ebbe's. Balliol College was half-deserted on Hopkins's first night, as most of the students were not due to arrive until Saturday or Sunday.[9]

Hopkins's set, of two rooms and a store-cupboard, was on the third and top floor of the black and crumbling building in Balliol's diminutive front quadrangle;[10] when there was a strong wind this 'scarred face' of the college would peel and flake. The roof sloped up to the middle of his ceiling; anyone but Hopkins would have called it a garret. The usual pattern was for undergraduates to occupy rooms within the college for their first three years, and then find approved lodgings in the town for their final one. The freshman spent his first term in inferior rooms; although disparaging his set in a letter to his mother because they lacked both a scout's hole and the traditional outer door or oak, Hopkins boasted that from four of his six windows he had the best views in Balliol, and that his staircase had the best scout in the college, Henry. Students were allowed to change rooms once during the three years, and Hopkins soon had his eye on the 'delicious' and spacious inner, or Garden, quadrangle, with its 'grove of fine trees and lawns where bowls are the order of the evening'.[11]

On his first morning he breakfasted in Mr Palmer's rooms, two floors below his own on No. 4 staircase, with Palmer and the Revd D. M. Owen, who had been the previous term's lecturer in Catechetics at Balliol. Owen was the Blundell Fellow, from Tiverton in Devon, the nearest town to Halberton, the village where his paternal grandmother had been brought up, and Owen had known her. Although Palmer spoke hesitantly, Hopkins found Owen's talk amusing; but he emphasized in a subsequent letter to his mother that Owen took only a minor role in college tuition, and was not half as important in Oxford as at Oak Hill.

Later that day Hopkins, with two other freshmen, was admitted to the College by the Master, who said the Latin formula, and the three names were entered in the Register of Admissions, in beautiful formal writing, under '1863 Termino Paschatis':

> Apr. 18 *Hopkins*, Gerardus Manley,
> f.n. max. Manley Hopkins, de Oak=
> hill prope circum Hampstead, com.
> Middlesex: admissus est Commen-
> salis. (Aet. 18—Highgate)

Some time afterwards the 'Commensalis' (Commoner) was altered to 'Exhibitionarius' (Exhibitioner), and after his father's name was added the abbreviation for 'bearer of a coat of arms'.[12]

Hopkins found ways of dealing with the nagging envy he felt towards the scholars. Secker was the Blundell scholar, and Hopkins, picking up the information that this title was for closed competition only in one school at Tiverton, found the name irresistibly suggestive and felt superior, since his own Exhibition had been won in open competition. He discovered that the 'dreadful and ghastly man' with 'grey goggle eyes', whom he had particularly noticed at the October examination, was E. M. Geldart, one of the scholars who had beaten him: 'If Cyril should see this he will gain some idea of him by imagining an exaggerated deformed brother of Worley's [a Highgate pupil]. ... I would not have had twenty Balliol scholarships to change places with him.' The other scholar who had beaten him was Barratt, described by Hopkins as looking 'commonplace'. (Barratt was to gain a brilliant treble First, in Literae Humaniores in 1865, in Mathematics in 1866, and in Law and History in the same year; Hopkins's First—in one school—was not gained until 1867, although he went up to Balliol only two terms later than Barratt.) On the staircase below Hopkins lived Ilbert, to whom the only response was hero-worship: 'He is the cleverest man in Balliol, that is in the University, or in the University, that is in Balliol, whichever you like.' As with Secker, Geldart, and Barratt, physical appearance was taken as guide to ability: 'He is also handsome and in fact is an admirable Crichton.' (The following year

Ilbert[13] duly obtained a First in Greats, won the Craven Scholarship, and was appointed to a Balliol Fellowship.) For a short time after he came up, Hopkins was nicknamed 'Poppy', which may refer to his physique.[14]

On Sunday morning Hopkins breakfasted with his father and Edward Bond, of St John's College, next to Balliol, then walked towards the delicate spire and cluster of pinnacles of the University church of St Mary the Virgin, on the High Street, to hear the University sermon.

Inside the church, the defaced moulding of one of the nave pillars showed where the platform had rested on which the three martyrs of the Protestant Reformation, Archbishop Cranmer and Bishops Ridley and Latimer, had been tried, before being burnt at the stake in the ditch a few yards away from Balliol's walls. On the opposite side of the nave was a hexagonal pulpit, from which, ten years before Hopkins was born, John Keble, a Fellow of Oriel, had preached the Assize sermon expressing his anxieties about the future of the Anglican Church. This was said to have marked the beginning of the Oxford Movement. In the 1830s, when Newman was vicar, it was to this church that the undergraduates flocked to hear the Tractarian sermons. Matthew Arnold remembered Newman

preaching in St Mary's pulpit every Sunday; he seemed about to transform and to renew what was for us the most national and natural institution in the world, the Church of England. Who could resist the charm of that spiritual apparition, gliding in the dim afternoon light through the aisles of St Mary's, rising into the pulpit, and then, in the most entrancing of voices breaking the silence with words and thoughts which were a religious movement, subtle, sweet, mournful.[15]

'For hundreds of young men', wrote Wilfrid Ward, '*Credo in Newmannum* was the genuine symbol of faith.'[16] The centre from which Newman's power went forth was the pulpit of St Mary's, 'with those wonderful afternoon sermons. Sunday after Sunday, month by month, year by year, they went on, each continuing and deepening the impression the last had made.' The service was simple, without pomp or ritualism. Its most remarkable feature was 'the beauty, the silver intonation, of Mr Newman's voice, as he read the Lessons. It seemed to bring new meaning out of the familiar words. Still lingers in memory the tone with which he read: *But Jerusalem which is from above is free, which is the mother of us all.*'[17] Among newspaper cuttings kept by Hopkins was one of a sequence of four sonnets, 'Outside St Mary's:

from the Oxford undergraduate's journal',[18] describing contradictory voices which seemed to be speaking in one church.

At five o'clock that afternoon, after his father had left, Hopkins walked the few yards from his rooms to the new Balliol chapel. Attendance at evening chapel on Sundays was compulsory. Instead of a sermon,

which I believe is never preached in our chapel—at all events there is no pulpit—after the second lesson, a lecture is delivered, on recondite metaphysical subjects. Questions are then set arising from the lecture, answers to which are shewn up to the Bursar on Tuesday morning. In fact the object is to see if we have been good and attended to the clergyman's sermon.

Unfortunately the service started at 4.30, and he missed it. 'I hope my catechecs., as they are called, may not betray me', he wrote to Oak Hill. (The term's report[19] on Hopkins shows that his absence was either excused or unnoticed.) Later that evening he wined with Brown, who had entered Balliol on the same day as himself. Brown impressed him because he was three years older, and spoke several languages. He was physically very unlike the small, schoolboyish Hopkins, large, tubby, with bulbous eyes, fashionable Dundreary whiskers, and a walrus moustache.

Hopkins had now to familiarize himself with the Oxford institutions. One of the most strange was that of the scout. The system dated back at least 150 years, and some of the Balliol scouts of the 1860s would have served the college for over thirty years. Each scout looked after one staircase, had a little room at the top or bottom of his stairs, and nearly always had a lad under him to do most of the rough chores, such as blacking boots and carrying coals. He laid out changes of clothes for students, brushed coats, supervised women bed-makers and cleaning of rooms, knocked up students before chapel in the mornings, brought them hot water for shaving, fetched breakfast and lunch for them from the buttery, and waited on them in Hall for the formal dinner each evening at half-past five. Valet and waiter, he was often also benevolent father. He had to call the students 'Sir', and they called him by his Christian name.[20]

There was a literature about the Oxford scout. Tom Brown's had been 'a stout party in black, of quiet, gentlemanly manners', who took 'the deepest interest in all my possessions',[21] while Verdant Green's, called Filcher, had 'cunning enough in his face to fill even a century of wily years', and was able to read a freshman at a glance.[22] Hopkins was soon sufficiently familiar with their characteristics to make his contribution in 'The Legend of the Rape of the Scout, Related in the Manner of Arnold and Liddell',[23] a parody of the first chapter of *The Student's Rome*, which he had read at Highgate:

It chanced that once while the younger men of Ballioli were sitting over their wine, being already, so runs the tale, heated with their cups, the discussion ran high on the respective excellences of their several scouts, each gentleman maintaining that the good fellow who served him, surpassed all others. Then, quoth one, what, Sirs, if we put our scouts to the proof. Let us plot to surprise them when they wot not we are near, and he whose serf is found most trusty he shall win the mead of glory and his catechetics shall be written for him for the term.

The 'Ballioli' men tested their scouts by returning unexpectedly to their rooms during a tedious siege 'at the room of Woolcombe':

One scout was found making away with coffee-cups that his master might get more of Hopkins, and he have a percentage, an other was decanting port in such wise that the decanter was but one third full, and another, who was a clerk, was reading Bohn's literal translations of the poet Ovid Naso's *Art of Love* on his master's shelves, and another used his master's tooth-brush and yet another was idling his time in unseemly dalliance with the washer-woman, and yet one more was quarrelling with his wife whether it were safe to take the fifth pot of Apricot Marmalade.

Only one scout proved trustworthy. On refusing a bribe to change staircases, he was threatened with the charge that he had cut his master's sofa, to reduce the room valuation. Forced to change, he 'went to Gurney's old rooms and there hanged himself'. The guilty man was sent down and had to go to the inferior Alban Hall, where he 'stirred up the minor colleges against Ballioli'.

The parody had an apparatus of etymological footnotes. One of them was a prolonged joke on the prominence of Scotsmen at Balliol, and the coincidence of the Master's name, Robert Scott. Balliol had been founded by the parents of a Scottish king and, since the seventeenth century, had always contained a small group of slightly older, experienced, sober, and learned undergraduates from Scottish universities, whose influence often seemed disproportionate to their small numbers. Immature English students sometimes felt self-protectively inclined to laugh at Gaelic pronunciation or engage in chauvinistic banter:

The original population was Scotch, but that it was reduced to subjection by the arrival of the English, and the Scots became slaves or attendants of the conquerors. Hence the name *Scot* or *Scout* became synonymous for servant. . . . *Scout* must be compared with *scuttle*—one who attends to the coals etc. . . . Doltz in his Animadversions against Püzler compares it with *scathe*, *scot*-free, so that it means a maimed or ill-used wretch. . . . In fact as the great Bentleius long ago remarked, the whole subject is wrapped in σκότος [darkness].

Another footnote recorded that one manuscript, instead of reading 'Room of Woolcombe', had 'the Room of Woolks'. The Revd E. C. Woollcombe, or 'Woolx', was, according to Hopkins in a letter to Oak Hill, 'a pinch-faced old man'—he was not yet fifty—'whom everybody likes as much as they yawn over his divinity lectures'. He was the Dean and senior tutor, and sometimes went by the name of 'Tay', because he stammered slightly over his Ts. He was considered by one of Hopkins's contemporaries to be 'the least really influential [tutor] in College. . . . of a gentle Tractarian type'. Hopkins found that in the coming term he had to attend the Divinity lectures on the Acts of the Apostles which Woollcombe was to give to a small group of freshmen; it was among this group, which included Hardy, Nash (the last of that term's four freshmen to come up), Brown, Entwisle, and Baillie (one of the college's Scotsmen), that most of Hopkins's early Balliol friendships were formed.

A less happy task of Woollcombe's was to mark off the name of each undergraduate entering the chapel at eight o'clock every morning. Hopkins found Butterfield's building, still only five years old, 'graceful', although many people regarded its colours and proportions as an obscene surrender to Balliol's desire for improvement at any cost. Its irregular horizontal bands of alternate purplish-red and yellowy-white stone were compared by Andrew Lang to streaky bacon, and several Fellows had been opposed to the neo-Lombardic Gothic style, with its priapic bell-tower. Although 'we have no choir, organ or music of any kind', Hopkins considered the building beautiful, 'and two of our windows contain the finest old glass in Oxford' (the remains of the early sixteenth-century St Catherine windows from the old, decadent Gothic chapel had been incorporated into Butterfield's building).

ॐ

In 1863 Balliol was a small college of ninety or so undergraduates, nearly all from the leading public schools. The other noticeable group was the ten from Scottish universities. Mackail's judgement that the students 'included wide diversities of upbringing' might seem myopic, but a quarter of all Balliol students during the period held a scholarship or exhibition won in open competition.[24]

Balliol's reputation, begun when Dr Jenkyns was Master (1819–54), stood high in most fields. Their tutors were considered by Balliol men, with some justification, to be the best in the university. A disproportionately large number of academic successes was gained in university examinations, and in rowing and cricket there were outstanding achievements.[25] The college was a self-sufficient society which (as Liddell said) 'consisted of a large circle of friends and acquaintances'. Whereas the larger colleges of 150 to 200 students tended to be divided into distinct sets, each leading its own life and hostile to that of the others, Balliol men claimed that theirs was a more intimate, family atmosphere. Wright-Henderson, who went up to the college the year before Hopkins, considered that

the lines which usually divide reading from non-reading men were faintly marked; both classes existed, for though all men were required to read for honours, yet some did not read very hard—nevertheless they played whist and billiards on equal terms with those who read. There was none of that suspicion and contempt, mingled with unreasoning admiration, with which the athlete and the future first-class man often regard each other, to the great loss of both.

A Balliol man was said to be recognizable by his keenness for and manner of argument. 'You could not enter a Balliol man's rooms', said Marett, 'without his offering you his theory of the universe while he likewise handed you a drink.' He would be likely to have a 'rooted tendency to question all things', and it was almost a Balliol tradition to 'flirt with what Carlyle called "the Everlasting No" before coming within reasonable distance of "the Everlasting Yes"'.

This society in which Hopkins was to move during the next four years was almost entirely male and unmarried; the only women to be seen regularly during term were the bed-makers and those in the Balliol kitchen. Oxford tutors, apart from heads of colleges, were celibate; nearly all were in orders. If a don wanted to marry he had to resign his position. They lived within their college walls on the same staircases as their students, dined in the college hall, and had few outside ties and interests. Besides facing their tutors in lectures and tutorials, students would see them at chapel, in hall, for extra tuition, and when they were invited to breakfasts or wines, besides casually passing them in the quadrangles and on the stairs.

'Young women of our own class', wrote A. G. C. Liddell, 'were a scarce commodity.' The love of women, said House, was considered 'either biological or sacramental'. There were prostitutes in the parks, and the occasional relationships, like those described in *Tom Brown at Oxford* and *The Adventures of Mr Verdant Green*, with Oxford women, besides various homosexual forms of behaviour carried over from the public schools. Some students gave the old monastical rationale for this *modus vivendi*, more or less convincingly: 'I think [the scarcity of females] was, on the whole, beneficial, as the claims of society and reading are not compatible. At any rate it suited my personal disposition.' On the other hand, R. L. Nettleship wrote in puzzled exasperation: 'There appear to be a great many people who have never really felt what it is to have "a war in their members".' The Oxford tradition of objecting to women and married dons is said to have continued well into the 1980s at All Souls.

George Saintsbury spoke of the characteristic 'curious "night wanderings" . . . from quad to quad and room to room after the gates were shut', in which 'the enormous superiority of a residential over a non-residential University consists'. Saintsbury's night wanderings at Merton in the 1860s took the form of 'a sort of hotch-potch of reading in your own or other people's rooms, playing cards, taking forty winks [or, in Oxford dialect, 'quiescing'] to put off sleep, brewing punch and drinking it. . . . discoursing on every possible subject on earth, and occasionally touching on things of Heaven'. Sometimes there would be formal and serious discussion meetings, called 'séances'.

'The older the institution and the buildings', said Saintsbury, the better for night wanderings, 'the more saturated they are with tradition'.[26] Balliol's buildings did not have the venerable unity of Merton's or Christ Church's, but apart from the Basevi block of 1825, Salvin's later buildings, and Butterfield's chapel, the college had remained largely unaltered since the eighteenth century, and its single-storied castellated group of the hall and the library–common room in the front quadrangle, with their grotesque heads carved at the top of both sides of each window, was of the fifteenth century.

Apart from afternoon walks and sporting activities, entertainment took place within college or at the Union. The Oxford world outside the college walls was one with which Hopkins had no contact. No serious theatre was allowed in Oxford during term, although there was a music-hall, the Old Vic, where the Great Vance, 'in an atmosphere of smoke and vulgarity, was wont to amuse his votaries with ribald lays'. The streets at night were often full of smock-frocked and corduroy-trousered men reeling home drunkenly, with slurred Oxford Cockney speech, to their dark, badly ventilated narrow courts in St Ebbe's, or to the mean brick cottages of Jericho, or, if they were domestic servants, to sleep in damp basements. St Ebbe's was afflicted with occasional typhoid and frequent consumption. Hopkins did not often stay out of his college after dark, except on Sundays, when there were church activities.

The Eton men at Balliol felt that Oxford was a continuation of school life. 'Eton friends and Eton ways were all around' Henry Scott Holland, for instance. Coming from a lesser school which he had gladly left, Hopkins had nothing to lose by entering a good college and all to gain. 'Everything is delightful,' he wrote in his first letter home, 'I have met with much attention and am perfectly comfortable. Balliol is the friendliest and snuggest of colleges.'[27]

# Freshman Allegiances

I do not suppose that life holds anything more enjoyable, except perhaps a successful honeymoon, than an undergraduate's first summer term at Oxford.

(A. G. C. Liddell)

He bought the usual things, attended the usual lectures, went to hear Pusey and Liddon, and so forth.

(Henry Scott Holland)

On Monday morning, 20 April, social and academic life started in earnest.[1] Hopkins had to work out a daily routine for himself:

7.15, get up, dress; 8, chapel; 8.30, breakfast; 10, lecture; 11, second lecture; 12, sometimes third ditto; 1–2, buttery open for lunch; afternoon, boating or walking and following your own devices; 5, evening chapel, which I have never yet attended; 5.30, hall; 6, the Union; 7 to bed-time, tea and preparing lectures.[2]

First came the meeting with his tutor, which took the form of a breakfast in the tower-room of Professor Benjamin Jowett. Hopkins shook the hand (said to be 'finny') of a cherubic man, who had 'a delicately rounded face, with its small mouth and chin, its great brow, and frame of snowy hair'; a mixture of 'revered schoolmaster' and an 'abbé of the old French type', a man with a high-pitched, piping voice, who was said to be 'hardly a man'.

Though not at the peak of his influence Jowett was already a legend, as a saint and sage or a heretic, depending on your viewpoint. He had been a Balliol tutor for twenty years, and had had an enormous influence on colleagues, pupils, the college's administration and reputation, and on academic and religious life. He had been refused the Mastership of Balliol on Dr Jenkyns's death in 1854, and for a time his reserve and isolation had increased. Balliol Fellows were divided into those for him and those against; there would be no majority for him for another few years. He was still 'the heretic in their midst', an 'apostate from the orthodox creed of Oxford'. Proceedings against him, instituted largely by Pusey, in the University Vice-Chancellor's Court, had recently been dismissed, but the storm over his book *The Epistles of St Paul*, and his article 'On the Interpretation of Scripture', in *Essays and Reviews*, would rage for a long time to come.

Hopkins went up to Oxford during the great years of the struggle between the High Church party of the University,[3] represented by Pusey, Canon Liddon, and Christ Church, and the liberal and utilitarian camp, represented largely by Jowett and Jowett's college. When Hopkins's contemporary Strachan-Davidson won his Balliol Exhibition, it had troubled his family's friends, to whom Oxford was chiefly 'the home of Tractarianism' and Balliol 'a hotbed of Latitudinarianism'. Mrs Humphry Ward saw 'Balliol versus Christ Church— Jowett versus Pusey and Liddon' as 'the field of battle', with both camps bearing 'the signs and symbols of mighty hosts, of great forces still visibly incarnate, and in marching array'. Jowett's salary of £400 a year as Regius Professor of Greek had been withheld from him for years on theological grounds—it came from the revenues of Christ Church, whose governing body included Pusey and Liddon. He had to exist on £40 per annum, which, as Geldart said, 'his predecessors had received in those olden times when money was worth more, when examinations were not, and when there was next to no work for the Professors to do'.[4]

Jowett 'expected his pupils to work hard, as he did. He would sometimes take their compositions after midnight. He did not spare them and he did not spoil them.' His students treated Jowett with a 'peculiar combination of awe and a desperate kind of affability', and many of them, such as Hopkins's friend Fearon, compiled dossiers of the Jowler's sayings and mannerisms. According to Geldart, Balliol students were 'man for man, on the side of their Professor. All shades of opinion, High, Broad, Low, and No-Church, united in denouncing the meanness, the malignity, the crooked perversity of the orthodox tactics.' At breakfasts, it was said, Jowett sat staring vacantly, eating little and sipping tea 'of the uncomforable college sort, lukewarm, out of a large metal pot, in big clumsy cups'. His student guests were 'stiff, awkward, shy, from their very reverence for Jowett. . . . The toast was heard crunching under desperate jaws of youths exasperated by their helplessness and silence. Nevertheless it was a great event to go— although nobody shone, neither host nor guest.' 'When you can get him to talk', said Hopkins after their first meeting, 'he is amusing, but when the opposite, it is terribly embar[r]assing.' Jowett advised him 'to be careful to have no debts beyond at latest the end of the term'.[5]

Besides being a tutor to individual students, Jowett lectured on Thucydides Book 1 to a group of freshmen which included Hopkins.[6] Other dons with whom he came into close contact in his first term were Henry Smith, the Revd Henry Wall (bursar of the college and that term's Catechetical lecturer), the Revd Edwin Palmer, and the Revd James Riddell. Smith was Savilian Professor of Geometry and Wall was Wykeham Professor of Logic. 'Oily' Smith, referred to by Hopkins as 'the mathematical master', had a 'flowing beard and flying gown', and 'an almost finicking silkiness of speech and manner'; he also had an international reputation as a mathematician; J. A. Symonds, who had left Balliol the previous year, considered him 'the greatest universal genius Oxford has'. He was known for the consideration he gave to such menial tasks as coaching freshmen for their first examination, Responsions, and it was in this role that he gave Hopkins a paper in algebra, to try his powers.

'Jimmy' Riddell, delicate in health, looks, manners, and scholarship, was well known as a Greek scholar and Christian gentleman 'almost too good for this world'. He had a quiet charm and gracious manner, which could be interpreted as diffidence, reserve, or 'extreme fastidiousness'. When he played rackets with students, the court echoed with 'his lamentations and anxious apologies for any bad stroke he made.' A student said: 'It was a pleasure to take composition to him, for a gentle sigh was his only comment on the most discreditable blunder, and he would substitute for some clumsy phrase or line an emendation which ... we should have thought to be a communication from Sophocles.' Hopkins was in Riddell's class for Aeschylus's *Eumenides*, and reported that the lectures were 'much thought of and popular'.

But Hopkins's most favourable comments concerned Palmer's lectures on Aeschines and the last six books of the *Aeneid*. Palmer's favourite method of delivering his Virgil lectures, a student said, was to 'run up and down the room with his eyes on the ground, and holding his pencil in front of him between his fingers'. He was an excessively shy man, who looked as if 'he longed every moment to bolt up the chimney'; but when he lectured, according to Hopkins, 'he does not hesitate, as in private, but reads long passages into the most beautiful fluent English'. He would 'pour forth in a quavering torrent of words a statement on the most complicated matter, delivered in a finished logical sequence, saying all that could be said on the subject'. Hopkins considered that his lectures 'shew a height of scholarship which makes me awestruck'.[7]

Balliol was renowned above other Oxford colleges for the amount and quality of the work expected from its undergraduates. Gone were the days when a Balliol tutor might say, as his did to a future Poet Laureate:

'Mr Southey, sir, my lectures are not likely to be of much value to you, so if you have any studies of your own you had better pursue them.' Its students were expected to sit for at least one honours school, and slack pupils were liable to be dismissed. Under the Balliol system, work could not be escaped. Lectures were still often 'the merely schoolboy construe-and-exercise business', though the method of teaching by individual tutorials was taking over. Composition and essay-writing for lectures and tutorials was additional.

Balliol also demanded, perhaps uniquely, the weekly essay, alternately in Latin and English, read to the Master every Saturday. At their first meeting Jowett advised Hopkins to take great pains with this essay, 'as on it would depend' his 'success more than on anything else'.[8] Most schools, including Highgate, had not valued essay-writing so highly. One ex-Etonian contemporary of Hopkins's at Balliol, A. G. C. Liddell, thought the essay 'a severe task',

and I found it uncommonly difficult to put together four pages on 'Casuistry' or the 'National Debt' in one or two hours on Friday evening. Like others of our set, I occasionally had recourse to Andrew Lang, whose good nature and extraordinary power of disquisition made him willing and able to knock off an essay on any subject in half an hour.

Scott's reputation as Master of Balliol would be overshadowed by that of his successor, but in Hopkins's time he was considered the finest scholar to have held the post. He had collaborated with Dean Liddell on the standard Greek dictionary, and his Mastership was said to be a triumph of tact at a difficult time. He was a 'handsome man, with a clear-cut somewhat bird-like face'. To some students he appeared 'stiff and austere', to others he had a 'quiet and kindly manner, under which lurked an irony which he seldom used'. He was more in evidence than most heads of colleges. The Warden of Merton kept up 'a certain godlike retirement, with occasional revelations, gracious or severe', but Scott took the weekly essay sessions, selectively: there were 'a good many of us together, [he] heard but one or two'. There were also the 'perpendiculars', hosted by Scott and his wife in the Master's lodge. Hopkins was soon aware that he would have to go to what he called 'a "wall-flower" evening at the Master's'; opinions differed as to how he would find it: 'some call it intensely stiff, others say every kindness is shewn you'.[9]

☙

On his first Monday in Oxford Hopkins was invited by Strachan-Davidson to wine in his rooms on the ground floor of the Garden quadrangle. Strachan-Davidson seemed destined for high academic honours, having won an award at both the Balliol examinations for which Hopkins sat. He had long brown hair, was very tall, not robust, quiet, courteous, and absent-minded. He and Hopkins got on well, and the next afternoon went boating on the upper river above Folly Bridge, 'Freshman's river', because its small boats were used by new students for pleasure, as opposed to the southern stretch of the Isis, where the serious boating men set off from College barges in their tub-pairs or Torpid fours or Eights to the shouts of cox and coach. Afterwards they took two of the popular canvas canoes on to the second of Oxford's rivers, the Cherwell. Hopkins conveyed his delighted sensations back to Oak Hill:

I know nothing so luxuriously delicious as a canoe. It is a long light covered boat, the same shape both ways, with an opening in the middle where you recline, with your feet against one board, your back against a cushion on another. You look, contrary of course to ordinary boats, in the direction in which you are going, and move with a single paddle—a rod with a broad round blade at either end which you dip alternately on either side. The motion is Elysian.

The Cherwell is narrow, 'satin-sliding', pensive with willows and green reflections; trees met in arches over young gentlemen sculling or punting, or supine with a book. Strachan-Davidson's canoe was low in the water, and 'the wind being very high and making waves, he shipped much water, till he said that it was more pleasant than safe, and had to get to shore and bale out the water, which had nearly sunk him'. Meanwhile Hopkins's canoe was 'washed onto the opposite lee shore', where he was comfortable but embarrassed, and 'could not get off for some time'. 'Altogether', Hopkins considered the experience 'Paradisaical. A canoe in the Cherwel [sic] must be the summit of human happiness.'[10]

The alternative way to spend summer-term afternoons was walking two or three miles along the roads from Oxford and on to country footpaths, south along the Isis towpath to Iffley and its Norman church, across the river to Bagley Wood and its wild hyacinths, south-west to the Hinkseys and Cumnor and Scholar Gipsy country, north along the river-bank, opposite the hedgeless expanse of Port Meadow, to Binsey and the ruins of Godstow Nunnery, and Wolvercote village, to suck cider-cup through straws at the Trout Inn, or north-east up the long haul to Elsfield, for its unrivalled views over several counties. Students returned with bunches of flag-flowers, the gruesome-beautiful fritillaries, hawthorn, and guelder-roses, and read until it was time for Hall.

On his first Wednesday afternoon in Oxford Hopkins walked with

W. E. Addis the three miles or so to the parish church of Saints Mary and Nicholas in the hamlet of Littlemore.[11] This walk was in the nature of a pilgrimage to the chapel Newman had built in 1836, when he was vicar of St Mary's. After the controversy over Tract 90 he had retired to his cottage at Littlemore, resigned the vicarage of St Mary's, and in September 1843 had preached his sermon on the Parting of Friends. 'The last public scene of the silent tragedy' had been enacted in Saints Mary and Nicholas. Newman had told

how he himself had found the Church of his birth and of his early affections wanting; how he was torn asunder between the claims of those he must leave behind him and those who would follow him; that he could speak to his friends no more from that pulpit, but could only commit them to God and bid them strive to do His will. His voice broke (so the tradition runs) and his words were interrupted by the sobs of his hearers as he said his last words of farewell.[12]

He had lived a life of monastic seclusion, self-denial, and simplicity, in his large, single-storied stone cottage at Littlemore, with close disciples. Two years later a Passionist monk, Fr. Dominic, heard Newman's confession, and received him into the Roman Catholic Church.

Hopkins revered this Littlemore church because it had been the setting for this moment in Newman's spiritual journey:

Littlemore Church . . . where was Newman's last sermon before the exodus. It is quite dark when you enter, but the eye soon becomes accustomed to it. Every window is of the richest stained glass; the east end, east window, altar and reredos are exquisite; the decorations being on a small scale, but most elaborate and perfect.[13]

Making the common assumption that architectural style reflected the mind of the builder, Hopkins's immediate aesthetic responses arose from his admiration for Newman. But he had assumed that the 'most elaborate' features were part of Newman's design, whereas the original interior had been plain. It had not been until after Newman's reception into the Roman Church that the coloured reredos, designed by Thomas Willement, had replaced the unpainted one of Newman's time, and the plain glass of the lancet and east windows gave way under the guidance of the Revd J. R. Bloxam, 'the father or grandfather of all ritualistics', to the yellow, red, and black praised by Hopkins. Whatever other sympathies Hopkins had with Newman, they did not share aesthetic tastes.

છ૭

It was common for undergraduates to spend the hours before or after Hall at the Union.[14] Hopkins planned to pass each evening from six to

seven o'clock there, and early in his first week he went to pay the
entrance fee which entitled him to most of the privileges of membership
without his having been elected. Although the Union had been founded
as a debating club, its other facilities were more important to most
students, in particular its extensive lending library, at the top of the
stairs of Benjamin Woodward's new building. Balliol did not have a
library for undergraduate use.

There were less imposing reading-rooms, one for newspapers, one
for weekly periodicals, and one for novels and other magazines; they
were like London clubs, with luxurious chairs. There were smoking-
rooms, and the Lower Reading-Room where coffee was served.
Hopkins was soon using the headed notepaper of the Union's writing-
room, where members' letters were stamped free, as another means of
showing off to his family, and sent off his mail from there rather than
Balliol. Most of his Balliol contemporaries had their school clubs in
Oxford, but Hopkins's school had not been sufficiently eminent to have
one.

Apart from clubs, Etonian culture, and sport, there was little from
which Hopkins could have felt himself excluded. A fortnight after
arriving in Oxford he wrote home: 'at the present rate it appears likely I
shall know all Oxford in six weeks. I have not breakfasted in my own
room for 10 days I think.' A 'breakfast' was a social institution of
Oxford university life. It took place in a student's or tutor's rooms after
Chapel; the recognized starting-time was not the usual breakfast-time
of 8.30, but 8.45, to allow the host to make sure his scout had brought
all the supplies from the buttery. The usual number present was six or
eight. J. A. Symonds described a Balliol breakfast of 1860:

Yesterday I had a very intellectual breakfast: Conington, Rutson, Green,
Tollemache, Dicey, Lyulph Stanley, and Puller. I find these breakfasts
formidable things; for there is a succession of meats, all of which I have to
dispense, to change plates, and keep people going with fresh forks and knives,
& c. It is not the custom for any scout to be in attendance, so that the host has to
do all menial offices. You would be amused to see these intellectual men begin
with fried soles and sauces, proceed to a cutlet, then taste a few sausages or
some savoury omelette, and finish up with buttered cake or toast and marmalade. Up to the sweet finale coffee is the beverage; and tea, coming when hunger
has abated, prolongs breakfast *ad infinitum*.[15]

After breakfast it was usual to bring out pipes and cigars, and the
occasion was considered the most pleasant way of having a meal and
starting the day.

Lunch was more casual and less sociable, taken in the student's
rooms if at all. The *Oxford Spectator* reported a typical frugal lunch of

1867: 'one o'clock upon each day finds me, seated at equal distances from the open window and the fire, sipping my sherry and crunching my biscuit.' It would be usual for a man to confine himself to 'bread, with cheese or butter, and beer', unless a friend dropped in. At Balliol soup was available, with cold meats, brawn, salad, pickles, and pastry. Dinner was called 'Hall'. Balliol's meals were solid and unexciting: roast beef 9*d*., rissoles 9*d*., steaks or stewed steaks 1*s*. 0*d*., curries 1*s*. 0*d*., stewed kidneys 1*s*. 3*d*. The most exotic dishes were roast duck (2*s*. 6*d*.) and half a goose (1*s*. 3*d*). Vegetables cost 2*d*., and radishes, watercress, and celery all cost 1*d*. For sweets there were jellies, creams, and ice puddings, at 4*d*. or 6*d*. George Saintsbury at Merton became a gourmet, but Hopkins merely developed a taste for his college's pastries.[16] After Hall there were 'wines', taking the form of dessert with port, sherry, or punch, and many pipes. They were less formal than breakfasts. At Merton 'men dropped in or not as they liked, and went out to billiards or cards or reading as their fancy or habit took them'. In his first term Hopkins enjoyed breakfasts, wines, and walks. 'Except for much work and that I can never keep my hands cool', he wrote to his mother, 'I am almost too happy.'[17]

ᘓ

Even in the small world of Oxford, a freshman in the 1860s had to choose his life. Although Balliol was said to be less divided into sets than other colleges, this opinion was expressed mainly by Balliol men. By his choice of set a man expressed his tastes, character, and public image. Each set was distinguished by its main interest, but also by leisure habits, friendship groups, behaviour, even clothes and speech. The lines and titles of the main sets had been established by custom and literature for several decades by Hopkins's time; the authors of *Tom Brown at Oxford* and *The Adventures of Mr Verdant Green* had lovingly delineated characteristics of the sets, and their portraits were taken as models by generations of students.

The 'fast set' was gaily dressed and monocled, and paraded the High, arm in arm. Stedman's description in 1887 is very like that of the *Oxford Spectator*'s in the 1860s, Cuthbert Bede's in the 1850s, and Thomas Hughes's Oxford in the 1840s: 'Next came three fast men, in coats and trousers of enormous and alarming patterns, with all about them of the newest and most advanced style.' The *Oxford Spectator* gave details of the 1860s set's 'gay apparel': 'The hat with curiously curved brim, the very spacious satin scarf, and the sealskin waistcoat.'

Horses were hired from Charley Symonds's stables on Holywell Street, hunters, hacks, and ponies for the two-wheeled dog-carts, easily transformed into the prohibited tandems. According to Hughes, an earnest Rugbeian meritocrat, the fast set were idle aristocrats, and during Hopkins's time a large number of the students who were sent down had distinguished names. To many students the fast set seemed creative and vivacious. But the *Oxford Spectator* dissuaded 1860s freshmen from joining them on practical grounds: 'First, a degree is seldom obtained by it; and secondly we may see, from the practice of lawgivers, that they make statutes against the peculiarities of the fast class.'

There were two sporting sets, because an earnest boating man was unlikely to be a cricketer as well. There was no serious rugby, soccer, or golf until the 1870s, and lawn tennis had not yet been invented. Racquets, fives, and real tennis were played, athletics competitions between Oxford and Cambridge began the following year, and students visited MacLaren's gymnasium for fencing and boxing. There were unrecognized sports, such as private horse races, and shooting water-rats 'from a bridge with a blow-gun'.

More students chose the river for their physical exercise, because of the surroundings and the influence of the Muscular Christians. Hopkins was not a sportsman, but before he settled into companionship with readers, walkers, and Ritualists, he showed some support for his college's physical prowess: 'We have great hopes that our boat may do brilliantly. Hopes, but hardly expectations, for one of our men [Allan Morrison] who was also in the Varsity eight has seriously injured himself, and cannot row.'[18] Balliol finished third, one place down on 1862, having been bumped by Brasenose on the first night of the eights, opposite the Cherwell, where Hopkins had gone canoeing. Canoeing, swimming, and walking were Hopkins's athletic activities at Oxford.

The reading set of the 1840s had been identified by Hughes as likely Tractarians, 'hopelessly at war' with the fast set. They had been 'quiet and studious men, such as were likely to remain up at Oxford', as opposed to 'men of more popular manners and active spirits, who would be sure to flit soon into the world'. But the reading set had been too unworldly for Hughes,

Too much like their tutors, men who did little else but read. . . . The best men amongst them, too, were diligent readers of the *Tracts for the Times*, and followers of the able leaders of the High-church party, which was then a growing one; and this led them also to form such friendships as they made amongst out-college men of their own way of thinking—with high churchmen. . . . They lived very much to themselves.

If Martin Geldart is to be believed—and there is an innocence about his first responses—Balliol students of 1863 were 'young and ardent, yet so utterly devoted to plain living and high thinking':

Never was I in an intellectual atmosphere so fearless and so free. I never knew what true tolerance without indifference was till I came to Oxford. It was a new experience to me altogether—to me, who had been brought up to regard Ritualism and Rationalism as the two right arms of the devil, to find myself suddenly launched among a lot of men who were some of them Ritualists of the deepest dye, some of them Rationalists, some of them Positivists, some of them Materialists, all eager in advancing their respective views, and yet all ready to listen with courtesy to their opponents. Nobody was shocked or offended by anything; every one was open to argument.[19]

Unlike their 1840s counterparts the Balliol reading men of 1863 were not to be identified with the High Churchmen. If there were a typical reading man he was more likely to be of the opposing party, like Strachan-Davidson, a supporter of Jowett and liberalism. There was a small High Church group in the college, and after the name of Strachan-Davidson ceased to be mentioned in Hopkins's letters home, the names of High Churchmen increased. The first of this group with whom Hopkins became friends was Addis, two years his senior, and on Sunday 3 May Hopkins commonized for breakfast with another prominent High Churchman, an Old Etonian, A. E. Hardy, who, though younger than Hopkins, had come up to Balliol the term before, and was in the same groups for Divinity, Greek, and Latin. Commonizing, Hopkins explained to his mother, was 'drawing your own commons at another man's rooms, and is very pleasant, as it enables you to enjoy a quiet meal with him and at the same time feel independance [*sic*]'. Showing off a little, Hopkins added: 'Hardy is the son of the M.P. for Leominster, of Hempsstead Hall, Staplehurst, in Kent, one of Lord Derby's government. We are great friends.'[20] In emphasizing Hardy's background, Hopkins was also preparing his mother to accept his plans for the long vacation.

The breakfast with Hardy went on so long that Hopkins became 'frightfully late', arriving at St Mary's just in time for the morning service, but missing the University sermon. After the Litany, Hopkins wrote, 'the congregation went partly into the Choir for the Holy Eucharist, partly out of church. I did the latter.'[21]

After lunch that day he walked out with Brown, having to return to Balliol for the 4.30 evening chapel. The weekly Catechetics lecture was given this term by Professor Wall. In his two more permanent college roles, as Logic Professor and Bursar, Wall was known to be 'short, clear, incisive'. His logic lectures, said Wright-Henderson, were 'not always appreciated as they deserved to be, for at that time Mill was predominant in the Oxford schools', but they were 'terse and clear', and 'enlivened by humorous illustrations, and questions suddenly addressed to the most inattentive or conceited in the lecture, exposing unknown depths of ignorance, to the comfort and delight of others no less ignorant than the victim'. Wall had a reputation as 'a strong Conservative'—'crusty old Wall', Hopkins called him—and 'found pleasure in puncturing Liberal windbags, of whom not a few, as well as windbags of the opposition persuasion, were to be found in those days ... among clever Balliol men'. Part of the spectacle this Sunday lay in seeing Jowett laugh at Wall's lecture. Wall's legendary conservatism extended to an antipathy towards organs, and Hopkins picked up the tale that, on hearing that the Master's wife 'was setting a subscription on foot for an organ for Ball. Coll. Chapel, [Wall] said that Mrs S. was not going to interfere in the affairs of the coll., and that while he was there, there shd. be no organ—and there is not'.[22]

After Hall Hopkins was invited to wine in Gurney's large expensive rooms, on No. 6 staircase in the Garden quad. Frederick Gurney, at the end of his third year at Balliol, was a senior member of the High Church group, most of whom were in their first year. Amcotts and Jenkyns, in the same lecture groups as Hopkins, were members, as well as Addis and Hardy. After the wine the group went along to St Edmund Hall, where the Revd H. P. Liddon was delivering a lecture in a series on the First Epistle to the Corinthians. Liddon was the idol of the High Church group at Balliol, as at every Oxford college. 'In the reaction which is undoubtedly taking place against Liberal opinions among the younger students at Oxford', wrote the Revd C. Kegan Paul in the *Guardian*, 'Mr Liddon stands out by the common consent of all as the man who has had the greatest sway.'

He exercises a personal open influence such as has not been known at Oxford since the days when the Heads of Houses were alarmed because the undergraduates flocked in troops to attend Mr Newman's lectures at St Mary's. .... What Newman was to the men of his time in his University, that is Mr Liddon to those of the present.

The Tractarian movement of the 1830s, instigated by Newman, had been intended to oppose 'the incoming tide of Rationalistic thought', or 'Theological Liberalism', which, starting in the early years of the century in Germany, had seemed to be threatening England. Rationalism should be opposed by 'reasserting and insisting upon the whole area of the Catholic Faith'. Although the direct work of the old Tractarians in Oxford had been more or less defeated by the joint forces of the University evangelicals and liberals, in 1863 the Tractarians' successors in Oxford, Liddon and Bishop Wilberforce, encouraged by Pusey, the surviving original Tractarian, who had reissued the famous Tract 90 in 1861 with a new preface, were renewing the fight

for the maintenance of the central positions of the Creed, not only against the teaching of those who directly denied the Faith, but also against any attempts to conciliate such opponents by surrendering any part of the Creed. Such attempts were commonly associated with the names and the teaching of Professor Jowett and Dr Stanley.

Liddon had returned to Oxford in the Lent term of 1863 after an absence, and was living in Pusey's house while his rooms at Christ Church were being made ready. He had no plans for his career, and his only regular work was preaching at All Saints', Margaret Street, and giving the Sunday evening lectures at St Edmund Hall. About three hundred undergraduates sometimes came to Liddon's 'Tea, Toast, and Testament'. Gurney was responsible for Hopkins's presence there that Sunday. Hopkins found the lecture 'I need scarcely say ... admirable'.[23] Geldart, dragged along by Hopkins to later lectures, described Liddon as 'a gaunt, cadaverous-looking man'. Mary Ward, on the other hand, observed an 'exquisite delicacy of feature', a 'brightness of eye', a 'slender willowy' body, and a 'dark head'. His message 'wore him out visibly as he delivered it. He came down from the pulpit white and shaken, dripping with perspiration. Virtue had gone out of him.' Hopkins saw Liddon's face as 'marred', a description Geldart interpreted as meaning bruised and chastised for other men's transgressions.

Liddon's voice Mary Ward found 'high and penetrating, without much variety ... but of beautiful quality, and at times wonderfully moving'. In spite of 'some awkward tricks of pronunciation, such as "jest" for "just"', Liddon's manner appealed to Geldart, and he and Mary Ward—neither of them sympathetic to Liddon's religion—liked his rhetoric and performance.

From Hopkins's letter home the next day it can be gathered that his family were not too well up in High Church politics: 'Liddon, perhaps you do not know, is Pusey's great protégé and is immensely thought of.' After the lecture, Gurney introduced Hopkins to Liddon; Hopkins wrote to his mother, 'I shall now go every Sunday evening.'[24] After a fortnight in Balliol, he was now a member of its Ritualist set, and of Liddon's wider circle of undergraduates.

Hopkins had missed the first lectures in Liddon's series. In subse-

quent weeks he took along his Greek New Testament and made notes
during the lectures, later copying out a fair version into the back of his
commonplace-book. He made detailed notes on chapters 5–7, where
Paul preached on sexual morality. Liddon seems to have assumed that
the questions asked by the Church members of ancient Corinth, to
which Paul replies, could stand for questions asked by Oxford undergraduates. It may have been the first time Hopkins heard such a serious
and reasoned advocacy of the strict Pauline code. 'Is it good for a man to
have sexual intercourse with woman at all? . . . *Answer*, If possible, it is
better not.' There were, of course, reasons for marriage, if it were
necessary: 'i. Procreation of the race; ii. the escape it affords from
fornication; iii. Mutual comfort', but Paul had advised the unmarried
not to marry, giving four reasons: '1. the impending calamities; 2. the
shortness of the time; 3. the transitoriness of all that meets the senses in
the world; 4. the alienation from religion which is in danger of being
produced by the cares of marriage'.[25]

Liddon did not appear to make any distinction between God and
Paul, or between Paul's injunctions and his own, and the prescriptive
nature of the text and emphasis of the lectures is plain: fornication was
'a sin against the body', and the body 'the temple of the Holy Ghost';
'we are not our own, to take our own pleasure—we are Christ's'.
Marriage might take place 'for the sake of avoiding fornication', but it
was morally better *not* to marry.

Also at the lecture was Sanday, who had been at Balliol before
winning a scholarship to Corpus. 'He is probably the most popular man
known to the college', said Hopkins, 'and Gurney considers him (and so
indeed does everybody else) "the most charming man" he knows. I
need not say that all I have seen of him is in accordance with this
estimate.' Sanday asked Gurney and Hopkins to his rooms in Corpus.
They arrived back at Balliol after the gate was shut, and were fined
sixpence, then they went to Hopkins's rooms, and stayed up talking.

ↄ

Jowett had advised Hopkins to be careful 'to have no debts beyond at
latest the end of the term'. Because of the relaxed credit system in 1860s
Oxford, it was easy to run into debt. For his first two years an
undergraduate could be persuaded to run up debts by importunate
tradesmen on Cornmarket or High Street, who might not send in their
bills until the third year. Manley Hopkins was taking no chances with
his son's expenditure, paying his bills, and trying to do so through

Hopkins's tutor; Hopkins had no bank account for another two years. His college buttery bill was slightly below average, and his rooms were almost the cheapest. From notes he made in subsequent years on his spending, it seems Hopkins was careful and scrupulous. But his financial dependence on Oak Hill irritated him, and his father had the annoying idea, gained from overseeing Marsland's bills at Cambridge, that Hopkins's tutor was his financial supervisor: 'Papa was really wrong about Oxford bills. The tutor does not see them, they come in to the undergraduates themselves. ... The system is quite different at Cambridge.'[26] 'I always find home so uncivilized,' Hopkins wrote later; 'they never seem to be acquainted with the ordinary luxuries or necessaries.'[27] He was at pains to prepare his father some months in advance of the Michaelmas term for a much better second set of rooms: 'I may state from numerous enquires that you cannot get decent second rooms under £35. Between this and £40 is ordinary, but if you like you may go up to £70 and £100, if you have money to spare and choose to inhabit a small palace. You get it nearly all back.'[28]

His letter to Coleridge the previous March showed that even before he went up to Oxford Hopkins felt held back by his family when he wanted to engage in new friendships. He wanted to meet Coleridge in the long vacation, 'far from Cyril', whom his family thought should be his close companion. His letters to Oak Hill in his first term try to impress by casual mention of social connections, and seek to establish a distance between Hampstead and his world, to shake off his parents' authority. He tries to diminish the Oak Hill world by denigrating Grandmamma's Oxford friend, or Cyril, or his father's knowledge of Oxford. His letters at the end of the Hilary term show strong resentment. In one he rejects his mother's pedantry: 'For 10 days I think; (*ten* days: I am afraid you will consider the numerals vulgar)', and this is followed by an ironic postscript, implying that his mother regarded his independent happiness as wilful unkindness: 'I hope you will not consider it unkind to say how happy I am, but in fact there are so many companions of my own age and so much liberty to see and do so much, that it ought not to make you think it unkind.'[29]

A fortnight after starting at Oxford he had sounded out his parents about the long vacation by a respectful letter, acknowledging that the decision about where he spent it was theirs, but insinuating that it was abnormal for an undergraduate *not* to go off on a reading party. His third and last letter that term started with a new sharpness. He had been blamed by his parents for not writing to Aunt Kate, widowed eighteen months before:

Dearest Mamma,—Then if Aunt Kate has not got the letter it is no fault of mine, but the Union's or the Post Office's. I posted it like any other letter, here, and put it in a foreign paper envelope directed to Warrington Terrace. If it has gone astray it is a thousand pities, but that is really no fault of mine. After this I cannot write an interesting letter; you have so put me out by your gratuitous blame.

To assert his rights he announced a decision to delay his return: 'I think I shall stay up to Commemoration; I do not rightly know when it begins.' A few lines further on resentment surfaces again:

Is Aunt Maria at Hampstead still? She is another of the people that make out I do not comply with little requests etc. Tell her please (if necessary, by letter when you are writing) that I came into the Angel and there waited some time to see them all, but in vain. I had intended to come in the evening but I could not get away till about eight, and then stupidly forgot all about them till just after nine when the college gates close. The next morning also I did not come at the first opportunity, and then when I did come they had just gone. I was much more disappointed than Aunt Maria, I will be bound.[30]

His new world had become all-important. At Hampstead, he wrote,

you can only see *The Times* and *Saturday* and nothing else, and the Church is dreary and friends talk of Oxford as if it were Samarkand or Bothnia Felix. . . . One of those thoroughly uneducated aunts one has (I do not mean in the vulgar sense, for she is deep in archaeology etc etc) thought College Chapels, ours at all events, were places where devotion was impossible on account of the unseemly giggling and so forth—cards behind the seats perhaps and all that.[31]

The closed gates of Balliol did not prevent Hopkins, Brown, and Hardy from proceeding 'to booze at the Mitre' eight days after the announcement that they had passed Smalls, which freshmen had to sit. For their late return they were fined threepence. Hopkins forgot to pay his share of the Mitre bill, 'but I believe Hardy meant to feast us, in his delight', having become 'light-headed, light-hearted, light-heeled', after the 'seizure of his *testamur*'.[32]

Towards the end of term a petition was got up among the liberals in the University to abolish religious restrictions on degrees. The reformers wanted to emancipate the university from the control of the Church of England, and their petition was signed by 106 college heads, professors, fellows, and other senior people. In response to this the undergraduates got up their own petition *against* the abolition of tests, and Hopkins reported: 'It has been numerously signed; there are more than 900, that is three quarters of the whole, names.' Hopkins signed, though he was 'not quite firmly convinced'.[33] His partisanship was ironic, considering the liberality with which Balliol later treated him over his conversion to Roman Catholicism.[34]

The year finished with Commemoration week. Then Oxford changed: it was not a place for dancing, said George Saintsbury, 'except at Commemoration, when the necessary objects [women] were imported'. On Show Sunday, after the Cathedral Service, there was the promenade in the Broad Walk, for all cap-and-gown Oxford, followed the next day by the procession of boats. There were balls, fêtes, and the undergraduates enjoyed themselves, as Rhoda Broughton described, 'in all the glory of their immemorial screeching'.

cಾ

During the first six months of 1863 England was optimistic. While other countries were in chaos, the prosperity and security of the royal house were reasons for self-congratulation. *Punch* viewed with superiority the Americans now 'murdering one another by the thousand', the 'sorry sight of Romans Pope-ridden by means of French physical force', the 'mournful struggle against the tyranny of the Russian bear in Poland', the king of Prussia's despotic rule without a constitution, and the crown of Greece 'going a-begging among the Royal Houses of Europe', and even felt itself licensed by the Prince of Wales's marriage to suggest that the Queen should leave off her mourning.[35]

Like the rest of Britain Oxford had been basking in the afterglow of the marriage during the summer term. On 7 March, three days before the wedding, Princess Alexandra had disembarked from the royal yacht *Victoria and Albert* at Gravesend. Newspapers and journals competed in laudatory adjectives; the *Illustrated London News* reported that a 'bevy of pretty maids, who, ranged on each side of the pier, awaited, with dainty little baskets filled with spring flowers, the arrival of the Princess, to scatter these, Nature's jewels, at the feet of the Royal lady'. Henry Nelson O'Neill, known for his ability 'to paint incidents to strike the feelings', made a crimson-flushed record of this scene (now in the National Portrait Gallery). To the rare cynics the stage-managing of these celebrations was politically astute: 'How much', reflected a Balliol don, T. H. Green, 'these festivities do to degrade people. I take it this one royal wedding postpones the chance of real reform a decade or more.' At least one of his students, Gerard Hopkins (born in the same year as Alexandra), was charmed by the 'Northern-rose-bud', and when the Prince and Princess visited Oxford for an honorary degree at the Commemoration, he took every chance to get a glimpse of her. His constancy was rewarded:

The Princess did not come. I might have known she would not. Whenever I wait on a contingency like that, inevitably I am disappointed. I am the victim of false alarms. . . . However, determined to see her once more I put myself in her way as she went to the station and got a good passing look, and, as I was alone at the particular spot, I think a bow. The Princess is different every time I see her, but in all her phases is beautiful.[36]

# 7

## Vital Truths of Nature: Hopkins and Ruskin

Hopkins spent the first week of the long vacation at Oak Hill, reading the *Georgics* with Edward Bond, whom he managed to bring round to his views on Virgil. Then the family and a cousin went to the Isle of Wight.[1] His parents considered that Gerard was not yet sufficiently established at Oxford to join a reading party, but he was able to break away at times from family amusements.

The journey took three-and-a-half hours from Waterloo to Ryde harbour. The Isle of Wight, with its land and sea views, was sometimes known as the Garden of England. When Keats stayed in Shanklin in 1817 and 1819 it was still 'a retired place', but in 1863 there were nineteen hotels, bathing-machines on the sands, and horse- and boat-trips. Visitors noticed 'a feeling of rapid expansion', particularly 'with some houses half-built, some plots vacant, and roads in a rough and ready state'. Growths of red-brick villas, disregarding the *genius loci*, stood 'in all their nakedness on the brink of the cliff'. In *Our Mutual Friend* Dickens made Shanklin the destination on their 'nuptial journey' of 'the mature young gentleman of property', Alfred Lammle, and his bride Sophronia, 'the mature young lady of property (powder and all)'.[2]

Well away from the growing residential quarter near the cliffs, the old village of leafy lanes and thatched cottages lay in a little valley sheltered by the downs. Manor Farm, the old Shanklin manor house, was at the heart of a wooded estate with hills ranged behind, just beyond the village outskirts. Francis White Popham, the sole landowner in Shanklin, who lived in the north of the island, leased it to a yeoman farmer, George Loe, who recouped some of his rent by letting part of the house for the summer to middle-class families such as the Hopkinses.[3] Manor Farm, the dominant building of a group which included a coach-house and a barn, was a large house with long casement windows and a heavily corniced roof. There were two ornamental ponds, and the house looked out over the Great Meadow. In the garden was a summer-house, said to have been a meeting-place of the Jacobite Pretender's supporters.

'Shanklin is a delightful place', Hopkins wrote to his fellow Balliol student Baillie, who had the misfortune to live in Edinburgh.

If you were here you would have soon

——forgot the clouded Forth,
The gloom that saddens heaven and earth,
　The biting East, the misty summer
And grey metropolis of the North,

where I do not envy you. The sea is brilliantly coloured and always calm, bathing delightful, horses and boats to be obtained, walks wild and beautiful, sketches charming, walking tours and excursions, poetic downs, the lovely Chine, fine cliffs, everything (except odious Fashionables). My brothers and cousin catch us shrimps, prawns and lobsters, and keep aquariums.

Hopkins's exuberance was not completely under control. His letter to Baillie continued:

I thought it would look strikingly graceful etc to wear sea-anemones round my forehead. (Mermaids do it, you know . . .). So I put a large one in the middle, and it fixed itself correctly. Now one had heard of their stinging, but I had handled them so often unharmed, and who could have imagined a creature stinging with its—base, you call it in sea-anemones? But it did, loudly, and when the pain had ceased a mark remained, which is now a large red scar.[4]

He never grew out of eccentric experimentation; after his death people remembered how as a Jesuit master he had shinned up a goal-post to cure a pupil's toothache, how he had rescued a monkey by climbing along a dangerous ledge, and how at a college meeting in Dublin he had blown pepper with a bellows through a keyhole.

He spent his mornings seriously, reading Tacitus, whom he found hard, 'and the *cruces* have a hopelessness about them which I do not think I find any where else in the classics'. He had brought with him Cicero's *Philippics* and some Greek works to study, but as he had forgotten to pack his Greek lexicon he had to stick to Latin.

While the younger members of the family—Milicent (aged fourteen), Lionel (nine), Kate (seven), Grace (six), and the youngest, Everard (still in frocks)—played on the sands and rocks, the older boys walked, sketched, and admired the scenery. Gerard and Arthur carried around pencils and tiny, gold-lettered, green, pocket sketch-books, which they had started over a year before at Hampstead. At school both Gerard and Marcus Clarke had been friendly with the drawing master, Mr Harley, but Hopkins either did not take lessons from him or dropped them when it became clear that he was of scholarship standard. In spite of the amateur sketching done by some of his relatives, Gerard does not seem to have had much practice or confidence in drawing before 1863. Arthur was the more advanced and accomplished artist, Gerard more tentative, still in the stage of trying to copy details from nature, and rarely spending much time on a sketch or finishing it.

Gerard completed an accurate but dull sketch of the farmhouse; one suspects it was done at the family's request. The early eighteenth-century house must have been attractive, with its creepered, spacious proportions and vast roof, chimneys like steamer funnels, and its doors and windows flung open to the July sun. But the drawing is heavy and clumsily precise, some lines drawn with the aid of a straight edge, and the angles of the side-wall to the right of the house are wrong. He did close and detailed indoor sketches of an iris and a carnation, with a sharply pointed pencil (probably too hard); the shape is good, but there is no ability to suggest texture. One day he walked westward to the Cliff Copse, making a delicate sketch on the spot, and some time afterwards preparing it carefully for display.

The 1863 Shanklin sketch-books show that the first joint sketching trip the brothers made was on 19 July, when they walked about five miles north, past Sandown to the Culver cliffs. This was a well-known view painted by several artists, including James Collinson, friend of the Pre-Raphaelites.[5] From the rocks below, on the edge of White Cliff Bay, both brothers sketched the striated cliff-face, where bands of flint intersected the chalk. Gerard's surviving sketch is perfunctory, showing the outlines of the cliff and the stripes, but little else, while Arthur made three separate studies, one of them beautifully finished. The same day Gerard made a stiff, hard-edged drawing of the buds of a white lily, probably taken from the circular pond in the ornamental garden of Manor Farm; again, he was more successful at suggesting outline than texture. Arthur waited two days and drew the same lily stem, after a circling group of the lower buds had opened. His softer sketch has more variety of texture and shape, and is more sensitive in observation.

Ruskin's *The Elements of Drawing* had finished with a stirring athletic exhortation:

But take knapsack and stick, walk towards the hills, by short day's journeys,—ten or twelve miles a day—taking a week from some starting-place sixty or seventy miles away: sleep at the pretty little wayside inns, or the rough village ones; then take the hills as they tempt you, following glen or shore as your eye glances or your heart guides, wholly scornful of local fame or fashion, and of everything which it is the ordinary traveller's duty to see, or pride to do. . . .

gradually the deeper scenes of the natural world will unfold themselves to you in still increasing fulness of passionate power.[6]

A walking tour of four days, from Wednesday 22 July to the following Saturday, can be plotted from two sketch-books which show a series of nearly identical locations stretching from Shanklin along the coast, 'the back of the Wight', to the Needles, the westernmost point of the island. The length of the trip may have been limited by the following Sunday's church service at St John the Baptist's, Shanklin, where all the family would be expected to turn out, and by the need to be back for Gerard's nineteenth birthday on the Tuesday.

The south coast of the Isle of Wight has luxuriant vegetation, and its scenery is wild and gentle. The famous chines, cliff-to-shore chasms, are not terrifying or sublime; the streams which run down to the shore would mostly be mere trickles in July. From Shanklin Gerard and Arthur took the high path on the outskirts of Luccombe through the hazel thickets and past the oaks of the Landslip, with its ferns, holly, and ivy, to emerge on the coastal path. After two miles they reached the village of Bonchurch, where Admiral Swinburne's twenty-six-year old son, Algernon, a protégé of Jowett's at Balliol, had that year begun a poem 'When the hounds of spring are on winter's traces'. On leaving the myrtles, fuchsias, clianthus, and verbena of Bonchurch they walked underneath the vast chalk St Boniface Down to Ventnor, overrun with holiday-makers and low-class lodging-houses, and then took the Undercliff walk of nearly seven miles, a series of irregular terraces detached from the cliffs above, with sea to their left and woods, secluding occasional cottages or a church, on their right.

In the recess of the village of St Lawrence lay the elegant Marine Villa of the Earl of Yarborough, and the brothers sketched a group of elms in the woods of the Villa. After the Undercliff they walked, by cornfields and blackberry hedges, along the coastal path to Walpen Chine, a chasm worn through the strata by an orange-brown streamlet, which eventually fell in a cascade over a ledge to the beach. There was no path down, and Arthur and Gerard stayed at the top looking out to sea. A gale did not deter Gerard from making a quick sketch of the Chine's main lines of rock. They had walked not much more than eleven miles that day. They probably lodged at the New Inn, Brighstone, the only inn between Walpen Chine and their first sketch-ing stop of the next day, the Long Stone at Mottistone, an ancient ceremonial sandstone pillar, thirteen feet high.

They walked along the cliff tops to Freshwater Gate, where the chalk was scored with parallel lines of black flint, running obliquely from base to summit of the cliff. On the shore, severed from its parent cliff, stood the Arched Rock, a curiosity said to resemble part of a ruined abbey. Perched on top of the crumbling high cliffs on patchy dry grass, the brothers peered down. The sketches they made from the 'Freshwater Cliff above' form a most interesting comparison. Arthur's two were simple shape and light-and-shade representations of the Arched Rock, not accurate, and probably completed at home. Gerard avoided the obvious view, and sketched the convergence of two masses of sea-water. Whereas Arthur intended a picture for an onlooker, Gerard concentrated intently on capturing what was happening. He felt his drawing was inadequate and wrote underneath

Note. The curves of the returning wave overlap, the angular space between is smooth but covered with a network of foam. The advancing wave already broken, and now only a mass of foam, upon the point of encountering the reflux of the former. Study from the cliff above.

Gerard's is the work of a Ruskinian student of nature rather than an artist; he needed the words to make the experience complete.

They continued their walk along the cliff-top, stopping at Sun Corner, a wave-worn bluff where Gerard made a study of the cliff's parallel black stripes, and finally reached the Needles, isolated chalk wedges dramatically rising out of the sea in a straight line with the island's final westward promontory. They sketched two of the rocks from the downs above, in an evening sun; the water was so still that the rocks were firmly reflected. For once the brothers' sketches were nearly identical. The following day they walked eastwards along the downs from Freshwater. On Shalcombe Down Gerard looked towards the pretty village of Brook, and sketched the church of St Mary the Virgin, which he mistakenly thought to be in ruins. This view is now obscured by trees, but inside the church hangs a small watercolour of the same view as Hopkins's, showing the church with its tower but without its present spire.

On Saturday they visited the fine ruin of Carisbrooke Castle, a mile south-west of the capital Newport, and climbed the flight of seventy-two broken steps to the Saxon keep. From the summit of the battlements there were remarkable views all around, but Hopkins chose to make a sketch looking down on two insignificant ruined parapet walls with a sickening fall immediately below. His sketching positions here and on the Freshwater Cliffs show that he had no fear of heights or precarious positions.

The journal Hopkins kept at this time was destroyed, and there are no records of his thoughts and feelings. We know that on the way back from Carisbrooke to Shanklin he visited Godshill and its church of All Saints, because in August 1868 he noted that 'one of the crosses [at St Albans] was a tree, as at Godshill, Isle of Wight'.[7] This pre-Reformation church was popularly known as 'the Church of the Lily Cross', owing to the medieval mural on the east wall of the south transept, which showed Christ crucified on a triple-branched flowering lily, symbol of purity and sinlessness. Just over a mile from the church was Appledurcombe House, seat of the Worsley family, whose monuments dominated the church; from Appledurcombe Hopkins made a sketch of a beech sapling growing on the mound in front of Godshill church, which has since become his most well-known drawing. There is now a fully grown beech tree on the spot.

After their sketching trip Gerard and Arthur made two further pairs of sketches together, one in the American woods near Shanklin, and the other of Shanklin Chine, which Keats had described as 'a cleft between the cliffs of the depth of nearly three hundred feet'.[8] It was a visitors' attraction; one you had to pay to see and to walk up the narrow path by its side. Gerard took up a position in the middle of the wooden bridgeway, at the foot of the topmost fall of the Chine. Like others of his, this sketch gives an outline idea of the area surrounding his main interest. His eyes became busily engaged only around the top of the waterfall, distinguishing complex items of interest and recording them in detail. Later he tried to emphasize the foreground detail by thickly blackening in the shadows, but his uncertainty shows up against the business-like drawing completed by his brother. Arthur filled in every bit of space, sacrificing the sense of the Chine's dramatic cliff-fall, which Gerard captured. Arthur had taken up a position fifteen paces further on up the Chine path, so that he was over the chasm, and had nothing to lead the eye into his drawing, but Gerard had placed himself on the path, and could use its lines to guide the onlooker. Gerard had a better sense of the delicately shimmering leaf-rafts above the gangway bridging the chasm, but Arthur avoided detail in order to finish the sketch.

A comparison of the other island sketches shows that Arthur attempted completed pencil pictures of conventional subjects, such as St John's church at Shanklin and a sailing vessel at sea, while Gerard took up, with more enthusiasm than science or persistency, the elementary Ruskinian subjects of sunset lineaments, with verbal colour annotations, and line-indications of wave- and sea-patterns. Often words obtrude onto the pages of the sketch-book; his mind's occupation could not be expressed solely by the sketch. Besides the drawing of overlapping waves at Freshwater Gate there is a sunset sketch annotated: 'N.B. As time went on, after sunset, clouds richer red purple, edges red gold and living orange. Dabblings of gold on the clouds.' He was interested in progression, a quality which in Victorian times visual art ignored; in other ways, too, his inclinations did not match the kind of training needed by a professional artist.

Hopkins's sketching was an expression of his way of looking at nature rather than a purely artistic occupation. The most detailed and delicate of all his extant sketches, and perhaps the only one which does not show impatience, is one of a hedgerow cluster of many different kinds of leaves and plants, done on Saturday 11 July. Later he framed it in a circle and highlighted details, as Ruskin suggested, by blackening the undergrowth background. When he made this sketch he had started a letter to Baillie which remarked the 'most deliciously graceful ashes' in the neighbourhood:

I think I have told you that I have particular periods of admiration for particular things in Nature; for a certain time I am astonished at the beauty of a tree, shape, effects etc, then when the passion, so to speak, has subsided, it is consigned to my treasury of explored beauty, and acknowledged with admiration and interest ever after, while something new takes its place in my enthusiasm. The present fury is the ash, and perhaps barley and two shapes of growth in leaves and one in tree boughs and also a conformation of fine-weather cloud.[9]

There is a page of studies of ash-twigs which may belong to this time. At the periphery of each group of twigs is a rough connecting curve, which resembles what Ruskin illustrated in a drawing and called 'the bounding curve': 'each [branch] has a curve and a path to take . . . and each terminates all its minor branches at its outer extremity, so as to form a great outer curve.'[10]

∽

Hopkins's arrogance, reinforced by stubbornness, surfaced when he pursued one of his compulsive lines of interest. He had to choose his own questions, work out judgements according to his own rules and impulses, and find answers in his own time. Those authorities which he accepted were chosen by intuition or sense of affinity, rather than by reason or respect for tradition. His obstinate independence of mind was constantly deflated by his recognition of areas of ignorance where he needed authority. His tendency was to find books more attractive than tutors; however authoritative it pretended to be, a book was a tool, which could be used as his impulse suggested. It was predictable that he would choose Ruskin.

After Hopkins's first term at Balliol, Oxford past and present offered him new standards and authorities. Oxford was the home of taste, and Hopkins was following in Ruskin's footsteps. Ruskin had been a gentleman commoner at Christ Church, one of the foremost of Oxford colleges and eventual home of the High Church leaders Pusey and Liddon; he won the Newdigate prize and spent his time drawing, studying nature and architecture, and writing. Leaving Oxford through bad health before graduating, he had been awarded an honorary degree, and by 1863 was famous, having published *Modern Painters*, *The Seven Lamps of Architecture*, 'Pre-Raphaelitism', and several *Notes on some of the principal pictures exhibited in the rooms of the Royal Academy*. *Modern Painters* was published under the pseudonym 'A Graduate of Oxford'. When he came to work out aesthetic questions in his dialogue 'On the Origin of Beauty',[11] Hopkins made the setting an Oxford one (the trees he spoke of are still there), and his Ruskin-like Professor of Aesthetics had been newly appointed to an Oxford chair.

Whether or not Hopkins realized the full extent of his debt, the source of many of his ideas about the laws of nature, although expressed in his highly idiosyncratic ways, was Ruskin. He had probably not read *Modern Painters* thoroughly in 1863, as the work appears in a list he drew up in February 1865 of books that he should read,[12] but he may have been familiar with *The Elements of Drawing*, which had been written in response to readers of the first volume of *Modern Painters* who asked Ruskin for a practical drawing manual. The whole book is crucial to Hopkins's ways of looking at nature and expressions of his reactions to it. Ruskin aimed at teaching to see, teaching to draw being secondary in importance; the aim of drawing was not learning a skill but learning to appreciate nature. From Ruskin's great principle, that art should be made, not by learning from general ideas or words, but by looking at natural objects, stem all Hopkins's debts to Ruskin.

Like Ruskin, Hopkins meant to record, and to 'obtain quicker [i.e. more alive] perceptions of the beauty of the natural world, and to preserve something like a true image of beautiful things that pass away'.[13] Ruskin's values became Hopkins's: the basic earnestness of response to nature, recording nature rather than inventing, and the elegiac inference which would become predominant in Hopkins's poetry, that natural beauty was unique, momentary, and vulnerable to time and man's impiety. In *Modern Painters* and *The Elements of Drawing* Ruskin expressed his faith in the significance and representative quality of a detail: 'If you can paint *one* leaf, you can paint the world.' Hopkins worked primarily through engaging the senses with detail, having come to Ruskin's conclusion about the grand significance implicit in nature's smallest part. Nature possessed superhuman subtlety, and in comparison man lacked imagination; man should be led by nature to look into the heart of things.

For example, man should see contrast rather than be satisfied with blandness: 'all natural shadows are more or less mingled with gleams of light. . . . in the darkness of foliage, the glitter of the leaves; . . . in that of a stone, granulation; in every case there is some mingling of light.'[14] Ruskin called attention to the productive clash of opposites in nature and art. He pointed to the importance of natural contrast-patterns by advocating 'drawing patterns, and any shapes of shade that you think pretty, as veinings in marble or tortoiseshell, spots in surfaces of shells, etc., as tenderly as you can'.[15] Ruskin also advocated imitating artificial patterns as 'introductory to the nobler complication of natural detail': 'the dead leaf-patterns on a damask drapery, well rendered, will enable you to disentangle masterfully the living leaf-patterns.'[16] In 'Spelt from Sibyl's Leaves' Hopkins used 'damask', taken from a pattern on woven cloth, to image a reduction of patterning in nature: 'Only the beak-leaved boughs dragonish damask the tool-smooth bleak light; black,/ Ever so black on it.'

Hopkins's 'fury' for the ash and 'two shapes of growth in leaves and one in tree boughs' comes from Ruskin. 'Draw first only two or three of the leaves', advised Ruskin, followed by 'larger clusters' and then 'more and more complicated pieces of boughs and leafage',[17] learning the shape of a tree-spray seen against the sky. The student should make 'careful studies of this kind of one bough of every common tree,—oak, ash, elm, birch, beech, etc.'.[18] Only after making drawings of sprays was the student ready to try 'the extremities of the real trees'. The form of a tree in its 'inimitableness' typified all natural objects, wrote Ruskin. 'If leaves are intricate, so is moss, so is foam, so is rock cleavage, so are fur and hair, and texture of drapery, and of clouds.'[19] The student should avoid 'all very neat things'—'Long live the weeds and the wilderness',[20] Hopkins agreed. Hopkins's close focus on texture and divergent growth was first a passion of Ruskin's: 'Choose rough, worn, and clumsy-looking things as much as possible.'[21] Hopkins's verbal sketches of natural details are his transference of Ruskin's precepts to the medium of words.

Foliage was the most important study to both Ruskin and Hopkins. Ruskin said,

First, that it is always accessible as a study; and secondly, that its modes of growth present simple examples of the importance of leading or governing lines. It is by seizing these leading lines, when we cannot seize all, that likeness and expression are given . . . and grace and a kind of vital truth to the rendering of every natural form. I call it vital truth, because these chief lines are always expressive of the past history and present action of the thing.[22]

The purpose of Dürer's lines was to give 'a true "signalement" of every nut-tree, and apple-tree, and higher bit of hedge'.[23] 'Signalement', the technical term in French law and science for a schedule of particulars serving to identify an individual or a genus, is the single word closest in meaning to 'inscape'. These 'leading lines' appeared in every natural object; in a wave or cloud they 'show the run of the tide and of the wind, and the sort of change which the water or vapour is at any moment enduring in its form, as it meets shore or counter-wave'.[24] Hopkins's sketch from 'Freshwater Cliff above' was that of a Ruskin student, while Arthur's belonged to common contemporary practice. The natural memoranda in Hopkins's journals are based on Ruskin. The man who could distinguish characteristic movement in nature was, to Ruskin, a more skilful artist than one who could not. The characteristic form of an object in nature could often not be seen in its momentary appearance, but it remained constant throughout the object's history, so finding this characteristic form depended on perceiving movement.

Ruskin's natural descriptions are full of verbs and nouns of movement: 'the boughs spring . . . stoop less and less', the 'plumy toss of the tree branches', a stem 'does not merely send off a wild branch here and there to take its own way', 'all the branches share in one great fountain-like impulse', 'each has a curve and a path to take', 'filling the united flow of the bounding curve', 'to throw the great mass of spray and leafage'.[25] The words are less distinctive than Hopkins's, but the referends and principles are the same. Foliage has not so much shape as lines of action.

It was probably Ruskin's constant advocacy of making memoranda which prompted Hopkins: 'make a hasty study of the effect' if time is short. 'If the subject seems to you interesting, try to get five spare minutes to go close up to it, and make a nearer memorandum . . . that you may thus perfect your experience of the aspect of things.' Although the notes Ruskin recommends are sketched outlines, not words, their result is close to Hopkins's verbal descriptions of nature: 'This kind of study is very convenient for carrying away pieces of effect which depend not so much on refinement as on complexity, strange shapes of involved shadows, sudden effects of sky, etc.'

It was Ruskin's discussion on the laws of unity in nature, mostly based on leaves,[26] which Hopkins reworked into his Platonic dialogue 'On the Origins of Beauty'. The 'great object of composition', Ruskin wrote, was 'always to secure unity', and he gave the chestnut-fan as example. In Hopkins's dialogue the Professor of Aesthetics uses a chestnut-fan in New College gardens to reach the Ruskinian conclusion that variety was preferable to uniformity. Hopkins added another Ruskinian remark, that trees form their natural shape only when uninfluenced by man, and the dialogue then becomes a muddled reiteration of Ruskin's better-ordered arguments.

Hopkins develops the argument in the dialogue by introducing other Ruskinian precepts, particularly the 'Law of Contrast', by which 'the character of everything is best manifested': 'every form and line may be made more striking to the eye by an opponent form or line near them.'[27] For both Ruskin and Hopkins continuity was associated with breaks in the series. Similarly, the law of interchange enforced 'the unity of opposite things, by giving to each a portion of the character of the other'.[28] It was a great help to Hopkins that Ruskin constantly universalized his observations by drawing parallels with other art-forms. In the concluding paragraph of the *Elements*, for instance, Ruskin wrote: 'All noble composition . . . can be reached only by instinct. . . .You may see it, and seize it, at all times, but never laboriously invent it.'[29] This process of 'seizing' is what Hopkins meant when he said 'I *caught* this morning morning's minion' in 'The Windhover'; he had not invented the falcon but had instinctively gathered it into his composition.

Ruskin did not have the same difficulty as most people in the 1860s in seeing the hyperphysical in the physical; there was no hyperbolic leap from the visual perception of an object to a moral vision. It was Ruskin who demonstrated to Hopkins how his aesthetic reactions to nature could be ethically justified. 'All nature is mechanical', Hopkins would write at Teignmouth in 1874, 'but then it is not seen that mechanics contain that which is beyond mechanics.'[30] Hopkins set out in his drawings, his journals, and then his poetry, to understand what Ruskin called 'the aspects of things', which were 'so subtle and confused that they cannot in general be explained', and determinedly to delve into their subtleties.

These interests seemed to be leading Hopkins towards a career as a professional painter, but in summer 1863 there was no urgency for him to make a choice. There is no indication that he considered following his father into the City, and Manley must have been influenced by the knowledge that his next youngest son, Cyril, who had left school to join Manley's firm, would provide the backbone the family needed. Arthur, still at Lancing, would join the family firm, though he left after two years to take up an artistic career. Hopkins's early wish to be a painter was romantic and unusual for an Oxford undergraduate; most of his Balliol contemporaries would train for the legal profession or the ministry, while others would enter public service or teaching.[31] It is likely that Ruskin's example again provided sanction. It may never have crossed Hopkins's mind that so reputable a system, given unstinted praise by everyone, including Wordsworth and Tennyson, would lead him into difficulties. But one of Ruskin's beliefs—that natural data must be *felt*, not learnt—was to cause profound disturbances for Hopkins and his poetry.

# Useful Information

Hopkins always needed someone with whom he could share creative discoveries. If there were no obvious candidate, he would force the role on someone. Opposition was sometimes more valuable than agreement. The acquiescent Canon Dixon would prove a less valuable critic than the robustly sceptical Bridges. During the long vacation of 1863 Mowbray Baillie was bullied into becoming Hopkins's sparring partner.

Baillie was the son of an Edinburgh doctor, and had been outstanding at his school, the Edinburgh Academy.[1] He gained a Balliol 'Domus' Exhibition, like Hopkins. His rational mind was said to have been 'a very valuable quality in him for those of his friends who possessed the "artistic temperament" '.[2] Hopkins was irritated by Baillie's intellectual stances, but this was an opposition to make him self-critical. Baillie made him see himself as motivated by irrational fits of enthusiasm, of which he wrote: 'I have told you that I have particular periods of admiration. . . . for a certain time I am astonished . . . when the passion has subsided . . . acknowledged with admiration . . . something new takes place in my enthusiasm. . . . the present fury . . . an insane fury induced me to ravage it—None, I think, but an idiot could.'[3] Baillie represented 'the so-called Logical Mind', which needed rational proofs; he distrusted general rules.

At first Hopkins did not know what to make of this Scotsman, only a year older than himself, but more mature and self-sufficient. He tried to provoke him out of his rationality with anti-Scots prejudice: the footnote on 'Scout', for example, seems designed for Baillie.[4] Baillie responded by saying that 'prejudices are *ipso facto weak* and foolish', to which Hopkins replied that they were, 'on the contrary, often a passive, and sometimes almost an active wisdom'.[5] He strongly resisted Baillie's belief that there could be no such thing as a great critic, trying not only to answer but to provoke him, saying with a pretence at logic that this was a prejudice uttered by one who denied the value of prejudices. He pointed to Ruskin as a critic whom Baillie admired, because he was one of those whose 'excellences utterly outweigh their defects', a man 'whose whole powers have been devoted to criticism, powers which in their time are perhaps equal to those of the men whose works he criticises'.[6]

But Hopkins needed Baillie as more than an opponent. He was put out by Baillie's refusal to offer an opinion on his translation of a chorus from *Prometheus Bound*; he needed Baillie's responses: 'I come under the list of those whom you anathematize so much, the writers of new unnecessary poetry, and need a critic often, and often am dispirited.'[7] He found himself thinking thoughts he recognized as having been expressed by Baillie:

I will be humble to you on one of your tenets, I mean General Rules. Although I had had opinions resembling yours before, yet you had arrived at a definite decision on them which I could not at first fully enter into. You were in advance. I am now seeing the truth of your objection to them. My daily experience is stumbling on them and rubs its shin cursing; if you see the force of the metaphor.[8]

A year later he found that Baillie had again anticipated a judgement of his, but instead of still feeling defensive enjoyed the coincidence of minds:

Do you know, a horrible thing has happened to me. I have begun to *doubt* Tennyson. (Baillejus ap. Hopk.) It is a great *argumentum*, a great clue, that our minds jump together even if it be a leap into the dark. I cannot tell you how amused and I must say pleased and comforted by this coincidence I am.[9]

'We are both right in this', he added, and his judgement had been confirmed when he read Tennyson's new volume, *Enoch Arden*.

In spite of Baillie's earlier response to his verse, Hopkins soon came to value Baillie as one of his two critics. The other was Edward Bond, whose role aroused a schoolboyish sense of rivalry in Baillie: 'You know', wrote Hopkins, 'I did not say you were "not such a pleasant critic to keep as Bond". On the contrary Bond would be, was in fact, much more severe; but he has not your great reticence, and blames and praises boldly, so that one knows what he means.'[10]

The shared enthusiasm was Art; Baillie was Hopkins's 'sole congenial thinker on art', and had to put up with lists of paintings Hopkins had seen and gushingly admired in the Royal Academy, the Junior Water-Colours, and Old Masters exhibitions. Later, a freshman, L. B. C. Muirhead, was 'said to spend his time in reading Art subjects', and Baillie and Hopkins thought of 'assuming him'.[11] It was to Baillie that Hopkins submitted his Ruskinese sketches of ash, barley, and 'two

shapes of growth in leaves and one in tree boughs and also a conformation of fine-weather cloud'.[12] Again he was hampered by Baillie's
reticence, but persevered, and Baillie became the audience that mat-
tered. He could understand Hopkins's sketches and his thoughts about
art and particular artists. In artistic disputes with Hopkins, Baillie said
later that he always took 'the common obvious uninspired view of the
"Man in the Street"'.[13]

Hopkins and Baillie read and admired Ruskin, and Hopkins's references to him in letters to Baillie are frequent, concerning several
different types of criticism. He accepted Ruskin's account of the birth
of Gothic architecture on the deathbed of Romanesque,[14] and started
writing comments on the lines of Ruskin's Royal Academy notes.
Baillie took over Marcus Clarke's role of someone to whom he could
praise Millais:

About Millais' Eve of S. Agnes, you ought to have known me well enough to be
sure I should like it. Of course I do intensely—not wholly perhaps as Keats'
Madeline but as the conception of her by a genius. I think over this picture,
which I could only unhappily see once, and it, or the memory of it, grows upon
me. Those three pictures by Millais in this year's Academy have opened my
eyes. I see that he is the greatest English painter, one of the greatest of the
world.[15]

Such admiration shows Hopkins's inexperience in looking at pictures:
he had insufficient knowledge of foreign painters to judge Millais, and
indeed his later judgements of paintings remain insular.

By the end of his first year at Balliol Hopkins's enthusiasm
for painting had grown, though he still preferred excited lists of
pictures and painters to detailed criticism: 'there were numbers of
Gainsboroughs, Sir Joshuas and Romneys. Romney is like them. Five
Velasquezes, a Murillo, a Zurbaran, many Canalettos, which I have
now unbared. ... There were also Carlo Dolces, a Sasso Ferrato,
Correggios, Rembrandt's Mill, Vandycks, Wouvermans, Tenierses,
Hobbimas, a charming Cuyp, Holbeins, and a fine early landscape
painter we have, Crome of Norwich.'[16]

During one vacation he met Christina and Maria Rossetti and
Holman Hunt at the Gurneys in Hampstead,[17] and started making notes
for an essay, 'Some Aspects of Modern Mediaevalism', by listing
members of the Pre-Raphaelite Brotherhood, together with Ford
Madox Brown and similar French and German painters; but he showed
by vaguenesses and mistakes that he was unfamiliar with all three
schools.[18] The essay was not to be confined to painters, as R. W. Dixon,
the Brownings, and Christina Rossetti were listed. Hopkins was feeling

so confident of his artistic abilities that he confided in Baillie: 'I have now a more rational hope than before of doing something—in poetry and painting. ... about the latter I have no more room to speak, but when I next see you I have great things to tell.' This news was probably about his meeting with the Irish painter F. W. Burton, who was familiar with German art, and would in 1874 become Director of the National Gallery. Hopkins had asked him questions about art history and the profession of painter; an entry in his diary reads: 'Mem. To ask Mr Burton about picture-frames, price of models, whether the pictures by W. S. Burton in the Academy are his, about the Preraphaelite Brotherhood, the French Preraphaelites, the Düsseldorf school etc'. Burton gave him the leading names of the modern medievalist schools, sketched architectural details in Hopkins's notebook to illustrate points about architects' drawing, and suggested that, instead of employing models for drawings, Hopkins should obtain *Fau's Anatomie*, a book of engravings for painters and sculptors.[19]

The lesson of his sketching exercises at Shanklin—that his talents did not lie in pictorial art—had not been absorbed. He was thinking of following in the footsteps of Oxford-educated artists such as Burne-Jones, who had been at Exeter College before becoming a painter, or Alfred William Hunt (highly praised by Ruskin), who had won the Newdigate Prize for English Verse and became a university Fellow before devoting himself to art. But there is no evidence that Hopkins followed up Burton's suggestions or devoted any subsequent time to painting.

ℰℐ

Hopkins came up for the Michaelmas term 1863 on Saturday 17 October, with the majority of the undergraduates. He found he had been allocated rooms in the Garden quadrangle, on staircase 6 in the ten-year-old Salvin buildings, a long, quiet, comfortable, honey-coloured stone block, in a medieval domestic style, where he would live for most of the next three years.

His outer door opened into a small hall, off which were sitting-room, bedroom, and the scout's hole. This arrangement, he wrote to his mother, 'gives me the advantages without the disadvantages of a ground floor room for I am able to run in and out without climbing a flight of stairs, while my window is too high to be looked into [seven feet above the level of the quadrangle] and yet comfortably placed so as to look and talk out of'.[20] His sitting-room window, of three arched lights, looked out on to the paths, flower-beds, trees, and lawns of the Garden quad. During the next Christmas vacation his sitting-room was repapered in 'a charming pattern', and the cornice painted. The mantelpiece was covered with 'a clot and fringe of the colour of stewed pears with white china-headed nails for nobs of cream'. His scout inveigled him 'into buying two new pairs of candlesticks of him, the old glass pair having cracked when the candles burnt down into their sockets'. Two of the new candlesticks were of 'black iron of a leafy, branchlike or wreathen kind', while the other pair was 'of shiny metal like silver'; they gave 'a *distingué* air' to the mantelpiece, and the room as a whole looked 'much more spruce'.[21] His bedroom was 'very good indeed, airy, light and comfortable'. Two narrow windows looked down on to St Giles, with St Mary Magdalene church to the left and the Martyrs' Memorial to the right. The Salvin building was said to be 'cold from being entirely of stone', but Hopkins found that his 'rooms get hot enough in the evening with the fire'. He had a fireplace in both rooms, and there were weekly deliveries of coal and faggots for firelighters.

Conveniently, in the room immediately above Jowett held classes. It was Balliol's first purpose-built lecture-room, with a raised platform at one end and a fireplace in the middle, pleasant, with large windows, one bay jutting over Hopkins's room which looked on to St Giles. The trees in front of his sitting-room windows 'make it rather dark, but in the darkest part of the year of course they are bare'. The darkness Hopkins felt to be justified, nature being more important than his convenience, but others, particularly Balliol infidels, thought differently:

They have cut down the beautiful beech in the Garden Quad, which stood in the angle of Fisher's buildings, because it was said to darken the rooms. This is a wicked thing; such a beech no doubt has not its like in Oxford, being a rare tree here. Its destruction is owing to the Fellows Green and Newman. The former is of a rather offensive style of infidelity, and naturally dislikes the beauties of nature.[22]

Much better to have pulled down the building and 'let the tree stand'.

Hopkins's daily path to Hall was a fifty-yard stroll through the quadrangle and through the entrance under the Salvin Tower. He was settling into the habit of spending less each week on buttery fare than the average student, having two entries most days instead of the usual three.[23] His weakness was pastries, in which he indulged more than most Balliol students. He did not feel completely settled in. Elizabeth, the nursemaid at Oak Hill whose job it had been to pack his luggage for Oxford, had left out his dumb-bells; he was not quite as self-conscious about size as he had been because there was 'a much littler person than I come to Balliol'.[24] This 'quite infantine' person was probably A. Anderson, a freshman that term, who posed for a photograph with Hopkins and other Balliol undergraduates later that Michaelmas term. He needed a new kettle-holder, and wanted portraits of 'Raphael, Tennyson, Shelley, Keats, Shakespeare—Milton, Dante, Albrecht Dürer'.[25] These names appear in the Pre-Raphaelite list of 'Immortals' with the exception of Dürer, championed by Ruskin in *The Elements of Drawing*.

Money was still a worry, though he was careful and not badly off: he had at least four sources—his school Exhibition, the Balliol Exhibition, his father, and Grandfather Smith, who the following Christmas gave him a 'most acceptable' present of cash.[26] On at least one occasion he received a gift of money from Grandmamma Hopkins. The estimated lowest rate at which an undergraduate could live for the six months in residence each year was £126; the average was said to be £177. His father still did not let him have his own bank account. 'I am sorry to say', he wrote to his mother, 'my scout has just told me that Wall the Bursar has remarked that he has struck my cross off but that I have not yet paid my fees (and caution-money). So I hope Papa will send the money as quickly as he can.'[27] Some time during his son's first terms at Oxford, Manley received a letter from 'All in the Downs. Oxon', addressed to 'Respected Father', and signed 'Arthur Flash de Wevunhoe'. It finished: 'I am sadly off for *rhino* for your last *cheque* could not *check* my expenses. And the bank *notes* being very *low* made me think you *base*. Please to *treble* the amount this *time* (say about 100 or 200 guineas) before I come down on Saturday. Be a brick and do it handsomely.'[28]

ও৲৩

During this first year, Hopkins was filling his diary with 'useful information', not making entries daily but as suitable items cropped up. The largest part of his notes concerns his discoveries and theories about words. From the first surviving entry, three weeks before he went up to Oxford for the Michaelmas term of 1863, these notes, though scholarly in form, are personal rather than purely linguistic. Although at one point in the diary he pretends to discuss etymology, his primary interest is in the *sound* of words and its putative psychological connection with meaning: for instance, he prefers strongly sound-effective words to 'puny' ones. Twelve years before 'The Wreck of the Deutschland' he is making lists of words whose similar sounds seemed to be signs of associations of meaning. He would use some piece of hit-or-miss etymological theory to lend weight to his selection of like-sounding words; whether he were right or wrong in his etymological speculations did not really matter. The power of the ear to insist that words of similar sounds have deeper associations than sound became a new territory. Here is one of his lists:

*Grind, gride, gird, grit, groat, grate, greet,* κρούειν, *crush, crash,* κροτεῖν etc. Original meaning to *strike, rub*, particularly *together*. That which is produced by such means is the *grit,* the *groats* or crumbs, like *fragmentum* from *frangere, bit* from *bite. Crumb, crumble* perhaps akin. To *greet*, to strike the hands together (?). *Greet,* grief, wearing, *tribulation. Grief* possibly connected. *Gruff*, with a sound as of two things rubbing together. I believe these words to be onomatopoetic. *Gr* common to them all representing a particular sound. In fact I think the onomatopoetic theory has not had a fair chance. Cf. *Crack, creak, croak, crake, graculus, crackle.* These must be onomatopoetic.[29]

During these days he formed a passionate attachment to particular words, and by putting them into his diary fixed them for future use. Words which he stared at in wonder in 1863 would be assimilated into poems of the 1870s and 1880s. His poetry did not need a pretence of etymological connection; two similar-sounding words placed next to each other did not merely have a doubling effect, but kept up a constantly reverberating relationship: 'The *ploughshare* that which divides the soil. *Share* probably = Divide ... *Shire,* a division of land. ... *Shower,* cf. shred, a fall of water in little shreds or divisions' (in the *Wreck,* 34: 'A released shower, let flash to the shire'; and *Wreck,* 11: 'sour scythe cringe, and the blear share come').[30] Other diary words later recalled include 'grind' ('in groans grind', in 'Spelt from Sibyl's Leaves'), 'wharf' (*Wreck,* 32: 'the wharf of it and the wall'), 'horn' (used in several different senses in poems). A large group of words and word combinations starting with *fl*: 'flick', 'flake', 'flint-flake', 'fled with a fling', 'flitches of fern', 'fleece of his foam/ Flutes', 'flange and the rail; flame,/ Fang, or flood' probably derive from notes made in late 1863 on words with initial *fl*.[31] The footnotes he wrote to his 'Legend of the Rape of the Scout' read as parodies of the verbal explorations in the diary.

Almost every diary entry shows him experimenting with language. He recorded Dr Dyne's explanation of the word 'premises'. He made many kinds of notes on *Twelfth Night*, from a comment on the meaning of 'tall' in 'as tall as any's in Illyria' to a discussion of the names of Sir Toby Belch and Sir Andrew Aguecheek: 'Sir A. A.'s name applies to the tremulous fat of his cheeks hanging down and shaking with his motions.'[32] He was interested in a Greek inscription noted by Jeremy Taylor on a circular fountain, which read the same clockwise and anti-clockwise. He recorded mistranslations from his Mods classes: 'Virginibus puerisque canto. I sing to the virginals and hautboys'; 'Ite domum saturae, venit Hesperus, ite capellae. Go home on Saturday, the Evening comes on, go to Chapel. A. E. Hardy.' He copied from the January 1864 *Cornhill* a list of Yorkshire rivers of British, Gaelic, or Erse origin, together with their original meanings; and he traced back a Celtic word *dhu* (black), which seemed to support his idea of words of similar sounds and meaning:

*Dhu.* in one or more of the Celt languages is *black.*—Gaelic *e.g.* Donuil Dhu—Donuil the Black. In above names it enters into *Dun* and *Dove*, perhaps *Douglas*, Dou—being *blue*, originally *black*. But perhaps *-glas* is blue, and we may compare *glastum* or *glassum* or *glessum*, Latin—or rather probably Latinizing of native word—for the *blue*-dye producing plant, woad.[33]

This spurred him on to record uncommon dialect words—'*duffer* in Cumberland means ass (literally)', 'clarty' was North Country for 'sticky', and in Isle of Wight dialect to 'gally' was to 'harry, annoy'. He noted phrases in which an apparently barren word could be vitalized by context—'*putting* the stone', 'the *good* ship', 'to *put* things, i.e. represent them'. He copied examples of an East African language that he came accross in Speke's *Journal of the Discovery of the Nile*; the language was based on euphony and required 'one to be possessed of a negro's turn of mind to appreciate the system, and unravel the secret of its euphonic concord'. He noted the words without having any idea or need of their meaning: 'U-sa-Gara, U-za-ramo, Dégé la Mhora, U-ra-guru, Maji ya Whéta, Jiwa la Mkoa, U-n-ya-muézi'.[34] He enjoyed Jacobean puns: 'Fast days I have found slow days; you do not know how long short commons will last.' And he met a man in London whose name he had to write down; 'Tito Télémaque Terenzio Themistoclés Théophile Paliardini'. He tried two experiments in sound. He wrote two lines and a bit of Sophocles' *Oedipus Tyrannus* as a continuous sound uninterrupted by spaces between words, punctuation, breathings, or separation into lines, and he wrote a comic representation of an undergraduate Latin verse composition:

> Aldiborontifostiformio
> Poluplosbiothalasses
> Spermagoraiolechitholaetanopolis
> Et pius Aeneas, quadrupetante putrem sonitu & c.

'From its *high sounding tone*', he suggested to his father, it would have won the Bell scholarship at Cambridge, 'but here alas—the less we say about it the better'.[35]

Throughout this year he kept close to nature in his walks and records. On every walk he must have encountered at least one river or canal; at some locks he tried to capture in words the actions and shapes of contained and released water. Sometimes he thought he could express the law of a particular portion of the fall by imagining the water's typical patterns as solid stone, and using the precise term Parker's *Glossary* had taught him: 'The water ... extends itself into three fans'; 'heaped up in globes and bosses'; and 'the shape of wave of course bossy, smooth and globy'.[36] He kept the Glossary in constant use by drawing examples from it of his favourite Decorated style of architecture and by analyses of architectural photographs given him by his Uncle George Giberne.

He often visualized and later wrote down a scene which would make a sketch. One Sunday in April he walked in Scholar Gipsy country with W. E. Addis, across the fields near Cumnor, his favourite Oxfordshire haunt:

Opening on the right ... in a hollow, on the road beyond Kennington, which runs below the plantations which border the other side of Abingdon Road to Bagley Wood. ... Dale in above plantation. Fir-grove on skirts of down beyond turnpike where Abingdon and the other road divide round Bagley wood. Opening in long avenue at Water Eton with view of the house. Cumnor and road thereto.[37]

He frequently wrote about birds and animals:

Two swans flew high up over the river on which I was, their necks stretched straight out and wings billowing.

... saw a snake glide through a hedge, thus [then a drawing] The curves being apparently formed by the twigs etc round which he drew himself.[38]

The bird and animal descriptions became infrequent, while the descriptions of water, leaves, foliage, flowers, and weather effects gradually became more vivid, elaborate, and expert.

In spring 1864 there were several short descriptions, some in verse:

Sheaves of bluebells with silver tails.

Snakes'-heads [snakes'-head fritillaries]. Like drops of blood. Buds pointed and like snakes' heads, but the reason of name from mottling and scaly look.

—and on their brittle quils
Shake the balanced daffodils.

Note on green wheat. The difference between this green and that of long grass is that first suggests silver, latter azure. Former more opacity, body, smoothness. It is the exact complement of carnation. Nearest to emerald of any green I know, the real emerald *stone*. It is lucent. Perhaps it has a chrysoprase bloom. Both blue greens.[39]

Some descriptions were less accurate but more poetic: 'Moonlight hanging or dropping on treetops like blue cobweb'; and 'Also the upper sides of little grotted waves turned to the sky have soft pale-coloured cobwebs on them, the under sides green'.[40]

Towards the summer of 1864, as his walks became longer and slower, there was more time to look calmly at the scene. Complete skyscapes made appearances in the diary, based on Ruskin's descriptions and occasionally using words from his lexis:

June 30. On this day the clouds were lovely. Opposite the sun between 10 and 11 was the disshevelled [sic] cloud on page opposite. The clouds were repeatedly formed in horizontal ribs. At a distance their straightness of line was wonderful. In passing overhead they were something as in the (now) opposite page, the ribs granulated delicately the splits fretted with lacy curves and honeycomb work, the laws of which were exquisitely traced. They in the zenith thus. There were squared odd disconnected pieces of cloud now and then seen thus [drawing], as if cut out from a lost whole.[41]

Drawings were not subordinated to words. Descriptions were more unified, musical, and strong in diction. In early May he walked with Addis to Stanton Harcourt:

Charming place, rather of my ideal Stratford-on-Avon kind; willows, lovely elms. Pool of inky black water with leaves in it. Vertical shortish grass. Orchards with trunks of trees smeared over with the common white mixture, whatever it is, rather pretty than otherwise. Primroses, large, in wet, cool, shady place.—On way fields yellow with cowslip and dandelion. Found purple orchis, which opens flowers from ground, then rises the stem pushing upward. Crossed Isis at Skinner's Weir, or as people about call it, *Wire*. Beautiful effect of cloud. Wild apple (?) beautiful in blossom. Caddis-flies on stones in clear stream, water-snails and leeches. Round-looking glossy black fieldmouse of some kind or water-rat in ditch on Witney Road. Cuckoo. Peewits wheeling and tumbling, just as they are said to do, as if with a broken wing. They pronounce *peewit* pretty distinctly, sometimes querulously, with a slight metallic tone like a bat's cry. Their wings are not pointed, to the eye, when flying, but broad, white and of a black or reddish purple apparently.[42]

He was showing interest in the theory of landscape perception. He made a note of an article by J. C. Shairp in the *North British Review* on Wordsworth, and copied into a notebook a passage from Shairp's *Studies in Poetry and Philosophy* which discusses Wordsworth's recognition of the relationship between an onlooker and the 'heart' or 'character' of a scene:

With regard to Wordsworth's 'ideal light' which 'brings out . . . vividly the real heart of nature, the inmost feeling, wh. is really there, and is recognised by Wordsworh's eye in virtue of the kinship betw. nature and his soul' Mr. Shairp adds in a note of defence: 'Each scene in nature has in it a power of awakening, in every beholder of sensibility, an impression peculiar to itself, such as no other scene can exactly call up. This may be called the 'heart' or 'character' of that scene. It is quite analogous to, if somewhat vaguer than, the partic. impression produced upon us by the pressure of each individ. man.[43]

There is more than a foretaste here of 'inscape' and 'instress'.

# Studies

Responsions (or 'Smalls'), the elementary test for all Oxford under-graduates, which Hopkins had passed in June 1863, was merely the qualification for entry to two sets of examinations which he had to sit in his four-year university career.[1] The emphasis on examinations as a framework for Oxford studies was symptomatic of a general stiffening of education in the second half of the nineteenth century. Competitive examinations, borrowed from the Chinese, provided objective evaluations of a student's progress for parents and employers. The growth of the modern State demanded competent administrators in vast numbers, which the old upper classes were unable to supply. The system of careful grading fostered the fashionable competitive spirit; the appearance of the class-lists was the climax of each year at Oxford, and success or failure branded a man.

The two sets of exams were Moderations and Finals (or the First and Second Public Examinations); in both there was a choice between the Pass and Honours schools, though the academically more demanding colleges, including Balliol, insisted that students enter for Honours in at least one school. In Honours Moderations, candidates took either Classics or Mathematics, and all had to pass also in Divinity. In Honours Finals the student had to offer one of the four schools: Literae Humaniores, Divinity, Mathematics, or History and Law. In the 1860s it was considered that 'the truest sons of Oxford' chose the Classical school in Honours Mods, and the Literae Humaniores in Finals. This was '*the* school *par excellence* of Oxford', and the one chosen by Hopkins. Some of the more energetic students tried for Honours in two schools either at Mods or Finals level (the examinations were not held concurrently), but Hopkins never showed any ambitions for this kind of versatility.

Classical Honours Moderations was the principal examination in Classics; Hopkins spent his first five terms working for it, and sat the exam at the end of the Michaelmas term. The major part was 'the minute learning of fixed portions of eight classical authors'. The emphasis was on poets and orators, rather than historians and philosophers, read in the Final schools. There were four compulsory authors: Homer, Virgil, Demosthenes, and Cicero. Hopkins studied the first six books of the *Odyssey*, the *Aeneid*, Virgil's *Eclogues* and *Georgics*, Demosthenes' *De Corona*, and Cicero's *Philippics*. In addition to the compulsory authors there were the 'specially offered' ones (four being a practical maximum), equally divided between Greek and Roman, with at least one Greek dramatist. The choice of Latin authors Hopkins studied in class seems to have been limited to Juvenal and Tacitus. In Greek he covered the first three books of Thucydides, and Aeschines' indictment of Ctesiphon (studied with the *De Corona*, the defence speech on the same cause); Hopkins had read the Demosthenes and the Aeschines in a single-volume edition before he came up to Oxford. From his Balliol timetable it appears that the special subject he offered was 'the history of the Greek drama', for which he was particularly well prepared, having read at least five Sophocles plays, four of Aristophanes, and two by Aeschylus. One of these must have doubled in the paper on specially offered authors.[2]

There were separate papers in Logic, and Prose and Verse Composition. For the Divinity exam Hopkins studied the Gospels and the Acts of the Apostles. Thus the main part of his studies until Christmas 1864 consisted (as H. S. Holland described it) of preparing for 'a long and rather pedantic examination, mostly in Greek and Latin, requiring strict accuracy of grammar and familiarity with set books'. The limitations of this system were underlined when sweeping changes were made in the 1880s. It was said that many candidates who had been perfectly prepared in the set authors had passed the examination without any 'real knowledge of the Greek or Latin language apart from them'. Editions of the prescribed authors were comprehensively annotated: discursive notes in Conington's edition of Virgil, for instance, came to be considered almost as part of the curriculum, and some students considered attendance at lectures unnecessary.

The Mods papers gave little space to questions on the 'contents, style, and literary history' of the set books. It is likely that the broadest-based question Hopkins faced in his Mods exam was: 'Trace the peculiar characteristics of the Greek mind as displayed in their vocabulary and modes of expression.' But the system fostered close attention to detail. A tutor presided over a table around which were seated twenty or so students, who construed aloud, with the tutor questioning and commenting. Of the nine Balliol students who passed Moderations in the Michaelmas term 1864, three were placed in the first class—Hopkins, Myers (another exhibitioner), and Paravicini, a scholar.

In the Lent term of 1865, Hopkins entered what—in spite of the recent setting up of the two modern schools in Natural Science and in Law and Modern History—was still considered the chief Honours school, that of Literae Humaniores, or 'Greats'. A first-class degree in this examination was the crowning achievement in the career of a classical student. 'Greats' was considered an unmatched training in clear thinking and singling out the essentials of a few well-tried texts. There were papers in History and Scholarship, but the school was pre-eminently philosophical. Hopkins's timetable shows a preponderance of Plato's *Republic* and Aristotle's *Ethics*. The only other Greek author was Herodotus, and the only Roman author studied in detail seems to have been Livy.³ The books Hopkins studied for the Ancient History paper were mainly Mommsen on Roman History (whom he found 'a brilliant historian'⁴), Grote's *History of Greece*, which he remembered in 1889 as 'so able, learned, and earnest a study'⁵ that it could hardly ever be antiquated, and Thomas Arnold's *Early History of Rome*. Other major texts were Hegel's *Philosophy of History* and Mill's *Principles of Political Economy* (for the paper on general Moral and Political Philosophy), and Bacon's *Novum Organon* (for the paper in Logic). For the Divinity paper he prepared two of the Gospels, two of Paul's Epistles, and five Old Testament books (Joshua, Judges, Ruth, II Samuel, and part of I Kings). The most important of all these books were Plato and Aristotle: 'Know your Republic and Ethics', it was said, 'and you are safe.'

The Balliol tutorial sysem consisted largely of discussion carried on in the spirit of the Socratic dialogues, the tutor assuming ignorance of the subject and asking deferential questions of his pupils, in ironic role reversal:

I remember, for instance, in reading a paper to Nettleship, I mentioned the distinction between form and matter. 'Excuse me for interrupting you,' Nettleship said, 'but this distinction you make, though it is no doubt most important, is one that I find a little difficult to grasp. If it is not troubling you too much, it would be a real kindness if you would try to explain it to me.'

'Oh, it's quite simple,' I answered patronisingly. 'There's the idea, say, in a poem, and there's the way in which it is expressed.'

Nettleship still seemed puzzled. 'Could you give me an instance?' he pleaded.

'Oh, nothing easier,' I answered. 'Take the lines, for instance, when Lovelace says:

> "I could not love thee, dear, so much,
> Loved I not honour more."

Now he might have said, "I couldn't be nearly so fond of you, my dear, if I didn't care still more for my reputation." The form, you see, is very different in both these sentences, but the subject of them—what they mean—is exactly the same.'

Nettleship seemed greatly discouraged. 'I'm afraid,' he said, 'I can't see that the meaning of the two sentences is the same. I'm afraid I'm very stupid, but to me they seem to say quite different things.'

He was, I thought, curiously stupid; but in my patient attempt to make my meaning clearer to him a dim suspicion began to waken in me that perhaps it was not Nettleship but I myself who was playing the part of the fool in the dialogue.[6]

This Socratic method of teaching had been perfected especially by Jowett, who was said to have believed it aimed at 'self-realisation, on the intellectual level', and elicited 'in a more rigorous form ideas that are already present in the student's mind'. It introduced students to 'the spirit of criticism', and hoped to eliminate 'the undue influence of teacher upon student'.[7]

But many Oxonians outside Balliol considered that the college's campaign for supremacy had resulted in a well-oiled teaching machine, which produced its crop of Firsts at too great a cost. Mark Pattison, in most matters a supporter of Jowett, argued that 'once involved in the great competitive struggle, it is superfluous and even dangerous for the welfare of his pupils for their teacher to say anything about the foundations of a subject, or to suggest that thoroughness and love of learning are the marks of true scholarship'. In practice the student was called upon to amass 'an assortment of ready-made propositions on the topics of philosophy, history, politics, and literature upon which the examinations are based'. Pattison found that the 'system has gradually become one which carefully excludes thoroughness. It is the exaltation of "smattering" into a method.' The Greats system did not produce intellectual discipline nor investigative abilities, but aimed rather at 'a clever answer to a question on a subject of which one has no real knowledge'.[8] Hopkins's ability to comment in an authoritative manner on subjects about which he knew nothing or had read a single article marks many letters he wrote. The musician Robert Stewart was to be one of the few people not bowled over by Hopkins's manner of argument:

I saw, ere we had conversed ten minutes on our first meeting, that you are one of those special pleaders who never believe yourself wrong in any respect. You always excuse yourself for anything I object to in your writing or music so I think it a pity to disturb you in your happy dreams of perfectability—nearly everything in your music was wrong—but you will not admit that to be the case.[9]

Though it would be crude to put the blame for this weakness of Hopkins on Balliol and the Greats system, there is a connection.

Pattison's strongest criticism of Greats is in 'Philosophy at Oxford', a paper written for the first issue of *Mind* in 1876.[10] After describing the astonishment he felt at the candidates' 'combination of scholarship, varied knowledge, command of topic and scientific vocabulary', he continued

A nearer acquaintance, however, with the whole result of the system dispels the illusion. If from the papers we turn to the minds from which all this clever writing has emanated, we shall find no trace of any philosophical culture in them. The question . . . is on a philosophical subject, but the process by which the question has been answered has been not a philosophical action of mind, but a purely literary or compositional process. . . . Memory is really almost the only quality called into play.

The Literae Humaniores graduate was 'an intellectual roué', according to Pattison, ill-prepared for research and the advancement of knowledge. Again, this bears on Hopkins's performance in his self-paced non-religious studies after he had left Oxford. Although we have to allow for his temperamental oscillation and conscientious uncertainty, it is striking that he started enthusiastically a large number of intellectual projects and finished few. When forced outside the neatly defined plots of the Greats system, he had difficulty in working out the parameter of a subject for himself, having an unreal confidence in his abilities and little practical experience of finding his own way in new territory. His initiating enthusiasms did not submit to the duller disciplines needed to carry through a project. Few of his surviving Greats essays cover more than four sides of paper.

౭౩

The prestige of Balliol was not yet at its peak. It would not be until after Hopkins's time that 'one-sixth of the Indian Civil Service was drawn from Balliol men', that three successive Governor-Generals of India were educated there, and nine Oxford colleges in succession elected graduates of Balliol as Heads. But two of the architects of its brilliance were already established there, and taught Hopkins. T. H. Green and Jowett profoundly influenced him, even when their thinking opposed his. Balliol's name had become synonymous with radicalism, although it was a cautious and comparative radicalism, and 'its liberal conscience ... usually stopped short of social democracy'. Though not yet widely influential, T. H. Green[11] was 'the great exponent of social conscience' in the college. As a Balliol undergraduate in the late 1850s he had been a member of the Old Mortality with Swinburne, and had subsequently become known as a partisan of radical causes as varied as Matthew Arnold's lectures, the Huxley faction in the great Evolution debate with Wilberforce in the new Oxford Museum, and Jowett's position in the *Essays and Reviews* controversy. He went to the meetings of radical political agitators, and organized an expedition to hear John Bright in Birmingham. Since visiting Germany in 1862 he had, according to Nettleship, 'definitely abandoned his belief in the miraculous, and therefore in the commonly accepted historical groundwork of Christianity'. He had never had 'the smallest sympathy' for Anglicanism or Roman Catholicism; indeed, Roman Catholicism 'had defined for him what must be excluded from his philosophy'. Yet although he was against all dogmatic theology, 'he would rather not express his own ideas at all, if by doing so he weakened anyone's faith'. But since succeeding in 1866 to James Riddell's place as college tutor and being appointed Senior Dean, Green had become a sober radical. 'His habitual dress of black and grey', said a friend, 'suited him well and was true to his character. He was drawn to plain people, to people of the middle and lower class rather than to the upper, to the puritans of the past and the nonconformists of the present, to Germans, to all that is sober-suited and steady-going.' The fashionable philosophy at Oxford, according to H. S. Holland, was 'that of the utilitarian school of Mill: while T. H. Green, who was at that time our chief teacher of philosophy in Balliol, was, as it is well known, the exponent of a very different system, of a more spiritual and less materialistic kind, founded upon the writings of Kant and Hegel.' Green, in all probability, took Hopkins's group of Greats students for the class on Mill's *Political Economy* in the Michaelmas term 1865, and on Hegel in Lent 1867.

Hopkins once proposed a motion at a Balliol debating club in support of the Fenians, but there is no other sign that he was ever on any but the opposite side in social and political responses. His earliest recorded reaction to Green, in autumn 1863, was a juvenile sneer of self-righteous antipathy, a slander of a man noted for honesty and integrity: Green was 'of a rather offensive style of infidelity, and naturally dislikes the beauties of nature'.[12] Green was known to depart in his lessons from the traditional procedure of emphasizing texts, in order to discuss their

philosophical issues, so that Hopkins would have been exposed directly
to the 'rather offensive style'. It may have been an unwillingness to face
Green directly that led Hopkins, in the term when Green was lecturing
on Mill, to write an essay for him, not on Utilitarianism, but on 'The
Position of Plato in the Greek World'.[13]

It was not that Hopkins did not hold opinions on modern philosophy.
Probably within six months of sitting his Final examinations he wrote a
deeply brooding essay for Robert Williams, a newly appointed Fellow
of Merton, on 'The Possibility of Separating ἠθική from πολιτική
ἐπιστήμη' (Ethics from Political Science).[14] In contrast with Hopkins's
later studies after he joined the Society of Jesus, it did not matter at
Oxford 'what philosophical views a man adopt, so long as he under-
stands them, and is consistent in them'. An account of Greats written
for undergraduates in the 1880s, for instance, emphasized that a
candidate who 'described Utilitarianism in his papers as "subversive of
all morality" ' was failed not because of his opinion but because he
'showed in his *viva voce* that he had no conception what Utilitarianism
meant'. Hopkins took advantage of this liberal opportunity to attack the
'Empirical and Utilitarian schools' failure of insight', which threatened
to 'overrun the whole field of thought'.[15] He also attacks the kind of
connection between politics and personal morality made by the English
followers (who included Green) of German idealism—'they overlook
this, that personal morality conditions political before political personal'. The essay shows Hopkins's hasty, unqualified rejection of
Green's ideal of personal involvement in social questions: to Hopkins,
inward virtue was of pre-emptive importance. One wonders if Hopkins
regretted his dismissal of Green's ideas when he was forced to face the
reality of industrial slum squalor in Liverpool in the 1880s.

When Hopkins was suffering from personal rejection because of his
self-imposed ideological isolation as a Roman Catholic convert, Green
was one of the few Oxford people outside his religion who lent a
sympathetic ear. And Hopkins later found himself able to call on Green
and his wife ('a very kind creature') when he returned to Oxford as a
priest in 1879.[16] Probably because his personal position was no longer
embattled Hopkins was able to be warmer towards Green. He wrote on
Green's death in 1882:

I always liked and admired poor Green. He seemed to me upright in mind and
life. I wish I had made more of the opportunities I had of seeing him in my 10
months at Oxford, for he lived close by. His fortune fell first on Knox and then
on Hegel and he was meant for better things. Probably if he had lived longer he
wd. have written something that wd. have done the same.[17]

The patronising tone shows an unattractive self-righteousness, and a crashing ignorance of Green's work, standing, and influence.

Jowett[18] held no other position at Balliol while Hopkins was there except that of Tutor; the *Essays and Reviews* controversy had resulted in his not being allowed to teach Catechetics or preach in chapel. He neither dined in hall nor attended the common-room. But he was the most influential person in the college; the appointment of Scott in 1854 had been made only to keep out Jowett. His reputation had been built not only on *Essays and Reviews*, his edition of St Paul's Epistles, his ideas for reforming Oxford and the Civil Service, and his friendships with eminent public figures, but also on the dedication and success of his tutoring at Balliol. Jowett was Hopkins's tutor for Greats. The thoroughness he required of his students can be seen from the Mods timetable in which Hopkins noted that he had to see him on Tuesday mornings at 8.30 a.m., after chapel but before breakfast; and on Tuesdays and Thursdays he was due to attend Jowett's lectures on Sophocles' *Ajax*, which took place between 1 and 2 p.m., whereas the normal practice was for lectures to finish at 1 o'clock.[19] At 9 o'clock on Wednesday nights Jowett sent Hopkins for Composition to a former pupil, Robinson Ellis, now a Fellow of Trinity. (Ellis lent him a manuscript copy he owned of D. G. Rossetti's 'The Blessèd Damozel', which Hopkins copied into his commonplace-book.[20])

Jowett was a teacher rather than a scholar, and the influence on his pupils was gained by 'his inquisitive and often sympathetic vigilance'. He worked students hard in techniques for passing examinations, 'a good deal of drill, memorising, and advance preparation of essays likely to be set'. He gathered them 'closely round him, and his care for them gave him, shy, reticent, even repellent as he sometimes was, a strong hold on the affection of many remarkable men'. The strictness of his concern for his pupils and his lack of charm is illustrated in the account of William Anson (a Balliol contemporary of Hopkins and later Warden of All Souls):

Jowett asked me to a solitary wine ... and then unfolded his plans for me for the term, which are, that I should read ten hours a day, which I don't think I shall do, that I should coach for a month with one of the most objectionable protégés, and, finally, that I should take a walk with him every Monday and breakfast with him every Friday, that he may see how I am getting on. .... It is very kind of Jowett to take so much trouble about me, but a tête-à-tête with him is rather a dismal thing.

Hopkins was never one of Jowett's favoured circle, and, except for the brief early acquaintance with Strachan-Davidson and a later one with Paravicini, he was not friendly with the Jowett group. After he had joined Liddon's group of Ritualist students in 1863, there was little possibility that he could approve of the moral and ecclesiastical principles which Jowett advocated. The Jesuits reported after his death that Hopkins had been 'the Star of Balliol';[21] if this were so the title would be conferred, not by Jowett (to whom the phrase is often attributed, through a mistake of Fr Lahey's[22]), but by Pusey, who would have meant that Hopkins was the one hope the Ritualist party had of gaining a foothold in heretical Balliol, dominated by Jowett: a star shining in darkness.

It is likely that Hopkins's reactions were as hostile as Henry Scott Holland's, who considered Jowett's religious stance to be 'just Platonism flavoured with a little Christian charity: Christianity is gutted by him. . . . there is not one atom of the feeling of prayer, of communication with God, of reliance on any one but self.' In March 1865 Hopkins recorded that he had spoken 'impertinently' about Jowett to Liddon, and in May that year was worried about his 'disrespectful feeling' towards Jowett.[23] It is also clear from his diary that at this time he was closely attached to Liddon, and envious when told that Liddon had called on Stuckey Coles and not on him. (In 1861 Liddon had voted against Pusey's proposal to raise the meagre salary attached to Jowett's Greek Chair, and objected 'to endowing Jowett in any way, direct or indirect'.) On one occasion Hopkins had to choose between the two. Early in the Lent term of 1865 he arranged to walk with Liddon at 1.30, at a time when he should have been at Jowett's lecture on Plato's *Republic*.[24]

To Hopkins, Jowett's moral shortcomings were of a piece with his aesthetic philistinism. Just as Green's infidelity had led him to condemn the beech tree, so Jowett's liberalism went with his condemnation of Ritualism, aestheticism, medievalism, and a preference for Waterhouse's crude architecture over Butterfield's pious and original Gothic: 'Waterhouse is to do the new buildings of the college. Ernest Geldart is up on the business. Jowett had him and the other man in to his rooms and held forth about proportion—after rejecting Butterfield.'[25] Yet, as House pointed out, Hopkins acknowledged the 'purity' of Jowett, 'as something which struck him more than in almost any other'. House's interpretation of this word 'purity' is subtle and convincing:

This curious verdict of a pupil on his teacher is an intuitive recognition of something in his personality which perhaps neither would have dared fully to explore. There is no evidence that Jowett was, like Hopkins, almost wholly homosexual; but it is clear from his deep interest in the personalities of young men, his preoccupation with the idea of marriage though he persistently remained unmarried, his many emotional friendships with women, that he was a person in whom the sexual impulse had not fully developed in the common way: even the portraits of his middle age show a face that has few of the typically male characteristics: it is a 'pure' face in that the shadow of ordinary desire does not seem to have passed across it. . . . There was enough likeness between them for both to be on their guard; both had this look of 'purity'.[26]

In the college of Jowett and Green the study of Plato led on to the German idealist philosophy, which many thought should rekindle the 'national glow of life and thought' (Arnold's phrase) so evident in the Athens of Pericles and so lacking in modern England. Hopkins did not share Arnold's admiration for the 'culture and a force of learning and criticism such as were to be found in Germany'.[27] He was opposed to and ignorant of German thought; in 1875 he wrote to Bridges: 'I have no time to read even the English books about Hegel, much less the original, indeed I know almost no German. . . . I do not afflict myself much about my ignorance here. . . . After all I can . . . read Duns Scotus and I care for him more even than Aristotle and more *pace tua* than a dozen Hegels.'[28] A leader of modern thought was rejected for a medieval theologian.

Hopkins accepted that Greek studies and modern thought were interdependent. His rejection of large elements of both was on narrowly moralistic grounds. Greek mythology and religion did not express truths that satisfied Hopkins. He wrote to Dixon in 1886: 'Could I speak too severely of [Greek mythology]? First it is as history untrue. What is untrue history? Nothing and worse than nothing. And that history religion? Still worse. I cannot enter on this consideration without being brought face to face with the great fact of heathenism.' His religious puritanism blinded him:

Now we mostly pass heathenism by as a thing utterly departed . . . but if for once we face it what are we to say of it? For myself literally words would fail me to express the loathing and horror with which I think of it and of man setting up the work of his own hands, of that hand within the mind the imagination, for God Almighty who made heaven and earth. Still he might set up beings perfect in their kind. But the Greek gods are rakes, and unnatural rakes.

He failed to understand the social and psychological functions of Greek myths; a god was justifiable only in so far as it resembled his idea of the Christian God:

Are the Greek gods majestic, awe inspiring, as Homer that great Greek genius represents them? They are not. . . . Indeed they are not brave, not self controlled, they have no manners, they are not gentlemen and ladies. They clout one another's ears and blubber and bellow. . . . At their best they remind me of some company of beaux and fashionable world at Bath in its palmy days or Tunbridge Wells or what not.[29]

A clue to this dismissiveness lies in the next sentence of this letter, which was in reply to Dixon's judgement of Greek mythology as 'very beautiful': 'Zeus is like the major in *Pendennis* handsomer and better preserved sitting on Olympus as behind a club-window and watching Danae and other pretty seamstresses cross the street—not to go farther.' Hopkins added: 'You will think this is very Philistine and vulgar and be pained.' Art had to be morally respectable, and the greatest art should be morally useful.

Greek art was not morally respectable, but medieval Gothic was. Hopkins's earliest description of architecture in his school-prize poem of 1860, 'The Escorial', shows that at sixteen he was aware of the acknowledged differences behind Gothic and Greek art: a Doric temple was 'a triumph of airy grace and perfect harmony', while the 'foliag'd crownals' of a Gothic building pointed 'how the ways / Of art best follow nature'. His reading of Parker on Gothic architecture had prepared him to be a disciple of Ruskin and Pugin in their battle against Greek architecture. To Ruskin, Greek perfection of architectural ornament, or 'absolute precision by line and rule',[30] was a sign of servility and lack of imagination, related to the degradation of machinery and other modern evils. Gothic architecture possessed 'a noble character', and 'a higher nobility still, when considered as an index . . . of religious principle'. Gothic was naturally English, but in the medieval spirit of England, where slavery 'is done away with altogether, Christianity having recognised in small things as well as great, the individual value of every soul'. The very imperfection of Gothic art, which admitted man's 'lost power and fallen nature' was at one with true Christian doctrine, and tended 'in the end, to God's greater glory'.

Ruskin's medievalist opposition to Greek art took in other dualisms. In *The Stones of Venice* his argument moves directly from Gothic's imperfect ornamentation to medieval awareness of imperfection in human nature, to irregularity as a source of beauty in leaves and branches. Ruskin could make a connection between such disparate ideas and feelings of Hopkins. Hopkins's hierarchy of poetic kinds— Delphic, Parnassian, and Olympian[31]—is markedly similar to Ruskin's division[32] of architectural ornament into Servile, Constitutional, and Revolutionary. Hopkins's mind often worked in similar ways to Ruskin's; areas of argument expand not by logical development but by enthusiastic rhetoric and imaginative association. Both would feel themselves increasingly isolated as the century wore on, and as confidence in making meaningful connections between different areas of knowledge waned and was replaced by specialization.

Hopkins would not have agreed with the second part of Newman's neat Hebraism/Hellenism division, in *The Idea of a University*, that 'Jerusalem . . . is the fountainhead of religious knowledge as Athens of secular knowledge'.[33] Whereas most of Oxford was assimilating the scholarly methods of the Germans, and slowly becoming modern, Hopkins had joined the counter-reformation forces. So far as Greek studies were concerned, his enthusiasm was limited and muted, but he did grant 'that Greek mythology is very susceptible of fine treatment, allegorical treatment for instance, and so treated gives rise to the most beautiful results. No wonder: the moral evil is got rid of and the pure art, morally neutral and artistically so rich, remains.'[34] Hopkins has unexpectedly changed his language, and assumed the mask of the 'aesthetic': 'fine treatment', 'most beautiful results','pure art, morally neutral and artistically so rich'. Even in Hopkins's case, the simplified party-terms of the age, expressed in such dualisms as Hebrew/Hellene, medievalist/modernist, Celt/Teuton, sometimes broke down.

Jowett had no medievalist tastes; he disliked barbarous beauty as much as Hopkins admired it, and like Plato was against poets. 'I shall shoot myself', Swinburne had sighed to Jowett, who, according to the story, replied 'Not on *this* carpet, Algernon'.[35] His first reaction to *Modern Painters* had been favourable—'the minute observation and power of description it shows are truly admirable', he had written in 1844; but his later attitude towards Ruskin was hesitant.[36] As early as 1865 he had condemned 'the beginnings of a movement that he promptly called "aesthetic"', which he linked with High Church ritualism 'as one of many strange "toys in the blood" '.[37] But although he deplored aestheticism, he was in some ways one of its progenitors, and a strong influence on elements of Hopkins's poetic style. Jowett knew that his task should have been to reconcile 'the methods of critical scholarship with Christianity as a revealed religion', but he escaped into editing Plato's *Republic*. His translation work nevertheless involved him in broader issues:

He managed always to direct the study of language so as to promote literary culture. . . . If there was less of exact scholarship imparted by him, than, for example, by James Riddell, the whole subject was surrounded with an air of literary grace and charm which had a more educative affect. As an interpreter, and above all as a translator, he seemed to his pupils to be unrivalled. He was never satisfied with any interpretation that could not be expressed in perfect English.[38]

Taught by Jowett from 1860 to 1862, Pater recalled 'a very dainty dialogue on language', the delivery of Plato lectures 'with many a long-remembered gem of expression'; Jowett seemed 'to have put the last refinements on literary expression'.[39]

It was not Jowett's individual style which was important to Hopkins but the attention he paid to style in classical texts and his students' essays. Before he left school Hopkins had felt the need for meticulousness and exactness of expression. Although preferring the dirges of Moschus and Theocritus ('say if there is anything so lovely in the classics', he demanded of Coleridge),[40] he spent part of the summer of 1862 in translating passages from Aeschylus' *Prometheus Bound*. Apart from false notes when he brings in a Jacobean phrase ('Ah well a day'), the thirty-six lines of Hopkins's verse are competent, graceful, and moving:

> The young chief of the bless'd of heaven
> Hath devised new pains for me
>   And hath given
> This indignity of chains,
> What is, and what is to be,
> All alike is grief to me;
> I look all ways but only see
> The drear dull burden of unending pains.

A compound adjective is elegantly rendered, 'fleet-feather'd'. When translation is faulty, it is due to a refusal to be dull: instead of 'with the light beat of wings' he writes 'with light pulse of pinions skirring'.[41]

Jowett's teaching was helping Hopkins to think more rationally and carefully about poetic style. His notes on Jowett's lectures on Sophocles and the *Republic* show that Jowett frequently digressed from the syllabus. He made comparisons with Shakespeare, commented on Greek words of colour, discussed metre, the collocation of words, loose grammar, characteristics of Sophocles' style. Hopkins was always confident of his own style, but at Balliol he grew self-critical: he wrote to Baillie in the long vacation of 1864: 'I am coming to think much of taste myself, good taste and moderation, I who have sinned against them so much.'[42] Under Jowett's tuition he came to admire Plato:

Plato the perfection of style. Perfectly equable, to be gathered from the whole page not from the word.

Perspicuity the first requisite. Difficult in proportion to the fineness of a style.
Must absolutely get rid of the Greek idioms in translating.
Perfect grace and freedom of his style. What cause?
Perfect purity of language, never falling below proper dignity.
Primary thing in translating him. This almost a matter of rhythm.
Prose depends on this almost as much as poetry.

Hopkins was one of the lucky students who had Jowett as personal tutor. From his other Balliol teachers he probably gained less academically, although he admired Riddell's life and character. When Riddell's classes were taken by a colleague, Hopkins remarked the difference, and wrote at the head of some notes: 'The following notes were taken down when reading the play with DuChavasse ... and have not Riddell's authority.' On Riddell's death in 1866, he took the trouble to copy out for Urquhart a long obituary.[43]

He developed fluency in Latin and Greek. He had to submit original Latin prose compositions, and knew the language well enough to obfuscate some of his private notes. He would find it easy to adapt to the crude dog Latin spoken every day in the Jesuit novitiate. In the English verse that he wrote at Oxford, there are fewer words of Latin derivation than one might expect from a Greats candidate; in the 'Soliloquy of One of the Spies Left in the Wilderness', for instance, he uses 'sandfield' instead of 'desert', although he seldom appears to be searching for words of Teutonic origin,[44] and did not often aim at sonorous Latinized vocabulary. Certain elements of adapted classical syntax which would be characteristic of his later poetry were already appearing in his Oxford verses. His word-order was sometimes adapted from the classical, for example, in preference to normal English usage, as though there were no different requirements in uninflected English from those of inflected Greek or Latin: 'Nostrils, your careless breath that spend/ Upon the stir and keep of pride'. He would also occasionally cut out prepositions ('And lily-coloured clothes provide/ Your spouse'). He used a kind of classical negative ('where springs not fail'), and sometimes cut out 'to' before infinitives. He was already dissatisfied with common adjectives and inventing adjectival clusters ('Fruit-cloistering hyacinth-warding woods').[45]

Though he reacted against aspects of classical civilizations, Latin and Greek gave him practice in thinking and writing about language, art, and poetry. He grew agile in making spirited linguistic connections and jumps from one language to another, and one word to another:

Lucretius IV, 1255. 'Crassaque conveniunt liquidis et liquida crassis.' And the quantity *iqu* in the various words *liqueo*, *liquidus*, etc. notoriously varies.

*Liquidus* is same as *limpidus*. Now *linquo*, of which the perfect is *liqui*, is certainly same as λείπω. We may conclude that the lengthening of *iqu* in the above verse arose from a (perhaps then no longer existing) form or pronunciation *linquidus* which was transmuted into *limpidus*. Perhaps λείπω may have passed through the form λείμπω. Compare in English *dank* and *damp*, *hump* and *hunk*.[46]

He read Max Müller's *Lectures on the Science of Language* and George Perkins Marsh's *Lectures on the English Language*, typical mid-century studies, but there is a refreshing innocent confidence and vigour in his notes on language. He is not cowed by the experts. As House says:

The time was kind for him; for he grew up just when philology had reached a stage in which it was prominent and yet still simple and fresh enough to be popular. ... The study of language was still free from the close and dry specialisation. ... Hopkins grew up before the mood ... was eclipsed by that of Skeat; and when in the eighties he wrote to Skeat about some of his own conjectures, the answer came from another world.[47]

# Dolben

Hopkins probably first met Robert Bridges, an undergraduate of Corpus Christi, at one of Canon Liddon's Sunday evening lectures in the Michaelmas term of 1863. They became good friends, and in February 1865 Bridges introduced Hopkins to Digby Mackworth Dolben,[1] who was entered for Balliol in 1866. Dolben was not quite seventeen, three-and-a-half years younger than Hopkins. He had 'fine dark melancholy eyes', was 'tall, pale, and of delicate appearance, and though his face was thoughtful and his features intellectual, he would not at that time have been thought good-looking'. He dressed neglectfully, and had an abstracted manner. He was short-sighted but did not wear spectacles, and 'though the dreaminess which it gave to his expression came to be a characteristic and genuine charm', wrote Bridges, 'it was, until it won romantic interpretation, only an awkwardness'.

At Finedon Hall in Northamptonshire Dolben had been brought up by his father in a stern Protestant tradition, though he had fallen under the influence of his Aunt Annie, a lady with 'strong ecclesiastical sympathies of a mystical sort'. At Eton he was in the Dame's house of which Bridges, a distant relative, was captain. Bridges enrolled him among his fags, and discovered 'the attraction of our similar inclinations and outlook on life'. In 'physical temperament' they were 'as different as boys could be'; Dolben was shortsighted and no athlete, while Bridges was a fine all-round sportsman, but they 'satisfied' a 'natural bias towards art by poetry', and responded to religious difficulties by becoming Puseyites. 'Neither of us at that time', wrote Bridges, 'doubted that our *toga virilis* would be the cassock of a priest or the habit of a monk.' Dolben became one of a group of Eton High-Church boys led by V. S. S. Coles, known as Stuckey and later Principal of Pusey House, Oxford. Coles later recalled a characteristic incident:

We had come to know that there was such a thing as a 'Retreat', though how to set about it rather puzzled us. We had reduced our food, and had settled down to devotions consisting eminently of prayers for the soul of K. Henry VI, but 'after four' our constancy broke down, and ... some one was sent for ices.

Dolben had little in common with the other Eton boys, and gained a reputation for peculiar religious opinions and extravagant behaviour. Instead of going to the hairdresser he burned his curly hair with a candle, 'gravely recommending the practice on the professional theory of sealing the ends of the hair'. Bridges and Dolben had many evening conversations in which they discussed their writing and found they had different literary tastes. Dolben had read more widely than Bridges in modern literature, and would talk of the Brownings, Tennyson, Ruskin, and Faber. Dolben had written imitations of Faber's hymns, and Bridges's disgusted response made Dolben reluctant to show them to him. Bridges was 'too ignorant of painting' to share Dolben's enthusiasm for Ruskin's 'sermonizing', and, like Mowbray Baillie, could not imagine 'how another could presume to tell me what I should like or dislike'. Dolben had little enthusiasm for Shakespeare, whom Bridges admired. Bridges carried Keats in his pocket, and studied Milton, having been 'dazed by the magnificence of the first book of Paradise Lost', but 'Milton was to Digby as Luther to a papist'. Dolben regarded poetry as 'the naïve outcome of peculiar personal emotion'; Bridges was drawn to poetry by 'the inexhaustible satisfaction of form'.

After writing 'a sentimental imitation of Spenser', Bridges's muse was 'silenced by my reading of the great poets', though he was hopeful of improvement; Dolben wrote prolifically and imitated with ease. His poems are pale imitations of Herbert, or dreamy Pre-Raphaelite scenes without the genuine precision of image. Bridges recorded one act which was not self-indulgent: 'One evening when I was sitting in his room and moved to pull out the drawer where he kept his poems, the usual protest was not made. The drawer was empty; and he told me that he had burned them, every one.' This may well have been the model for Hopkins's similar act four years later.[2] (As with Hopkins's juvenilia, it turned out that only one copy of each poem had been burnt, and several survived in second copies.)

Dolben's behaviour at school was unconventional and imprudent. He developed a 'passionate attachment' to a fellow member of the High-Church group, Martin Le Marchant Gosselin, disguised in Bridges's Memoir as Archie Manning. Dolben realized that they were bound to separate, because Gosselin 'was destined to go out into the world ... while he was pledged to renounce the world and all its delights'.

Gosselin was coming between Dolben and his religious faith. Dolben's 'perpetual vision of the Man of Sorrows calling him out from the world could not be so vivid as this actual image of living grace that made mortal existence beautiful'.

Bridges's gentle, careful account does not mention the sexual implications of the relationship, which would have been clear then as now. J. A. Symonds's diaries and *Boys Together* have described the indecorous life beneath the respectable surface of nineteenth-century public schools: 'As early as 1840', writes John Chandos, 'social sensitivity was keen enough for potential blackmailers to spread rumours of "immorality" at Eton, with the object of extorting hush money from the head-master.'[3] When Dolben's tutor and Domini (housemaster) decided that Dolben was unsuited to Eton they were unlikely to have been referring only to his religious practices, though Bridges implied that they were.

The most unorthodox area of Dolben's behaviour was his religion. It was not just that he 'crossed himself at meals', and 'left his queer books about'. A compulsory period called 'Sunday questions' 'gave him a grand opportunity of airing his mediaeval notions', and Sunday became 'altogether a field-day for Digby'. According to Bridges, Dolben dragged in his medievalisms because he 'enjoyed exercising his malicious ingenuity', taking a natural delight in whatever was 'out of place', and in the 'perplexity that he knew it must cause'. Visits to various Anglican or Roman Catholic establishments 'owed a great part of their pleasure to their being disapproved or forbidden'. At different times he visited 'an Anglican Priory at Ascot', Beaumont Lodge (a Jesuit house at Old Windsor), a Roman Catholic chapel at Slough, and a High-Church community at Clewer, where he probably made confessions. It was 'a stolen visit to the Jesuits' which was the immediate cause of his expulsion from Eton in sumer 1863. At the end of the summer holidays, his father persuaded Dolben's tutor to take him back, as he had overcome his 'silly fancies'. A promise of improved behaviour was extracted, but it was only a convenient gesture: 'Of course I shall be very discreet', he wrote to Bridges just before he returned to school,

and generally unexceptionable (I hope) but, alas, who can tell. The frailty of human nature is so great. Isn't it? My last frailty was to go to see a Catholic chapel at Bangor, and as a low mass was just beginning, can I be blamed if I remained on my knees until it was concluded?

By this time he was dating his letters by Roman Church feast-days, in Latin ('Inf. Oct. S Laurentii. Di'), sometimes put a cross by his name, and wrote his address in a letter as 'Eton College near Windsor (and Old

Windsor, and Clewer and Slough)', though he was confirmed in the Church of England, and seemed to be 'quieting down'.

He was developing 'a profound sense of personal unworthiness', and fasted rigorously in preparation for his Confirmation and first Communion. He 'exerted himself to make other boys in his Dame's house attend seriously to their preparation, even assisting them so far as to steal their breakfast-rolls away from them, so that they might go to the Chapel fasting'. Early in 1864 he was introduced to the Revd J. L. Lyne, who had founded his personal version of a Benedictine monastery, within the Anglican communion, at Claydon in Suffolk. By Easter of that year Dolben, now just sixteen and still at school, had joined the Order of Saint Benedict, and signed letters '✠Dominic O. S. B. iii'. He wrote to Bridges at Oxford, enclosing a copy of the Order's rules, a description of the joys of Heaven composed by Br. Ignatius (as Lyne called himself), and four pages about Ignatius' activities. 'Is it not marvellous? Is it not glorious? Is it not miraculous?' asked Dolben. A printed tract gives a clear idea of the Order's rhetorical style and appeal:

and now Jesus is all, and all in all to them—they are *close* to His side, His Pierced Side—they are languishing in the intensest ecstasy of love, they are burning, and glowing, and glittering, and dazzling—in a flood of light. . . . And, oh devoted monk, this is for EVER—for EVER—for EVER! . . .
P.S. The brothers are in the greatest need of assistance—being in the extremest poverty.[4]

Dolben now had a monastic habit, 'imagined himself a mediaeval monk', and considered it 'well nigh impossible to attain to anything of the Saintly Life' at Eton. He wrote poems expressing the conflict between human and divine love, and worldly and mystical pleasures:

> For here before the altar there is given
> The peace I sought for long and wearily
> Through all the peaceless world and never found,
> Although I ransacked all its richest stores.
> Dreaming the breath of poetry divine
> Could heal my sin-sick soul, dreaming that art
> Could rest these aching eyes, that Nature's voice
> Conscience, imagination, feeling, sense
> Could help me.

'The reading of these poems', commented Bridges, 'makes one see why schoolmasters wish their boys to play games.'

Bridges said in his memoir of Dolben that he himself had been unimpressed by Brother Ignatius' rhetoric and his *carte de visite* portrait 'with extravagant tonsure and ostentatious crucifix', though Dolben thought Bridges 'seemed inclined to join' the order. Dolben left Eton in December 1864, to prepare for Balliol.

♄

Dolben's encounter with Hopkins at Oxford was their only meeting, though Bridges thought they must have seen a good deal of each other in this short period. Just as Hopkins came to recognize in Coventry Patmore expressions of his own inhibited political reactions, and in Walt Whitman aspects of his own temperament which he dared not name, so Dolben's flamboyant leanings towards Rome incarnated Hopkins's suppressed spiritual inclinations. They also suggested a solution to his increasing self-dissatisfaction. Hopkins found Dolben attractive, and like many others succumbed to his charm; it was this infatuation that probably caused him to understate the flirtatiousness and provocativeness in Dolben's religious attitudes.

Their mutual interests were religion and poetry. Hopkins was temperamentally closer to Dolben than Bridges, and they shared objects of enthusiasm. Perhaps the most important was Savonarola. At Christmas 1863, Dolben had written to Bridges: 'Read "Romola" by George Eliot (as the authoress calls herself). Be enthusiastic about Savonarola, I am. Read also a new "Life of Savonarola" just come out.' During the Christmas vacation of 1864 Hopkins had also read *Romola* and at least dipped into Horner's translation of Villari's history of Savonarola. On 5 January he told Baillie: 'I am reading *Romola*. I made an effort not to accept it at first; but now think it is a great book.'[5] Five days later he reported to Urquhart that he had been in bed with a severe cold, and 'there I have finished *Romola* and made myself wretched over the fall of Savonarola'.

I did not know much about the latter events of his life except that the *Arrabiati* and Pope Borgia overthrew and burned him, and in especial nothing about his confession. I must tell you he is the only person in history (except perhaps Origen) about whom I have a real feeling, and I feel such an enthusiasm about Savonarola that I can conceive what it must have been to have been of his followers.[6]

He had come to the conclusion that because George Eliot was 'pagan' she could not understand Savonarola, 'clever as she is'. But he put *Silas Marner* and *The Mill on the Floss* on his next reading-list.[7]

Hopkins may have disliked Eliot's account of the psychological subtleties of martyrdom:

But the worst drop of bitterness can never be wrung on to our lips from without: the lowest depth of resignation is not to be found in martyrdom; it is only to be found when we have covered our heads in silence and felt, 'I am not worthy to be a martyr; the Truth shall prosper, but not by me.' (*Romola*, ch. 66)

He would have preferred a more conventional assessment of a martyr's motivations. He may also have shrunk from the comparison between Romola, 'The Visible Madonna', and 'The Unseen Madonna', the Pitying Virgin Mother. (It is likely that by this time he had a statue of Our Lady in his room, and kissed the floor in front of it every morning.[8]) But it is ironic that he should have accused Eliot of misunderstanding Savonarola when his own image was so clearly created by emotional needs:

I can conceive what it must have been to have been of his followers. I feel this the more because he was followed by the painters, architects and other artists of his day, and he is the prophet of Christian art, and it is easy to imagine oneself a painter of his following.[9]

(Later that year Hopkins was told by Addis that his 'arguments are coloured and lose their value by personal feeling', and determined to repress this in future.[10]) Hopkins also thought Villari's portrait of Savonarola defective because Villari's unpoetical mind could not appreciate 'the poetical and picturesque character' of Savonarola's mind. To Hopkins, Savonarola was an ascetic reforming martyr, and an artistic prophet.

For Hopkins Savonarola's 'mystic religious ardour' seems to have provided a model analogous to that of the Counter-Reformation: 'How strangely different is the fate of two reformers, Savonarola and Luther! The one martyred in the Church, the other successful and the admired author of world-wide heresy in schism.'[11] Savonarola wanted to restore the Church by returning it to its former glorious state, while Luther wanted to reform by destruction of the Church's unique essence. This is the first clue in Hopkins's writings to his choice of a Counter-Reformation order rather than a pre-Reformation one.

ℰℐ

At the start of that 1865 spring term, Hopkins had sometimes attended several breakfasts or dinners in a week:

Dine with A. Spooner on Monday.
Breakfast with Addis on Tuesday.
Dine with Wood tomorrow, Sunday. Name off hall.

Breakfast with Lake on Thursday.
Wine with Muirhead on Thursday.
Breakfast with Fyffe on Wednesday.
Breakfast with Macfarlane on Monday.
To breakfast with me on Thursday, Urquhart, Muirhead, Marshall, Madan.
To ask Whitaker, Hood, Addis, Plummer, Macfarlane, Wood, No not Hood
and Whitaker.[12]

On his first shopping-list of the term wine appeared, as well as
toothbrush, clothes-brush, slippers, chalk and drawing-paper.[13] He
decided that his armchair needed to be re-covered or replaced, bought a
new necktie and waistcoat, and described the first spring flowers—
bluebells ('delicious shine'), hyacinths ('crystal-ended'), and 'the
dented primrose'.[14] After his meeting with Dolben, changes appear in
his notebook. He finds out the name and address of the London print-
seller who can supply a copy of Fra Bartolommeo's portrait of Savonarola, and plans to put up statuettes in his room, on brackets, with 'green,
or green and purple silk or cloth backs'. The reading-list made within a
week of Dolben's visit includes the second volume of Villari's account
of Savonarola and Browning's 'Paracelsus'—Browning's style had been
imitated by Dolben but disliked by Hopkins. Also in the reading-list
were two of the basic controversial texts in mid-century ecclesiastical
disputes, *Tracts for the Times* and *Essays and Reviews*.[15] After two years
at Balliol Hopkins had not even read Jowett's famous contribution to
the latter volume, so he obviously knew little of the prevailing liberal
arguments.

His poetry in the next two months turns to new subjects, perhaps
influenced by poems Dolben had sent him—'Homo Factus Est/ (Hic
Genuflectitur). BREV. ROM.' and 'Strange, all-absorbing Love, who
gatherest', which he copied into his commonplace-book. He wrote a
processional hymn for Death, faintly anticipating the 'Death on drum'
stanza in 'The Wreck of the Deutschland' ('O Death, Death, he is
come./ O grounds of Hell make room'); there was an attempt to
romanticize the martyrdom of St Dorothea; and he wrote 'Barnfloor
and Winepress', elaborating and particularizing Old Testament metaphors of harvest. This last poem was published in the *Union Review*,
whose editor, Revd F. G. Lee, a 'doctor of Salamanca', called by
Bridges 'a notoriously eccentric high-church clergyman', had published Dolben. Hopkins created images of torture—'Sheaved in cruel
bands, bruised sore,/ Scourged upon the threshing floor', and 'rackèd
from the press', but pain was stronger in another poem, 'Easter
Communion', with its savouring of Lenten austerities:

Pure fasted faces draw unto this feast:
God comes all sweetness to your Lenten lips.
You striped in secret with breath-taking whips,
Those crookèd rough-scored chequers may be pieced
To crosses meant for Jesu's . . .

The reward for 'sackcloth and frieze/ And the ever-fretting shirt of punishment' would be, wrote Hopkins, God's gift of 'myrrhy-threaded golden folds of ease'. Purity is associated with sensual deprivation and self-inflicted punishment, but the rewards are forms of delayed and spiritualised hyper-sensuousness.

It can be assumed that Hopkins was practising some of the austerities evoked in 'Easter Communion', and may have been influenced by Dolben. Some of his profound experiences in this period can only be guessed. The 12th of March, for instance, he recorded as 'A day of the great mercy of God', and then on Saturday, 'Lady Day, March 25', he made a confession, almost certainly to Canon Liddon, who became his regular confessor. That day he started making confession notes covering every day but not necessarily written daily. Though it was probably Dolben's practice which prompted this, he had thought about making a record of his sins during the previous year, when he had made occasional diary notes of nocturnal losses of semen, noting whether they were voluntary or involuntary, and in making this distinction, separating sins from acts of chance. According to the custom of the time he sterilized his admissions by resorting to Latin ('scelus Onanis'), but was influenced by prevalent medical fictions: 'Indulgence is fatal', said Thring, headmaster of Uppingham, in a sermon. 'The pale complexion, the emaciated form, the slouching gait, the clammy palm, the glassy eye and averted gaze indicate the lunatic victim to this vice. ... The wretched victim either sinks down to a lower level and lives on, or often finds an early grave, killed by his own foul passions.'[16] The reading-list which Hopkins drew up for the Easter vacation included Dr Pusey's 'Sermon on Everlasting Punishment, and on the Remedy for Sins of the body'.

Hopkins wrote his lists of sins in his diary, in gaps between notes on architecture, poems, notes of things to do, lists of people he had to write to, and addresses.[17] Not many of his 'sins' would be recognized by the Church. A number show Hopkins's self-dissatisfaction, particularly with his use of time. (The precisely detailed daily regimen of every Jesuit suggests another reason for Hopkins's choice of the Society of Jesus.) He frequently records wasted time, often having sat too late talking in a friend's room. 'Idleness' and 'idling' are two of his most frequent words. He gets up late—a habit he never completely conquered, even after years as a Jesuit. He does not start work when he should, or spends time on architectural drawings or scribbling patterns, not concentrating properly on his work. Sometimes he spends too long at the Union. Another group of his faults is concerned with 'inattention' at morning chapel or evening service at St Philip and St James, the new High Anglican church designed by Street, at which he now regularly worshipped, or not reading the scriptural lesson which he set himself as a daily task.

Hopkins was over- rather than under-scrupulous in detecting weaknesses of the flesh, and his list of sexual immoralities is probably shorter and less intense than the complete record of an average adolescent. Nothing goes beyond glances, awareness, and 'temptations': the objects of attraction remain at a distance. Most instances of sinful attraction involve males, usually boys or young men: he was frequently attracted to college friends, C. A. Fyffe in particular, and once felt temptation while sketching Baillie.

When he gave up the idea of being a professional painter, because it placed too great a strain on his emotions, he was probably basing his decision on such temptations: 'evil thoughts' occurred to him while he was drawing, particularly when he drew a crucified arm, and a crucifix of his Aunt Kate's stimulated him in the wrong way. In the Easter vacation 1865 he visited 191 Piccadilly, where 'Mr Ford Madox Brown's Exhibition' was being held, and after looking at the painting 'Work', with its foreground focus on the manly forms and bare arms of navvies labouring on Heath Street Hampstead, he had looked in a sinful way at navvies in Swiss Cottage Fields. He often recorded that he found illustrations, such as those in *Once a Week*, temptingly attractive.

He records looking up 'dreadful words' in his lexicon or dictionary, reading 'dangerous things' in *The Saturday Review* and once in *Love's Labour's Lost*, and looking at anatomical diagrams in *The Lancet*. This part of his diary also fills in details of his college and home life during 1865. His particular friends were Addis, Baillie, Urquhart, and—increasingly—Stuckey Coles. That term he and Coles joined a High-Church essay society called 'The New Vitality', probably at the instigation of Geldart, already a member.

At the end of the Easter vacation 1865 he got Dolben's address at his new tutor's, Revd C. Prichard, South Luffenham, in Leicestershire, and wrote it in his diary.[18] Almost every day that summer term he spent some time with Coles, who knew Dolben well—better than Bridges had known him—from Eton. On the day Hopkins recorded Dolben's address he also committed the sin of 'dangerous talking' about Dolben, probably to Coles. Dolben had become a 'forbidden subject'. It seems likely that Hopkins's confessor, Canon Liddon, forbade him to have contact with Dolben, except by letter; the 'forbidden subject' and 'dangerous things' occur in the confessional notes several times within this period, which includes the noting of Dolben's address and the writing of the sonnet 'Where art thou friend?'[19] Perhaps on the day he wrote this poem he recorded that he had brought up the forbidden subject in Coles's room, and one or two days before admitted that he had talked dangerously to Coles about Dolben. 'Where art thou friend?' was written in the middle of confession notes, many of which relate to Dolben, and House's connection of Dolben with this poem, as well as with the religious crises and confessional notes, seems correct. The separation is clear: 'Where art thou friend, whom I shall never see,/ Conceiving whom I must conceive amiss?' The imagination attempts a substitute for the real presence of the friend, but cannot quite succeed. In spite of the awkward recall of Shakespeare's sonnets, the autobiographical pressure is clear, as personal love and longing are masked as a religious plea:

> Thou who canst best accept the certainty
> That thou hadst borne proportion in my bliss,
> That likest in me either that or this.

Hopkins understood and shared Dolben's conflict between secular and divine love. A day or two later he wrote another sonnet, 'Confirmed beauty',[20] on writing a memorial to a beloved, which concluded that he would lay poetry aside, 'and freshly turn instead/ To thy not-staled uncharted memory'.

On 3 May he was again broaching 'dangerous things' to Coles, and two days later dawdled in Coles's room, hoping to hear things 'connected with forbidden subjects, as questions about Dolben'. The next day he started drafts of the three sonnets together called 'The Beginning of the End'. The first wishes desire away: 'My love is less, my love is less for thee./ I cease the mourning and the abject fast', but the wish-fulfilment is passionately contradicted: 'That *less* is heavens higher even yet/ Than treble-fervent *more* of other men'. The beloved is cold— 'Even your unpassion'd eyelids might be wet'; and a fragment of verse which follows is about jealousy and envy. Hopkins may have learnt from Coles or Bridges of Dolben's passion for Gosselin. The next two days he suffered from what his college tutors would have called 'languidness'—he missed chapel on two successive mornings, wasted time both morning and evening, scribbled instead of working, was inattentive at compline, missed the evening lesson, and went to bed later than was good for him.

The second of the three poems which make up 'The Beginning of the End' shapes despondency and unworthiness: his passion had been 'begun/ In the worst hour that's measured by the sun,/ With such malign conjunctions as before/ No influential heaven ever wore'. His hopes were 'evil-heaven'd'. The third sonnet continues the miserable picture: the poet's 'bankrupt heart has no more tears to spend', or else there would be 'fiercer weepings of these desperate eyes/ For poor love's failure'. Mental anguish has led to physical weariness: 'now I am so tired I soon shall send/ Barely a sigh to thought of hope forgone.'

The middle of June 1865 was a time of despondency and inertia. He could not get up in the morning or go to bed at night, missed chapel, and grew dilatory about his devotions. A poem written in mid-May, 'The Alchemist in the City', expresses a self-disillusionment in personal relationships:

> Yet it is now too late to heal
> The incapable and cumbrous shame
> Which makes me when with men I deal
> More powerless than the blind or lame.

Solitude seems preferable to company: 'Then sweetest seems the houseless shore,/ Then free and kind the wilderness'. He continues to note slacknesses and self-disgust. An unfinished poem asks 'But what indeed is ask'd of me?', and comes to a negative conclusion, of 'unworthiness'.

Just before the end of term he copied from *The Spectator* into his diary a poem 'I am! yet what I am who cares or knows?',[21] which John Clare had written in Northamptonshire Asylum. It contains the lines 'And e'en the dearest—that I loved the best—/ Are strange—nay, rather stranger than the rest'. Hopkins was experiencing his first estrangement; exiled in Dublin twenty years later, he wrote 'To seem the stranger lies my lot, my life/ Among strangers', which recalls Clare's words and emotions. And in 1865 Hopkins, like Clare, felt he was an exile.

ও১

Before going home for the long vacation Hopkins made a list of the term's bills, tipped his scout two pounds and the college porter five shillings.[22] Within two days of being back at Hampstead he had written another sonnet of self-denigration:

> Myself unholy, from myself unholy
> To the sweet living of my friends I look—
> Eye-greeting doves bright-counter to the rook, . . .

This was the first of many identifications he made with the rook or crow, culminating in his adoption of the *nom de plume* of 'Brân Maenefa', the crow of Maenefa. Eventually he came to use the image self-disparagingly and wryly.[23] The speaker finds that each of his friends is imperfect, but has one fault or another, while he has them all, and his confidence has been replaced by 'the sultry siege of melancholy'. This simplification of a depressed state concludes with the solution: 'No *better* serves me now, save *best*; no other/ Save Christ: to Christ I look, on Christ I call.' In another poem written in the same week, 'See how Spring opens with disabling cold', he again explores self-denigration, anticipating poems written twenty years later. There is disgust with 'the waste done in unreticent youth', a sense of bitter truth, and a resolve to win 'with late-learnt skill uncouth' some yield from poor soil.

In the first week of July Hopkins went to stay with Martin Geldart and Nash at Geldart's home in Bowdon, near Manchester, and there he wrote poetry of a different kind. He went back to his pastoral drama *Richard*, left unfinished from the previous year, and wrote a continuation of Garnett's poem 'Nix', a children's tale of witches and maidens. On 20 July he travelled back to Hampstead, where he spent the next week. He was not in a good temper, arguing with Cyril, and mimicking the St John's curate, Mr Herclots. He made his mother unhappy about his poems, and was unkind to her when he left for Devon on 28 July.[24] He was off to Chagford, to join a reading party (in contrast to the summer of 1863, when his parents had forbidden it). On his way he visited the village of Halberton, at whose Norman parish church of St Andrew's his grandparents, Anne Manley and Martin Edward Hopkins, had married in 1814. Inside the church were memorials to his great-great-grandparents, Henry and Mary Manley, and to his grandmother's brother, Henry, who had died in the year Hopkins had been born. He went in by the west door and climbed up the steeple. Just outside the village he met an old man driving a donkey-cart, who talked about the Manleys, the Eagles, and the Wemysses (his grandmother's sisters and brothers-in-law), in 'pure Devonshire', which, to Hopkins's surprise, reminded him of his grandmother.[25]

Hopkins found the original Manley well off the main road, and was disappointed that it was only a farmhouse in the middle of red-clay fields. He walked by the Grand Western canal, recently sold to the railway, until he reached Tiverton, in the valley of the Exe. He stayed that night at the Lamb Inn, and called on acquaintances of his grandmother's, the Miss Barneses, in St Peter Street. Next morning he attended matins at the parish church of St Peter's, opposite the Lamb, and heard the organ on which Mendelssohn's music for *A Midsummer Night's Dream* had first been played as a wedding-march, thirty years before. By the main church porch was a Manley family tombstone. After church, Hopkins went to see the Patches of Broomfield, on St Andrew Street. The two Miss Patches were his second cousins, and he found them (he wrote to his mother) 'pretty lively girls'. (His diary records that he looked sinfully at a Tiverton boy that day, but does not mention the girls.) After lunch at Broomfield the girls played duets on the piano and harp, and walked with Hopkins into Tiverton, 'shewed me my road, and left me under a pleasing sense of what charming country cousins I had'. The elder sister had 'beautiful eyes, a bright complexion, black hair tied with blue bands, and a pretty figure all in muslin'. The other was 'more of the Charles II beauty in character, with cherry lips'. He added: 'I am so glad I have seen them.' Hopkins found the road south 'most beautiful', and the Exe valley, gradually widening towards Exeter, 'delightful', with its oaks, thatched cottages, red Devon soil, and green meadows. After the walk of over fifteen miles he reached Exeter, 'a pleasant town, old but flourishing', and stayed at the Royal Clarence Hotel on the Cathedral Green.[26]

On Sunday he crossed the cobbles from his eighteenth-century hotel to attend morning service in the twelfth-century Exeter Cathedral, but felt that his thoughts and feelings were not concentrated on worship. In the afternoon he took the old-fashioned coach for the seventeen miles to the small market town of Chagford,[27] by then becoming known as a centre for excursions into the picturesque Teign gorge or the wilder moor scenery. Hopkins signed the visitors' book at the Three Crowns Inn, a low Tudor building, across the cobbled High Street from the parish church of St Michael the Archangel,[28] and met his study companions, Edward Bond and W. G. F. Phillimore; Phillimore, a year younger than the others, was a historian at Christ Church, and a member of the Hexameron Essay Society.

They probably divided the average day into three: mornings for study, afternoons for walking, and evenings divided between study and informal leisure, with set times for prayers. The first day, Monday 31

July, was spent in catching up on news and talking until late in the night. Hopkins's conscience was troubled by the frivolous day, and he wrote tersely: '31. Idling. Self-indulgence. Old habits [i.e. masturbation]. No lessons. Talking unwisely on evil subjects. Wasting time in going to bed.' By daily identification of shortcomings, Hopkins hoped for self-improvement, but weaknesses continued to show themselves during his month in Dartmoor. On the following Saturday evening he had to record constant idleness, deviations from his work timetable, and loose talking to Bond and Phillimore. He did not feel he had prepared himself properly for Holy Communion, and the following Sunday was marred by inattention at church, and passing the holy day frivolously.

But his liveliness of mind and response to nature had been so stimulated by his surroundings that he was sketching, and writing disciplined description. Chagford had not changed much during the last three hundred years. There were medieval lanes and cottages, undatable walls, casement windows, dark courtyards, and gasless streets at night. Hopkins thought of writing an Elizabethan play, *Castara Victrix* or *Castara Felix*, and drew up a preliminary list of characters: 'Silvian, the king, and his two sons Arcas and Valerian. Carindel. The fool. Carabella. Pirellia. Piers Sweetgate. Daphnis. Daphne.' A stray line occurred to him: 'The melancholy Daphnis doats on him.'[29] But it was not so easy to escape the modern world, and the superficiality of Hopkins's immersion in Chagford's pastoral atmosphere shows in the pedantic names and affected spelling.

In a modern mood, Hopkins, like Ruskin, was noting sunrises and sunsets. One morning at about half-past five, from his window in the east-facing front of the Three Crowns, he saw the sun rise over the row of sycamores bordering St Michael's churchyard on the opposite side of the street:

Sunrise at Chagford. There was a remarkable fan of clouds traced in fine horizontals, which afterwards lost their levels, some becoming oblique. Below appearing bright streaks which crowded up one after another. A white mist in the churchyard, trees ghostly in it.[30]

This description might, he thought, come in handy for a scene from *Floris in Italy*. The second week in Chagford repeats these patterns. There is observation and description; 'The butterfly perching in a cindery dusty road and pinching his scarlet valves'; occasionally there are watery attempts to carry the process further and make literature from the description: 'O what a silence is this wilderness!/ Might we not think the sweet and daring rises/ Of the flown skylark, and that traverse flight/ At highest when he seems to brush the clouds . . . ?' Sometimes the observations—of streams, trees, leaves, skyscape—are translated into quick pencil drawings, meditations on the image, rather than serious art. But among the stilted lines and too-sweet cadences of Hopkins's Chagford verse there is the occasional glimpse of a more specifically Devonshire sight, showing how he was becoming attached to the district. Dartmoor is well characterized by 'stony air', and Becky Falls caught in the lines 'As the wood-sorrel and all things sensitive/ That thrive in the loamy greenness of this place'. It might have been the slim oaks in the woods surrounding these falls whose roots Hopkins observed as 'silvery, smooth, solid and muscular', and in the same spot he could have done his quick sketch of shallow water (he was there in the summer) falling between smooth boulders, or made the technical observation that 'Water rushing over a sunken stone and hollowing itself to rise again seems to be devoured by the wave before which it forces up,/ Reverted, with thrown-back and tossing cape'. About this time he wrote the playful architectural descriptions 'Bossy water' and 'Glazed water vaulted o'er a drowsy stone'.[31]

The nagging, scrupulous part of Hopkins caught up with him each night as he catalogued the day's deficiencies. Of the first fifteen days of his study holiday, he had studied for only five. 'Idleness', 'waste of time', and 'lateness to bed' are written repeatedly, and he felt his religious preparation was not all it should be. It was also on his mind that he had not succeeded in controlling his 'old habit' for longer than two days at a time.

There was a disastrous culmination on Monday, 14th August. In church the previous day he had not attended to the service, while attracted by the sweetness of the singing. He had wasted more time later in the day, gone to bed late, and indulged in 'old habits'. The new week had started inauspiciously with 'no lessons' and 'old habits'. There was some disagreement with Bond and Phillimore. As a result he was almost in despair, and despair was a moral fault. He was sexually tempted when he recalled a boy he had seen, and while drawing Phillimore felt another temptation. Finally that day he had to record 'Loss of faith in God'.

The next day the three went to the neighbouring Moreton Hampstead, and visited the church. St Andrew's was typically Devonian, with battlemented porch, granite tower with lichened pinnacles, and wagon-style roof. Among the names of rectors painted on the wall was that of a Robert Manly, an Oxford University man who had been incumbent in the late seventeenth century. Hopkins looked at some men in church in a way he considered immoral, and duly recorded this in his account of the day's shortcomings, along with 'lateness to bed', 'no lessons', 'sharp temper', and 'O.H.'

On Friday they were invited to dine at the Rectory, with the Revd Hayter Hames.[32] The visit may have contributed to another lapse in study and reading penitential psalms that day. Hopkins felt he had over-indulged at dinner at the Hameses, since it was his habit to be abstemious on Fridays. It was about the time of this visit to the parson, in his happy family circle but newly bereaved,[33] that Hopkins wrote six lines of verse in which he imagined what it would be like to renounce family life and become a celibate priest, devoted to a heavenly realm:

> Mothers are doubtless happier for their babes
> And risen sons: yet are the childless free
> From tears shed over children's graves.
> So those who . . . of Thee
> Take their peculiar thorns and natural pain
> Among the lilies and thy good domain.[34]

For the remainder of this stay Hopkins became more dissatisfied, and especially troubled by his outbreaks of bad temper towards Phillimore. A picnic was spoilt by his affectation and self-indulgence, he thought. But he sketched leaves and trees, and walked to the magnificently steep Whyddon Park, at the foot of the Teign gorge. He developed his passions for ash-clusters and skylarks, and made the oddly false observation that the rainbow is 'almost invisible when looked at with one eye'. Towards the end of August he moved to south Devon, for a stay at Frederick Gurney's cottage in Torquay. Gurney had left Oxford the previous year with a third-class degree, and was training for the Anglican priesthood. He had recently married a delicate young woman, Alice, whom Hopkins considered dangerously attractive. At Torquay Hopkins found a letter from Bridges, inviting him to stay in Rochdale vicarage, the Bridges–Molesworth home, to meet Coles and Dolben. But the invitation came too late. He had arranged to leave Torquay for Hampstead, so replied that he wished the invitation had reached him in July, while he was near Rochdale: 'Nothing cd. have been so delightful as to meet you and Coles and Dolben. . . . Give my love to [Coles] and Dolben. I have written letters without end to the latter without a whiff of answer.'[35] It had been six months since he had seen Dolben, and he had been fervently hoping for renewed contact.

# *Religion*

When Hopkins travelled from Torquay to Oak Hill on Monday 28 August, there were six weeks before the Michaelmas term. For the first ten days of this period his diary is split between terse notes on reprehensible actions and fragments of soliloquy, song, and dialogue from *Castara Victrix*:[1]

> CASTARA. And how long was the way?
> ESQUIRE.                     This shorter way?
>                 Two miles indeed.
> C.                     We have come four, do you think?
>                 Somewhere we slipt astray, you cannot doubt.
> E.         True, madam. I am sorry now to see
>                 I better'd all our path with sanguine eyes.

Neither his heart nor mind were in this writing, filled with faint echoes of verses from another mind and time, without personality or urgency. Characters are indistinguishable, situations not thought out, rhythms dull. Only one stanza in Daphne's pastoral song has images of any power:

> His cap shall be shining fur,
> And stained, and knots of golden thread,
> He shall be warm with miniver
> Lined all with silk of juicy red.

Even at its best this verse is nothing like the recent scraps of sharply engaged poetry, or the experimentally patterned notes on sounds.

Feeling a sudden 'fascination about the dramatic form', Hopkins took up *Floris in Italy*, started fifteen months earlier as a poem and later turned into neo-Shakespearean drama, composing a speech in which Floris argues against reciprocating Giulia's love, since true love must be spontaneous, not anticipated or designed—'New love is free love, or true love 'tis not'. The speech is less about love than aesthetics; though Hopkins's outline states that Giulia's 'beauty is urged', 'beauty' is discussed in the abstract, and Giulia forgotten:

> Say beauty lies but in the meet of lines,
> In careful-spacèd sequences of sound. . . .
> Allow at least it has one term and part
> Beyond, and one within the looker's eye.

Hopkins is crudely breaching a phonaesthetic ideal which would be fully developed ten years later, as well as laying the groundwork for his theory of perception.

While writing these fragments he was reading *Love's Labour's Lost* and daunted by comparison, gave up the task, putting the experience into a poem, *Shakspere*, whose tone and imagery echoes Arnold's 1844 sonnet 'Shakespeare':

> In the lodges of the perishable souls
> He has his portion. God, who stretch'd apart
> Doomsday and death—whose dateless thought must chart
> All time at once and span the distant goals,
> Sees what his place is; but for us the rolls
> Are shut against the canvassing of art.

So he gave up the Elizabethan/Jacobean mode.

His curt confessional notes are repetitive. He is dully caught up in the round of petty habits he knows are wrong but has no power to discontinue. Day after day he records lateness in getting up and going to bed and idleness, and obliquely notes minor sexual transgressions. His casual reading is a waste of time or done for the wrong reasons, he looks at 'tempting pictures' in *Once a Week*, reads Walter Savage Landor 'with wicked curiosity', and catches himself out 'weakly reading a stupid story'. He still has not conquered the habit of looking up suggestive words in the dictionary.

It is difficult to judge how he fitted in with family life during these weeks, as the only records are the notes he made when he felt himself in the wrong. He argued and disagreed more with his mother than with his father, but this may have been because his father was in his office most of the day. Hopkins seems to have entertained his brothers and sisters regularly by mimicking his father, and they emulated his imitations. He recorded the mimicry as reprehensible, but went on doing it. He also recorded the odd squabble with Kate, and frequent arguments with Cyril.

Every Sunday he attended at least one service at St John's with the family, but sometimes felt a lack of faith, and on 7 September wrote:

My prayers must meet a brazen heaven
And fail and scatter all away.
Unclean and seeming unforgiven
My prayers I scarcely call to pray.
I cannot buoy my heart above;
Above I cannot entrance win.
I reckon precedents of love,
But feel the long success of sin.

My heaven is brass and iron my earth:
Yea, iron is mingled with my clay,
So harden'd is it in this dearth
Which praying fails to do away.
Nor tears, nor tears this clay uncouth
Could mould, if any tears there were.
A warfare of my lips in truth,
Battling with God, is now my prayer.

The structuring images of the poem are Homeric: the brazen dome of the ancient Greek heaven, and the four stages in Man's moral deterioration, gold to silver to bronze to iron (perhaps borrowed from Arnold's essay 'Heinrich Heine'). If his heaven is of brass, then his earth must be the lowest stage of all, iron, and himself clay. The poem describes Hopkins's personal religious practices: prayer, need for confession and absolution, and repentance. Hopkins is stifled by the values of liberal Balliol, and longs to transcend the sordid secular round.

On 10 September he started a difficult letter to Baillie,[2] still one of his frequent companions after two years at Balliol. He was aware that compared with Baillie he seemed an impulsive gusher: 'My fear was once that my extravagances (and perhaps also my pugnacity) might indispose you towards my opinions and I might stand in the way of truth.' Baillie had written to tell Hopkins of 'a great change' that had taken place in him: a 'Catholic principle' had 'approved itself' to him, and he knew that Hopkins had already accepted some Catholic beliefs. Hopkins trod cautiously, careful not to dislodge any new tenet of faith:

In whatever I have said in this letter—and generally—pray pardon any assumption, wh. I am afraid I must often have offended you with in old times when yr. opinions were not altogether fixed in shape, it being, though very wrong, a natural consequence fr. time to time of the irrepressible sense of holding the truth however unworthy one really was to hold it.

He was afraid that he expressed the 'effervescence and enthusiasm given by noble principles', rather than 'their moral and essential parts', like the writers in the Roman Catholic *Dublin Review* and the Anglican *Church Times*. Having recognized these values 'in a conscious and deliberate shape' longer than Baillie, he felt able to speak 'of the difference the apprehension of the Catholic truths one after another makes in one's views of everything'. Catholicism seemed to him to be the remedy for his troubles:

the *sordidness* of things, wh. one is compelled perpetually to feel is perhaps . . . the most unmixedly painful thing one knows of: and this is (objectively) intensified and (subjectively) destroyed by Catholicism. If people cd. all know this, to take no higher ground, no other inducement wd. to very many minds be needed to lead them to Catholicism and no opposite inducement cd. dissuade them fr. it.

Though an agnostic, Baillie later said that Hopkins 'enormously influenced me, so that to this day [1917] I am often inclined to think that [the traditional Christianity of the Middle Ages] is the only form of Xtianity worth considering'.[3]

Although Hopkins was reading with varying degrees of criticism and sympathy journals inclining to Roman Catholic, Tractarian (the *Union Review*), and Anglican positions, which would all call themselves 'Catholic', by 'Catholic truths' and 'Catholicism' in his letter to Baillie he was referring to the Roman Church. In the same letter he gave further hints of his religious sensibility: the particular 'Catholic truths' which influenced his 'views of everything' were 'those of course of the blessed sacrament of the altar', and Catholicism provided a sufficient bulwark against the erosion of new knowledge: 'I am amused to find how very far the advance of thought or science is fr. being on every side an encroachment on Christianity. I think I see them retiring fr. old positions before it in important parts.'

A more credulous and romantic facet of Hopkins's religious feeling is shown in his recording of a vision of Edward the Confessor:

that England should be afflicted and not restored to God's mercy till 'a green tree, cut down from the root, and removed three furlongs distant from its own stock, should, without the help of any man's hand, return to its own root again, and bring forth fruit and flourish.' . . . Taking 1525 as the date of the Reformation and a furlong as 125 years, that is the 8th of 1000 years which might well stand for a mile, three furlongs would = 375 years and bring the date of reunion to 1900.[4]

With the impulsive logic with which he often interpreted numbers, Hopkins is expressing faith in numerical coincidence as a sign of

Providence, and a hope for the reunion of the Anglican and Roman Churches.

He became doubtful of the efficacy of Anglican Holy Communion, and for weeks worried about his preparation for receiving Communion. The Sunday services at St John's were unsatisfactory, and his Sundays generally ill-spent; he felt contempt for the sermons, and doubted the Anglican version of divine revelation. Once he imagined himself preaching a form of Catholic truth unacceptable to Anglicans, and afterwards castigated himself for spiritual pride and self-will. On 5 October he spoke out (unwisely, he later thought) about leaving 'our Church'; next day he spoke of apostasy. The following Sunday he was inattentive during the St John's service, laughed at the sermon, felt ill will towards Herclots, again forecast that he might one day join the Church of Rome, and at dinner talked about Dr Newman 'in a foolish way likely to produce unhappiness and pain'.

The poetry he had written during the previous fortnight gives an unfinished and uncharacteristically sparse articulation of spiritual barrenness:

> Trees by their yield
> Are known; but I—
> My sap is sealed,
> My root is dry.

The sense of barrenness was to recur for the rest of his life. (In 1889 he would write: 'birds build—but not I build; no, but strain,/ Time's eunuch, and not breed one work that wakes'.[5]) He copied into his diary Newman's 'The Pillar of the Cloud', written in 1833, while Newman was an Anglican:

> Lead, Kindly Light, amid the encircling gloom,
>   Lead Thou me on!
> The night is dark, and I am far from home—
>   Lead Thou me on!
> Keep Thou my feet; I do not ask to see
> The distant scene,—one step enough for me.

In the revised edition of *Apologia Pro Vita Sua*, published in 1865, Newman had associated 'Lead, Kindly Light' with an earlier memorandum in which he had spoken of himself as 'now in my rooms at Oriel College, slowly advancing, & c. and led on by God's hand blindly, not knowing whither He is taking me'. In the second stanza of 'Trees by their yield' Hopkins had argued:

> although
> Self-sentenced, still
> I keep my trust.
> If He would prove
> And search me through
> Would he not find
> (What yet there must
> Be hid behind . . .

At this point he broke off the poem.

In the *Apologia* Newman had written of the three 'original points of belief' which kept him an Anglican: 'the principle of dogma, the sacramental system, and anti-Romanism'. Newman had been more learned and passionate an anti-Romanist than Hopkins, but by the time he went up to Oxford on 13 October, Hopkins was doubtful of Anglican dogma and its sacraments. An essential step of Newman's advance towards Rome was his wish 'for union between the Anglican Church and Rome, if, and when, it was possible'. Within a fortnight of returning to Balliol, Hopkins had written two more poems about his conflict. In a sonnet 'Let me be to Thee as the circling bird', the narrator has found 'the authentic cadence', after imagining 'each pleasurable throat that sings', and 'every praisèd sequence of sweet strings'; the poem's resounding conclusiveness has a decision behind its strength:

> I have found the dominant of my range and state—
> Love, O my God, to call Thee Love and Love.

The other poem, 'The Half-way House', takes its title from Newman's image of the Church of England as half-way between Roman Catholicism and atheism. One of the most Herbertian of Hopkins's poems, its tone has a new calm and satisfaction:

> Love I was shewn upon the mountain-side
> And bid to catch Him ere the drop of day.
> See, Love, I creep and Thou on wings dost ride:
> Love, it is evening now and Thou away;

The Church of England, 'my national old Egyptian reed', has been replaced by the true Church, 'a cross-barred rod or rood', which is waiting:

> You shall have your wish; enter these walls, one said;
> He is with you in the breaking of the bread.

During this Michaelmas Term Hopkins found himself speaking unwisely to Coles about Romanizing. His most frequent companions now were the Ritualists Coles and Urquhart. According to J. A. Symonds, who had known him when they were both Balliol undergraduates, Urquhart was 'a Scotchman of perfervid type', who 'had High Church proclivities and ran after choristers'.[6] He was curate at Saints Philip and James, where Hopkins worshipped regularly. Hopkins's diary records his speaking ill of that church and, during one week in October, 'laughing at Urquhart' on no fewer than five days. Sometimes he found himself arguing angrily with Coles. His feeling for Dolben flared briefly on one occasion at the end of October. On 6 November he wrote 'On this day by God's grace I resolved to give up all beauty until I had His leave for it;—also Dolben's letter came for which Glory to God.'[7] ('Glory to God', besides being meant literally, seems to have been a personal exclamation of Hopkins's.) Dolben's letter is likely to have been connected with the vow to give up beauty. Perhaps it brought word of Dolben's ascetic self-restrictions, encouraging emulation, but certainly the vow—not kept for long—was a Dolben-like gesture. Despite guilt, Hopkins found himself 'going on with a letter to Dolben at night agst. warning', and on 14 December he wrote another letter, about which he recorded feeling some conceit.

On 16 December, the day before he returned to Hampstead, he confessed to Pusey. He recorded having laughed at 'the dear Doctor', suggesting that his admiration was no longer unmixed. Early in the new year he recorded details of a review by Frederick Oakley, a Roman Catholic priest, of Catholic reactions to Pusey's new work *Eirenicon*, as though seeking Roman Catholic support against Pusey.[8] At home he unwisely pursued arguments about Catholicism. During the first week of the vacation he composed some more of 'A Voice from the World' especially for Dolben, started eighteen months earlier, and now retitled 'Beyond the Cloister', and on Christmas Day he wrote a simple poem of dedication, rather like a prayer composed by his father for recitation by the children of the St John's Sunday school:

> Moonless darkness stands between.
> Past, the Past, no more be seen!
> But the Bethlehem star may lead me
> To the sight of Him Who freed me
> From the self that I have been.
> Make me pure, Lord: Thou art holy;
> Make me meek, Lord: Thou wert lowly;
> Now beginning, and alway:
> Now begin, on Christmas day.

During the second half of 1865 Hopkins thought he had passed through a crisis of identity. The old self was repudiated, but he had not yet knitted together the valuable pieces of his past. It is doubtful if he ever achieved complete coherence—he seems always afraid of his unconquered demons, and took strong measures to keep them down. But at this time he was confusing dissatisfaction over his instability with a growing alienation from the Anglican Church, the more easily repudiated values of Oak Hill and St John's, and the powerful spirit of Balliol liberalism. He knew that he was ready for a new identity. It is probable that the change was less one of basic beliefs than a development of existing ones, but in the fiercely partisan religious battleground of the 1860s his conversion was bound to look like a complete transformation. It was a time when apostasy from a creed involved social and personal repudiations. Beneath the simple and apparently external form of Hopkins's apostasy lay a complex act of repudiation, involving an inability to come to terms with his own temperament. Oxford offered strong ideological models, from which he chose the strongest and most comprehensive.

His notes on personal behaviour show that his reaction to his indiscriminate sexual feelings was a desire not to resolve but to crush them. His judgement by absolutes combined with sexual inexperience to produce a standard of female purity that was narrow even by the standards of the 1860s. His religious career strengthened and sanctioned such ignorance. Shakespeare's Beatrice to Hopkins was not only 'vain' but 'impure minded . . . (I do not know that I may not call her a hideous character)'; whereas 'in my own [experience], it seems to me that nothing in good women is more beautiful than just the absence of vanity and an earnestness of look and character which is better than beauty'.[9] The innocence and fear that lay behind such judgements is sometimes exposed in his mature poetry, where he wrenches ethical argument to justify the appeal of physical beauty.

Though he went on making confessions within the Anglican Church, his confession notes ended on 23 January 1866. On that day he made a list of personal regulations:

For Lent. No pudding on Sundays. No tea except if to keep me awake and then without sugar. Meat only once a day. No verses in Passion Week or on Fridays. No lunch or meat on Fridays. Not to sit in armchair except can work in no other way. Ash Wednesday and Good Friday bread and water.[10]

The next entry shows he has broken his vow to give up beauty, and that, despite his attempt at sexual suppression, the response to natural beauty is not asexual:

Lobes of the trees. Cups of the eyes. Gathering back the lightly hinged eyelids.

Bows of the eyelids. Pencil of eyelashes. Juices of the eyeball. Eyelids like leaves, petals, caps, tufted hats, handkerchiefs, sleeves, gloves. Also of the bones sleeved in flesh. Juices of the sunrise. Joins and veins of the same.[11]

In the middle of January he wrote 'The Habit of Perfection', a poem not so much about asceticism as about the sensuous gratification to be gained by deprivation. Ears, eyes, palate, nostrils, and skin are deprived of satisfaction to experience greater fulfilment;

> Palate, the hutch of tasty lust,
> Desire not to be rinsed with wine:
> The can must be so sweet, the crust
> So fresh that come in fasts divine!

Such romantic ideas of cloister life had been portrayed in Pre-Raphaelite paintings of the 1850s. The reality of asceticism was still distant from Hopkins's imagination.

About this time Hopkins also copied out for Dolben another, similar poem, knowing that it would appeal to its recipient:

> *Fair Havens—The Nunnery*
>
> I have desired to go
>     Where springs not fail,
> To fields where flies not the unbridled hail,
>     And a few lilies blow.
>
> I have desired to be
>     Where havens are dumb,
> Where the green water-heads may never come
>     As in the unloved sea.

In a letter to Coleridge, who was due to start at Balliol next term, Hopkins, without mentioning Catholicism, expressed the contrast he felt between his daily life and the religious life. Even such severe doctrines as that of eternal punishment served to 'correct and avenge the triviality of this life'. Such triviality needed a strong corrective, a belief which made 'ordinary goings on look more ridiculously trivial than they wd. otherwise'. In this letter Hopkins used the word 'trivial' thirteen times in a paragraph of eleven sentences, declaring that 'the trivialness of life is . . . done away with by the Incarnation'.[12] Despite his confidence in the answer to the new scientific and philosophical questions, Hopkins felt an urge that spring to write in 'Nondum' his own version of contemporary doubt, using echoes from *In Memoriam* and recent sonnets by Charles Turner Tennyson:

And Thou art silent, whilst Thy world
Contends about its many creeds
And hosts confront with flags unfurled
And zeal is flushed and pity bleeds
And truth is heard, with tears impearled,
A moaning voice among the reeds.

The expressions of doubt and prayer ('Speak! whisper to my watching heart/ One word') are unoriginal, and 'Nondum' should be placed beside 'The Nightingale', written earlier in 1866, as a pale imitation of Tennyson's 'Enoch Arden'.

*છ*

At the start of the Trinity term, on 2 May 1866, Hopkins and Addis went into lodgings at 18 New Inn Hall Street. Hopkins started a new journal, the first one which still exists. That term it was filled with accounts of his walks in Oxford and its neighbourhood. The descriptions show a tender sense of the setting, as well as a fascination with odd details:

May 3. Cold. Morning raw and wet, afternoon fine. Walked then with Addis, crossing Bablock Hythe, round by Skinner's Weir through many fields into the Witney road. Sky sleepy blue without liquidity. From Cumnor Hill saw St. Philip's and the other spires through blue haze rising pale in a pink light. . . . over the green water of the river passing the slums of the town and under its bridges swallows shooting, blue and purple above and shewing their amber-tinged breasts reflected in the water, their flight unsteady with wagging wings and leaning first to one side then the other. Peewits flying.

May 4. Fine. Alone in Powder Hill wood. Elms far off have that flaky look now but nearer the web of springing green with long curls moulds off the skeleton of the branches. Fields pinned with daisies. Buds of apple blossoms look like nails of blood. Some ashes are out.

June 3. . . . With Garrett in Binsey Lane. The green was softening with grey. The meadows yellow with buttercups and under-reddened with sorrel and containing white of oxeyes and puff-balls. The cuckoo singing one side, on the other from the ground and unseen the wood-lark, as I suppose, most sweetly with a song of which the structure is more definite than the skylark's and gives the link with that of the rest of birds.—Yellow meadows shining through the willow-rods pretty.[13]

It was the custom for potential First-Class Honours students to take a term's intensive coaching in the year before their Finals, and Hopkins was sent to a protégé of Jowett's, Walter H. Pater, a Fellow of Brasenose for the past two years. Hopkins took a walk with him on the last evening in April, a fine, bitterly cold night. At that time Pater represented to him 'Bleak-faced Neology'. A month later, on another cold day Pater talked 'two hours against Xtianity'.[14] The other surviving record of Pater's coaching is an essay on 'The Origin of Our Moral Ideas', which shows Hopkins at his least strident and moralistic. As he compares art and morality, he is taking care not to fall foul of an authoritative opponent known to abhor 'vulgarity of expression, over-emphasis, exaggeration'. The style is sensitively balanced and donnish, rather than undergraduate:

In art we strive to realise not only unity, permanence of law, likeness, but also, with it, difference, variety, contrast: it is rhyme we like, not echo, and not unison but harmony. But in morality the highest consistency is the highest excellence. The reason of this seems to be that the desire of unity is prior to that of difference and whereas in art both are in our power, in moral action our utmost efforts never result in its perfect realisation, in perfect consistency.[15]

One would not guess that the writer of this had experienced struggles with self-disgust, nor that he was thinking of becoming a priest. Hopkins shows here that he has given up the fight to unite morality with art, a fight with which Pater is still occupied in *Marius the Epicurean* (1885), where Marius speculates that morality may be 'in effect, one mode of comeliness in things—as it were music, or a kind of artistic order, in life'.

The day before he left Oxford for the long vacation of 1866, Hopkins visited the Botanical Gardens. He probably used the gate in the west wall, as he first noted 'vines silver on walls', and there was a vine next to that gate. Today the plants are still arranged in much the same order 'of kinship and descent' as in 1866. He may have absorbed material for the details of his theory about variegation in beauty from the scientifically laid-out beds of patterned, mottled, and pied beauty in the Gardens. Some of his favourite flowers belonged to the lily and iris families;[16] on this visit to the Gardens he noticed some yellow and orange tall-stemmed lilies just beyond the west gate near the north-west corner; they were 'most like amaryllises, but the name of the yellow sort was *hemerocallis*, I believe'.[17] The *Hemerocallis fulva* is still by the west wall, 'in chaplets', as Hopkins described, 'and curled sometimes at the upper, sometimes the lower, side, most beautiful'.

On 15 June Hopkins and Addis set out on a walking tour of western English cathedrals. (Ruskin had praised medieval cathedrals as England's most glorious architecture.) They took the train from Oxford to Glastonbury, and after looking at the abbey walked to Wells, where they stayed overnight. The next day they walked over the Mendips to

Bristol. During the next three days they heard a Gregorian setting of a psalm or canticle at St Raphael's, a High Anglican church near the Bristol docks, walked from Chepstow to Tintern Abbey, then to Ross-on-Wye and on to Hereford. From there they went 'to the R. C. Benedictine Monastery at Belmont two miles up the river, first he, then by his direction I, partly along the river, partly inland amidst oaks, which grow richly here. The sky at that time was grey and moulded in long flutings.' One of the Benedictine monks, probably Dom P. R. Raynal, 'was very kind and showed me over everything'. The footsore Hopkins took the train for Gloucester, and after seeing the 'very sadly done' cathedral, went home to Hampstead in a rain-storm.[18]

He visited the Water-Colours and Royal Academy exhibitions, stayed at Blunt House for two days, and wrote letters to A. W. Garrett and W. A. C. Macfarlane, High-Church friends of his, planning their forthcoming reading holiday.[19]

# Perversion and Estrangement

The Sussex Downs was a seductive place to go for a reading party, Walter Pater suggested to Hopkins.[1] Hopkins put forward Salisbury as an alternative, because it was near a cathedral, with good country, and not far from George Herbert's Bemerton, Lord Herbert's church, Salisbury Plain, Stonehenge, and Avebury.[2] But he and his friends took Pater's advice and rented Whiting's Farm, near Horsham, from Mr Henry Ings, for the last fortnight in July 1866.[3] In bed on the night of 17 July, Hopkins 'saw clearly the impossibility of staying in the Church of England', but resolved 'to say nothing to anyone till three months are over'. He also decided that he would not be received into the Roman Catholic Church until after he had taken his degree.[4]

On 19 July, while Garrett and Macfarlane went to Evensong, Hopkins walked alone in the woods and the Nuthurst Lodge park, where there was a view over the South Downs to Shoreham harbour. In the park Hopkins

found the law of the oak leaves. It is of platter-shaped stars altogether; the leaves lie close like pages, packed, and as if drawn tightly to. But these old packs, which lie at the end of their twigs, throw out now long shoots alternately and slimly leaved, looking like bright keys. All the sprays but markedly these ones shape out and as it were embrace greater circles and the dip and toss of these make the wider and less organic articulations of the tree.[5]

The next day, on a fine afternoon, Macfarlane and Hopkins strolled in 'a delightful wood of tall oaks', on the other side of the Nuthurst Lodge wood. Hopkins noted: 'The boughs spare, just roughed with lichen, and gracefully and muscularly waved, checking each other as well as the whole grate of one tree those of its neighbours, are jotted with light and shadow by the sunlight.' They attended evensong and returned to the farm for tea. On Saturday Macfarlane found Hopkins 'rather disagreeable' during the day, and went off with Garrett into Horsham. When they returned Hopkins had tea ready for them, but did not join them on their evening stroll, going on his own to study 'a large-leaved kind of ash which grows in tall close bushes: when the wind blows it the backs of the sprays, which are silvery, look like combs of fish-bones, the leaves where they border their rib-stem appearing, when in repetition all jointed on one rib, to be angularly cut at the inner end'.[6]

This holiday is the only time in Hopkins's life of which there are two accounts, one by himself and the other by a companion:

*22 July* [Macfarlane] Strolled out with G. and H. and H. deserted us. Church at Horsham, ambitious but rather futile sermon. Full choral service. Tea on returning and we had a serious talk with Hopkins about his manners etc. Compline at 10.45 and so to bed.

*22 July* [Hopkins] Bright, sky a beautiful blue. [then the symbol signifying that he had taken Holy Communion that day]

*23 July* [Macfarlane] Very fine day. . . . Invented a cypher for Hopkins and set him to decypher it in which he did not succeed before tea. Walked all three after tea. Read Trench Parable of Labourers. Compline.

*23 July* [Hopkins] The same [weather], but blighty in morning.

*24 July* [Macfarlane] Fine day. . . . Walked out with Hopkins and he confided to me his fixed intention of going over to Rome. I did not attempt to argue with him as his grounds did not admit of argument. Went to Evensong alone. Tea delayed till past 8 owing to non appearance of Garrett & Hopkins not providing eggs. Hopkins found out the cypher.

*24 July* [Hopkins] Dull, sky breathing open in blue splits and a little sunlight.— Spoke to Macfarlane, foolishly.—The wild parsley (if it is that) growing in clumps by the road side a beautiful sight, the leaf being delicately cut like rue. There is a tree that has a leaf like traveller's-joy, curled, and with brick-like veinings. It has clusters of berries which are flattened like some tight-mouthed jars. . . .[7]

Hopkins's moodiness shows in a letter he wrote that day to Bridges: 'the place is rather a fool's paradise for the church is not what we expected and we are a long way off. The farm is ugly as can be but the country very pretty.'[8]

Three days later they had their photographs taken together in Horsham. They look comically uncomfortable, overdressed in waist-coats, collars, and ties, carrying hats and canes, in the long grass under a blossoming tree at the bottom of the photographer's garden. Macfarlane sits huge, serious, bearded and bespectacled, on a dining-room chair in the uncut grass, Garrett stands stiff and severe, looking into the distance, with his fist on the top of the chair, and Hopkins—a Chaplinesque figure with baggy and crumpled, light-coloured trousers, long, dark jacket and waistcoat—clasps a bowler to his chest, leaning uncomfortably inwards, with his elbow on Macfarlane's neck, and staring hostilely at the camera, his lips taut under a tiny moustache, as though the photographer has just asked him to close his mouth.

From a certain crispiness in Macfarlane's diary for that fortnight, and the fact that they often separated to do different things—Macfarlane to play the organ, Hopkins to sketch and walk alone—it does not seem to have been a very sociable holiday. There was little reading done, and desultory strollings every day to and from a church they didn't like. They parted on 2 August, Garrett going to London, Macfarlane to Oxford, and Hopkins to stay with his family at Shanklin again, where they had rented Cintra, a large villa in its own grounds in the old town. It was not a happy holiday there either for Hopkins, and he felt that his work for Greats had been so inadequate that he would have to read hard for the rest of the vacation. Bridges invited him to come to Rochdale, to stay with him and his mother and step-father, Dr and Mrs Molesworth, saying that Hopkins could study. Hopkins replied that he would 'like nothing so much as to stay at Rochdale, more especially ... when you hold out the possibility of Dolben being there', but explained that first he had 'some business ... to do some time' in Birmingham.[9]

The day after he arrived back at Oak Hill, Hopkins wrote a letter kept secret from the family:

Reverend Sir,—I address you with great hesitation knowing that you are in the midst of yr. own engagements and because you must be exposed to applications from all sides. I am anxious to become a Catholic, and I thought that you might possibly be able to see me for a short time when I pass through Birmingham in a few days, I believe on Friday. . . . I do not want to be helped to any conclusions of belief, for I am thankful to say my mind is made up, but the necessity of becoming a Catholic (although I had long foreseen where the only consistent position wd. lie) coming upon me suddenly has put me into painful confusion of mind about my immediate duty in my circumstances.[10]

The letter was addressed to the Revd Dr John H. Newman, at the Oratory, Edgbaston, Birmingham.

By Friday morning, when he was due to catch the train for Birmingham, he had received no reply from Newman, and set out for Rochdale. At the Molesworths' vicarage he was in an anxious state, which grew acute one day as he and Bridges were filling an aquarium. Hopkins later paid a tribute to Bridges's personal gentleness and sympathy over that period: 'His kindness at that time when he did not know what was the matter with me I perpetually thank God for.'[11]

In the middle of September, while he was still at Rochdale, Hopkins received a letter from Newman, redirected from Oak Hill, apologizing for the delay in replying, caused by his absence abroad, and saying that he would gladly see Hopkins if he would fix a day. Hopkins arranged to meet him at the Oratory on 20 September. Having received a mysterious letter postmarked 'Edgbaston', and then having to announce suddenly that he had to go urgently to Birmingham, made it impossible for him to conceal from Bridges the news about his conversion and visit to Newman. Despite the fact that he had moved during his years at Oxford from ritualistic Anglo-Catholicism to agnosticism, Bridges was sympathetic towards Hopkins's problems, though surprised and sorry that Hopkins had not trusted their friendship sufficiently to confide in him earlier. Hopkins made a flustered attempt at rationalizing:

I am most distressed to think that the news of my conversion, if [Dr and Mrs Molesworth] hear it, may give them pain and alarm for you, but you must remember that when I came to Rochdale I did not look upon my reception as to be so soon as it really was to be. You see the point of what was on my mind at the vicarage was chiefly this, that my wishes about you cd. not be gained except at your own and their trouble and grief.

When the letter from Newman arrived, Hopkins hastily packed his bags and said goodbye to Dr Molesworth, but did not catch Mrs Molesworth to thank her. At the Oratory,

Dr Newman was most kind, I mean in the very best sense, for his manner is not that of solicitous kindness but genial and almost, so to speak, unserious. And if I may say so, he was so sensible. He asked questions which made it clear for me how to act; I will tell you presently what that is: he made sure I was acting deliberately and wished to hear my arguments; when I had given them and said I cd. see no way out of them, he laughed and said 'Nor can I': and he told me I must come to the Church to accept and believe—as I hope I do. He thought there appeared no reason, if it had not been for matters at home of course, why I shd. not be received at once, but in no way did he urge me on, rather the other way. More than once when I offered to go he was good enough to make me stay talking.[12]

In Newman's room he saw a bird's eye view of Oxford, on the frame of which were the words from Ezekiel: 'Fili hominis, putasne vivent ossa ista? Domine Deus, tu nosti.' ('Son of Man, do you think these dry bones live? Lord God, thou knowest.')

As a result of this visit, Hopkins changed his mind about the timing of his entry into the Catholic Church: 'I am to go over fr. Oxford to the Oratory for my reception next term—early in the term I must make it.' Newman thought it 'both expedient and likely that I shd. finish my time at Oxford'. The importance of Newman's advice that Hopkins should enter the Church and stay to finish his degree cannot be overstated. If Hopkins had chosen Manning, rather than Newman, as his mentor, Manning would have said—as he did later on to one of Hopkins's Jesuit colleagues, Henry Browne—that a Catholic could not remain at Oxford.[13] Newman offered Hopkins, or so the latter understood, a retreat at the Oratory during the Christmas vacation.[14]

After the meeting Hopkins returned to Oak Hill, having decided to keep his conversion a secret from his parents until the time of his reception, when he would let them know by letter from Oxford. On the day of his return home he wrote to Urquhart telling him of his conversion, but asking him to let no one know until after he had been received; he was praying for and expecting Urquhart's own conversion. H. W. Challis had recently gone over, and he was expecting Addis to 'in not a very long time'. Urquhart was the only friend whom Hopkins deliberately told of his conversion, though three days after seeing Newman he admitted to Urquhart that Macfarlane and Garrett knew through his 'incaution', and one of his brothers, probably Cyril, 'forced' it from him 'by questions'. 'Dr Newman of course and one or two other Catholics know',[15] and he would have told Addis except that he did not want to break up Addis's holiday at Birchington. Bridges wrote promising to keep silent, but still puzzled at being kept in ignorance. Hopkins replied that it would have been unkind to have told him, again evading an answer:

Though you call yourself 'of a plain blurting disposition' I think you wd. however agree that silence is an excellent discipline and especially during the process of conviction (this of course is neither here nor there to my silence at Rochdale)—indeed you have several times said as much. In fact it occurs to me that you are unusually reticent and certainly have a great respect for reticence.[16]

Apart from this anxiety over trust, the relationship had deepened over the period of Hopkins's conversion and reception.

કત

Letters from Hopkins to Bridges just before the start of the Michaelmas term 1866 describe men by whose appearance Hopkins is fascinated:

[24 September] I saw too another Oxford man, whose name I do not know, with a delightful face (not handsome), altogether aquiline features, a sanguine complexion, rather tall, slight, and eager-looking. . . . His face was fascinating me last term: I generally have one fascination or another on. Sometimes I dislike the faces wh. fascinate me but sometimes much the reverse, as is the present case.

[28 September] . . . the Corpus man whose name I wanted to know. I met him riding in one of our roads a few days ago and I stared at him in order to note his features but not very comfortably, for he plainly recognised my face. As far as I can give it this is the description of him: he has plenty of thick rather curly dark auburn hair parted in the middle and εὐφυέας [shapely] whiskers of the same; his eyes are deep set and I think rather near together; the fault of his face is that the features are too broad and depressed; his forehead is wide across and narrow upwards to the hair; he looks happy. I drew him when I got home but some touches destroyed the likeness at last.[17]

At the start of the Michaelmas term Hopkins's mind was on his reception and its consequences. Urquhart was worried that he had pushed Hopkins towards Rome. Hopkins reassured him:

The difference between your stake and mine is very great and besides you have had this subject so long before you that it has no doubt come to turn on a great many points and got much complexity, whereas to me it was pretty simple— now of course I think, very simple. In fact as I told you my conversion when it came was all in a minute. Again I cd. not say that your talk influenced me in that direction: to see or hear 'Romanising' things wd. throw me back on the English Church as a rule.[18]

Hopkins probably went up to Oxford on 11 October. He had asked to see Pusey at Christ Church to tell him of his conversion, but Pusey sent a grim note:

I thank you for the personal kindness of your letter, It would not be accurate to say, that I 'refused to see' you. What I declined doing was to see you simply 'to satisfy relations'. I know too well what that means. It is simply to enable the pervert to say to his relations 'I have seen Dr P, and he has failed to satisfy me', whereas they know very well that they meant not to be satisfied, that they came with a fixed purpose not to be satisfied. This is merely to waste my time, and create the impression that I have nothing to say. It has, in fact, when done, been a great abuse of the love I have for all, especial[l]y the young.

I do not answer what you say, in a note, because it would be still more useless. You have a heavy responsibility. Those who will gain by what you seem determined to do, will be the unbelievers.[19]

The last words echoed Hopkins's feeling the day after he had seen Newman: 'I feel that wherever I go I must either do no good or else harm.'

It was 'a deeply painful thought'[20] that Canon Liddon would learn of Hopkins's 'perversion'. The news was spreading fast. T. A. Eaglesim of Worcester College, a fellow member of 'The New Vitality', wrote in his diary for Monday 15 October:

Tait [Dr R. C. Tait, later Archbishop of Canterbury] has today informed me of an event which has produced a strong impression on my mind, & made me almost wish I had not heard of it. As we were going out of his room after lecture, he kept me behind the rest, & said to me, after I had sat down, 'I suppose you have heard the news about Addis.' I said, 'No, not all.' 'Addis has just been received into the Roman Church, and Hopkins is to received [*sic*] this week. Garrett of Balliol & Wood of Trinity are, I believe, to go with them.' . . .

I said that I was not altogether surprised that Addis had gone. . . . Hopkin's [*sic*] case, I confessed, suprised me a little more; for I could not so well imagine how he should have been able to satisfy himself so soon.[21]

Liddon heard from Coles, and wrote a letter to Hopkins which must have hurt them both: 'after our intimate friendship with each other, I cannot bear to be silent, even though you should not be willing to listen. . . . Let me entreat you once more *not* hastily to take a step wh. unless it be certainly God's will, *must be* a most serious mistake.'[22] Liddon's pleadings must have been harder for Hopkins than Pusey's rejection. Pusey's 'yours faithfully' ended any dialogue between him and Hopkins, but Liddon's 'Ever aff'', suggested importuning, and two days later (Hopkins not having replied) came another pleading letter. This time Hopkins replied immediately and patronizingly: 'I wish to thank you for your kindness and even for the trouble you took to prevent my reception, for of course to you it was the right thing to do.' He ended 'Do not trouble yourself to write again: this needs no answer and I know how precious your time is.'[23] The letter contained a long justification, arguing his new Church's case against the Anglican schism, and denying Liddon's charge that he believed he had a personal illumination: 'I can hardly believe anyone ever became a Catholic because two and two made four more fully than I have.' Next day there was a third plea:

As it is dear friend what have you done, but shut your eyes, and under the impression that you have had a call from heaven, escaped from all further examination of the points at issue? . . .

Your father has written to me,—of course in very deep sorrow. I have replied to his letter, by saying that I shall hope to see you on my return to Oxford: I wish I could have told him that I thought you would listen to what I have to urge. The moral duty of delay appears to me so very plain, that you will I hope and trust not have gone to Birmingham today.[24]

Liddon's letter was posted on Friday 19 October.

As soon as he had settled into 18 New Inn Hall Street, Hopkins wrote to his mother and father announcing his conversion. 'Their answers were terrible', he wrote to Newman, 'I cannot read them twice.' His parents urged him to wait until he had taken his degree, but this seemed impossible. So he asked Newman: 'Wd. you therefore wish me to come to Birmingham at once, on Thursday, Friday, or Saturday?'[25] He may well have wanted a *fait accompli*. Eaglesim recorded that Hopkins 'seems much distressed at present about the estrangement of his relatives',[26] but Hopkins's letter to Newman explains:

You will understand why I have any hesitation at all, namely because if immediately after their letters urging a long delay I am received without any, it will be another blow and look like intentional cruelty. I did not know till last night the rule about *communicatio in sacris*—at least as binding catechumens, but I now see the alternative thrown open, either to live without Church and sacraments or else, in order to avoid the Catholic Church, to have to attend constantly the services of that very Church. This brings the matter to an absurdity and makes me think that any delay, whatever relief it may be to my parents, is impossible. I am asking you then whether I shall at all costs be received at once. . . . And if you shd. bid me be received at once will you kindly name the day?

The reply is a masterpiece of tranquillizing style: 'It is not wonderful that you should not be able to take so great a step without trouble and pain. There is no reason you should not travel on Sunday.' There would be no difficulty in Hopkins continuing to attend college chapel if the authorities did not give him leave to absent himself, 'but I can explain all this when I see you. Meanwhile you have my best prayers that He who has begun the good work in you may finish it—and I do not doubt He will.'[27] But Hopkins got into difficulties with the Balliol authorities about his attendance at chapel. On 16 October the Master sent for him, and said he could not grant him leave of absence without an application from his father. So Hopkins wrote to his father:

As the College last term passed a resolution admitting Catholics and took a Catholic into residence it has no right to alter its principle in my case. I wish you therefore not to give yourself the pain of making this application, even if you were willing: I am of age moreover and am alone concerned. If you refuse to make the application, the Master explains that he shall lay my case before the common-room. In this case there is very little doubt indeed that the Fellows wd. take the reasonable course and give me leave of absence from chapel. . . . I want you therefore to write at once, if you will,—not to the Master who has no right to ask what he does, but to me, with a refusal: no harm will follow.[28]

Acting on a college rule, Scott duly wrote to Manley Hopkins 'asking him leave to permit his son to go to the Roman Catholic chapel'. Manley Hopkins wrote his refusal to the Master. The college, however, gave Hopkins leave to go to Birmingham, and a meeting of the Fellows on 23 October passed a resolution that the Master be 'requested to give Exhibitioner Hopkins a dispensation from attendance at Chapel & Divinity Lectures'.[29] Hopkins would not find persecution easily.

Manley Hopkins had asked his son to delay his reception, but he replied: 'I must either obey the Church or disobey. . . . if I were to delay and die in the meantime I shd. have no plea why my soul was not forfeit.' (Three friends whose conversions were later than his, Garrett, Addis, and Wood, had already been received.) This is a long, unattractive letter, anticipating some of Hopkins's harsh stands on dogma after he became a priest. It is not without a childish petulance, and a certain pride in having the Law on his side:

You are so kind as not to forbid me your house, to which I have no claim, on condition, if I understand, that I promise not to try to convert my brothers and sisters. Before I can promise this I must get permission, wh. I have no doubt will be given. Of course the promise will not apply after they come of age.

His father asked him if he had no thought of the estrangement it would mean from his family. Hopkins replied that if his father shrank from approaching Christ 'in a new way in which you will at all events feel that you are exactly in unison with me', then 'you will see you are prolonging the estrangement and not I'. Mingled with self-righteous devotional protestations are strains of adolescent assertiveness:

I am most anxious that you shd. not think of my future. It is likely that the positions you wd. like to see me in wd. have no attraction for me, and surely the happiness of my prospects depends on the happiness to me and not on intrinsic advantages. ... My only strong wish is to be independent.[30]

His father's reply is moving, particularly after a letter showing no sensitivity to his feelings. He sees the futility of persuasion:

There are one or two things I should like to say to you though you will perhaps not regard them. At least the tone of your letter is so hard & cold, it gives me little encouragement. ... Can you really put aside all our claims upon you by saying that it rests with us to think as you do? ... All we ask of you is for your own sake to take so momentous a step with caution and hesitation; have we not a right to do this? Might not our love & sorrow entitle us to ask it? & you answer by saying that as we might be Romanists if we pleased the estrangement is not of your doing. O Gerard my darling boy are you indeed gone from me?[31]

On Saturday 20 October Hopkins wrote to his mother:

I am to be received into the church tomorrow at Birmingham by Dr Newman. It is quite the best that any hopes should be ended quickly, since otherwise they wd. only have made the pain longer. Until then the comforts you take are delusive, after it they will be real. And even for me it is almost a matter of necessity, for every new letter I get breaks me down afresh, and this cd. not go on. Your letters, wh. shew the utmost fondness, suppose none on my part and the more you think me hard and cold and that I repel and throw you off the more I am helpless not to write as if [it] were true. In this way I have no relief. You might believe that I suffer too. I am your very loving son,

Gerard M. Hopkins[32]

He bought a copy of the Vulgate and signed it 'Gerardi Manley Hopkins. Octobris XXXI, in vigil. omn. sanct. MDCCCLXVI.'[33]

Following Hopkins's reception the family letters stop for a time.

Hopkins must have had some of the peace of mind he needed to read for Greats. 'Gerard's abandonment of the church in which he was born', wrote Cyril Hopkins afterwards, was 'at first, a great blow to [Mrs Hopkins]. This has always ... rather astonished me, for her religious opinions had always been of what was then regarded as of a very "High Church" order, & would now, I suppose, have been labelled "Anglo-Catholic". But Gerard was her first-born & she was very proud of him & they were in close sympathy together, so that I suppose she felt estranged.' Although she distressed herself over Gerard's conversion 'very much for a time', she 'of course became reconciled eventually'.[34]

A different reaction came from Jowett, who wrote to Florence Nightingale:

You may have seen in the newspapers, perhaps, that three foolish fellows at our College & three at other Colleges have gone over to Rome. There is no great harm in this really. For the youths are under much better guidance now than that of Pusey and Liddon. It is said that some more are going & those who like Lady Castlemaine don't like travelling in a crowd must make haste.

I think that an Ecclesiastical storm is getting up which like a commercial panic seems to return about once in seven years: Ecclesiastic titles—Essays and Reviews—Ritualism. But it is very miserable that at Oxford or elsewhere there should be so little of moral strength & so little regard for truth. I quite agree with you in the comparison of this age & the last. The poor old drunken eighteenth century has great injustice done to it by the smooth sleek religionism of this.[35]

Hopkins wrote to Newman that he was on easier terms than he had expected with his parents and would go home for Christmas. Newman then cleared up a misunderstanding about his invitation for Hopkins to stay at the Oratory—he had proposed it on the assumption that Hopkins would have broken off relations with his family. He had not meant that Hopkins should necessarily make a retreat—there was no rush: 'Your first duty is to make a good class. Show your friends at home that your becoming a Catholic has not unsettled you in the plain duty that lies before you.' Newman's tone and advice are just right. He added, 'And, independently of this, it seems to me a better thing not to hurry decision on your vocation. Suffer yourself to be led on by the Grace of God step by step.'[36]

In a subsequent letter Newman suggested that Hopkins might spend a week at the Oratory before term started in January. At Oak Hill Hopkins was making some necessary practical preparations. 'If you happen by any chance', he wrote to Bridges, 'to have the statutes by you will you kindly look out for me what in the way or stead of Divinity is to be taken for Greats by those who are not *in gremio Ecclesiae*

*Anglicanae?*'[37] He planned to move to 12 Holywell, where he would share rooms with Garrett, another convert. On Christmas Eve he went to midnight mass, and on 17 January, during a severe frost, went to stay at the Birmingham Oratory. He had received an offer from a Mr Darnell of a coaching post after taking his degree, but some time after his stay at Birmingham Newman invited him, despite Hopkins's telling him that he 'disliked schooling', to teach from the following September at the Oratory School. He would offer the same terms as Darnell, the work would not be hard, and 'I think you would get on with us, and that we should like you'. Hopkins would find it much better 'to be in a religious house than with Mr Darnell in the country'.[38]

In January of the new year, Hopkins and Garrett moved into the new lodgings in a three-storied house, over two hundred years old, of timber beams and thin lathes bound together with plaster and horsehair. It had spacious rooms, high ceilings, large windows, and was four minutes' walk from Broad Street. At the end of the Easter term Garrett and Hopkins moved back into Balliol to study for most of the vacation. Macfarlane came to stay with them for a while. At the end of term Jowett put Hopkins through a two-day examination, 'a most trying thing'. Then Jowett went abroad, and only a few men besides Hopkins were left in college to look at the construction of Waterhouse's new buildings:

The outer quadrangle and the Master's house are a wreck. There seems to be no conservative spirit at work at all in the buildings that are to be. It is very doubtful whether the fine old groined roof of the gateway, the finest in Oxford, will be kept. . . .[39]

If Riddell had still been alive 'things might have been arranged better'. (He had died the previous September, and Hopkins had heard the news from Newman.) His father sent Hopkins £20 for the vacation's extra expenses, as he would not be at Oak Hill, and there had been a delay in the payment of his Highgate School Exhibition money. With his application for each payment from the school governors Hopkins had to send a certificate of good behaviour and progress signed by the Master of Balliol. On the April certificate, after the words 'conducted himself soberly and piously', Dr Scott had inserted 'so far as he has come under my cognisance'. The treasurer to the governors had written to Hopkins requesting an explanation, and he had replied that he 'had become a Catholic'. (This answer was probably unnecessary: what Scott meant was that Hopkins had lived out in lodgings.) At the governors' meeting of 17 April, the treasurer reported the correspondence, adding that by 'Catholic' Hopkins meant 'Roman Catholic'; at the next meeting it was decided that he had not forfeited the award, and the cheque was forwarded.[40] On Monday 15 April Hopkins went to spend Holy Week and Easter with the Benedictines at St Michael's Priory, Hereford, 'a delightful place in every way',[41] and on Easter Monday went to Oak Hill for the last four days of his vacation.

Hopkins took a First in Greats. Hardy made up for his poor showing in Mods and also had a First, but Geldart got a Second. During 'that preoccupied time of reading for the schools' Hopkins had made a rule 'to have nothing to do with versemaking', but revised one poem. On 9 July he caught the night Channel steamer for France, with Poutiatine, a Christ Church man who had just taken a Second in Greats. Travelling through northern France, Hopkins wrote notes:

Flames of mist rose from the French brooks and meadows, and sheets of mist at a distance led me to think I saw the sea: at sunrise it was fog. Morning star and peach-coloured dawn. . . . The trees were irregular, scarcely expressing form, and the aspens blotty, with several concentric outlines, and as in French pictures.[42]

They stayed in the Latin Quarter of Paris, at the Hôtel de Saxe, visited the Louvre and Notre Dame, saw Paris from the river, and the Universal Exhibition on the Champ de Mars. Hopkins went to High Mass on Sunday at St Eustache, to the Madeleine at night, and saw a Nadar balloon.

On 17 July he went home on his own by Dieppe and Newhaven. On his return he found a letter from Coles, waiting since the day he left for Paris. Dolben was dead. He had arrived at South Luffenham rectory, to be tutored by Mr Prichard, on 15 June. On 28 June, having previously spoken of 'the great beauty of the descriptions in the Œdipus Coloneus', he construed 'the speech of Ajax taking leave of the world before his death', which he found 'very beautiful'. It was late in the afternoon and he went to bathe with Prichard's son Walter, two miles away, in the river Welland:

The boy could not swim, but had learned to float on his back. Digby was a good swimmer. They had bathed together before, and there was so little thought of danger that no apprehension was felt when they did not return. . . . What happened was that when they were bathing Digby took the boy on his back and swam across the river with him. Returning in the same fashion he suddenly sank within a few yards of the bank to which he was swimming. The boy, who was the only witness, had the presence of mind to turn on his back and keep himself afloat, and shout to some reapers in the riverside meadows. They did not at once take alarm, but on the boy's persistently calling they ran to the bank and got him out with difficulty and delay: the water was deep, and none of them could venture in.[43]

The body was not found for some hours; he was buried a week later, under the altar at Finedon.

'I looked forward to meeting Dolben', Hopkins wrote to Bridges,

and his being a Catholic more than to anything. At the same time from never having met him but once I find it difficult to realise his death or feel as if it were anything to me. You know there can very seldom have happened the loss of so much beauty (in body and mind and life) and of the promise of still more as there has been in his case—seldom I mean, in the whole world, for the conditions wd. not easily come together. At the same time he had gone in a way wh. was wholly and unhappily irrational.[44]

Newman wrote to Hopkins saying that he had heard about Dolben:

The account was very pleasant. He had not given up the idea of being a Catholic—but he thought he had lived on excitement, and felt he must give himself time before he could know whether he was in earnest or not. This does not seem to me a wrong frame of mind. He was up to his death careful in his devotional exercises.[45]

Bridges did not think Newman's words 'at all measured Dolben, though of course he cannot have known him at all.' 'Did you not think', Bridges wrote to Hopkins on 12 September, 'that there was an entire absence of strength in Dolben? It always seemed to me so in spite of his great moral courage as people would call it, in carrying out his "views".' Hopkins had left one of his notebooks at Rochdale vicarage, and Bridges looked into it, finding a vivid recall of Hopkins, 'thanks to your style,', and he told Hopkins, 'I had a curious dream the other night in which your D$^r$ Newman, Dolben, and a strange Roman Catholic priest and myself had the most wonderful discussion possible.'[46]

'Some day', wrote Hopkins, 'I hope to see Finedon and the place where he was drowned too.' Among his copies of Dolben's poems Hopkins found a translation from an Italian tomb; 'Digby might have written it', he suggested to Bridges, 'for his own restless, lonely, life':

> I, living, drew thee from the vale
> Parnassus' height to climb with me.
> I, dying, bid thee turn, and scale
> Alone the hill of Calvary.[47]

# Decision: Bovey Tracey and Birmingham

In the morning of Friday 23 August, Hopkins's parents and Milicent left for Brittany, which they had visited the previous year. After seeing them off on the boat-train, Hopkins went to call on Baillie's friend, Mrs Cunliffe, but as she was out walked a little in Hyde Park, noticing 'a fine oblate chestnut-tree with noble long ramping boughs more like an oak'. From there he went to Notting Hill, and in the chapel of the Poor Clares–Colettines took the first step in making the decision 'to be a priest and religious'. It was taken in a 'cautiously conditional form', and in his journal he qualified it: 'but now, Sept. 4, nothing is decided'. That evening, searching for company in the absence of his parents, he spent at Aunt Kate's. There was a fiery sunset.[1]

The next day dawned bright; it was spent with his family, first in the garden at Oak Hill. Lionel, aged thirteen,

had a piece of sky-blue gauze for butterfly-nets lying on the grass. . . . It was a graceful mixture of square folds and winding tube-folds. But the point was the colour as seen by sunlight in a transparent material. The folds, which of course doubled the stuff, were on the sun's side bright light blue and on the other deep blue—*not shadow-modified*, but real blue, as in tapestries and some paintings. Then the shadowed sides had cobweb-streaks of paler colour across . . .

While the younger children set off for Rottingdean, on the Sussex coast, Gerard and Cyril spent a last afternoon together by the Thames at Richmond, Gerard using the occasion to record: 'What I most noticed was the great richness of the membering of the green in the elms, never however to be expressed but by drawing after study.'[2] Hopkins had given up the idea of becoming a professional artist: he felt that his senses would be dangerously engaged. But a certain quality in these elms could be recorded only in visual art; the wistful cadence in this sentence is valedictory. In future, words would be the only means of describing the appearance and activity of the natural world.

On the following Monday he took the Great Western Railway to

Bovey Tracey[3] in the West Country. Newman had agreed to take him on as master in mid-September. Hopkins had declined Pater's invitation to join a secular reading party at Sidmouth, on the south Devon coast, that August, and had come to stay with Urquhart.

On leaving Oxford, Urquhart had been appointed to one of the three Bovey Tracey curacies by Canon C. L. Courtenay, a controversial figure in the Church, who brought the Oxford Movement struggles into this tiny town to the east of Dartmoor. On being appointed Vicar of St Peter and St Paul, Bovey Tracey, Courtenay planned a second church, St John's at the lower end of the town, so that 'the surplice could be worn in the pulpit instead of a black preaching gown'. The new church soon aroused cries of 'Romanism' and 'No Popery' in Bovey Tracey— accusations which have continued to the present day. The year after Hopkins's visit, Urquhart was joined as curate by another Oxford High-Church friend of Hopkins, Frederick Gurney (whose tomb is now next to the door of St John's church).

Courtenay had strong Oxford connections, and most of his curates were Oxford men. In 1867 he had three who shared his High-Church convictions, the most recently appointed being Urquhart, who had moved with his mother and sister into a house on the north side of East Street, which ran in front of the old parish church. Hopkins's room was in the top storey. The house was near the top of the Bovey valley, and at its back a long garden rose above the roof level. Hopkins spent some mornings in the summer-house at the highest point of the garden, which commanded views of towering rocks and tors on the opposite side of the valley. To his mother Hopkins wrote: 'Mrs Urquhart is a nice person: I do not care so much for Miss Urquhart.' He gave two accounts of his first day's reactions to the Bovey district's trees. He said to his mother that it was a 'teeming climate and the oaks and elms grow straighter than elsewhere in fact the latter overshoot their nature and run up like poles'.[4] In his journal he wrote a more serious, precise, and full technical observation, using his peculiar vocabulary:

Oaks as well as elms grow straight here: it is a new mood in them to me: they are tall and upright, sided well and ricked distinctly, the focus (?) of their enclosing parabola being near the top instead of leaning over to the N.E.; trunks white and clean; isles of leaf all ricked and beaked.[5]

His eleven days at Bovey were spent in a more relaxed way than those on the study holiday at Chagford, two years before. They were occupied with walks to nearby beauty spots, where he sketched or wrote descriptions. He visited local Anglican churches, in which he developed a close interest, went to mass in Roman Catholic churches, visited several houses and made friendships. One day Hopkins and Urquhart met a Miss Warren and her nephew, a Fellow of St John's, Oxford, and they walked to Bullaton Rocks. The sun 'came out in gleams over the tors and vallies', and they sketched, Hopkins drawing the tree-heads in a copse down below in a cleave, then returned to Hazelwood House, north of Bovey, for tea with the two Miss Warrens who knew the Giberne family, related to Hopkins. The elder Miss Warren, Charlotte, superintendent of the local parish school, was 'a curious oldfashioned old lady who shewed us some portfolios—full of early water-colours by her father'; he had known Charles Lamb in the last year of his life. Miss Warren also told Hopkins of an old woman's vision:

She saw, she said, white doves flying about her room and drops of blood falling from their 'nibs'—that is their beaks. . . . The room was full of bright light, the 'nibs' bathed in blood, and the drops fell on her. Then the light became dazzling and painful, the doves gone, and our Lord appeared displaying His five wounds.

Four days later Hopkins used this new word, 'nibs', in his description of the Dartmoor furze. It is a sign of his purposeful limiting of interests at this time that, although he was reading William Henderson's *Notes on the Folk Lore of the Northern Counties of England and the Borders*, and staying in one of the richest areas of England for stories and legends, this is the only piece of folklore he wrote up in his journal, apart from a passing reference to pixies.[6]

The nearest Roman Catholic church was the chapel of the Cliffords at Ugbrooke Park, about six miles east of Bovey parish church. For mass on the first Sunday at Bovey he walked to Ugbrooke, on a 'bright and beautiful' day, with 'great climbing white wool clouds, and swathes of grass flying behind'. Although a private chapel, it was open for public worship; but a new face would have been noticed, and some of Lord Clifford's staff invited Hopkins for breakfast. He was shown over the park, where he noticed planes, oaks, a poplar, wych-elms, and a beech. Afterwards he returned to the chapel for the benediction. He had been given directions for returning to Bovey by a less direct route, and struck out across Ugbrooke Park to Gappah and the heathfields, barren common land except for the heath-plant and a whitish clay, from which bricks were made for the local pottery. In the middle of Knighton Heathfield he observed 'the wholeness of the sky and the sun like its ace; the colours of Dartmoor were pale but else the common was edged with a frieze of trees of the brightest green and crispest shadow'.[7]

There are journal entries for every day, sometimes long ones; he was enjoying working experience into prose. Two days' entries are longer than the rest. On Sunday 8 September he reported his talk with Kenelm Vaughan, mission-priest at Newton Abbot, and the day after his visit to Ugbrooke he recorded a full and vivid day out of doors. The day was fair, sometimes sunny, and they drove along narrow roads and unmetalled tracks west out of Bovey to Haytor Vale, and on to the huge tumbled mass of Haytor Rocks, where they walked up the grassy path to the 1500-ft. tor. From the summit there was a view over Dartmoor, with prehistoric hut-circles and cairns, modern mine-workings and quarries, and the recently closed granite railway, which had carried stone in horse-drawn carts. These traces of human labour interested Hopkins less than the gorse:

The composition of the bloom is this—the head of a spike has, let us say, eight flowers, the nibs of which—I do not know the botanical name—point outwards, arranged as below, thus suggesting a square by way of Union Jack; the wings or crests rising behind make a little square with four walls, as in the drawing, these crests being those of the bigger flowers and those of the smaller, I fancy, being suppressed; these little walls are like the partitions in honeycombs; the nibs when looked down upon are as in the diagram, something like a Jew's-harp, enclosing a split tongue; the whole makes a pretty diaper.[8]

There is only rarely a lyrical smooth delight: the eccentric persistence of the Victorian explorer is dominant. Hopkins's mature poetry never came easily, and much of the long wrestling that lay behind its muscled strength was tried in his early prose. There is scarcely a trace of it in the poetry of this time.

From Haytor they continued their drive west around Top Tor, and descended the steep hill to the village in the valley, Widecombe-in-the-Moor. Widecombe was dominated by its church of St Pancras, the Cathedral of the Moor, and the church by its broad and tall steeple, ashlar-built and 135 feet high. Hopkins wondered why 'the steeple half-blinded the west-side windows', and Urquhart, perhaps jokingly, attributed the disproportion to the church's Somerset character. The most plausible explanation was the far-flung nature of the parish over all of which bells had to be heard, and the deadening acoustic effect of wind in the moorland trees. Hopkins was appalled by the bad condition of the fabric and the lack of reverence for the medieval screen: 'Moses and Aaron at the east end, the cieling [*sic*] falling in, a piece of handsome painted rood-screen cut down and put in a pew etc.' The recent convert was over-sensitive: he saw half the medieval rood-screen in its original position, and although some of its figures of martyrs and saints had been defaced in the Reformation, the upper part of this particular screen had not been destroyed by anti-Papists, but removed forty years before Hopkins's visit, when its wood was found to be beyond repair. It had been replaced only then by figures of Aaron, dressed as a rabbi, and Moses in Roman toga.

They drove out of the compact village and up the steep, cultivated vale of the East Webburn River, where Hopkins noted 'many syco-mores, now browning. Everywhere here hollies abound and flourish, growing into sided rocky shapes.' They continued along a rough road between Easdon Tor and its Whooping Rock to their left, and the impressive Bowerman's Nose and Hound Tor on the right, to the unspoilt village of Manaton, where there were more 'long cripples'—giant adders—than anywhere in Devon. They passed through plane-trees to the lych-gate of St Winifred's church. Under the fan-vaulted roof of the church porch were the remains of a holy-water stoup. The ancient door of St Winifred's was locked. They peered in through the diamond-leaded windows of the north side of the church, Hopkins on tiptoe. He saw a well-preserved rood-screen—without its rood—stretching across the chancel, and painted with apostles and saints, well-known and local, with their heads brutally defaced, reputedly by Cromwell's troops. The images of the four Doctors of the early Church had been completely disfigured. Hopkins did two sketches of the hanging shoot of an ash-tree which overlooked the village cricket-field. In the distance were the granite piles of Hound Tor, which he and Urquhart sketched together. On the way back they made the obligatory stop at the local beauty spot, Becka Falls. From the hills overlooking the woodland of the Bovey valley, they could see down into Devon combes and cleaves, formations which Hopkins drew on for the rest of his life.

The next day was foggy and rainy, and Hopkins went with Urquhart to the annual flower show and industrial exhibition of the Bovey Tracey Horticultural Society, and found that the night's rain had 'got through the tents and spoilt some of the industry'. He wrote to his mother in Brittany:

from Newton Abbot it is said that 1000 people were coming; only 200 came as things went. One man had exhibited stuffed animals but the rain melted the birds off their perches and they were found twice dead. The poor man got up in the middle of the night and walked over seven miles from Newton [actually only six miles away] to save them. There were some good things to be seen. The show was wide, ranging from Palissy ware to ornamental penmanship.[9]

This was the tone of the letters to his mother for the rest of his life—affectionate, informative, but whimsically oblique, patronizing, and unserious. His journal shows his real interests at the exhibition:

N.B. handsome green earthenware Russian jug; jug of, I suppose, 17th century—I do not know the name of the ware—in dark blue and brown richly patterned, with cover and purchase; dish of Palissy ware with a pike; old tiles of 13th etc centuries, one having an architectural design, which is uncommon, another a handsome fleur-de-lys with a checker border; etc.[10]

An important part of his daily record was 'a regular weather-journal'. Each day's account starts with a quick summary of weather developments, giving the impression that activities were determined by them. He had his own measuring scale: gloomy/dull/fair/fine/bright/sunny, and showers/hard showers/spitting rain/rain. It rained most days at Bovey, but he seems to have been undisturbed, though a few years later bad weather weighed on his mind. The frequent rainbows were gifts: 'Rainbow on dark ground of cloud crimson and green; on light ground it is the dun red and blue'. And rain created more subtle aesthetic effects:

I saw where rainwater had run through one of the cuttings made to carry it off in the turf by the side of the road, and the gully being sandy, it had carried the sand down into the road, throwing it in clear expression into a branched root or, if you looked at it from above downwards, a 'treated' tree head: it ended definitely, in (roughly speaking) a horizontal, and each runnel was rounded at the end.

He delighted in skies and they offered opportunities for a new vocabulary:

Aug.26 . . . silver lights and cobweb and blown-flix weather clouds; then white sweep.

Aug.30 . . . the clouds had a good deal of crisping and mottling.

Sept.2 . . . sometimes grey with mouldings; bright sand frettings.

Sept.7 . . . blown-flix clouds and especially a tuft of the most graceful curled and waved locks.

Sept.8 . . . fretted moss clouds.[11]

He was free to experiment in vocabulary and to re-experience his confrontation with nature. He senses danger in the shapes, texture, and movement of human beauty, but his responses to sky could be indulged. Hopkins had found a conventionally acceptable way of expressing, and perhaps masking, some of his most powerful sensuous responses. He was still an artist, but now his medium was words:

In Babbicombe bay the cliffs were glowing with red, the beach ash-white, the sea in-shore chlore green above these same white pebbles, the outer blue purpled by fringed cat'spaws. . . . On the way I saw from the road hollow coombs filled with upright dressed elms gilt sometimes with bright sprays of new leaves, a beautiful sight.[12]

At other times he responded to nature almost as though it were human: 'copses with slim bare stems, sometimes leaning and falling apart; elms too I saw with more liquid in their growth than elsewhere, slimmer and falling towards one another'. He apparently never experienced guilt-free sexuality, but by the time of this stay in Bovey Tracey he had managed to bypass the insistent guilt that had so frequently disturbed his 1865 holiday.

Journal-writing completed his solitary communion with nature, but it was balanced by a full social life. The journal records many meetings, with Urquhart, the Miss Warrens and their nephew, people of Lord Clifford's, the Monros and Miss Bowies at Ingsdon, Gurney and Bright at Torquay, the Morrises at Watcombe, Kenelm Vaughan and Mr Spenser at Newton, and the Harrises of Plumley, local gentry into which Urquhart was to marry five years later, and whose son, William Augustus, had been at Balliol with Hopkins. At Plumley, 'they told me that the people here fully believe in Pixies; they call fairy-rings pixy-rings, and a field near Shap Tor where there are some is called Pixies' Meadow, and there is a cave called Pixies' Parlour'. The directory for Bovey at this time still divided the town's inhabitants into gentry and tradespeople, not mentioning others, and Hopkins's reference to 'the people' is a reminder that his social round was among the gentry, though he did have the odd chat about dialect words with Cleave, the carpenter, who lived in Fore Street.

An essential constituent of the middle-class tourist itinerary was a visit to parish churches and other pre-eighteenth-century buildings, to look at them with an antiquarian and aesthetic eye, and perhaps to feed patriotism by marvelling at past native workmanship. As a new Roman Catholic, Hopkins's accounts of visits to Anglican churches usually contain at least a tinge of partisan feeling. He had more than an aesthetic and antiquarian interest in pre-Reformation churches, and a more than ordinary attachment governed his response to medieval church furnishings, and their destruction. Near the end of his stay at Bovey, for example, Hopkins visited the church of Saints Peter and Paul, said to have been rebuilt by Sir William de Tracey as penance for his part in the murder of Thomas à Becket in 1170, and noticed

a damaged but rich screen, painted with saints, but poorly: below the saints is a row, as often, of quaterfoils centered with four-cornered bosses, and of these bosses two were delicately worked in a way I have never seen before. Also a rich and now restored carved pulpit.[13]

Devonshire was known for its rood-screens, and this was one of the most richly carved, dating from 1427, and restored ten years before

Hopkins's visit. Its figures, considerably older than on most Devon screens, were of the twelve apostles reciting the Apostles' Creed, each supported by a prophet confirming doctrine from his writings. The pulpit, carved and decorated in free-stone, was one of the few in England surviving from the Catholic Middle Ages; it was lavishly coloured and decorated with 'in each panel, two figures above each other and bossy leaf strips up the angles between the panels'. Hopkins makes no mention in his journal of the other Anglican church in Bovey, the new, undistinguished, modern Gothic St John's, though he would have visited it.

For his second and last Sunday mass, Hopkins walked to Newton, having missed the train; his long account of that day's events shows a concentration on Catholic devotion. Mass was said by a mission priest, Kenelm Vaughan. Afterwards Hopkins breakfasted with Vaughan, who drove him in a mule-cart to St Augustine's Priory, Abbotsleigh, where they spent most of the day. Vaughan related stories of the pious Italian poor, and told Hopkins that he had once been dying of consumption:

The sisters had a *novena* for him and he was drinking from St Winifred's well: one Sunday he had crept down to say mass, when, there being no rain, before the consecration a quantity of water fell on him and the altar so that he sent to ask the Canon whether he should consecrate or not: he was told to do so and Mass went on: after Mass he was perfectly well. He had two enthusiasms—for the B. Sacrament and for the bible. He has a silver lamp to burn before the bible in his room to make reparation to God for the desecrated use that has been made of it for these 300 years.

Vaughan's influence may have been instrumental in Hopkins's decision about his vocation. Certainly St Winefride and her Well proved to hold more than a passing interest for him. Two days later, on Tuesday 10 September, he set out for Birmingham.

જી

Hopkins missed his train at Bovey 'through the slowness of the Bovey clocks', and had to walk to Newton. Punctuality was not one of his strong points.[14] After 'a wild tear' he caught the Exeter train, and had a pain in his back for several days. At Exeter station he saw Tracy of Christ Church with H. N. Oxenham, an old Oxford acquaintance, who wore 'a remarkable cap like an ancient helmet with *bucculae*'.[15] For his first week at Birmingham he stayed with the community in the Oratory, then moved into one of the school's boarding-houses, on Plough and Harrow Road, off the Hagley Road, near the back entrance to the Oratory.

The Oratory School started in 1859 and soon ran into trouble, when its first headmaster, Fr Nicholas Darnell, over-ambitious to create a rival to the public schools, took the running largely out of Newman's hands. The crisis came in the winter of 1861–2, after Darnell demanded the resignation of the matron, Mrs Wootten, over what he called her 'excessive coddling of sick or delicate boys'. The quarrel ended when the congregation of the Oratory gave a vote of confidence to Newman's views. The school survived the crisis, and opened for the spring term of 1862 only a few days late. Newman took a more active role, teaching, adapting Latin comedies for the boys to act, and, worried by the gossip that the boys did not receive a proper religious training, himself giving them instruction. It was largely because of this crisis that Newman decided to write a literary work to gain converts, which became the *Apologia Pro Vita Sua*. Kingsley's slander, that Newman had taught that truth was no virtue, was merely the pebble which started an avalanche. Hopkins, of course, had been exactly the type of convert Newman had hoped to catch.[16]

Newman's aim was 'to influence the tone of thought and opinion prevalent in the various circles of society, high and low, to recommend Catholicism, to expose Protestantism, & especially to take care of young men'.[17] In his reply to an address presented by the Oratory School Society, he outlined his school's ideals: 'A school such as ours is a pastoral charge of the most intimate kind. ... Day schools are not schools except in school hours, but the superiors in a school such as ours live with their pupils, and see their growth from day to day ... and they are ever tenderly watching over them that their growth may be in the right direction.'[18]

The question was whether Hopkins was the right man for the Oratory School. A letter to Baillie written before he had seen any of his pupils suggests a clash between the practical reality of Newman's ideals and Hopkins's wishes: 'I want to read almost every thing that has ever been written.' Term started on Tuesday 17 September, a dull day, and Hopkins reported that school went on 'but languidly till Friday'. By then his box (borrowed from Mrs Ridley, his landlady on Holywell Street) had arrived from Oxford. The daily routine came as a shock to Hopkins's constitution and habits:

Fancy me getting up at a quarter past six: it is however done with a melancholy punctuality nearly every morning. The boys' mass is at seven; then what they call Preparation fr. 7.45 to 8.30; then breakfast in Hall, so to speak; at 9.30 school till 12; dinner in Hall at 1; school fr. 2 to 3; then the boys and sometimes I go to their field, which they call Bosco, for a game, just now hockey but soon football; at 6 tea in Hall; from 6.30 to 8.30 school.

He taught the fifth form, but he was given charge of two private pupils, only five years younger than himself, W. J. Sparrow and Richard Bellasis, the first boy to enter the school. They came to him from 8.45 to 10 every night except Saturday, and from 5 to 6 on the half-holidays, Tuesdays, Thursdays, and Saturdays. These long hours were almost the same as those he would keep in the Jesuit novitiate. Not surprisingly, he wrote to Urquhart, 'with reading the class books and looking over exercises (which takes a long time) I find all my time occupied'.[19]

He was soon looking for relief. He could see no newspapers and received no letters, and nothing interesting happened, although the country around the Oratory was 'really very good for so near Birmingham.' He corresponded with Oxford friends, demanding Oxford news, photographs, complaining with some humour, as he would throughout his Jesuit career: 'Today however is Sunday and the boys are playing fives like good ones: I wish they wd. play all the other numbers on the clock all the other days of the week.' Other masters must have considered him fortunate in his duties: he had the top form, of five boys, so his total number of pupils was only seven. He was able to develop friendships with individual boys, some of which would last for several years: 'I feel as if they were all my children, a notion encouraged by their innocence and backwardness.' He became very fond of his 'spiritual children', even though 'the fattest and biggest' of them lamed him with a kick on the ankle at football. His boys never swore, except one who said 'Con-found you, you young fool'. As for his colleagues: 'The master's table appears to be the dregs of Great Britain.' He tried to tone down this judgement, partially succeeding: 'When I say dregs I only mean that they come fr. all quarters indiscriminately and I include myself: it is sweepings, not dregs I mean.' It was the kind of rough mixture he would have to put up with all his Jesuit life. Another feature of institutional life to which he was being introduced was lack of privacy: 'every leisure time of Sunday was interrupted by people coming in', he wrote to Bridges; 'an oak is a great device, do you know, but I have none and cannot tell how to supply its place.'[20] He consistently needed a mental oak, against the spirit of institutional life.

After less than a fortnight he considered leaving: 'I wonder', he wrote to Urquhart on 30 September, 'if there is anything I cd. do, though the income were less, wh. wd. give me more time, for I feel the want of that most of all.' A fragment of a draft letter exists, in which he wrote: 'I do not expect to be long here: if I get a vocation to the priesthood I shd. go away (I shd. . . . to be an Orato[rian] . . . and if not I s[hould] . . . better

myself ... I knew for cer[tain] ... was not to be.' Coleridge, still at
Balliol, responded to a letter by asking if he could come over for a day
and perhaps hear Newman preach. Hopkins's replies dither, and it is
probable that the visit did not take place:

if you like to come some Sunday and agree to let me convince you that F.
Ambrose St. John is Dr. Newman and overlook the fact that he is fat, rosy,
short, and very audible instead of all the opposite it will be very jolly, but if in
your realist way you shd. insist on historical accuracy in envisaging Dr.
Newman why there you have me again.[21]

After a time he had achieved a kind of friendship with Newman,
though his journal entry for 14 September, four days after his arrival in
Birmingham, registers awe: 'The Father came from Rednal.' (Newman
liked to be called 'the Father', and later, 'His Eminence the Father'.)
Despite the sympathy Hopkins felt for the *Apologia*, he must soon have
become aware of differences in taste and temperament. Like Hopkins,
Newman believed in credulity and prejudice, as against cold utilitarianism and the 'encircling gloom' of liberalism. Newman had never been
the naïve imperialist that Hopkins was, nor an advocate of neo-
Gothic—he called the Middle Ages 'barbarous', and said 'my heart has
ever gone with Grecian'. (The Oratory church must have been a sad
disappointment to Hopkins, consisting mainly of four plain brick walls
and a roof bought second-hand from a disused factory.) Newman and
Hopkins had a similar background in the London professional classes,
and there were likenesses in the reactions of their parents to their
conversions, but Newman had a stubborn resistance to harsh blows,
while Hopkins was more cloistered in training, and less resilient.

Hopkins probably started writing as many books as Newman, but
finished none. Newman considered the post of Oratory School teacher a
'pastoral office' which required 'sustained attention' and 'unwearied
services', but Father Ambrose, the prefect of studies, soon made an
arrangement by which Hopkins could get time for private reading.
Hopkins's old Oxford acquaintance Challis, 'once of Merton, a great
swell and friend of mine before the Flood', started teaching at the
school early in November, and took over from Hopkins the tutoring of
Sparrow and Bellasis at late hours. Hopkins was given the fourth form
instead. But as he complained to his journal: 'Occasionally, when
Stokes was away, I had the second too. I did a great deal of work,
clinched with the exam. papers, and am much tired.'[22] He saw little of
the Oratory Fathers, except for Ignatius Ryder, the youngest of the
priests.

He wrote to Bridges, 'I have scarcely any leisure at all.' Nevertheless he had begun the violin, 'and if you will write a trio or quartet I will some day take the first or second part in it'.[23] This venture came to nothing, but he wrote a six-stanza poem, 'The Elopement', a tired echo of Keats's 'Eve of Saint Agnes', for a weekly journal of three copies, handwritten at the school, 'The Early Bird or The Tuesday Tomtit'. His pupils Bellasis and Sparrow parodied it with a better poem, 'The Robbery'. 'An interest in philosophy', Hopkins wrote to Baillie, 'is almost the only one I can feel myself quite free to indulge in still.' He wrote short essays in a notebook headed 'Notes on the history of Greek Philosophy etc', and in one of them, on Parmenides, explores his ideas of *inscape* and *instress*, using these terms for the first time, though with a sense of familiarity and confidence:

all things are upheld by instress, and are meaningless without it. . . . [Parmenides'] feeling for instress, for the flush and foredrawn, and for inscape/ is most striking and from this one can understand Plato's reverence for him as the great father of Realism. . . . indeed I have often felt when I have been in this mood and felt the depth of an instress or how fast the inscape holds a thing that nothing is so pregnant and straightforward to the truth as simple *yes* and *is*.[24]

Bridges invited Hopkins to Rochdale for Christmas, but Hopkins was suspicious of enjoyment: 'the very pleasure I had in my stay last year is part of the reason why I do not wish to make another, if you can understand. I do not know what you will think of all this.'[25] There is a pained anticipation that Bridges may not sympathize with his asceticism, and after Bridges announced that he and Muirhead would be sailing to Egypt and Syria after Christmas, Hopkins added a postscript: 'You sometimes now address me by my Christian name and I like it but I do not you by yours, for first it wd. not feel natural to me and secondly it wd. be unnecessary, for your surname is the prettier.'[26] The previous November he had asked for and received a photograph of Bridges, and in one letter changed from 'Dear Bridges . . . yr. ever affectionate friend' to 'Dearest Bridges . . . yr. very affectionate friend', but then reverted to the old style.

Two or three days before he sailed Bridges visited Hampstead to see Hopkins, but he was making the rounds of his relatives. The family at Oak Hill redirected him to Westbourne Villas, but by the time he got there Hopkins had moved to the Smiths at Blunt House. From Croydon Hopkins wrote:

The year you will be away I have no doubt will make a great difference in my position though I cannot know exactly what. But the uncertainty I am in about the future is so very unpleasant and so breaks my power of applying to anything that I am resolved to end it, which I shall do by going into a retreat at Easter at the latest and deciding whether I have a vocation to the priesthood.[27]

Hopkins' patience was running out. His first and last period of independence, during which he earned a living by his own merits, had not been a success:

I must say that I am very anxious to get away from this place. I have become very weak in health and do not seem to recover myself here or likely to do so. Teaching is very burdensome, especially when you have much of it: I have. I have not much time and almost no energy—for I am always tired—to do anything on my own account.[28]

Hopkins knew himself so little that he put down his mental fatigue to 'uncertainty . . . about the future', but his complaints anticipate, almost exactly, those made in similar states of depression twenty years later in Dublin. His complaint that he had no time for reading was also repeated twelve years later, when working at St Aloysius', Oxford, and at other times in his Jesuit career. Another constant complaint, before and after becoming a Jesuit, was the lack of desirable books.

In a letter to Baillie of 12 February 1868 he discusses his reasons for becoming a professional religious. They are expressed in terms of self-created limitations, and stress negative results, such as his mother's grief, and his own hurt at that grief. Asceticism is opposed to the 'unsafe' regions of painting, which are nevertheless its 'higher and more attractive parts'. He thinks—illogically—that the remedy for depression caused by burdensome teaching lies in a tightening of discipline:

I am expecting to take orders and soon, but I wish it to be secret till it comes about. Besides that it is the happiest and best way it practically is the only one. You know I once wanted to be a painter. But even if I could I wd. not I think, now, for the fact is that the higher and more attractive parts of the art put a strain upon the passions which I shd. think it unsafe to encounter. I want to write still and as a priest I very likely can do that too, not so freely as I shd. have liked, e.g. nothing or little in the verse way, but no doubt what wd. best serve the cause of my religion. But if I am a priest it will cause my mother, or she says it will, great grief and this preys on my mind very much and makes the near prospect quite black. The general result is that I am perfectly reckless about things that I shd. otherwise care about, uncertain as I am whether in a few months I may not be shut up in a cloister, and this state of mind, though it is painful coming to, when reached gives a great and real sense of freedom.[29]

His use of the personal word 'happiest' is unconvincing, and its juxtaposition with the ethical 'best' sadly wilful. It is apparent that if he is to become a priest it will be at great cost, but there is something masochistic in his meditations on being 'shut up in a cloister', and on pain's 'great and real sense of freedom'. There was something too tame for Hopkins in the secular priesthood of the Oratory.

On 30 December Newman had written: 'It seems to me you had

better go into retreat at Easter, & bring the matter before the Priest who gives it to our boys.' By February Hopkins was looking for a tutorship, 'as I am anxious to leave this place then and also not to leave it without having secured something to live upon till, as seems likely, I take minor orders'. He had told Newman of his difficulties, and the reply suggests that he had been less than frank: 'You need not make up your mind till Easter comes, as we shall be able to manage matters whether you stay or we have the mishap to lose you.' On Palm Sunday, 5 April, Fr Henry Coleridge of the Society of Jesus, a cousin of E. H. Coleridge and a friend of Newman's (he had first published 'The Dream of Gerontius'), took the retreat for the boys. It ended on the 9th with high mass. On Easter Sunday, 12 April, Hopkins heard Newman preach for the last time, and three days later left the Oratory for good, going to Oak Hill.

On 27 April he went to the Jesuit Manresa House, at Roehampton, and made a ten-day retreat. Half-way through he resolved to write no more verse, and to destroy what he had written. On a cold day, 5 May, he 'resolved to be a religious'. The bald statement hides an experience of passionate submission that his later poetry conveys:

> I did say yes
>    O at lightning and lashed rod;
> Thou heardst me truer than tongue confess
>    Thy terror, O Christ, O God;
> Thou knowest the walls, altar and hour and night:
> The swoon of a heart that the sweep and the hurl of thee trod
>    Hard down with a horror of height:
> And the midriff astrain with leaning of, laced with fire of stress.
>
>    The frown of his face
>    Before me, the hurtle of hell
> Behind, where, where was a, where was a place?
>    I whirled out wings that spell
> And fled with a fling of the heart to the heart of the Host.
> My heart, but you were dovewinged, I can tell,
>    Carrier-witted, I am bold to boast,
> To flash from the flame to the flame then, tower from the grace to
>            the grace.[30]

On 7 May he returned to Oak Hill, 'after having decided to be a priest and religious but still doubtful between St. Benedict and St. Ignatius'. Four days later he made a bonfire of his verses, 'Slaughter of the innocents' he called it in his journal.[31] He had, however, sent copies of most of them to Bridges, and held back from the flames corrected copies of poems Bridges did not have in their latest versions. And it was only three months later, on 8 August, that he remarked to Bridges with pride on 'the peculiar beat I have introduced into St. Dorothea. The development is mine but the beat is in Shakespeare.'[32] There were signs that Hopkins's literary holocaust was a romantic indulgence.

Within the next day or so he decided on St Ignatius, and sealed his decision by writing to Newman, and formally applying to the Society of Jesus in Farm Street, London. On 19 May he was interviewed by Fr Weld, the English Provincial, head of Jesuits in the English Province. On 28 May he went to Oxford and on the next day took his degree, when he met Simeon Solomon the painter, and saw Swinburne. On arriving home on the 30th he found the acceptance for the Jesuit novitiate. 'I do not think there is another prospect so bright', he wrote to Liddon, with a trace of maliciousness, because he must have known how Liddon would be hurt by the news. He told Urquhart that the Jesuits' acceptance had brought him 'the first complete peace of mind I have ever had'.[33]

# Swiss Swan-Song

Edward Bond and Hopkins had arranged to start in the early hours of Friday 3 July for a month's tour of Switzerland.[1] Alpine scenery had played a part in the education of the Romantic poets, and it would be Hopkins's last opportunity to see Switzerland because (Bond said) Jesuits were forbidden to enter the country.[2] The day before they were due to depart Hopkins was still worried about how he would pay for the tour. With his previous earnings from *Once a Week* in mind, he had started an article on the medieval school of poets and, in particular, William Morris's *The Earthly Paradise*, published two months previously. Difficulties brought him to a standstill, in a manner which was to become habitual:

I meant the *North British [Review]* at first: one of our Balliol Fellows writes in it and wd. perhaps recommend me—but now I have thought of the *Dublin* too. I am afraid though Ward wd. read a page and then use some pious profanity. . . . To make matters worse *The Earthly Paradise*, the poem in question, I cannot get. So far as I have got I am dull and abstruse. The worst is that an article must be (i) written, (ii) accepted—the first requires time, of which I have so little and perseverance, of which I have so none at all; the second is doubtful. . . . I am afraid the thing will really never be done.[3]

About twenty years later he wrote from Dublin:

I am now writing a quasi-philosophical paper on the Greek Negatives: but when shall I finish it? or if finished will it pass the censors? or if it does will the *Classical Review* or any magazine take it? All impulse fails me: I can give myself no sufficient reason for going on. Nothing comes.[4]

Hopkins kept a verbal and pictorial record of his travels, in the gentleman-amateur tradition. Since the first paintings of the Alps had been exhibited in England around 1770 there had been an increasing number of British visitors to Switzerland, clutching their Baedekers. Wordsworth and Robert Jones crossed the Alps in 1790, and *The Prelude* portrayed the mountains as assertions of harmony and the human imagination. Ruskin taught Alpine travellers to devote themselves to 'the certain facts' of nature, in the hope of creating 'imaginative topography'. Hopkins's drawings of mountains, falls, and glaciers are Ruskinian foreground studies, but show his limited talents. To put a Hopkins sketch beside Ruskin's of the same Swiss scene shows his inferiority and imitation.[5] Even in written descriptions a comparison with Ruskin is sometimes to Hopkins's detriment. Though his new vocabulary made precise descriptions, it could also deaden the prose. Hopkins's natural descriptions do not convey as often as Ruskin's an emotional involvement, though they show bursts of enthusiasm.

Hopkins' process of building up a personal vocabulary and dialect had been more self-conscious and pedantic than Ruskin's. Now, after four years at Oxford, noting information, working out ideas in essays, and writing verse and journals, he had almost completed his word-hoard. The word *inscape* is prominent in his Swiss journal and *instress, scape,* and *outscape* are also used. He has a long list of semi-private terms, which he fluently employs in description: boss, brassy, cluster, coil, comb, cream, crest, crisp, cuff, damask, fan, flake, flue, flush, flute, foil, fret, horn, huddle, jut, knot, modulate, mould, peak, pierce, plane, precipitate, quain (quoin), rib, rick, ruck, rut, shaft, spray, swell, tackle, tret, wimple. For colours he was already using *black, rose,* and *yellow* idiosyncratically and forcefully. He had come to see how the juxtaposition of two ordinary words could be extraordinary: 'the *sea* . . . became . . . *fat*', and '*fat* and gleaming *dandelion*', and ordinary words if used with observational precision could be visually sharp: 'the pale grey *shaven* poles . . . on the railway'.

Visual accuracy can be lifeless, when too insistent:

all the women sat on one side and you saw hundreds of headdresses all alike. The hair is taken back and (apparently) made into one continuous plait with narrow white linen, which crosses the lock of hair not always the same way but zigzag (so that perhaps there must be more than one linen strip) and the alternation of lock and linen gives the look of rows of regular teeth. The fastening is by a buckle (Bädecker calls it) or plate of silver generally broadened at the ends or sometimes by a silver or gold pin, wavy and headed by a blunted diamond-shaped piece gracefully enamelled.

Fortunately Hopkins had brought his careless-Romantic-fool mask with him—the one which let him, in order to appear 'strikingly graceful', fix a large, stinging sea-anemone on his forehead.[6] As this was not the Shanklin sands but the Swiss mountains he wore his 'pagharee [a silk scarf wound Indian-fashion round the head, and falling down behind at the neck] and turned it with harebells below and gentians in two rows above like double pan-pipes'.

The first exhilarating Swiss experience was

Basel at night! with a full moon waking the river and sending up straight beams from the heavy clouds that overhung it. We saw this from the bridge. The river runs so strong that it keeps the bridge shaking. Then we walked about the place and first of all had the adventure of the little Englishwoman with her hat off. We went through great spacious streets and places dead still and came to fountains of the clearest black water through which pieces of things at the bottom gleamed white. We got up to a height where a bastion-shaped vertical prominence shaded with chestnut trees looked down on the near roofs, which then in the moonlight were purple and velvety and edged along with ridges and chimneys of chalk white. A woman came to a window with a candle and some mess she was making, and then that was gone and there was no light anywhere but the moon. We heard music indoors about. We saw the courtyard of a charming house with some tree pushing to the windows and a fountain. A church too of immensely high front all dead and flush to the top and next to it three most graceful flamboyant windows. Nothing could be more taking and fantastic than this stroll.

Such a passage makes one regret the infrequency with which Hopkins relaxed moral constraints when writing. This is not countryside, not nature—which Hazlitt had called 'the last refuge of the misanthropist'—but civilization, and yet he finds nothing objectionable here. The dangerous areas have not been censored or disguised, neither is there the sentimentality or shrillness that occur in many of his poems about humans. He exposes himself to all experience. Two women appear in the passage, emphasizing the absence of women elsewhere in Hopkins's writings, except for virgin martyrs. There is nothing sexually explicit or even implicit in 'the adventure of the little Englishwoman with her hat off' or 'a woman came to a window with a candle', but the *possibility* of sexuality in the scene has not been denied. Both those phrases could occur in an episode of Sterne's *Sentimental Journey*. Even the windows are not judged as architecture, but are enjoyable and enjoying themselves—'most graceful flamboyant windows'. The phrase 'We heard music indoors about' is an extension of the benevolent tone into the unseen human interior of the dark houses. Clearly focused perceptions take their place in a continually unfolding scene, and are not abstracted from a human context: 'the river runs so strong that it keeps the bridge shaking', and 'the near roofs, which then in the moonlight were purple and velvety . . . and chimneys of chalk white.' Rhythms evolve naturally from events, and do not seem to be authorially imposed: 'A woman came to a window with a candle and some mess she was making, and then that was gone and there was no light anywhere but the moon.'

Although a large proportion of Hopkins's vocabulary in these descriptions is architectural, it is rarely over-solemn. When over-precise, it may be for a humorous climax: 'the spraying was baffling and beautiful, like netting pulled horizontally and in places broken. In fact horizontally prolate gadroons.' There is the constant shock of an unexpected image: 'a very low rainbow against the sides of the lake colouring the trees, red, green, and purple, and the red being prominent it looked like a slice of melon'. This is one of a large number of domestic images which give this journal a homely, happy, and human quality:

all was mist and flue of white cloud, which grew thicker as day went on and like a junket lay scattered on the lakes

curled edges dancing down, like the crispiest endive

clusters of water like the moistened end of a pocket handkerchief

clusters of water . . . at a distance they are like the wax gutturings [*sic*] on a candle and nearer . . . like rockets when they dissolve and head their way downwards

coffee-foam waterfalls

the Giessbach falls . . . like lades of shining rice

the fine pleatings of the snow . . . sometimes cut off short as crisp as celery

the mountains . . . shaped and nippled like the sand in an hourglass

the blue colour [of the upper Grindelwald glacier] . . . looks like starch in ruffs

the snow on the hills . . . looks like rags of cambric drying

at the take-off [the upper of the three Reichenbach cascades] falls in discharges of rice or meal

the great limbs [of a fall] . . . are tretted [*sic*] like open sponge or light bread-crumb where the yeast has supped in the texture in big and little holes

the Monte Rosa range are dragged over with snow like cream

peach-coloured sundown

a blade of water looking like and as evenly crisped as fruitnets let drop and falling slack

the second stage [of the Rhône glacier] . . . appeared like a box of plaster of Paris or starch or toothpowder, a little moist, tilted up and then struck and jarred so that the powder broke and tumbled in shapes and rifts

Hopkins's imagery was peculiarly inventive on this holiday. There are strong visceral images: 'rich big harebells glistening like the cases of our veins when dry and heated from without'; the Grindelwald glacier was 'haggard and chopped', and 'becoming deep within it looks like deep flesh-cuts where one sees the blood flush and welling up'. There are the expected alliterative couplings: 'shires of snow', 'the highest and furthest flaked or foiled like fungus', 'ribbon of rainbow'. And there is imaginatively comic imagery: 'melodious lines of a cow's dewlap', and 'the edges of broken spray ... toss like thousands of little dancing bones'. His invention joyfully expands from the object to further imaginative reaches:

the fall of the Gelner—like milk chasing round blocks of coal; or a girdle or long purse of white weighted with irregular black rubies, carelessly thrown aside and lying in jutty bends, with a black clasp of the same stone at the top ... or once more like the skin of a white snake square-pied with black.

His most fanciful image is of the end of a glacier by the Jungfrau:

If you took the skin of a white tiger or the deep fell of some other animal and swung it tossing high in the air and then cast it out before you it would fall and so clasp and lap round anything in its way just as this glacier does and the fleece would part in the same rifts: you must suppose a lazuli under-flix to appear. The spraying out of one end I tried to catch but it would have taken hours: it was this which first made me think of a tiger-skin, and it ends in tongues and points like the tail and claws: indeed the ends of the glaciers are knotted or knuckled like talons.

He is delighting in his own inventiveness, reaching beyond the Ruskinian aim of presenting the object as it is.

The only saying of Bond's which Hopkins thought worth recording was 'the grasshoppers are like a thousand fairy sewing-machines'. Many other people appear in this journal: the little Englishwoman, the young Englishman who had been to see Charlotte Brontë's school in Brussels, a 'liberalising Swiss guide who clinked glasses at lunch with "à votre santé, monsieur!" and approved of E.B.'s *dicta* and epigrams', a Frenchman 'of cultivation and a great mountaineer', Wilson, a young American, who went up the Faulhorn with Hopkins and Bond, the guide who said when Hopkins would not let him take his knapsack, 'Le bon Dieu n'est pas comme ça', a 'strange party of Americans' at Guttanen, a guide who sprang up the side of a hill and brought down for them bunches of Alp-roses, 'in the valley a girl with a spindle and distaff tending cows', the guides Gasser and Welchen, and 'young Mr. Pease of Darlington', who climbed the Breithorn with them in brilliant starlight, John Tyndall, the eminent natural philosopher and mountaineer, an atheist who prescribed treatment for Bond's sickness ('I hope he may come round', Hopkins generously said, some time later), the monks and dogs of St Bernard ... There was also 'that repulsive type of French face':

The outline is oval but cut away at the jaws; the eyes are big, shallow-set, close to the eyebrows, and near, the upper lid straight and long, the lower brought down to a marked corner in the middle, the pupils large and clear; the nostrils prominent; the lips fleshy, long and unwaved, with a vertical curling at the end (in one case at any rate); the nose curved hollow or so tending; the head large; the skin fair—white and scarlet colour.

There were several human scenes: at the *tables d'hôte* at inns, mass at churches, dancing in the *salle à manger* of the Trois Couronnes at Vevey, the 2 a.m. mass for the guides going up the Matterhorn with Tyndall: 'I got up for this, my burnt face in a dreadful state and running. We went down with lanterns. It was an odd scene; two of the guides or porters served; the noise of a torrent outside accompanied the priest. Then to bed again.'

But the narrative Mrs Hopkins received is non-expansive and informative, full of 'nexts':

Brussels the first day, to Cologne the next, up the Rhine to Mainz the next, by train to Basel the next. Basel we liked immensely and saw it by moonlight. Next day we reached Lucerne by train. . . .

Oak Hill was still a pressure foreign to his feelings and needs. 'How fond of and warped to the mountains it would be easy to become!' he wrote in his journal. But 'even with one companion', says his journal in another part, 'ecstasy is almost banished: you want to be alone and to feel that, and leisure—all pressure taken off'. People spoiled the summit of the Breithorn for Hopkins: 'the cold feet, the spectacles, the talk, and the lunching'. Six weeks later he was due to join the Jesuit community at Roehampton, where he would have to live in institutional proximity to a number of people, and where he would have to keep a close-pressured curb on his senses, his selfishness, and his behaviour.

# PART III

# The Jesuit, 1868–1874

I did say yes
O at lightning and lashed rod

# Novitiate: Roehampton, 1868–1870

During the fortnight before Hopkins entered the novitiate[1] he said goodbye to friends and relations. Bridges came over to Oak Hill one day,[2] and Hopkins presented him with the Aldine edition of the Earl of Surrey's poems, which his father and mother had given him the previous Christmas. He would not be allowed personal books in the novitiate. It was later said, however, that he 'expressed surprise at not being allowed to keep by him Swinburne's *Poems and Ballads*' while he was a novice.[3] On the evening of 7 September, a 'dim, fine, and very hot' day, he said goodbye at home and set off to Manresa House, arriving late at the Georgian mansion, with its fine Doric-pillared portico.

Roehampton was a village of villas and mansions, five-and-a-half miles south-west of Hyde Park Corner. Like Hampstead, it was one of the highest and healthiest suburbs of London, and even wealthier. Roehampton Park, formerly the estate of the Earl of Bessborough, was at the south-west extremity of the village, and in 1861, when the Jesuits took possession, consisted of 42 of the original 110 acres. There were fine trees—elms, poplars, huge cedars, chestnuts, Turkey oaks, and a specimen of a Japanese tree said to be the largest of its kind in Europe, shrubberies, and secluded landscaped walks, called by the Jesuits St Aloysius' and St Stanislaus'. Also in the grounds were a farm and a brick-walled kitchen garden, 150 yards long and 60 wide, which contained hot-houses, cucumber-houses, melon-pits, and cold frames, left over from the time of the original owners and now decayed. On its west side Manresa's grounds bordered on Richmond Park, with which, at the front, it appeared to be continuous, separated only by a sunken fence. The only building in the wide expanses of royal parkland visible from the house was the White Lodge; deer sometimes fed at the ha-ha. It was perfect for a Jesuit novitiate, in large, secluded grounds but near a great city: St Ignatius Loyola, founder of the order, had said that its work was in large towns.

Six other novices entered with Hopkins; each would have had the same kind of examination on entering:

He is asked about the age, health, and position of his parents in the world; whether they are Catholics; whether they are likely to need his help in their old age. He has also to give a full account of himself; whether he suffers from ill-health or other infirmity, hereditary or acquired; whether he owes money, or is under any other obligation; what studies he has made and what are his literary attainments, whether he has lived a virtuous life, how long he has been entertaining the idea of entering the Society, and what is his motive for wishing to do so; whether it has been suggested to him by any one else or springs entirely from himself.[4]

It was written in the Society register that Hopkins's parents were Protestant, he had spent eight years at the grammar school in Highgate and four at Balliol, had taken the degree of BA, and when admitted as a novice had been a Catholic for two years.[5] It was not mentioned that he owed money to Balliol: at midsummer 1867, the bursar's arrears book shows he owed £7 10s. With interest, the sum outstanding unpaid had become £20 9s. by 1876, when the debt was finally settled. This debt might have barred Hopkins from the Society.[6] Unlike the other novices he was to be called by both his names: one of the others was called Frederick Hopkins, he wrote to his mother, 'so that we must keep our Christian names to avoid confusion and on the other hand I must keep my surname because there is already a brother Jerrard with a J.'.[7]

After supper that first night the novices would have visited the Blessed Sacrament, then gone to community recreation up a wide flight of stairs to the *aula*, the novices' hall, which had been one of the grandest parts of the old mansion, dating from 1761; it was a high room, having 'a fine ceiling, with baroque plaster work and a place where once a crystal chandelier had hung'. Past splendours stopped at the ceiling: tradition said the bleak pine panelling had been put in seven years ago to cover classical frescoes of 'bare limbs and voluptuous bosoms'.[8] Part of the evening would be taken up with the recitation of litanies in the chapel:

On a small prayer desk in front of the sanctuary a single candle lighted the pages of an open book. When we were all kneeling in our places ... a priest came forward from the back of the chapel and knelt at the prayer stool. We newcomers in the ignominy of lay attire knelt at the very back, behind everybody.

The novice porter closed the door when everyone seemed to have come in. ... The Litanies of the saints, recited nightly in Jesuit houses ... are a curiously soporific devotion. ... The priest went through the various invocations and the longer prayers at the end in a rapid Latin. ... After a few nights' practice I was able to come in at the right moment with the appropriate *Miserere nobis, Ora pro nobis*, and *Libera nos, Domine*, without time to think much about the meaning of the various petitions.

The whole of this evening devotion took only some fifteen minutes, and then we all trooped out.[9]

There would probably have been a talk from Fr Fitzsimon, novice-master and Rector of the community: besides the new novices or postulants, there were senior novices, lay brother novices, lay brothers, and two fathers. Hopkins was given a bedroom of his own, 'but in a short time shall move into one of the dormitories or, as they call them, Quarters'. He told his mother they had to keep their rooms tidy 'to an extraordinary degree'.[10]

During the first week or so the new novices were separate from the others, shepherded around by two 'angel-guardians'. One of these was John Walford, Bridges's friend, whom Hopkins had met at the Oratory in Birmingham. During this first period:

the rules of the Society are put into their hands, and are explained to them; they are instructed as to the kind of life they will have to live, and the difficulties that they will have to encounter. They have to study the 'Summary of the constitutions', in which is set forth the end and object of the Society, the spirit that must animate its members, the obedience they must be ready to practise, the sacrifice of their own will and judgment that they must be prepared to make; in fact, they have every possible opportunity given them of ascertaining what it is that they are undertaking when they declare their intention of serving God in the Society according to its laws and constitutions.[11]

A retreat followed, in which the novice-master gave a series of 'instructions on the fundamental truths of religion' to the postulants, who had to keep perfect silence, then meditate for an hour on the main points. After this probationary retirement the postulants were received as novices and clothed in the Jesuit dress.

We went to a large room where an old lay brother, making a guess at our height and weight, took two gowns from a rack where large numbers were hanging. They were all secondhand, some neatly patched, others whose pristine black had become a dark bottle-green. ... The gown of the English Province is a simple garment, not much more than knee-length, with two buttons, and two streamers or hanging wings at the shoulders. It has no sleeves. ... There were two pockets, to be used only for such things as a handkerchief, a rosary, and a little book for daily examens of conscience. No novice was supposed to keep his hands in his pockets at any time. Out of doors you might tuck your hands in the ends of your sleeves as monks do. It wasn't satisfactory, because our coats were ordinary secular ones, not the monk's full-sleeved affair.[12]

Hopkins would have been given what looked like a rosary, but of an unfamiliar kind. It consisted of 'a piece of wire about four inches long, turned up at the lower end into a circle holding some black beads. They could be pushed from the circle to the straight part, or vice versa.' These examen beads, a symbol of the Spiritual Exercises of St Ignatius, were 'to help you keep count of the number of times you fell into a fault you were trying to overcome'. They were fastened with a safety-pin to a special place on the inner side of the gown. When you committed a fault,

you shifted a bead from the upright part of the wire to the circle. At midday and night examinations of conscience you counted the beads and then made marks to record the number in your little grey book [about two inches by three, carried in the pocket and written in during the day, and taken to chapel for these examens]. There are two lines for each day. They get progressively shorter as the weeks go by and your self-conquest improves—in theory.[13]

Hopkins was probably introduced to another Jesuit custom, and may have found the experience similar to Denis Meadows's:

'And now,' [the brother] said, 'here is something else.'
He glanced at each of us in turn, almost roguishly, were not the word too incongruous. He held up before our eyes a pair of what looked like circlets of galvanized barbed wire with slightly blunted points, and two little scourges, or 'disciplines', each of knotted cords with a rope handle.
'Well, I'm jiggered!'
Brother Hunsdon disregarded Jenkins' exclamation.
'We have bodily penances—not as much as some religious orders, because our chief mortifications are of our own will and judgment, by means of obedience.' . . .
'We use the discipline'—Brother Hunsdon held one up for our inspection—'twice a week, in our cubicles before going to bed. You may give yourself twelve strokes, and—'
'Do you have to give yourself twelve strokes?' asked Brother Jenkins.
'You're supposed to. You must ask Father Rector's permission if you want to do more. It's not recommended.' We waited for the reason.
'Because of vainglory. You see, the novices in the other cubicles can hear you and count the strokes.' . . .
'And now the chain.' He held up one of the wire circlets, and then demonstrated it by putting one foot up on a chair and fastening the chain round the upper part of his right leg.
'You put it on when you get up, and take it off after breakfast—twice a week. If you want to do more, you must ask—'
'Do you wear it outside your trousers?' Brother Jenkins broke in.
'No, Brother, of course not. I'm only showing you how to put it on.'[14]

The instruments of penance were kept in the drawer of the washstand in the dormitory cubicle. The dormitories were lofty rooms with large windows, sparsely furnished, and with a big fireplace. The cubicles were 'like stalls in a well-kept stable', except for the curtains at the front. There was little room 'for anything more than a single iron bedstead, a washstand with a pitcher and basin, and a "Charley", or chamber pot, shoved modestly away underneath. An oblong piece of carpet of indeterminate color lay on the floor boards beside the bed.' The windows were left open at night, and 'a foggy air from across the Pen Ponds and Beverly Brook' seeped into the room. All members of the Society of Jesus rose at 5.30 a.m.:

There was a confusion of sounds in what I thought was the middle of the night. The door handle rattled, some unintelligible words were shouted, there were answering responses from most of the cubicles, heavy footsteps in the room were echoed in the hall outside, and then the incandescent lights went up, one after another. I looked at the watch lying by the pitcher and basin—half-past-five. The foggy air had filled the room during the night, and I felt as though in cold storage. The lay brother, whose heavy footsteps and shouted 'Deo gratias' had awakened me, passed along to another room and I heard the same sounds again, faint beyond the dividing wall. I washed quickly in ice-cold water and scrambled into my clothes, brushing my hair and doing my tie with half-frozen fingers in such light as came over the top of the cubicle; the red curtain was quite opaque. I had been warned that I should have twenty minutes in which to wash, dress, and empty the slops. Then I must throw the bedclothes over the curtain rod of the cubicle to air.

Each novice carried out his slops, lining up to empty them at the sink. If you bumped into anyone in the queue you apologized in Latin, 'Veniam frater'. By this time the dormitory windows had been shut and a fire lit, although it was considered self-indulgent to warm chilly hands above the fireguard, and cold was endured as a mortification.[15]

From the previous evening's litanies until breakfast was the *maximum silentium*, the great silence, when you did not speak, even in Latin. Then the loud bell went for morning oblation; everything was done by the precisely timed hand-ringing of the novice-bell. The larger community bell, with its different note, was the voice of the superiors, which meant the voice of God. It had been a strict rule of St Ignatius that his spiritual soldiers should stop what they were doing on hearing the bell, even if they were in the middle of writing or speaking. Morning oblation, private prayer to begin the day, was in the chapel. At the end of ten minutes the porter banged the ledge in front of him with his knuckles three times as a signal, and the novices would go back to their dormitories for meditation, as the clock struck six. In front of each cubicle was a desk, with a chair placed just inside so that no novice could see his neighbour, but visible to the senior novice who would wake him if he were drowsy. The points for this meditation had been studied for a quarter of an hour before going to bed on the previous evening. The novices found it a very long hour and it was divided into quarters by knuckle-raps on a desk. For the first fifteen minutes they knelt on their small shiny black kneeling-stool stuffed with horsehair; they were not allowed to sprawl on the desk or lean on their elbows. For the next quarter-hour they sat on a chair, which was such a relief that they often dozed off. Then the senior novice would rap loudly, or pull at a wing of the offending novice's gown (Jesuits were strictly forbidden to touch another person, 'even in jest, apart from the accolade or embrace before going on a long journey'). For the third fifteen minutes they had to stand, not leaning on anything, and the last quarter was spent kneeling. At 6.55 the bell would ring for community mass in the chapel; communion was conducted in hierarchical order: senior novices first, then postulant novices, lay brothers, lay brother novices, laymen. It lasted half an hour, and the last quarter before breakfast at 7.45 a.m. was spent in reconsidering the morning meditation.[16]

In the refectory were long tables covered in white cloths, the laid places 'all geometrically alike'. There was 'a reader's pulpit, with a large crucifix above it, lofty windows along the opposite wall, and a wide serving hatch open at the further end, where aproned lay brothers stood in silence waiting to hand the food out to the novice servers.' Meadows thought the refectory the most monastic-looking part of Manresa House, which otherwise was rather like a boarding-school. A typical breakfast was porridge, bacon, bread and butter, and tea or coffee.[17]

At 8.30 a.m. the novices were again at their desks, for a half-hour's reading of *Rodriguez on Christian Perfection*, followed at 9 o'clock by instruction on the rules from the master of novices. After this they had 'to make their beds and arrange their little cells, and, when this is done, to repair to some appointed place where one of their number, appointed for the purpose, assigns to each a certain amount of manual labour, commonly known as "indoor works"'. This might be washing up in the butler's pantry (called the *cella poculorum*): scraping the leavings into a bucket for the pigs, and rinsing the dishes, tumblers, cups, and saucers in hot soapy water with washing soda, not pleasant to cold hands in winter. Other tasks were laying the refectory tables for dinner, or 'a secretis'—swilling disinfectant over the latrine floor, or sweeping the hall and dormitories with brooms and wet sawdust. Most of the work which would have been done by servants in a private house was done by the novices, with the exception of cooking and skilled jobs, done by the lay brothers. This domestic regimen, like much else, resembled the basic training of a soldier recruit. At 10.15 they had to learn by heart part of the Society's rules, or a prayer, psalm, hymn, or papal bull. There was then about half an hour's *ad lib*, or free time, which they used to read a spiritual book or saint's life, pray in the chapel, or walk in the grounds, in solitude and silence.

At half-past eleven they reassembled for 'outdoor works'. For this the novices took off their gowns and wore old clothes and shoes, or were issued with the thick-soled, strong Stonyhurst boots, but they were not allowed to work in shirt-sleeves. One of the older novices, 'master of outdoor works', allotted jobs from an oblong board with the names on pegs. *'Visne secare ligna, quaeso frater'* was an order to work at the wood-pile, near the kitchen yard where the tramps came, or a novice might be ordered *'colligere folia'*, to rake up the fallen leaves and carry them off in a wheelbarrow. Other duties included digging or weeding, cutting grass, or picking fruit. After an hour they returned to the house, washed and tidied, and at 12.40 the bell summoned them to fifteen minutes of prayer in the chapel, and examination of the morning's duties.

Dinner at 1 o'clock was formal, starting with a long Latin grace:

A priest recited the versicles and everyone the responses. It was not chanted as in monastic orders. From the pulpit under the big crucifix a novice read a few verses of the Bible in Latin, and then went on with a modern book of church history [or a saint's life, or the history of the Society]. Halfway through dinner he was relieved by another reader. Occasionally one of the priests ... at the rector's table corrected errors in the reading.[18]

When they finished eating 'the rector gazed up and down the tables to make sure everyone had finished. Then he raised his eyes to the reader in the pulpit. "Satis, frater" (It is enough, Brother).' Then the novice read from a leather-bound folio the Roman martyrology, the next day's date was announced (translated into Latin), with a list of all the saints to be commemorated. After another long Latin grace, everyone walked in single file to the chapel, to pray in silence. On the porter rapping with his knuckles everyone stood up, genuflected, and left.

An hour's recreation followed. 'You recreated', says Thomas, 'with the first brother encountered.'[19] Afternoon occupations were largely a repetition of the morning, but

on three days in the week a walk of about two hours has to be taken in companies of two or three. No one is allowed to choose his companions, but the master of novices arranges the various companies. Sometimes a game of cricket or football is substituted for the walk. At 6 a second hour of meditation of half an hour has to be made in the chapel [an 'hour' in the Jesuit sense could mean a 'period' of time, just as a 'week' of the Spiritual Exercises did not mean a period of seven days] after which the recital of some vocal prayers, and some free time which they can dispose of for themselves, bring them on to supper at 7.30. After this they have an hour's recreation, during the first half of which Latin has to be spoken.[20]

At nine night prayers in the chapel were followed by fifteen minutes' work on the meditation for the next morning, then they reviewed their day. Finally

the ... curtains were all drawn across the fronts of the cubicles and from within came sounds of washing—in cold water—tooth-cleaning, and the thud of shoes dropped on bare boards as the novices changed into the felt-soled slippers worn only at night and for serving in the refectory. The fire had died away to a red glow, the windows had been opened. ... [They] undressed hurriedly and slipped into bed, between sheets that were stiff and icy cold. The fire gave a last dying splutter and threw a rosy light on the Earl of Bessborough's baroque plasterwork. ... Then a clock boomed in ten slow measured strokes.[21]

℃℈

Nine days after his arrival Hopkins and other first-year novices began the Long Retreat, lasting thirty days, and conducted according to St Ignatius' famous *Spiritual Exercises* of 1541. It is divided into four 'weeks', each consisting of meditations, prayers, rules for praying, and other spiritual rules. 'Five times a day the master of novices gives points of meditation to the assembled novices, and they have subsequently to spend the following hour in a careful pondering over the points proposed to them.' Between each 'week' of retreat there was a recreation day, 'spent in long walks, and in recovering from the fatigue which is caused by the constant mental strain involved in the long time of meditation and prayer'. Apart from those days, there was no recreation, and silence was 'strictly kept throughout.'[22] No letters could be written or received: the retreatant was cut off from all secular interests.

The first 'week' (eight days) was to reform the sinner, *deformata reformare*, its subjects 'the end for which man was created, the means by which he is to attain that end, the evils of sin and its consequences, and the four last things, death, judgment, heaven, and hell'. The second 'week' (ten days) was the most important and characteristically Ignatian of the Exercises, aimed at *reformata confirmare*, consolidating the reformation: 'the Kingdom of Christ, His Incarnation, Nativity, and His life on earth ... with separate meditations on the two standards of Christ and Satan, under one of which every one is fighting, on the tactics of the evil one, the choice that has to be bravely made of a life of hardship under the standard of the Cross, and other subjects akin to these.' The third 'week', its aim *confirmata confirmare*, to confirm more strongly 'the repentant sinner already confirmed in his penitence', lasted for seven days, during which 'the Passion of Christ is dwelt upon in detail.' The concluding part, lasting five days, suggested emotions of joy and comfort missing from previous weeks, its subjects 'the Resurrection, the appearance of our Lord to his disciples, the Ascension, with one or two concluding meditations on the love of God and the means of attaining it', and the object *confirmata transformare*, to transform the confirmed repentant sinner.[23]

On the last day, Sunday 18 October, the *Te Deum* was sung at Benediction 'in thanksgiving for all graces received during the Spiritual Exercises'. The exhausted novices were given 'the brief respite of "long sleeps", that is, of getting up in the morning half an hour later' (at 6 a.m.).[24] Cardinal Wiseman summed up the ideal behind the Long Retreat's progression:

A man is presumed to enter into the course of the Spiritual Exercises in the defilement of sin, under the bondage of every passion, wedded to every worldly and selfish affection, without a method or rule of life, and to come out of them restored to virtue, full of generous and noble thoughts, self-conquering and self-ruling, but not self-trusting, on the arduous path of Christian life. Black and unwholesome as the muddy water that is poured into the filter, were his affections and his soul; bright, sweet and healthful as the stream that issues from it, they come forth. He was as dross when cast into the furnace, and is pure gold when drawn from it.[25]

The eulogy does not do justice to the terrifying intensity of the ordeal, physical and mental; it is an experience which mature professional religious are known to dread. Meadows describes that part of the Exercises called the Composition:

St. Ignatius, born before Columbus discovered America, and dying soon after the middle of the sixteenth century, believed as well as felt about hell in the mode of his generation. The exercise on hell was a contemplation rather than a meditation. You had to apply the five senses to the place of torment. The nature of this exercise, and the invariable use of a picture or composition of place at the beginning of a meditation make it clear that St. Ignatius had an active and vivid imagination.

Our composition of place now was to picture the length, breadth, and depth of hell. Then we were to pray that if the love of God grew cold within us, at least the fear of hell should keep us from sin.

We must take each of the senses in turn. First, says St. Ignatius, you see the fire, and the souls as though in bodies of fire. With your ears you hear the wailing, howling, and blasphemy of the lost ones. You smell the sulphur, smoke, and putrescence of hell. Then you taste in imagination the bitterness of tears, sadness, and conscience ever remorseful, ever unabsolved, yet ever in rebellion. Last of all, you feel the fire touching and burning even an immaterial entity like the soul. Afterward you are to pray to Christ, bringing to mind all the souls in hell, including those who did not believe in Him. We are to thank Him that so far He had been merciful, not cutting us off in mortal sin, in which case we should infallibly have joined all those for whom there could be no pity nor ever an end to their pain.

This meditation was not made at our desks. We were told to carry our kneeling stools into our cubicles, draw the curtains, and meditate in private. The silence in the dormitory as we went back to it seemed more intense than before. We drew the curtains across the open ends of the cubicles. The senior novice went down the room lowering the window blinds as he had been instructed. In the dim light we set to work applying our five senses to the pains of hell.[26]

Another commentator, Boyd Barrett, who directed many retreats, came to be severely critical:

It introduces a spirit of military discipline and coercive thinking into prayer. It reduces praying to something not remotely unlike a cross-word puzzle. It raises conscious thinking, goaded to activity by will efforts above normal semi-conscious thinking. It aims at producing by force emotions and affections. It sounds the death-knell of simple, unsophisticated praying, and introduces an atmosphere of strain and tension. It leaves little or nothing for the Holy Spirit to do.[27]

He was especially critical of the Long Retreat for inexperienced novices:

Novices are carefully 'worked up' to a high pitch of excitement. They are told that their whole future lives depend upon how they make this thirty days' Retreat. They are not allowed to read or hear a single word about the 'Exercises' before they begin, but it is suggested to them that these 'Exercises' are the most holy and wonderful form of spirituality in the whole world and that if they correspond fully they will become saints. When the evening arrives on which the 'long retreat' is to commence, and when the noviceship bell signals the opening of the 'long retreat', the novices enter the chapel trembling with excitement and pent-up emotion. The journey to heaven has begun. Day by day as it proceeds the novices become more strained, more absorbed, more abnormal. ... At night in the dormitory, or corridor in which the novices' sleeping-alcoves are placed, there are strange signs of restlessness. Voices are raised in self-accusation, or in plaintive calls for home, and few enjoy more than broken sleep at such times of intense spiritual strain.[28]

'It is not to be wondered at', wrote Barrett, 'that many novices break down and become unnerved during retreats.' Those who did not break down, however, were 'gripped by the retreat and make the most fervent resolutions to devote their whole lives to attaining perfection'. The following year, when the new novices were making the Long Retreat, Hopkins recorded:

They were reading in the refectory Sister Emmerich's account of the Agony in the Garden and I suddenly began to cry and sob and could not stop. I put it down for this reason, that if I had been asked a minute beforehand I should have said that nothing of the sort was going to happen and even when it did I stood in a manner wondering at myself not seeing in my reason the traces of an adequate cause for such strong emotion—the traces of it I say because of course the cause in itself is adequate for the sorrows of a lifetime.[29]

ભ્

The noviceship was aimed at 'putting the novice's vocation to the test'. The thirty days of spiritual exercises were 'the chief test of a vocation, . . . also in epitome the main work of the two years of the novitiate and for that matter of the entire life of a Jesuit'. The novitiate had the purposes of acquainting a man with the Ignatian mould, training him to regulate his own submission to that mould, and ensuring perpetual conformity by training his will into 'blind obedience'.

There were formalized ways of subjecting the novice to constant scrutiny and correction by superiors, by peers, and self, of the smallest details of behaviour and thought. Most of the methods originated in the culture and psychology of a distant age, and are foreign to twentieth-century practices and sympathy: penances and public humility, for example, willingly undertaken, then possibly taken one stage further by being denied, seem masochistic:

Most of the novices wished to do extra penances . . . but the rector was sparing of permissions. The devout, however, might go in for spiritual mortification by penances in the refectory. They were not physically onerous. After grace and before the reading began, you 'told your fault' in the framework of a formula: 'Reverend Fathers and loving Brothers, by order of holy obedience I tell my fault [then you named it], for which fault holy obedience enjoins on me the penance of [whatever it was].' The faults were usually small violations of rule or carelessness about property of the house. We broke a good many plates and dishes in our two years, and that was a fault against religious poverty. The penances were minor humiliations, like kissing the feet of the novices at the nearest table, or taking your own meal on bended knees at the 'little table'. This last was rather trying, as you were immediately under the eyes of your superior a few feet away.[30]

A less sympathetic observer described the scene differently:

Were one to glance through the window of a Jesuit Refectory at the beginning of dinner or supper on an ordinary Friday or on the vigil of a feast, one would see quite a number of Jesuits saying grace on their knees, with outstretched arms; kissing the floor; crawling around under the tables and kissing the toes of those already seated at table. Others they would hear calling out in a loud voice that they were guilty of some breach of order or of charity.[31]

But even Meadows registered bizarre aspects of the regular penances: 'When we rose at the caller's five-thirty "Deo gratias", we clamped our chains onto our right legs before dressing. A certain stiffness was noticeable as we genuflected and knelt for Holy Communion. I think we must have looked as though we all had a touch of rheumatism.' The chains were worn for three hours, together with 'those galvanized spikes gripping [the] thigh muscles'.[32]

More frightening must have been an exercise in humility called 'rings':

The procedure was simple, but rather frightening, if you were nervous or hypersensitive. We sat around the hall, two rows on each side. . . . Father Rector was going to call on two novices in turn to receive public admonitions. He did not follow alphabetical order, so you never knew when you might be the victim. . . . At length the rector named one of the novices.

The young man rose to his feet, walked slowly to the middle of the room, and knelt on the floor. I felt sorry for him. . . . He looked unhappy.

On these occasions the rector sat very still, very erect. I do not remember seeing him relax in a chair. After a few seconds he turned his head to the left and asked the porter what he had 'observed' in Brother So-and-So.

After six novices described minor faults or were non-commital, one accused him of being 'conceited', adding, 'Just a little, Father.'

I don't think it was true, even with the qualification.

Father Rector did not seem to take the qualifying words into account. Perhaps 'conceit', as first cousin to pride, was more than a matter of rule or decorum. It was a moral fault. Or, on the other hand, the rector, who was an experienced director, may have had a higher opinion of the novice than we had, and been determined to help him by giving him occasion for humility. . . . He delivered a scathing diatribe against the poor novice's 'fault'. Who was he to give himself airs or think himself better than his companions in the noviceship, which should be a school of humility? Had his meditations on the hidden life of Our Lord taught him no more than that? It was meant to be morally bracing, but it was too much for the recipient. His lips trembled, he blinked, rubbed his eyes, and the tears began to roll down his cheeks. He fished out a handkerchief and wiped his eyes, but he could not stop his tears. I think we all felt embarrassed and rather shocked. . . .

Father Rector was stern.

'Stop that snivelling, Brother,' he said. 'Put up your handkerchief at once. Now, Brother Jenkins, what have you observed?'

Brother Jenkins hadn't observed anything. He was the last in the back row.

'Very well, Brother. Return to your seat.'[33]

The Rector described here, Fr Daniel Considine,was a fellow-novice of Hopkins's.

Another exercise in self-conquest was 'private admonitions': for a period, each novice had another appointed to watch over and reprimand him; this practice was common to all Jesuits in every house, however senior. Besides correcting faults, the training tried to inculcate 'the difficult habit of abstaining from any mental criticism of the order', a habit said to be 'the distinctive feature of the obedience of the Society of Jesus'.

More extroverted skills, such as preaching, were also taught. Novices delivered sermons, or 'tones', in the community refectory. Hopkins's first sermon, however, was delivered in the chapel, in November of his second year, on the Feast of St Stanislaus, the special feast of the house. In his obituary, written twenty years later, it was said that 'his fellow-novices well remember his panegyric of St Stanislaus, which was as brilliant and beautiful as it was out of the usual routine of pulpit deliveries'. The novices were also tested as catechists, going to instruct the children of local parishes. Hopkins's catechizing duties over the two years took him to Isleworth, Homer Row, Fulham, and Brentford. Homer Row involved a four-mile walk and a train journey; a contemporary account reads:

On the arrival of the catechists the doors of the school were thrown open, and there flocked in up the stairs into a large room on the first floor a crowd of children, boys and girls, whom piety or curiosity had attracted from the neighbourhood. These children had first to be sorted into their respective classes in two large rooms, then new-comers, of whom there were often many, were examined by the head catechist and assigned to what seemed their proper division, and the work of teaching began.[34]

Each class consisted of a dozen or more

little Cockneys, lively as fleas and unstable as quicksilver. Harassed novices, at their wits' end to keep the children attentive and well-behaved until the benediction service, would eke out the matter of the Penny Catechism with pious stories. A 'tale', however moralistic, would hold the youngsters, so long as it was gruesome enough—St Lawrence on his grid-iron, St. Bartholomew flayed alive, martyrs torn apart with red-hot pincers. The children learned to exploit the situation. They would start their nonsense early in the class, and . . . would besiege the novice with appeals to 'Tell us a tyle, Bruvver, tell us a tyle.'[35]

Although there were no general studies, the novices learned to speak fluently in dog Latin, 'their second mother tongue'. They had to keep silent most of the time, and if they had to speak it was in Latin. This led to curious incidents: 'Returning once from some ceremony at Farm Street, and arriving at Fulham Bridge, a novice wishing to descend from the top of the bus, the vehicle having begun to move on, amazed the conductor by crying out, "Siste paulisper, velim descendere".[36]

One of the few entertainments was 'indoor recreation', which took the place of walks in bad weather:

We were divided into little groups and had to sit in a number of separate circles in the novices' hall. . . . For about two hours we sat on hard wooden chairs with nothing to look at but the faces of our companions or the rain-washed windows. There were no indoor games of any kind, and we might not read even the pious books kept in the *arca*, a bookcase standing between two of the windows. All we were allowed to do was talk, but soon became desperate for matter of conversation. We knew nothing of topical events, read only religious literature, never saw a play or went to a concert. 'Worldly' conversation was discouraged.

Long before the first hour of this recreation was over, I listened eagerly for every sound of the big clock as it struck the quarters.[37]

A time of recreation anticipated with enthusiasm was the hay season:

The hay season was the nearest thing to a summer vacation for us. Even after supper, when the twilight was fading, we went to have a last look before going upstairs for recreation and the *pia fabula*.

Then, one morning, when the sunlight was streaming over the red curtains of our cubicles, and the birds began singing before the caller's '*Deo gratias*', we heard the whirr of a mowing machine and the voice of the man in charge of it calling to his horses. The hay season had started.

When we went down to the chapel for morning oblation, even the recollectedness of the greater silence could not prevent some of us peeping through the glazed door of the Long Gallery to look at the tiny swaths of new-cut hay waiting for our rakes and pitchforks.

Daily until the hay was all dried and carted we turned out in our oldest clothes after dinner to work in the field. Toward teatime we assembled at . . . a picnic spot. There were benches under the trees, and a big garden table. We called the place the Temple, because it was near Lord Bessborough's classical summerhouse. Tired and hot, with our shoes and trouser legs yellow with buttercup pollen, we sat and listened to a novice reading a religious book. This took the place of our private spiritual reading.[38]

Hopkins resolved early in his first year to keep 'no regular weather-journal but only notes', but fortunately, after the end of the year his journal expanded considerably, and he described sunsets, the scaping of leaves, the natural sculpting of snow, stories the lay brothers told him during a week he spent in the kitchen, a visit to Kew Gardens, the causes of dreams, gathering mulberries and bluebells:

I do not think I have ever seen anything more beautiful than the bluebell I have been looking at. I know the beauty of our Lord by it. It is strength and grace, like an ash. The head is strongly drawn over and arched down like a cutwater. The lines of the bells strike and overlie this, rayed but not symmetrically, some lie parallel. They look steely against paper, the shades lying between the bells and behind the cockled petal-ends and nursing up the precision of their distinctness the petal-ends themselves being delicately lit.

This passage was originally much longer, but Hopkins went over it, excising weak words. The third sentence first read: 'Its inscape is mixed of strength and grace, like an ash tree.'[39] The artist was alive, even though the novices were supposed never 'to forget the distinction between the supernatural and the "merely" natural'.[40] His journal entries were observations of nature, and only occasionally, as in this passage, did he attempt, a connection of supernatural with natural.

બ

In the fortnight before his first Christmas as a novice, Hopkins was visited by his Balliol contemporaries Lewis Nettleship and Henry Scott Holland. Holland wrote of the visit to T. H. Green, who commented:

I am glad that you and Nettleship saw Hopkins. A step such as he has taken tho' I can't quite admit it to be heroic, must needs be painful, and its pain should not be aggravated—as it is pretty sure to be—by separation from old friends. I never had his intimacy, but always liked him very much. I imagine him— perhaps uncharitably—to be one of those, like his ideal J. H. Newman, who instead of simply opening themselves to the revelation of God in the reasonable world, are fain to put themselves into an attitude—saintly, it is true, but still an attitude. . . . The 'superior young man' of these days . . . hugs his own 'refined pleasures' or (which is but a higher form of the same) his personal sanctity. . . . It vexes me to the heart to think of a fine nature being victimised by a system which in my 'historic conscience' I hold to be subversive of the Family and the State, and which puts the service of an exceptional institution, or the saving of the individual soul, in opposition to loyal service to society.[41]

Green's reactions included personal sympathy, judgement, psychological description, and common English prejudices about the Society of Jesus, typifying the various responses of family, friends, and acquaintances.

Hopkins's had been no sudden or simple impulse. Just as the path to his reception into the Roman Catholic Church could be traced back to his walk to Newman's church three years earlier, and before that to his medievalist interests at school, so his choice of the Jesuits depended on complex motivation, including behaviour patterns, reactions to academic and religious environment, and personal emotions. He did not have many religious orders to choose from: he had a limited knowledge of the Benedictines, and a thorough acquaintance with Newman's Oratorians, but he was probably ignorant of Jesuits until the year before he joined them. But the Jesuits were the best known Catholic clergy in

Britain: a list of converts to Catholicism who became priests between the Tractarian Movement and 1899 shows that 78 became Jesuits, the next most popular group being the Oratorians (26), followed by the Dominicans (23).[42]

Mid Victorian England, largely ignorant of Catholic beliefs, had not rid itself of the old 'No Popery' phobias. On a railway journey Pugin once 'crossed himself while engaged in private prayers . . . to the horror of a lady, alone with him in the compartment, who cried out: "You are a Catholic, Sir;—Guard, Guard, let me out." '[43] In popular imagination the Jesuits were a secret organization bent on subverting liberal countries and enslaving people's minds. To Hopkins they probably appeared the most likely modern means of restoring England to her old spiritual unity, from her present state as the 'City of Confusion' (Newman's phrase). They also presented the most complete rational framework for resolving the problems of personality. Hopkins was hoping to impose on a 'sordid' and unpredictable existence a sense of rightness and order, even at the price of putting himself out of joint, in some respects, with personal and national culture.

The Spiritual Exercises of St Ignatius, the foundation on which the Jesuit organization had been built, had some aspects which would appeal to Hopkins, and others of potential disadvantage to him and his poetry. Behind them was the strong protest against divided beliefs and slack spiritual habits. No other religious order offered such practical teaching and aims: 'to conquer oneself and regulate one's life, and avoid coming to decisions through the impulse of disordered passion'. Hopkins's confessional diaries of 1865 showed his dissatisfaction with the frequent petty lapses; and during his two terms at the Oratory school he still had no satisfactory day-to-day way of life. The Exercises had the attraction of being a complete, self-contained system; a methodological counter to insecurity, uncertainty, and guilt, they were capable of transforming the psychic and moral life. In Ignatius' predilection for technique, obsession with methodology, and minute directions about behaviour, nothing was left to chance.

Critics of the Exercises objected to their fundamental doctrine, 'that strategy must be used in religion, and that victory is to be won less by love, as Christ taught, than by craft and guile'. There were, however, more imaginative aspects of the Exercises, like their visualizations of fights between angels and devils; these would have presented no difficulty to Hopkins, who had a natural tendency to what William James, in *Varieties of Religious Experience*, called 'overbelief'. And Ignatius' class-consciousness, his denial of equable rights to women and servants, and his praise for ascetic practices, also accorded with Hopkins's pre-Jesuit thinking.

Two particular aspects were less congenial to Hopkins. One is the doctrine of 'indifferentism', implying complete detachment, 'not only from what is evil, but also from what is in itself harmless or indifferent':

One must grow cold to all things: love of friends, country, parents; particular interests; kinds of learning. . . . In fine the ideal put forward is that of a soldier held by no tie of affection . . . utterly detached from all natural desire. . . . The beautiful things that grow . . . human love with its impulses; music, dance and song; the conquering of nature; art and dreams, have no value in themselves, and must be bartered for whatever helps piety.[44]

The Exercises emphasized the benefits of going against nature. They were not healthy or helpful for a temperament predisposed to melancholia. It was assumed that normal minds would be purged, and emerge refreshed, but some were turned to self-loathing and morbid pessimism.

It took a special personality to survive happily the tensions of a religious community. Hopkins was considered 'a little odd' by the Jesuits, said Herbert Lucas; 'few really appreciated him'. To another contemporary Jesuit, Joseph Rickaby, he was 'too delicate' and 'too whimsical'.[45] A vow of obedience killed many aspects of the self. Community life constricted individual personality. There was a lack of privacy, the constant proximity of other people, which in the Jesuit system of supervision could be—or seem—'a world of espionage, delation and intrigue'.[46] Men were expected to live without normal emotional sustenance: 'love' was permitted only in the large sense, and there was a morbid fear of 'special friendships'. A Jesuit seminary was an institutional asylum, sharing characteristics with army barracks and prisons. Such a community provided a self-justifying and well-defined corporate structure, but the cost was paid in impersonal routines, habits, and disciplines.[47]

# Philosophate: St Mary's Hall, 1870–1873

Hopkins's two years as a novice ended on Thursday 8 September 1870. At the close of an eight-day retreat, four out of the original seven novices, Thomas McMullin, Charles Wilcock, Frederick Hopkins, and Gerard Hopkins, took their vows. It was two years since their first full day in the Society: 8 September was the day each year dedicated by the Church to the Nativity of the Blessed Virgin Mary.

After dinner the previous night they were each given a large sheet of poor-quality paper. After it was folded in half, Hopkins made a copy of his two Latin vow formulae, on the first and third of the four sides.[1] On the third side he copied the shorter probationer-scholastic vow, and on the front the vow of admission to the Society: 'A.M.D.G./ Omnipotens sempiterne Deus, ego Gerardus Manley Hopkins licet . . .':

Almighty and eternal God I, Gerard Manley Hopkins, though altogether most unworthy in Your divine sight, yet relying on Your infinite goodness and mercy and moved with a desire of serving You, in the presence of the Most Holy Virgin Mary and Your whole heavenly court, vow to Your Divine Majesty perpetual poverty, chastity, and obedience in the Society of Jesus; and I promise that I shall enter that same society in order to lead my entire life in it, understanding all things according to its Constitutions. Therefore I suppliantly beg Your Immense Goodness and Clemency, through the blood of Jesus Christ, to deign to receive this holocaust in an odour of sweetness; and that just as You gave me the grace to desire and offer this, so You will bestow abundant grace to fulfil it. In the Novitiate at Roehampton on the eighth day of the month of September, in the one thousand eight hundred and seventieth year.

Gerard Manley Hopkins[2]

The data was written in dog Latin, ecclesiastical style, and Hopkins started writing 'sept. die' (the day on which he wrote the copy) and had to cross it out and substitute 'die octavo', 'the eighth', the day when he took the vow.

Soon after sunrise the ceremony of the vows took place in the tiny novices' chapel, lit by a diamond-paned skylight, on the top floor of Manresa House. The secrecy was due to the penal clause in the Catholic Emancipation Act of 1829:

in case any person shall, after the commencement of this Act, within any part of the United Kingdom, be admitted or become a Jesuit . . . such person shall be deemed and taken to be guilty of a misdemeanour and being thereof lawfully convicted, shall be sentenced and ordered to be banished from the United Kingdom for the term of his natural life.

The Roman Catholic Relief Act had admitted Catholics to the same political rights as Protestant dissenters. Nearly all public official posts, and the privilege of sitting in Parliament, denied them since the Reformation, were now open to Catholics. But Wellington and Peel, who forced the bill through to avoid civil war in Ireland, had to placate their own 'Protestant and High-Church party' with sops like this clause.[3]

The threat in the clause was real enough, and preserved a sense of the Penal Days. (As late as 1902, a Protestant clergyman applied for a summons at Marlborough Street police court against Frs Sydney Smith, Herbert Thurston, and John Gerard, in order to have the Jesuits declared illegal.) For seven years from 1854, when the novitiate had been moved from Hodder House in remote Lancashire down to Beaumont Lodge near London, it had been known as Mr Clarke's Finishing Academy, after its rector Tracy Clarke. So throughout the 1870s the novices at Roehampton pronounced their vows in secrecy.

They entered the room singly, as though going to confession, and knelt at a prie-dieu, facing the Rector and novice-master, Fr Gallwey, who sat at a small table on which stood a crucifix. The vows were pronounced; Fr Gallwey answered 'Amen', and received the written formula of the vows.

Hopkins discarded the lay clothes he had worn for the last two years—the shabby and patched gown, his own black tie, and Cyril's black coat. Wearing for the first time a Roman collar, a new black suit of the kind worn by secular clergy, loose academic gown with wings, and biretta, he took leave of the novices at a reception with wine held after dinner in the refectory. At this, on the rector saying '*Deo gratias*', the rule of silence was suspended, and Fr Gallwey made gifts, including a crucifix, to each new scholastic.[4]

As a novice, Hopkins had followed the community life and customs, but was free to return to the world, just as the order was free to reject him. As an approved scholastic, he was bound by vows which forbade him to leave the Society without the consent of his superiors. Before entering the novitiate, candidates had been divided into two groups: those who at the end of the two years' training would become 'temporal coadjutors' (the 'brothers' who fulfilled domestic duties, a servant class), and those intended for eventual priesthood, who became known as the 'scholastics'. There were five stages to a scholastic's training based on the Jesuit *Ratio*, or educational method: the novitiate (two years); the juniorate (two years); the philosophate (three years); the theologate (three or four years—at the end of the third year the Jesuit entered the priesthood); and the tertianship (one year).

The next stage for the four new scholastics was the juniorate, a two-year course of academic, mainly classical, studies, which showed the traditional Jesuit attachment to a Latin-based humanist culture, and which was designed to prepare for teaching in the Society's schools. Because of his Oxford degree and training, however, Hopkins went straight from the novitiate to Stonyhurst, for three years of 'philosophy'.

☙

Roehampton, because of its proximity to London, had been close to the world of Hopkins's first twenty years, and Manresa House helped to preserve the comfortable shelter and privilege of his southern middle-class background. Despite the strict personal routine and domestic chores, there had been genteel assumptions in the House. The Georgian architecture of the mansion, its pastoral setting, its royal associations, and the upper-class background of many novices buttressed the distinction in intellectual and spiritual rank between the future lay brothers and the future priests.

Now Hopkins was moving to the north country. Stonyhurst,[5] a large parkland estate in Lancashire, was about 225 miles north-west of Roehampton, over half the length of England. It included three Jesuit institutions: a preparatory school (Hodder Place), a second-level school (Stonyhurst College), and the seminary for Jesuit philosophers, St Mary's Hall. His train journey took Hopkins into another world, a northern world, probably not the one in his imagination. Nineteenth-century Lancashire had highly populated and slum-filled industrial towns, exposed to Irish immigration, like Manchester, Liverpool, Preston, and Bolton. It must have been with some surprise that, on leaving Manchester, where he took midday dinner at the Jesuit house and saw the new church being built, Hopkins passed through the russets and browns of the Lancashire millstone moors, and saw the heather-covered fells and richly wooded river valleys.

The Stonyhurst area, within easy reach of a clustered band of industrial towns, was little known by southerners, because it was at the southernmost tip of a wild upland region, the Forest of Bowland, which contained only one hilly road. The main roads north from industrial Lancashire veered away to skirt the forest before they reached Stony-hurst. A horse and trap with a driver and small child were waiting at Whalley for Hopkins's train, and as they were driving away the child, pointing back to the viaduct, told Hopkins 'Yon brig's over the Cauder'—a phrase and pronunciation he found so picturesque that he put it in the letter he wrote to his mother next day.[6] The trap drove the four miles up and down hill, along damp and narrow lanes overhung with chilling trees, over bleak hill-country, until they came to Wood-fields, a small group of thick stone houses, where College employees lived, then turned off into a cluster of trees, which secluded the Hall from the road and the College. The seminary was an austere block, often compared to an army barracks, but lacking the concessions to grace or comfort which military architects sometimes allowed. It had been planned in 1830 by a Jesuit, Fr West, who had distrusted art, outside contractors, and his own workmen; these last had named it 'Thin-Drink Hall', to memorialize the poor quality of the home-brewed ale supplied by their priest-overseer. Fifteen years later it was christened St Mary's Hall. There was a short wing at each end of the main block, the west wing containing the tiny chapel, and the east the kitchen wing, two extremes of spirit and flesh. All other functions of the seminary were carried on in the main block.

There were three floors and a large attic. On the ground floor, on either side of the front door, were parlours for visitors. There were lecture rooms, called the logic room (for first-years) and the ethics room (second- and third-years), refectory, the scholastics' library, assembly hall, recreation room, and a special Shoe Place, a round-the-year necessity in muddy Lancashire. At one end of the ground floor were rooms occupied by the *cur vals*, elderly priests against whose names in the Province's Catalogue was written '*Curat valetudinem*', indicating that they had retired, and were waiting to die. On the two floors above were study bedrooms, distributed impartially among the three profes-sors and thirty-five scholastics. In the attic a collection of mainly theological books bequeathed to the philosophate by an ecclesiastical lawyer, Edward Badeley, a friend of Newman, and known as the Badeley, or the 'upstairs' Library.

The thick Seminary Wood almost surrounded St Mary's Hall, but the front was exposed, looking down over the Ribble valley to the distant Pendle Hill. Hopkins was lucky to be at the front, in a room with the view: if he had been given one at the back his surviving journal for 1870–1 would have been different. His room was similar to this:

It had two doors, an inner and an outer. There was a window overlooking the terrace and garden in front of the building. In the window embrasure was a wooden seat with a hinged top. This was a coal scuttle as well as a seat. You needed to keep it well filled in the winter. The Lancashire winter is raw, cold, and wet—and we had no central heating in our rooms.

In an alcove was a small iron bedstead, and by the bed a piece of carpet—a drugget, the lay brother called it—that may once have been of a definite color, but now was merged into the prevailing greyness. There was a fireplace in the middle of one wall, a table with two bookshelves on it, a plain wooden chair at the table, and by the fireplace a Windsor chair. A deal chest of drawers with a small mirror over it stood cattycorner to the right of the window. Against the wall opposite the fireplace was a deal washstand with the usual crockery. Near the foot of the bed there was a prie-dieu, and by it a kneeling stool. There were a few clothes hooks on the back of the door.

He was shown where the brooms and sawdust were kept, for sweeping his room every third day, and the sink for slops. 'My personal possessions were few', wrote Meadows, 'because of my vow of poverty':

I had a very scanty stock of clothes, my vow crucifix (which is so called because every Jesuit receives one on taking his first vows), and several books—the Jesuit's *Thesaurus*, containing the Rules and Spiritual Exercises, a Roman Missal, and a Latin prayer book. These are all a Jesuit normally can call his own in the way of books. If, for reasons of study or research, he is allowed volumes for his private use more or less permanently, he writes a note to that effect on the front endpaper—'in usum So-and-So.'

I put my clothes away in the chest. The crucifix and books I put on the prie-dieu. My two bookshelves were empty.[7]

Hopkins reported to his new superior, Fr Charnley, who was at the end of his term at St Mary's Hall; and he would probably have gone to the Shoe Place for a pair of Stonyhurst boots, necessary for the uneven roads and the fells. The second- and third-year scholastics were on holiday, but among the first-year students, or Logicians, were three he had known at Roehampton: Ignatius Gartlan and Sydney Morgan, four years younger than him, and a former naval commander, Henry Kerr, six years older. These familiar faces, together with the comforting moonlight, after a day of rain and harsh winds, helped Hopkins overcome his uneasiness at the strangenesses around him. Even the movements of people were welcoming, and in a letter to his mother next day there is relief at finding the 8 o'clock supper pleasant and sociable. There would be a comforting sense of community and familiarity at the first devotion in the half-empty chapel, the evening recitation of the litanies, a quarter-hour of invocations to various saints, each followed by an appropriate response, and finishing with longer prayers. Later that night, alone, after he had gone to bed and turned out the gas, the sense of companionship was replaced by feelings of strangeness and sleeplessness, and a consciousness of the exposed position of the house, high on Longridge Fell, in an inhospitable climate.

In the dark, at half-past five the following morning, Hopkins replied '*Deo gratias*' to the brother whose duty it was to open the two doors of each room and call '*Deo gratias*' until the words were repeated by the occupant. He lit the gas-lamp, washed and shaved in cold water poured from his large jug into the basin, and dressed. At about ten to six he went downstairs to the chapel for the morning oblation, an offering of the day to God, then back to his room for an hour's meditation, before attending community mass in the chapel downstairs. From there he walked with the other scholastics the length of the house to the refectory for breakfast. After breakfast he tidied his room, cleaned his shoes, and perhaps made a fire.

Later that day he wrote the first of his infrequent letters home. It consisted of a single long paragraph, for the most part an ordered account of his arrival and first evening. He told his family he had taken his vows, and concluded, perhaps with conscious provocativeness: 'I can speak more freely now because I have bound myself to our Lord for ever to be poor, chaste, and obedient like Him and it delights me to think of it.'

There were signs that all was not well. The letter said:

It has rained many times already and I know it will go on to the end of the chapter. I can feel that summer is but diluted here. They say it is mild in winter compared with places more south and I partly believe it; that is I believe it is mild in winter compared with places more north. But a Scotchman told me Argyleshire was the mildest part of Great Britain and that trees etc grow there which will grow no where else. At all events both are near the sea and in the eye of the west wind.

The humour does not hide his heaviness. Many of his letters over the next three years sound the same complaint against perpetual winter and lack of spring. Within a few hours of arriving at Stonyhurst, Hopkins had become enmeshed in the obsessive pessimism about the climate, prevalent among the Stonyhurst people and the villagers: rain, dampness, and rheumatism were the subjects most frequently discussed. But despite the climate Hopkins enjoyed his view of the countryside: 'The window of the room I am in commands a beautiful range of moors dappled with light and shade.'

Further on in the letter is another ominous sign:

By daylight I feel the strangeness of the place and the noviceship after two years seems like a second home: it made me sad to look at the crucifix and things Fr Gallwey gave me when I was going. He was very very kind. But the brotherly charity of everyone here can be felt at once: indeed it is always what you take for granted.[8]

Hopkins was trying to cling to the novitiate, as though it were a surrogate home for the one he had rejected.

അ

Besides three priests and two lay-brothers, there were thirty-five men in St Mary's Hall, sixteen in their first year as philosophers. For the first part of their three years they studied pure and applied logic and mathematics, and in the second and third years 'psychology, ethics, metaphysics, general and special, cosmology, and natural theology'. In his first year (according to Thomas), Hopkins 'would have attended lectures in logic and mathematics every morning except on Thursdays and Sundays.[9] On Mondays, Wednesdays, and Fridays there were also logic lectures in the evening, and on Monday and Wednesday after-noons at half-past three there were "circles".' These 'circles' were considered to be among 'the most valuable elements in the philosophi-cal and theological training of the Society', and were said to provide those who passed successfully through the system 'with a complete defence against difficulties which otherwise are likely to puzzle the Catholic controversialist'. They lasted an hour,

during the first quarter of which one of the students has to give a synopsis of the last two lectures of the professor. After this, two other students, previously appointed for the purpose, have to bring against the doctrine laid down any possible objection that they can find in books or invent for themselves. Modern books are ransacked for these objections, and the 'objicients' do their best to hunt out difficulties which may puzzle the exponent of the truth, who is called the 'defendant'. Locke, Hegel, Descartes, Malebranche, John Stuart Mill, Mansel, Sir William Hamilton, and other modern writers, are valuable contributors for those who have to attack the Catholic doctrine. . . . When the two objicients have finished their attack, there still remains a quarter of an hour before the circle is over. This time is devoted to objections and difficulties proposed by the students.[10]

Lectures were in Latin; the professors, who were Italian and German, were non-specialists: Fr Capaldi lectured in 'logic, general and special metaphysics, and ethics', and at one time taught Church history to theologians. The philosophy teaching was based on that of St Thomas Aquinas, and every argument had 'to be brought forward in syllogistic form, and to be answered in the same way'. Lectures began on 3 October. The day was cut up into units, each activity having a fixed starting and finishing time from the rise at 5.30 a.m. to the 'Gas out' at 10.30 p.m.; the students had only seven hours for sleep. Each man had catechist duties at one of six local centres.

Hopkins found the course hard and wearisome. In April of his first year he wrote to Baillie: 'I am going through a hard course of scholastic logic . . . which takes all the fair part of the day and leaves one fagged at the end for what remains.' He had little time for writing or reading, 'so that I can seldom write and when I do I have nothing to say'. He found the life 'painful to nature'. He begged for letters from home, and from Bridges and Baillie, though saying to the latter, 'your letters are always welcome but often or always it is more pleasant to get them than easy to see how they are to be answered'. He had at last realized *how* to read, but too late: 'now I see things, now what I read tells, but I am obliged to read by snatches'. It was 'mainly about books and so on that I shd. be writing and I read so few'. He was glad to hear literary and other news from Baillie, 'as I am here removed from it and get much behind'.[11]

Everything at St Mary's Hall was 'as dank as ditchwater', he wrote to his mother.[12] 'Early in the year they told me there wd. be no spring such as we understood it in the south. When I asked about May they told me they had hail in May. Of June they told me it had one year been so cold that the procession could not be held on Corpus Christi.' (The *Stonyhurst Magazine* of 1888 reported that 'no month has been completely free from frost during the last forty years'.) 'Perpetual winter smiles', he told Baillie. 'I hope you find yourself happy in town: this life here though it is hard is God's will for me as I most intimately know, which is more than violets knee-deep.'

But though the countryside was 'bare and bleak', it was nevertheless 'fine scenery, great hills and "fells" with noble outline often, subject to charming effects of light (though I am bound to say that total obscuration is the commonest effect of all), and three beautiful rivers'. He wrote in his journal:

Oct. 20—Laus Deo—the river today and yesterday. Yesterday it was a sallow glassy gold at Hodder Roughs and by watching hard the banks began to sail upstream, the scaping unfolded, the river was all in tumult but not running, only the lateral motions were perceived, and the curls of froth where the waves overlap shaped and turned easily and idly.—I meant to have written more.— Today the river was wild, very full, glossy brown with mud, furrowed in permanent billows through which from head to head the water swung with a great down and up again. These heads were scalped with rags of jumping foam. But at the Roughs the sight was the burly water-backs which heave after heave kept tumbling up from the broken foam and their plump heap turning open in ropes of velvet.

He found the clouds 'more interesting than in any other place I have seen'. Once spring came, he started writing accounts of what he saw looking towards Pendle:

[16 April] Pendle dappled with tufted shadow; west wind; interesting clouding, flat and lying in the warp of the heaven but the pieces with rounded outline and dolphin-backs shewing in places and all was at odds and at Z's, one piece with another. Later beautifully delicate crisping.

[22 April] But such a lovely damasking in the sky as today I never felt before. The blue was charged with simple instress, the higher, zenith sky earnest and frowning, lower more light and sweet. High up again, breathing through woolly coats of cloud or on the quains and branches of the flying pieces it was the true exchange of crimson, nearer the earth/ against the sun/ it was turquoise, and in the opposite south-western bay below the sun it was like clear oil but just as full of colour, shaken over with slanted flashing 'travellers', all in flight, stepping one behind the other, their edges tossed with bright ravelling, as if white napkins were thrown up in the sun but not quite at the same moment so that they were all in a scale down the air falling one after the other to the ground.

[1 May] Very clear afternoon; a long chain of waxen delicately moulded clouds just tinged with yellow/ in march behind Pendle. At sunset it seemed to gather most of it to one great bale, moulded as Br. Bacon said like a brain, and I have said a bale because its knops are like the squeeze outwards of the packed stuff between the places where a network of many cords might bite into it.[13]

The extended descriptions record joyful experiences, although they were nothing to do with his course or with any Jesuit parts of his mind. By the middle of June, although they had not 'had one hot day', his health was 'in the main robustious'; and 'we bathe every day if we like now at a beautiful spot in the Hodder and between waterfalls and beneath a green meadow and down by the greenwood side O. If you stop swimming to look round you see fairyland pictures up and down the stream.'[14]

&

The first-year examinations in philosophy and mathematics were over by the end of July 1871. At the beginning of August, St Mary's Hall was needed for the Salford diocesan clergy retreat, so the seminarians went to live for a fortnight in the College, in the rooms left empty by the lay philosophers, whose term had finished with the annual speech-day, or 'Academy'. The seminarians, released from formal studies for the summer, and with increased leisure, enjoyed the riches provided for the lay philosophers: their own recreation room, the College garden, a billiard table set up in a long room in the front of the College, boats, cricket, and salmon-fishing.

None of these philistine treats was likely to have raised Hopkins's spirits. But on Sunday 6 August he and Henry Kerr climbed up the Longridge Fell to Jeffrey Hill. Looking across to the ridge opposite, Hopkins noticed: 'the folds and gullies with shadow in them were as sharp as the pleats in a new napkin', and made out, 'appearing as clearly outlined flakes of blue, the Welsh coast, Anglesey, and Man, and between these two the sea was as bright as brass'.[15]

The seminarians' annual holiday, or *villegiatura*, always called the 'Villa', was held that summer at Innellan, in Argyllshire. They travelled by train to Liverpool, and there embarked on the *Bison*, which set sail at 11.30 a.m. for Greenock, on the Firth of Clyde.[16]

It was a calm voyage, with a glorious sunset at sea; a small group in a quiet corner on deck prepared for the next morning's meditation. Hopkins saw a mirage, in which the headlands of the coast appeared to be lifted above the sea. Off the Isle of Man he noticed

high near the zenith and above the sun not a halo but the arc of a bow just like a rainbow unless rather smaller. It was convex to the sun. No rain was then or at any time falling. A sailor who said it was a rainbow did not make much of it but said it was a sign of wet weather in the morning and fine in the evening, in fact the common weather-saw about the rainbow. The time was towards sunset.[17]

The boat landed at a quarter-past five in the morning at Greenock, where they attended mass at St Mary's on Patrick Street. Having breakfasted 'sumptuously', according to the beadle's journal, at the Tontine Hotel, they took a steamer for the hour's voyage back down the Firth of Clyde and across to the Argyllshire coast, where they landed at Innellan at half-past ten in the morning. Innellan was a small village and summer resort for Glasgow families. They were to stay at Broom Lodge, a large house facing over to Wemyss Bay; it was set in beautifully laid out grounds, with a separate fruit garden.

The next day Hopkins went on a hurried trip to the Island of Arran, admiring from the boat the island's scenery, 'Goat Fell and the other mountains enclosing Glen Sannox', but disappointed at not having time to explore a glen on the island. The next evening he climbed the brae behind Broom Lodge—'much beautiful after-sunset clouding and all round the lochs and sea'. On 21 August, a party walked twelve miles through the Corlarach Forest to Loch Egg (or Eck), 'walking barefoot over the low-water sands of Holy Loch and fording "a big burn"'.

Then Hopkins and Francis Bacon, a seminarian with whom he struck up a friendship, left the group to climb one of the braes, 'by which the opposite heights looked nobler; else I was rather disappointed'. At other times during the Villa boats were taken out under Henry Kerr's instruction—mainly rowing-boats, as the weather was wet and windy.

On 24 August a party of fifteen travelled to Edinburgh, where they were met by Lord Henry Kerr, father of William and Henry Schomberg Kerr. Lord Henry gave them lunch at the station, and his son guided them around Edinburgh. Once again Hopkins felt the disadvantage of being a member of an organized group, unable to pursue his own objects: 'I should like to stay there long enough to let the fine inscape of the Castle rock and of Arthur's Seat and Salisbury Crag grow on one.' The party had time to visit only the castle and the abbey and palace of Holyroodhouse. At Holyroodhouse, Hopkins was interested only in what was called 'the Chapel Royal', at the north-east corner of the palace. The ruined and roofless nave of the abbey kirk was all that remained of the early thirteenth-century abbey of Holyrood, destroyed at the Reformation. Hopkins was attracted by 'two low arches looking as if 3rd Pointed over the gateway foiled with downward fleurdelys'.[18]

At four o'clock they caught the train back. Their boat, according to Hopkins, was tossed in the crossing of the Firth, 'and the rain, which I took for hail, cut one's ears and somebody said was like pebble-stones'. They reached Broom Lodge at eight, and their supper, 'with meat, mutton chops etc.' was washed down with punch. That evening Hopkins noted the northern lights, 'beautiful but colourless, near the horizon in permanent birch-bark downward streaks but shooting in streamers across the zenith and higher sky like breath misting and then being cut off from very sensitive glass'.

The last day of the Villa was the first fine one. A party took a boat up the Clyde to Glasgow, and spent so much time at the Govan shipbuilding yard of Robert Napier—of little interest to Hopkins—that they did not see Glasgow Cathedral 'till when it was shut and almost dark'. The Protestant cathedral of St Mungo's, the patron saint of Glasgow, dated back to the twelfth century. Although its stone was black with industrial smoke and dirt, Hopkins found it 'very complete and well preserved'. He noticed in an arch of the choir-screen what he took to be another foil ending in a fleur-de-lys, like that at Holyroodhouse. But his mind was creating a false trail, and the dim dusk-light deceived him: each of the cusps in the trefoiled arches of the choir arcade ended in a carved plant with berries. He was annoyed that he had no time 'to study the tracery well from within nor at all from without'.

Because of the weather there were not many outdoor excursions during the fortnight, and journal entries are few and short. When he writes he often expresses frustration: 'We landed at Brodrick and had only time for a rush to the entrance of Glen Rosa' (19 August); 'else I was rather disappointed' (21 August); 'I should like to stay there long enough to let the fine inscape ... grow on one' (24 August); 'We ... mismanaged things so as not to see the Cathedral till when it was shut and almost dark' (28 August—the exasperated 'mismanaged' is masked by 'We').

On Monday 28 August they had a rough voyage back to Liverpool, arriving at half-past four in the morning. They caught a train to Preston, and drove to Stonyhurst, and that night they were again indulged with punch, at their supper of cold meat.

ɕʍ

The day after they returned they went into retreat, which ended on 8 September. On that day Cyril came to visit; he stayed for two nights, then Gerard and he travelled to Blackburn, where their paths separated. Cyril went back to Liverpool, where he worked in the branch office of Manley Hopkins's firm, and Gerard to Hampstead, where he found his father and Milicent, his mother and the others having gone for the summer holidays to Bursledon, near Southampton. After visiting his grandmother and Aunt Annie at St John's Wood, the next day he took the train to join the rest of the family for a week in Bursledon. He found 'things pleasanter than they have ever been since my conversion, which is a great comfort'. In the garden with a view over the river Hamble, he noticed the difference between the Stonyhurst countryside and this 'elm and oak country', whose woods 'have the rich pack look in the distance one notices in southcountry landscapes'. His past holidays in Devonshire and the Isle of Wight contributed to this sense of distinctive southern inscape, which he found confirmed in Hampshire. Next day he made the distinction between 'constant' or 'running' instress, and present instress, a relationship of contradictory rather than confirmatory impressions:

On this walk I came to a cross road I had been at in the morning carrying it in another 'running instress'. I was surprised to recognise it and the moment I did it lost its present instress, breaking off from what had immediately gone before,

and fell into the morning's. . . . And what is this running instress, so independent of at least the immediate scape of the thing, which unmistakeably
distinguishes and individualises things? Not imposed outwards from the mind
as for instance by melancholy or strong feeling: I easily distinguish that
instress. I think it is this same running instress by which we identify or, better,
test and refuse to identify with our various suggestions/ a thought which has
just slipped from the mind at an interruption.[19]

Behind the terms 'inscape' and 'instress' lay not just a student's
desire for explanatory laws, but a personal hesitation and guilt at
acknowledging perceptions unless they were validated by objective
standards. 'Inscape' made the qualities he described originate with the
object, rather than in his reactions, and 'instress' transferred the
onlooker's feelings to the object, freeing the onlooker from responsibility.

Protected by these concepts, Hopkins indulged his desire to record
powerful experiences, sometimes resorting to the words 'inscape' and
'instress'. His individual response is noticeable in the experiences he
records, even though he attributes feeling to scene or object: 'I could
not but strongly feel in my fancy the odd instress of this, the moon
leaning on her side, as if fallen back, in the cheerful light floor within
the ring, after with magical rightness and success tracing round her the
ring the steady copy of her own outline.'[20] This description of a lunar
halo is made personal by the creative personification and the confession
of feeling. When he describes the Bleeding Heart flower, he has selected
his four angles of observation, though to the average observer there
would be only one: 'in the full-blown flower there are at least four
symmetrical "wards" all beautiful in inscape—the broadside, the
birdseye, underneath, and edgewise, besides what can be seen in the
unopened bud'.[21] The inscapes he sees and instresses he feels depend on
his ways of looking or feeling, in spite of the pretence that they are
buried in nature, waiting to be called out by some sensitive perceiver: 'I
thought how sadly beauty of inscape was unknown and buried away
from simple people and yet how near at hand it was if they had eyes to
see it and could be called out everywhere again.'[22] In a guilty reaction
against his schoolboyish pride in authorship (which remained with
him), he tried to disguise responsibility for his own feelings.

A description of sky or other natural sight may be drawn out, with
many pictures, metaphors, and types of vocabulary, to form a fluctuat-
ing and subjective vision. Returning from Southampton to Bursledon
one evening after confession, Hopkins caught the transitory effects of
sunset, which for him, as for Ruskin, was a favourite time for observing:

the sky in the west was in a great wide winged or shelved rack of rice-white fine pelleted fretting. At sunset it gathered downwards and as the light then bathed it from below the fine ribbings and long brindled jetties dripping with fiery bronze had the look of being smeared by some blade which had a little flattened and richly mulled what it was drawn across. This bronze changed of course to crimson and the whole upper sky being now plotted with pale soaked blue rosetting seized some of it forward in wisps or plucks of smooth beautiful carnation or coral or camellia/ rose-colour.[23]

Many of the nature entries Hopkins made in his journal at St Mary's Hall were of extraordinary atmospheric and climatic occurrences, of the kind that many people record: parhelion (mock sun), northern lights, lunar rainbow, thunderstorms, double rainbow, and lunar eclipse. But Hopkins's journal records the intense and concentrated experiences of a lonely spectator whose vision and expression are so peculiar that they make him a part of what is happening. He often becomes a character who physically appears in the scene, leading the reader in through his presence and eyes:

A lunar halo: I looked at it from the upstairs library window. It was a grave grained sky, the strands rising a little from left to right. The halo was not quite round, for in the first place it was a little pulled and drawn below, by the refraction of the lower air perhaps, but what is more it fell in on the nether left hand side to rhyme the moon itself, which was not quite at full.[24]

Towards the end of his second year at St Mary's Hall, when he had changed his room to one at the back of the house, looking towards Longridge, he wrote another account of a sunset:

When the sunlight near sunset falls on the wall of my room I can see the fuming of the atmosphere marked like the shadow of smoke: I have seen it once with the light coming through leaves, and this got less and less distinct on white paper which I moved towards the windows and once coming without a break from the brim of the fells.[25]

He is like a monk in his cell, rather than a member of a community; and there is an occasional trace of disharmony with the people around him: 'A parhelion seen after dinner, the mock sun being almost as bright as the true. I was not there: they did not take the trouble to tell anyone.'[26] The community was a handicap, rather than a help to his relationship with nature and art. Sometimes, instead of anger at other people's insensitivity, a sense of sadness and loss came over him:

Stepped into a barn of ours, a great shadowy barn, where the hay had been stacked on either side, and looking at the great rudely arched timberframes— principals (?) and tie-beams, which made them look like bold big **A**s with the cross-bar high up—I thought how sadly beauty of inscape was unknown and buried away from simple people.[27]

The Shireburn tithe barn, over fifty yards long and forty feet wide, was a wall-less structure of oak beams ('principals', with grooved-in spars), springing from the ground to form a gothic arch; it was the oldest building on the Stonyhurst estate, and dated back to before the Reformation. None of its pattern had been built since the Middle Ages.

A pre-Reformation practice officially encouraged among the seminarians was that of placing 'May Lines', on the first of May each year, by the statue of the Virgin Mary. Before entering the Jesuits Hopkins thought poetry 'wd. interfere with my state and vocation', but there could be no harm in such a sanctioned act. He wrote two poems for the occasion during his three years at St Mary's Hall, 'Rosa Mystica' and 'Ad Mariam'. Neither of these suggests more than a dutiful exercise, but the latter shows one surprising influence. In the novitiate Hopkins expected to be allowed to keep by him Swinburne's *Poems and Ballads*; and 'Ad Mariam', besides showing no originality (as Schneider says), reads like a parody of the famous chorus from *Atlanta in Calydon*, in stanza, anapaest, and diction:

| (Swinburne, 11. 1–2) | When the hounds of spring are on winter's traces,<br>The mother of months in meadow or plain |
| (Hopkins, 1–2) | When a sister, born for each strong month-brother,<br>Springs one daughter, the sweet child May |
| (Swinburne, 17) | Wherefore shall we find her, how shall we sing to her |
| (Hopkins, 33) | Wherefore we love thee, wherefore we sing to thee |
| (Swinburne, 25) | For winter's rains and ruins are over |
| (Hopkins, 9–10) | We have suffered the sons of winter in sorrow<br>And been in their ruinous reigns oppressed. |

The influence is the more remarkable because, as Hopkins had written to Baillie, it was impossible for him 'not personally to form an opinion against the morality of a writer like Swinburne'. Despite disapproval of his morals (in 1877 he would call him 'a plague of mankind'), and later of his diction, imagery, and rhythm, Hopkins showed an interest in Swinburne's poetry until the end of his life, calling his genius 'astonishing'.[28]

# 17

## Seascapes: The Isle of Man

On Saturday 3 August 1872, when the second-year examinations were over, the seminarians, with Fr Parkinson, their Spiritual Prefect, set out to the Isle of Man[1] for the Villa at Douglas, the island's main town and a popular resort for the manufacturing towns of northern England and the Potteries. Hopkins's group of about thirty was to stay at Derby Castle, at the northern end of Douglas Bay. Derby Castle (pronounced Dirby) was sheltered under the cliff, on the water's edge, at the Onchan end of Douglas, quieter and more select, beyond the popular promenade. A winding path led to the cliff's summit through a mass of shrubs and flowering hedges. The shore was shingle, with jagged rocks which made it dangerous for bathing, but a secluded nearby cove was suitable for gentlemen bathers.

One of the disadvantages of being a member of a religious community was that even during holidays the community rules and practices governed personal behaviour and activities and companions. Hopkins's itinerary for his fortnight's stay in the Isle of Man, as for all holidays after he entered the Society, followed a conventional pattern of boat- and fishing-trips, and visiting by well-trodden paths the most well-known sights and beauty spots. One day his party walked north to Ramsey; another day they travelled to the Norse and medieval ruins at Peel, after making the routine stops to inspect the ancient Kirk Braddan crosses, the ruins of St Trinian's church, and the four-tiered Tynwald Hill at the Norsemen's parliament field.

Another trip was planned, thirteen miles south-west to Port Erin, but 'a thick haze and heavy dew' discouraged Hopkins and Walter Ratcliff when they were a mile or so beyond Douglas Head, so they left the group, turned off the main road on to a lane, and downhill between high hedges to the grey-pebbled beach of Port Soderick. Hopkins saw 'hawks and gulls and cormorants and a heron, I think, that alighted on a rock with easy beating wings'. They spent the day among the rocky outcrops and caverns. Hopkins became fond of the spot and the day before they returned to Liverpool went back:

This time it was a beautiful day. I looked down from the cliffs at the sea breaking on the rocks at high-water of a spring tide—first, say, it is an install of green marble knotted with ragged white, then fields of white lather, the comb of the wave richly clustered and crisped in breaking, then it is broken small and so unfolding till it runs in threads and thrums twitching down the backdraught to the sea again.[2]

Hopkins had to rely largely on what was presented to him, but the Isle of Man was congenial. His descriptions are marked by hyperbole, comparatives, and superlatives: 'The people are the most goodnatured I think I have ever met'; 'the flowers in the island are plentiful and strongly coloured . . . the brambles were often doubled. The flower was bigger, purplish pink'; 'a higher average of heat in winter than Rhodez or Milan. Fuchsias, strawberry trees, and tamarisks do well'; 'the Laxey waterwheel . . . said to be the biggest in the world'; a churchyard was 'as beautiful as any I ever saw', and in it a wychelm's leaves were 'happy', a pathetic fallacy not typical of Hopkins. Once, looking at 'dimpled foamlaps' from the cliff-top, he was reminded of that Isle of Wight holiday nine years before, when he and Arthur sketched from the Freshwater cliffs.

He was able to use his interest in mechanics on a visit to the Lady Isabella waterwheel, built to pump water from the Laxey zinc and lead mines under Snaefell. On another day, while walking in the same part of the island, he heard a little girl sing a song in Manx, which was fast being replaced by English, but he was not able to grasp its characteristics. At the end of his stay he met another Manx speaker near Snaefell, and recorded that the old man 'complained that now a days the young people were too proud to talk Manx and would talk nothing but English and it was not English at all'.

From the cliffs above Derby Castle, Hopkins saw no crowds, only the occasional fisherman digging for worms in the wet sand. Two miles away, he could see Douglas as part of a sunset scene:

Very beautiful sunset; first I think crisscross yellow flosses, then a graceful level shell of streamers spreading from the sundown. The smoke of the steamers rose lagging in very longlimber zigzacs of flat black vapour, the town was overhung and shadowed by odd minglings of smoke, and the sea at high tide brimming the bay was striped with rose and green like an apple.[3]

In a similar way, two years later, looking from the summit of Maenefa over the Clwyd valley, he could assimilate the industrial smoke, from lime-kilns, to the landscape's 'beautiful liquid cast of blue'.

One day, when they were bathing at a nearby secluded cove, Port Jack, Hopkins recorded 'a big hawk flew down chasing a little shrieking bird close beside us'. (Nearby was Falcon Cliff.) One Monday there was an excursion to Peel Castle and Cathedral, on St Patrick's Isle, over on the west coast; the community probably hired the popular two-horsed roundabout waggonettes, known as Hi-Kelly carts. 'On the way', Hopkins wrote,

we went into the churchyard of Kirk Braddan, as beautiful as any I ever saw: fine and beautiful ashes and a wychelm with big glossy happy and shapely leaves, spanish chestnuts and other trees surround it and others stand in groves beyond; the ground slopes down to the road with tier upon tier of thick black gravestones.[4]

The party did not go inside the austere Protestant church, but looked at the twelve crosses in the churchyard, dating from the sixth or seventh century to the twelfth. Hopkins reported seeing 'runes engraved and curious work containing dragons and monsters, more odd than pretty and a little Japanese in look', probably referring to Thorlief Hnakki's Cross, worked in the distinctive Manx design of Gaut, the finest of the early island sculptors. The closely packed gravestones and graceful deciduous trees singled out by Hopkins are noticeable today.

Henry J. Holding's 'Peel Castle Isle of Man', in the Manx Museum, painted the year of Hopkins's visit, shows fishing vessels and crude huts on the shore, and pounding seas. Hopkins's account starts baldly: 'Peel castle is a ruin. It is built wholly or partly of red sandstone. . . .', and ends, 'And in other ways the Castle has historical interest'. What caught his interest was nature, not art:

What pleased me most were the great seas under a rather heavy swell breaking under the strong rocks below the outer side of the castle—glass-green, as loose as a great windy sheet, blown up and plunging down and bursting upwards from the rocks in spews of foam, but in a great gale, our funny meek old guide told us, it is a grander sight than we saw.

He is intensely concerned with waves and rocks—God's living architecture.

೮೨

The greater part of his Isle of Man journal is given to seascapes. The unique feature of this holiday was the presence of sea. Like other people who lived inland, he saw the sea only at holiday time, and throughout his life it remained for him a treasured sign of change from routine: 'I am in a sort of languishing state of mind and body', he wrote during his worst period in Dublin, 'I should like to go to sea for six months.'[5]

At the start of this holiday he wrote:

At this time I had first begun to get hold of the copy of Scotus on the Sentences [*Scriptum Oxoniense super Sententiis*] in the Baddely library and was flush with a new stroke of enthusiasm. It may come to nothing or it may be a mercy from God. But just then when I took in any inscape of the sky or sea I thought of Scotus.[6]

It is tempting to connect Scotus with the journal's brilliant Manx seascapes; but since he was nineteen Hopkins had been noticing and attempting to describe similar things, in words and drawings, and Scotus did not noticeably alter his habits of looking at nature, although helping to reinforce and sanction them.

His words can convey extraordinary excitement: 'It is pretty to see the dance and swagging of the light green tongues or ripples of waves in a place locked between rocks.' Original discoveries of image, shape, and texture in particular scapes are joyfully recorded in words grouped in expressive rhythm. Isolated images in the Manx journal have an intensity and creativeness, produced by colouring, metaphor, repetition, and animation:

that work of dimpled foamlaps—strings of short loops or halfmoons

[the sea] was of a strong smouldering green over the sunken rocks water, which seems bound over or lashed to land below by a splay of dark and light braids

[the breakers] are scrolled over like mouldboards or feathers or jibsails seen by the edge

the looped or forked wisp made by every big pebble

the great seas ... glass-green, as loose as a great windy sheet, blown up and plunging down and bursting upwards from the rocks in spews of foam ...

when the wave ran very high it would brim over on the sloping shelf below me and move smoothly and steadily along it like the palm of a hand along a table drawing off the dust

how the laps of foam mouthed upon one another

Most of Hopkins's images could not be contained by a poem; in a journal they are allowed space and time to develop.

Sometimes syntax is subordinated to more important compulsions:

with the brinks hidden by the fall of the hill, packing the land in/ it was not seen how far, and then you see best how it is drawn up to a brow at the skyline and stoops away on either side, tumbling over towards the eye in the broad smooth fall of a lakish apron of water, which seems bound over or lashed to land below by a splay of dark and light braids: they are the gusts of wind all along the perspective with which all the sea that day was dressed.[7]

More often the continuity between various stages of natural process is represented by the syntax: a sentence is not just a list of images flashing out in the order in which objects are experienced, but an individuated representation of impressions and moments:

It is pretty to see the hollow of the barrel disappearing as the white combs on each side run along the wave gaining ground till the two meet at a pitch and crush and overlap each other.

then I saw it run browner, the foam dwindling and twitched into long chains of suds, while the strength of the backdraught shrugged the stones together and clocked them one against another.

I looked down from the cliffs at the sea breaking on the rocks at high-water of a spring tide—first, say, it is an install of green marble knotted with ragged white, then fields of white lather, the comb of the wave richly clustered and crisped in breaking, then it is broken small and so unfolding till it runs in threads and thrums twitching down the backdraught to the sea again.

Sometimes the inscape captured is the observer's capturing act, not the thing observed: 'The shores are swimming and the eyes have before them a region of milky surf but it is hard for them to unpack the huddling and gnarls of the water and law out the shapes and the sequence of the running.'[8] There are other remarkable passages besides those concerned with the sea, but very few.

⁊

One effect of life at St Mary's Hall was to enlarge the ordinary event into something extraordinary. Nothing happened, constantly. The daily dinner, Hopkins said, became a 'great circumstantial Olympiad of the twenty four hours'. The common refectory joke of 'the dullards who lunch upon an annual jest and thrive and bloom on it' was not to his taste, nor did he appreciate 'their joke which was never a joke even when it was new'.[9] When writing to Baillie he insists that his life is duller than that of his friends: 'I can tell you nothing of the least interest but you could have told me, over and above personal news, a great deal which would have been fresh and interesting to this retirement.'[10] While the Tichbourne Claimant's case ('whether he = Sir Roger Tichbourne or only the Ditchborn Dodger', as Hopkins summarized the issue) was being heard, it was the topic of refectory conversation, but Hopkins was uncertain how important it was to the outside world, half afraid to mention it to Baillie in case he should be 'fuming at a letter ... which only thrums at the most worn-out and wearisome talk of London'.[11] He was sometimes doubtful as to what was considered normal among his peers in the Jesuits, too. Once he came into the refectory for breakfast to be asked why his hair was arranged in such a peculiar style, replied that he wanted to look like Dante, and was told by the Jesuit in charge to return to his room 'and not reappear until you look like everyone else.'[12]

Occasionally a journal entry on a domestic subject shows a childish compound of self-aggrandisement and incredulity:

This month here and all over the country many great thunderstorms. Cyril, in bed I think, at Liverpool after a simultaneous flash and crash felt a shock like one from a galvanic battery and for some time one of his arms went numbed. At Roehampton Fr Williams was doubled up and another Father had his breviary struck out of his hand. Here a tree was struck near the boys' cricketfield and a cow was ripped up.[13]

The deaths he experienced did not give rise only to sadness: there is a morbidity about the way he collected and begged for details. His interest in Fletcher's death, for instance, is not entirely accounted for by friendship and shared religion:

About this time I heard from Addis and Baillie of the death of Fletcher of Balliol. Baillie says 'He had a house in some very out of the way place and I fancy was not well off. He started off a walk of some 10 or 12 miles to a town to try and get a servant and on returning was caught by a snowstorm. He was found dead only a few hundred yards from his own house. Is it not sad? He had only been married a few months.' But Addis says 'Do you remember Fletcher a Scotch Catholic? He was a penitent of one of our FF, and used to spend a great deal of time in our church. He married a young lady of good family whom he converted from the Scots Kirk and went out with her to the Red River. There he was the great support of the Catholic chapel. One morning he said to his wife "I have made my meditation this morning on the best way to spend the last day of my life." That same day he was frozen to death in the snow.'[14]

Hopkins is interested in comparing the accounts, partly because they represent a Catholic and a non-religious point of view, but also because the details make good death-stories.

An even more interesting death was that of Basil Poutiatine, his former Balliol friend, in the summer of 1872, which Hopkins related after Alexander Wood visited him at Oak Hill the next Christmas:

Wood told me the particulars of Poutiatine's death last summer. He wanted to marry a Greek girl a doctor's daughter. The Admiral disapproved because of the inequality of rank but his opposition seems to have been more or less got over. But Poutiatine's own doctor said the marriage was impossible on the score of his health. The girl's father, as if with authority being himself a doctor, treated this as a shift to get off the match, the girl herself seems to have fallen in with her family, and then gave Poutiatine who was in the same hotel in Paris, so much annoyance that he took to flight. . . . His dead body was found in a pool or horse- or cattle-trough by the roadside only a few feet deep. His hat was on the bank. They think from this that he had stooped to drink, been seized with a fit, and fallen in—or fallen in and been seized with a fit. But this is hard to understand. The bank was steep on the side he fell in from and two others but on the fourth there was a slope for the beast to go down by. The pool, as I have said, was quite shallow. On his body was found a cross. His name they could find nowhere but in his boots and for some time they thought it was the maker's. Wood and Gladstone convinced themselves it was not suicide.[15]

During his time at St Mary's Hall he recorded deaths among the main Stonyhurst community, and that of one of his fellow seminarians, Br Boefvé. He described Scriven's death from consumption: 'In the night he had a great struggle in which he started up in bed and caught hold of the Rector with both hands. Afterwards he was calm.'[16] He wrote a graphic account of a Stonyhurst College boy's death:

One day about this time, I think during the retreat, Wm. Stanton one of the cleverest boys they had at the College died by hanging, at Chorley in the Woods in this county. He had been reading a novel of Trollope's in which a hanging is described and it was believed he was trying to act it. His body was naked except that his shoes were on. He was not throttled but died by some shock to the spine, which had been injured some years before at Stonyhurst. Mr. Cyprian Splaine had tears in his eyes as he told us about it.[17]

Victorian death-scenes belong to the psychology of that age, but there are special emphases in Hopkins's death narratives, which search for aesthetic qualities. In his accounts of the deaths of animals, the conventions of human death stories are irrelevant:

They told me that when the young birds in a nest under one of their windows were nearly ready to fly a wasp coming into the nest stung them in the throats so that they died and then was seen in the nest feeding on them.

Under a stone hedge was a dying ram: there ran slowly from his nostril a thick flesh-coloured ooze, scarlet in places, coiling and roping its way down, so thick that it looked like fat.[18]

His imagination often worked with such naïve strength: abstract fascination with texture and colour could make him oblivious of moral or emotional restraints.

His susceptibility made him liable to displays of emotion when unexpectedly provoked:

After a time of trial and especially a morning in which I did not know which way to turn as the account of De Rancé's final conversion was being read at dinner the verse *Qui confidunt in Domino sicut mons Sion* which satisfied him and resolved him to enter his abbey of La Trappe by the mercy of God came strongly home to me too, so that I was choked for a little while and could not keep in my tears.[19]

When his brothers Cyril and Arthur were going through the usual processes of seeking wives, engaged to Harriet and Rebecca Bockett, Gerard was forbidden close relationships with people of either sex. Although his relationship with his family was easier than it had been since his conversion, his opportunities for seeing them and showing affection were limited. He was very moved by signs of affection:

Dec. 17–18 at night—Rescued a little kitten that was perched in the sill of the round window at the sink over the gasjet and dared not jump down. I heard her mew a piteous long time till I could bear it no longer; but I make a note of it because of her gratitude after I had taken her down, which made her follow me about and at each turn of the stairs as I went down leading her to the kitchen run back a few steps and try to get up to lick me through the banisters from the flight above.[20]

His sensibilities were heightened when he fell ill during his final year at St Mary's:

That fever came from a chill I caught one Blandyke [monthly holiday] and the chill from weakness brought about by my old complaint [piles], which before and much more after the fever was worse than usual. Indeed then I lost so much blood that I hardly saw how I was to recover. Nevertheless it stopped suddenly, almost at the worst. This was why I came up to town at Christmas.[21]

That Christmas he underwent an operation for piles at Oak Hill, by Mr Prance, the family doctor, and a surgeon, Mr Gay. Grace Hopkins remembered that when she 'was allowed to see Gerard, he said, jokingly, that as he lay awake the night after the operation, he kept thinking of the lines—"Puts the wretch that lies in pain/ *In remembrance of a shroud*." '[22]

The operation lasted half an hour, although to him it seemed only ten minutes. During his fortnight recuperating in bed two Jesuit Brothers came from Roehampton to see him, and he was visited by Addis, Wood, Bond, and Baillie. He made two visits to the Old Masters' exhibition at Burlington House. On 21 January he went to see the Provincial at Manresa House, and next morning was sent by Fr Gallwey to Dr Fincham, the doctor who attended the Roehampton Jesuits. As a result his work was lightened and the Rector forbade him to fast during Lent, but by the time of the Villa he had still not quite recovered his health.

∽

On Friday 1 August 1873, the St Mary's seminarians went again for their Villa to Derby Castle. The first weekend was marred by bad weather. Hopkins complained of the cold, caught up on his letter-writing, and read, not being able to concentrate properly because the people around him were engaged in less demanding activities, and would talk to him, repeating a joke he made the previous night, and reading out snippets from the *Manx Sun*.[23]

He had brought with him *Empedocles on Etna, and Other Poems*, by another Balliol man who had visited the Isle of Man; he read Matthew Arnold's poems 'with more interest than rapture . . . for they seem to have all the ingredients of poetry without quite being it . . . but still they do not leave off of being, as the French say, very beautiful'. In a letter to Bond he appraised Arnold's moral frame of mind: 'Besides he seems a very earnest man and distinctly seeing the difference between jest and earnest. . . . But then very unhappily he jokes at the wrong things, as I see by a very profane passage quoted from his new book.' The objectionable passage may have been Arnold's description in ch. 10 of *Literature and Dogma* (published earlier that year) of the Trinity as 'the fairy-tale of the three Lord Shaftesbury's', with God as 'a sort of elder Lord Shaftesbury . . . infinitely magnified'. Arnold also refers to God as 'the Supreme Governor'. Hopkins attempted to integrate his two contradictory opinions: 'however that passage though profane is not blasphemous, for we are obliged to think of God by human thoughts and his account of them is substantially true.'[24]

*Literature and Dogma* often mentions Newman, whom Arnold saw as representative of pre-modern Oxford. Arnold praises 'this exquisite and delicate genius', while criticizing Newman's religious stance for its use of dogma to authenticate 'abstruse metaphysical conceptions', and for failing to apply tests of reason and science. Hopkins's letter gives a general judgement on Newman's writing, based on his reading of *A Grammar of Assent*. His reactions are more mixed than might be expected:

The justice and candour and gravity and rightness of mind is what is so beautiful in all he writes but what dissatisfies me (in point of style) is a narrow circle of instance and quotation—in a man too of great learning and of general reading . . . and a want, I think a real want, of brilliancy (which foolish people think every scribbler possesses, but it is no such thing). But he remains nevertheless our greatest living master of style . . . and widest mind.[25]

&

Parts of the holiday were spoilt by uncertain health, and this journal is briefer than the one for the previous Villa. The group went mackerel-fishing from Douglas harbour, but Hopkins was 'in pain and could not look at things much', though he left a vivid record:

When the fresh-caught fish flounced in the bottom of the boat they made scapes of motion, quite as strings do, nodes and all, silver bellies upward. . . . Their key markings do not correspond on the two sides of the backbone. They changed colour as they lay. There was sun and wind. I saw the waves to seaward frosted with light silver surf but did not find out much, afterwards from the cliffs I saw the sea paved with wind—clothed and purpled all over with ribbons of wind.

Another day he conducted a less willed sensuous experiment:

Some yellow spoons came up with the tumblers after dinner. Somebody said they were brass and I tasted them to find out and it seemed so. Some time afterwards as I came in from a stroll with Mr Purbrick he told me Hügel had said the scarlet or rose colour of flamingos was found to be due to a fine copper powder on the feathers. As he said this I tasted the brass in my mouth. It is what they call unconscious cerebration, a bad phrase.[26]

Only once, except for the day they left, did he write an extended description of the sea:

Walking along the cliffs towards Growdle. Sun and wind; sea dark blue, yet one can always see the dimness in the air shed upon the offing and stealing the distant waves. Painted white cobbled foam tumbling over the rocks and combed away off their sides again. The water-ivybush, that plucked and dapper cobweb of glassy grey down, swung slack and jaunty on the in-shore water, plainer where there was dark weed below and dimmer over bare rock or sand.— On the cliffs fields of bleached grass, the same colour as the sheep they feed, then a sleeve of liquid barleyfield, then another slip of bleached grass, above that fleshy blue sky. Nearer at hand you see barley breathe and open and shut and take two colours and swim.

On Tuesday 12 August a party of seminarians took a carriage to the Hibernian Inn, ten miles north of Derby Castle on the Ramsay road. While some probably climbed up the North Barrule or walked into Ramsay, Hopkins and a first-year student, Anselm Gillett, four years younger, went off down the pretty, narrow road to 'the beautiful little mill-hamlet of Balaglass in the glen and started a shining flight of doves to settle on the roof. There is a green rich thickleaved alder by the bridge and ashes and rocks maroon-red below water up the glen.'[27]

The hamlet was the mill-house, a cottage, and the old Cornaa Mill. From there they followed a footpath over a ridge through ash and beech woods, along the side of a Lancashire-like clough down to the 'little shingly bay' of Port Cornaa, 'where above the beach there stretches a small plain of grass flooded by the springtides, through which the brook runs to the sea'. After bathing, Gillett and Hopkins returned to the hamlet, then turned aside from the road they had taken, to enter the Ballaglass Glen. Following the river 'up under groves' formed by trees arching over water, Hopkins picked out beech and spirally twisted sweet or Spanish chestnut from the canopy of birch, elm, sycamore, oak, and rowan. The river fell in a series of steep cascades over boulders, sometimes passing through deep channels:

The rock is limestone, smooth and pale white, not rough and gritty, and without moss, stained red where the water runs and smoothly and vertically hewed by the force of the brook into highwalled channels with deep pools. The water is so clear in the still pools it is like shadowy air and in the falls the white is not foamed and chalky, as at Stonyhurst, but like the white of ice or glass.

At one part of the glen was 'the water chute', at the foot of which the water fell into a deep pool. Here Hopkins made these observations:

Round holes are scooped in the rocks smooth and true like turning: they look like the hollow of a vault or bowl. I saw and sketched . . . one of them was in the making: a blade of water played on it and shaping to it spun off making a bold big white bow coiling its edge over and splaying into ribs. But from the position it is not easy to see how the water could in this way have scooped all of them.

(It was actually not the water which scooped out the potholes, but stones spun round for a long time in one place.) At the point where Hopkins stopped to sketch, the path was twenty feet above the river, with a canopy of ash and Spanish chestnuts. It was raining, but this did not matter, and Hopkins 'jumped into one of the pools above knee deep'. When the two, one drenched more thoroughly than the other, reached the high road, Gillett turned right to return to the carriage in the inn-yard, while Hopkins, 'to keep warm', turned left and walked towards Douglas, until the carriage caught him up.

'We got home in heavy wet', Hopkins recorded in his journal, 'and Mr Sidgreaves covered me under his plaid.' Edward Sidgreaves, though a first-year student, was four years older than Hopkins; there was a rule that they were not to use Christian names, to speak to or refer to other students. A week earlier Hopkins had replied to Edward Bond's invitation to spend part of the holidays with him:

I am afraid that I must not avail myself of your kindness. On the score of time indeed there wd. be no difficulty on my side but leave for invitations to stay with friends who are not kindred without some more pressing reason than I could shew is so seldom given that I should not wish even to ask it. But it would have been a great pleasure to me if it had been possible.[28]

On the Saturday morning of their departure the group got up at four, to find the weather stormy. From the castle, Hopkins saw 'duncoloured waves leaving trailing hoods of white breaking on the beach', and he went to the secluded cove of Port Jack:

I took a last look at the breakers, wanting to make out how the comb is morselled so fine into string and tassel, as I have lately noticed it to be. I saw big smooth flinty waves, carved and scuppled in shallow grooves, much swelling when the wind freshened, burst on the rocky spur of the cliff at the little cove and break into bushes of foam. In an enclosure of rocks the peaks of the water romped and wandered and a light crown of tufty scum standing high on the surface kept slowly turning round: chips of it blew off and gadded about without weight in the air.[29]

At 8 o'clock the packet left for Liverpool in wind and stinging rain. Hopkins noticed 'a good-looking young man on board that got drunk and sung "I want to go home to Mamma"'. He wrote in his journal that he 'did not look much at the sea', but, knowing that it would probably be a year before he saw it again, made some notes:

the crests I saw ravelled up by the wind into the air in arching whips and straps of glassy spray and higher broken into clouds of white and blown away. Under the curl shone a bright juice of beautiful green. The foam exploding and smouldering under water makes a chrysoprase green.

On this holiday and the last he had been constructing a new vocabulary to describe the sea.

At Liverpool they caught the train to Blackburn, and Hopkins and others walked the twelve miles to Stonyhurst, across 'infinite stiles and sloppy fields, for there had been much rain. A few big shining drops hit us aslant as if they were blown off from eaves or leaves.' Another part of Hopkins's stored vocabulary, for sunset effects, was being pondered and extended:

Bright sunset: all the sky hung with tall tossed clouds, in the west with strong printing glass edges, westward lamping with tipsy bufflight, the colour of yellow roses. . . . The sun itself and the spot of 'session' dappled with big laps and flowers-in-damask of cloud.

By the time they reached Stonyhurst everything seemed wrong. The seminarians had been thrown out of St Mary's because the building was wanted as a retreat-house for secular priests. They had to go to the vast, almost deserted, College. The gas-retorts were being mended:

therefore candles in bottles, things not ready, darkness and despair. In fact being unwell I was quite downcast: nature in all her parcels and faculties gaped and fell apart, *fatiscebat*, like a clod cleaving and holding only by strings of root. But this must often be.[30]

The Provincial's decision to give Hopkins a year's 'rest' from next September was much needed.[31]

# Teaching: London and Devon, 1873–1874

Some German Jesuit students of theology, expelled by Bismarck's Kulturkampf, were spending their Villa at the College, and put on concerts for their hosts; and on 21 August the seminarians returned the compliment with an after-supper entertainment consisting of 'music, comic and half-comic pieces etc', which the beadle's log reported 'was mainly got up by Mr G. Hopkins, and was a decided success'. On 27 August Hopkins went down to Whalley to see off the Germans, who were returning to Ditton Hall near Widnes, and afterwards walked with Herbert Lucas by the river, and 'talked Scotism with him for the last time'. He had known for some time that in September he would be posted to teach for a year in one of the Jesuit schools, perhaps Stonyhurst College. His Provincial had decided that the year's teaching would be a rest, and Hopkins thought it 'as good an arrangement as could have been made'. That evening he received orders to go to Roehampton, to teach rhetoric to the juniors, and the next day set out for Manresa House.[1]

At Roehampton he met his former novice-master, now the Provincial, Fr Gallwey, who 'spoke most kindly and encouragingly', and began his annual eight-day retreat, directed by Fr George Porter, Rector of Manresa House and his new Superior. During the retreat he 'received as I think a great mercy about Dolben'; this probably means (as House says[2]) that Hopkins thought he had some heavenly sign of Dolben's salvation. The new set of nine novices arrived, and at the close of the retreat fourteen novices who had completed their two-year course took their first vows. That day Uncle Charles Hopkins was married to 'Helena Marian, only d. of Mark Coindet de Marcichy, late Captain in the Swiss Cavalry'. Hopkins spent some of the day talking to Brother Duffy as he ploughed, asking him the names of the various parts of the plough and its tackle—'the cross, side-plate, muzzle, regulator, and short chain'; and the brother talked 'of something *spraying* out, meaning splaying out and of *combing* the ground'.[3]

The next day Hopkins met his class of juniors for the first time, and set them a trial paper in Greek and Latin, choosing passages from Virgil's Georgics and Aeschines' Against Ctesiphon, books he had studied at Balliol. His job was one of the Province's easier ones, 'as compared with the more hectic rough and tumble of teaching in one of the large schools'. He was asked to teach for one year before proceeding to his theology training, whereas some of his contemporaries would teach for as many as seven or eight; 'all in all', says Fr Thomas, 'he can be said to have got off lightly.'[4]

The juniorate stage of the Jesuit training system was the one Hopkins had escaped because of his degree. Although the juniors remained in Manresa House with the novices, their life was quite different. The emphasis on religious exercises was replaced by courses in classics and rhetoric. It was similar to a freshman course in classical studies at a university, Latin and Greek language and literature, essay-writing, mathematics, and rhetoric. There were twenty-eight juniors, and although Hopkins had the title Professor of Rhetoric, he was more of a classroom teacher, dealing with Latin, Greek, and English. Br O'Neill, a junior himself, taught mathematics. Lectures were in the mornings and evenings, and Hopkins had Sundays and Thursdays completely free.[5]

On 18 September, when the juniors had their Blandyke (day's holiday), Hopkins went to the Kensington Museum (the Victoria and Albert), and spent a long time in the musical instruments section, making comparative notes on the distinguishing features of the harpsichord, the spinet, the virginals, dulcimers, theorbos, and viols. He was struck by Michelangelo reproductions: 'the *might* . . . seems to come not merely from the simplifying and then ~~instressing or~~ amplifying or emphasising of parts but from a masterly realism in the simplification, both these things.'

That night he had a nightmare:

I thought something or someone leapt onto me and held me quite fast: this I think woke me, so that after this I shall have had the use of reason. This first start is, I think, a nervous collapse of the same sort as when one is very tired and holding oneself at stress not to sleep yet/ suddenly goes slack and seems to fall and wakes, only on a greater scale and with a loss of muscular control reaching more or less deep; this one to the chest and not further, so that I could speak, whispering at first, then louder—for the chest is the first and greatest centre of motion and action, the seat of θυμός [life].

He had lost all sense of power in his muscles, but not feeling, and could remember thinking that 'I could recover myself if I could move my finger . . . and then the arm and so the whole body':

The feeling is terrible: the body no longer swayed as a piece by the nervous and muscular instress seems to fall in and hang like a dead weight on the chest. I cried on the holy name and by degrees recovered myself as I thought to do. It made me think that this was how the souls in hell would be imprisoned in their bodies as in prisons.[6]

Hopkins did not keep his journal with any regularity at Roehampton, but every now and then made notes on the Manresa trees, particularly cedars, poplars, and elms, and on events in the sky:

Two taper tufts of vapour or cloud in shape like the tufts in ermine, say, touched with red on the inside, bluish at the outer and tapering end, stood on each side of the sun at the distance, I think, the halo stands at and as if flying outward from the halo. The lefthand one was long-tailed and curved slightly upwards. They were not quite diametrically opposite but a little above the horizontal diameter and seemed to radiate towards the sun.

He constantly looked out to the ha-ha. In October a doe came there to be fed: 'she eats acorns and chestnuts and stands on the bank, a pretty triped, forefeet together and hind set apart.' It was the mating season, and the bucks grunted all night, fighting and clashing their antlers.[7]

At 6.15 on Christmas Eve the community assembled in the chapel, and after the Martyrologium (a list in Latin of the day's martyrs, with brief notices of their lives and deaths), sung by Br Blount, proceeded to the crib. The carol 'See Amidst the Winter's Snow' was sung, and supper followed. At 7.15 the Rector gave meditation points to the community, they went to bed, then at eleven they rose again for meditations, and just before midnight 'Adeste Fideles' was sung. After midnight mass there was cocoa and soup in the refectory.[8]

Later that morning, after high mass at the local church, Hopkins went off to spend Christmas at Oak Hill. He went with Arthur to the Water-Colours winter exhibition, and took some of his most detailed notes on any picture—a watercolour version of Frederick Walker's 'Harbour of Refuge'. He was not uncritical, seeing the rough execution, and the inconsistency between parts of the picture which had to be seen at close quarters, and others only effective at a distance. But he liked the figure in the right foreground:

The young man mowing was a great stroke, a figure quite made up of thew and grace and strong fire: the sweep of the scythe and swing and sway of the whole body even to the rising of the one foot on tiptoe while the other was flung forward was as if such a thing had never been painted before, so fresh and so very strong.[9]

During the remaining seven months he had opportunities of visiting museums, galleries, and exhibitions. He went to the Sir John Soane

Museum, and was particularly interested by its collection of gems, and returning to the Kensington Museum in April made a list of the gems on display there and their characteristic colours. It is a list which conveys excitement:

chalcedony/ some/ milky blue, some/ opalescent blue-green, some/ blue-green with sparkles, some/ dull yellow green, dull olive, lilac, white; jacinth/ brownish red, dull tawny scarlet; chrysoprase/ beautiful half-transparent green, some/ dull with dark cloudings; sardonyx/ milky blue flake in brown; topaz/ white, madder, sherry-colour, yellow, pale blue, wallflower red; 'dark sard' seemed purplish black; jaspar (or chalcedony)/ dull flesh brown; chryso-lith/ bluish with yellow gleam or *vice versa*, also pale yellow-green, also yellow—transparent; cymophane/ beautiful stone and name.[10]

He visited the National Gallery, went twice to the Royal Academy exhibition, several times to the Houses of Parliament, and to Wimbledon army camp, where he watched 'a man who fired on his back with one arm', and the pretty action of flags 'folding and rolling on the wind; the figures seemed to glide off at one end and reappear at the other'. He re-opened his interest in the Tichbourne trial, and heard the Lord Chief Justice's summing up. He went to All Saints' in Margaret Street, 'to see if my old enthusiasm was a mistake', and though recognizing a lack of zest in some of the work, he found the lines of Butterfield's tracery and 'the touching and passionate curves of the lilyings in the ironwork under the baptistry arch marked his genius to me as before'.[11]

At the exhibitions he made rough notes, and later edited them into more finished prose accounts for the journal. His notes on the summer exhibition at the Royal Academy show that he went with fixed inten-tions about what he would see and what he would think. His notes on the four Millais paintings and the three Leightons are the longest. In almost all his notes the word 'inscape' occurs. He judges each canvas by whether it has that quality, though the word shifts its meaning. The leopards in Briton Rivière's 'Apollo' showed 'the flow and slow spraying of the streams of spots down from the backbone and making this flow word-in and inscape the whole animal and even the group of them'. Alma-Tadema's 'Vintage Festival' is held together by 'vigorous rhetorical but realistic and unaffected scaping', though 'no arch-inscape is thought of'. There is a similar 'want of arch-inscape' in Millais's 'North-West Passage', but 'true inscape' in the same painter's 'Day-dream'. Millais had been Hopkins's first artistic loyalty, and though he records the 'casual' and 'aimless' qualities (in 'Scotch Firs' and 'Winter Fuel', two of Millais's more sophisticated and impressionistic mood-pictures), Hopkins becomes intensely involved with his oil landscapes, as though they were tracts of real nature: 'There was a beautiful spray-off of the dead oak-scrolls against dark trees behind with flowing blue smoke above. Toss or dance of twig and light-wood hereabouts.' In Millais's 'Daydream' he responds to 'the fall away of the cheek' (which five years later became 'The dappled die-away/ Cheek' in a poem). Hopkins dutifully describes some minor paintings in the Ruskinian manner, Henry Moore's 'Rough Weather in the Mediterranean', a 'fine wave-drawing', and Archibald Wortley's 'In Wharncliffe Chace'. Brett's 'Summer Noon in the Scilly Isles' was a 'not quite satisfying picture but scarcely to be surpassed for realism in landscape'. The most interesting comments he makes are of paintings whose voluptuousness is outside his usual range, and involve him unawares. He describes Tissot's 'atmospheric women in clouds of drapery with mooning-up eyes and mooning-up nostrils of oddly curved noses'. The 'gem of the exhibition' he judged to be Leighton's 'Old Damascus: Jews' Quarter':

There was in the picture a luscious chord of colour (which grew on me)— glaucous (blue, with green and purple sidings) browns (with reds to match). In the green scale, which was part of the glaucous or blue faction, were the lemontree, the duller-green striped and flowered sort-of-dressing gown the flowerpot woman wore, her pinks, and the bluer green flowerpot plants behind her; purple appeared in the roundels. ... In the red scale were the same women's scarf and drawers, the child's skirt, which was rosier, the flowers in the pots, some mosaic and the brown marble framing of the braced windows, in which ... there was a beautiful flush of dark.

As if to compensate for indulgence he added 'but after much looking [at the arabesques on the picture-frame] I did not find much inscape in them'.[12]

With the exceptions of the exotic works of Tissot and Leighton, Hopkins did not allow the paintings to overwhelm him, but imposed ideals and measured accordingly. With nature there need be no holding back. Summer had started in Manresa Park, after having delayed so long that Hopkins had a recurrence of chilblains at the end of May:

Heat has come on now [a rhythm echoed in a later poem, 'Summer ends now']. The air is full of the sweet acid of the limes. The trees themselves are starrily tasselled with the blossom. I remark that our cedars, which had a warp upward in the flats of leaf, in getting their new green turn and take a soft and beautiful warp downwards: whether it is the lushness or the weight of the young needles or both I cannot tell.

Later that week, he noted the smell of a big cedar, not when he was passing it but always at a particular patch of sunlight on the walk: 'I found the bark smelt in the sun and not in the shade and I fancied too this held even of the smell it shed in the air.'[13]

23 July was the Rector's Day at the neighbouring Beaumont College, and Hopkins, with Fr Porter and Fr MacLeod, the Prefect of Studies for the juniors, walked to the celebrations, passing 'beautiful blushing yellow in the straw of the uncut ryefields, the wheat looking white and all the ears making a delicate and very true crisping along the top and with just enough air stirring for them to come and go gently'. He wanted to look at the scene again on the return journey, but 'during dinner I talked too freely and unkindly and had to do penance going home'.[14]

During that year Hopkins frequently made contact with friends outside the order. In July he had 'made the acquaintance of two and I suppose the only two Scotists in England in one week'. In March Alexander Wood came to see him, having just published a book on London's ecclesiastical antiquities; later, Challis and Bellasis came from the Birmingham Oratory. Bond corresponded with him and they probably met at least once. He became slightly less ascetic over fasting for Lent, pleasing his mother:

You remember how you would have it I should take wine. Well so I do. 'The Lenten Festivities', as someone among us said, have begun for me, but in general, besides me, those who teach do not fast, as is but reasonable. (This is obscure and might mean the opposite of what it does. I mean that I in particular do not fast and that those who teach in general do not.)[15]

He had the satisfaction of feeling his prejudices justified when the Conservative Party won the general election in February: 'The Conservative reaction what a reality it is! The *Spectator* says the Liberal party is smitten hip and thigh from Dan even unto Beersheba: some think it is Beersheba at both ends.'

Another event which should have made him happy was the renewal of his friendship with Bridges after two-and-a-half years. Bridges had not replied to a letter Hopkins wrote in August 1871 from Stonyhurst, saying that he was 'always thinking of the Communist future', was afraid 'some great revolution' was 'not far off', and that the Communist 'ideal bating some things is nobler than that professed by any secular statesman'.[16] Although opposed to the Communists' means of achieving aims, Hopkins considered it

a dreadful thing for the greatest and most necessary part of a very rich nation to live a hard life without dignity, knowledge, comforts, delight, or hopes in the midst of plenty—which plenty they make. They profess that they do not care what they wreck and burn, the old civilisation and order must be destroyed. This is a dreadful look out but what has the old civilisation done for them? As it at present stands in England it is itself in great measure founded on wrecking. But they got none of the spoils, they came in for nothing but harm from it then and thereafter.

Hopkins assumed that Bridges's silence came from a Conservative disgust 'with the *red* opinions [the letter] expressed'. If this were the reason, Bridges had ignored Hopkins's admission of remoteness from political reality ('I must own I live in bat-light and shoot at a venture') and his ultra-conservative opinion that 'the hands of the powers that be' should be strengthened. The 'old civilisation', against which the agitators rebelled, consisted of an 'iniquitous order', Hopkins had written, but it embodied 'another order mostly old and what is new in direct entail from the old, the old religion, learning, law, art, etc and all the history that is preserved in standing monuments'. Because the working classes had not been educated, they 'know next to nothing of all this and cannot be expected to care if they destroy it'. Hopkins's diagnosis of the social condition is not very different from Disraeli's account of the Two Nations, and his solution would probably be Disraeli's—to expand opportunities within a still essentially Conservative social framework, so that revolutionaries would have less material to work on.

In the *Academy* of 17 January 1874, Hopkins had seen an appreciative review by Andrew Lang of 'a Mr. Bridges' poems, Robert Bridges the title shewed'. He could not remember ever having seen any of Bridges's poems, and this gave him 'an occasion to write again'.[17] He coaxed a response: 'I think, my dear Bridges, to be so much offended about that red letter was excessive.' Shortly after Hopkins left Roehampton a reply came from Bridges.

The year of comparatively easy duties ended with examinations. On the morning of 29 July the examination in rhetoric and the Latin theme were held, and the next day was taken up with orals. The feast of St Ignatius, on the last day of July saw Hopkins 'very tired', and he 'seemed deeply cast down' until he had 'some kind words from the Provincial'.[18] His professional duties were the root cause of depression. Anticipation of the next day's teaching load caused him constant anxiety, and he taught rhetoric 'so badly and so painfully'. He looked forward eagerly to intervals in the Manresa routine, and the springiness in his journal and letter-writing suggests that his dulled mind was released by personal enthusiasms. Looking back on the year he wrote:

'Altogether perhaps my heart has never been so burdened and cast down. . . . The tax on my strength has been greater than I have ever felt before.'[19]

On Thursday 6 August Hopkins travelled with the Beaumont community to spend a fortnight's Villa with them at Teignmouth,[20] on the south Devon coast. He was feeling weak and able to do little. On his first day there he wearily brought his journal up to date after writing nothing for a fortnight. It records pettish self-preoccupation: 'This seems a dull place . . . the sand on the shore flies and stings you': and the landscape is described with a journeyman dullness: 'The cliffs are of deep red sandstone . . . the vegetation is rich; the Teign is an estuary where it meets the sea and as far up as Newton Abbot.'

That evening he and Stephen Hayes, another thirty-year-old Jesuit in training, walked west out of Teignmouth, unadventurously taking the main Newton Abbot road, past the remains of a bishop's palace, four miles to Kingsteignton. The next morning Hopkins again walked into the countryside, with Fr Beiderlinden. There were sharp showers, but the sun shone in between. They were not sure of their whereabouts, but came to a pretty farmyard, where a thatched roof cast 'sharp shadow on whitewash'. Hopkins saw 'a village rising beyond, all in a co[o]mb'. That evening, on his own, he left the flat seaside town of genteel retired people and holidaymakers to climb up the red cliffs, then into the hills towards Bishopsteignton, on a private quest to trace the visionary coomb, and came upon a village which a little girl told him was called 'Ke-am', or 'Ku-am', in other words Coombe.

Before reaching that, just out of Teignmouth, I looked over a hedge down to a row of seven slender rich elms at a bottom between two steep fields: the runs of the trees and their rich and handsome leafage charmed and held me. It is a little nearer the sea in the same coomb the little girl spoke of indeed. Then near Bishopsteignton from a hilltop I looked into a lovely coomb that gave me the instress . . . which all the west country seems to me to have: soft maroon or rosy cocoa-dust-coloured handkerchiefs of ploughfields, sometimes delicately combed with rows of green, their hedges bending in flowing outlines and now misted a little by the beginnings of twilight ran down into it upon the shoulders of the hills; in the bottom crooked rows of rich tall elms, foreshortened by position, wound through it: some cornfields were still being carried.[21]

Hopkins's feelings towards these two views are extraordinary; they are almost sexual in their intimate and intense surrender, as he acknowledges the sensuousness of shape, colour, and texture, and their relationships. The range of his strongly engaged responses is shown in the vocabulary. The harshnesses he was sometimes guilty of when eye and mind combined to express natural movement or construction are absent.

Within easy walking distance of Teignmouth were several coombs—Holcombe, Luscombe, Smallacombe, Hamblecombe, Sharracombe, Combeinteignhead, Haccombe, Charlecombe, and Rocombe, and when there were no planned excursions Hopkins frequently went out among the Haldon slopes, looking for old or new coombs to savour and possess. One day he walked near the same spot with Considine, who had been a fellow-novice:

I looked into this same and other coombs. I saw how delicately beautiful the orchards look from far above: the wrought-over boughs of the appletrees made an embroidery and whole head and wood a soft tufting and discolouring which were melted by the distance and the rain.[22]

He was trying to make Haldon his own, proving his love by description and definition, like Constable with Dedham and East Bergholt. For no other landscape at any other time did Hopkins record such an intense feeling.

One day he crossed the mouth of the Teign to Shaldon by the wooden bridge, nearly a mile long, which swung open in the channel to let small vessels through. He recorded the fact that it had been built by a namesake, Roger Hopkins. From Shaldon he climbed up the hills towards Torquay, 'seeing all around me the sea and coast and valley of the Teign and getting fresh glimpses at every gate as I mounted', and from the Beacon, above Smugglers' Cove and Labrador Bay, he saw to the north the coastline running beyond the mouth of the Exe into Dorset, and to the south Hope's Nose at the furthest point of Babbacombe Bay. To the west, beyond the villages of Stoke- and Combe-in-Teignhead lay the four miles of the Teign estuary, then the valley 'backed and closed by Dartmoor', with the Haytor rocks, which he had climbed in 1867, visible in the distance. Even the holiday town of Teignmouth, at the corner of the estuary, seemed amenable from that viewpoint—'an irregular, not unpicturesque jaunt of white walls and lavender slate gables'. In Babbacombe Bay the sea was 'striped with splintered purple cloud-shadows'. From here he 'marked the bole, the burling and roundness of the world'.[23]

As well as these large landscape features, he noted—not altogether characteristically—smaller details which he enjoyed. Joy took over from analysis: 'Many butterflies fluttering in the lanes, burnet-moths loafing on heads of scabious; hedges of whitehorn, and blackthorn thick with sloes, blackberries, flags in seed, tall yellow fennel starred with flowers.'

Sometimes he wrote less fluently. On 13 August, when there were heavy seas, he walked along the sea wall towards the Parson and Clerk rocks, and wrote a laboured description:

The seawall is picturesque and handsome from below—it is built of white and red and blue blocks and with a brim or lip or cornice or coping curved round to beetle over and throw back the spray without letting it break on the walk above: this shape and colour give it an Egyptian look.—The laps of running foam striking the sea-wall double on themselves and return in nearly the same order and shape in which they came.[24]

He added: 'This is mechanical reflection and is the same as optical: indeed all nature is mechanical, but then it is not seen that mechanics contain that which is beyond mechanics.' Occasionally there are painterly colour notes: 'On the barrow-hill were rich purple-red ploughfields: where the green tufts of the elm-heads stood up against them I could catch the lilac in the red.'

One Monday a party went from Teignmouth to Ugbrooke, an Adam mansion on the other side of Haldon, at the invitation of Charles, eighth Lord Clifford of Chudleigh. The first Lord Clifford had been a member of the Cabal which encouraged Charles II to sign the treaty with Louis XIV of France, agreeing to become a Roman Catholic and work for the reconversion of England,[25] so until the Emancipation Act of 1829 the Cliffords had been barred from public office. The Ugbrooke chapel, in which Hopkins had attended mass in 1867, had once been disguised as a hall, and its entrance concealed, during the years when it was illegal to celebrate mass. The Cliffords were now one of the most prominent Catholic families in England, and conscious of it. Mary, Lady Monkswell, an Anglican visitor to Ugbrooke, wrote in her diary: 'I am reminded at every turn that they are Roman Catholics. On the programme of the day in my bedroom is written first of all "Mass, 8.30", there are pictures & busts of relations that are Bishops & Cardinals, one of the bedrooms is called the "Cardinal's Room", in the drawingroom you find the *Tablet*: R.C. almanacs full of saints I never even heard of. There is a Chapel in the house & a priest appears occasionally.'[26]

Lord Clifford took the party on a tour, first to Chudleigh rocks, 'which are a cliff over a deep and beautiful cleave quite closed with ashtrees into which we looked down', to the site of the camp occupied by the Danes when they fought Alfred, a boundary oak called Great Rawber, and the spot said to be where Dryden wrote 'The Hind and the Panther', and where white hinds were kept in the park in memory of the poem. It was a fine day, and they were taken over the park, landscaped by Capability Brown, which Hopkins found 'beautiful, especially from the falls of ground—great brows falling over to the lakes, and clothed with fern and clumps of trees and woods'. Inside the house were footmen in livery, with powdered hair. The Jesuits were introduced to the Clifford family, and Hopkins liked the 'very frank and simple way' in which the children spoke, which 'shewed innocence as well as good breeding. As we drove home the stars came out thick: I leant back to look at them and my heart opening more than usual praised our Lord to and in whom all that beauty comes home.'[27]

&

On 15 August Hopkins went on a day's excursion to Exeter, to see the cathedral, but was annoyed to see it under restoration. The choir was boxed off by a makeshift screen of boards, and he could not distinguish the old from the new. He made a few notes by which to remember the cathedral, but they did not show a very live interest until he noticed the 'long, richly carved corbels, like long strawberry pottles, especially rich and beautiful in choir (I think they have been recut there)'. The huge presbytery corbels consisted of superbly carved naturalistic foliage of mugwort, hop, oak, vine, ivy, hawthorn, and hazel. He noted the new choir-stalls, furnished by Sir Gilbert Scott, who was later severely criticized for his alterations here.

Then Hopkins's dissatisfied, wandering eye fixed on what he called 'the most beautiful thing I saw'. In the North Presbytery aisle, he squatted on the gravestone set into the floor of Edward Drew, a Protestant archdeacon of Cornwall, and made two quick attempts at sketching the side-panel of the tomb-chest, dating from around 1210, of Henry Marshall, bishop when the cathedral had been still in pure and unbroken Catholic descent. The stone tomb was worn, so that most of the details of three monks sitting reading on a continuous ledge in their cloister, framed by swirling foliage, had been obliterated, but in spite of battering by time, the figures kept a devotional power: 'The flow of the main lines of tracery enclosing the panels or medallions and the foliation filling the spandrils and vacant field is original, flush, sweet, and tender, and truly classical, as befits and marks a flush and hopeful age.' A work of art showed Hopkins the ideal connection between nature and God in the past.[28]

Three days later, accompanied by one of his juniorate students, John Lynch, Hopkins looked at a church which was a mere seven years old: All Saints' Babbacombe, on the outskirts of Torquay.[29] He had visited this High Anglican show-piece of Butterfield's while staying with the

Gurneys in 1867, but, surprisingly, had not then commented on the unfinished church, although Butterfield's architecture had been a great passion. Expensive and exclusive, it stood in an open park, surrounded by trees and villas. Hopkins noted the exterior:

It is odd and the oddness at first sight outweighed the beauty ... the steeple rather detached, not, I thought, very impressive, with an odd openwork diaper of freestone over marble pieces on the tower/ and on the spire scale-work, and with turrets at corners.

This reaction echoes conventional conservative opinion. Charles Eastlake criticized the tower and spire of All Saints' for being 'of a shape and proportions which puzzled the antiquaries, scandalized the architects, and sent unprofessional critics to their wit's end with amazement'. Hopkins had picked on one of Butterfield's most notable innovations, the transference of diaperwork—surface decoration of a small repeated pattern—from its traditional brickwork to stone ribbing. It was thus, as Eastlake declared, 'not a new style, but a development of previous styles'.[30] Perhaps deliberately, Hopkins did not mention the prominent and distinctive gargoyles, and ignored the lectern designed by Butterfield, but commented on out-of-the-ordinary shaped openings, the use of many coloured marbles, and several of the outstanding patternings. He responded to strong juxtapositioning of opposites in architecture, as in nature, and it was this aspect of Butterfield which most appealed to him. Surprisingly, he admired the elaborate pulpit, fashioned like a miniature shrine from a number of violently clashing coloured marbles.

They came out of the church and sat on the cliffs above Babbacombe bay. Behind them, rising over the top of the down, were the three tiers of All Saints' spire. The town of Teignmouth was beyond the headland to their left, Exmouth just visible in the distance. The sea was 'like blue silk. It seemed warped over towards our feet. Half-miles of catspaw like breathing on glass just turned the smoothness here and there.' The cliffs were pink in places and elsewhere so red they were almost purple. Below them to their left was the 'white ashy shingle' of Oddicombe Beach. Then

green inshore water, blue above that, clouds and distant cliffs dropping soft white beams down it, bigger clouds making big white tufts of white broken by ripples of the darker blue foreground water as if they were great white roses sunk in a blue dye.[31]

The next day Hopkins made a farewell climb up the heights of Haldon, of whose beautiful tall and slender elms he had become fond. As a soldier in Christ's Company he could only love and leave. The weather was sultry:

I looked down into a coomb full of sleepy mealy haze; the sun, which was westered, a bush of sparkling beams; and below/ the trees in the hollow grey and throwing their shadows in spokes/ those straight below the sun towards me, the others raying away on either side—a beautiful sight; long shadows creeping in the slacks and hollows of the steep red sandstone fields.[32]

# PART IV

# The Poet, 1874–1877

All things counter, original, spare, strange

# St Beuno's

Before returning to Roehampton on 21 August, Hopkins spent two days at Bristol, and a further few days at Beaumont. He still had a day or two to spare, in which to indulge for the last time in delights only London could provide. He had arranged to dine with the Jesuit Fathers at Westminster on Tuesday evening, and earlier that day visited Westminster Abbey. He went round the pre-Reformation cloisters, taking in 'the beautiful paired triforium-arcade with cinqfoiled wheels riding the arches', and discovering 'a simplicity of instress in the cinqfoil'. At the National Gallery, he hurried at first from painting to painting, having lost the habit of looking at pictures; then the words 'studious to eat but not to taste' occurred to him, and he relaxed, and started making notes.

The next day he heard that he was to go on Friday 28 August to St Beuno's College, in North Wales, to make his theology, which would in all likelihood mean he would spend the next four years there.[1]

ↄﾉᴑ

On the morning of his departure Hopkins got up half an hour earlier than usual. His last fixed impression of his year at Manresa House was of 'the full moon of brassyish colour and beautifully dappled hanging a little above the clump of trees in the pasture opposite my window'.

He probably caught the Irish Mail to Chester, where he crossed the Dee into Wales. At St Asaph station he found two of his future fellow theologians waiting with pony and trap to meet him. Bodoano was a stranger, but the other was an old acquaintance, the bearded and exuberant former naval commander Henry Schomberg Kerr. The station was at the edge of the town and, turning right under the bridge into the Holywell and Chester road, they were immediately in the countryside. Descending into the valley Hopkins had his first sight of the narrow River Clwyd. The straight road climbed gently for a mile, a sea bay gradually appearing in the distance to the left, over the roof-tops of Rhyl, and the densely wooded Clwydian Hills across the skyline drawing nearer. The road twisted, the range separating into two long hills, to the left Y Foel (the bare hill) and Mynydd y Cwm (Cwm mountain) and to the right, Moel Maenefa (the bare hill Maenefa). At the Rhuallt crossroads the trap turned by a plain, red-brick Methodist chapel on to a narrow road, with Maenefa looming above over trees to the left, and on the right a view over a patchwork of fields into a valley, beyond which were hills and mistier mountain ranges.

A fifty-yard drive led to the St Beuno's College entrance and courtyard. The college's skyline proliferated with roofs and roof-parts, chimneys of varying shapes, gables, gothic decorations, a belfry, a corner of a tower, cramped on a small plateau on the steep hill. There were other familiar faces to make him welcome, including that of Francis Bacon, a year ahead of Hopkins at Manresa House. Hopkins was shown to the room of Fr Murphy, the Minister, in charge of running the house, and was taken to his own room. It contained the expected iron bedstead, dark brown varnished wooden prie-dieu, with worn and pressed knee-cushion, chamber-pot, crucifix above his bed, working table, with inkwell and a candle in a holder and a wax taper, chair, indeterminately coloured mat, bookrests, dark brown chest of drawers, side-table with enamel wash-basin and jug, folded towel draped over the jug, mirror on the wall above, and some bright scarlet geraniums, which Bacon had picked for him. The room was probably a good-sized and well-lit one in Mansions or Hamlets Gallery, looking down over the valley. 'Everyone was very kind and hospitable', Hopkins wrote in his journal. He was shown the refectory, chapel, the one bath which served the community of sixty or so, and reported that night to his Rector, Fr James Jones, whom he already knew slightly, as it was he who had given the annual retreat at St Mary's Hall in 1872.

He was about to exchange the position of teacher for that of taught. But the theologians' year did not officially start until the beginning of October; he had arrived during the holiday period, when most of the community were away at Aber House, the College's vacation villa at Barmouth, on the west coast. He had five weeks in which to get used to his surroundings, the almost deserted college and the countryside.[2]

The house was planned in ten-feet-wide corridors, called galleries, each fifty yards long with a low ceiling. They enclosed two small courtyards, one a secluded rose-garden, and the other the entrance-yard. Newcomers were confused because staircases were hidden behind doors which looked the same. 'The staircases, galleries, and bopeeps are inexpressible', Hopkins wrote to his father on Saturday, 'it takes a fortnight to learn them.' He considered the architecture 'decent outside, skimpin within, Gothic'. It had been built by the designer of Birmingham town hall, who was to achieve wider fame as the inventor of the hansom cab. The college had pioneered a primitive hot-water and hot-air system of central heating, conveying 'lukewarm water of affliction to some of the rooms', but those whose rooms had only coal fires were considered more fortunate.

The best feature of the college Hopkins found to be its steep hillside gardens and walks. 'The garden is all heights, terraces, Excelsiors ['higher'], misty mountain tops, seats up trees called Crows' Nests, flights of steps seemingly up to heaven lined with burning aspiration upon aspiration of scarlet geraniums: it is very pretty and airy but it gives you the impression that if you took a step farther you would find yourself somewhere on Plenlimmon, Conway Castle, or Salisbury Craig.'[3] From the highest point of the gardens was a vast prospect over the long-drawn valley of the Clwyd, and beyond was the Snowdonian range which, Hopkins wrote, was sometimes 'bright visible but coming and going with the weather'. On the St Beuno's farm, Tŷ-Mawr, just below the road, were noises of cows and sheep; and the college donkeys, who with their carts did most of the necessary hillside hauling, were continually braying in a field near the gate; sometimes students took the place of donkeys between the wooden shafts.

On Hopkins's first Sunday at St Beuno's, Bacon suggested a walk to Cŵm (the same word as the Devonshire *coomb*, to which Hopkins had so fondly responded that summer). They retraced the trap-journey back to the Rhuallt crossroads, then walked on to the winding Dyserth road and along the side of the Clwydian range, which later became the 'pastoral forehead of Wales' to Hopkins; on their left was the wide Vale. The valley's qualities had always been attractive to visitors, and the description had not varied much since Defoe's in the 1720s:

descending now from the hills, we came into a most pleasant, fruitful, populous, and delicious vale, full of villages and towns, the fields shining with corn, just ready for the reapers, the meadows green and flowery, and a fine river with a mild and gentle stream running through it.[4]

Cŵm parish church was dedicated to local Saints, Mael and Sulien. Despite the English churchyard cypress and conifers, services were in Welsh in this stone barn, with a belfry like a chimney on one end of the roof. Its Sunday bell echoed around the Cŵm valley, whereas St

Beuno's was silent, Catholics being forbidden to ring bells. Christian names recognizable to English eyes were on the tombstones, but a large proportion were in Welsh: 'Ymay Gorwedd/ Cathrine/ Merch Luke a Jane Denman/ Bu farw Ion 20 1857/ Oed 5 mlwydd'. The language first appeared to Hopkins to be all consonants; after a longer time in the district he found that it was 'almost all vowels'. He realised the anomalous position of an English-speaking community in the heart of a remote Welsh-speaking countryside, and had (he told his father) 'half a mind to get up a little Welsh: all the neighbours speak it'.[5]

They returned across the St Asaph road and by the ten-year-old British School, whose red-brick awkwardness emphasized its alien purpose of educating native Welsh-speakers in English culture. The children of the district were commonly 'plump and rosy enough', wrote a St Beuno's Jesuit, but the men grew up 'stunted and with an eager, hungry look, as if their life was very hard; yet both they and their wives appear well though plainly dressed on Sundays and holidays'. They were mostly small farmers, getting a poor living out of twenty acres and a few cows.

The next day Hopkins walked with Henry Kerr in the opposite direction, past the tiny Rock Chapel which crowned the summit of a wooded hill above them. It had been built fifteen years before by a corps of volunteer Irish navvies, in their spare time from constructing the local railways, and was intended 'to make reparation to Our Lady for the sanctuaries that had been snatched from her in the Vale of Clwyd'. It could be seen distinctly for miles from the valley below, and in the distance produced all the effects of a larger and statelier Continental shrine. They reached Tremeirchion, like Cŵm a hill-village of rough-stone, two-storey houses and labourers' cottages with thick, white-washed walls and flourishing gardens. Hopkins and Kerr came upon a lodge-keeper's cottage, at the end of a wooded drive which wound to Brynbella, a house which Mrs Piozzi, Dr Johnson's friend, and her husband had built a hundred years before. Hopkins was introduced to the lodge-keeper, an old woman who would be eighty-nine that September (about his grandmother's age, he thought), and who had been servant to the previous owner Mrs Piozzi, who had been Mrs Thrale. She did not remember seeing Johnson, but she gossiped about her life with the Piozzis, and told the two men she came from Tremeirchion. All the towns and villages around there had their characteristic beast: she was a Tremeirchion Cow, and there were Cŵm Calves, Caerwys Crows, and Denbigh Cats.[6] Hopkins was to remember this eighteen months later, when he adopted as his Welsh bardic signature 'Brân Maenefa', the Crow of Maenefa.

The next day he visited the village-city of St Asaph, and the smallest of all the English and Welsh cathedrals. In the past the cathedral had suffered at the hands of the Welsh, who under Owen Glendower had burnt it to the ground in 1402, and the choir-stalls that Hopkins noticed had been used for horses in Cromwell's time. The modern vandals were the gothic restorers. When Hopkins visited it, St Asaph's was 'restoring and restored, with the usual consequence that its historical interest is gone and you cannot tell what is old, what new'.[7] It had the inscape of neither the old nor the modern. It was in the hands of the prolific restorer, Sir Gilbert Scott, 'a certain obliterator of historic records who had run down from London and back in a day', as Thomas Hardy later characterized him.[8] Scott could, however, earn Hopkins's admiration. Two days later Hopkins walked with James Purbrick to the village of Trefnant, nearly three miles beyond Tremeirchion, where they entered the church built in the Decorated style, to Scott's designs, in 1855. In contrast to the churches of his favourite, Butterfield, this one was quietly and delicately decorated.

The next Sunday, Kerr took Hopkins up Moel-y-parc, 'a furze-grown and heathy hill' of 1305 feet, behind Maenefa; it was seven miles from St Beuno's and well known for the views from its summit. Hopkins looked up the Clwyd valley south towards the town of Ruthin on its hill, and down the valley to where the river entered the sea by Rhyl. The cleave made by the Afon Chwiler, the river Wheeler, in which lay the villages of Bodfari and Caerwys, was close below:

It was a leaden sky, braided or roped with cloud, and the earth in dead colours, grave but distinct. The heights by Snowden were hidden by the clouds but not from distance or dimness. The nearer hills, the other side of the valley, shewed a hard and beautifully detached and glimmering brim against the light, which was lifting there. All the length of the valley the skyline of hills was flowingly written all along upon the sky. A blue bloom, a sort of meal, seemed to have spread upon the distant south, enclosed by a basin of hills. Looking all round but most in looking far up the valley I felt an instress and charm of Wales.[9]

On a September walk with Bacon Hopkins discovered the beauty of the second river valley. They climbed the hillside to the Cefn Rocks, from where

the view of the deep valley of the Elwy, the meeting of two, which makes three, glens indeed, is most beautiful. The woods, thick and silvered by sunlight and shade, by the flat smooth banking of the tree-tops expressing the slope of the hill, came down to the green bed of the valley. Below at a little timber bridge I looked at some delicate flying shafted ashes—there was one especially of single sonnet-like inscape—between which the sun sent straight bright slenderish panes of silvery sunbeams down the slant towards the eye and standing above an unkept field stagged with patchy yellow heads of ragwort.[10]

In the fortnight before the scholastic year started, Hopkins walked among the beautiful woods near Caerwys, once a Roman station, and climbed Maenefa with his fellow theologian Joseph Rickaby, noticing from the summit how the many-coloured smokes from the kilns in the valley below did not spoil the beautiful liquid cast of blue which all the landscape had. One evening he watched

a lovely sunset of rosy juices and creams and combs; the combs I mean scattered floating bats or rafts or racks above, the creams/ the strew and bed of the sunset, passing north and south or rather north only into grey marestail and brush along the horizon to the hills. Afterwards the rosy field of the sundown turned gold and the slips and creamings in it stood out like brands, with jots of purple. A sodden twilight over the valley and foreground all below, holding the corner-hung maroon-grey diamonds of ploughfields to one keeping but allowing a certain glare in the green of the tufts of grass.[11]

℘

Before the term started, there had been an event of great importance in his religious life: his reception of the tonsure and of the four minor orders of Doorkeepers, Readers, Exorcists, and Acolytes. Although, as Hopkins wrote to his mother,[12] their use was almost obsolete, they were a sign of progression in his profession, and so should have been a source of encouragement. On 1 October the summer vacation came to an end. In the three hours before breakfast that morning, apart from the *Veni Creator*, mass, and benediction, there was a Latin discourse in the recreation room by an Italian dogmatic theologian, Fr Luigi Tosi. The single-sentence entry in Hopkins's journal that day patronizingly refers to Fr Tosi's unusual pronunciation, 'an interesting composition but a little amusing'.[13]

His daily theologate pattern at St Beuno's was similar to that of the St Mary's philosophate. Private meditation, community mass, and breakfast were followed on most weekday mornings by two lectures, on moral and dogmatic theology, given by Fr Jones, the Rector, and Fr Tepe, a German. On Monday, Wednesday, and Friday afternoons, there were three additional lectures, from Fr Morris on canon law or church history, dogmatic theology again, and Hebrew with Fr Perini, an Italian who had been forced to leave Rome by the 1870 uprising. This last lecture lasted only half an hour. Fr Morris used to

read his lectures for half an hour in the evening in English. He would not allow us to take notes during them; so you had simply to give yourself up to listen, and a very pleasant half hour it was, an interval of sunshine in a day otherwise neither stormy nor gloomy, but certainly trying, the school-day, namely, of the theologian.[14]

On these three days there was a 'circle', presided over by the Rector and lasting an hour, during which students were tested on their understanding of Fr Jones's recent theological lectures, and their ability to argue in syllogistic form in support of Catholic doctrines. On Tuesday evenings was held the 'case of conscience'. The procedure was the same every week: 'The case to be discussed—hand-written or chromographed—was displayed on the notice-board about mid-week, two Theologians were instructed to prepare solutions, and a third would study it, and be ready to give his opinion if asked; all were expected to have studied it in advance.' One theology student was given the task of deciding 'what course of action should be pursued by a flabbergasted Bishop who had just heard the confession of a dying priest to the effect that he (the priest) had never had the slightest faith in any of the Sacraments which he had administered for thirty years, and was in fact a complete Atheist.'[15]

It was important that Jesuits be trained in argumentative method and practised in defending their religion. During their comparatively brief existence they had been controversialists and the subject of controversies. They had enemies within their own Church, and were often attacked by Protestants as the most representative and conspicuous body of that Church. Persecution had been an everyday occurrence, and even in the nineteenth century not a decade passed without a community in some country being attacked. While Hopkins was at St Beuno's there were violent attacks abroad, with printed and pulpit criticisms at home. Hopkins attempted to soothe his mother's worries about attacks in two issues of *The Quarterly Review*:

I am glad you have not such an altogether unfavourable opinion of the Society. If those 'very bad things' done by it in its time are historical actions, such as the iniquitous charges of instigating Gunpowder Plot, murdering Cardinal I forget who in China, or introducing brandy among the Canadian Indians, incredible and well shewn up as such charges are, I cannot undertake to speak to their falsehood out of my own examination, for I have no time for the history of the Society or any other history. But if they are doctrines and moral teaching set your heart at rest about them: I live in the midst of all that and I know or can easily ascertain what we do and have taught.[16]

There was no time for history, and no time even for philosophical reading outside course requirements: 'it was with sorrow I put back Aristotle's Metaphysics in the library some time ago feeling that I could not read them now and so probably should never.'[17] (One day a week was set aside for recreation, and they were 'free to go out for the day with sandwiches, but without money'.) On Sundays 'tones' were preached. These were sermons delivered to the community in the refectory. Then in the afternoon there was first 'companies', a walk with a companion chosen at random, nicknamed 'lotteries'. Benediction followed, then usually a debate, supper, and the dominical (a half-hour's practice sermon).[18]

The list of St Beuno's debating club subjects[19] shows a judicious mixture of course material, topical matters of parish and school policy, and the kind of subject discussed in national reviews. One week the motion might be: 'That it is lawful and expedient to baptize an heretic at the point of death even though he has expressed no desire to be received into the Church', where the students' training and professional judgement would be tested; another week the debate would be framed to rehearse viewpoints on a subject of practical interest, like future teaching: 'The boys in our colleges should attend a late Mass with sermon on Sundays'. Sometimes a topic discussed in secular journals was chosen, so that Jesuit policies could be spelt out: 'That it is a subject for congratulation that the Queen has assumed the title Empress of India' (where the attitude of the Society towards temporal monarchs would be bound to enter into the debate).

The polemical nature of debate was underlined by presentation and seating arrangements. Nevertheless, the students were free to back which opinion they chose. Hopkins, for instance, advocated music as a more powerful aid to religion than painting, which may have been justification of his own rejection of painting. Conscience rather than inclination may also explain his support for the motion that 'A theological student should eschew all literature not bearing on his studies'. This topic probably originated in a complaint the Superior General of the Jesuits had heard about St Beuno's and passed on as instructions to the English Provincial: to take care that the students 'spend more time on serious study (and less time on light reading)'. In January 1877, the Rector decreed that 'all students should gain the approval of a professor and of the Minister (the Assistant Rector) before taking a book from the library'.[20]

℘

There was little time to spare, and Hopkins's journal became sparse. News of friends and relatives was quickly and briefly written down. Bond's sister, the superior Susan, of whom all the Hopkins family were fond, got married. Mowbray Baillie was threatened with consumption and was spitting blood; he had been ordered south and was going up the Nile.[21] The weather became bleaker, but the countryside's charm remained, and Hopkins's delight in word-painting:

The day was rainy and a rolling wind; parts of the landscape, as the Orms' Heads, were blotted out by rain. The clouds westwards were a pied piece—sail-coloured brown and milky blue; a dun yellow tent of rays opened upon the skyline far off. Cobalt blue was poured on the hills bounding the valley of the Clwyd and far in the south spread a bluish damp, but all the nearer valley was showered with tapered diamond flakes of fields purple and brown and green.[22]

Hopkins's enthusiastic moods seldom lasted long. His journal also noted the death at Stonyhurst of his late pupil, Br Richard O'Neill: 'There was, I now remember, a sad and wistful look he had, a sort of mark of early death stamped upon him; I interpret after the event.' He had recorded seven such deaths in his journal during the last two and a half years. There was (as Ritz observes[23]) a morbid element of compliance in Hopkins's accumulation of painful pieces of news and distressing details; he loved the dangerous presences which sapped his energy.

Life in his first year at St Beuno's was, as Fr Thomas puts it, one of 'sustained uneventfulness'; he kept back letters he was writing to Oak Hill 'in case anything should turn up but nothing has'. From time to time, despite frail physique and frequent poor health, Hopkins managed long and arduous walking expeditions, one of about twenty miles, in bad weather, including a climb up a mountain covered in snow. Before Christmas there was skating on Llyn Helyg, 'tempered by catastrophes and wettings to the middle'. His mother sent jerseys for Christmas, as the old ones had to be discarded. 'On coming here they shrank at the wash to that degree that the pain of wearing one for a day lasted round the chest for two days after. I got pieces put in but they were still so uncomfortable that I cast them: besides they were almost worn out.' The laundress at St Beuno's, 'unlike the admirable and queenlike Miss Holden at Stonyhurst', did not know her trade, 'and I am afraid some harm will happen to the new jerseys too'.[24]

In February Bridges wrote, trying to interest Hopkins in Hegel, but he replied: 'the close pressure of my theological studies leaves me time for hardly anything: the course is very hard, it must be said.'[25] Throughout his first year at St Beuno's he rarely felt relaxed happiness.

The weather, his health, and his studies were sources of unhappiness and tension. 'Such a backward spring I cannot remember', he wrote in April 1875: 'Now things begin to look greener and the cuckoo may be heard but our climate on the hillside is a touch Arctic. I have recovered from a cold I caught lately and am well but for daily indigestion, which makes study much harder and our shadowless glaring walks to my eyes very painful.' In reply Mrs Hopkins sent him a parcel, which came packed in so much sawdust that 'it will serve to sweep my room for weeks. This morning I meant to handsell it but have found nobody about to give me a spoon. It is a queer medicine and is like eating death and cremation: I hope it may be an effectual one'.[26]

Besides suffering ill-health, he found that the pressure of the yearly examinations made him 'unwilling to do more correspondence than necessary just now'.[27] He passed the two July exams, in moral theology and dogma; in the half-hour's oral examination in dogma, on 27 July 1874, three of the four examiners put him in the third grade and one in the fourth, the lowest grade necessary for a pass. He had performed adequately, not brilliantly; neither he nor his superiors can have been entirely satisfied with his year's performance, but he was promoted to second-year theological studies.

# Welsh and Wells

One bright day soon after his arrival at St Beuno's Hopkins had walked
with Bacon to Ffynnon Fair,[1] in a meadow by the Elwy. Ffynnon Fair
or Mary's Well was one of nearly a hundred wells dedicated to the
Virgin Mary in Wales. She had been so real to the medieval Welsh that
a tradition had arisen that she had come to Wales. Some of the roofless
stone remnants of the chapel walls were still high enough to show the
outline of simple gothic windows and doorways, with a profusion of
fiercely competing tangled plants making a wilderness where its floor
used to be. The well itself had formed the western arm of the cruciform
medieval chapel; it was three sides of a square, with a large bath into
which the well-water flowed, forming an irregular fourth side. At the
centre of each of the three sides an extra triangle had been added,
making, with the two corners of the square, five points towards which
the spring-water gushed up from the bottom of the well, breaking the
surface with wellings-up and bubbles. Steps led down into the bath,
and a strong stream ran out of it, curving round until it flowed just
inside the south wall of the chapel. To enter through the south doorway
one trod on a stone slab which bridged the stream. The five points of
the well towards which the water flowed represented, as Hopkins
thought, the five porticoes of Bethzatha or Bethesda, the 'house of
mercy' in St John's Gospel, under which the crowds of sick people
waited to be healed when the waters moved. Hopkins noted 'the basis of
pillars (which would have supported a canopy having five openings in
circuit and two at the side between the well and the trough or bath)'.
Only the pillar-bases remained after the chapel and well had been
despoiled in the sixteenth century.

 To many nineteenth-century travellers with their guide-books, the
well and weed-choked chapel by the river would be a romantic ruin. To
Catholics there would be a poignancy, as in all ruins of Catholic holy
places no longer reverenced. The history of Catholicism in Britain

would be brought home to them; they could relive the Reformation. Hopkins's journal entry is touchingly restrained: 'we said a prayer and drank the water'.

A month later, on a bright and beautiful day, when 'crests of snow could be seen on the mountains', Hopkins and Clement Barraud walked to Holywell, and bathed at St Winefride's Well:

The sight of the water in the well as clear as glass, greenish like beryl or aquamarine, trembling at the surface with the force of the springs, and shaping out the five foils of the well quite drew and held my eyes to it.

The priest in charge, Fr John Baptist di Pietro, told them how a young man from Liverpool, Arthur Kent, had recently been cured of a rupture by bathing in the water. Hopkins wrote in his journal:

The strong unfailing flow of the water and the chain of cures from year to year all these centuries took hold of my mind with wonder at the bounty of God in one of His saints, the sensible thing so naturally and gracefully uttering the spiritual reason of its being (which is all in true keeping with the story of St. Winefred's death and recovery) and the spring in place leading back the thoughts by its spring in time to its spring in eternity: even now the stress and buoyancy and abundance of the water is before my eyes.[2]

As with many of his obsessions, precursory thoughts and feelings about the well had been with Hopkins for some time before he actually saw it. His first impressions of it dated back to September 1867, after he had been received into the Catholic Church, when he had walked from Bovey Tracey to Newton Abbot for mass and breakfasted with Kenelm Vaughan, who had been cured of consumption by drinking water from St Winefride's Well. It may have been on that day, inspired by Vaughan, that Hopkins had decided on his vocation, so that St Winefride and her well held more than a passing interest.

By Hopkins's time Catholic priests had developed an ambivalent attitude towards Winefride's story, first written down by monks in the twelfth century, about five hundred years after her death. Winefride, or Gwenfrewi, was the daughter of a chieftain, Tewyth ap Eylud, and his wife Gwenlo. One Sunday, when her parents were at mass in the church built by her uncle Beuno, a chieftain, Caradoc, tried to seduce her. She escaped towards the church; Caradoc pursued and beheaded her, and a spring welled up from the spot where her head fell. Beuno restored the head to the body; Winefride came alive again, became a nun, and lived for another fifteen years with no sign of a wound except for a white scar round her neck. The story reads like a compendium of details from Celtic hagiography, and even Hopkins, who could be credulous, added, when advising the sceptic Bridges to read the story in Butler's *Lives*, 'you should treat it as a fable'.[3]

The spring-water was artificially directed so that the main gush came up from the earth through static water, emerging to splay outwards from its centre in a ragged shape, which was formalized into a five-pointed star by a surrounding recessed stone structure. Like the Ffynnon Fair at Cefn, it represented the five-porched healing Pool of Bethesda. Arches arose to form a well-chamber, which was the crypt of a small chapel. Having escaped destruction at the hands of Henry VIII and Thomas Cromwell because of its valuable offerings, during Elizabeth's reign the chapel had been secretly placed in the care of the hounded and itinerant Society of Jesus, and its well had become an important centre of Catholic resistance. Jesuits associated with the well had been hunted, tortured, or executed, and people had made pilgrimages to the shrine in increasing numbers. The chapel had remained undamaged, while the Jesuits continued to keep a record of the cures. In the 1860s a convent and hospice had been established, and in the two or three years immediately before Hopkins's first visit, Fr di Pietro and the Holywell mission had added wooden cubicles and screens for pilgrims.

Cures at the well had never died out. During the next six months Hopkins followed up the alleged cure of Arthur Kent, and promised to report the result to his father. The final answer to his queries never came, but he 'heard of another cure having just been worked in London by the moss or water and am going to enquire into that'.[4] There is no further mention of this. On the green dank wall behind the well hung crutches, leg-irons, and other medical aids left by cured pilgrims, though tombstones on the hill above recorded invalids who had died uncured.

The well came to mean more to Hopkins than anything else in Wales. It 'fills me with devotion', he told Bridges, 'every time I see it and wd. fill anyone that has eyes with admiration, the flow of ἀγλαὸν ὕδωρ [bright water] is so lavish and so beautiful.'[5] God showed his glory to man through nature, and man responded with worship and gratitude. As pilgrimages to the shrine had never died out, the well was a sign to God that Hopkins's native land had not been completely false; the ambiguity of whether it were an English or Welsh shrine would not have worried Hopkins, who had recently acknowledged that his father's ancestors had been Welsh. The responsibility of the Jesuits for keeping it alive was an additional source of pride, and the saint's martyrdom in defence of her virginity was a sanctification of religious chastity.

Hopkins wanted to express his feelings about the well in poetry. Traditionally it had inspired Welsh poems celebrating the coincidence of God's purpose and Nature's acquiescence, and the Jesuit custom of placing polyglot verses by Our Lady's statue at Stonyhurst on Mayday offered another precedent. Hopkins started composing Latin elegiacs, to be placed in St Winefride's shrine on 3 November 1874, the day she was commemorated in the diocese of Shrewsbury.

Taking his journal of the visit he and Barraud had made to the well on 8 October he translated and extended some of its thoughts. His sixteen lines fell into four disconnected groups,[6] and, perhaps because he was rushed and could not immediately see how to combine them into a unified poem, he chose four lines, polished them, added two more, and wrote them out in fair on a separate sheet, to stand on their own, headed by 'A.M.D.G.', and followed by 'L.D.S.', as though they were an official classroom exercise. In addition he made a free translation of them into English, recalling a phrase 'Sweet soul' he had used several years before in a poem on another virgin martyr, St Dorothea:

### On St. Winefred
*besides her miraculous cures*
*filling a bath and turning a mill*

As wishing all about us sweet,
She brims her bath in cold or heat;
She lends, in aid of work and will,
Her hand from heaven to turn a mill—
Sweet soul! not scorning honest sweat
And favouring virgin freshness yet.

These two six-line poems were probably both offered at the statue; well-crafted epigrams rather than the poem which the original elegiacs suggest was his first intention. They are occasional poems, whose taut and restricted style conveys the censorship Hopkins was placing on his poetry.

This is a translation of the central section of the Latin poem:

And first [take] the fact that the river issues from three springs: this is the nature, as we believe, of our threefold God; and take the fact that these springs join together and increase with a clear level surface: there you have the singleness of heart which you nourish, gracious faith. What of the fact that the spring, rising from a hidden source, makes its way into the sunlight and into the sight of men?[7]

The imagery of the well's springs clearly anticipates 'The Wreck of the Deutschland':[8]

I steady as a water in a well, to a poise, to a pane,
But roped with, always, all the way down from the tall
Fells or flanks of the voel, a vein
Of the gospel proffer, a pressure, a principal, Christ's gift.

In this discarded Latin, hidden God is revealed to men through a natural phenomenon, as the storm delivers the stress in 'The Wreck of the Deutschland', and there is also a symbolic coincidence of number, three here and five in the 'Wreck'. Singleness of heart in the elegiacs becomes 'there was a heart right!/ There was single eye' in the 'Wreck'.[9] Hopkins is occupied with more complex feelings, thoughts, and images than emerge in the six-line verses, but they were a matrix for his first major poem.

ℰↃ

The other great stimulus during his first year was the Welsh language. 'A Divine has quite enough to do', wrote a Jesuit, emphasizing the utilitarian nature of the St Beuno's training,

if he will learn his theology well, and the few leisure moments he may have to spare will never suffice to acquire such a proficiency in Welsh as will be of any service to him. Besides, he is a mere bird of passage, and ought not to waste his time and energies in acquiring a language which will be of no earthly use to him after he has finished his course of theology.[10]

Nevertheless, from his first day in Wales Hopkins had been keen to learn the language. All his neighbours spoke Welsh by preference, even if they understood English, and it was the exception to find English understood outside the larger towns or the northern coastal resorts which had been colonized by Liverpool and Lancashire people. By his fourth day in Wales he had already heard the language, telling his mother: 'It is complicated but euphonious and regular. People think it has no vowels but just the contrary is true: it is almost all vowels and they run off the tongue like oil by diphthongs and triphthongs—there are 20 of the latter and nearly 30 of the former.'[11] He had always looked on himself as half-Welsh, he added.

On the first day of his annual retreat he consulted the Rector, who discouraged his learning the language 'unless it were purely for the sake of labouring among the Welsh'.[12] Hopkins realized that his interest in Welsh was not 'pure'; his motivation was not to effect conversions, so he gave it up, reluctantly. But with him the wish was often father to the thought: 'I had no sooner given up the Welsh than my desire seemed to be for the conversion of Wales and I had it in mind to give up everything else for that.'[13]

Since the founding of St Beuno's a desire to convert the local people had been a common reaction of newcomers. The first Jesuits at St Beuno's had eagerly set out to convert the mainly Wesleyan natives, and in the early 1850s several professors and scholastics began to learn Welsh. A Welsh service and sermon in the chapel were instituted, but soon abandoned as the audience diminished. 'Discourses in Welsh from an alien, and a Saxon at that', wrote a Jesuit, 'would never be regarded by the Welsh mind with any other feelings than one of amused patronage, even derision. . . . Such academic exercises are apt to be feeble instruments for the dislodging of centuries of deeply ingrained prejudice and national animosity.'[14] On 23 March 1851, the congregation at the Welsh service consisted of two laundry maids and a child.

Since the 1850s little attempt had been made to convert the Welsh or to learn Welsh. The number of converts had been negligible, though there was the occasional sensation, as in 1854, when Miss Smalley, daughter of the parson of Cŵm, had been received into the Catholic Church.[15] Sham conversions could 'readily be secured for a small sum of money'.[16] It was predictable that a St Beuno's debate of April 1876, in which Hopkins took part (against the motion, of course), resolved that 'The sooner Welsh dies out the better'.[17] An enthusiasm such as Hopkins's had come to be regarded as naïve by older Jesuits. He weighed up his motives by St Ignatius' rules of election, and resolved not to take up Welsh again.

His other great interest was music, but the only available instrument was 'a grunting harmonium that lived in the sacristy'; he had 'made singularly little way' with that, and so his music 'seemed to come to an end'. This double surrender, of Welsh and music, affected him deeply. It 'disappointed me and took an interest away—and at that time I was very bitterly feeling the weariness of life and shed many tears, perhaps not wholly into the breast of God but with some unmanliness in them too, and sighed and panted to him'.[18] Two of his strongest inclinations thus ran counter to prescribed Jesuit behaviour.

Hopkins's St Beuno's journal does not chart the life of a professional religious, but the intense preoccupations of a separate life, kept and chronicled apart, in his spare time. As yet his way of looking at nature had no place in his Jesuit life, his interests were not worthy for their own sake, and his 'treasury of stored beauty' was apparently useless. The instress and charm of Wales which he experienced did not correspond to anything in his Jesuit training. It was not the Jesuit way to say with Ruskin that we may learn of the profoundest values through the eye.

But in spite of his Rector's discouragement, his own scruples, and the decision to give up Welsh, Hopkins's journal for 7 February 1875 shows him taking Welsh lessons from a Miss Susannah Jones. There is no evidence of how and why the change took place. In the St Beuno's records and his own references to these Welsh studies there is no mention of Hopkins's undertaking a mission among the Welsh, speaking Welsh from the pulpit, or going among the Welsh-speaking people. Yet its important place even in his strict and harassed timetable of theological studies is shown in a letter to Bridges in February 1875:

I have had no time to read even the English books about Hegel . . . it was with sorrow I put back Aristotle's Metaphysics in the library some time ago feeling that I could not read them now. . . . The close pressure of my theological studies leaves me time for hardly anything: the course is very hard, it must be said. Nevertheless I have tried to learn a little Welsh, in reality one of the hardest of languages.[19]

His journal[20] shows him enthusiastically exploring the new language, which he associated with poetry and mythology. It must have been a curious Welsh lesson: a Welsh Catholic 'good woman' (as Hopkins called her), of local farming stock, teaching the nervous Oxford-English priest how to translate *Cinderella* into Welsh. It was not straightforward tuition. He encouraged her to stray from mere grammar and exercises. On his asking her the Welsh for fairy,

She told me *cĭpenăper* (or perhaps *cĭpernăper*, *Anglice kippernapper*): the word is nothing but *kidnapper*. . . . However in coming to an understanding between ourselves what fairies (she says *fairess* by the way for a she-fairy) and kippernappers were, on my describing them as little people 'that high', she told me quite simply that she had seen them.

℅

Probably for the saint's feast-day of 3 December 1875, Hopkins made two verse translations of Francis Xavier's well-known Latin hymn, 'O Deus, ego amo te'. One, headed 'A.M.D.G.', is in English, the other in Welsh.[21] This translation predicts ways in which he would manipulate and transform Welsh poetic technique in 'The Wreck of the Deutschland'. The Welsh hymn shows a collision, not a reconciliation. The chosen metre is English. There are linguistic errors: the wrong conjugation of an irregular verb, the misuse of a reflexive verb, and a lack of familiarity with common idioms. But there are two deviations from common Welsh practice which show Hopkins pressuring Welsh to suit his poetic purposes. In stanza 3 he uses a Welsh device *sangiad* in lines 1 and 2 to change the syntactical structure from the normal prose word-order: 'Aneirif ddolur darfu it,/ A phoen, a chwŷs eu dwyn'. He wants *ddolur* and *darfu* next to each other, and has also created a structure of parallels with 'A phoen, a chwŷs'. In so doing he offends against correct Welsh practice, which requires that the two parts of the compound verb *darfu* and *dwyn* should be put close together. Similarly, in stanza 5 he has omitted a conjunctive pronoun, and altered the structure of a normal Welsh sentence by bringing next to each other the two parts of the verb 'to love', *garaf* and *garu'r*, so that their simultaneous similarity and difference can be pointed.[22] His comparative ignorance of Welsh helped him to use it to form abstract sound- and rhythm-patterns for his own poetic purposes. The loneliness of his Welsh studies may have helped, too, for he had only one or two outdated books and Miss Jones to inhibit his pattern-forming. If correct grammar and the desires of the Muse were opposed, the Muse could win.

Besides learning the spoken language and practising poetic exercises on pious subjects, he studied classical Welsh poetry. In July 1875 he cut out from a local newspaper, *The Montgomery Mercury*, a printing, with translation and commentary, of the sixteenth-century bard Tudur Aled's *Cywydd i Wenfrewi Santes* (*Cywydd* to St Winefride).[23] Some of the Welsh-language echoes in his own 'St Winefred's Well' were to come from this example of the Welsh metrical form, including the Welsh for 'Winefred', which he transliterated into his play as 'Gwenvrewi'.[24] Similarities between Tudur Aled's and Hopkins's *cywydd* on his Bishop's Silver Jubilee, in which he makes use of the legend of Beuno and Winefride, show how he took the poem as a model. But Hopkins's *cywydd* is accurate only in the comparatively simple metre. In his attempt at including *cynghanedd*, a complex patterning of internal rhyme and alliteration, he is strictly correct in only two of eighteen lines. He was not attracted for long by the *cywydd* form, which demanded the same number of syllables—seven—in every line. Hopkins's new rhythm in 'The Wreck of the Deutschland' worked by disciplining the stresses in a line, but allowing freedom in the number of syllables, as many or as few as were wanted. What attracted him in the *cynghanedd* was its variety of enriching and binding systems; it foregrounded the inscape of sound-patterns. The danger, as he later acknowledged, was that sense would 'get the worst of it'. But he insisted his poetry had to be read aloud, so that the full effect of the consonance was the first thing the audience ('those who hear') took in.

The discoveries about Welsh poetry confirmed and strengthened emphases already evident in lecture notes made during his teaching year at Roehampton. For lessons to the Jesuit juniors, he wrote down his ideas on the principal features of verse. His lecture on 'Poetry and Verse'[25] emphasized that poetry was a form of spoken sound; a printed or written version of a poem was its representation, not its actuality. Poetry was 'speech only employed to carry the inscape of speech for the inscape's sake'. The inscape of words had to be emphasized over and above matter and meaning; 'the inscape must be dwelt on'. To ensure that the inscape would be understood, 'repetition, *oftening, over-and-overing, aftering* of the inscape must take place in order to detach it to the mind'. Poetry, as Hopkins saw it, had to be 'speech couched in a repeating figure'. The importance of repetition in Hopkins's mature poetry went back to early days at Oxford, when he made those lists of words with similar sounds or meanings. This view of the nature of poetry is prescriptive, the language of a practitioner rather than a teacher. Hopkins had in mind what his own poetry might be like.

In his lecture notes on 'Rhythm and other Structural Parts',[26] Hopkins distinguished one group of 'repeating figures', which he called 'lettering of syllables': 'Likeness or sameness of letters [,] and this some or all [,] and these vowels or consonants [,] and initial or final'. The word 'rhyme' had a 'more special or narrower sense', and he described this likeness with the word 'chime', or 'widely rhyme'. Alliteration, assonance, and 'skothending' (final half-rhyme), were forms of this 'rhyme in a wide sense'. Among his examples is a translation from Norse poetry:

> Softly now are sifting
> Snows on landscape frozen.
> Thickly fall the flakelets,
> Feathery-light together.

The lectures on poetry, the study of Welsh, the use of sanctioned occasions for verse, and the exercises in Welsh, Latin, and English poetry, were preparations for something greater.

# 21

## 'The Wreck of the Deutschland'

A shipping disaster is a godsend . . .

The story of the composition of 'The Wreck of the Deutschland' is familiar. Reading *The Times* one day in early December 1875, Hopkins was strongly affected by its account of the wreck: because of severe conditions and negligence, the *Deutschland*, carrying some nuns who had been expelled from Prussia, foundered on a notorious sandbank in the mouth of the Thames. 'Happening to say so to my rector he said that he wished someone would write a poem on the subject.' Using this hint as sanction, Hopkins 'set to work'.[1] With his age's concern for factual details, his first thought was to collect eyewitness descriptions from *The Times*. Being unable to cut the house's newspapers, he asked his mother to send him all she could find,[2] but before the cuttings arrived from Oak Hill he was already writing and even planning the publication of an imaginative, inventive, and complex poem.

He immediately saw religious and doctrinal implications in the event, and the possibilities it presented for a poem on the subject of a modern Catholic martyrdom. Particular aspects of this martyrdom appealed to him, and the event seemed to contain hidden messages and symbols: the German and English national implications, the reported cry of the tall nun, the number (five) of the nuns.

From his earliest days in the novitiate Hopkins learnt the reality of persecution of Catholics in mainland Europe, through constant news of expulsions of Jesuits, and meetings with the exiles. Despite the legal inhibition of the Penal Clause in the Emancipation Act, which, though never invoked, forbade the presence of Jesuits in the country, the English Province of the Society was able to offer sanctuary to their persecuted fellows. Two months after arriving at Roehampton for his novitiate, Hopkins had met Fr Joachim Forn from the Aragon province, one of the Jesuits expelled from Spain in the revolution of 1868;[3]

and in February 1869, after reading an account in *Letters and Notices*, Hopkins dramatized with childish relish some of the livelier Spanish experiences in a letter to his mother:

Some had to escape in disguise. At Cadiz the Admiral though belonging to the revolution stood their friend and marched them through the town to the fleet. They all had the power of going to their homes but most chose exile and those who did go back seem to have done so against their will and by the advice of their superiors. A boy of 14 who was to be sent home begged with tears to go with the rest into exile and at last his wish was granted.[4]

To secular minds, exile might be taken as a humiliating defeat and rejection, but since Christ's execution as a criminal had been mythologized into a triumphant pattern for martyrdoms, the Society of Jesus had inverted defeat into victory. Appalled and enthusiastic responses to martyrs' fates joined. Hopkins commented on the expulsions from Spain: 'To be persecuted in a tolerant age is a high distinction.' Seven weeks after that he read out to the Roehampton novices a letter that was sent to the Spanish exiles at Angers in France; written in Latin, it was probably composed by Hopkins.[5]

On 25 October 1870 he wrote in his journal: 'A little before 7 in the evening a wonderful Aurora, the same that was seen at Rome (shortly after its seizure by the Italian government) and taken as a sign of God's anger.'[6] Rome had been captured by Victor Emmanuel on 20 September, and for the rest of that year the life of the Stonyhurst seminary had been disrupted by the arrival of Italian and Irish exiles from Rome. The reference library, parlour, and workshop were filled with beds, special prayers were said, and refectory readings about the Italian revolution were held. The world leader of the Jesuits, Father General Peter Beckx, requested that there be an Exposition of the Blessed Sacrament on Friday evenings, and the scholastics watched, two at a time.[7]

Only seven months before the *Deutschland* sank, Hopkins had given his mother an account of Russian persecution of Polish Catholics, with a naïve enthusiasm:

The United Greeks, who are Catholics, are being forced to return to the Russian Church. Cossacks are sent into the village, the peasantry are driven by the knout to the Church, when they refuse they are scourged to blood, then put into the hospital till their wounds are healed sufficiently for them to be flogged again. Some have died under the lash. Women and children are flogged too. In one village the people being brought to the altar and refusing to communicate, their mouths were forced open with the sword and the Precious Blood poured down.[8]

The desire to impress and the righteous savouring of violent details show that for Hopkins there was a sensuous pleasure about martyrdom.

On 4 July 1872 an Act had been passed in the Reichstag which ordered all Jesuits to leave Germany within six months. At the end of his time at St Mary's Hall, Hopkins came into contact with victims of Bismarck's *Kulturkampf*. He organized the entertainment for the group of exiled Germans continuing their Jesuit training near Stonyhurst; he had found the Germans 'kind, amiable, and edifying people', and saw them off at Whalley station.[9] Most of England, however sympathized with Bismarck. 'The British people', said a leader in *The Times*,

are not very hard hearted or wholly without fairness or utterly irreligious; yet the Roman Catholics will not find it easy to enlist their sympathies on behalf of the Jesuits. . . . Bismarck wishes to abate a very great nuisance, the nuisance of an unscrupulous conspiracy bent on dissolving society in order to accomplish certain impossible ends of its own.[10]

Bismarck's aim was to unite Germany, and since the Churches were an obstacle, he expelled the Jesuits. By the Religious Orders Act of May 31st 1875, aimed particularly at the Roman Catholic Church, 'all religious orders were banned from Prussia, except those that devoted themselves to nursing the sick'.[11] Among the victims were the Franciscan Sisters of Salzkotten, the Motherhouse of the *Töchter der heiligsten Herzen Jesu und Maria*. In response to earlier laws, offshoot houses of the Order had been founded in the United States, and three groups of sisters had already emigrated there. A fourth group, of five sisters, left Salzkotten on 3 December 1875, and on 4 December boarded the iron single-screw steamer, the *Deutschland*, belonging to the North German Lloyd's line, at Bremerhaven. Among them was Sister Maria Henrica Fassbaender, chosen to be the Superior of the American province.

ℰℛ

'The Wreck of the Deutschland', in so many ways original, is unmistakably a Victorian sea-disaster poem. Britain was supremely conscious of being a maritime power, dependent on the sea for trade, empire, and military supremacy. Jane Austen's Emma was typical of inland people at the beginning of the century in never having seen the sea; but with the spread of cheap railway travel people of all classes were going to the seaside resorts.

Sea-fever extended to arts and entertainment. Bowdlerized versions of sea-ballads and chanties were sung in drawing-rooms, together with modern sea-songs like 'Hearts of Oak', 'The Arethusa', 'Tom Bowling', and 'The Death of Nelson', popular long after Trafalgar. There were lower-class penny weeklies, like *Tales of Shipwreck and Adventures at Sea* (1846–7), and popular novels such as Marryat's *Mr Midshipman Easy* (1836), and R. H. Dana's *Two Years Before the Mast* (1840), which Hopkins enjoyed.[12] Many painters specialized in marine subjects: Turner's wrecks and storms contributed to the myth of the ocean as a dangerous, unstable element, personifying moral and natural forces. Poets used the image of a turbulent sea to express the powerlessness and solitude of the individual: 'Dotting the shoreless watery wild,/ We mortal millions live *alone*', and Arnold connected this with the incomprehensible distance of God.

Shipwrecks were an ever-present reality and a staple ingredient of news. William Whiting's hymn 'Eternal Father, strong to save', still used in Anglican churches, conveys the fear of Victorian coastal communities, and the Revd R. S. Hawker, vicar of Morwenstow, a Cornish community used to wrecks, wrote shipwreck poems with a moral, such as 'The Fatal Ship'. Shipwreck was a recurring theme in sentimental verse for popular recitation:[13] George R. Sims's second most popular ballad, after 'In the Workhouse: Christmas Day', was 'The Lifeboat', and Clement Scott, drama critic of *The Daily Telegraph*, wrote such pieces as 'The Women of Mumbles Head' and 'The Wreck of the Indian Chief'.

More serious poets learned the popular iconography, and exploited sentiments aroused by real situations. Tennyson wrote 'The Wreck' after reading in the *Pall Mall Gazette* of a catastrophe which happened to the *Rosina* on her way to New York. Perhaps the best-known shipwreck poem was Longfellow's 'The Wreck of the Hesperus', written in December 1839, after a disaster in which twenty had perished. It has elements in common with Hopkins's poem: vivid and repeated descriptions of the storm ('The snow fell hissing in the brine,/ And the billows frothed like yeast'), heroic drama, prayer, a powerless crew, dangerous proximity to the shore ('It was the sound of the trampling surf,/ On the rocks and the hard sea-sand'), and horrific detail ('With his face turned to the skies,/ The lantern gleamed through the gleaming snow/ On his fixed and glassy eyes').

Hopkins was drawing on literary convention for subject, details, emotion, and vocabulary. There was also a personal context for the poem's genre in his family experience. The prosperity of the Hopkins family was built on shipwrecks. 'A shipping disaster is a godsend', an article on ship insurance started, 'to some member of a very useful class of the business community—the average staters or average adjusters.'[14]

The subject also gave him opportunities to exploit his developed powers of observing water, sea, and weather.

∽

'The Wreck of the Deutschland' drew on Hopkins's classical learning: it rewrote the Greek choral ode.[15] Pindar, the most imitated Greek ode-writer, was heroic, exalted, bold, and allusive; and out of knowledge and intuition Hopkins chose the Pindaric ode as appropriate to encompass the variety of elements he needed to incorporate in his poem: a story of heroic victory against odds, the narrative of a shipwreck, and a shaping of his personal crisis, argument, and prayer. The highly wrought and stylized Pindaric ode was the ideal form to express Hopkins's determination to carve a shape out of the shapeless details of the *Deutschland*'s and the nuns' fate. As opposed to the incoherent, protracted disaster of the wreck, the ode traditionally exalted humanity and emphasized purposeful fate.

Pindar's Epinician odes started from the occasion of a particular victory in the Games, and enlarged to praise the gods for victory, proclaiming exemplary life and predicting immortality. There is a similar expansion in Hopkins's poem, from a particular occasion to idealizing and generalizing exemplariness. Hopkins, like Pindar, enlarges the significance of a single human occasion until it becomes myth.

Pindar's passion and impetuosity were bridled by strict craftsmanship, and in this way also he was a perfect model for Hopkins. Hopkins did not choose Pindar's triadic form, however, but a monostrophic form close to that of Milton's 'On the Morning of Christ's Nativity', which built up, through a sequence of shorter lines of contrasting lengths, to a weighty concluding alexandrine.

Hopkins took his account of the nun's cry from *The Times* of 11 December 1875, which reported that 'the chief sister, a gaunt woman 6 ft. high' called loudly and often "O Christ, come quickly!" till the end came'. In his sermon at the burial service, Cardinal Manning, as Van Noppen says, 'enlarged upon' the accounts of the final moments:

these holy souls, these good sisters, were so resigned in the tranquillity of their confidence in God, that they showed not the smallest sign of agitation or fear. They remained quietly in their cabin, and when at length they were asked to mount the riggings, as a last chance of safety, they refused—they were already prepared for the great voyage of eternity—life and death were the same to them. When at length a means of escape was at hand they allowed others to take their places and to save themselves.[16]

Hopkins would have known the text of this sermon, and must have made a conscious choice not to have used such a doubtful interpretation of the event. The most detailed eyewitness account was that in *The Daily News*, which gave a different emphasis:

There were five nuns on board who, by their terror-stricken conduct, seem to have added greatly to the weirdness of the scene. They were deaf to all entreaties to leave the saloon, and when, almost by main force, the stewardess (whose conduct throughout was plucky in the extreme) managed to get them on to the companion ladder, they sank down on the steps and stubbornly refused to go another step. They seemed to have returned to the saloon again shortly, for somewhere in the dead of the night when the greater part of the crew and passengers were in the rigging, one was seen with her body half through the sky-light, crying aloud in a voice heard above the storm, 'O, my God, make it quick! make it quick!'[17]

Hopkins could not have checked beyond the immediate accounts in *The Times* or he would have found this and other discrepancies: the tall nun, it emerged later, was not in fact the 'first' of the five, the Superior designate Maria Henrica Fassbaender, but one of the other four. What is important is his determination to find a significance in the tall nun's cry. In stanza 28 the speaker makes the discovery, brilliantly imitating the hard process of arriving at a solution:

> But how shall I . . . make me room there:
> Reach me a . . . Fancy, come faster—
> Strike you the sight of it? look at it loom there,
> Thing that she . . . There then! the Master,
> *Ipse*, the only one, Christ, King, Head:
> He was to cure the extremity where he had cast her;
> Do, deal, lord it with living and dead.

The process of poetic discovery is presented more memorably than the nun's discovery. And at the moment when Hopkins needs to be most explicit, there is some uncertainty as to what he means; commentators vary in their conclusions because it is difficult to see the connection of stanza 28 with 'O Christ, Christ, come quickly!'. What is plain is the method by which Hopkins urges the connection between this event and the personal religious experiences with which the poem starts; the references back from lines 4 and 7 of this stanza to the first in the poem—'Thou mastering me/ God', and 'Lord of living and dead'—are unmistakeable. Just as the poet 'did say yes' in confessing Christ's terror not with his tongue but 'with a fling of the heart', so in the nun 'there was a heart right'; to both the poet and the nun Christ was the 'heart's light'. Hopkins is advocating, not the truths of the logician, but the warmer truths of the poet.

The poem seems to me to look forward less to the joyful Welsh poems than to the tragic Dublin poems. It is a poem about unmaking, unfathering, unchilding; compassion is begged for rather than described; and the acknowledgement of the nature of God (reality) only comes about after harsh and bitter personal torment, physical and mental. 'The jay-blue heavens . . . of pied and peeled May' are there but subordinate to the infinite, unkind air, 'God's cold':

> And the sea flint-flake, black-backed in the regular blow,
> Sitting Eastnortheast, in cursed quarter, the wind;
> Wiry and white-fiery and whirlwind-swivellèd snow.

Delicate and aesthetic, humanly controlled ways of acknowledging God are put forward as counter-suggestion:

> I kiss my hand
> To the stars, lovely-asunder
> Starlight, wafting him out of it; and
> Glow, glory in thunder;
> Kiss my hand to the dappled-with-damson west.

But a more insistent emphasis is given to the confrontations between the protagonist and God's terror: 'I did say yes/ O at lightning and lashed rod', and

> The frown of his face
> Before me, the hurtle of hell
> Behind, where, where was a, where was a place?

The poem is at its most particular and sensuous in articulating violence; stronger than the plea of the final stanza, 'Our King back, Oh, upon English souls!', is the death-stanza:

> 'Some find me a sword; some
> The flange and the rail; flame,
> Fang, or flood' goes Death on drum,
> And storms bugle his fame.
> But we dream we are rooted in earth—Dust!
> Flesh falls within sight of us, we, though our flower the same,
> Wave with the meadow, forget that there must
> The sour scythe cringe, and the blear share come.

Behind the poem's ostensible message of a divinely balanced justice lie echoes of fatalism, disenchantment, and pessimism. There are two counterbalances. One lies in the personal excitement conveyed by Hopkins's idiosyncratic version of the conventional sea-disaster poem. The other is offered by the poem's texture, the vigour of its language, in individual natural images like 'cobbled foam-fleece', 'rash smart sloggering brine', 'bower of bone', and extended metaphor:

> I am soft sift
> In an hourglass—at the wall
> Fast, but mined with a motion, a drift,
> And it crowds and it combs to the fall;

And there is the brilliance of the complete scene:

> They fought with God's cold—
> And they could not and fell to the deck
> (Crushed them) or water (and drowned them) or rolled
> With the sea-romp over the wreck.
> Night roared, with the heart-break hearing a heart-broke rabble,
> The woman's wailing, the crying of child without check—
> Till a lioness arose breasting the babble,
> A prophetess towered in the tumult, a virginal tongue tolled.

The vastness of Hopkins's achievement in breaking away from poetic conventions into such dramatically truthful art is ultimately not ascribable to any influence outside Hopkins himself.

☙

While writing it, Hopkins read parts of 'The Wreck of the Deutschland' to one of his St Beuno's friends, Clement Barraud, the son of a Royal Academician and with artistic leanings. A closer friend of Hopkins, Bacon, a fellow poet who would have been a more sympathetic and painstaking listener, had by this time left St Beuno's, and did not see the poem until later. Barraud 'could understand hardly one line of it', and said later that, although Hopkins's poetry was 'full of tremendous power', it was 'rough and often rudely grotesque'. He should have 'condescended to write plain English', but he 'wilfully set all tradition at defiance'.[18] It may have been Barraud's inability to scan the poem which persuaded Hopkins to mark in accents, and to write a Note on its rhythm and scansion to be printed with the poem.[19]

Preliminary ideas about 'sprung rhythm' had been written into Hopkins's Roehampton lectures, for which he had thought carefully about the different nature and effects of accentual and quantitative verse, and under the heading of 'Rough English accentual verse' had given examples:

Ín Julý   He prepáres to flý,
Ín Augúst   Gó he múst.[20]

Discussing 'The Wreck of the Deutschland' Hopkins said: 'I had long had haunting my ear the echo of a new rhythm which now I realised on paper.'[21] As that implied, this rhythm could be understood only by a correct hearing of the poem. This account is the clearest Hopkins ever wrote, but is still at times difficult, and not always reconcilable with his practice in the poem. The important features have been summarized by Van Noppen: 'A fixed number of rhythmic units per line; each unit is dominated by one speech accent; the accent may be accompanied by any number of weak or slack syllables, or stand alone. There is no metrical substructure.'[22] When a line of the poem is being read, each rhythmic unit in it should last the same amount of time; the number of rhythmic units being, in each stanza, line by line, 'as the indentation guides the eye', wrote Hopkins, 'namely two [in Part the Second three] and three and four and three and five and five and four and six'. The beats (or stresses) had to be strongly marked, Hopkins told his readers.

In the late spring of 1876 he completed the poem. In May he wrote to Fr Henry Coleridge, his 'oldest friend in the Society' and probably the first Jesuit he ever met, and told him about his poem. Coleridge had been editor of *The Month* since 1865, soon after it had been bought by the then Provincial Fr Weld in the hope that it would help the formation of a community of Jesuit writers. Coleridge had been a Fellow of Oriel in his Anglican days, and was a friend of Newman; in 1865 *The Month* had been the first to publish *The Dream of Gerontius*. Coleridge was said to be 'a scholar of the old-fashioned classical type'. Without sending a copy of 'The Wreck of the Deutschland' Hopkins asked Coleridge to accept it for publication, 'but I had to tell him that I felt sure he wd. personally dislike it very much, only that he was to consider not his tastes but those of the *Month*'s readers'. Coleridge replied that 'there was in America a new sort of poetry which did not rhyme or scan or construe; if mine rhymed and scanned and construed and did not make nonsense or bad morality, he did not see why it shd. not do'. On receiving this rash approval, Hopkins sent a copy of the poem (with accents to aid scanning), and the long note for readers; he hoped that he would see it in print in the July 1876 number of *The Month*.

There was a long delay; not until 28 June did Hopkins hear from Coleridge that the poem was too late for July, but would appear in August. There was a snag:

He wants me however to do away with the accents which mark the scanning. I would gladly have done without them if I had thought my readers would scan right unaided but I am afraid they will not, and if the lines are not rightly scanned they are ruined. Still I am afraid I must humour an editor but some lines at all events will have to be marked.[23]

The delay was not so simply explained. According to an account written seventy-eight years later by a friend of a friend of Fr Coleridge, Coleridge had 'read the poem and could not understand it, and he did not relish publishing any poem that he himself could not master'. The poem was not printed in the August *Month*, and Hopkins felt let down and suspicious: 'Whether it will be in the September number or in any I cannot find out', he wrote to his father, 'altogether it has cost me a good deal of trouble.'[24]

By the middle of September he had resigned himself to its rejection. At least, resignation was the mask he chose to confront the outside world: 'About the Deutschland', he told his mother, '"sigh no more", I am glad now it has not appeared.'[25] Apparently an acceptance, but the quotation from *Much Ado About Nothing*[26] significantly continues:

> Sigh no more, ladies, sigh no more,
>   Men were deceivers ever;
> One foot in sea, and one on shore,
>   To one thing constant never.

He must have felt deeply disappointed: *The Month* was not just one possible place of publication, as it would have been to a non-Jesuit; it represented the sanctioned orthodoxy. Even if he could bring himself to offer the poem to another journal, and obtain the necessary permission from his superiors, there would remain the feeling of a rejection by his community. Any answer to the question why Hopkins never again attempted a poem even half as ambitious as 'The Wreck of the Deutschland' has to start with this rejection.

We cannot know the nature of the conversation betwen Hopkins and his Rector in December 1875. Why did Hopkins say to Dixon two years later that *The Month* 'dared' not print the poem?[27] The mask he adopted to cover his hurt became increasingly useful over the following years, as he fitted in less with the standard picture of a Jesuit. By the time he reached Dublin in 1884 he was already regarded as 'eccentric', an unsympathetic and evasive word. In Dublin he was seen as a 'droll jester'. The rejection of 'The Wreck of the Deutschland' began to set up the barrier between Hopkins's central self and the public image, which in Dublin would have become so alienating that he would be forced to express it in the loneliest of poems, written for himself and seen by no one else while he lived: 'To seem the stranger lies my lot. My life/ Among strangers'.

# 'Light, amid the encircling gloom'

Early in 1876 Hopkins was also engaged on the three Silver Jubilee poems.[1] The Catholic hierarchy had been restored to Britain in 1850, and in the following year a bishop had been appointed to the diocese of Shrewsbury, which included the six counties of North Wales. In 1876 the silver jubilee of the first Bishop, James Brown, was celebrated. It was a time for rejoicing over the past and hope for the future.

The mystical value of anniversaries was an aspect of Catholicism which Hopkins, even before his conversion, found congenial. There is a naïvety in his welcoming of anniversaries and numerical coincidences as inscapes of divine origin, which displayed to mankind the connectedness of apparently haphazard aspects of experience. His consolatory letter of October 1877 mentions to his mother the 'happy token' that her father had died on the Feast of the Holy Rosary:

It is a day signalised by our Lady's overruling aid asked for and given at the victory of Lepanto. This year the Anniversary is better marked than usual, for Lepanto was fought on the 7th of October but the feast is kept on the first Sunday of the month whatever this day: this time they coincide. I receive it without questioning as a mark that my prayers have been heard.[2]

The coincidence of two fives is a pivotal point of 'The Wreck of the Deutschland'. Additional proofs of divine synchronism were that the day of the jubilee, Friday 28 July, was Hopkins's thirty-second birthday, and also—he mistakenly, perhaps wilfully, believed—the jubilee of the restoration of Catholicism to North Wales. The Bishop came to stay for a few days at St Beuno's, to honour the Jesuits by celebrating with them the feast of their founder St Ignatius Loyola. At mass on the Sunday morning a special sermon was preached by the Professor of History at St Beuno's, Fr John Morris, and a formal presentation took place in the chapel. The community presented the Bishop with a cheque for £100, and a thick ornate album containing a prose address and compositions, chiefly verse, in many languages penned and decorated in varieties of script and coloured ornament.[3] Hopkins noticed particularly Chinese and Manchoo contributions 'by a little German very very learned, with a beaky nose like a bugle horn . . . beautifully penned by himself'.[4]

Hopkins was responsible for poems in English, Latin, and Welsh. It was not surprising that he was chosen to compose the Latin poem: though it was compulsory at certain times for all St Beuno's theologians to speak the language, good written classical Latin would be hard to find, let alone the linguistic skills practised for Oxford Latin verse compositions. For the Welsh verse, Hopkins wrote, 'they had to come to me, for, sad to say, no one else in the house knows anything about it'.

More significantly, he was chosen from fifty or so highly educated men to compose one of the four English poems. Despite his reluctance to compose unless called for by occasion, and his authorial modesty, shown in his disguise of the authorship of 'The Wreck of the Deutschland' by the pseudonym 'Brân Maenefa', Hopkins must have been known to his colleagues as a poet. This reputation probably followed him from Stonyhurst, where he had written the Marian poems, and 'The Wreck of the Deutschland' would of course be known to the Rector.

Hopkins's reputation among the Jesuits as a writer would be enhanced by 'The Silver Jubilee', which was set to music and performed by the community choir during the dessert at Sunday's high dinner. It 'was set effectively', Hopkins wrote to his father,[5] 'by a very musical and very noisy member of the community and was sung as a glee'. To cap this honour, the largest Catholic publishers in Britain, Burns and Oates, had at the Bishop's request printed a twenty-page pamphlet on white laid paper, containing the sermon, the address, and, on page 19, 'The Silver Jubilee', signed 'G.M.H.'. Hopkins had protested against his poem being included, but Fr Morris had gracefully persuaded him that he needed its publication in order to entitle the sermon 'The Silver Jubilee'. Hopkins told his father about this in a modest letter which failed to disguise excited pride. It was the first work he had published since entering the Society of Jesus, and it was also the only serious complete English poem written after he became a Jesuit which he would ever see in print.

He later wrote to Bridges that, though it was a 'popular' piece 'in which I feel myself to come short', the 'Silver Jubilee I do not regret: it seems to me to hit the mark it aims at without any wrying'.[6] The opening couplet in each stanza has a classical English sound, like that of

Comus' opening speech, but the third line is an imitation of a Welsh measure, called Gorchest-Beirdh by Gray, who used it in 'The Bard':

> Though no high-hung bells or din
> Of braggart bugles cry it in—
>   What is sound? Nature's round
> Makes the Silver Jubilee. . . .

> Then for her whose velvet vales
> Should have pealed with welcome, Wales,
>   Let the chime of a rhyme
> Utter Silver Jubilee.

In these first and last stanzas the device of the internal rhyme fits unobtrusively, with particular success in the last, where sound and meaning joyfully, humorously, and reflexively support each other. The sparseness of the form makes Hopkins happily forgo any descriptive concentration or expansion.

Hopkins also wrote twenty-two Latin couplets for the occasion, but the first nine were found unintelligible, and only thirteen were included in the album. These translate into conventional pieties, but the discarded nine, despite an over-laboured image, show Hopkins meditating imaginatively on the circular rhythms of the universe: a revolving urn with a face on it is compared with the constellation Cassiopeia.[7]

As far as we know, Hopkins wrote only two poems in Welsh, the translation of St Francis Xavier's Latin hymn, and his *cywydd* on Bishop Brown's jubilee. Of the three, it is the Welsh poem which, despite grammatical faults and a loose use of *cynghanedd* in eighteen of its twenty lines, conveys most deeply and directly Hopkins's response to Wales. This comes through even in translation:

Our focal point here is bright and glad with the streamlet of many a fountain, a holy remnant kept for us by Beuno and Winefred. Under rain or dew, you will hardly find a country beneath heaven which is so luxuriant. Weak water brings a faithful testimony to our vale, but man bears no such witness. The old earth, in its appearance, shows an eternal share of virtue; it is only the human element that is faulty; it is man alone that is backward. Father, from thy hand will issue a spring from which will flow the beautiful prime good. Thou bringest by faith a sweet healing, the nourishment of religion; and Wales even now will see true saints—pure, holy, virgin.

> Brân Maenefa sang this
> April the twenty-fourth 1876.[8]

Hopkins expressed similar thoughts a year later in 'In the Valley of the Elwy': 'Lovely the woods, water, meadows, combes, vales,/ All the air things wear that build this world of Wales;/ Only the inmate does not correspond'. This English poem expresses the thought behind the conclusion to the Welsh one: 'Complete thy creature dear O where it fails'.

The image of himself as a rook or crow had been in Hopkins's mind since before his twenty-first birthday, when he had compared his 'unholy' qualities with the 'sweet living' of his friends: 'Eye-greeting doves, bright-counter to the rook',[9] perhaps suggested by Hood's poem 'The Doves and the Crows'. It might have originated at Highgate, where the hero of Clarke's 'The Lady of Lynn' 'puffed out his big black gown/ As he mouthed out the text from a big black book/ He looked like some big, black, eldritch rook'. The idea of himself as a bird of the traditionally 'low' crow family stayed with Hopkins for the rest of his life. Maenefa had its birds, kestrels, and its human inhabitants, its Crows: a common term among Jesuit schoolboys (at Stonyhurst and elsewhere) for their masters was 'crows', because of their black garb and flapping sleeves. When Hopkins later needed a pseudonym for a trio of triolets he had written for the *Stonyhurst Magazine*[10] he chose just 'Brân'.

If the Silver Jubilee poems of April 1876 showed a retreat within narrow poetic limits which allowed little opportunity for Hopkins's most original skills, the two poems written soon afterwards are vividly free-ranging explorations of natural inscape, and unfinished. 'Moonrise June 19 1876' is a solitary, concentrated, and complex meditation on moonlight. Off the north end of Mansions Gallery, where Hopkins's room was probably located, the rooms looked over roofs, chimneys, vegetable plots, and fruit-trees to Maenefa:

I awoke in the midsummer not-to-call night, in the white and the walk
    of the morning:
The moon, dwindled and thinned to the fringe of a fingernail held to the
    candle,
Or paring of paradisaïcal fruit, lovely in waning but lustreless,
Stepped from the stool, drew back from the barrow, of dark Maenefa
    the mountain;
A cusp still clasped him, a fluke yet fanged him, entangled him, not quit
    utterly.
This was the prized, the desirable sight, unsought, presented so easily,
Parted me leaf and leaf, divided me, eyelid and eyelid of slumber.

Solitary awareness is uttered in the opening grandeur of a personal assertion without parallel in any of his previous poetry. The fragment conveys the joy of being able to put into verse the simple affirmation of a direct meeting between himself and nature, 'presented so easily', rather than achieved through will or intellect.

In contrast, 'The Woodlark', written a fortnight later, labours for a medieval ingenuousness:

> 'I am the little woodlark. . . .
> The skylark is my cousin and he
> Is known to men more than me . . .'

Its central section shows Hopkins trying for more concentrated and emotionally heightened descriptions of nature than he put into his journal, more directly suited to his genius than the personification in 'Moonrise':

> The blue wheat-acre is underneath
> And the corn is corded and shoulders its sheaf,
> The ear in milk, lush the sash,
> And crush-silk poppies aflash, . . .

Barraud, possibly the only person to hear Hopkins read 'The Wreck of the Deutschland' at the time of its composition, did not appreciate what he called Hopkins's 'wild freaks'. He preferred those poems which Hopkins wrote 'at times with charming directness'. 'Is it not strange', he wrote, 'that ["The Wreck of the Deutschland"] and "Penmaen Pool" should have come from the same workshop?' 'Penmaen Pool' is a community poem, in fact written 'For the Visitors' Book at the [George] Inn', while Hopkins was on the villa at Barmouth in the second half of August. It is a piece of jolly Victoriana. It steals from William Barnes and from an Emerson poem Hopkins copied down at Balliol; Hopkins was trying to adopt the persona of a bar poet while attempting more ambitious things than the throwaway form allowed:

> And ever, if bound here hardest home,
> You've parlour-pastime left and (who'll
> Not honour it?) ale like goldy foam
> That frocks an oar in Penmaen Pool.

Landlords of the George Inn have been persecuted over the last fifty years by people asking if the 1876 visitors' book still exists.[11] It was probably thrown away.

Another poem of the same period as 'The Wreck of the Deutschland' was a verse paraphrase of a passage from the *Life and Revelations* of St Gertrude, the German mystic. (In 'The Wreck of the Deutschland'

Hopkins had interpreted the coincidence that Luther's birthplace had been the town near which Gertrude had lived in her convent.) This modest piece is seldom commented on, but it came to mean a great deal to Robert Bridges:

> To him who ever thought with love of me
> Or ever did for my sake some good deed
> I will appear, looking such charity
> And kind compassion, at his life's last need
> That he will out of hand and heartily
> Repent he sinned and all his sins be freed.

ତ

At Christmas 1876 Hopkins had written 'without any necessity', he informed Baillie, 'interesting letters of Wellwish' to his 'blackguardly aunts and other kinsfolk and friends'; but did not get 'a line of answer from any one of them', not even from Arthur, who never replied to 'a long letter with criticisms about his Xmas drawings'. Baillie had re-established contact on his return from Africa, where he had gone for his health. Hurt by his relatives' neglect, Hopkins was grateful to Baillie, and as sometimes happened when he received a personal generosity, the usual guard on his emotions was lowered:

I think I had better also do at once what I might have done at any time and that is to say how very kind you have always been to me, how much kinder than I deserved, and that as I am of a blackguardly nature and behaviour (I believe it from my heart and clearly see it) so as compared with you in particular I appear to myself in the light of a blackguard: it is the word that hits my meaning and I must employ it.[12]

Baillie had a more controllable temperament than Hopkins and could also pursue his serious spare-time interests. Besides being proficient in Latin and Greek he had always been interested in living languages, and came back to London eager to follow up his recent acquaintance with Arabic and Egyptian. Hopkins admired Baillie for taking up Arabic, and admitted: 'I fear I shall never know any Arabic, for I do not see my way to going on with my Hebrew even, which is more necessary to me—yet go on with it I feel I must.'

Hopkins's worrying studies were in preparation for his last examination in moral theology at the beginning of March 1877. Moral theology 'covers the whole of life and to know it it is best to begin by knowing everything, as medicine, law, history, banking'. 'If you were to come to learn moral theology', he advised the agnostic Baillie, 'you wd. find your knowledge of law very advantageous. Emphyteusis, laudemium, mohatra, antichresis, hypotheca, servitus activa et passiva . . . these and the like would be pleasant technicalities for you: I have taken them from the treatise on Contracts I am reading.'[13] Behind the humour there is a wish to impress Baillie with the intellectual breadth and validity of his theology, and also a bid for sympathy.

Even when writing to his mother for her birthday on 3 March,[14] his self-preoccupation darkens the celebratory letter: 'going over moral theology over and over again and in a hurry is the most wearisome work, and tonight at all events I am so tired I am good for nothing.' But despite a 'very sharp frost with bitter north winds', there were 'prim-roses about us', and 'in a freak the other day' he had written two sonnets, 'The Starlight Night' and the one he eventually called 'God's Grandeur'; both of these he copied out and sent as a birthday present. Part of the force behind 'The Starlight Night' could have been his disappointment, expressed in the same letter, at having missed the total eclipse of the moon on 28 February because of the community's lack of interest in the night sky: 'Someone on the spot excused himself for not letting us know sooner by saying it was in all the almanacks.'[15]

In both poems the narrator is exasperated at the inability of people to see the grandeur of God in nature:

> Generations have hard trod, have hard trod;
>     And all is seared with trade; bleared, smeared with toil;
>     And bears man's smudge and wears man's smell. The soil
> Is barren; nor can foot feel being shod.[16]

He is determined to reawaken his audience to the energies which drive the God-made world, to nature's expressive outbursts: 'It will flame out, like shining from shook foil'; but the poet needs to goad his listeners to open their eyes:

> O look at all the fire-folk sitting in the air!
> The bright boroughs, the glimmering citadels there!
> Look, the elf rings!

The language changes in the sestets of each sonnet. 'The world is charged' finishes with complex imagery of nature's renewing power, hopeful dawn succeeding dark dusk. The Holy Ghost assumes the physicality and tenderness of a bird enlarged to super-terrestrial size:

> the Holy Ghost over the bent
> World broods with warm breast and with ah! bright wings.

In 'The Starlight Night', after the transformation of the stars into supramundane beings and realms, there is an abrupt descent to abstractions—'Prayer, patience, alms, vows'—spoken by the contrasting voice of religious tradition, which has less emotional force and resonance. Then the 'look, look!' excitement is taken up again:

> Buy then! bid then!—What?—Prayer, patience, alms, vows.
> Look, look: a May-mess, like on orchard boughs!
> Look! March-bloom, like on mealed-with-yellow sallows!

In the last three lines there is again a change of imagery and language; but the drop in tension produces an awkwardly telescoped and obscure metaphorical picture of the barn and its corn-stooks:

> These are the barn, indeed: withindoors house
> The shocks. This pale and parclose hide the spouse
> Christ and the mother of Christ and all His Hallows.

In both octaves there is a vivid sense of Hopkins's urgency to communicate his state of perceptual excitement and the qualities of the natural things which have excited him; but in the sestets it appears to me as if a different, authoritarian voice, representative of tradition, has superimposed an alien framework onto the novel and personal emotions and sights. It is as if the poet's urgent responses have been not just dampened down but blotted out and replaced; as though the poet's demand that the new process of urgent looking be accepted has been answered by a victorious counter-demand that the conventional response, as represented by the traditional currency of 'Prayer, patience, alms, vows', should be reinstated.

❧

Bridges had always been suspicious that Hopkins would compromise his powers when he joined the Jesuits. Among the traditional Protestant prejudices against the Society—that they were prevaricators, dissemblers, and practised in subtle casuistry—was a belief that their educational system repressed individuality in thoughts and expression. This prejudice had seemed to Bridges to be established as a truth by what Hopkins had said about the censorship system just before he entered the novitiate: 'the letters will of course be read and I doubt whether I shall be able to write in answer'.[17] Bridges's irritation that his letters to Hopkins might be read by a Jesuit official was constantly aroused during the twenty years of their relationship. Hopkins tried various ways of calming this reaction of Bridges, by humour, sarcasm, appeals to commonsense, and minimizing the possibility that a letter would actually be looked at. In February that year, for instance, he wrote:

as for your letters being opened—you made that an objection before, I remember—it is quite unreasonable and superstitious to let it make any difference. To be sure they are torn half open—and so for the most part as that one can see the letter has never been out of the envelope—but how can a superior have the time or the wish to read the flood of correspondence from people he knows nothing of which is brought in by the post? No doubt if you were offering me a wife, legacy, or a bishopric on condition of leaving my present life, and someone were to get wind of the purpose of the correspondence, *then* our letters would be well read or indeed intercepted. So think no more of that.[18]

Bridges was defending both prejudice and his right to privacy—a principle which later would cause him to discourage his own prospective biographers: the protective aspect of his affection for Gerard was also strong. It was not in him to be easily convinced. He wrote back huffily, hiding many of his thoughts, and lamely said that he disliked Jesuits; at which Hopkins asked him, reasonably enough, 'Did you ever see one?'[19]

ᘍᕝ

On Saturday 3 March Hopkins underwent 'a very serious examination', 'ad audiendas confessiones', and having passed it with positive votes from all four professors, was now officially knowledgeable and skilful enough to hear confessions. It was probably shortly afterwards that he wrote 'The Lantern'. The previous year he had written humorously to his mother that 'the changes in the Province are like Puss in the Corner and the September ones are sometimes called General Post'. Although constant removal was a basic condition of Jesuit life, the process still wounded:

Much change is inevitable, for every year so many people must begin and so many more must have ended their studies and it is plain that these can seldom step into the shoes left by those, so there is an almost universal shift. . . . Add deaths, sicknesses, leavings, foreign missions, and what not and you will see that ours can never be an abiding city nor aný one of us know what a day may bring forth.

He added in professional justification: 'and it is our pride to be ready for instant despatch'.[20]

The subject was not so quickly dismissed as he pretended to his mother. People were *not* merely parcels for despatch; the separation, by 'death or distance', from a person he had come to be fond of, affected him deeply in his loneliness. (Bacon, one of the few Jesuits who showed appreciation of Hopkins's poetry while he lived, had left.) Such a person was like a lantern in the night, he wrote, in his own adaptation of the image made popular by Newman, the 'Kindly Light, amid the encircling gloom':

> Sometimes a lantern moves along the night.
>    That interests our eyes. And who goes there?
>    I think; where from and bound, I wonder, where,
> With, all down darkness wide, his wading light?
> Men go by me whom either beauty bright
>    In mould or mind or what not else makes rare:
>    They rain against our much-thick and marsh air
> Rich beams, till death or distance buys them quite.

The narrator, prey to unspecified sadness, lives in a timeless darkness, palpable like some black substance. His only healthy relief is the 'wading light', signifying a person rare to his eyes, 'beauty bright/ In mould or mind'. The narrator is stationary and subdued by the hindering atmosphere, yet his mind gains purpose and vigour when greeted by a rare arrival. This vulnerability is suggested by the powerlessness of the 'beams' he sends out, even 'rich' ones, raining against thick air, and also by his inevitable 'death or distance'. The power of the exceptional men (by 'men' Hopkins means *vires* rather than *homines*) is somehow not of this world; it is not surprising that Hopkins would one day half-hope that his Bugler-Boy, 'breathing bloom of a chastity in mansex fine', would be killed prematurely in Afghanistan,[21] passing to a realm which would preserve his unearthly qualities, nor that he praised young geniuses, Keats or Fred Walker, killed before their maturity. Hopkins is thinking in terms of his own kinds of lonely remove (as in the 1885 poem 'To seem the stranger'):

> Death or distance soon consumes them: wind
>    What most I may eye after, be in at the end
>    I cannot, and out of sight is out of mind.

There is a poignancy in the utterance of total deprivation by 'death or distance'. Another biographical significance lies in the importance of eyes and the sense of sight, with the implication that other means of communication are barred ('out of sight is out of mind'). The *seeing* of something dear is everything. Contrary to the spiritual ideal of dis-

1. Hopkins aged about 18.

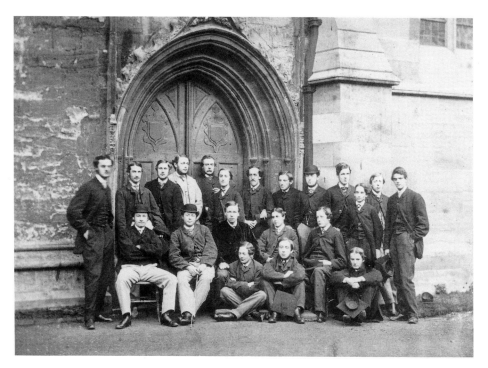

2. A group of Balliol students in 1863, in front of the doors to the Chapel passage. Hopkins is standing sixth from the left, between W. A. Brown and A. Entwisle. A. E. Hardy is seated furthest right, and A. Barratt is the central one of those seated on the ground.

3. Robert Scott, Master of Balliol.

4. Revd Edwin Palmer.

5. T. H. Green.

6. Benjamin Jowett, sketched by Hopkins (enlarged).

7. Garden Quadrangle, Balliol College, north-west corner; Hopkins's room on left, ground floor.

8. Canon H. P. Liddon.

9. Dr E. B. Pusey, by Ape.

10. Manor Farm, Shanklin.

11. Hopkins's sketch of Manor Farm.

12. Hopkins, 'Lord Massey's domain, Co. Dublin. April 22, 1889'.

13. Ruskin, 'Junction of the Aiguille Pourri with the Aiguille Rouge'.

14. 'The present fury is the ash': 'At Manaton . . . I sketched a hanger of ash' (2 September 1867).

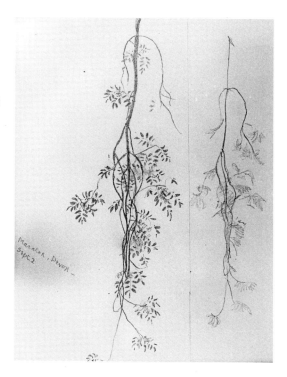

15. 'In a wood of oak and ash. Shanklin. July 11. 1863.'

16. A. W. Garrett, W. A. Comyn Macfarlane, and Hopkins,
photographed on 27 July 1866.

17. Hopkins, photographed by George Giberne.

19. R. W. Dixon.

18. Robert Bridges, 1884.

20. Coventry Patmore.

21. A. W. M. Baillie, *c*.1916.

22. Hopkins in 1880.

23. Oxford Catholic Club in front of St Aloysius', Oxford, 1879. Hopkins stands second from left; Revd T. B. Parkinson is seated second from left.

24. 'Brothers': Henry George Broadbent and James Broadbent, Mount St Mary's College.

25. Revd William Delany SJ, President of
University College, Dublin.

26. Archbishop William J. Walsh.

27. Katharine Tynan.

28. Sir Robert Stewart.

29. Hopkins in April 1888, 'not shopdone but artistically better'. 'The other day as I was walking in our backyard . . . somebody did me instantaneous.'

counting physical presence, the narrator cries out in need of loved and familiar presences.

Many of Hopkins's 1877 sonnets seem to be advocating an acceptance of the *rightness* of the physical world as opposed to the spiritual, while purporting to open people's eyes to the spiritual. This poem dramatizes in a muted way a dependence on his physical meeting. Perhaps the poet had just become able to articulate this complaint through his discoveries in 'The Wreck of the Deutschland' of his new voice and the rationale for using it; in the final three lines the prescribed answer is given:

> Christ minds: Christ's interest, what to avow or amend
> 　There, eyes them, heart wants, care haunts, foot follows kind,
> Their ransom, their rescue, and first, fast, last friend.

It might be argued that the concentration and length of the first eleven lines are more forceful than the counteraction of the final three. The poem's second voice, which speaks the intended clinching argument of Christ's interest, could be said also to lack a dramatic link with the first.

Although in the future he would frequently suffer emotional pain similar to that described in this poem, Hopkins now had solid evidence that he was able to use poetry to define, if not resolve, that pain.

cro

One Sunday evening, soon after the March examination, it was his turn to preach a dominical at supper in the community refectory: 'While by eating the body is refreshed', stated a rule of Ignatius' in the Jesuit Constitutions, 'let the soul also have her food.' The Gospel for the day had been St John's account of the feeding of the five thousand, and Hopkins took as his text: 'Then Jesus said: Make the men sit down.'[22] One of the least pregnant sentences in the account, its ordinariness must have been seen by Hopkins as a challenge to his powers of imaginative transformation and expansion. To fix the minds of his audience he started with a conventional Ignatian composition:

Let us do as we are accustomed—return to the story, turn it over and dwell on it, go in mind to that time and in spirit to that place . . . go along with me, in mind, I say, and in spirit, not in the body, for you are as when Our Lord said: make the men sit down.

Attempting to make his seated audience part of the composition he again repeated the key phrase: 'let the men sit down', adding 'that is/ be at rest be still, be attentive, listen for what is to come'. His audience were asked to imagine the scene of Christ's miracle, the Sea of Galilee, which Hopkins tried to bring home by transposing to the Clwyd valley, almost the same length. If the maps of the two areas were superimposed, their local Welsh villages and towns could be in equivalent positions to the Bible places:

St. Asaph would be where the Jordan enters the valley; Bethsaida Julias would be Rhuddlan . . . Tiberias would be Denbigh; Chorozain might be Bodfari; and the place of the miracle seems to have been at the north end of the lake, on the east side of the Jordan, as it might be at this very spot where we are now upon the slope of Maenefa.

Nothing could better illustrate the ingenuity and directness of Hopkins's imaginative powers, and the naïvety with which he sometimes applied them. Though this transposition from Galilee to north Wales was made with geographical neatness, the list of equivalent place-names crowds too much detail into the attention of men at table at the end of a day's work. The speaker weakened his narrative thread further by suggesting that they think of the sea's shape as 'something like a bean or something like a man's left ear', without anticipating ludicrous associations. Hopkins's intention to 'say what may be useful to you in thinking of places where our Lord often was' was jeopardized by fussy asides, such as over the name Philip and the 'boy' with the food: 'There is a boy here—*a little boy* it is in the Greek, *just a boy* in the Latin: certainly a little boy . . . to be sure a little boy, just a boy.'

Hopkins's eye was sometimes more on himself than on his audience: when dealing with Andrew's name he had written 'Manly' not 'manly'. He was turning over words and ideas already expressed in 'The Wreck of the Deutschland': 'Crown Him now who can crown you then, kiss the hand that holds the dreadful rod'; and the Galilee scene, like that at the Kentish Knock sandbank, 'was full of the sense of royal majesty, of more than prophetic power, of divine glory'. Occasionally the language rose to poetic heights: 'this world's studs and steeds and splendour, its chivalry and chariots and chargers'.

The sermon was not a success. After fifteen minutes he had dealt with only the first nine short verses of the biblical account, and had clarified neither argument nor purpose. He tried to rectify the situation by repeating the key phrase, hoping to generate power and significance by iteration:

The lord and master spoke now: *Make the men sit down.* . . . the gentle but great and undeniable word was in their ears driving them down into the thousands below: *Make those men sit down.* . . . Suddenly the thunder had rolled over their heads . . . and all the place was full of the sense of royal majesty . . . of divine glory: *Make the men sit down.* . . . Down fell the men to table . . . fifty in this company, a hundred in that; not one man more, not one less; down I tell you, the master has spoken.

Hopkins's voice was inclined to become shrill and lose authority when raised. His ineffective dramatization proved too much for the audience, and he recorded:

People laughed at it prodigiously, I saw some of them roll on their chairs with laughter. This made me lose the thread, so that I did not deliver the last two paragraphs right but mixed things up. The last paragraph, in which *Make the men sit down* is often repeated, far from having a good effect, made them roll more than ever.

The last five minutes of the sermon were not delivered.

છ

When Hopkins described Philip's failings in his sermon he added, as examples of human shortcomings, some of his own: 'I speak', he said, 'of what I know in myself':

if we are sad we think we shall never be happy more, though the same thing has happened to us times and times; if we are sick we despair of ever getting well, though human nature every day is in some one or other sickening and recovering. . . . if tired we complain as if no sleep or rest would ever refresh us.

Although his examinations were over for the time being, he did not have enough energy for a prompt reply to Bridges; when he did write he felt drained, and replied testily: 'You have no call to complain of my delay in writing, I could not help it: I am not a consulting physician and have little time and now I am very very tired, yes "a thousand times and yet a thousand times" and "scarce can go or creep".'[23] (Bridges was now working in the casualty department of St Bartholomew's Hospital, where during 1878 he treated 30,940 patients.[24]) Hopkins was also worried about a paper he had to prepare, and told his mother: 'I have a cold and cough just now, things I seldom have, but they are going away; and I am thinner, I think, than ever I was before now, but hope to be all right with summer.'[25]

His Holy Week holidays had not gone as planned. Since his Welsh lessons had stopped the previous year, Hopkins's struggles with the language had been frustrating: 'I can read easy prose and can speak stumblingly', he told Baillie, 'but at present I find the greatest difficulty, amounting mostly to total failure, in understanding it when spoken and the poetry . . . I can make little way with.'[26] At the end of

March he went to Caernarvon to improve his Welsh, with an old Oxford acquaintance, Fr J. H. Jones, the priest in charge of SS Peter and Paul, on the rocky Twt Hill, overlooking the town. Fr Jones had been received into the Catholic Church by Newman the year before Hopkins and left Oxford without taking a degree; he was reputed to be the only Catholic priest who could preach in Welsh. Hopkins intended to stay for a fortnight, but had to return after three days 'on account of a misfortune which overtook my host's servant'.[27] As some compensation, the minister at St Beuno's sent Hopkins and two others for a Saturday jaunt with pony and trap, an occasional indulgence allowed to those run down in health.

Towards the end of April Hopkins was very busy. He had been asked for a poem to commemorate the visit to St Beuno's of the famous Dominican preacher, Fr Thomas Burke, itinerant in the Order of Preachers' tradition. His methods were legendary:

When Fr. Burke ascended the pulpit, he looked around on the vast congregation, and throwing out his right hand he cried three times in crescendo: 'To hell with the Jesuits.' So intense was the effect that the bated breath of the congregation was almost visible. Even his dramatic pause, after his astounding statement, increased anxiety. 'Such', he remarked quietly, 'is the cry of today.'[28]

He had achieved great success in the United States, where he aroused American sympathy and English antipathy by fierce criticism of British policy in Ireland.

Though unsuccessful in his preaching, Hopkins must have been building up a reputation as someone who could be relied on for occasional verse. He duly produced, on St George's Day, a thirty-eight line poem in Latin, 'Ad Reverendum Patrem Fratrem Thomam Burke O.P. Collegium S. Beunonis Invisentem';[29] but this was no ordinary presentation piece. It started with a private joke: 'In the whiteness of his clothing he was nearer than we are to the guileless doves'—'we' being, Hopkins implying, black-clothed crows. The poem continued with a description, a shade too objective, of the strange appearance of the monk among the St Beuno's Jesuits: 'by his dress was such as might call to mind a sheep'. References followed to the Dominican tradition of St Thomas Aquinas, the approved theologian of the Jesuits.

Before the eighteenth century, scholastic philosophers had been divided into Scotists and Thomists. There was bitter war between them. This had died down, with scholasticism generally, in the eighteenth century: 'Scotists and Thomists now in peace remain./ Amidst their kindred cobwebs in Duck Lane', Pope had written. In the nineteenth century Scotus had been neglected, Catholics being encouraged to follow Aquinas' teachings. Hopkins tried to reopen the pre-eighteenth-century controversy. Full of enthusiasm for the great Franciscan opponent of Thomism, he could not resist an impolitic assault on eminent Dominican theologians who had been apologists for Aquinas against Scotus's attacks:

[Burke is] one skilled at interpreting the oracular words of Thomas Aquinas, if indeed there is still anything obscure in the utterance of him whom Gudinus [Antoine Goudin], Godatus [Pedro de Godoy], Gonetus [Jean Baptiste Gonet] and Cajetanus [Tommaso di Vio] strive to make so clear, who has already long endured countless interpreters, and whom each man twists, without hesitation, to suit his own conceptions.

This is the first indication that his increasing allegiance to Scotism involved some antagonism towards the prescribed Thomist teachings, as well as revision of his own recent training.

He may have hoped that his Latin and covert allusions would mask his feelings. The poem finished with a personal confrontation, its defensive jingoism perhaps prompted by St George's Day: 'Such a man I should now warmly greet; but one doubt keeps me hesitant, namely, whether he would wish to be praised by me, an Englishman he who (in controversy) lays my countrymen low throughout the world.' Such prickly panegyric was not ingratiating. A month afterwards, a group of Franciscans from the nearby Pantasaph Monastery came to dine at St Beuno's, and a recitation in honour of St Francis was given,[30] but Hopkins was apparently not asked to contribute.

He expressed disagreement with Aquinas and sympathy for Duns Scotus in a more open and personal way in an untitled poem he wrote about this time. One of the features which distinguished Scotism from Thomism was its emphasis on the importance of being as being, rather than essence, and on Man's ability to know a particular object by intuition rather than ratiocination:

> As kingfishers catch fire, dragonflies draw flame;
>     As tumbled over rim in roundy wells
>     Stones ring; like each tucked string tells, each hung bell's
> Bow swung finds tongue to fling out broad its name;
> Each mortal thing does one thing and the same:
>     Deals out that being indoors each one dwells;
>     Selves—goes itself; *myself* it speaks and spells.
> Crying *What I do is me: for that I came.*

Behind this impassioned advocacy of the individuality of objects lies an indictment of colder methods of perception, of certain emphases in the official Thomist theological course; there is an assertion that the rightness of the senses should be recognized. The poem is a determined plea that physical beauty be acknowledged to have moral value, that attraction to aspects of the physical world may be sanctioned by a recognition of their moral status; there is surely also a defence of the poet's practice.

The final three lines make a more personal plea for the sanctification of human beauty:

> I say more: the just man justices;
>   Keeps grace: that keeps all his goings graces;
> Acts in God's eye what in God's eye he is—
>   Christ. For Christ plays in ten thousand places,
> Lovely in limbs, and lovely in eyes not his
>   To the Father through the features of men's faces.

Hopkins was dissatisfied with the poem; it never got beyond the draft stage, and was not sent to Bridges.

# 'In my salad days, in my Welsh days'

In April 1877 the architect William Butterfield had sent, in reply to a request from Hopkins, a complete list of his buildings, and in a letter of thanks Hopkins expressed his affinity with Butterfield's work, though he disliked some of its oddnesses:

... yr beautiful and original style. I do not think this generation will ever much admire it. They do not understand how to look at a Pointed building as a whole having a single form governing it throughout, which they *would* perhaps see in a Greek temple: they like it to be a sort of farmyard and medley of ricks and roofs and dovecots. And very few people seem to care for pure beauty of line, at least till they are taught to.[1]

It is tempting to think that by 'a sort of farmyard and medley of ricks and roofs and dovecots' Hopkins was referring to the lazily higgledy-piggledy groupings of Joseph Hansom's St Beuno's buildings, and contrasting them with the secretive, scholarly, centripetal unity of Butterfield's works, which people found so difficult to understand. There is more than a hint of fellow-feeling in Hopkins's disparagement of a public which looked for and could see only the most simplified form of unity; 'this generation' were quite unable to see the more subtle, deeper unity which came from a single organic governing principle. He felt allied with Butterfield, standing up for principled originality, at however great a cost in immediate recognition, but he conceded, if grudgingly, that it might be necessary to help the public appreciate difficult art.

A few days later he was creating a work of art in which, he later admitted, 'the sense gets the worst of it ... it exists but is far from glaring'.[2] The second week in May, in a conventional rather than thoughtful gesture of his superiors, he was sent to Rhyl for five days. Rhyl was a flat, dull town of terraced houses, populous with holiday-makers from Manchester, Liverpool, and the Midlands manufacturing towns, who were attracted to its long beach and undemanding amusements. Feeling 'this shallow and frail town' to be shamed by the purity of nature, he composed a poem which became 'The Sea and the Skylark':

### Walking by the Sea

On ear and ear two noises too old to end
  Trench—right, the tide that ramps against the shore;
  By flood, by fall, low-lull-off or all: roar
Frequenting there while moon shall wear and wend;

Left hand, off land, I hear the lark ascend
  With rash-fresh more, repair of skein and score,
  Race wild reel round, crisp coil deal down to floor,
And spill music till there's none left to spend.

In a letter to Bridges some years later Hopkins wrote that this poem was 'the greatest offender in its way that you could have found. It was written in my Welsh days, in my salad days, when I was fascinated with *cynghanedd* or consonant-chime.'[3] The waves' in-and-out motion and the lark's rise are actualized with a wonderful freshness.

On this occasion, as so often, Bridges represents the bewildered reader. He objected to the lark-description—who could say what was meant by 'rash-fresh more', 'repair', 'skein', 'score', 'reel', 'crisp coil', 'deal'? Hopkins's gloss provides an interesting contrast to any innocent-ear interpretation:

The word is *more* and is a midline rhyme to *score*, as in the next line *round* is meant in some way to rhyme to *down*. 'Rash-fresh more' (it is dreadful to explain these things in cold blood) means a headlong and exciting new snatch of singing, resumption by the lark of his song, which by turns he gives over and takes up again all day long, and this goes on, the sonnet says, through all time, without ever losing its first freshness, being a thing both new and old. *Repair* means the same thing, *renewal, resumption*. The skein and coil are the lark's song, which from his height gives the impression (not to me only) of something falling to the earth and not vertically quite but tricklingly or wavingly, something as a skein of silk ribbed by having been tightly wound on a narrow card or a notched holder or as fishingtackle or twine unwinding from a reel or winch: [or as pearls strung on a horsehair] the laps or folds are the notes or short measures and bars of them. The name is called a score in the musical sense of scores and this score is 'writ upon a liquid sky trembling to welcome it', only not horizontally. The lark in wild glee races the reel round, paying or dealing out and down the turns of the skein or coil right to the earth floor, the ground, where it lies in a heap, as it were, or rather is all wound off on to another winch, reel, bobbin, or spool in Fancy's eye by the moment the bird touches earth and so is ready for a fresh unwinding at the next flight.[4]

As Hopkins said ruefully, there was 'plenty meant'. When he revised the poem later, he felt he had lost 'the freshness I wanted'; but some of the images and rhythms in the revised version keep this freshness— 'crisps of curl off wild winch whirl'.

His descriptions of sea and skylark told of something much more idiosyncratic and complex than 'purity', however. The motivation for complaint is puzzlingly distant from his summarized statement:

> How these two shame this shallow and frail town!
>     How ring right out our sordid turbid time,
> Being pure! We, life's pride and cared-for crown,
>
>     Have lost that cheer and charm of earth's past prime:
> Our make and making break, are breaking, down
>     To man's last dust, drain fast towards man's first slime.

'Our sordid turbid time' is a rejection of his everyday life, of everything man-made and man-ordered; in the disgust of the last two lines, and in the contrast of the shallow seaside town with fresh nature, Hopkins showed how far he was from being in sympathy with the common world and its emotions.

He returned from Rhyl on 14 May, and on the following Saturday began the five-day Whitsun holiday, walking and writing poetry. 'Spring' starts with a burgeoning sound, a hyperbole, which is followed by an ecstatic scene of movements, shapes, sounds, textures, and colour:

> Nothing is so beautiful as Spring—
>     When weeds, in wheels, shoot long and lovely and lush;
>     Thrush's eggs look little low heavens, and thrush
> Through the echoing timber does so rinse and wring
> The ear, it strikes like lightnings to hear him sing;
>     The glassy peartree leaves and blooms, they brush
>     The descending blue; that blue is all in a rush
> With richness; the racing lambs too have fair their fling.

The contrast of the sestet's interpretation is startling:

> What is all this juice and all this joy?
>     A strain of the earth's sweet being in the beginning
> In Eden garden.—Have, get, before it cloy,
>
>     Before it cloud, Christ, lord, and sour with sinning,
> Innocent mind and Mayday in girl and boy,
>     Most, O maid's child, thy choice and worthy the winning.

Tone, pace, and imagery have changed. The poem's success depends on an acceptance of a world of significance beyond the physical. First there is a withdrawal from the excruciatingly sharp experience of spring's phenomena—from the meeting of nature's lush textures and vivid communication to open and receptive human faculties. The voice of the removed commentator, absent since the opening line, asks what lies behind these excitements of the season, and the answer comes that it is what is left of the God-given, innocent paradise of the Garden of Eden. In the simplicity of this answer lie its strength and its weakness. To some people the poem is moving and powerful; to others the interpretation of the spring phenomenon appears incomplete, naïve, or extraneous.

In 'Spring' the poet was unable to go on facing the human world, picturing it as fallen and degenerate. In a poem possibly written during the same Whitsun holiday, man's fate is described as 'in drudgery, day-labouring-out life's age':

### The Caged Skylark

As a dare-gale skylark scanted in a dull cage
    Man's mounting spirit in his bone-house, mean house, dwells—
    That bird beyond the remembering his free fells,
This in drudgery, day-labouring-out life's age.

Though aloft on turf or perch or poor low stage,
    Both sing sometimes the sweetest, sweetest spells,
    Yet both droop deadly sometimes in their cells
Or wring their barriers in bursts of fear or rage.

Not that the sweet-fowl, song-fowl, needs no rest—
Why, hear him, hear him babble and drop down to his nest,
    But his own nest, wild nest, no prison.

Man's spirit will be flesh-bound when found at best,
But uncumberèd: meadow-down is not distressed
    For a rainbow footing it nor he for his bones risen.

'The Caged Skylark' is one of the few poems written at St Beuno's which achieves a complex, passionate argument. The imagery beautifully conveys the mind's-eye translations of body and bird. Hopkins's imagery for man's lot ('This in drudgery, day-labouring-out life's age') and his physical condition ('in his bone-house, mean house, dwells') is more fully realized and of more immediate power than the imagery for spiritual aspirations and possibilities ('mounting spirit'). The 'sweetest, sweetest spells' on a 'poor low stage' engage the listener's sympathetic faculties less than 'droop deadly sometimes in their cells/ Or wring their barriers in bursts of fear or rage'. ('Sweet' is, I suggest, one of Hopkins's overdone words, seldom used in his poems with precision or power.) The poet is plainly affected by man's condition, but drawn, dragged within it, whereas the spiritual possibilities of escape from that human condition are envisaged less confidently, despite the lovely 'rainbow footing' image.

එ∂

On the last day of his Whitsun holiday, Hopkins wrote another sonnet, possibly his third within the four days:

### In the Valley of the Elwy

I remember a house where all were good
  To me, God knows, deserving no such thing:
  Comforting smell breathed at very entering,
Fetched fresh, as I suppose, off some sweet wood.

That cordial air made those kind people a hood
  All over, as a bevy of eggs the mothering wing
  Will, or mild nights the new morsels of Spring:
Why, it seemed of course; seemed of right it should.

Lovely the woods, waters, meadows, combes, vales,
All the air things wear that make this house, this Wales;
  Only the inmate does not correspond:

God, lover of souls, swaying considerate scales,
Complete thy creature dear O where it fails,
  Being mighty a master, being a father and fond.

Receiving another request from Bridges for elucidation, Hopkins explained:

The kind people of the sonnet were the Watsons of Shooter's Hill [on the edge of Greenwich Park, south-east of London], nothing to do with the Elwy. The facts were as stated. You misunderstand the thought, which is very far fetched. The frame of the sonnet is a rule of three sum *wrong*, thus: As the sweet smell to those kind people so the Welsh landscape is NOT to the Welsh; and then the author and principle of all four terms is asked to bring the sum right.[5]

Besides the explicit contrast between the unworthiness of the people who dwell in Wales and the beautiful natural world they inhabit, there is a hidden biographical comparison between the sweet and comforting peace of the household and the harsh institutional surroundings that were Hopkins's habitat. The 'mothering wing' in the second stanza is a reminder that Hopkins was un-mothered in the Jesuits.

eʌɔ

A week later, at the end of May, a month during which he had already composed probably four poems, Hopkins wrote 'The Windhover'. It became his favourite poem of this creative year. Many happinesses seem to be behind the poem: it was his recreation day, the weather was seasonal, he was in a congenial place, he had been successful in his examinations (and the next one was some way off), and there were those completed poems.

The kestrel was very much a Clwyd bird (common around Cŵm and, to a lesser extent, on Maenefa). Hopkins saw it as an exotic bird, particularly when he heard it given the appropriate name 'windhover':

### The Windhover

I caught this morning morning's minion, king
  Of daylight's dauphin, dapple-dawn-drawn Falcon, in his riding
  Of the rolling level underneath him steady air, and striding
High hung so and rung the rein of a wimpled wing
In an ecstasy; then off, forth on swing
  As a skate's heel sweeps smooth on a bow-bend: the hurl and gliding
  Rebuffed the big wind. My heart in hiding
Stirred for a bird,—the achieve of, the mastery of the thing!

Brute beauty and valour and act, oh, air, pride, plume, here
  Buckle! AND the fire that breaks from thee then, a billion
Times told lovelier, more dangerous, O my chevalier!

  No wonder of it: sheer plod makes plough down sillion
Shine, and blue-bleak embers, ah my dear,
  Fall, gall themselves, and gash gold-vermilion.

Two actions of the falcon are represented: his riding of the wind, holding his forward action steady, as though motionless, by using the rapid wing movement as a rein, and his sweep into a glide. The excitement and high-pitched intensity of the octave is effected by a madrigal medley of sound devices: nearly every line has its characteristic one, two, or three consonants. The bird's hovering is imitated by the long first sentence continuing from line to line, and the elaborate adjectival clusters preceding 'Falcon' and 'air', the bird's incessant, tense activity by the pressure of the narrator's exclamatory voice, and the immediacy by the first-person-singular opening, whose Herbertian casual conversational entrance introduces a more intense scene. At the transformation point, the repetition of 'morning', the bird's action is enlarged into acts of a chivalric herald.

At moments in the octave Hopkins is at his best: meaning, expression, rhythm, and emotion seem to be simultaneously perfect—'how he rung upon the rein of a wimpling wing/ In his ecstasy' (in the revised version), 'dapple-dawn-drawn'. His special kind of earnestness over the exact representation of an action triumphs in 'the rolling level underneath him steady air'.

The bird's state of ecstasy, in tension and stasis, is like the perceptive onlooker and non-participant, appreciating mortal beauty with quivering sensitivity and apprehensive understanding, yet held at the invisible wall of religious rule, never allowing the natural forces of mingling and communion to overcome his plodding, dogmatic will. The onlooker who cannot participate—'my heart in hiding stirred'—Hopkins cannot himself make the kind of display he admires in others.

In the sestet, the constituents of the falcon's performances are metamorphosed into parts of armour, which the chivalric lord Christ is entreated to buckle on, that he may appear in his glory, the windhover's qualities being merely one minute, exemplary part of the infinitely greater glory of God ('Ad maiorem Dei gloriam'). The two images of the last three lines form a magnificent ending; and in the fond address, 'ah my dear', Hopkins again borrows from his favourite Herbert.

જ્જી

The strain of study for the July examinations in dogmatic theology is evident in the terse letter to Bridges on 13 June:

I see I must send a line to 'put you out of your agony'. Want of convenience of writing was the only cause of my delay. Having both work here to do and serious letters to write I shrank from the 'distressing subject' of rhythm on which I knew I must enter. I could not even promise to write often or answer promptly, our correspondence lying upon unprofessional matter. . . . I cannot write more now.[6]

Jesuit theology students were examined orally at the end of every year of the course, for half an hour for their first two years, and for an hour in the third-year examination. In the previous year, the Superior General of the Jesuits had listed certain complaints he had heard about the examinations at St Beuno's: 'The examiners were too indulgent, the students were ill-prepared in moral theology, in dogmatic theology they could not adequately discriminate among various doctrinal positions, and passing grades were given too easily'. As a result, 1876–7 had been a year of academic reform and tightening of standards.

On Sunday 22 July Hopkins was examined for an hour by four professors, Fathers Perini, Tepe, Frins, and Hayden. They awarded him two low positive and two negative votes, noticeably lower grades than those of previous years. He needed at least three positive votes to enter the fourth year of theology. Of the fourteen classmates, ten were allowed to enter their fourth year. According to one of his contemporaries, Joseph Rickaby: 'in speculative theology [Hopkins] was a strong Scotist, and read Scotus assiduously. That led to his being plucked at the end of his third year: he was too Scotist for his examiners.'[7] As Thomas says, 'since he was examined orally any differences between him and his teachers would have been more likely magnified than diminished'.[8] Fr Lahey, interviewing people who had known Hopkins, recorded that his 'avocation for Scotism eventually became a passion with him . . . so that he was often embroiled in minor duels of intellect'.[9] Irish colleagues wrote that his 'obstinate love of Scotist doctrine . . . got him into difficulties with his Jesuit preceptors who followed Aquinas and Aristotle'; and concluded that 'the strain of controversy . . . had marred his earlier years'.[10]

Hopkins's keenness for Scotus was at its height in 1877. Several years later he looked back nostalgically to the days when he 'used to read [Scotus] with delight'. Hopkins's sympathy for Scotus was like that he felt for Butterfield:

He saw too far, he knew too much; his subtlety overshot his interests; a kind of feud arose between genius and talent, and the ruck of talent in the Schools finding itself, as his age passed by, less and less able to understand him, voted that there was nothing important to understand and so first misquoted and then refuted him.[11]

Three days later Hopkins set off for a fortnight at Oak Hill. He visited Bridges at Bedford Square for dinner, and stayed the night; they discussed music, and each other's poetry. After the visit he wrote half-humorously about Bridges's poems: 'It seems that triolets and rondels and rondeaus and chants royal and what not and anything but serving God are all the fashion.'[12] Nevertheless, he recommended *The Growth of Love* to his mother, 'for they are very beautiful sonnets, designedly written in Miltonic rhythms but not violent like mine'. He added, 'I feel quite proud of them'. As no one at St Beuno's was interested in Bridges's poems, he would try to send his own copy to Oak Hill.[13] He made sure that Bridges had a complete set of his own sonnets, corrected up to date, and as soon as it arrived from St Beuno's, he sent him a copy of 'The Wreck of the Deutschland', with accents. Bridges was keen that they should meet again while Hopkins was in London, but after seeing the Provincial at Farm Street, Hopkins cut short his stay to return to St Beuno's. 'Much against my inclination', he wrote sadly to Bridges, 'I shall have to leave Wales.'[14] On his temporary return to St Beuno's to await news of his next posting, 'no sooner were we among the Welsh hills than I saw the hawks flying and other pleasant sights soon to be seen no more'.[15] In the village of Tremeirchion, he composed a curtal sonnet celebrating his joy at these brilliant sights. As though making sure that its theological purpose should be seen to be above reproach, the poem was framed—like all pieces of work done in Jesuit schools and colleges—by A.M.D.G. (Ad maiorem Dei gloriam) at its head, and L.D.S. (Laus Deo semper) at its finish, except that the initials were expanded and the Latin, translated into English, became the first and last words of the poem:

### Pied Beauty

Glory be to God for dappled things—
  For skies of couple-colour as a brinded cow;
    For rose-moles all in stipple upon trout that swim;
Fresh-firecoal chestnut-falls; finches' wings;
  Landscape plotted and pieced—fold, fallow, and plough;
    And all trades, their gear and tackle and trim.

All things counter, original, spare, strange;
  Whatever is fickle, frecklèd (who knows how?)
    With swift, slow; sweet, sour; adazzle, dim;
He fathers-forth whose beauty is past change:
                    Praise him.

It is a poem of self-display, the narrative voice carrying a pride of achievement at the great generalized discovery of 'dappled things', and the marvellous words representing them. The voice is somewhat at odds with that of the earlier 1877 poems, where its role had purported to be a more priestly one of guiding the onlookers or readers to enlarge their *own* perceptions. Hopkins is praising and advocating a group of qualities not merely unusual but contrary to the orthodox: the poem might be seen as an attack on the idea of God as the god of the conventional.

The poem is an organised, summarized version of the Ruskinian description of contrast patterns in nature: 'Then you approve of variety over absolute uniformity. And variety is opposed to regularity, is it not?' the Professor of Aesthetics had asked Hanbury in 'On the Origin of Beauty'. 'Certainly', replied Hanbury.[16] Like the Impressionist painters, Hopkins realized that vividness was brought about by the conjunction of opposites. The poem proceeds by listing the speaker's likes. The line 'And all trades, their gear and tackle and trim' extends nature to that art made by nature, and enables us to read 'All things counter, original, spare, strange' as including the poet's pride in his words.

ↄ

Bridges sent a long letter criticizing 'The Wreck of the Deutschland' and enclosing a parody. He found the poem full of licences, although he knew that that would not disturb Hopkins, who could justify anything if he wanted to. He objected to some of the rhymes and quantities, to the poem's 'outriding feet', and to 'sprung rhythm'. Was such an invention necessary? The poem might be called 'presumptious juggl-ery'; it was obscure, and should be altered. Not for any money would he read it again.

Hopkins replied with a long and measured defence of his own practices, not revealing, except by an occasional sharpness, any hurt he felt. Bridges's reactions were no worse than those of others who had seen the poem: 'Your parody reassures me about your understanding the metre. Only remark as you say that there is no conceivable licence I shd. not be able to justify, that with all my licences, or rather laws, I am stricter, than you and I might say than anybody I know.'[17] His rhymes were true to the ear, if not to sight: 'apparent licences are counter-balanced, and more, by my strictness', and 'all English verse, except Milton's almost, offends me as "licentious". Remember this.' Bridges was mistaken about outriding feet, of which there were none in the 'Wreck'. As for sprung rhythms Hopkins did not claim to have invented them, but to have 'enfranchised them as a regular and permanent principle of scansion'. He employed sprung rhythm because 'it is the nearest to the rhythm of prose, that is the native and natural rhythm of speech'. It combined 'markedness of Rhythm' and 'naturalness of expression'. Why, he asked, 'if it is forcible in prose to say "lashed: rod", am I obliged to weaken this in verse, which ought to be stronger, not weaker, into "láshed birch-ród" or something?'

He repeated that 'my verse is less to be read than heard ... it is oratorical, that is the rhythm is so'. As for its 'presumptious jugglery', it could not be called that, 'only for this reason, that *presumptious* is not English'. He could not think of altering anything: 'Why shd. I? I do not write for the public. You are my public and I hope to convert you.' Reference to himself was 'all strictly and literally true and did all occur; nothing is added for poetical padding'. He finished the letter with a plea that Bridges would reread the poem in a more sympathetic and serviceable spirit; his present criticism was useless, being 'only a protest memorialising me against my whole policy and proceedings':

You say you wd. not for any money read my poem again. Nevertheless I beg you will. Besides money, you know, there is love. If it is obscure do not bother yourself with the meaning but pay attention to the best and most intelligible stanzas, as the two last of each part and the narrative of the wreck.[18]

&

Hopkins's last poem before leaving Wales for good was, as he later told Bridges, 'the outcome of half an hour of extreme enthusiasm as I walked home alone one day from fishing in the Elwy':[19]

### Hurrahing in Harvest

Summer ends now; now, barbarous in beauty, the stooks rise
Around; up above, what wind-walks! what lovely behaviour
Of silk-sack clouds! has wilder, wilful-wavier
Meal-drift moulded ever and melted across skies?

I walk, I lift up, I lift up heart, eyes,
Down all that glory in the heavens to glean our Saviour?
And, eyes, heart, what looks, what lips yet gave you a
Rapturous love's greeting of realer, of rounder replies?

And the azurous hung hills are his world-wielding shoulder
Majestic—as a stallion stalwart, very-violet-sweet!—
These things, these things were here and but the beholder
Wanting; which two when they once meet,
The heart rears wings bold and bolder
And hurls for him, O half hurls earth for him off under his feet.

Hopkins's most ecstatic poem has one of his best beginnings. A strong stress on 'ends' is followed by the almost silent dropping away of 'now'; and the repeated low 'now' prepares for the shooting up of the emphatically 'barbarous' stooks of corn. The textures and meanings of 'barbarous' and 'beauty' play against each other, in a vivid pieing process. The ecstatically heightened involvement of the narrator is shown by the exaggerated textural description of the clouds as 'silk', a word which elevates and changes 'sack'. This is not objectivity but fondness. The emotion carries the verse forward in its enthusiastic exclamatory speech, intensified by the repeated 'I' in Hopkins's most egoistically assertive line: 'I walk, I lift up, I lift up heart, eyes'. The poet realizes the sexual nature of the responses, but hides it by saying that this response is more powerful than a sexual one: 'What looks, what lips yet gave you a/ Rapturous love's greeting of realer, of rounder replies?' 'Lips' suggests kisses, not words.

There is a lowering of tension in the middle of the sestet—'these things were here and but the beholder/ Wanting' (similar to 'only the inmate does not correspond' in the Elwy Valley poem). This increases the effect of the ending, in the magnificent climax of the ideal meeting between nature's glory and the beholder, when—if it were to take place—the heart would finally come out of hiding.

လ

All Jesuit activities had to be directed 'To the greater glory of God'. In 'The Wreck of the Deutschland' Hopkins had worked out the rationalization he needed to take up poetry seriously again, and now he had the ostensible purposes of praising God (in His creation), and persuading non-Catholics to acknowledge the Catholic truth. But his 1877 English poems were by no means all of one kind: other purposes were evident which had varying degrees of connection with the main proselytizing motive. Sometimes his unconscious drives seemed to be opposed to his conscious ones; idealism was constantly undermined by disillusion.

Throughout these 1877 poems, Hopkins's knowledge of the joys of nature in its uncorrupted freedom serves to throw into relief his misanthropy and loneliness. There is no relationship between the order in which the poems were written and their place on the scale of positive to negative emotions; Hopkins's spirits rose and fell in no predictable pattern that year. He reacted most constantly to place: while the Welsh countryside charged his optimistic spirits, the town of Rhyl provoked his disgust at Man: in 'God's Grandeur' and 'The Lantern' Hopkins is not conscious of the countryside and it is not visualized. Another biographical factor important, if not directly apparent, in these poems is the distinction between daily professional duties and holidays. His daily theological work and the examinations are always mentioned in Hopkins's letters in connection with emotions of worry, tiredness, and tension; not once during the year did he write enthusiastically about his professional studies. He could focus his mind and emotions on nature only when he was off-duty, on half-days, Blandykes, and vacations, officially let loose from work.

෭

Three weeks after writing 'Hurrahing in Harvest', Hopkins was ordained to the priesthood, towards which he had been working and studying for nine years. On 15 September he went into retreat, and then on successive days, 21, 22, and Sunday 23 September, with fifteen others, he received the major orders of subdeacon, deacon, and priest-hood. The minister's journal for Sunday reads:

Ordinandi sleep until eight [.] Breakfast (meat for all) by special order of the Rector, 7.30. Ordinations 10 (over at 12.5) all those yesterday made deacons . . . were today made priests. . . . Three were appointed to conduct people to their seats [,] keep order &c in the Chapel [,] three to lead them from hall door to Chapel. Lunch laid out in refectory [;] five tables placed crosswise gave fifty places [;] sweets [,] fruit & flowers placed on tables. Six of Schol[astics] served. Roast Mutton, Soup, ham & fowls was the lunch provided together with tongues, peas, French beans, &c. After the lunch the guests strolled about the grounds and the community took a meat lunch. Then there was an Impromptu concert in the recreation room. . . . After that Solemn Te Deum and Benedic-tion. Then the guests nearly all departed. . . . After dinner according to tradition . . . the senior ordinatus proposed the Bishop's health. He that of the ordinati. . . . After this music in the recreation room.

None of Hopkins's family were present at the ceremony or celeb-rations.[20]

Before another week passed Hopkins was confined to bed. Dr Turnour was sent for, and came from Denbigh with a surgeon; they performed the operation of circumcision. It was successful, and after a few days in bed and another visit from Dr Turnour he was allowed up. 'In a few days' time', he wrote to his mother, 'I shall be completely recovered, and am then to go to Mount St. Mary's College, Chester-field, Derbyshire.'[21] At 9.30 on Friday morning, 19 October 1877, Hopkins took his last look at St Beuno's.

# PART V

## Fortune's Football, 1877–1884

'And they have made him give up his art?'

'For a time—yes—perhaps altogether. Of course it has been his great renunciation. His superiors thought it necessary to cut him off from it entirely. And no doubt during the novitiate he suffered a great deal. It has been like any other starved faculty.'

The girl's instincts rose in revolt. She cried out against such waste, such mutilation. The Catholic tried to appease her; but in another language. He bade her remember the Jesuit motto. 'A Jesuit is like any other soldier—he puts himself under orders for a purpose.'

'And God is to be gloried by the crushing out of all He took the trouble to give you!'

'You must take the means to the end,' said Helbeck steadily. 'The Jesuit must yield his will—otherwise the Society need not exist. In Williams' case, so long as he had a fascinating and absorbing pursuit, how could he give himself up to his superiors? Besides'—his grave face stiffened—'in his case there were peculiar difficulties. His art had become a temptation. He wished to protect himself from it.'

(Mrs Humphry Ward, *Helbeck of Bannisdale*, bk. iv, ch. 2)

# 24

## 'Cobweb, soapsud, and frost-feather permanence': Mount St Mary's, Stonyhurst, Farm Street, Oxford, 1877–1879

Although its postal address was Chesterfield, in Derbyshire, Mount St Mary's College[1] was nearer to Sheffield in Yorkshire, on the edge of a remote country village, Spinkhill, with coalmines nearby. Mount St Mary's had been opened as a school in 1842, in buildings adapted from Park Hall, residence of the old Catholic family, the Poles, one of whose ancestors, St Margaret Pole, had been executed by Henry VIII. A Gothic church, designed by Alfred Hansom, who had converted Park Hall, was seventy yards away, perched on the edge of the hill. When Hopkins arrived new college buildings were being put up. The plan for the block included school-rooms, areas for recreation and for private study, and a dormitory at the south side of a quadrangle; the front of the college was to overlook the valley towards Eckington. The new block stood stark in a miry field between the college and the church, with a long covered way of corrugated iron, known as 'the Tin Gallery'. Hopkins's room was on the ground floor of a brick block built on to the house in 1859.

The Rector, Fr Thomas Dykes, was a cheerful man, a Cambridge graduate who had been an Anglican clergyman before his reception into the Catholic Church in 1851. He had expanded the number of boys to over 150, introduced Chemistry and Natural Philosophy, and entered on a building programme which soon overran its funds. His Prefect of studies was Fr Ryan, and Hopkins was the replacement for Fr Peter Prestage as sub-minister. While he was at St Beuno's Hopkins described his job at Mount St Mary's not optimistically: 'The work is nondescript—examining, teaching, probably with occasional mission work and preaching or giving retreats attached.' The community was

'moderately small and family-like', the countryside 'not very interesting but at a little distance is fine country'.[2]

When he arrived at the college, Hopkins found that the air was 'never
once clear in this country, not to see distances as in Wales or even at
Hampstead'. Apart from his work in the college and as assistant to the
parish priest, he taught religion to two senior classes, Syntax and
Poetry. The prescribed books were the theological treatises *De Princi-
piis*, *De Religione Christiana*, and *De Religione Revelata*, together with
the study of 'Church History down to the Reign of Constantine'. He
heard confessions and gave Sunday sermons. He probably did no
examining as, according to the *Ratio Studiorum*, this was one of the
duties of the Prefect of Studies. He was given stopgap jobs, and by the
spring term 1878 was reacting much as he did at the Oratory School: 'I
am so fallen into a mess of employments that I have given up doing
everything whatever but what is immediately before me to do.' One of
the masters, Mr Hepburne, was ill for some weeks and Hopkins had to
take his place 'without diminution of . . . former occupations'. Even
Sunday was busy, with 'work both in the school and at the church'.[3]

In the hexagonal schoolroom his new 'Figures' class of eleven- to
thirteen-year-olds welcomed the young priest with a reputation for
scholarship, after the fierce Mr Hepburne. Once Hopkins set them
Byron's 'The Destruction of Sennacherib' ('The Assyrian came down
like the wolf on the fold') to put into Latin verse, and must have
wondered why they were delighted: it had been set before. A boy in that
class, William Lee, wrote of another occasion:

Until quite recently I had kept my priceless effort in this paper amongst some
similar rubbish, and I remember I had included two or three verses of the crib
amongst my native production. Fr. Hopkins's lead pencil had been very busy
amongst the latter, but under the former were his firm wavy strokes of
commendation and the side note 'extraordinarily good'. He had found the
wheat among the tares, but was too trustful to have suspected me of borrowing,
and I feel ashamed to have deceived him. My only wonder, now, is whether the
rest of the class availed themselves of the same tap and if Fr. Hopkins found
any similarity of wording.[4]

Another time Hopkins asked the class to write an account of the Lisbon
earthquake:

'It was a fine bright day' they say 'when at ten o'clock a picture of extreme
suddenness came on'. After the earthquake 'an old ruffian of a mob ran about
killing everyone he met'. Finally 'this catastrophe has left many a mark on the
minds of learned men.'

'A batch of copybooks', Hopkins ruefully wrote to his mother, 'lies before me with no doubt more of the same sort on the Earl of Nithsdale's escape.'[5]

Hopkins's favourite pupil was Hubert Berkeley, who won a prize competed for amongst several Catholic schools. Hopkins was 'more pleased than I should have thought possible'. Berkeley was 'clever and hardworking', and 'I shall not easily have so good a pupil again'. He was a born actor, 'a very amusing low comedian and still better in tragedy', and during the Christmas holidays he acted the part of Fergus, Macbeth's younger brother, in the Jesuit version of Shakespeare as it should have been—without female characters. (In the Jesuit common rules, the *Monita Generalia*, it was forbidden in school and college plays for any female-like person [*persona ulla muliebris*] to appear or for female clothing [*habitus*] to be worn on stage. At Stonyhurst Lady Macbeth became 'Uncle Donald'.) Hopkins wrote a prologue:

It was a scene of a farce and consisted in the speaker seeming to forget all the points, but Berkeley did it so naturally that he overshot the mark and most part of the audience thought he had forgotten in earnest and that his strange behaviour was due to 'refreshments' behind the scenes.[6]

The Rector gave permission for the actors to have 'coffee twice and porter once'. (Despite Berkeley's gifts, a friend reported, 'He had no idea of value in goods or money, direction, distance. . . . In after life . . . he never made the headway he should, and he died, disappointed, in 1899, at the early age of forty.'[7])

At Shrovetide 1878, another pupil, James Broadbent, played Salingophalos, a herald, in a one-act burlesque *A Model Kingdom*, (adapted from Henry Carey's *Chrononhotonthologos*), in the school theatre, which doubled as a study place. Hopkins was struck by the reactions of James's brother Henry, in the audience. He seems not to have written anything down at the time, but over two years later, at Oak Hill, he composed a poem 'in Wordsworth's manner'[8] on the incident:

> Our boys' plays brought on
> Part was picked for John,
> Young John; then fear, then joy
> Ran revel in the elder boy.
> Now the night come; all
> Our company thronged the hall;
> Henry, by the wall,
> Beckoned me beside him.

While John acted in a 'brass-bold' way, Harry 'hung on the imp's success', and finally 'in his hands he has flung/ His tear-tricked cheeks of flame/ For fond love and for shame'; and the poet comments: 'Nature, bad, base, and blind, / Dearly thou canst be kind.'

Pope Pius IX died early in the New Year, 1878; a Solemn Requiem was held in the church, and 25 February held as a holiday in honour of the new Pope, Leo XIII, who had been a pupil of the Society of Jesus. Hopkins was feeling too sick and melancholy to make much effort, and used the free day to write thanking Bridges for having called with his mother to see Hopkins's parents. He liked to think of those he loved getting together, even when away from him, and frequently tried to bring friends of his into contact. 'Nothing pleasanter could have happened', he wrote. 'Remember me very kindly to [your mother] and say how glad I was.' 'Write me an interesting letter', he begged, 'I cannot do so. Life here is as dank as ditch-water and has some of the other qualities of ditch-water.' By this he meant that he had been 'reduced to great weakness by diarrhoea, which lasts too, as if I were poisoned.'[9] Bridges at once offered to come to Spinkhill and treat him, to which Hopkins replied: 'very kind indeed, but I should have lost all shame if under any circumstances I had allowed such a thing to be as for you to come hundreds of miles to cure me.'[10]

Hopkins's muse had 'turned utterly sullen in the Sheffield smoke-ridden air',[11] and he had not written a line, until on 24 March HMS *Eurydice*,[12] an elderly frigate of 900 tons, returning to Portsmouth after a training cruise to the West Indies, with 368 seamen and boys, capsized off the south-east coast of the Isle of Wight, near the Culver Cliffs, which Hopkins had sketched fifteen years earlier in the long vacation. The ship was struck by a squall, so that she heeled to starboard, with her mizzen topmast snapped and her sails bursting under the violent wind. The whipped-up sea poured through open hatches, trapping the men below. A snowstorm had so reduced visibility that no one onshore realized she had sunk until the squall passed and the sun shone on the mastheads. There were two survivors.

Hopkins's response was, as with the *Deutschland*, to take little notice of the newspaper reports, but to find those aspects which stirred his heart. What started Hopkins was probably not the wreck, but the fact that Hubert Berkeley was going in for the Jesuit Inter-Collegiate English verse competition, and the subject was 'The Loss of the *Eurydice*'. Several poems on the subject, some with the same title, were published in newspapers and journals in April 1878.

One of Bridges's criticisms of 'The Wreck of the Deutschland' had been that there was too little narrative. Hopkins wrote to him: 'The Deutschland would be more generally interesting if there were more wreck and less discourse, I know, but still it is an ode and not primarily a narrative. ... This poem on the Eurydice is hitherto almost all narrative however.'[13] The final version, incorporating many suggestions of Bridges and Dixon, shows that he had taken note of reactions to the earlier poem. But he still had to train his audience; he wrote to Bridges:

To do the Eurydice any kind of justice you must not slovenly read it with the eyes but with your ears, as if the paper were declaiming it at you. For instance, the line 'she had come from a cruise training seamen' read without stress and declaim, is mere Lloyd's Shipping Intelligence; properly read it is quite a different thing. Stress is the life of it. Take breath and read it with the ears, as I always wish to be read, and my verse becomes all right.[14]

He creates speedy narrative in 'The Loss of the Eurydice', with a simpler stanza than in the 'Deutschland', shorter lines, and simple commentary:

> The Eurydice—it concerned thee, O Lord:
> Three hundred souls, O alas! on board,
>     Some asleep unawakened, all un-
> warned, eleven fathoms fallen
>
> Where she foundered! One stroke
> Felled and furled them, the hearts of oak!
>     And flockbells off the aerial
> Downs' forefalls beat to the burial.
>
> For did she pride her, freighted fully, on
> Bounden bales or a hoard of bullion?—
>     Precious passing measure,
> Lads and men her lade and treasure.
>
> She had come from a cruise, training seamen—
> Men, boldboys soon to be men:
>     Must it, worst weather,
> Blast bole and bloom together?

There is powerful compounded sea-imagery, such as 'Hailropes hustle and grind their/ Heavengravel', and 'champ-white water-in-a-wallow', but the pace and short stanza form do not build complex sound structures. Hopkins's sadness at the loss of young male beauty ('he was all of lovely manly mould') does not come through strongly, and certain feelings seem like muttered asides, rather than major strands in the structure. His disgust at the moral state of England is uttered in three lines: 'Day and night I deplore/ My people and born own nation,/ Fast foundering own generation.'

Shortly after the letter which was to bring Hopkins back into contact with his former master, Canon Dixon, Hopkins sent him the poem. Dixon replied: 'The Eurydice no one could read without the deepest & most ennobling emotion.'[15] Bridges, Hopkins wrote, gave him not only 'words of praise' but 'monstrous and indecent spiritual compliments',[16] and began his own ode on the subject. *The Month* rejected Hopkins's poem for publication, but although he must have been affected by this second official refusal, he gave no hint. He made alterations on his friends' recommendations, but was becoming hardened to rejection, more confident in his self-justification, and less tolerant of fools: 'Obscurity', he wrote to Bridges,

I do and will try to avoid so far as is consistent with excellences higher than clearness at a first reading. . . . As for affectation I do not believe I am guilty of it: you should point out instances, but as long as mere novelty and boldness strikes you as affectation your criticism strikes me as—as water of the Lower Isis.[17]

By the end of April Hopkins had become 'very fond of the boys I have had to do with as pupils, penitents, or in other ways. I think they lead a very happy life with us, though the discipline is strict.' He took some boys to Clumber Park, and went with a community party to see 'the most beautiful little Norman ruin you can imagine', and Cresswell Crags, 'a cleft between cliffs with water between'. These trips made him long to see the great houses of Derbyshire—Chatsworth, Haddon Hall, and Hardwick Hall; but before May he left for Stonyhurst, just when the neighbourhood of Mount St Mary's was 'gayest and prettiest, as vermilion tiles and orchard blossoms make it'.[18]

එ∕ට

Hopkins's change of post was unexpected; the Provincial had visited Spinkhill to give the decision only ten days before. A meeting of the community's priests, planned for the last day of April, with Hopkins expounding a fictitious case of conscience, was called off.

He was sent to Stonyhurst College for three months, to coach a few students for external degrees of the University of London. He arrived there on 27 April, in time to compose a May poem in honour of the Virgin Mary, to be placed before her statue in the Stonyhurst garden on the first of May—if it passed scrutiny. In the twelve stanzas of 'The May Magnificat' Hopkins saw 'little good but the freedom of the rhythm'.[19] His superiors saw less, and refused permission for it to be placed with the others. After the previous rejections of the two shipwreck poems, it seems perverse of Hopkins to have written to

Dixon eighteen months later, 'You say truly that our Society fosters literary excellence'.[20] Whatever it had done for Hopkins, the Society had not recognized his excellence, rejecting his poems for publication and imposing absolute censorship on everything he published. Hopkins's subsequent precautions against letting his poems be published are explained by this Jesuit barrier: he knew that if he said all he wanted to about Scotus and his theories he would incur official disapproval, and that those with the power to accept or reject his poems could not understand them, let alone appreciate their originality. There was an unhealthy atmosphere, in which Hopkins thought that the slightest move towards publication except through official channels might be misinterpreted. He was unable to tell outsiders what he meant, and dropped dark hints about 'enemies'. He had an almost impossible prohibition placed on him: 'It is the habit, the difficult habit of abstaining from any mental criticism of the order given that is the distinctive feature of the obedience of the Society of Jesus.'[21] Hopkins's nature, as he emphasized, needed constant encouragement, even though his belief in his poetry was strong and assured.

The literary standard which the Society fostered can be judged, as MacKenzie says, by a quotation from May verses composed by Newman and printed later in *The Stonyhurst Magazine*:

> Green is the grass, but wait awhile,
>    'Twill grow, and then 'twill wither;
> The flow'rets, brightly as they smile,
>    Shall perish altogether.
> The merry sun, you sure would say,
>    It ne'er could set in gloom;
> But earth's best joys have all an end,
>    And sin a heavy doom.[22]

The poem rejected by Hopkins's superiors has awkward passages which show haste: 'Is it only its being brighter/ Than the most are must delight her?' but the easily flowing form conveys a poet's lively delight:

> When drop-of-blood-and-foam-dapple
> Bloom lights the orchard-apple
>    And thicket and thorp are merry
>    With silver-surfèd cherry
>
> And azuring-over greybell makes
> Wood banks and brakes wash wet like lakes.

&#8766;

It may have been a sense of active discouragement that was responsible for Hopkins writing the letter of remarkable sympathy and prescience that revived his acquaintance with Canon R. W. Dixon. It was to be an important friendship for Hopkins. On 6 June 1878, a forty-five-year-old Church of England clergyman, living in a remote country village near Carlisle, must have been surprised to receive a letter from a dimly remembered former pupil. Canon R. W. Dixon's was 'a tallish, elderly figure, its litheness lost in a slight scholarly stoop, . . . wearing unimpeachable black cloth negligently, and a low-crowned clerical hat banded with twisted silk'. Gracious, gentle, shy, ingenuous, generous and idealistic, as an undergraduate he had been a companion of Burne-Jones and Gabriel Rossetti, but had taken Anglican orders on leaving Oxford, and after a spell of teaching had settled in the living of Hayton. He was a devoted parish priest, a published though little-known poet, and had begun the task of writing the *History of the Church of England from the Abolition of the Roman Jurisdiction*, which he worked on for the rest of his life.

Hopkins's letter began:

Very Rev. Sir,

I take a liberty as a stranger in addressing you, nevertheless I did once have some slight acquaintance with you. You will not remember me but you will remember taking a mastership for some months at Highgate School, the Cholmeley School, where I then was. When you went away you gave, as I recollect, a copy of your book *Christ's Company* to one of the masters, a Mr. Law if I am not mistaken. By this means coming to know its name I was curious to read it, which when I went to Oxford I did. At first I was surprised at it, then pleased, at last I became so fond of it that I made it, so far as that could be, a part of my own mind. I got your other volume and your little Prize Essay too. I introduced your poems to my friends and, if they did not share my own enthusiasm, made them at all events admire. And to shew you how greatly I prized them, when I entered my present state of life, in which I knew I could have no books of my own and was unlikely to meet with your works in the libraries I should have access to, I copied out *St. Paul, St. John, Love's Consolation*, and others from both volumes and keep them by me.

Two aspects of this letter must have made a direct, perhaps uncomfortable, appeal: Hopkins's open-hearted praise of the poetry, and his estimate of its undervaluation—'I thought the tenderness of *Love's Consolation* no one living could surpass. . . . if I were making up a book of English poetry I should put your ode to Summer next to Keats' on Autumn and the Nightingale and Grecian Urn. . . . The extreme delight I felt when I read the line "Her eyes like lilies shaken by the bees" was more than any single line in poetry ever gave me.' Hopkins's appreciation of Dixon's lack of audience is personally felt:

and then I knew what I should feel myself in your position—if I had written and published works the extreme beauty of which the author himself the most keenly feels and they had fallen out of sight at once and been (you will not mind my saying it, as it is, I suppose, plainly true) almost wholly unknown; then, I say, I should feel a certain comfort to be told they had been deeply appreciated by some one person, a stranger, at all events and had not been published quite in vain.

This is as close as he came to speaking about his own case: 'It is not that I think a man is really the less happy because he has missed the renown which was his due, but still when this happens it is an evil in itself and a thing which ought not to be and that I deplore, for the good work's sake rather than the author's.'[23] (His emphasis on the work, rather than the author, underlines chagrin by trying to hide it.)

Dixon replied: 'I received your Letter two days ago, but have been unable to answer it before, chiefly through the many and various emotions which it has awakened within me.'

You cannot but know that I must be deeply moved, nay shaken to the very centre, by such a letter as that which you have sent me: for which I thank you from my inmost heart. I place and value it among my best possessions. I can in truth hardly realise that what I have written, which has been generally, almost universally, neglected, should have been so much valued and treasured. This is more than fame: and I may truly say that when I read your Letter, and whenever I take it out of my pocket to look at it, I feel that I prefer to have been so known & prized by one, than to have had the ordinary appreciation of many.

About three years previously, Dixon had received a letter from D. G. Rossetti which said that he was 'one of the most subtle as well as varied of our poets', and that 'the neglect of such work as yours on all hands is an incomprehensible accident'. Beside that letter he placed Hopkins's.[24] It was an opening to the friendship of the two men.

Hopkins's second letter again took up the subject of poetic fame:

When I spoke of fame I was not thinking of the harm it does to men as artists: it may be do them harm, as you say, but so, I think may the want of it, if 'Fame is the spur that the clear spirit doth raise To shun delights and live laborious days'—a spur very hard to find a substitute for or to do without.

What he did regret was 'the loss of recognition belonging to the work itself'. His idea of the artist's purpose is an expression of what he felt his poems were about: 'And the world is full of things and events, phenomena of all sorts, that go without notice, go unwitnessed. ... And if we regret this want of witness in brute nature [cf. 'and but the beholder/ Wanting'] much more in the things done with lost pains and disappointed hopes by man.' His acceptance of rejection and lack of recognition is articulated: 'But since there is always the risk of it, it is a

great error of judgment to have lived for what may fail us. . . . For
disappointment and humiliations embitter the heart and make an
aching in the very bones.'

Hopkins recommended to Dixon's attention 'my friend Dr. Bridges'
poems', in particular 'a set of sonnets, a tiny anonymous work no bigger
than a short pamphlet of two dozen pages, they are called *The Growth of
Love*', and he closed by announcing his change of address in July to '111
Mount Street, Grosvenor Square, London W., where I am to be
stationed'.[25]

crs

The Church of the Immaculate Conception, in Farm Street, Mayfair,
was the principal Jesuit church in the English Province; 111 Mount
Street, at the side of the church, was the residence of the Jesuit Fathers,
and the headquarters of the Province. The large church, in fourteenth-
century decorated Gothic, had been built in 1849 on the site of a back-
street mews in the most fashionable area of London. The altar and
reredos were by Pugin. The church's services, missions, and sermons
played a prominent part in the life of Catholic London, and converts
received at Farm Street averaged about a hundred a year. The church
had a reputation for fine music (though not to Hopkins's taste), the
choir sometimes being assisted by an orchestra.

The Superior at Farm Street in July 1878 was Fr Peter Gallwey,
Rector and Professor of Moral Theology at St Beuno's during
Hopkins's last year in Wales. Gallwey had been 'much struck by the
originality of a sermon [Hopkins] gave in the Refectory' at St Beuno's,
and was responsible for bringing him to Farm Street to preach.
Hopkins's duties at first consisted of 'writing 3 sermons to be preached
in August; I have little else to do (of duty) and so employ myself in
making up my theology, but my work will soon thicken'. He told
Bridges, 'I am, so far as I know, permanently here, but permanence
with us is ginger-bread permanence; cobweb, soapsud, and frost-
feather permanence.'[26]

On hearing of Hopkins's move to London, Bridges had immediately
sent a dinner invitation, but with his impractical mixture of scruple and
dithering, and the crossed lines and misunderstandings which seemed
to attend on his appointments with friends, Hopkins delayed acceptance. On Sunday 4 August Hopkins preached his first sermon at Farm
Street, with Bridges in the congregation. Hopkins felt afterwards that
he had not learnt it as well as he should:

I was very little nervous at the beginning and not at all after. It was pure forgetting and flurry. The delivery was not good, but I hope to get a good one in time. I shall welcome any criticisms which are not controversy. I am glad you did not like the music and sorry you did not like the mass.[27]

Bridges and Hopkins did eventually meet, in Bridges's elegant Georgian house on the south side of Bedford Square. Their conversation was about literature, except during a few minutes before they parted. Hopkins regretted that they did not speak 'on any more important subject', and, crudely and uningratiatingly, he tried to question the reserved Bridges on his morals, as though he were Bridges's parish priest. He assumed he knew about Bridges's inner life: 'Now you may have done much good, but yet it may not be enough: I will say, it is not enough.'[28]

Hopkins's duties increased. In October he wrote to Dixon that 'a visit to Great Yarmouth and pressure of work has kept me from answering before yr. very kind letter. ... I have no time for more pressing interests. I hear confessions, preach, and so forth; when these are done I have still a good deal of time to myself, but I find I can do very little with it.'[29] He wrote long letters to Dixon, pressing him to read Bridges's poems (later, from Oxford, he urged Bridges to read Dixon's and to send Dixon a copy of his). He gave a detailed account, in response to Dixon's question whether he wrote verse himself, of the burning of his early poems, the writing of the two 'Wrecks' and the St Beuno's sonnets, and a clear account of his new rhythm. He gave Bridges copies of his poems, but at the end of October, before going on his yearly retreat, he was informed that he had been posted away from Farm Street. 'I daresay', he wrote to Bridges from the retreat house in Old Windsor, 'we may not meet again for years.'[30]

⁓

In October 1878 Hopkins wrote to his new friend Dixon that he was very fond of Oxford. 'I became a Catholic there. But I have not visited it, except once for three quarters of an hour, since I took my degree. We have a church and house there now.'[31] Four months later he was able to report: 'You will see that I have again changed my abode and am returned to my Alma Mater.'[32] After his eight-day retreat at Beaumont Lodge, he had been sent for a week in the middle of November as curate to St Mary's on the Quay, Bristol, and then posted to St Aloysius', Oxford. He was now thirty-four.

There had been no centre for Roman Catholics in Oxford throughout the eighteenth century, until in 1793 a Jesuit missioner, Fr Leslie, built the small chapel of St Ignatius, in the district of St Clement's, then just outside the city boundary. It had been there, on 12 October 1845, that a group of four Catholic neophytes, including Newman, having walked from Littlemore, attended their first Mass. The mission had never been productive, and in 1871 a legacy of Baroness Weld enabled a new church to be built in the centre of Oxford, in St Giles, not far from Balliol. The ubiquitous Catholic architect Joseph Hansom made a neo-Gothic design of the fifteenth century, 'with stone fan-vaulting and a tower to rival Great Tom', but the church of St Aloysius[33] dedicated in 1875 showed little resemblance to his plan. It was mainly yellow brick, to most people cheap and nasty in the context of Oxford buildings. The window shapes were featureless, and the design lacked intricacy and originality. It had been placed in the hands of the Society of Jesus, and at the laying of the first stone, the Jesuit Fr Morris had sounded hopeful: 'I am sure that the Catholics of Oxford have felt that it has been for them hitherto a long winter, and although all we have before us this day is but a promise, still it is a promise of the riper, better time coming.'[34] At the service of dedication in 1875, however, Cardinal Manning, taking as the text of his sermon the University's motto, *Dominus Illuminatio Mea*, had attacked its teaching, thereby underlining his policy (the opposite of Newman's) of discouraging Catholics from attending the university. Among those at the ceremony had been Oscar Wilde, reported to have come away 'feeling rather depressed'.[35]

Although Roman Catholicism was not popular in England, in Oxford the High-Anglican Ritualists were still fashionable, conducting services which in fervour and ceremonial appeared to many indistinguishable from Roman Catholic practice. Their centre of worship was the new Italianate church of St Barnabas, in the poor area called Jericho, near the canal and railway station. Sometimes to be seen in the streets, dressed like medieval monks, were the Cowley Fathers, living examples of the old virtues of poverty, chastity, and obedience. Pusey was still at Christ Church, and he, Liddon, Bright, and Scott Holland were leaders of the Oxford High-Anglican party, who, according to Hopkins, were 'up to some very dirty jesuitical tricks'.[36] St Aloysius' congregation was described towards the end of the century as being a 'huddled little flock, very thinly recruited from the university, with one or two remnants of old Catholic families, and for the rest drawn from modest commercial and industrial circles'.

The parish was large and varied, extending to Witney in the west and Temple Cowley in the south and east; it included the labouring-class areas of Jericho, St Ebbe's, and St Clement's. Hopkins found that the parish priest and his one curate had to serve the old St Clement's church as well as St Aloysius', and minister to the Catholics in Oxford Prison, in the barracks at Cowley, and at the Radcliffe Infirmary. They also had to run various parish organizations, including the Catholic Club recently founded for undergraduates.

The priest in charge was Fr Thomas B. Parkinson, a fifty-nine-year-old Cambridge graduate, and a former clergyman of the Church of England. Nicknamed by his Jesuit contemporaries 'Truly Benevolent Parkinson', or sometimes '*Extreme* Unction', he was described by one of his first university students as 'both in appearance and character. . . . the most typically English, John Bullish person I have ever known'. He was plump, 'always unwieldy in sacred vestments', and considered 'rather dull' and 'somewhat tedious' in the pulpit. 'He used sometimes to stretch himself slightly with much deliberation (he was already sufficiently large) and to say slowly, with great distinctness of utterance—as unlike an Italian as anyone possibly could be: "And they say that *I* am a Roman".'[37]

Fr Parkinson had bought the three adjoining houses which had largely concealed the church from the street, and in their place built parish rooms and a presbytery, on the second floor of which Hopkins was given a spacious and airy room, which he found 'comfortable'. From his window there was the church on his right, the start of the Woodstock Road on the left, and in front the west side of St Giles. The priests' quarters were divided from the servants' quarters by doors which were plain on one side, elaborately carved on the other. Water was piped only to the basement, and a dumb waiter conveyed water to the upper stories. There was a belled cat.

Hopkins was not happy during his second period in Oxford. 'Often I was in a black mood, "but still," I used to say to myself like the people in Euripides, "I see the sun," not only the literal sun but nature and the many things which make Oxford attractive.'[38] In his ten months' stay he found the townspeople 'very deserving of affection—though somewhat stiff, stand-off and depressed'.[39] The Young Men's Association were 'shopkeepers and so on, a fine wellmannered set of young men, but their peculiarity and all our congregation's (excepting the University men and some of the gentry) is that they have a stiff respectful stand-off air which we can scarcely make our way through nor explain'. Hopkins's upbringing made it hard for him to make contact with 'the town'. The tone of his apology for awkwardness explains why he was not a success among his working-class parishioners in northern England:

We believe it to be a growth of a University, where Gown holds itself above and aloof from Town and Town is partly cowed by, partly stands on its dignity against Gown. These young men rally to us, frequent and take parts in our ceremonies, meet a good deal in the parishroom, and so on, but seem as if a joke from us would put them to deep and lasting pain.[40]

His account of 'a small parochial concert' is patronizing: 'Neither voices nor choice of music was very good, still the effect is humanising, as they say.' He felt more at home in a different class of audience, with different tastes:

Sir Gore Ouseley came up the other day to give the last of a course of lectures on organ-music (illustrated) at the Sheldonian Theatre. The organ is new; the organist said to be a genius: he cries (like Du Maurier's man) over his own playing. The audience, which was large and brilliant, included Miss Lloyd in a black bonnet and yellow ribbons. Sir Gore (ghastly as this is, what else can you say?—his name in a book of Mallock's would become Sir Bloodclot Reekswell) wanted us to agree with him that such and such an example was in a better style than such and such another, livelier, one, but we were naughty and would not; the more griggish the piece the more we clapped it.[41]

But during his stay Hopkins saw comparatively little of the University: 'I could not but feel how alien it was, how chilling, and deeply to be distrusted.' His attitude was ambivalent: 'I could have wished, and yet I could not, that there had been no one that had known me there.'[42] He used to fear 'that people wd. repeat against me what they remembered to my disadvantage'.[43] However, 'as a fact there were many and those friendly, some cordially so, but with others I cd. not feel at home'. His religion proved to be his 'peace' and his 'parting'. 'Religion, you know', he wrote to Baillie (who was probably less likely than Hopkins to notice it), 'enters very deep; in reality it is the deepest impression I have in speaking to people, that they are or that they are not of my religion.'[44] This letter, written some months after he had left Oxford, showed how he was pulled in opposite directions. Ten years before, he had gone against most of his friends and teachers by entering the Roman Catholic Church, yet felt that 'not to love my University would be to undo the very buttons of my being'. He emphasized that the impression people made on him depended on their religion, but there are signs that he was less at ease with Catholic acquaintances outside the university than with his former Balliol friends who were not Catholic. He said of the St Aloysius congregation that 'they criticised what went on in our church a great deal too freely' (in contrast to his previous opinion of their 'stiff respectful stand-off air'), and judged this attitude as 'd—d impertinence of the sheep towards the shepherd'. If this kind of behaviour 'had come markedly before me I shd. have given them my mind.'[45]

He visited his old Balliol teachers. He dined with the Paters, invited
Pater to dine with him, and wrote that he 'was one of the men I saw
most of'.[46] He called on the Greens, and found Mrs Green 'a very kind
creature'.[47] The man he saw most of was Francis de Paravicini, now a
Fellow of Balliol (characterized in *The Masque of Balliol* as a 'little
cynic' and an 'oddity'), and his only Oxford acquaintance who offered
religious sympathy and academic affinity. The Paravicinis were 'very
kind', and became fond of him. Mrs Paravicini, a devout convert, was 'a
very sweet good creature'.[48] Many of his old contemporaries at Oxford
were up ('I used to come on more and more of them'[49]), including
Stuckey Coles, Willert, and Bridges's friend Muirhead.

Hopkins's main task was 'parish work and left no time, that was of
any use, for reading'; it was 'very tiring . . . and makes letterwriting
hard', but he wrote several postcards and long letters to Bridges and a
few to Dixon. At Hopkins's request, Bridges had sent Dixon his last
copy of *The Growth of Love* and one of the first of his new *Poems*. To
help with this volume Hopkins sent Dixon a long and complex
explanation of 'sprung rhythm', which must have added to Dixon's
difficulties:

To go a little deeper, it supposes not only that, speaking in the abstract, any
accent is equal to any other (by accent I mean *the* accent of a word) but further
that each accent may be considered to be accompanied by an equal quantity of
slack or unaccented utterance, one, two, or more such unaccented syllables; so
that wherever there is an accent or stress, there there is also so much
unaccentuation, so to speak, or slack, and this will give a foot or rhythmic unit,
viz. a stress with its belonging slack. But now if this is so, since there are plenty
of accented monosyllables, and those too immediately preceded and followed
by the accents of other words, it will come about that a foot may consist of one
syllable only and that one syllable has not only the stress of its accent but also
the slack which another word wd. throw on one or more additional syllables,
though here that may perhaps be latent, as though the slack syllables had been
absorbed. What I mean is clearest in an antithesis or parallelism, for there. . . .[50]

After this meandering account Hopkins went on to give the perfect
concise explanation: '*one stress makes one foot*, no matter how many or
few the syllables'.

A fortnight later he sent Dixon copies of the 'Eurydice', the
'Deutschland', and some recent sonnets. Dixon ignored the whole
subject of sprung rhythm but replied with the highest praise: 'I have
your Poems and have read them I cannot say with what delight,
astonishment, & admiration. They are among the most extraordinary I
ever read & amazingly original. . . . It seems to me that they ought to be
published. Can I do anything?' Dixon was at the time working on the

next volume of his *History of the Church of England*, and proposed to add 'an abrupt footnote about your poems, if you thought good. . . . You may think it odd for me to propose to introduce you into the year 1540, but I know how to do it.' His object would be 'to awaken public interest & expectation in your as yet unpublished poems.'[51]

Hopkins replied that the footnote reference 'would not at all suit me'. He had 'no thought of publishing until all circumstances favour, which I do not know that they ever will, and it seems that one of them shd. come from one of our own people'. He felt that 'to allow such a notice would be on my part a sort of insubordination to or double dealing with my superiors.'[52] Dixon was not skilled in paying close attention to Hopkins's words, and the matter had not closed.

Since their meeting in London, Hopkins had been storing up thoughts about Bridges's spiritual state, and now he asked Bridges to communicate his thoughts on important subjects. 'You understand of course that I desire to see you a Catholic or, if not that, a Christian or, if not that, at least a believer in the true God (for you told me something of your views about the deity, which were not as they should be).' Hopkins also counselled Bridges to give alms:

I lay great stress on it. . . . It may be either in money or in other shapes, the objects for which, with your knowledge of several hospitals, can never be wanting. I daresay indeed you do give alms, still I should say give more: I should be bold to say/ give, up to the point of sensible inconvenience.

Four days later, finishing off the letter, Hopkins admitted 'it is very bold, as it is uncalled for, of me to have written the above. Still, if we care for fine verses how much more for a noble life!'[53] But he sent his less than tactful advice, and Bridges soon sent three letters objecting to Hopkins's suggestions. Hopkins countered that he had been misunderstood, and was 'not only surprised but put out. For amongst other things I am made to appear a downright fool.' He gave further explanations of what he had meant, and finished by enclosing two poems that Bridges had not seen, 'and though the subject [the Bishop's Silver Jubilee] may not interest you the lines may and may take tastes out.' He added, 'I have nothing newer.'[54]

Hopkins's discussions with Bridges and Dixon about their poems made him formulate his attitude to his publication, and he gave a hint which Bridges took as a sacred charge: 'All therefore that I think of doing is to keep my verses together in one place—at present I may not even correct copies—, that, if anyone shd. like, they might be published after my death.' As to writing more poetry:

I cannot in conscience spend time on poetry, neither have I the inducements and inspirations that make others compose. Feeling, love in particular, is the great moving power and spring of verse and the only person that I am in love with seldom, especially now, stirs my heart sensibly and when he does I cannot always 'make capital' of it, it would be a sacrilege to do so.[55]

A week later Bridges sent a copy of his new volume. Hopkins criticized some of the poems on moral grounds—'The meaning is bad', 'The meaning is very bad', and 'The vulgar verses about Anne leave a bad taste', but offered detailed critiques and some praise. The 'Hymn to Nature' he thought 'fine'; it had 'much impressed the mind of my chief, Fr. Parkinson, the Parkinsonian mind, I shd. prefer to say; who read it murmuringly out over tea, with comments and butter'.[56]

He also wrote: 'I have two sonnets soaking, which if they shd. come to anything you shall have.'[57] In January he had sent Bridges a poem by his father, 'called forth by the proposal to fell the trees in Well Walk (where Keats and other interesting people lived) and printed in some local paper'. He thought his father's lines 'choicely phrased', and wrote to his mother that he hoped 'the Well Walk trees are saved'. (He used to see them every day in his last year at Hampstead on his way from Oak Hill across the Heath to school at Highgate.) A month afterwards—at the end of a bitter winter which had seen a 'long frost, severer, it is said, at Oxford than elsewhere', and floods so high that 'the great expanse of Port Meadow was covered over'—he had taken a walk to his favourite Oxfordshire haunts, along the river bank north from Folly Bridge. He 'need not go far', he told Dixon, 'to have before my eyes "the little-headed willows two and two" and that landscape the charm of Oxford, green shouldering grey . . . the Wytham and Godstow landscape (as I take it to be) of "Love's Consolation" and "Waiting" ',[58] poems in Dixon's volume *Christ's Company*. Willows and aspens shaded stretches of the river in summer to a degree impossible south towards Iffley, where it was too wide for trees to dominate. On the afternoon of 13 March 1879 he went up to Godstow, and 'am sorry to say that the aspens that lined the river are everyone felled'.[59] In the bitter winter of that year, when Oxford was 'but its own skeleton', he felt that 'that landscape the charm of Oxford' had been 'abridged and soured and perhaps will soon be put out altogether'. These feelings developed into 'Binsey Poplars' and 'Duns Scotus's Oxford'. Hopkins might have written both poems standing on the Iron Bridge, built in 1865, and embodying the harshly metallic insensitivity of the new Industrial Age. West of the bridge were the meadows, trees, and streams which surrounded Binsey village, and to the east a view across Port Meadow. The low, wide landscape gave an impression of Oxford being 'enisled', cut off in remote perfection. 'Now at Oxford', Hopkins wrote to Bridges, 'every prospect pleases and only man is vile.'[60] Both these poems are expressions of modern man's insensitivity to landscape. To the west the aspens had once 'dandled a sandalled/ Shadow'. To the east 'that neighbour-nature' that Oxford's 'grey beauty is grounded/ Best in' was soured by the 'base and brickish skirt' of Jericho's cheap, working-class houses. Above the brick in the distance rose grey stone towers haunted by Duns Scotus, he 'who of all men most sways my spirit to peace'. (Hopkins does not mention the brash prominence of the new Keble and St Barnabas towers.)

It was not just Oxford which had changed but Hopkins. As an undergraduate, fourteen years earlier, he had written of his increasing and unquenchable love for the city:

> More sweet-familiar grows my love to thee,
> And still thou bind'st me to fresh fealty
> With long-superfluous ties, for nothing here
> Nor elsewhere can thy sweetness unendear.
> This is my park, my pleasaunce . . . .

In March 1879 the fondness is still there: 'Towery city and branchy between towers;/ Cuckoo-echoing, bell-swarmèd, lark-charmèd' ('by the way', Hopkins had written to Bridges the previous month, 'you should write *crabbed*, not *crabbèd*, which is as wrong as *blessèd*, *learnèd*, *crookèd*, *wickèd* would be'). The 'rural rural keeping' which in the Middle Ages had enabled Oxford to be in fellowship with 'folk, flocks, and flowers' was confounded by the modern 'graceless growth'. Oxford was no longer Hopkins's Oxford, though parts of it, 'these weeds and waters, these walls', were now reminders of Scotus; and the poem changes to its more lasting subject—Scotus as a vital source of comfort to Hopkins's troubled spirits. Scotus was 'the rarest-veinèd unraveller' of 'realty'—not of the actual scene (his world had passed away) but of 'insight', of a way of looking at individual objects, which provided some kind of comfort by justifying in moral terms the practice of looking at Beauty.

'Binsey Poplars' is also concerned with the passing away of beauty, but with no comfort offered. Hopkins is again putting his argument for the vital importance of the senses—'After-comers cannot guess the beauty been.' An intellectual feat was no substitute for physical perception of the poplars. The cutting down of the beautiful beech at

Balliol had been 'wicked' and due to 'infidelity'. Both poems express deep rejection of modern religion and modern civilization. (One reason why he was so sympathetic towards Dixon's poetry was that Dixon was a living example of what Hopkins called 'the "prescientific" child'.)

As though further arguments were useless and the sight too painful, 'Binsey Poplars' ended in sad and hypnotic dreaminess, the speaker closing his eyes to go back nostalgically to original perfection:

> The sweet especial scene,
> Rural scene, a rural scene,
> Sweet especial rural scene.

This lament for destruction of 'being' was followed by 'Henry Purcell', a sonnet praising the musical utterance of 'the very make and species of man'. Purcell's music seemed to Hopkins, like Milton's verse, 'something necessary and eternal'.[61] Hopkins was now going well beyond conventional Catholic taste and argument. Despite his ill-considered moral rebukes to Bridges, he seemed able to blind himself at times to his own deviation from the orthodoxy required of him. Although he once said that Christ was the only just literary critic, he could praise the works of people damned by the Church. Milton's art, for instance, was 'incomparable, not only in English literature but, I shd. think, almost in any'; yet 'Milton was a very bad man'. Swinburne was one of 'those plagues of mankind', yet his style could be copied for a Stonyhurst Marian poem, and the critical vocabulary of his 1878 *Poems and Ballads* could be used in discussing literature with Dixon (Tennyson's poetry appeared 'chryselephantine'). Although Hopkins makes passing reference to Purcell's damnable moral state ('listed to a heresy'), he can identify with him and utter a paean in honour of his music's individual power: 'It is the forgèd feature finds me; it is the rehearsal/ Of own, of abrupt self there so thrusts on, so throngs the ear.' The enthusiasm for Purcell's art expands the imagery of his praise. Purcell was 'low-laid' by the outward moral sentence, but his music was the 'air of angels'— moral creatures. Purcell becomes a being like 'some great stormfowl', to whom moral criteria are inapplicable; what is valuable about Purcell is what he dynamically conveys through his art: 'meaning motion fans fresh our wits with wonder'.

On 28 March, to his curate's chagrin, Fr Parkinson had 'thought well to break his collarbone and be laid up in a charming country house commanding the White Horse Vale, throwing the whole of the work at the hardest time of the year on his underling'.[62] In a particularly downcast mood Hopkins wrote 'The Candle Indoors', a sonnet of self-examination, suggesting that he needed to pay more attention to his own disrupted state, before looking at his parishioners: 'Come you indoors, come home; your fading fire/ Mend first'. The thoughts of the sestet anticipate 'Patience, hard thing' and 'The times are nightfall'. After Fr Parkinson returned he was 'laid up with another complaint', 'has sprung a leak (exema) in his leg', and Hopkins was 'laid on all the harder'.[63] His health suffered. The 'kind and gentlemanly' Dr Tuckwell 'thought it was not so much dysentery I had as an irritation due to the remains left by the operation for piles, though that was some years ago'. The doctor gave him a comforting prescription, which 'did the required work and rather more, so I gave up taking the bottle half through, but keep it by me'. Near the end of June he was 'now well, barring fatigue, which easily comes over me'.[64]

Despite overwork and illness, Hopkins wrote 'The Handsome Heart', about two boys of the congregation who helped him in Holy Week: 'I offered them money for their services, which the elder refused, but being pressed consented to take it laid out in a book. The younger followed suit.' When Hopkins asked him what he should buy he answered, 'Father, what you buy me I like best.' (His father, Hopkins recorded, 'is Italian and therefore sells ices'.[65]) His 'gracious answer' caused Hopkins to reflect that on the heart 'falls light as ten years long taught how to and why'. His parish work was tiring and dispiriting, but he found in 'professional experience now a good deal of matter to write on'. When some fresh incident touched him, he could seize it in verse, using as models Wordsworth's poems which transformed ordinary occurrences. 'The Bugler's First Communion' and the unfinished 'Cheery Beggar' were based on incidents which Hopkins also used in a sermon. The scene of 'Cheery Beggar' was the Plain, an open space where the medieval church of St Clement had once stood; it was now surrounded by houses and was near St Ignatius', the little chapel with a circular window and small pediment, where Hopkins preached the Sunday sermon several times during the summer of 1879. There he had given a few pence to a beggar,

> in a burst of summertime
> Following falls and falls of rain,
> When the air was sweet-and-sour of the flown fineflour of
> Those goldnails and their gaylinks that hang along a lime.

On the last day of August Hopkins preached a sermon on the Ten Lepers, which finished on the subject of the relationship between the destitute and their benefactors.[66]

On the Feast of the Precious Blood, 6 July, he preached at St Ignatius' on the blood of Christ as having *'the noblest lineage in the world. Beauty and perfection of his body*, its health untouched by any sickness or ache'. The same blood which made for bodily perfection also promoted the performance of 'nobler offices than any other blood can do'.[67] The primitive idea of looks and health mirroring inner qualities appears again in the Ten Lepers sermon:

the man or woman, the boy or girl, that in their bloom and heyday, in their strength and health give themselves to God and with the fresh body and joyously beating blood give him glory, how near he will be to them in age and sickness and wall their weakness round in the hour of death![68]

and in the summer 1879 poems 'Morning, Midday, and Evening Sacrifice' and 'The Bugler's First Communion'.

Beyond the Plain and almost three miles from St Aloysius' were the Cowley Barracks, headquarters of the Oxfordshire and Buckinghamshire Light Infantry. The 'little drummer boy' was a popular figure (a common story was that of the seven-year-old British soldier in the Napoleonic Wars, Drummer James Wade of the Ninth Foot), boys being commonly used to play the drum or fife or bugle. Like the 'two beautiful young people', subjects in a later poem, Hopkins's bugler-boy[69] has an Irish mother and an English father. The naïve and powerful feelings for the boy are imaged and dramatized through the roles of priest and first communicant:

Here he knelt then in regimental red.
Forth Christ from cupboard fetched, how fain I of feet
    To his youngster take his treat!
Low-latched in leaf-light housel his too huge godhead.

There! and your sweetest sendings, ah divine,
By it, heavens, befall him! as a heart Christ's darling, dauntless;
    Tongue true, vaunt- and tauntless;
Breathing bloom of a chastity in mansex fine.

The rawness and vulnerability of Hopkins's emotions stand starkly displayed in this most Victorian poem. The difficulties of many of his poems lie in expression, but here the subject-matter probably keeps modern readers at a distance. In some ways the feeling towards the end of the poem is similar to that in 'Binsey Poplars'. The unique moral qualities of the boy, like his attractive looks, would be certain to degenerate, so the poet wants to close his eyes to the destructive future: 'Let me though see no more of him, and not disappointment/ Those sweet hopes quell'. Hopkins wrote to Bridges: 'I am half inclined to hope the Hero of [the poem] may be killed in Afghanistan', consigning his goodness to God.[70]

A month before he left Oxford, Hopkins wrote the sonnet 'Andromeda', trying for a plainer, more Miltonic style, to answer his correspondents' criticisms. It is difficult to recapture or understand the sense of importance that the Victorians attached to the Andromeda myth. Kingsley, who had published *Andromeda, and other poems* in 1858 had found that 'the beauty of that whole myth is unfathomable; I love it, and revel in it more and more the longer I look at it'. To Kingsley, Andromeda was rescued from 'the dark powers of nature' by the more human Greek religion, but Hopkins's poem makes no correspondences or interpretations.

'Peace' was composed when Hopkins was about to leave Oxford. It expresses sadly but plainly his lack of inward ease and comfort. As in 'Patience, hard thing', the consolatory ending is less powerful than the complaining start:

> When will you ever, Peace, wild wooddove, shy wings shut,
> Your round me roaming end, and under be my boughs?
> When, when, Peace, will you, Peace?—I'll not play hypocrite
>
> To own my heart: I yield you do come sometimes; but
> That piecemeal peace is poor peace. What pure peace allows
> Alarms of wars, the daunting wars, the death of it?

# 'So fagged, so harried and gallied up and down': Bedford Leigh, Liverpool, Glasgow, 1879–1881

In October 1879, after ten months in Oxford, Hopkins was appointed to Liverpool. First he had to go on supply to St Joseph's, Bedford Leigh,[1] possibly to take the place of Fr Charles Karslake, brother of his schoolfriend Lewis Karslake. One bad aspect of the posting was its stopgap nature; he did not know what work faced him in Liverpool and came to doubt whether he should ever get there. There was no constancy even about his work in Leigh—he was liable to be sent for the odd day or week to nearby parishes, such as St John's, Wigan, or the town of St Helens. St Helens he found 'probably the most repulsive place in Lancashire or out of the Black Country. The stench of sulphuretted hydrogen rolls in the air and films of the same gas form on railing and pavement.'[2] Leigh itself was not much better, 'a darksome place, with pits and mills and foundries'.[3] It was smaller and less dignified than nearby Rochdale, where Bridges's mother lived: 'the houses red, mean, and two storied; there are a dozen mills or so, and coalpits also; the air is charged with smoke as well as damp'.[4]

As far as the Catholic Church was concerned Leigh was a shining example, in the most Catholic of English counties. Over half the town's inhabitants were officially Catholic. Rooms in old farmhouses where mass had been celebrated during persecutions were still pointed out, there were secret passages in mansions, and the 'holy head' of the Lancashire martyr, Fr Edmund Arrowsmith SJ, 'rescued from the mutilated body', was preserved in the nearby church of Ashton-in-Makerfield. Two and a half years before Hopkins arrived in Leigh, at the solemn requiem mass for the much-loved parish priest, Fr Middlehurst, between seven and eight thousand people, Catholic and Protestant, had paid their last tribute of respect. The present priest, Fr James Fanning, had been at St Joseph's for a year. His church was a massive and magnificent Gothic stone building, with a capacity of over 1,200 people.

Hopkins soon experienced the parish's reputed piety: 'The place is very gloomy', he wrote to Dixon, 'but our people hearty and devoted.' He called the Leigh people 'hearty' in a letter to Bridges, whereas 'at Oxford every prospect pleases and only man is vile, I mean unsatisfactory to a Catholic missioner'. He had been fond of his parishioners at Oxford, but they lacked 'the charming and cheering heartiness of these Lancashire Catholics, which is so deeply comforting'.[5] Another clue to his preference for the Leigh Catholics lay in his account of the freely critical St Aloysius' flock. Hopkins preferred his people to be unquestioningly devoted to authority, a quality more likely to be found among the poor, uneducated Lancashire classes. Hopkins's support for the hierarchical structure of his religion is clearly related to his attitude towards political levellers and freethinkers, expressed to Baillie:

Bradlaugh spoke here lately and Mrs Annie Besant gave 3 lectures on Sunday last. To think I could ever have called myself a Liberal! 'The Devil was the first Whig.' These two are at large (I mean Bradlaugh and Besant) and the Government is arresting Irish agitators, that will do far more harm in prison than on the stump.[6]

'Gerard was no politician', his contemporary Joseph Rickaby wrote after Hopkins's death.[7]

Baillie protested that it was 'something of an affectation' for Hopkins 'to run up the Lancashire people and run down . . . the Oxford ones', and Hopkins answered,

I felt as if [I] had been born to deal with [the Lancastrians]. . . . And then it is sweet to be a little flattered and I can truly say that except in the most transparently cringing way I seldom am. Now these Lancashire people of low degree or not of high degree are those who most have seemed to me to welcome me and make much of me.[8]

Perhaps the closest link he established with the Leigh people was in his sermons, eight of which survive. Fr Devlin, editor of the sermons, praises them for 'homely touches' and 'happy piety', and says that the two December ones 'have all the warmth of assurance that is kindled by the sympathy of an audience'.[9] On the printed page they do not seem outstanding, and the effect on a congregation is difficult to judge. Certain passages have biographical interest. In his sermon on the Immaculate Conception, to open a triduum celebrating the twenty-fifth anniversary of Pius IX's definition, he uses the occasion to praise Duns Scotus (without naming him):

It is a comfort to think that the greatest of the divines and doctors of the Church who have spoken and written in favour of this truth came from England: between 500 and 600 years ago he was sent for to go to Paris to dispute in its favour. The disputation or debate was held in public and someone who was there says that this wise and happy man by his answers broke the objections brought against him as Samson broke the thongs and withies with which his enemies tried to bind him.[10]

Another sermon singles out the Lancashire martyr Margaret Clith-eroe, about whom he was writing a poem, but his most interesting sermon is that on Christ as hero and pattern. Christ is discussed under the three attributes of body, mind, and character, of which the first section overshadows the other two by its power and unexpectedness. Using traditional, non-scriptural sources Hopkins gives a startlingly exact and personal physical description:

In his body he was most beautiful. . . . They tell us that he was moderately tall, well built and tender in frame, his features straight and beautiful, his hair inclining to auburn, parted in the midst, curling and clustering about the ears and neck as the leaves of a filbert, so to speak, upon the nut. He wore also a forked beard and this as well as the locks upon his head were never touched by razor or shears; neither, his health being perfect, could a hair ever fall to the ground. . . . I leave it to you, brethren, then to picture him, in whom the fullness of the godhead dwelt bodily, in his bearing how majestic, how strong and yet how lovely and lissome in his limbs, in his look how earnest, grave but kind. In his Passion all this strength was spent, this lissomness crippled, this beauty wrecked, this majesty beaten down. But now it is more than all restored, and for myself I make no secret I look forward with eager desire to seeing the matchless beauty of Christ's body in the heavenly light.[11]

Part of this sermon had been worked out in a letter to Bridges the previous month. Hopkins had been so discouraging that Bridges wondered if there were any good in his going on writing poetry. Hopkins replied by going over the criticism in detail, modifying it, and trying to get to the roots of Bridges's self-disenchantment:

You seem to want to be told over again that you have genius and are a poet and your verses beautiful. You have been told so, not only by me but very spontaneously by Gosse, Marzials, and others. . . . You want perhaps to be told more in particular. I am not the best to tell you, being biassed by love, and yet I am too.

The next stage of the argument—that his love for Bridges is partly for bodily beauty—is omitted by Hopkins. But he continues:

I think then that no one can admire beauty of the body more than I do, and it is of course a comfort to find beauty in a friend or a friend in beauty. But this kind of beauty is dangerous. Then comes the beauty of the mind, such as genius, and this is greater than the beauty of the body and not to call dangerous. And more beautiful than the beauty of the mind is the beauty of character, the 'handsome heart'.

After a long excursus on the Aristotelian theory that the soul is the form of the body, Hopkins makes his point: 'If I were not your friend I shd. wish to be the friend of the man that wrote your poems. They shew the eye for pure beauty and they shew, my dearest, besides, the character which is much more rare and precious.'[12]

This letter was one of the longest he wrote to Bridges, and its writing took twenty-seven days. The day before he started the letter he had assisted at the wedding of Mr John Fairclough to Miss Maggie Unsworth in St Joseph's, and composed a three-stanzaed celebratory poem, 'At the Wedding March'. It was the only poem he completed at Leigh, though he started 'a tragedy on St. Winefred's Martyrdom' and one on Margaret Clitheroe, 'who suffered by pressing to death at York on Ouse Bridge, Lady Day 1586 (I think): her history is terrible and heartrending'. He confessed to Bridges once that he felt a 'great spooniness over weddings', and thought everyone should get married. After blessing the couple and entreating them to 'Each be other's comfort kind', the poet speaks personally:

> Then let the March tread our ears:
> I to him turn with tears
> Who to wedlock, his wonder wedlock,
> Deals triumph and immortal years.

In a sermon he wrote the following month, Christ is 'the true-love and the bridegroom of men's souls'.

He had been having trouble with Canon Dixon's admiration of his poetry, and with his intention to insert that 'abrupt footnote' about Hopkins in his next volume of Church history. Hopkins wanted to wait until circumstances favoured publicity—if they ever would—and did not want to appear to be insubordinate. He added: 'The life I lead is liable to many mortifications but the want of fame as a poet is the least of them.' His attitude to publication of his poems varied from time to time, and Dixon did not take him at his word. In October 1879 Hopkins received a brief note:

I feel that I have kept your Poems longer than I ought; but I am unwilling to send them back without doing something.

Should you be angry that I sent your Loss of the Eurydice, or part of it, to one of the Carlisle Papers, giving your name, and a line or two of introduction from myself?

Hopkins *was* angry:

I am troubled about it because it may come to the knowledge of some of ours and an unpleasant construction be put upon it. It would be easy to explain it to the Provincial, but not so easy to guard myself against what others might say. . . . You would not, I hope, think I secretly wished to steal a march upon my superiors: that would be in me a great baseness.[13]

Dixon's reply has been lost, but it produced a fussy and uncontrolled letter from Hopkins: 'Pray do not send the piece to the paper: I cannot consent to, I forbid its publication. You must see that to publish my manuscript against my expressed wish is a breach of trust. Ask any friend and he will tell you the same.' Hopkins dreaded 'private notoriety'. The Society 'could not approve of unauthorised publication', then again 'if you were to print my piece you would surely not mutilate it. And yet you must; for with what grace could you, a clergyman of the Church of England, stand godfather to some of the stanzas in that poem?' Besides he wanted to alter the last stanza. If the paper published the poem, it would be sure to misprint it, and 'few will read it and of those few fewer will scan it, much less understand or like it'.[14] Four days later—the details are not known—everything had 'blown over and no harm done'. Dixon's appreciation of Hopkins's poems was not only well-meant and sincere, but wholehearted:

I have read [your poems] many times with the greatest admiration: in the power of forcibly & delicately giving the essence of things in nature, & of carrying one out of one's self with healing, these poems are unmatched. The Eurydice no one could read without the deepest & most ennobling emotion. The Sonnets are all truly wonderful. . . . The Deutschland is enormously powerful.[15]

Perhaps to gain local inspiration for his play, Hopkins spent Christmas at St Beuno's. His mother sent him gloves, mittens, and a comforter (the last he gave away). The vale of Clwyd was looking beautiful, and on St Stephen's Day he bathed in St Winefride's Well, which was 'lukewarm and smoked in the frosty air'.[16] But on New Year's Day, 1880, he was in Liverpool.

જી

He had been appointed one of several curates to the large, poor parish of St Francis Xavier's, Salisbury Street, Liverpool.[17] It came as a shock to this patriotic southerner to see the ghastly cost of his country's prosperity, to which Liverpool had largely contributed. Liverpool's population had grown rapidly during the Industrial Revolution, and the overcrowding had been increased by large immigrations from

Ireland in the potato-famine years of the 1840s. The river Mersey was
an unrelieved symbol of industrial gloom. Liverpool was perhaps the
most blatant example of the extremely poor and the extremely rich
living within a few yards of each other, sometimes divided only by a
street. Rodney Street, Mornington Terrace, and other bright, spacious,
and beautifully laid-out streets to the east of the city centre were grimly
neighboured by the Everton slums to the west.

Hopkins lodged in Everton, in Salisbury Street, which stretched
along the brow of the hill off Islington. It was not as bad as some areas
of Liverpool; there was a repetitive pattern of streets, leading down to
the canal and dock, of flat stone setts. The narrow houses were on top of
one another; there were fixed iron water pumps outside in the badly lit
streets. Yet half a mile down Islington Hill was one of the grandest and
proudest groups of civic buildings in England, the magnificent Corinthian temple called St George's Hall, with its twin equestrian statues of
Albert and Victoria, the Free Public Library, and the Public Gardens,
opposite the London and North-Western Railway station on Lime
Street. The artisan classes could walk into the Walker Art Gallery,
which had been opened three years before Hopkins arrived, and see
images remote from their own lives—Greek, Roman, Eastern, medieval
English, Arthurian, and pastoral.

Hopkins's first message from Liverpool was on a postcard, and
flurried: 'I have been here a day or two and am settled. I cannot write
more and shall have less time than ever.'[18] The tone of his subsequent
letters from Liverpool is similar: (to Baillie) 'my Liverpool work is very
harassing and makes it hard to write'; (to Dixon) 'the parish work of
Liverpool is very wearying to mind and body and leaves me nothing but
odds and ends of time. There is merit in it but little Muse, and indeed
26 lines is the whole I have writ in more than half a year, since I left
Oxford.'[19] His work was the ordinary parish drudgery—confessions,
catechism classes, house and hospital visits, and occasional sermons—in
a depressing area: 'Jenkinson Street and Gomer Street and Back Queen
Ann Street and Torbock Street and Bidder Street and Birchfield Street
and Bickerstaffe Street and the rest of my purlieus'.[20] He tried to
transfer to his Liverpool parishioners the sentimental warmth he had
felt towards the people of Bedford Leigh. He had to assert positive
feelings in order to carry on work for which he had no talent or
inclination. And he made the occasional piece of poetry out of his parish
work.

On 21 April 1880 a thirty-one-year-old horse-shoer or farrier, Felix
Spencer, died. Hopkins visited him in his Birchfield Street slum during

his consumptive illness. On the following Sunday the name was read out from the St Francis Xavier pulpit, and Hopkins preached that morning's sermon.[21] He wrote his poem 'Felix Randal' on 28 April. 'There is something highly poetical about a forge', George Borrow had written, and seeing the farrier racked by coughing and wasting lungs, Hopkins pictured the former glory of this 'mould of man, big-boned and hardy-handsome', 'when thou at the random grim forge, powerful amidst peers,/ Didst fettle for the great grey drayhorse his bright and battering sandal!' The poem has an amazing structure of image and sound, but some readers have felt distaste for its romantic distance from the human subject, and reject the poem for the picture Hopkins paints of himself as a fatherly parish worker.[22] 'I do not think I can be long here,' he wrote to Baillie, after he had been in Liverpool for five months; 'I have been long nowhere yet. I am brought face to face with the deepest poverty and misery in my district.'[23]

Hopkins was chosen for the honour of giving four Sunday evening sermons in St Francis Xavier's pulpit. The Sunday evening sermon was an event in the district, with established traditions of unloading trams and queuing crowds.[24] Hopkins took as his subjects 'Thy will be done', 'Thy Kingdom come', 'God's Kingdom in the Earthly Paradise', and 'On the Fall of God's First Kingdom',[25] the governing analogy being between God's kingdom and an earthly one. The second sermon was densely written, and full of qualifications, the line of thought neither simple nor direct. Hopkins was neither himself nor a popular preacher. He tried to speak according to his idea of what a popular preacher would say. However, it was not style over which he came to grief but his theology. Scotus was to blame: his theory of the Incarnation led to Hopkins's title 'The Fall of God's First Kingdom'. Hopkins's note, written beneath the title on the manuscript, tells the story: 'I was not allowed to take this title and on the printed bills it was covered by a blank slip pasted over. The text too I changed to last week's, and had to leave out or reword all passages speaking of God's kingdom as falling.'[26] When he preached the sermon again, in January 1882, he added two paragraphs of explanation.

He was not asked to preach again for the next three months; when he did, his Rector, Fr Clare, talked to him about the art of the sermon, and there is a pained remark 'it seems that written sermons do no good' at the head of his notes, followed by 'However the Rector wishes me to write'.[27] By this time the preacher was Fr William Dubberley, who had come to St Francis Xavier's at the same time as Hopkins. The parish historian, as Devlin remarks, 'recalls Fr Dubberley's sermons in glowing terms, but of Hopkins as a preacher he has no record'. After the four January sermons, Hopkins preached only another nine in his remaining eighteen months in Liverpool, and four of these were mid-week. Even then all did not go smoothly. A note of Hopkins's of 25 October 1880 reads: 'In consequence of this word *sweetheart* I was in a manner suspended and at all events was forbidden . . . to preach without having my sermon revised. However when I was going to take the next sermon I had to give after this regulation came into force to Fr Clare for revision he poohpoohed the matter and would not look at it.'[28]

Writing to his mother for her birthday in March, Hopkins explained: 'Every week one of our community goes to Lydiate, to a Catholic country house the residence of the Lightbound family, so as to say mass next morning and return.' The Lightbound country house near the small village of Lydiate was Rose Hill. Walking from there to the train in September 1880 Hopkins wrote a poem, to which he later began a plainchant air:

> *Spring and Fall:*
> to a Young Child
>
> Margaret, are you grieving
> Over Goldengrove unleaving?
> Leaves, like the things of man, you
> With your fresh thoughts care for, can you?
> Ah! as the heart grows older
> It will come to such sights colder
> By and by, nor spare a sigh
> Though worlds of wanwood leafmeal lie;
> And yet you *will* weep and know why.
> Now no matter, child, the name:
> Sorrow's springs are the same.
> Nor mouth had, no nor mind, expressed
> What heart heard of, ghost guessed:
> It is the blight man was born for,
> It is Margaret you mourn for.

'Spring and Fall' is one of Hopkins's most Victorian poems and one of his most successful. Almost every year after he became a Jesuit Hopkins recorded in his journal or letters the annual crisis of spring: he knew he would gain strength from the fresh season's arrival, but sometimes doubted if it would come. Spring was nearly always late, and then did not carry the power he expected. Part of the beauty of 'Spring and Fall' lies in its indulgence and detachment, its sad interplay between the sorrowing girl and melancholy adult speaker. The poem keeps Hopkins's natural description compressed, while creating inscapes with a new haunting quality: 'Though worlds of wanwood leafmeal lie'.

Apart from 'Spring and Fall' and 'Felix Randal', he was almost unable to write: 'time and spirits were wanting; one is so fagged, so harried and gallied up and down.' His work seemed of little use: 'the drunkards go on drinking, the filthy, as the scripture says, are filthy still: human nature is so inveterate. Would that I had seen the last of it.'[29] He occasionally joked about his writing:

The teapot of inclination has been tilted several times till the spout of intention very nearly teemed out the liquor of execution (I am speaking of myself now ... and must point out the extraordinary merit of the figure I am employing: I shall work it up), but till now it has not filled the cup and saucer of communication. Time indeed is scanty.[30]

Again and again Hopkins comes back to the awfulness of Liverpool, which drains him of energy and time: 'Liverpool is of all places the most museless. It is indeed a most unhappy and miserable spot. There is moreover no time for writing anything serious—I should say for composing it, for if it were made it might be written.'[31]

'Every impulse and spring of art seems to have died in me', Hopkins wrote to Bridges, 'except for music, and that I pursue under almost an impossibility of getting on.' But he still wrote airs, and sent some of them for his sister Grace to harmonize: 'Tell Grace I am really getting on with the two pieces of music set to Bridges' spring Odes and they will be ready in a day or two.'[32] His music, the occasional Hallé orchestral concert, and the exchanges of poems and comments with Dixon and Bridges were the only constant pleasures. In March 1880 he was 'knocked up': 'the work of Easter week (worse than Holy Week) was so hard, and I had happened to catch a bad cold, which led to earache and deafness.' He felt wretched for some time:

Neither am I very strong now [30 April] and as long as I am in Liverpool I do not see how I can be; not that I complain of this, but I state it. There are many Italians here, organ grinders and so on: I do not know how they can bear such an air and sky. No, I see nothing of the Spring but some leaves in streets and squares. It is good, and all advise it, to get out of town and breathe fresh air at New Brighton or somewhere else, but I find it almost impossible. I have done it but once, barring the necessary run to Lydiate. ... Work and sickness have stood in the way of the music.[33]

By September that year he was, if anything, worse: 'I take up a languid pen to write to you, being down with diarrhoea and vomiting, brought on by yesterday's heat and the long hours in the confessional. Yesterday was in Liverpool the hottest day of the year.'[34]

Nature was absent. In Oxford he used to say to himself 'but still . . . I see the sun', whereas 'now at Liverpool one can *not* see the sun'. But there is one exception, which stands out strangely in his writings from the city. In January of the new year he went 'down to see the ice in the Mersey and the infinite flocks of seagulls', and wrote for Bridges an account which is different from his usual descriptive prose; it has the broad-canvas, objective life of a novel:

Well, I went. The river was coated with dirty yellow ice from shore to shore; where the edges could be seen it seemed very thick; it was not smooth but many broken pieces framed or pasted together again; it was floating down stream with the ebb tide; it everywhere covered the water, but was not of a piece, being continually broken, ploughed up, by the plying of the steam ferryboats, which I believe sometimes can scarcely make their way across. The gulls were pampered; throngs of people were chucking them bread; they were not at all quick to sight it and when they did they dipped towards it with infinite lightness, touched the ice, and rose again, *but generally missed the bread*: they seem to fancy they cannot or ought not to rest on ground.—However I hear the Thames is frozen and an ox roasted whole. Today there is a thaw, and the frostings, which have been a lovely fairyland on the publicans windows, are vanished from the panes.[35]

Hopkins was grateful to Dixon for high praise of his poems, but another generous piece of encouragement from Dixon came to nothing. Hall Caine had asked Dixon's permission to reprint a couple of his sonnets in an anthology he was making, and with his reply Dixon had sent Hopkins's 'The Starlight Night' and 'The Caged Skylark', and wrote to Hopkins asking if he would agree to have one of his poems published with his name on it. Surprisingly, Hopkins immediately sent off to Caine a choice of three sonnets,[36] which Caine acknowledged 'in a somewhat effusive postcard and promised to write more fully in 2 or 3 days, but did not'. Hopkins also recommended to Caine a little volume of sonnets by Richard Crawley, an Oxford contemporary. Eventually, he reported, Caine wrote.

He is not going to print me, because the purpose of his book (or introduction or prefatory essay to it) is to 'demonstrate the impossibility of improving upon the acknowledged structure whether as to rhyme-scheme or measure'. Poor soul, he writes to me as to a she bear robbed of her cubs. I am replying now and reassuring him and smoothing down.[37]

In the same letter to Bridges Hopkins commented on his own 'eccentricities': 'Alas I have heard so much about and suffered so much for and in fact been so completely ruined for life by my alleged singularities that they are a sore subject.'[38] Lent and Easter week being on him again, Hopkins was 'much jaded', and disappointed by the Mayday procession of horses:

The procession was not so very good: some people had thought it shd. be on Monday and so everybody and every horse did not come. A busman or cabman consoled me by declaiming in a voice hoarse with professional passion that he cd. not get on for this damned show. While I admired the handsome horses I remarked for the thousandth time with sorrow and loathing the base and bespotted figures and features of the Liverpool crowd. When I see the fine and manly Norwegians that flock hither to embark for America walk our streets and look about them it fills me with shame and wretchedness. I am told Sheffield is worse though.[39]

'What will befall me I do not know', Hopkins wrote to Bridges on 15 May 1881, 'but I hardly think I shall be much longer in Liverpool'.[40]

*ొ*

On 10 August that year, Hopkins was sent, as temporary replacement for Fr Bernard Winkler, to the parish of St Joseph's, Glasgow,[41] for a fortnight or so, it was thought, but his stay was prolonged to two months. He found things pleasanter at Glasgow. 'Like all great towns', he wrote to Bridges, Glasgow was a 'wretched place', and 'repulsive to live in', but there were alleviations: 'I get on better here, though bad is the best of my getting on.'[42] The streets and buildings were 'fine', and 'the people lively':

The poor Irish, among whom my duties lay, are mostly from the North of Ireland, scarcely distinguishable in tongue from the Scotch and at Glasgow still further Scoticised. They are found by all who have to deal with them very attractive; for, though always very drunken and at present very Fenian, they are warm-hearted and give a far heartier welcome than those at Liverpool.[43]

He found himself very much at home with them, he wrote to Baillie.

St Joseph's was in a densely populated district of Glasgow. Large numbers of the parishioners came from Donegal; they lived in crowded tenements, and were mainly employed in the factories and at a local whisky bond-house. There was enough parish work to keep four Jesuit priests busy, at baptisms, marriages, funerals, confessions, catechism classes, schoolwork, visits, and instruction. Hopkins was soon performing baptisms;[44] occasionally there was the hurried baptism of a newborn baby not expected to live, or the baptism of an illegitimate child, with the space for the father's name blank on the register. At the beginning of October Hopkins's touch is noticeable in the Latin column of the register, where—in contrast to his colleagues, who did not attempt to translate names more difficult than John or William—he transforms Louisa into 'Ludovica'. He performed twenty-eight baptisms during his two months in Glasgow.

In Liverpool and Glasgow he was constantly frustrated in his desire to write, not only poetry but letters. At Glasgow, however, he did start an ode on the sixteenth-century Jesuit martyr Edmund Campion. The 300th anniversary of the execution at Tyburn of Campion and his companions Sherwin and Briant would fall on 1 December next, 'from which I expect of heaven some, I cannot guess what, great conversion or other blessing to the Church in England'. The poem had not been hard to start: 'thinking over this matter my vein began to flow'; by the middle of September he could report to Bridges 'I have by me a few scattered stanzas, something between the *Deutschland* and *Alexander's Feast*, in sprung rhythm of irregular metre'.[45] But his time for completing the poem was limited, and he felt a sense of urgency. (He had resolved that once at Roehampton, where he was due to go in October for his tertianship, the third year of his noviceship, 'I will altogether give over composition for the ten months, that I may *vacare Deo* as in my noviceship proper.') He feared he would not finish the ode: 'the vein urged by any country sight or feeling of freedom or leisure (you cannot tell what a slavery of mind or heart it is to live my life in a great town) soon dried and I do not know if I can coax it to run again.' One night, as he lay 'in a fevered state', he 'had some glowing thoughts and lines, but ... did not put them down and I fear they may fade to little or nothing'. Sometimes he was surprised 'how slow and laborious a thing verse is', while 'musical composition comes so easily, for I can make tunes almost at all times and places'.[46] (Nothing of the Campion ode exists.)

Hopkins even found it difficult to write a letter to Dixon who, he told Bridges, 'lies like a load on my heart. To him I am every day meaning to write and last night it was I began, but it would not do.' In January that year Dixon had sent Hopkins some of his poems in manuscript, with blank pages opposite each for Hopkins's comments. Hopkins kept them by him in Liverpool, but as the year wore on and he had not looked at them, their presence weighed on his mind.

Some of the poems Hopkins had brought with him to Glasgow, and on 16 September, after completing his letter to Bridges, he eventually sat down to write to Dixon. As a first stage he copied out most of the poems, and three of them he liked so much that he learned them by heart. All of these were song-like, and Hopkins found tunes for two,

'Sky that rollest ever', and 'Fallen Rain', whose delicate and poignant little air is Hopkins's most appealing music. On 17 September he wrote to Dixon of the third poem, 'Does the south wind?', 'this is one of those interpretations of the meanings of nature of which you have the secret, like those princes and people in fairytales who "knew what the birds were saying" '. The last stanza 'breathes a lovely touching pathos', and one phrase in particular 'lingers on the mind'.[47]

He had been promised that before he left Glasgow he could have two days to see something of the Highlands. As it turned out though, he 'never had more than a glimpse of their skirts'. On 28 September, at the end of his stay in Glasgow, he took a hurried trip to Inversnaid, on the eastern shore of Loch Lomond, in the Trossachs, a mountain region deserted except for a lone sheep farm or hunting lodge. Hopkins's probable reason for going there was Wordsworth's poem 'To a Highland Girl/ (At Inversnayde, upon Loch Lomond)', written there at the same time of year. Inversnaid had been famous as a summer resort for Glaswegians since the publication in 1807 of the poem, and there was now a large hotel on the loch shore, by the side of the Inversnaid Falls, catering for the summer boatloads of visitors. Despite its popularity, Inversnaid was isolated, and even during its short summer season very beautiful.

'The day was dark', wrote Hopkins afterwards, 'and partly hid the lake, yet it did not altogether disfigure it but gave a pensive or solemn beauty which left a deep impression on me.'[48] While on the boat he 'was delivered of an air' to Dixon's 'Does the south wind?'—'a very good tune to some lovely words',[49] he later said. He could spend only a few hours there, but the spot inspired a poem. Wordsworth's poem had described

> these grey rocks; that household lawn;
> Those trees, a veil just half withdrawn;
> This fall of water that doth make
> A murmur near the silent lake;
> This little bay; a quiet road
> That holds in shelter thy Abode . . .

At this time Hopkins considered Wordsworth and the other Lake poets 'faithful but not rich observers of nature'.

Arklet Water[50] was wider and fuller than a burn; its peaty-brown waters, descended from Loch Arklet, were added to by burns, noticeably Snaid Burn, and over a course of a mile and a half through narrow valleys of heather and ladder-fern to oak forests, with the occasional birch, ash, and, hanging over the water, rowan, gradually steepened and quickened. There were smaller falls and side pools, with froth, foam, bubbles, and whirls, in rocky basins, before the final, magnificent, high but broken fall into a larger pool just before it entered Loch Lomond. Hopkins first saw the fall from the steamer, and on landing at the pier climbed up the mossy and rocky side of the stream to the narrow road, and then walked along the road inland, following the course of the stream uphill.

Hopkins began with an echo of Wordsworth's procedural method, 'This . . .'. But Hopkins's is a richer observation, and more limited, as it concentrates on describing the stream and the fall. It is his only Scottish poem and mixes Scottish words, like 'burn' and 'brae', with words which he surely imagined spoken by a mid-Scots voice, so dominant are the *l*s and *r*s, which would be formidably exaggerated if pronounced by a Glaswegian. But behind the Scottish sounds his own lexis is present, in 'coop', 'comb', 'fleece', 'foam':

> This darksome burn, horseback brown,
> His rollrock highroad roaring down,
> In coop and in comb the fleece of his foam
> Flutes and low to the lake falls home.

Wordsworth's calm tetrameter is transformed into a rollicking ride, with subtle variations in its well-marked rhythm, and with more physical images and hard-consonanted, strange words.

The final stanza enlarges and unifies. In Oxford, two-and-a-half years previously, Hopkins had composed 'something, if I cd. only seize it, on the decline of wild nature, beginning somehow like this—

> O where is it, the wilderness,
> The wildness of the wilderness?
> Where is it, the wilderness?'[51]

And he now used that musical fragment, worked at and tightened until it formed a moral plea and conclusion to his Inversnaid stanzas:

> What would the world be, once bereft
> Of wet and of wildness? Let them be left,
> O let them be left, wildness and wet;
> Long live the weeds and the wilderness yet.

Hopkins was not satisfied with the poem, and did not mention it to either Bridges or Dixon, neither of whom saw it until after his death.

☙

Hopkins was due to present himself at Manresa House, Roehampton, on 10 October, to begin the tertianship, 'the third year', as he explained to Bridges, '(really ten months) of noviceship which we undergo before taking our last vows'. After Liverpool and Glasgow he felt he needed the noviceship: '[I] shall be every way better off when I have been made more spiritual minded'.[52]

# 26

# 'Surely one vocation cannot destroy another?': Roehampton Tertianship and Stonyhurst, 1881–1883

Hopkins came to Manresa House on 8 October. As he explained to Canon Dixon, the tertianship was not a noviceship. At the end of the noviceship proper, before he had left Manresa in 1870, he had taken vows which were perpetually binding, and renewed them every six months after that until he was professed or took the final degree he was to hold in the Society. The tertianship prepared for these last vows, which would be pronounced at its close. At this stage Hopkins considered he still had a chance of making up his lost fourth year of theology and becoming a professed father, the only rank eligible for the major Jesuit offices.

The tertianship, he went on, was 'meant to enable us to recover that fervour which may have cooled through application to study and contact with the world'. Its exercises were nearly the same as those of the noviceship proper. 'As for myself', he told Dixon,

I have not only made my vows publicly some two and twenty times [that is, twice a year for the eleven years since he had left the novitiate] but I make them to myself every day, so that I should be black with perjury if I drew back now. And beyond that I can say with St. Peter: To whom shall I go? Tu verba vitae aeternae habes.

He drew the ideal picture of the withdrawn life:

Besides all which, my mind is here more at peace than it has ever been and I would gladly live all my life, if it were so to be, in as great or a greater seclusion from the world and be busied only with God. But in the midst of outward occupations not only the mind is drawn away from God, which may be at the call of duty and be God's will, but unhappily the will too is entangled, wordly interests freshen, and worldly ambitions revive. The man who in the world is as dead to the world as if he were buried in the cloister is already a saint. But this is our ideal.[1]

It was Newman's also: his self-composed epitaph reads: 'ex umbris et imaginibus in veritatem'—'from shadows and images passed into reality'. Hopkins's statement of this chilling ideal does not acknowledge the passionate attachments which his writings show were part of his nature.

The opening of the tertianship was celebrated by double tables in the refectory and a cold-meat breakfast.[2] After a week and a half Hopkins felt the strain: he wrote to Bridges, 'I shd. have written before, but it is no easy task meeting one's out of door liabilities (any how writing letters is what I mean) with a day so sliced up into the duties of a noviceship as this life is. I see no newspapers, read none but spiritual books.'[3] The tertian has to

repeat all the experimental tests and trials of the first two years of his religious life. He has to sweep and dust the rooms and corridors, to chop wood, to wash plates and dishes, besides going over again the spiritual work of the novice, the long retreat of thirty days included. He has also during this year to study the institute of the Society, and during Lent to take part in some one of the public missions which are given by the various religious orders in the large towns.[4]

The Manresa community consisted of about a hundred, of whom nine were tertians; their tertian master was Fr Whitty. It was miserable weather, 'raining very heavily, thro' a white fog'. A great gale 'left a scene of havoc, and knocked all round our neighbourhood tall trees down like ninepins'. But although Manresa's grounds had suffered from natural decay and more from human hands, they were still beautiful, Hopkins felt; and 'it is besides a great rest to be here and I am in a very contented frame of mind'.[5]

The Long Retreat began on 7 November. An account of an earlier tertianship said:

We have got through the long retreat with very little fatigue. I found the midnight meditations (of which we had sixteen) not at all tiring, and they did not unfit one for the meditations of the day, as I rather expected. Of course I felt tired from time to time, but the day's repose when it came freshened one up again for a new beginning. We had three such repose days.[6]

Hopkins made several notes during the Retreat, mainly on the implications of biblical texts.[7] One of these takes Christ as the example for a hidden life, 'sacrificing, as he did, all to obedience his very obedience was unknown', and draws an interesting corollary, in view of Hopkins's own abhorrence of certain places he was stationed at, of the 'repulsiveness' of Nazareth.[8] On 8 December, the feast of the Immaculate Conception, the tertians finished their Long Retreat. After dinner they had two glasses of claret with the other fathers in the refectory, and the day finished with solemn benediction. Three days afterwards, on Sunday 11 December, Hopkins said the 11 a.m. mass at the local parish church of St Joseph's.⁹

In spite of his resolve to give up non-professional writing for the ten months, he wrote four long letters to Dixon, on 12–17 and 23–5 October, 29 October–2 November, and 1–16 December,¹⁰ including detailed criticism of Dixon's poetry, poem by poem, an account of the music that he had written to four of Dixon's poems, and a long lecture on the sonnet form. He felt guilty about these letters, and near the end of the third one wrote: 'This must be my last letter on literary matters while I stay here, for they are quite out of keeping with my present duties.' While in this frame of mind, which belongs to the attitude of self-subjugation fostered by the tertianship, Hopkins gave an account of ideal attitudes to writing his poetry:

The question then for me is not whether I am willing . . . to make a sacrifice of hopes of fame . . . but whether I am not to undergo a severe judgment from God for the lothness I have shewn in making it . . . for the waste of time the very compositions you admire may have caused and their preoccupation of the mind which belonged to more sacred or to more binding duties.¹¹

There can be no doubt about the conflict between the priest and the poet, since the time devoted to poetry is not only a 'waste of time' but liable to 'severe judgment from God'. The conflict had been present from the time of 'the destruction of the innocents', and though never resolved in practice, was renewed in each retreat: 'I destroyed the verse I had written when I entered the Society and meant to write no more; the *Deutschland* I began after a long interval at the chance suggestion of my superior, but that being done it is a question whether I did well to write anything else.' Hopkins was a compulsive poet: even repressed by a severely ascetic moral culture, his compulsiveness created space for itself, however restricted and eroded:

However I shall, in my present mind, continue to compose, as occasion shall fairly allow, which I am afraid will be seldom and indeed for some years past has been scarcely ever, and let what I produce wait and take its chance . . . . But I can scarcely fancy myself asking a superior to publish a volume of my verses and I own that humanly there is very little likelihood of that ever coming to pass.

The argument wavers; once he has come down firmly on the official side, he objects: 'And to be sure if I chose to look at things on one side and not the other I could of course regret this bitterly.' There can be only one conclusion, particularly during the tertianship: 'There is more peace and it is the holier lot to be unknown than to be known.—In no case am I willing to write anything while in my present condition: the time is precious and will not return again and I know I shall not regret my forbearance.'[12]

Dixon's muted reply acknowledged the sacrifice: 'the regret that much of it gives me: to hear of your having destroyed poems, & feeling that you have a vocation in comparison of which poetry & the fame that might assuredly be yours is nothing. I could say much, for my heart bleeds . . . .' Dixon had seen the conflict: 'Surely one vocation cannot destroy another: and such a Society as yours will not remain ignorant that you have such gifts as have seldom been given by God to man.'[13]

Writing on Christmas Eve, Hopkins told his mother of an article appearing in January's *Month*, on a thirteenth-century manuscript of a hymn to the Blessed Virgin in Latin and English: 'The Latin and English texts are carefully reproduced; and a modernisation of the latter follows, made originally by me but altered since, perhaps not altogether for the better. The footnotes on the old english are mostly by me.' Just before Christmas his brother Lionel had come to Manresa House and stayed to dinner:

We had a pleasant afternoon together, somewhat clouded however by the inordinate and inexpressible smoking of the chimney of the guest-room. But after he had gone I had a worse misfortune in my own room, where the gale blew the soot all over the place and made things miserable. This only happens when the wind is in that one quarter. He and I may now hope to meet again.

Although near home, Hopkins had to spend Christmas at Manresa. The community of tertians had become 'much diminished: some have been called off altogether and others have been despatched for Christmas duty here and there'. There was 'a general topsy-turvy cheerful air, Christmas is being hung everywhere'.[14] For Christmas dinner there were bacon and eggs for the first dish, 'three glasses of wine (one during dinner) with dessert, apples, oranges & biscuits. Pousse & coffee for Fathers who were joined by the Tertians.'[15] Hopkins, however, was 'quite crippled with a chilblain and can only hobble. It is a serious nuisance. It is not broken, I wish it would break'.[16]

On New Year's Eve Hopkins went to supply at Brentford, but was 'hourly expecting orders to return to Liverpool':

One of our Fathers [William Hilton], who was for the best part of two years my yokemate on that laborious mission, died there yesterday night after a short sickness, in harness and in his prime. I am saddened by this death, for he was particularly good to me; he used to come up to me and say 'Gerard, you are a good soul' and that I was a comfort to him in his trouble. His place must now be supplied and it must be by one or two, both in this house; I feel little doubt it will be by me and that this is probably the last night I shall spend at Roehampton.[17]

Hopkins was wrong. He wrote at the beginning of February to Bridges, who, after 'a sudden and wonderful recovery' from serious illness, had gone to Italy for the winter, 'At the beginning of Lent I am to take duty at Preston'.[18]

On 2 February, a holiday, he visited the South Kensington museums, was bewildered by the 'wealth of beautiful things', and thought of the advantage Bridges had in Italy, 'for which nothing can completely make up . . . of seeing these things on the spot'.[19] At the beginning of Lent he was sent to St Wilfrid's, Preston, Lancashire, 'to stop a gap and do some parish work'.[20] Then, on 12 March, the feast of St Gregory the Great, Apostle of England, a mission began at the Benedictine church of Our Lady and St Patrick in Maryport, conducted by Hopkins and Fr White. The *Maryport Advertiser* commented:

During the past fortnight mission services have been conducted . . . and have been largely attended. On Sunday evening last the inauguration of the 'Children of Mary' took place. The candidates wearing white veils occupied seats in the lady chapel. The Rev. Father Hopkins preached an appropriate and eloquent sermon. The choir having been strengthened by some professional singers, the Benediction service was exceedingly well sung, especially the 'Tantum Ergo'. Upwards of 750 persons were present at the service.[21]

It was 'something like a Revival without the hysteria and the heresy', Hopkins told Bridges; 'and it had the effect of bringing me out and making me speak very plainly and strongly (I enjoyed that, for I dearly like calling a spade a spade): it was the first thing of the sort I had been employed in.'[22]

On his way from Maryport he stopped off at Carlisle to meet Dixon, probably the only time they met. Dixon gave him dinner and showed him round the cathedral. Partly because of this sightseeing, but 'more through shyness on his part (not on mine) we did not get much intimate or even interesting talk'. 'I wish our meeting cd. have been longer for several reasons', Hopkins wrote to Dixon afterwards, 'but to name one, I fancied you were shy and that time would have been needed for this to wear off.' 'I dare say I seemed "shy" ', Dixon replied; 'I have an unfortunate manner: & am constantly told that I am too quiet. . . . You must therefore forgive it: it is not from want of feeling or affection.'[23]

Hopkins returned to Manresa on 5 April, and was told to go on supply at St Elizabeth's, in Richmond, Surrey, where the parish priest had been taken ill. At the end of the month Hopkins gave an eight-day retreat to an elderly gentleman, Mr Plant.[24] On 18 May, Ascension Day, Bridges came to Manresa with his young nephew, son of his sister Maria, who made conversation difficult:

My heart warmed towards that little Bertie Molesworth (I do not mean by this that he is so very small), so that if you were to bring him again I shd. be glad to see him. (But I am afraid he felt dull. He is shy I dare say.) . . . It cannot be denied nevertheless that the presence of a third person is a restraint upon confidential talk.

They walked around Manresa's beautiful grounds and Bridges asked the gardener Davis to let him buy some peaches,[25] but Hopkins's scruples would not allow it. Almost fifty years later, when Hopkins had been dead for forty of them, Bridges wrote this incident into *The Testament of Beauty*:

> when the young poet my companion in study
> and friend of my heart refused a peach at my hands,
> he being then a housecarl in Loyola's menie,
> 'twas that he fear'd the savor of it, and when he waived
> his scruple to my banter, 'twas to avoid offence.[26]

Hopkins's fear of the peach's savour is familiar and poignant. 'Davis the gardener', he wrote to Bridges, 'was discontented that I would not let you buy his peaches: he wd. have let you have them on reasonable terms, he said.'

On 8 June Bridges again visited Manresa, and saw a Corpus Christi procession, which Hopkins admitted was 'heavy and dead'. Bridges's cynical reaction hurt Hopkins: 'It is long since such things had any significance for you. But what is strange and unpleasant is that you sometimes speak as if they had in reality none for me and you were only waiting with a certain disgust till I too should be disgusted with myself enough to throw off the mask.'[27]

On odd days during the rest of that ten months Hopkins was sent off to do various jobs—hearing confessions at Brentford, supplying for the Sunday haymaking at Horseferry Road, Westminster, and saying mass at St Joseph's. Just before his tertianship ended there was a retreat, during which he wrote sixteen pages of a commentary on St Ignatius' Spiritual Exercises. Then on 15 August, the feast of the Assumption, eight fathers pronounced their last vows, during 9 o'clock mass celebrated at St Joseph's by the Provincial, Fr Purbrick. Three of the eight repeated the four vows of the Professed, followed by the other five, including Hopkins, who took the simple vows of Spiritual Coadjutors.[28] Hopkins had completed his formal training as a Jesuit, fourteen years after he had first entered Manresa as a novice.

∽

On Thursday 31 August 1882, Hopkins went to Stonyhurst College to teach classics. The Provincial had given him leave to stay until term began in any of the province's Jesuit houses. He went for a week to Worcester, but felt uneasy and thought it better to go on to Stonyhurst immediately. His appointment was to teach the class that Stonyhurst called the 'philosophers', for the London University Intermediate and BA examinations, which he likened to Moderations and Greats at Oxford. Hopkins knew the college well from his stay of three months in 1878, and his three-year philosophate at the neighbouring St Mary's Hall.

When Hopkins arrived, new building was in full swing. There were 'contractors, builders, masons, bricklayers, carpenters, stonecutters and carvers, all on the spot; a traction engine twice a day fetches stone from a quarry on the fells; engines of all sorts send their gross and foulsmelling smoke all over us; cranes keep swinging; and so on'. Although he could see no real beauty in their design, Hopkins found the new buildings imposing, and liked the furniture and fittings. He climbed on to the flat roof, and found that, when the air was not thick, as it mostly was, it commanded 'a noble view of this Lancashire landscape, Pendle Hill, Ribblesdale, the fells, and all around, bleakish but solemn and beautiful'. 'I wish I could show you this place', he wrote to Bridges. He had taken upon himself the job of showing it to visitors, the tour taking anywhere from an hour and a half to three hours—'I do it with more pride than pleasure'. The college was proud of its sights: 'The garden with a bowling green, walled in by massive yew hedges', and 'a bowered yew-walk', gloomy and geometrical, the trees severely chopped into symmetrical blocks. The college observatory was in the charge of Fr Stephen Perry, an internationally known astronomer, whose Jesuit superiors had allowed him 'to follow the natural bent of his mind, and to devote himself wholly to science'. Stonyhurst prided itself on its Arundell Library and permanent exhibitions, which told the history of English Roman Catholicism and Jesuitism, from the Middle Ages to the present day, by means of objects. Its collection included early breviaries and manuscripts on fine vellum, books from secret sixteenth-century presses, a first edition of the work for which Pope Leo X had conferred on Henry VIII the title of Defender of the Faith, and works of Fr. Robert Persons SJ, first Superior of the English Jesuit Province. Other items exhibited were black wooden stocks, a bracelet of beads used in persecution times as a rosary, a miniature of Bonnie Prince Charlie, a lock of hair given by Mary Queen of Scots to George Douglas for saving her life at Lochleven Castle in 1568, and a pack of cards dating from 1679, which represented an anti-Catholic view of the Popish Plot, each card depicting a different scene.

Other things visitors might like to see, according to Hopkins, were: 'schoolboys and animation, philosophers and foppery (not to be taken too seriously), a jackdaw, a rookery, goldfish, a clough with waterfalls, fishing, grouse, an anemometer, a sunshine guage [*sic*], a sundial, an icosihedron, statuary, magnetic instruments, a laboratory, gymnasium, ambulacrum, studio, fine engravings, Arundel chromos, Lancashire talked with *naïveté* on the premises (Hoo said this and hoo did that)'. In the neighbourhood were 'the two other dependent establishments, one a furlong the other ¾ a mile off [St Mary's Hall and the preparatory school]; the river Hodder with lovely fairyland views, especially at the bathingplace, the Ribble too, the Calder, Whalley with an abbey, Clitheroe with a castle, Ribchester with a strange old chapel and Roman remains'.[29] Hopkins does not, however, seem to have seen much of the countryside during the school year; the natural scene is surprisingly absent from nearly all the letters. There is an occasional reference to a solitary walk; 'And now I think I am going out by woods and waters alone', he wrote to Bridges in May 1883.

'Knowing Stonyhurst',[30] it was said, 'you start to know the Jesuits.' During the early years of the nineteenth century Stonyhurst had been more than a Catholic school with a seminary attached: it had been the mother-house of the Society of Jesus in England, and the repository of the Society's history and traditions. The English Jesuits had been known as 'the gentlemen of Stonyhurst' since they and their pupils from the English missionary college at Liège had taken possession in 1794 of the derelict Elizabethan house with collapsed roof in 'one of the rudest districts of the kingdom'. The school had curious traditions. Stonyhurst boys entered the school at Elements, and moved up through Figures, Rudiments, Grammar, Syntax, and Poetry, to Rhetoric, which corresponded to the sixth form. The rooms were called Washing Place, Study Place, Dick's Place, Tailor's Place, Stranger's Place, Shoe Place. The school had its own versions of cricket and football which preserved many features of common Elizabethan games. The college curriculum was strictly dependent on the classics, and of course concentrated on religious instruction and practices. There was a high proportion of Irish pupils, and in the 1880s football matches were often played between the Irish and the rest.

Discipline was severe even by English public-school standards. Arthur Conan Doyle, who spent seven years as a boy at Stonyhurst before leaving in 1875, wrote: 'They try to rule too much by fear—too little by love and reason', and he said he would never send a son of his to the college because of its psychological pressures, the constant scrutiny by spying prefects and masters 'whose presence secures that training in orderliness, self-control and obedience to law, that is a chief object in education'. Dormitories were patrolled at night by a master, and the boys 'never left to themselves for a moment, the priests taking part in their games, their walks, and their talks'. Methods of discipline included the 'penance-walk' in which a boy 'was compelled to walk in silence and isolation up and down the playground for up to an hour'. There was the instrument called a 'ferula' or 'tolly', 'a piece of india-rubber of the size and shape of a thick boot sole. . . . One blow of this instrument, delivered with intent, would cause the palm of the hand to swell up and change colour.'[31]

Fr Purbrick wrote some time later that he had given Hopkins the post 'with fear and trembling', but he was sympathetic to Hopkins's temperamental problems, and on the occasion of his appointment told him that what time was left over from teaching Hopkins 'might employ in writing one or other of the books' Hopkins had told him about. One of these was on Greek lyric art, or 'the art of the choric and lyric parts of the Greek plays'. Hopkins wanted it to be in two parts, one on metre, the other on style:

My thought is that in any lyric passage of the tragic poets . . . there are usually . . . two strains of thought running together and like counterpointed; the overthought that which everybody, editors, see . . . the other, the under-thought, conveyed chiefly in the choice of metaphors etc used and often only half realised by the poet himself, not necessarily having any connection with the subject in hand. . . . Perhaps what I ought to say is that the underthought is commonly an echo or shadow of the overthought, something like canons and repetitions in music.[32]

This original structural and linguistic insight anticipates modern work on iterative imagery, but was doomed to failure. It is unlikely that Hopkins could have kept to a plan for such a large project, cutting out the ramifications his mind was in the habit of making. The few lines of plan, in the letter to Baillie, are extracted from passages of qualification and self-doubt, like this:

My thought is that in any lyric passage of the tragic poets (perhaps not so much in Euripides as the others) there are—usually; I will not say always, it is not likely—two strains of thought running together and like counterpointed; the overthought that which everybody, editors, see (when one does see anything— which in the great corruption of the text and original obscurity of the diction is not everywhere) and which might for instance be abridged or paraphrased in square marginal blocks as in some books carefully written; the other . . . .

There was no precedent in Hopkins's writings for such an extended work. His surviving Balliol essays are short, and a curt, epigrammatic style seems to have been encouraged rather then the exploratory language of speculation and analysis. His habit of assuming an attitude of instant mastery of a subject may have been—as suggested—fostered at Oxford. Clement Barraud once wrote to Hopkins 'from Demerara, describing the Feast of Lanterns, as celebrated there by the resident Chinese. His reply was a learned disquisition on Chinese music, God save the mark! discussing its peculiar tonality, and claiming for it merits which had certainly escaped my observation.'[33]

In spite of lively comments on a vast range of topics in his letters, he was not familiar with current work in any scholarly field outside religion, though he was well-read in modern English poetry. The Jesuit system of education had its own aims: Hopkins's ignorance of contemporary classical scholarship shows in his vague remark: 'There are, I believe, learned books lately written in Germany on the choric metres and music, which if I could see and read them would either serve me or quench me.' Hopkins was not working in an institution which offered him the kind of facilities and encouragement needed for scholarship. And a final impediment was self-doubt: 'It is I am afraid, too ambitious of me, so little of a scholar as I am. . . . it is a laborious business and why shd. I undertake it?'[34] Even before his teaching for the year at Stonyhurst started, he was predicting 'very little time will be left over and I cd. never make time. Indeed now, with nothing to do but prepare, I cannot get forward with my ode.'[35]

Once the academic year at the college was in full swing, although he liked his pupils and did 'not wholly dislike the work', he was dispirited:

I fall into or continue in a heavy weary state of body and mind in which my go is gone. . . . I make no way with what I read, and seem but half a man. It is a sad thing to say. I try, and am even meant to try, in my spare time (and if I were fresher or if it were anyone but myself there would be a good deal of spare time taking short and long together) to write some books; but I find myself so tired or so harassed I fear they will never be written.[36]

As he took the élite class, he was spared the punishing schedule of most of the masters, who had five hours of class daily, as well as at least one hour of extra assistance, and extra work for honours students, presiding over study, and daily marking. 'The system', said an otherwise approving commentator, 'is one which sacrifices the teacher to his pupils', and 'deprives the Professors of the opportunity of much useful reading and study'. Hopkins feared 'I shall not have time even for necessities, let alone luxuries or rather bywork'. Dixon tried to soothe him by saying his own experience was 'any teaching any literary work is good for the mind provided that it be literary'.[37]

But early in October Hopkins had finished his maidens' song, 'The Leaden Echo and the Golden Echo', meant for his drama of St Winefride's Well. He sent it to Bridges, settling in his new house at Yattendon, in Berkshire. As Hopkins said, it was 'very highly wrought', and musical, though not lazily so: 'the long lines are not rhythm run to seed: everything is weighed and timed in them'.[38] Hopkins told Dixon four years later 'I never did anything more musical'. It is possible that the two choruses, the second echoing and then answering the first, were intended to be sung. Hopkins meant them to be 'popular'; they are less demanding than most of his mature poems, but depend on performance to bring out subtleties of feeling, humour, morality, and tenderness, as well as music. Hopkins intended that the choruses should sound like 'the thoughts of a good but lively girl':[39]

> Come then, your ways and airs and looks, locks, maidengear,
>     gallantry and gaiety and grace,
> Winning ways, airs innocent, maidenmanners, sweet looks, loose
>     locks, long locks, lovelocks, gaygear, going gallant, girlgrace—
> Resign them, sign them, seal them, send them, motion them with
>     breath,
> And with sighs soaring, soaring sighs, deliver
> Them; beauty-in-the-ghost, deliver it, early now, long before
>     death
> Give beauty back, beauty, beauty, beauty, back to God beauty's
>     self and beauty's giver.

Bridges suggested that Whitman's influence was clear, to which Hopkins replied that, 'Although I always knew in my heart Walt Whitman's mind to be more like my own than any other man's living', he had read only 'half a dozen pieces at most' of Whitman's. Whitman's rhythm was 'in its last ruggedness and decomposition into common prose', but his own was more like the sprung rhythm of Greek tragic choruses or of Pindar: 'wait till [the long lines] have taken hold of your ear and you will find it so.'[40] Hopkins did not deny all poetic resemblance to Whitman, who shared his liking for the alexandrine. Some years later, when he sent Bridges a copy of 'Harry Ploughman', it crossed his mind that it might be like Whitman.

At the end of the autumn term 1882 he was 'in a state of weakness, I do not well know why', and even after a few days' rest at Christmas he reported to Bridges: 'Since our holidays began I have been in a wretched state of weakness and weariness, I can't tell why, always drowzy and incapable of reading or thinking to any effect.'[41] He had kept up a good rate of letters to Bridges, however, writing ten in the four months since he arrived at Stonyhurst, and had written the occasional letter to Dixon. He gave detailed criticism of Bridges's *Prometheus the Firegiver*, discussed William Barnes's linguistic experiments, and his own sonnets, giving valuable explications in answer to Bridges's difficulties. Since coming north he had finished a sonnet and three triolets by the end of March. The triolets, not outstanding examples of that virtuoso exercise, were printed in the school journal, *The Stonyhurst Magazine*, for March 1883; it is ironic that three of his least characteristic, least mature pieces were among the handful of his works published in his lifetime.

His interest in the sonnet form was reawakened by the correspondence over Bridges's poems. He wrote 'Ribblesdale', and sent copies to both Dixon and Bridges, but admitted to Bridges, 'I am always jaded, I cannot tell why, and my vein shews no sign of ever flowing again', and to Dixon:

My time, as I have said before this, is not so closely employed but that someone else in my place might not do a great deal, but I cannot, and I see no grounded prospect of my ever doing much not only in poetry but in anything at all. At times I do feel this sadly and bitterly, but it is God's will and though no change that I can foresee will happen yet perhaps some may that I do not foresee.[42]

Intended as a companion piece to 'In the Valley of the Elwy', 'Ribblesdale' has little of the earlier poem's balance between place and message; it does not create individuality for Ribblesdale, but seems a product of misanthropic broodiness, written in distinctive style, but without passion or urgency:

> And what is Earth's eye, tongue, or heart else, where
> Else, but in dear and dogged man?—Ah, the heir
> To his own selfbent so bound, so tied to his turn,
>
> To thriftless reave both our rich round world bare
> And none reck of world after . . .

For Stonyhurst's Mayday celebration Hopkins produced 'The Blessed Virgin compared to the Air we Breathe', in three-foot couplets. He felt it was 'part a compromise with popular taste, and it is too true that the highest subjects are not those on which it is easy to reach one's highest'.[43] The metre, perhaps borrowed from Dixon's poem 'Blue in the mists all day', does not encourage originality, and the poem lacks power:

Be thou then, O thou dear
Mother, my atmosphere;
My happier world, wherein
To wend and meet no sin;
Above me, round me lie
Fronting my froward eye
With sweet and scarless sky.

After announcing to Bridges that he is writing this poem he adds, 'The cold half kills me'.

He had taken up music again:

I fumble a little at music, at counterpoint, of which in course of time I shall come to know something; for this, like every other study, after some drudgery yields up its secrets, which seem impenetrable at first. If I could get to accompany my own airs I should, so to say, enter into a new kingdom at once, for I have plenty of tunes ready.[44]

Modesty was not one of Hopkins's virtues, and though he had taken no elementary music lessons he suggested to Bridges that he might like to ask his friend John Stainer, the eminent musician, at present organist of St Paul's Cathedral, to look at Hopkins's 'exercise in the second species in two parts on "Pray, Goody, please to moderate" ', and let him know 'if it is correct and if not where'.[45] It had taken him a long time, 'and I shall never write anything so long again by way of exercise'. Bridges suggested a less eminent adviser, and the exercise was sent off.

Another pleasant way of occupying himself at Stonyhurst was in visiting the observatory; he had come to know Fr Perry well. Perhaps Perry encouraged Hopkins to read *Nature*, edited by Perry's friend Norman Lockyer. *Nature* contained many reports of unusual sky phenomena, and in November 1882 Hopkins joined in the correspondence with a letter on 'beams of shadow meeting in the east at sunset'. Two further letters written while he was at Stonyhurst were printed in *Nature*, the most interesting of which are those written after the Krakatoa eruptions in 1883, which produced the loudest noise ever heard on the earth's surface, probably 100,000 deaths, and vivid green and blue sunsets graphically described in English papers. Hopkins's skyscape descriptions on this occasion are not as vivid and singular as his 1870 journal entries, but are remarkable (as Patricia Ball says) for 'their range of reference and a suggestiveness going beyond the ambition of the other correspondents':[46]

The glowing vapour above [the horizon] was as yet colourless; then this took a beautiful olive or celadon green ... and delicately fluted; the green belt was broader than the orange, and pressed down on and contracted it. Above the green in turn appeared a red glow, broader and burlier in make; it was softly brindled, and in the ribs or bars the colour was rosier, in the channels where the blue of the sky shone through it was a mallow colour. Above this was a vague lilac.

On 4 December 1883 the glow was 'more like inflamed flesh than the lucid reds of ordinary sunsets', and 'the fields facing west glowed as if overlaid with yellow wax'.[47]

Two accounts of Hopkins at Stonyhurst in the 1880s,[48] written long afterwards, stress his eccentric public image. A boy called Alban Goodier had toothache:

His class-master told him to go out into the playground and amuse himself since he would not be able to follow the class. He was wandering all alone in a vast playground, in pain and quite disconsolate. After some time Fr Hopkins appeared, walking from the Observatory (which is on the far side of the playground) towards the college. Fr Hopkins came up to the small boy and asked why he was there at all alone. Goodier explained, and then Hopkins said: 'Watch me.' He took off his gown and proceeded to climb up one of the goal-posts. . . . Hopkins reached the top of the post and then lowered himself down. He put on his gown and then walked away.

The other anecdote also involves Hopkins the climber. Fr Perry had brought from his travels a tame monkey:

One day the monkey escaped out of the window on to the leaden gutter which ran along the West Front of the building. Fr Hopkins, who was a near neighbour, climbed out and walked along the narrow ledge to where the monkey was cowering in panic at the end of the building. He coaxed it to within reach and then led it back through the window. Those who know the West Front at Stonyhurst will know what steadiness of nerve that involved.

# 'Careful and subtle fault-finding':
## Patmore and Hopkins

At the end of July 1883 Hopkins's first year of teaching classics at Stonyhurst was ended, and he did not expect to see his name on the next year's appointment list, to be published on 1 August. On that day the old college year was to be rounded off by 'Great Academies', Stony-hurst's annual speech-making and prize-giving ceremony, to which parents and distinguished speakers were invited. There were good reasons for doubting whether he would be kept on at Stonyhurst. Apart from his compulsory training periods—the novitiate at Roehampton, the philosophate at St Mary's Hall, and the theologate at St Beuno's—Hopkins had not once, since leaving Oxford sixteen years before, lived anywhere or held any professional position for longer than a year. He had lived in Spinkhill, Stonyhurst, London and Oxford in 1878, and in Liverpool, Glasgow, and Roehampton in 1881. It was to be one of the ironies of his life that the least congenial of his many postings, Dublin, would be his longest stay in one place.

On 26 July he wrote to Bridges,[1] enclosing a prayer which he had composed at his friend's request for a collection being edited by Mrs Elizabeth Waterhouse. She was Bridges's new neighbour at Yattendon, would soon become his mother-in-law, and she was the wife of Alfred Waterhouse, the architect who designed the east and south sides of Balliol's front quadrangle. Bridges probably thought that in contribut-ing to this *Book of Simple Prayers* Hopkins would have none of his usual misgivings and scruples about publication. But Hopkins found himself unable to respond to Bridges's generous opportunism by making the compromises Mrs Waterhouse wanted, and his prayer was rejected. Sending a copy of the book to Hopkins in May 1886, Mrs Waterhouse said: 'You will think [the book] sadly undogmatic and perhaps when I was gathering it together I was a little too much afraid of dogma.'[2] She intended the prayers 'to be such as can be used from the heart by all who in the simplest way are "sure of God"'.[3] The professional focus of Hopkins's prayer and its stern Augustinian tone were too uncompromising for a book aimed at people looking for uncomplicated poetic sentiment:

We have grievously come short of thy glory; nay worse, [we own] that we have been rebels and many many times in small things and in great broken thy holy law and not kept thy commandments. We are ashamed, we look at ourselves and thee and are confounded. We wither at thy rebuke, we faint at thy frown, we tremble at thy power and threatened punishments.[4]

Bridges's expectation of a different kind of prayer from Hopkins is surprising. Being something of an Anglican as well as something of an agnostic, he would not have been attracted by its tone and Catholicity, but he loyally pasted it, after its rejection, in his book of Hopkins's poems called 'A', and indexed it as 'A prayer that protestants might use', a title which Hopkins probably gave it.[5] Hopkins thought the prayer was rejected because its religious truth was unpalatable: 'now in that [book-buying] public I regret, and surely I may, that it can no longer be trusted to bear, to stomach, the clear expression of or the taking for granted even very elementary Christian doctrines. I did not realise this well enough, did not realise that distinct Christianity damages the sale and so the usefulness of a well meant book.'[6] He was hurt by being cut off once again by his religious stand.

On 26 July he gave a melancholy account of his situation:

Our year begins with autumn and the appointments for this college will be made public on the 1st of next month. It seems likely that I shall be removed; where I have no notion. But I have long been Fortune's football and am blowing up the bladder of resolution big and buxom for another kick of her foot. I shall be sorry to leave Stonyhurst; but go or stay, there is no likelihood of my ever doing anything to last. And I do not know how it is, I have no disease, but I am always tired, always jaded, though work is not heavy, and the impulse to do anything fails me or has in it no continuance.[7]

Hopkins avoids thinking of the human agencies involved in his move from Stonyhurst; he is one of the 'obedient men'. 'Fortune' may seem a strange factor for a Jesuit to believe in, and 'Fortune's football' an odd description of himself. But Hopkins was using a phrase already associated with English Jesuits. In the college library would probably be found Mrs Ogden Meeker's four-volume *Fortune's Football*,[8] a historical tale of Jesuit martyrdoms in Elizabethan England, which attempted a Catholic corrective to the picture of the Jesuit common in mid-Victorian Protestant fiction as a villain of 'the blackest dye, a spy, a secret agent, suave, supercilious and satanically unscrupulous, laying his cunning plots for the submission of England to "Jesuitocracy" '.[9] Her subject and approach would be suitable for the boys of a Jesuit school brought into being largely by the determination of Queen Elizabeth I to stamp out Catholicism.[10] In saying he is 'Fortune's football', Hopkins is acknowledging that he is a Jesuit in the traditional English pattern.

ᘓ

During the next month his mood lightened. On 30 July the Rector of Stonyhurst gave him a common college assignment, looking after a distinguished visitor. Coventry Patmore had come to speak at Great Academies two days later. Five years previously, Hopkins had written to Dixon admiringly of Patmore's poetry: 'Mr. Coventry Patmore, whose fame again is very deeply below his great merit, seems to have said something very finely about the loss of fame in his lately published Odes.'[11] The subject was discussed by Hopkins and Patmore, in letters, when they knew each other better. They saw a lot of each other during the four days Patmore was at Stonyhurst, and talked about poetry, particularly Bridges and Dixon. On 12 August Hopkins gave a detailed account to Dixon of Patmore's responses to Dixon's and Bridges's poetry. For once Hopkins had met a poet who expressed his opinions more forcefully than he did: 'I suppose I am more tolerant or more inclined to admire than he is, but in listening to him I had that malignant satisfaction which lies in hearing one's worst surmises confirmed.'[12] Patmore's visit revived Hopkins's spirits, and they were raised further when he learned on 1 August that he had been re-appointed to Stonyhurst for another academic year, until the end of July 1884. He announced this in letters to Bridges and Dixon, playing down the news.[13]

After Patmore had left Stonyhurst, Hopkins was granted leave of absence for the fortnight's holiday, starting on Thursday 9 August. He intended going to his parents at Hampstead for a week, and arranged that Bridges would come up from Yattendon to see him on the 13th. He planned to go with his parents to Holland to fetch home his sister Grace. She had travelled to see the grave of her fiancé, Henry Weber, at Sensburg in East Prussia. A doctor's son in frail health, he had died at the beginning of June, having known Grace for less than a year, most of which they had spent apart.[14] On first hearing of Weber's death Hopkins had written to Grace, attempting to put her loss in a religious perspective. His letter reads coldly, even taking into account contemporary conventions, using more stilted language than he usually does in letters to close relatives:

> is it not plain that God our Lord knows what he does and in striking so hard pitied your poor heart and meant for you something far better, the brighter that seeming future was the better this real one? But you are not to think, my dear, that you are somehow to be made happy some day for being unhappy this: there is no sense in that. What God means is that you shall greatly gain if you will be humble and patient.[15]

After staying with the Weber family in Prussia, Grace was to meet her parents and Gerard in Holland. But at the last moment an emergency arose at the Jesuit church of the Holy Name, Manchester, thirty-five miles from Stonyhurst, and Hopkins was sent there for a week. From Manchester he went to London, reaching Hampstead on 16 August. There he was visited by Bridges; then, taking the poems of Bridges, Dixon, and Patmore, he went to Holland for the last week of August, to join his parents, Kate, and a cousin. Kate recalled:

> when my cousin & I were laughing over [the] day's experiences, the door opened & in came my brother smiling & asking 'What are you girls laughing at?' wishful to join in our merriment; & how we spent a happy $\frac{1}{2}$ hour leaning [out] of our window watching the bats flitting to & fro, hearing their tiny voices & throwing little bits of plaster into the air to cheat them into diving at it believing it food.[16]

&

On 3 September Hopkins started his annual seven-day retreat, at Beaumont Lodge, under the direction of Fr Kingdon, a Cambridge convert who for a brief period, ten years before, had been Hopkins's colleague at Stonyhurst. In a note written during this retreat he determinedly made a place in conventional theology for his own terms 'instress' and 'scape': 'God is good and the stamp seal, or instress he sets on each scape is of *right, good*, or of *bad, wrong*.' The sinner is he who matches his own self with God's, and as eternal punishment he is 'carried and swept away to an infinite distance from God', and suffers 'the stress and strain of his removal'. And yet that same note had started with Hopkins allotting a brave and vital role to man's individuality and its free nature, that faculty which enables man to apprehend God:

> the tendency in the soul towards an infinite object comes from the *arbitrium*. The *arbitrium* in itself is man's personality or individuality and places him on a level of individuality in some sense with God; so that in so far as God is one

thing, a self, an individual being, he is an object of apprehension, desire, pursuit to man's *arbitrium*. There would be no apprehension, desire, action, or motion of any kind without freedom of play, that play which is given by the use of a nature, of human nature, with its faculties.[17]

Sympathy towards human nature changes within that short passage to an awareness of the ways in which he should be framing his thoughts. The section concludes with a statement about Judgement Day: 'And the true position of things between man and God appears by an immediate light at death, when man's self is set face to face with God's.' A year later, similarly prolonged and concentrated contemplation produced 'Spelt from Sibyl's Leaves', which projects a terrified vision of the unreality of life's variety and energy, nullified by the judgements of the Day of Wrath.

These 'lights on the Particular Judgment', as Hopkins called them, may have clarified his mind on theological points, but dragged his spirits towards unhappiness. The prescribed retreat often seems to have left him in a dejected state. The deliberate psychological operations of Ignatius's Exercises do not take into account a mind like Hopkins's, but assume confusion which needs to be ordered, and selfishness which needs to be chastened. In Hopkins they seemed to disrupt self-esteem, and the constructive process meant to follow the breaking down of the old self fails to work.

Two days before the end of the retreat he was saddened by 'the thought of the little I do in the way of hard penances', but comforted by the idea given him by a previous mentor, Fr Whitty, 'how a great part of life to the holiest of men consists in the well performance, the performance, one may say, of ordinary duties'.[18] Increasingly he realized that he had set his sights romantically high and would have to accept a lower level of professional fulfilment. When the opportunity arose, five years later, of celebrating the canonization of Alphonsus Rodriguez, a lay brother who had been given the humblest of roles, Hopkins characterized him as fighting 'the war within', during 'years and years' of 'world without event'. The day before the retreat ended, in a meditation on the Crucifixion, he saw that 'asking to be raised to a higher degree of grace was asking also to be lifted on a higher cross'.[19]

In the thanksgiving after mass, despite feeling that he had gained 'insight in things' during the retreat, he experienced 'much bitter thought', and his meditation that morning on the walk to Emmaus, from Luke's gospel, was made 'in a desolate frame of mind'. Towards the end of the meditation there was some relief, as his concluding notes suggest:

I was able to rejoice in the comfort our Lord gave those two men, taking that for a sample of his comfort and them for representatives of all men comforted, and that it was meant to be of universal comfort to men and therefore to me and that this was all I really needed; also that it was better for me to be accompanying our Lord in his comfort of them than to want him to come my way to comfort me.[20]

But this sounds like self-persuasion, rather than the record of a comfort achieved.

The next day he had arranged to meet Bridges at Yattendon, before travelling on to Oxford. In spite of experience he was not very good at dealing with trains, and Bridges received a postcard the day after, explaining that 'The train at Reading did certainly seem earlier than there was any need but I got into it without suspicion: I was whirled past Pangbourn [the nearest station to Yattendon] and by the time you were there, if you went, was almost at Oxford.' It was, he said, 'a dreadful disappointment, but it was to be'. Hopkins had a wilful belief in providence. He had written in his consolatory letter to Grace the previous June: 'But the firmest and most fruitful ground of comfort is to look on everything that has happened ... as things providential, always meant ... by God to be'; but it does seem excessive to attribute his carelessness over trains to divine will. 'The worst of it is', he added, 'I do not even see how another opportunity is ever to occur.'[21] His close friends were few, and their meetings far between.

Back at Stonyhurst for the autumn term, he found waiting for him a parcel from George Bell's, Patmore's publisher, and he began an intensive correspondence with Patmore. During the next four months he wrote thirteen letters, more than he wrote to anyone else in a similar period. He had sent Patmore a copy of Bridges's *Prometheus*, recommending particular passages, though he felt that as an advocate he was 'like the *Guide to North Wales*: "on the extreme right the visitor will not fail to observe" etc.'[22] Having persuaded him to buy Dixon's *Mano*, he feared Patmore would have 'a surfeit of my friends'. But his recommendations were not undiscriminating, and in their pointing to faults, to anticipate negative responses, they are like Bridges's 1918 Preface to Hopkins. The style of *Mano* 'is more archaic than I approve; I look on archaism as a blight'. Dixon had 'a hateful and incurable fancy for rhyming *Lord* to *awed*, *here* to *idea* etc.'.[23] Patmore was disappointed with *Mano*, and Hopkins largely agreed with him that it lacked 'a leading thought to thread the beauties on'.[24]

The parcel from Bell's contained the four handsome volumes of Patmore's poems, and Hopkins reread *The Angel in the House*, as asked by Patmore, who was planning revision. 'Much of it I remember without reading (I do not say word for word)', he wrote to Patmore, 'and of the rest there is little I do not at least remember to have read.' He felt that criticism was 'a dangerous and an over-honourable [task] and perhaps it was presumptuous to accept it.' He had to do so quickly, to meet author's and publisher's deadlines, and within twelve days sent two letters of comments, 'hurriedly put together', to Patmore.

Hopkins began with modest disavowal:

In making them first I blush at my own boldness; next I know that they may be mistaken and that your judgment on the matter is better than mine and even where you may be ready to agree with me, still some flaws are flies in amber, embedded in excellence which must perish in removing them.[25]

But the tone is astringent and uncompromising: 'I have one serious fault to find and on that I lay so much stress that I could even wish you were put to some inconvenience and delay rather than that the poem should go down to posterity with it.' Naming the fault would be put off until the end of the letter. There followed a list of thirty-two mistakes of detail, ranging from infelicities to errors, like ' "link catching link": only goods trains do this; passenger trains are locked rigidly'.[26] At the end, Hopkins discovered he had run out of time, and left Patmore in suspense about the 'one serious fault'.

Hopkins revealed this in the next letter. He objected on moral grounds to the poem's idea of womanhood. Patmore had asked a Jesuit priest to criticize a poem on 'the heart's events', the love between a man and woman, which included scenes of flirtation, jealousy, and pride, and in which there is constant erotic appeal:

> Her dress, that touch'd me where I stood;
>     The warmth of her confided arm;
> Her bosom's gentle neighbourhood;
>     Her pleasure in her power to charm;
> Her look, her love, her form, her touch,
>     The least seem'd most by blissful turn.

The poet maintained that his intention was to emphasize the divine nature of human love, and there are frequent insistences that this is not just the personal record of a sexually enraptured man. But the poem is largely a glorification of one man/woman relationship, as Patmore suspected: 'Yourself, and love that's all in all'. Rather like Hopkins in 'To what serves Mortal Beauty?', Patmore was trying to reconcile erotic experience with religion:

> Happy, if on the tempest's gloom
> Thou seest the covenant of God;
> But far, far happier he on whom
> The kiss works better than the rod.

'The truth seems to me', responded Hopkins, 'that in writing you were really in two inconsistent moods, a lower and a higher.'[27] He must have been pained, not just by the 'inhaling of love's delighted breath', but by the dismissals of religious practices:

> We fast, give alms, pray, weep, and wake,
> And wear our hearts out, o'er the Word:
> Ah, less of this, and let us make
> More melody unto the Lord!

The representative phrase to which Hopkins particularly responded was 'Women *should* be vain':

In the midst of a poem undertaken under a kind of inspiration from God & to express what, being most excellent, most precious, most central and important and even obvious in human life, nevertheless no one has ever yet, unless passingly thought of expressing you introduce a vice, the germ of widespread evils. . . . In particular how can anyone admire or (except in charity, as the greatest of sins, but in judgment and approval) tolerate vanity in women?

Not only arguing against Patmore's experience, he also offers examples from his own domestic experience:

It seems to me that nothing in good women is more beautiful than just the absence of vanity and an earnestness of look and character which is better than beauty. It teaches me (if I may give such an instance—I cannot easily give others) in my own sisters that when they let me see their compositions in music or painting . . . they seem to me to be altogether without vanity—yet they might be with reason vainer of these than of their looks. . . . It is the same in literature as in life: the vain women in Shakspere are the impure minded too, like Beatrice (I do not know that I may not call her a hideous character).[28]

Such revulsion from the heroine of *Much Ado About Nothing* must be rare.

On 'The Woman Question', in particular the wife, Hopkins is more anti-reformist than Patmore:

[In *The Angel in the House*] it is said that a wife calls her husband lord by courtesy, meaning, as I understand, only by courtesy and 'not with her least consent of will' to his being so. But he *is* her lord. If it is courtesy only and no consent then a wife's lowliness is hypocrisy and Christian marriage a comedy, a piece of pretence. . . . And now pernicious doctrines and practice are abroad and the other day the papers said a wretched being refused in church to say the words 'and obey': if it had been a Catholic wedding and I the priest I would have let the sacrilege go no further.[29]

'If I have written strongly', Hopkins closed the letter, 'I am sure it is in a zeal for the poem.' His attitude towards women was not likely to be contradicted by the official theologian, Aquinas, to whom woman was a 'failed man' (*mas occasionatus*) created 'to help men, but only in procreation'.[30]

Patmore replied mildly, to Hopkins's relief, as he had begun 'to fear I had, as people say, "done it this time". For you might not have taken my remarks, I am afraid intemperately expressed, in so gentle a spirit.'[31]

Patmore thanked him over-gratefully: 'Your careful and subtle fault-finding is the greatest praise my poetry has ever received. . . . 'Tamerton Church Tower' and 'The Sign of the Prophet Jonah' are incorrigible.'[32] Again Hopkins feared his criticism had been devastating; he answered: 'it would be a calamity in literature if *Tamerton Church Tower* were suppressed and a consummation devoutly to be wished against'. He tried to make amends in his next letter by comparing the poem to *Love's Labour's Lost* 'and others of Shakspere's plays, which are faulty though they teem with genius and could never be spared'.[33]

In his discussions of his friends' work, Hopkins was more likely to blame than to praise, and to show insensitivity to personal feelings. Patmore's reactions to Hopkins's criticisms were like those of Bridges four years earlier. Hopkins was more careful when Patmore asked him to glance over the verses of his son Henry, who had died, aged twenty-two, nine months earlier: 'In your son Henry you have lost a mind not only of wonderful promise but even of wonderful achievement.' He felt 'astonishment at a mind so mature, so masculine, so fresh, and so fastidiously independent', and he saw 'the unnatural maturity of consumption and the clearsightedness of approaching death'. He praised the father's qualities in the son's: 'Naturally, being who he was, to write poetry came to him first; his mind had been cradled in it; and even the metres he employs are those he was familiar with in you.'[34] The poems had their faults, 'in flow, in the poetical impetus, and also in richness of diction', and if published 'are not likely to have any wide success; they would be caviare to the general'. (In a letter to Muirhead of 1878 Bridges had judged Hopkins's own poems 'magnificent but caviare to the general.')[35] Hopkins's moral over-sensitivity had been irritated by a comment of Patmore's that his son had, 'though idle, easily carried off the first prizes and places among his school-fellows', and he remonstrated with the over-fond parent: 'You seemed to say this in his praise, but it is not to his praise. It is a fault which now he must repent of.'[36]

Patmore's reply to Hopkins's rigid moralizing was dignified and gentle, and Hopkins again half-withdrew his ill-considered words: 'I was much afraid after my last letter that the words about idleness would have given you pain and by their coarseness justly displeased you.' On politics, Hopkins's voice sounded deceptively moderate when compared with the tone of Patmore, who wrote in *The Angel in the House*:

In the year of the great crime,
When the false English Nobles and their Jew,
By God demented, slew
The Trust they stood twice pledged to keep from wrong.

Hopkins remonstrated:

'Their Jew': this is a hard saying, all politics apart. Many people speak so, but I cannot see how they can be justified. For *Jew* must be a reproach either for religion or for race. It cannot be for religion here, for Disraeli was not by religion a Jew ... It must be then for race. But that is no reproach but a glory, for Christ was a Jew.

Disraeli, 'a Jew born', was 'above all things a British patriot'; and that was the sentiment behind the Primrose League. Patmore replied that 'the political action and inaction of England ... during the last twenty years or more' filled him with 'an actual thirst for vengeance ... and I sometimes long for some hideous catastrophe ... which should wake the country from its more hideous sleep'. He hated 'in all charity' Disraeli 'more, if possible, than I hate Gladstone, and "Jew" or *any* stone seemed good enough to throw at such a dog'. His Reform Bill of 1867, originating to stem 'the tide of revolution', ended 'in actually consummating the revolution wh. the Radicals were only dreaming of'.[37] Hopkins responded that Patmore should present his political reactions as historical responses rather than as considered judgements. However, Hopkins appeared moderate only compared with Patmore's extremism, and his opinions differed in degree and expression rather than in substance: 'I do not want to controvert', he added, 'especially as I scarcely dispute the facts.'[38]

Hopkins sympathized with Patmore on seeing that his name did not appear in the *Spectator*'s list of living poets and prose writers:

I saw your name nowhere. Indeed I believe you were not in the running. And when I read *Remembered Grace*, *The Child's Purchase*, *Legem Tuam Dilexi* and others of the volume I sigh to think that it is all one almost to be too full of meaning and to have none and to see very deep and not to see at all, for nothing so profound as these can be found in the poets of the age, scarcely of any; and yet they are but little known and when the papers give a list of the contemporary English poets your name does not appear.[39]

The pathos of unvalued genius had struck Hopkins in the past, when he read Duns Scotus with delight, and felt the feud 'between genius and talent' which condemned Scotus to misunderstanding and rejection. A sense of the gap between fame and merit remained with him.

# PART VI

## The Stranger, 1884–1889

> Lét life, wáned, ah lét life wínd
> Off hér once skéined stained véined varíety upon, áll on twó spools;
>     párt, pen, páck
> Now her áll in twó flocks, twó folds—bláck, white; ríght, wrong;
>     réckon but, réck but, mínd
> But thése two; wáre of a wórld where bút these twó tell, eách off
>     the óther; of a ráck
> Where, selfwrung, selfstrung, sheathe- and shelterless, thoúghts
>     agáinst thoughts ín groans grínd.
>
> ('Spelt from Sibyl's Leaves')

Gerald Hopkins was at an opposite pole to every thing around him: literary, political, social & c. (a thorough John Bull incapable of understanding Rebel Ireland). No one took him seriously; he played the part rather of the droll jester, in the medieval castles.

(Fr J. Darlington)

# An Irish Row

Since the first week in December 1883 Hopkins had been keeping a secret from his family and friends. He knew he would probably have to leave Stonyhurst for Ireland. On 7 March 1884, he wrote to Bridges on notepaper headed 'University College, 85 & 86, Stephens Green, Dublin': 'Remark the above address: it is a new departure or a new arrival and at all events a new abode. I dare say you know nothing of it, but the fact is that, though unworthy of and unfit for the post, I have been elected Fellow of the Royal University of Ireland in the department of classics.' He added: 'There was an Irish row over my election.'[1] Hopkins had been thrust as a pawn into a controversy of far-reaching importance to Ireland.

Though Ireland was officially part of Great Britain, its history, customs, and feelings were distinct; and the Irish Province of the Jesuits had been legally separate from the English since the 1860s. In a country of intrigues, Hopkins's appointment had been a party matter and a lasting grievance to the defeated faction. For much of the time this Dublin controversy[2] appeared to be about rival educational politics; at other times it seemed to be a dispute between the Irish bishops (the Hierarchy) and the Jesuits. As often happens with any ideological battle in Ireland, the debate sometimes concerned rival methods of achieving national independence, and turned on personalities.

The main personalities were Fr William Delany, President of the University College on St Stephen's Green, Dublin, and Dr William Walsh, President of St Patrick's College, Maynooth. Hopkins's appointment to Dublin was engineered by Delany and opposed by Walsh. Hopkins's reactions to the Irish political scene, frequently expressed in letters during his five-and-a-half years in Dublin, were largely a personal and anglicized version of views represented by Delany, while his most bitter antagonism would be reserved for the causes championed by Walsh and Parnell, with Gladstone's support.

The history of Irish Catholic higher education was long and bitter by the time Hopkins's name was first mentioned in Dublin. The desire for a national Catholic university overlaps the rise of Irish aspirations to national independence in the nineteenth century. Before the 1880s the Catholic bishops had adopted a conservative line of trying to win support for social and educational legislation from British politicians who, with the exception of Gladstone, proved uninterested or uncomprehending. The foundation of the Royal University of Ireland, a purely examining body, which gained its charter in 1880, was the most recent ineffective measure, which shelved demands for higher education rather than satisfied them.

One institution whose students sat for the Royal University examinations was the dilapidated remnants of Newman's old Catholic University, in two houses on the south side of Dublin's largest square. It had been owned and administered by the bishops since the 1850s, but by January 1882 the majority of the bishops agreed that the college should be handed over to a religious teaching order, and sent for Fr Delany, a successful headmaster of Jesuit schools, who outlined an educational programme.

Delaney was an idealist with an independent streak. His purpose was to organize a Catholic rival to Trinity College Dublin, the prestigious Protestant foundation from Elizabethan days, and to achieve this he would staff his college with well-qualified foreign Jesuits. Fr Tuite, the Jesuit Provincial in Ireland, tried to dissuade him: 'I look upon Dr. Newman's selection of English professors and officials as the first cause of failure of the Catholic University. I am afraid the same might happen with regard to us. ... We must not hurt *national prejudices* on any account.'[3]

Delany received enthusiastic support from Fr George Porter, the English assistant to the Jesuit General in Rome, who guaranteed the warm support of the Father General. So Delaney felt able to ignore Fr Tuite's warning that he might be sent men 'other provinces were not anxious to hold on to'. Tuite dreaded Englishmen 'on account of the present feeling in the country, and particularly English converts who are sometimes—well let us say—unsuited to this country and its thoroughly Catholic people'.

Delany asked about likely Jesuits in England, France, Germany, and Italy, particularly those qualified in mathematics and classics. In autumn 1882 he wrote to the English Provincial, Fr Edward Purbrick, asking for men and suggesting seven names, which included J. T. Walford, a fellow of King's College, Cambridge, for eleven years before his conversion; Joseph Rickaby, a brilliant mathematician and philosopher, ordained at St Beuno's on the same day as Hopkins; Herbert Lucas, expert on Savonarola and Byzantine architecture, who used to walk by the river at Stonyhurst with Hopkins, talking Scotism, and Gerard Hopkins.

These names might have been suggested by Porter, who knew the seven more intimately than Delany, having taught at St Beuno's and St Mary's Hall, and having been Rector at St Francis Xavier's, Liverpool, and at Roehampton during the year Hopkins taught there. Porter wrote to Delaney in 1882 that he 'might get Hopkins or Walford but certainly not Rickaby or Lucas'. It was his opinion that Hopkins 'is clever, well trained, teaches well but has never succeeded well: his mind runs into eccentric ways'.

On 10 November Purbrick replied. Six of the seven names on Delany's list were 'just the cream of the province', and though he wished to help 'in so great and important a work', he could not spare them. That left Hopkins; he warned: 'Fr. Hopkins is very clever and a good scholar . . . but I should do you no kindness in sending you a man so eccentric. I am trying him this year in coaching B.A.s at Stonyhurst, but with fear and trembling'. It looked as if Fr Tuite's prediction was coming true: other provinces would send their good wishes but not their best men.[4]

Through the Jesuit General's support, the Provincial was instructed to accept the bishops' offer, if it were made, and Delaney pressed on with his plans for recruiting staff. He had already provoked antagonism. He had gained the General's support through the influence of an English Jesuit in Rome, against his Irish Provincial, and gone against the Provincial's advice in advocating English teachers. Among the many disadvantages of the old Catholic University he had inherited, there was one he had underestimated: its local reputation as an English college. Delany sometimes misjudged the strength and nature of the new political feeling in Ireland. After Hopkins's appointment, Delany was frequently attacked for being in league with Dublin Castle (seat of British government) and for not 'conceiving any other than a University of the English type', meaning an exclusive cramming institution, as opposed to a teaching establishment with a more open entrance policy.

On 26 October 1883 the University College on St Stephen's Green changed hands. The bishops were divided over whether it should be handed to the Jesuits or to the Holy Ghost fathers of Blackrock, but the Jesuits narrowly won, and Delany assumed the Presidency. On 12 July it was announced that there were eight unfilled Fellowships of the

Royal University, each worth £400 per annum, including one in Natural Science and one in Classics. Delany assumed these would be granted to his new college, and went ahead with his plans to nominate his two candidates for automatic election by the Royal University Senate.

എ

But at the Senate meeting Dr William Walsh had taken his seat for the first time as one of the eighteen Roman Catholic members.[5] Walsh had different ideas from Delaney on the allocation of Fellowships, and spoke out for a multi-collegiate system of Catholic higher education, as opposed to the concentration on University College. Walsh made public attacks on the unbalanced distribution of Fellowships within the Royal University, and started lobbying each Senator, but his efforts met with refusals and evasions. The Vice-Chancellor, Lord O'Hagan, told Walsh that any change in the pattern would lead to 'embarrassment and confusion. . . . I do not feel warranted to interfere.' The O'Hagan family had close connections with the Jesuits, and Lady O'Hagan helped the new University College to overcome its financial troubles.

The crucial Senate meeting at which the elections would take place was on 30 January 1884. Delany had settled on Robert Curtis, a brilliant Irish Jesuit mathematician, who had been a scholar of Trinity College Dublin, as his candidate for the Natural Science Fellowship. He was more doubtful about his Classics candidate, and wrote for advice to his friend Dr James Kavanagh, a Royal University Senator. Kavanagh replied: 'Take Hopkins, if you cannot get a better. The £400 a year you will find useful, being an S.J.' Kavanagh had laid his finger on the crucial point: it was essential that Delany should secure these two Fellowships for his college to balance the books, if for no other reason. The Stephen's Green College was short of money (a loss of £700 had been reported for the previous year); if a lay Fellow were elected it meant a teacher at no cost, but if the Fellow were a Jesuit, the college not only got a free teacher, but an extra income of £400 a year, as the Jesuit would transfer his salary to the college's funds. (To put this in perspective: the college cook in 1884 was paid £20 per annum, the butler £16, the hall-porter £13, and the bedroom-porter £12.[6])

Delany wrote to the English Provincial asking for Hopkins, and on 29 November Purbrick replied:

As far as I am concerned I have no objection to your inviting Fr Gerald [*sic*] Hopkins to stand as a candidate for a Fellowship. He is the only man *possible*.

You know him. I have the highest opinion of his scholarship & abilities—I fancy also that University work would be more in his line than anything else. Sometimes what we in Community deem oddities are the very qualities which outside are appreciated as original & valuable. . . . I have not said anything to Fr Hopkins because I thought an invitation direct from you with my sanction more complimentary & appetizing to him.[7]

Purbrick knew Hopkins well, having been his Rector at St Mary's Hall, and his judgement is acute. Never one to delay, Delany set out for Stonyhurst and probably saw Hopkins on 4 December. Hopkins probably travelled back with Delany for a brief introduction, visiting Clongowes Wood College, near Naas, as well as Dublin.

The applications were vetted by a Standing Committee, and it looked as though Hopkins would be the only candidate for the Classics Fellowship. The committee were impressed by the fact that Benjamin Jowett, who had succeeded to the Mastership of Balliol in 1870 and was now also Vice-Chancellor of Oxford University, was supporting Hopkins's candidacy, and that R. L. Nettleship, his other referee, now a Fellow and Tutor of Balliol, had written about Hopkins in glowing terms: 'I should say that he was one of the cleverest and most original men in the College at that time. He was an excellent classical scholar, combining great care and accuracy with a curiously delicate perception in the use and criticism of language. I should expect him to be a conscientious and stimulating teacher.'[8] Nettleship's careful warning contained implications which perhaps ought to have been more closely examined: how suitable were Hopkins's peculiar skills for that particular post? Nor was it mentioned, apparently, that in his career as a teacher in Jesuit schools he had not been considered successful.

Dr Walsh had also been busy: he persuaded the Episcopal Education Committee, almost at the last minute, to nominate the Revd J. E. Reffé, Dean of Studies at Blackrock College, a respected teacher, and author of a pamphlet advocating dispersal of the Fellowships, though he was not well qualified in Classics.

છ૭

During the week before the election there was a flurry of meetings, journeys, dinner invitations, and letters, with both sides trying to resolve the issue to their own advantage, while keeping up appearances. The letters between Delany and Walsh are models of calculated diplomacy, masking thrusts, manœuvrings, and iron determination. On Tuesday 22 January Delany called on Cardinal McCabe to present

Curtis. The Cardinal was affable at first, but Delany reported to Walsh that the Cardinal said:

a propos of Fr. Hopkins's name, that he disliked having Englishmen, and thought this place had had too much of Englishmen in its past history. I [Delany] replied that unfortunately there were hardly any qualified Irishmen, and that the only two whom I knew of were already engaged here . . .'[9]

The Cardinal's vacillations puzzled both sides during the next days, and Delany left the Cardinal not knowing whether he could count on the support of the Primate or not. He asked Walsh if he knew the Cardinal's mind, and enclosed a financial statement showing how much his college needed the money from the Fellowships if it was to remain solvent. Before he had set foot in the country Hopkins was being attacked because of his nationality, and supported because of his monetary value.

On the afternoon before the Senate meeting, an Episcopal Committee unanimously adopted a resolution asking the Jesuits to withdraw Hopkins before the election. The Secretary of the Committee, Dr Woodlock, was requested at 5 o'clock to inform the Jesuit Provincial of the decision, and of the fact that 'his Em. [Cardinal McCabe] was in perfect accord with the resolution'. There are two versions of what happened then. Fr Brown, the new Irish Provincial, wrote in the aftermath of the election that he had not received official information of the Committee's views, and that the Cardinal had communicated to him a different opinion. It appears the message had reached Fr Delany that evening, but that he refused to withdraw Hopkins's name owing to the lateness of the hour, because he would be unable to contact Hopkins. Blackrock College maintained that this was merely an excuse.

Walsh insisted that McCabe propose Reffé at the Senate meeting the next day, in the hope that a proposal by the Cardinal would prevent open conflict among the Catholic Senators, but he underestimated the independence and conservatism of those who he later called 'plausible Catholic Whigs like Lords O'Hagan and Emly'.[10]

℘

On 30 January the Senate met at noon in Dublin Castle. The fifth item on the agenda was the election of Fellows. The minutes read:

For the vacant Fellowship in Classics His Eminence Cardinal McCabe proposed, and Rev. Dr. Walsh seconded, Rev. J. E. Reffé. The Right Hon. The Lord Emly proposed, and Mr. Redington seconded, Rev. G. M. Hopkins.
  Upon a division there voted—

For Mr. Reffé ........ 3
For Mr. Hopkins ........ 21

Rev. G. M. Hopkins was accordingly declared elected.[11]

Curtis, proposed by Cardinal McCabe and seconded by Lord Emly, was elected to the Natural Philosophy Fellowship.

Hopkins entered into residence at St Stephen's Green the following week. The Royal University Returns for the academic year 1883–4 record that he and Curtis were paid, not the full £400, but £187 13s. 4d., the 'proportionate parts of their respective salaries'. The Returns also state: 'as a Professor had been already appointed for the whole Session to teach the subjects assigned to Professor Hopkins, Professor Hopkins's services during the remainder of the Session were utilised chiefly in examination work.' In the column showing the number of lectures delivered by each Fellow for the year ending 1 October 1884, Robert Curtis has 105 lectures, while Hopkins has none.[12] No wonder that Hopkins continually complained of examination-marking.

The week after Hopkins's election one of the Episcopal Committee, Dr Gilooly, wrote to the Jesuit Provincial, deploring the Senate's actions, and requesting Hopkins's resignation. Fr Brown refused. The Fellowship was debated vociferously in the Dublin press for the next few months, and the rumpus took a long time to die down. Cardinal McCabe resigned from the Senate in protest. (Later, after a personal request from the Lord Lieutenant, Earl Spencer, he withdrew his resignation, but never again attended a Senate meeting.) Walsh had intended to remain on the Senate to secure some equity in the distribution of the remaining fellowships, but his efforts were in vain, and the fellowships were all assigned to Delany's college. Walsh resigned in June, and a friend of Delany's appointed in his place. A final attempt was made to oppose Delany's principle of importing foreign teachers: a motion was proposed that existing vacancies for Fellowships 'be restricted to the Graduates of the [Royal] University, and be filled by examination'. Perhaps as a safeguard Hopkins and other teachers at University College were given honorary degrees by the RUI.

℺

Delany and Walsh had now parted company; the difference in their educational principles was symptomatic of the gulf between their socio-political standpoints. After Cardinal McCabe's sudden death the following year, Walsh was appointed to the See of Dublin, in response to Irish nationalist agitation, and with the enthusiastic support of Charles Stewart Parnell. Croke, the openly nationalist archbishop, wrote to Walsh: 'no news ever pleased me more', and the *Freeman's Journal* declared that the people of Dublin were determined that 'an appanage of Dublin Castle' should not take McCabe's place. The appointment was made despite undercover diplomacy by the British Government in Rome, and although the Irish bishops were informed by the Vatican Propaganda that the Papacy was opposed to the involvement of clerics in politics. Throughout his subsequent career Walsh was regarded with suspicion by Rome—he never received the Cardinalate which his position as Primate should have gained him.[13]

Whereas Walsh was the first Irish Primate to have been educated entirely within Ireland, Delany had studied in England at Stonyhurst and had been for two years in Rome. He came to be firmly associated with the governing class in Ireland, and belonged to 'a well-marked type of Irish ecclesiastic of the nineteenth-century ... [and] to a generation which had been taught to distrust the work of political agitators. ... None the less ... [he had] a sense of the wrongs that had been inflicted on the people of Ireland, and a very earnest and patriotic resolve to work for the righting of those wrongs.'[14] Delany's views have much in common with one of Hopkins's more paradoxical attitudes: his belief in the inevitability of Home Rule expressed in the same breath as his condemnation of Gladstone's dispersal of the Empire, and of the archbishops' support of land and tax agitation. Delany could not adjust to the new emphasis of Home Rule under Parnell, or to the shift in ecclesiastical life represented by the new type of influential prelate, such as Walsh and Croke. Hopkins's acquaintance with those two historically significant figures helped him to place his over-strong reactions to political events in some perspective, though the circumstances of his appointment, together with his inbred patriotism, closed his mind to the ideals which motivated not only Walsh but the majority of Irish Catholics.

℀

'Dublin itself is a joyless place and I think in my heart as smoky as London is; I had fancied it quite different',[15] Hopkins wrote to Bridges. Like other Englishmen he had probably pictured Dublin[16] as it had been been in the late eighteenth century: the second city of the British Empire, elegant Georgian streets and town houses, brilliant social life, magnificent military reviews, and animated cultural life. But the city he came to had the air of a deposed capital in economic decline and with a falling population. It was impoverished, unhealthy, and gloomy. The old Parliament House in College Green was a bank. 'The weary, the woebegone, the threadbare streets', wrote George Moore, '—yes, threadbare conveys the moral idea of Dublin.'[17]

Since the Act of Union in 1800, the Irish landed gentry had disappeared from Dublin. Their houses became working-class tenements, or were occupied uneasily by the middle classes, as combined residences and offices. The souls of middle-class Dubliners harmonized with their squalid surroundings. The fashions were London's of a past age. Idle servants and other dependents of the departed civilization joined the increasing numbers of peasants coming in from the country, to create large-scale unemployment, poverty, and misery. The city had failed to respond to the industrial revolution and had been overtaken by expanding cities of mainland Britain, like Liverpool, Manchester, and Birmingham, and by Belfast in northern Ireland. The major social problems included drunkenness and ill-health. Country people were afraid to visit the city because of the high mortality rate from infectious diseases such as typhoid, tuberculosis, and other respiratory diseases. The river Liffey was the city's major sewer, and house drains were in an appalling state, particularly those of properties on low-lying soil.

St Stephen's Green was low-lying, and the drains of No. 86 were infested with rats. 'The house we are in, the College,' wrote Hopkins, 'is a sort of ruin.' Since the 1850s, when Newman moved into them, the buildings had 'fallen into a deep dilapidation. They were a sort of wreck or ruin when our Fathers some months since came in and the costly last century ornamentation of flutes and festoons and Muses on the walls is still much in contrast with the dinginess and dismantlement all round.'[18] Other houses on Stephen's Green were also decaying. Only one, that of the Church of Ireland Archbishop of Dublin, was still put to its original use.[19] In the centre was the park, laid out by a newly ennobled member of the Guinness brewing family, with a lake, mounds, trees, and gravel walks, partly to provide an open recreational space for the poor; it looked, thought Moore, 'like a school-treat set out for the entertainment of charity children'.[20] For most of the year the gardens were desolate, and when it rained 'all the flower-beds and walks confronted the grey of the sky with a truculent sodden brown'.[21] On the north side of the Green was the fashionable Shelbourne Hotel; the same side, says Daly, was notorious 'for its congregation of beggars or nominal beggars: children pretending to sell flowers, matches or newspapers'.[22]

A visitor in 1884 to the Shelbourne, with its winter garden, fountain, ferns, and stone frogs, and sitting-room with painted Swiss scenery and invalid ladies on ottomans, might have been startled to be told of violence and political unrest in the country. The Phoenix Park murders of 1882 were fresh in people's minds; there were outrages, evictions, and the activities of the Land League, above all the campaign for Home Rule. Loyalties were polarized on political and religious lines. Hopkins's patriotic instincts were on the side of conservative English policies, against Gladstone and Parnell. His political sympathies should have been with the Protestant Unionists, in retreat, making their homes no longer in Dublin but in the self-contained southern suburbs of Rathmines, Monkstown, and Blackrock,[23] or living in intellectual isolation in Trinity College, said to be 'the only English foundation that ever succeeded in Ireland'.[24] But as he was a Catholic Hopkins could belong to neither camp. As Daly says,

Already by the 1850s, and to an even greater degree by the 1880s, the links between catholicism and nationalism had been so forged that for many Dubliners, indeed many Irishmen, a patriotic, English catholic who lacked sympathy with Irish nationalism would have seemed an unfathomable incongruity.[25]

౸

A relative of Hopkins, the Revd Sydney Smith, said in 1807: 'The moment the very name of Ireland is mentioned, the English seem to bid adieu to common feeling, common prudence and common sense, and to act with the barbarity of tyrants and the fatuity of idiots.' The English and Irish viewed each other largely as national stereotypes rather than as individuals; prejudices had built up during centuries of military, political, and religious confrontation. It was common for Victorian Englishmen to picture the Irish as inferiors: they lacked enterprise, as was shown by the absence of industry and industriousness; they were 'brawling' and 'unreasonable' (Carlyle); they lacked self-control and emotional stability—their wildness made them unfit for self-government; they became drunk on whiskey and dreams.[26] They were priest-ridden beyond all bearing, said Thackeray: 'the society is under-educated—the priests as illiterate as boors'.[27] The Irish joke, well-established in England by the 1880s, mocked Paddy's alleged failure to grasp cause and effect. The Irish retaliated by depicting John Bull as the epitome of a philistine, with 'bulging eyes and paunch and heavy jowls'.[28] Racial consciousness featured more prominently in everyday Irish than in English life, and was bound to rub off on Hopkins: his examples of 'mortal beauty' in an 1885 poem written in Ireland were Angles, though he considered his two 'beautiful young people' in another poem as mixtures of John Bull with Paddy and Biddy.

ᏇᏏ

Hopkins's periods of Jesuit training had been spent in sympathetic places—Roehampton, Stonyhurst, and St Beuno's—and his professional appointments had been for one year at the most. But the Professorship of Greek was a permanent appointment. Before he went to Ireland he had achieved only a 'cobweb permanence', so that he built no sense of belonging; but the place where he was doomed to stay was the least congenial. For an Englishman of Hopkins's situation and constitution, the sense of being Fortune's football would certainly be exacerbated. It was a country where he would feel that conversations were conducted on two levels: the surface words, flowing musically and easily, and the hidden thoughts. The silent interrogations would start when a name was mentioned. Was the name of Irish or English origin? Though originally a British name, 'Hopkins' had become absorbed into Ireland by the nineteenth century, and 'Gerard' is a Catholic saint's name, as common in Ireland as in Britain. But unfortunately for him his voice, a south-eastern, English, middle- to upper-class one, its traditional ruling-class characteristics exaggerated by public school and Oxford, would have a powerful stereotype associated with it: the British, the upper class, the gentry, the aristocrats, the strangers, perhaps the usurpers. Sympathy would be impossible unless this barrier, set up by centuries of British domination in Ireland, were brought down. Newman is spoken of in Ireland today as almost a saint, but the image is that of a figure walking alone in the distance on Stephen's Green. Surviving descriptions of the English professors at the college from Newman's day to the setting up of the National University in 1908 suggest specimens of a strange breed.[29]

Since the college's opening under its Jesuit management in November 1883, it had been plagued with difficulties. The terms of the agreement with the Catholic bishops, owners of the Stephen's Green buildings, had been less than favourable to the Jesuits. They had to pay rent, rates, and taxes, their tenancy could be terminated at any time, and they were responsible for repairs and alterations to the dilapidated buildings. Although Fr Delany saw the institution as the heir to Newman's Catholic University, the bishops showed both parsimony and suspicion of the college. Newman's University church, his 'large barn' decorated 'in the style of a Basilika, with Irish marbles', was now a parochial church under diocesan control, not available for the college's use; so they had to turn the main drawing-room, or salon, of No. 85 into a chapel, its rich Corinthian style and decorative plaster-work hidden under the chocolate-brown paint which covered the whole room.

It had been planned that the college should be spread over three houses, Nos. 84, 85, and 86. No. 84 was a modest but smart Georgian town-house, 85 a little Venetian villa, built by a German Huguenot, and decorated with exuberant and weighty plasterwork, and 86, called by Newman 'that beastly old Georgian house', was the square block of a mansion built by a *nouveau riche* vulgarian, Buck Whaley, who had decorated it largely with swooping plaster birds; by 1883 it had become, in Delany's words, a 'neglected old barracks', full of dry rot. Space was cramped. The tenant of 84 refused to move, and the ground and first floors of 86 were occupied by the Rector of the phantom Catholic University, Dr Molloy, so only the top two floors, consisting mainly of small rooms, could be used. In this space were accommodated class-rooms, chapel, dining-rooms, and kitchen, and residences for the community and a few students. There were no laboratories or apparatus for scientific studies, and just before the Jesuits moved in the library of the Catholic University had been removed. In spite of protests over subsequent years, the books were never returned by the bishops, and members of the college were sent out to the second-hand bookshops on the Liffey quays with small sums of money, to pick up what they could. The purchases were then arranged on the staircase landings. The college was crucially short of endowments and money in general, the bishops having washed their hands of responsibility for its finances. The old Catholic University had had an annual subvention, from the bishops and from special collections at mass, of about £7,000 a year. Delany had to beg constantly. He was forbidden to call his college the 'Catholic' University College, with the result that it lost a substantial legacy.

Despite its new name and management, the college looked exactly as it had done in the days of the Catholic University, whose long tradition of failure seemed to be continuing. Delany inherited the staff of the old Catholic University, men who belonged to another age, and were unsuited to the new conditions. Two of these were holders of the

Classical Chairs senior to Hopkins's, Professors Robert Ornsby and James Stewart. They were Tractarians, in their sixties, and infirm; the students objected to attending their classes. Ornsby had to be carried in to his classes and propped up in a chair; Stewart, who had held three Anglican parishes before his conversion, was now practically unable to do any work; he taught nothing for the first year of the Jesuit tenure and very little in the second.[30] The Professor of English, Thomas Arnold, was Matthew Arnold's younger brother and had heard Wordsworth read his poetry; he had first been offered a post in Newman's University in 1856, and was understood to have been the original of Philip Hewson, the young radical poet of Clough's *The Bothie of Tober-na-Vuolich*. Now he was reduced to a 'tall figure stooped at the reading-desk', with a slight stammer and slow of speech, 'clear-cut features with wide mouth', and a 'fringe of side whiskers which he wore in the fashion of men of his generation'.[31] Among the new Jesuit staff were John J. O'Carroll, said to be able to speak eighteen languages, Denis Murphy, an Irish historian, Bursar and Librarian, and Tom Finlay, a 'long-bodied man, fleshy everywhere', with 'russet-coloured face ... insignificant nose, short grey hair', direct speech and rough clothes, who at different times held Chairs of Classics, Philosophy, and Metaphysics.[32] The most exotic figure was the Frenchman Père Mallac; there was 'a haggard look in his strong, well-cut, swarthy features, and sometimes the glance from his black eyes was so terrifying that he was yclept "Mephistopheles" '. He had been a free-thinker before his conversion, and was 'a fierce follower of Aristotle'. He was said to study in his room all day and most of the night, 'often absenting himself from community meals and taking alone some black coffee and a biscuit'.[33]

☙

His spiritual notes and letters from Ireland testify to Hopkins's pessimism and depression during most of 1884. A fortnight after arriving in Dublin he wrote:

In the events which have brought me here I recognise the hand of providence, but nevertheless have felt and feel an unfitness which led me at first to try to decline the offer made me and now does not yet allow my spirits to rise to the level of the position and its duties. But perhaps the things of most promise with God begin with weakness and fear.[34]

There are personal implications in a note he wrote at the beginning of March on the Gospel of the Temptations: 'He was led by the spirit into the wilderness. Pray to be guided by the Holy Ghost in everything.

Consider that he was now led to be tempted and the field and arena of the struggle was a wilderness where the struggle would be intenser but not perhaps more really perilous.' A note on the feast of the Lance and Nails reads: 'Seeing Christ's body nailed consider the attachment of his will to God's will. Wish to be as bound to God's will in all things, in the attachment of your affections to Christ our Lord and his wounds instead of any earthly object.'[35] The same day he wrote to Bridges that his appointment to Dublin was 'an honour and an opening and has many bright sides, but at present it has also some dark ones and this in particular that I am not at all strong, not strong enough for the requirements and do not see at all how I am to become so'.[36]

By the middle of April 1884, in spite of a short period away at Clongowes Wood College, there were signs that his depression was worsening: 'I cannot spare much time . . . . I wish, I wish I could get on with my play. . . . it would be tedious to explain how, AND WHAT DOES ANYTHING AT ALL MATTER? . . . The East wind is worse than in England. I am in a great weakness. I cannot spend more time writing now.' At the end of the month he wrote a short and bright letter congratulating Bridges on his engagement to Monica Waterhouse, but added after his signature: 'I am, I believe, recovering from a deep fit of nervous prostration (I suppose I ought to call it): I did not know but I was dying.' At the beginning of summer he made notes on his condition: 'Take it that weakness, ill health, every cross is a help. . . . I must ask God to strengthen my faith or I shall never keep the particular examen. I must say the stations for this intention. Resolve also to keep it particularly even in the present state of lethargy.'[37]

At the beginning of July a holiday in the west of Ireland buoyed him up, and he wrote a cheerful letter to his father describing the people of Castlebar, in County Mayo:

Every one in the country parts and most markedly the smallest children, if asked a question, answer it by repeating the words without yes or no. 'Were you at school on Friday?'—'I was, sir,' 'You would be afraid to go in where the bull is!'—'I would not, sir.' The effect is very pretty and pointed.[38]

But even such a pleasant holiday was marred by small dissatisfactions, not disguised by Hopkins's humorous expression: 'Great part of the population are very pleasantly shod in their bare heels and stockinged in their bare shins. How gladly would I go so! The struggle I keep up with shoemakers, murderers by inches, I may say ever embitters my life.' His new argosy braces never allowed him to 'draw an easy breath'.

His holiday in the west lasted for over a fortnight. One day he was taken in a *púchan*, a little fishing-boat, across Galway Bay to County

Clare, where he saw the cliffs of Moher; on the way back across the bay a storm nearly overwhelmed the boat, and, Hopkins told Bridges, 'we were in some considerable danger of our lives'.[39] Yet in spite of the 'fine scenery' of Connemara, and the 'beautiful woods' surrounding Furbough House, where he stayed with an old Catholic family, the Blakes, he had only gained a temporary relief:

The weakness I am suffering from—it is that only, nervous weakness (or perhaps I ought not to say nervous at all, for I am not in any unusual way nervous in the common understanding of the word)—continues and I see no ground for thinking I can, for a long time to come, get notably better of it, but I may reasonably hope that this pleasant holiday may set me up a little for a while.[40]

He assured Bridges that there was 'no reason to be disquieted about me, though weakness is a very painful trial in itself'. Bridges asked him to be best man at his wedding, but Hopkins declined, giving as his main reason that he would be beginning his examination work and could not leave Ireland. He added that he liked men to marry, because 'a single life is a difficult, not altogether a natural life'. To cope with it 'special provision, such as we have, is needed'.

On 30 September, St Michael's Day, Hopkins wrote in his notebook: 'Consider your own misery and try as best you can to rise above it, by punctuality, and the particular examen; by fervour at office, mass, and litanies; by good scholastic work; by charity if you get opportunities.'[41] The same day a postcard to Bridges identified the immediate cause of his misery: 'I am in the very thick of examination work and in danger of permanently injuring my eyes. I shall have no time [free of duties] at all till past the middle of next month and not much then, for I have to begin lecturing and cannot now prepare.'[42] From the beginning of his time in Dublin, Hopkins was dismayed at the prospect of so much examining: 'I have a salary of £400 a year, but when I first contemplated the six examinations I have yearly to conduct, five of them running, and to the Matriculation there came up last year 750 candidates, I thought that Stephen's Green (the biggest square in Europe) paved with gold would not pay for it.'[43]

Confronted with endless piles of examination scripts, he was shocked by the poor standard of answers, and by their grammar, expression, and spelling. He made lists of notes on peculiar things that caught his eye;[44] his frustrations are plain from his comments: candidate 420 'translates *money/ munniam*', number 445 was 'raving throughout'; the Caesar translation of another student was 'mere jargon'. Hopkins's bewildered and hopeless remarks reveal the fastidious distance between his standards and those of the students: 'Most do not try, the rest do wrong the scanning of two common hexameters'; and 'Two candidates, girls I think, being asked to give Caesar's words *as spoken* give an extraordinary jargon like "The of the butcher wife of them the tails with knife off cut"; I suppose they mean it for a word for word rendering of Latin. And this when they have translated the Latin right.'

In the battered exercise-book called Hopkins's 'Dublin Notebook' there are pages and pages containing thousands of examination ticks, marks, and occasional comments. Interspersed among the marks are his spiritual notes; often the text of the day leads Hopkins to indicate his present low state, either directly (as in the St Michael note) or by some sudden sign of abnormality or disturbance: in a note on the Creation written about 8 September, for instance, he enlarged a word 'created' to several times its normal size, then crossed it through, and wrote, again much enlarged, 'cr crea'.

On 25 October he wrote to Dixon that he was much better after the summer, though 'drowned in the last and worst of five examinations'. He had '557 papers on hand: let those who have been thro' the like say what that means'. At 'this most inopportune time' he had been asked by Thomas Arnold to write a short account of Dixon's life and work for the fifth edition of his *Manual of English Literature*. Taking time off from marking, but summarizing comments already made in letters, he hurriedly wrote an essay of four paragraphs, which overpraised Dixon's work—'the very rare gift of pure imagination', 'a truth and splendour not less than Keats' own'—but finished by pointing to faults of 'a certain vagueness of form, some unpleasing rhymes, and most by an obscurity ... suggesting a deeper meaning behind the text without leaving the reader any decisive clue to find it'.[45]

❧

Hopkins needed more than ever the correspondence of people who understood him. 'It is a great help to me to have someone interested in something (that will answer my letters), and it supplies some sort of intellectual stimulus', Hopkins later told Baillie. 'I sadly need that and a general stimulus to being, so dull and yet harassed is my life.'[46] Congratulating Hopkins on his new post, '& on the honours that your learning has won for you', Dixon showed how little he knew Hopkins's situation: 'The prospect of reading for examining others would be a pleasant one to me: at least if it involved re-reading books that I once read with the other motive of being examined: for nothing seems more to refurnish the mind than reading old books again.'[47] In December 1882 he wrote, 'My own experience is that any teaching, any literary work is good for the mind.'[48] To Hopkins his October examining was an illness—he was, he told Grace, 'just over a bout of severe work' which had left him 'jaded'. The so-called 'lectures' which replaced the examinations in his timetable were 'no more than lessons',[49] for which he had to teach at an elementary level, take the names of absentees, and put up with schoolboy pranks. Dixon's ideas on poetry were also somewhat removed from Hopkins's; he had been trying 'to spell out a few Canons of Poetry'. Among the opinions which he asked Hopkins to comment on were: 'For the two highest kinds of poetry, dramatic & heroic, blank verse is the only proper vehicle', and 'Poems in any stanza are of inferior form to poems in the continuous measure of blank or even couplet verse.' Hopkins's reply is missing, but his own poetry had moved far from Dixon's, in practice and precept, since the days he had admired Dixon's *Christ's Company*, and had written versifications of Bible stories. Dixon's appreciation of Hopkins's recent poems was too generalized and uncritical to be useful or encouraging: 'I like the Sonnet on Earth the Creature ['Ribblesdale'], which you sent, very much, as I do all your work: it has the rareness, the sweetness that is in all.' But at least he responded positively, although Hopkins's increasing consciousness of his own distance from other people may have caused a wry response when Dixon wrote that 'Ribblesdale' could 'have been written by none other'.[50]

The friendship with Bridges, however, retained much of its original ease, openness, and breadth of mutual interest. Hopkins's affectionate pleasure at Bridges's marriage shows in his letter of 2 September 1884 to 'My dearest Bridges and my dear Mrs. Bridges', 'to wish you the happiest of days tomorrow and all the blessings of heaven on that and all the days of your wedded life'. He posted it too late: 'the consequence is that these wishes must, like the old shoe, be sent *after* you', and added, 'there is no harm in that if when they overtake you they ever after attend you'. He felt he could not ask permission to be present at the wedding, 'much as I desire to see you and your wife and her mother and Yattendon itself'. Perhaps the wedding-day would not be such a good day for him to visit 'as some other. Only unhappily I do not see when that other is to be.'[51]

When the October examinations were over, Hopkins's daily life became less arduous and there were pleasures and enthusiasms. But he was constantly aware of surrounding hostility—'indeed what is Ireland' (he asked his mother) 'but an open or secret war of fierce enmities of every sort?'—and the college was 'really struggling for existence with difficulties within and without'; it was 'poor, all unprovided to a degree that outsiders wd. scarcely believe', and life there was 'like living at a temporary Junction and everybody knowing and shewing as much'. Fr Delany had 'such a buoyant and unshaken trust in God and wholly lives for the success of the place', that Hopkins felt the college might weather its difficulties. If Delany was 'as generous, cheering, and openhearted a man as I ever lived with', the person who gave him greatest happiness was Robert Curtis. He wished that his mother could some day see Curtis, 'for he is my comfort beyond what I can say and a kind of godsend I never expected to have'.[52]

Curtis was Irish and eight years younger than Hopkins.[53] After a brilliant mathematics and science career at Trinity College Dublin, where he had been the first Catholic entrant after Gladstone had abolished religious tests, he entered the novitiate. There had been doubts about his appointment to University College because of his health. He had an epileptic condition which prevented his ordination as a priest; during one of his fits he had fallen on spikes in Stephen's Green. It was known before his candidature arose that his health was 'indifferent', and it was thought that 'the work of preparing and examining papers would be too much for him.' A doctor suggested he should be allowed 'at most three hours *quiet* work per day'. Like Hopkins, Curtis was considered an enthusiast and an eccentric. He was reputed to stay up into the small hours working on mathematical problems; this became such a difficulty that while he was a teacher at Clongowes Wood College a man was deputed to turn off his gas at 10 o'clock each evening. (Hopkins became known for keeping Curtis up late at night.) Curtis was renowned for his rapid walking pace, and the story was told how he would suddenly jump over a fence during a walk; Hopkins was supposed to have commented: 'I think there must be a hare in that man's pedigree.' Hopkins often used to visit Curtis's parents in their large Georgian house just north of the Liffey, 'and shd. more if I had time to go there'. Curtis's father was a prominent barrister and Queen's Counsel, and so, like most of the non-Jesuit friends Hopkins made in Dublin, on the British side in politics.

With the beginning of the academic year Hopkins started giving lectures, which he liked 'well enough, that is rather than not'.[54] With Michaelmas term came new interests. One evening in October he was much taken with a sunset: 'the sun of a ruddy gold, which colour it kept till nothing was left of it but a star-like spot; then this spot turned, for the twinkling of an eye, a leaden or watery blue, and vanished.' There followed a glow almost as bright as those after Krakatoa. Between 6.15 and 6.30,

it was intense: bronzy near the earth; above like peach, or of the blush colour on ripe hazels. It drew away southwards. It would seem as if the volcanic 'wrack' had become a satellite to the earth, like Saturn's rings and was subject to phases, of which we are now witnessing a vivid one.

Realising the relevance of his observations to the correspondence in *Nature* about a corona or halo surrounding the sun, Hopkins wrote a fourth long letter to the editor (printed on 30 October 1884), confidently contradicting another correspondent, and ridiculing a Professor Piazzi-Smyth who had argued that the colours seen around the sun were due to a weakening of the sun's rays: 'To set down variations in light and heat to changes in the sun', wrote Hopkins, 'when they may be explained by changes in our atmosphere, is like preferring the Ptolemaic to the Copernican system.' He preferred to assign the phenomena to optical effects, such as those he had noticed in North Wales several years before the eruption of Krakatoa.

Another interest he took up again was music. Perhaps the only good thing to come out of the October examinations for him that year was his meeting with the examiners in music. Dr Joseph Smith, known as 'Joe', was 'one of the most thorough "tykes" I ever met and an Englishman, yet not from Yorkshire, the land of tykes, but from Worcester'. The other examiner was Sir Robert Stewart, who had 'a pleasant hearty undisguised snubbing way'. Stewart interested Hopkins because he was a great admirer of Purcell. He decried Thomas Arne: ' "the pedantic and ungenial Arne" he said twice, out of some lecture, I shd. guess; as if it were some kind of Lord Chief Justice's sentence and no more to be said.' Stewart did not believe in Greek music, nor in other aspects of Hopkins's musical interests, but Hopkins hoped 'to know more of him.'[55] Stewart introduced him to Stainer's *Theory of Harmony*, and before long Hopkins had 'a great light on the matter of harmony myself, new, I need not say'. Before leaving Stonyhurst he had begun to compose a Gregorian setting to Collins's 'Ode to Evening'. 'Quickened by the heavenly beauty of that poem I groped in my soul's very viscera for the tune and thrummed the sweetest and most secret catgut of the mind.' What came out seemed to its composer 'very strange and wild', and with the addition of harmony 'was so delightful that it seems to me . . . as near a new world of musical enjoyment as in this old world we could hope to be.' It was in three movements, 'something like a glee', and was meant to be performed by a soloist singing in unison with a double choir, while an accompanying organ or string band played the harmony.[56]

A more ambitious project was his hope to publish 'a new and critical edition of St. Patrick's "Confession"', a work Hopkins thought 'worthy to rank (except for length) with St. Austin's Confessions and the Imitation'.[57] Like so many of his Dublin projects, this one disappeared without trace, but it is an example of his early desire to do well by Ireland. Another aspect of his interest in his new country was the fascination he felt for its forms of English. In a letter to Bridges he recounted 'a humorous touch of Irish Malvolio or Bully Bottom, so distinctively Irish that I cannot rank it: it amuses me in bed'. Playing in a cricket match, a Jesuit scholastic, William Gleeson, from Nenagh in County Tipperary, 'was at the wicket and another bowling to him. He thought there was no one within hearing, but from behind the wicket he was overheard after a good stroke to cry out "Arrah, sweet myself!"' Hopkins put this phrase into the list of Irish dialect words he was collecting.[58] He tried his hand at imitating Irish speech to his sister Kate:

And now, Miss Hopkins darlin, yell chartably exkees me writin more in the rale Irish be raison I was never rared to ut and thats why I do be so slow with my pinmanship, bad luck to ut (savin your respects), but for ivery word I delineate I disremember two, and that's how ut is with me.[59]

In the same letter he told his sister 'I have a kind of charge of a greenhouse.' The college accounts book from 7 to 11 October[60] shows a flurry of activity, costing over £17, including the repair of the greenhouse at the back of No. 86, and the purchase of garden supplies. This activity, however, seems soon to have stopped. It looks like another sudden enthusiasm. With another potential interest Hopkins lacked the spirit even to start:

A dear old French Father, very clever and learned and a great photographer, who at first wanted me to take to photography with him, which indeed in summer would be pleasant enough, finding that once I used to draw, got me to bring him the few remains I still have, cows and horses in chalk done in Wales too long ago to think of, and admired them to that degree that he is urgent with me to go on drawing at all hazards; but I do not see how that could be now, so late: if anybody had said the same 10 years ago it might have been different.[61]

❦

Hopkins just about kept up his correspondence with Oak Hill, but by the end of the year felt ashamed that he had not written to his mother for a long time. He had written to Grace, who claimed that writing to him was like throwing letters into a well. He did not know Milicent's address, now that she had joined an Anglican religious order: 'I am sure I do not know what in the world, in which we scarcely ever meet, we gain by not writing.' He had not written to Lionel since his brother had gone out to China. He found letter-writing, though 'so pleasant in doing', 'a most harassing duty to set to with other work on hand'. Despite these attempts to keep in touch he felt disinclined to spend Christmas at Hampstead. 'You can easily understand reasons', he told his mother, somewhat tetchily:

If I came now I could not again so soon. Travelling long distances in winter is harder, more tiring, and the broken sleeps are a great trial to me. Then Grace is away. Then it is so soon after coming to Ireland; it does not look so well. Then the holidays are short and I have an examination at the end of them. Altogether I do not welcome it.[62]

He had an invitation to spend that Christmas at the home of Lord Emly, a Catholic Senator of the Royal University who had supported Hopkins's nomination; he was an anti-Gladstonian Liberal, who had known Newman when they were together at Oriel in the 1830s. The note Hopkins wrote in his spiritual diary, probably while staying at Lord Emly's, suggests—though reticently—a less than happy mood:

Dec. 24, Christmas Eve—
Mary and Joseph were poor, strangers, travellers, married, that is to say respectable, honest. . . . Their trials were hurry, discomfort, cold, inhospitality, dishonour.
    Their comfort was Christ's birth. Thank God for your delivery of today. Here think the Gloria in excelsis and bring yourself to leave out of sight your own trials rejoicing over Christ's birth. Wish a happy Christmas and all its blessings to all your friends.[63]

# 'Dapple at end'

Dies Irae, dies illa
Solvet saeclum in favilla:
Teste David cum Sibylla.

*The Fifth Exercise* is a meditation on hell . . . The first point will be to
see with the eye of the imagination those great fires, and those souls as
it were in bodies of fire.

(St Ignatius, *Spiritual Exercises*, First Week)

The lost now lying in hell are Devils without bodies and disembodied
souls, they suffer nevertheless a torment as of bodily fire. Though
burning and other pains afflict us through our bodies yet it is the soul
that they afflict, the mind: if the mind can be deadened, as by
chloroform, no pain is felt at all: God can then if he chooses bodily
afflict the mind that is out of or never had a body to suffer in. No one
in the body can suffer fire for very long, the frame is destroyed and the
pain comes to an end; not so, unhappily, the pain that afflicts the
indestructible mind. . . . Let all consider this: we are our own
tormentors.

(Hopkins's meditation notes on the Fifth Exercise)

Many poets in the 1870s and early 1880s were obsessed by the mystical
significance of twilight and sunset, almost constituting a sub-genre,
which included parts of *In Memoriam*, the elegiac songs in Tennyson's
*The Princess*, and the popular drawing-room song by C. Lloyd Stafford,
'Watchman, what of the night?'. This kind of Victorian neo-Sublime,
reacting against Darwinism and science, sentimentally exalted faith
over reason. In such poems there were usually dimly seen pleasures,
sparks among the fading ashes, predictions of the glorious dawn when
night should be no more, the hope of meeting in Heaven the loved one

who had gone before. Towards the end of 1884 Hopkins began his own twilight elegy, a sonnet, 'Spelt from Sibyl's Leaves', which he did not complete until two years later. Hopkins's poem was not compromised or distanced by comforting diction, rhythms, or sentiments; its subject was the imminence and terror of Judgement Day. The tone and much of the imagery derives from the medieval tradition of associating Doomsday with the pagan Sibyls: Pope Julius II had ordered that the Sibyls appear on the Sistine ceiling among the prophets and patriarchs of the Christian era.

The poem makes a modern reiteration of the Sibyl's vision, using the Sibylline mode of divination. 'Spelt from ... Leaves' implies the normal method the Cumaean Sibyl used for prophesying, which was to shuffle her palm-leaves on which oracles had been written down, and draw one leaf at a time at random (as a tarot pack is used for fortune-telling). The Cumaean Sibyl was the votaress of Apollo, the sun-god; the Greek gods are now dead, but the message of the sunset remains the same, except that now the seer is a Christian priest. Hopkins is taking hints and disordered fragments from his responses to a sunset which seems portentous, and fitting them together gradually until the meaning becomes clear. The sunset does not yield its meaning easily, and so the first line is of apparently disconnected Sibylline fragments, oracular epithets without the noun which explains their existence. Larger pieces are added, building to the climax when the subject and significance suddenly become plain to the seer-poet: 'Our tale, O our oracle!' An evening passing into night is seen by the poet as such a complex and vast transition that the natural scene is metamorphosed into a cosmic paradigm, of the night into which time will dissolve:

Earnest, earthless, equal, attuneable, vaulty, voluminous, . . . stupendous
Evening strains to be tíme's vást, womb-of-all, home-of-all, hearse-of-
    all night.
Her fond yellow hornlight wound to the west, her wild hollow hoarlight
    hung to the height
Waste; her earliest stars, earlstars, stars principal, overbend us,
Fíre-féaturing héaven. For éarth her béing has unbóund; her dápple is
    at énd, as-
Tray or aswarm, all throughther, in throngs; self ín self stéepèd and
    páshed—qúite
Disremembering, dismembering all now. Heart, you round me right
With: Óur évening is óver us; óur night whélms, whélms, ánd will énd
    us.

Only the beakleaved boughs dragonish damask the tool-smooth bleak
     light; black,
Ever so black on it. Óur tale, O óur oracle! Lét life, wáned, ah lét life
     wínd
Off hér once skéined stained véined varíety upon, áll on twó spools;
     párt, pen, páck
Now her áll in twó flocks, twó folds—bláck, white; ríght, wrong; réckon
     but, réck but, mínd
But thése two; wáre of a wórld where bút these twó tell, éach off the
     óther; of a ráck
Where, selfwrung, selfstrung, sheathe- and shelterless, thoúghts
     agáinst thoughts ín groans grínd.

  More than any other of Hopkins's poems this one demands a
dramatic vocal reading, carefully planned to incorporate Hopkins's
markings. The sounds are orchestrated to express a vast terrestrial
movement, broken up into a variety of successive effects which build
towards the terrible climax. The ponderous, carefully spaced beat of the
first line establishes an inexorability, succeeded by an articulation of the
process in which the vulnerable aesthetic properties of Nature are
strained away by the forces of Doomsday. The complementary natures
of the twin, delicately beautiful, areas of the evening sky are expressed
in the balanced sounds of the two halves of the third line. This is
followed by the unexpected cancellation, 'Waste', showing the transitory earthly joys replaced by unyielding values of morality. The varied
and replaceable rhythms at the start of the poem are gradually forced
into a starkly insistent beat, which first takes over with the unnatural
emphasis on 'Óur . . . óur . . . óur . . . óur', and ignoring more and more
the usual emphasis of words forces them into an uncomfortable
discipline, 'thoúghts agáinst thoughts ín groans grínd.'
  The poem's close conformity to Christian orthodoxy, in particular
the *Dies Irae* and the Sibylline framework, provides sufficient ambiguity and indirectness to mask biographical significance. In 1884
Hopkins experienced one of his most prolonged and profound periods
of pessimism. He felt his physical and mental powers were unreliable,
and his religious profession—for which he had given up so much—was
unrewarding. For the first time since his reception into the novitiate
sixteen years earlier, his duties seemed of doubtful value. He lacked
almost every comfort. In 'Spelt from Sibyl's Leaves' Hopkins's poetry
became a vehicle for this pessimism. He could no longer find the
psychic strength to observe and experiment with reality. Weakness had

made him reject disquieting enquiry, of an almost Protestant[1] kind, to revert to the orthodox certainties of Catholicism, supported by the antique prophets. Stars were no longer the whimsical Victorian fire-folk of 'The Starlight Night', but Ptolemaic portents of despotism and doom.

The poem attempts a terrible annihilation of Hopkins's idiosyncrasies of person and poetry. The marvelling exploratory vision and language in the Welsh poems, which discovered new ways of showing God's design in nature, had depended on the generous argument of belief through providential design. Now Hopkins was forced to attempt an argument, not from creation, but from destructive dissolution. The carefully designed individualities in nature are of no account; they will be swept away. The most positive enriching elements of Hopkins's life—dapple, earth's being, self—are not just destroyed but morally invalidated, worth nothing compared with the old earthless, selfless, medieval message of traditional, doom-laden morality. God disposes, and does not leave man room to propose.

In joining the Jesuit order Hopkins had inhibited himself as a poet writing about people. When the poems show an encounter between his private self and the outside social world it is seldom a happy one. 'Landscape painting', Hazlitt had said, 'is the obvious resource of misanthropy'. It now looked as though external nature was also shut off, and he never again wrote about nature with unqualified joy, though he was opening up a new range of non-doctrinal expression for his poetry.

&

The 1880s was a period of transition, insularity, and nationalism, with Catholic Ireland possessing no sophisticated culture or educational standards, compared with most of Europe. The conditions at 86 Stephen's Green not only were different from those Hopkins had been accustomed to at Balliol but did not conform to European ideas of a university. The college's teaching consisted of cramming for examinations, and impersonal lectures on an elementary level to students who mostly lived at home, without the advantage of collegiate life and tutorials. Academic standards would have seemed shockingly low to Hopkins.

The prospective artist Stephen Daedalus found the same college, a few years later, 'a day-school full of terrorized boys, banded together in a complicity of diffidence. They have eyes only for their future jobs: to secure their future jobs they will write themselves in and out of convictions, toil and labour to insinuate themselves into the good graces of the Jesuits'. Hopkins's pupils would not be interested in the classics for their own sake or for the mental training they gave. The students' utilitarian attitudes extended also to art, in which they were uninterested, regarding it as a continental vice:

It was all very well to be able to talk about it but really art was all 'rot': besides it was probably immoral; they knew (or, at least, they had heard) about studios. They didn't want that kind of thing in their country. Talk about beauty, talk about rhythms, talk about esthetic—they knew what all the fine talk covered.[2]

Stephen found that the students' reactions to art were largely a product of the college's teaching, which tended towards a narrow moralistic outlook, and did not encourage original thought. In *Stephen Hero* Father Butt (the Professor of English) and the President are Joyce's portraits of Fathers Darlington and Delany, Jesuit colleagues of Hopkins's. Reading through *Twelfth Night* Fr Butt 'skipped the two songs of the clown without a word', and, when Stephen forced them on his attention, showed that he had no idea of their serious artistic purpose: 'It was a custom at that time for noblemen to have clowns to sing to them . . . for amusement'. Hopkins was also interested in songs from Shakespeare's plays, and in 1886 translated several into Greek and Latin, an exercise which demanded understanding of every detail. (Two from *The Tempest* were published in Fr Matthew Russell's *Irish Monthly* in 1886 and 1887.) Stephen Daedalus tells how Father Butt

took *Othello* more seriously and made the class take a note of the moral of the play: an object lesson in the passion of jealousy. . . . We see the conflict of these human passions and our own passions are purified by the spectacle. The dramas of Shakespeare have a distinct moral force. . . . [Stephen] was amused to learn that the president had refused to allow two of the boarders to go to a performance of *Othello* at the Gaiety Theatre on the ground that there were many coarse expressions in the play.[3]

When Darlington had been appointed to the English Fellowship he found he was expected to teach and examine in all English literature, all modern European history, and all geography—'and I had done at Oxford no English literature whatever, no history, no geography'.[4]

There was 'little or no interest in pure literature in the College' in the 1880s, said a pupil of Hopkins.[5] Daedalus's teachers saw art as an escape from life; Hopkins's colleagues and students soon developed a picture of him as a 'detached aesthete'. He could be understood in Dublin only as an example of English aesthetic Catholicism, with which the Irish had no sympathy.[6] Many of his characteristics—appearance, way of talking, Newmanite conversion, shyness and reclusiveness, educated upper-class Englishness and Oxonian mannerisms, scrupulous habits, interests in music and the visual arts, poetic composition—appeared typical facets of an English aesthete. His known friendships with modern English poets like Patmore and Dixon, and his interest in nature, confirmed the impressions.

Hopkins became known in Dublin as 'a small, shy, almost insignificant man'; a student remembered him as 'a very slight man'. He was considered effeminate but (said an acquaintance) 'did *not* look like a woman'.[7] Fr Darlington, in his declining years, remembered Hopkins as 'holy, gentle and feminine'.[8] A resident student at No. 86, John Bacon, described him as 'a man looking probably older than his age, a lean ascetic with a long V-shaped face, lined, and the look of a contemplative, mouse-coloured hair going grey'. Bacon had the impression of 'a rather saintly character', shy, and 'in speech refined and very precious'. Darlington said 'one could not help noticing him, so original was he in appearance and in speech, and in what he wore, and how he wore it, and in all his actions; e.g. the very slippers he wore; the kind little girls of 10 or 12 used then to wear: with ancle straps'.[9]

Darlington, an Oxford man himself, said Hopkins 'brought Baliol [*sic*] and Oxford into our College'.[10] Fr Tom Finlay was another colleague who saw him as 'the typically "Oxford" man'. Hopkins came over to Ireland, Finlay recalled, with the kind of Irish sympathies a young man of the 'Oxford' type would have, and set out to learn the local language—Hiberno-English. He amused Finlay by coming out with 'I'm after being down in Westmoreland Street, begob' ('Westmoreland' pronounced not as in England, with emphatic first syllable and slurred remainder, but as the Irish say it, with the stress on 'more'). Once when he was staying at Clongowes Wood College in County Kildare he went for a walk in a wood, and according to the Rector, Fr Conmee, came back shouting 'She said it, she said it!' Asked to explain who said what, Hopkins replied 'Faiks, I'm getting sticks for me fire'; he had asked a woman what she was doing, and had been thrilled to hear someone say 'Faiks'. Hopkins was not, Finlay thought, concerned with the affairs of ordinary mortals, and never came to look on Irish politics in an Irish way: from his early vague sympathy with the Home-Rulers Hopkins's mind was changed by the people he associated with, mainly of the landowning classes, with English sympathies. His sympathy with the Home-Rulers was 'legalistic'. One St George's Day he appeared with a rose in his buttonhole and Fr Mallac said 'Look what Gerry

Hopkins is wearing'; Hopkins took this as a serious insult, and angrily exclaimed 'Lâche!'[11] It became the common view that Hopkins was 'quite out of place in University College', he was 'much too "refined and cultured" for the roughness of Ireland at that time'.[12] Fr Darlington considered that

No 'squarer' man could be in a 'rounder' hole than was G.H. in University College, and in the work there to be done then. He was so much too good for the pioneer roughness of it all . . . Gerald [sic] Hopkins was at an opposite pole to every thing around him: literary, political, social & c. (a thorough John Bull incapable of understanding Rebel Ireland). No one took him seriously; he played the part rather of the droll jester, in the medieval castles.

One of his pupils, Martin Maher, also got the impression that Hopkins felt strange in Ireland, and decades later remembered how one day, when people were claiming Kitchener for an Irishman, Hopkins responded, 'You Irish—you drag everything into your own net over here'. John Bacon said that Hopkins was 'very strongly anti-Home Rule and no doubt regarded his students as wild Irish barbarians'. Hopkins's letters, on the other hand, show that, although he was strongly opposed to Irish 'disloyalty' and many republican and Land-League activities, he thought Home Rule was inevitable and believed Ireland had been grievously wronged by England. Bacon thought that Hopkins's antipathy for Père Mallac was provoked by Mallac's fierce republicanism: 'Mallac would say "I don't like that little Englishman" and Hopkins would confide "When I see Mallac's face I always think of the devil".' This does not square with Hopkins's account of Mallac as 'a dear old French Father, very clever and learned', and the many friendly references to him in letters from Ireland.[13]

Darlington once attended a meeting in a college room: 'suddenly everyone began to sneeze violently', and the meeting had to be broken up. 'On inquiry I found Fr Hopkins had got some cayenne pepper, and then taught a mischievous errand boy in buttons we had in the hall . . . how to turn it under the door.' Another time Hopkins amused the community by 'begging clothes for a poor beggar woman, who in rags with 2 nearly naked little children, and a baby in arms . . . used to stand pursuing her trade outside the College; when the set of poor wretches got the clothes, these last were pawned at once; and the woman explained to G. H. that he knew nothing of her business; her trade would be ruined if she carried it on in any other way than that she adopted.' It was noticed that he spent much of his time strumming with one finger on the piano, though he could play neither the piano nor any other instrumental, and George O'Neill laughed at him for this.[14]

Hopkins was given one of the college's best rooms, large and plainly decorated, with a fireplace, on the second floor of No. 86 (now room 18).[15] James Gaffney, a student who read Greek with Hopkins, used to go into Hopkins's room, next to his own, and find him lying on his back on the floor, 'with his arms outstretched to straighten his back'. The sheets in Hopkins's room often became dirty, and this used to worry him. Eventually he discovered that the boy bed-maker threw the bedclothes on the floor. Hopkins may have found the Jesuit régime rather strict, said Fr Maher. The general rule in Irish Jesuit houses was to get up at 5.30 in the morning, which Hopkins found difficult. A special concession of an extra half-hour may have been made to him. He used to say his rule was 'to *begin* to get up at the right time'.[16]

In the classroom he was unable to cope with discipline, said a student, and 'never really won the confidence and affection of his pupils'. They were 'crudely disposed to rag anybody, and him particularly'. William Magennis (who later taught at the college) 'would make deliberate mistakes in his translation in the style of Artemus Ward', in order to hear Hopkins solemnly put them right. 'They were like schoolboys', said the same student. Hopkins used to come into the classroom with a bundle of books. He 'spent a long time', said Bacon, 'over a short passage of Greek, dwelling perhaps with little success upon its poetic quality'. Maher said that Hopkins's criticisms were 'not of much marketable value'. When reading Tacitus in language classes he would bring in the history of the texts 'in an aloof sort of way, as a reverie of his own'. In the Tacitus classes, Hopkins 'did not, as other Jesuit professors were known to do, skip over passages about rapes etc.', but he would 'let the class read them through in the ordinary way—and afterwards hold up his hands and say "O those poor girls!"' Another tale was that to demonstrate the death of Hector he had lain on his back on the floor and got a student to drag him round the table.[17]

Hopkins was always being misinterpreted. He was 'so naïve and simple', said John Howley, one of his students, that he 'neither suspected he was being ragged, nor [was] able to see that remarks of his were open to misreading'. He once said that 'he regretted that he had never seen a naked woman: this said in all simplicity opened up a new chance for "ragging", and was perhaps even solemnly misunderstood'. Howley considered it 'a great piece of good fortune' that they did not know he was a poet, because if they had known 'they would have parodied him and ragged him still more'. Hopkins was 'twitted by his Jesuit colleagues in the same sort of way as he was ragged by his pupils', said Howley. None of them intended to hurt him, and 'probably did not realize how sensitive he was'.[18]

Hopkins's scrupulosity as an examiner was talked about. It was said that he was horrified at a particular examiner who gave one man 100 per cent and another 105 per cent in a paper. He was so scrupulous about the unfair examination advantages his own students had over candidates from other colleges that at the beginning of the year he undertook not to teach his class anything which would be asked in exams, so students came to his classes to find out what *not* to study.[19] Although many of Hopkins's letters from Dublin picture him as overworked, Darlington considered that he was given 'very light work indeed as a Greek teacher', and that his trouble was that 'he never seemed to enter into the great works to be done—or think of it'. He never 'seemed to regard the real work of the College, as anything but a mere joke: he never seemed to take any serious interest in the aims, and purposes of things: he did what he was told like a child might, so far as he could, but without any appearance of responsibility in the material order'.[20]

Hopkins seldom talked about his poetry to his colleagues: Fr Tom Finlay, for instance, never saw any of his poems while he was alive. The few responses he did receive were not encouraging. 'Now look here! What you're bringing me isn't poetry at all', the classicist Professor Stewart is supposed to have said. He sometimes read his poems to Maher and O'Neill, especially the latter. Maher said afterwards that he didn't understand them. Darlington, the Professor of English, said after Hopkins's death that 'there was no heart, or passion in his poetry, or in anything he said or did'. His sonnets, to Darlington's mind, were 'mere grammatical, acrobatic feats of juggling, and word combination. . . . G. H. was a merely beautifully painted sea-shell. I never found any mollusc inside it of human substance.'

Hopkins's headaches began, Darlington reported, after Hopkins had been in Dublin some time. Once he described them to Darlington: they were accompanied by the visual images of blocks which had to be fitted together. Darlington associated this with the fitting together of the words and phrases of the poems, which he deplored. Hopkins 'let himself be guided by Bridges . . . who taught him to meddle with the English grammar and mere word settings'. Hopkins's vocation in Dublin, Darlington believed, was 'to give his energies to pushing the University business ahead—*which he did not do*: he did his routine teaching well and was "a very holy fellow, and all that", but wasn't really concerned about university politics'.[21]

☙

In the sonnet which acts as the preface to its companions, Hopkins summed up his lot—'To seem the stranger lies my lot, my life/ Among strangers'. Like a man reading the epitaph on his own tombstone, he saw his destiny. He might have been reading his own name, 'P. Gerardus Hopkins', among the Irish ones, on the Jesuit memorial cross in Glasnevin cemetery. No longer can he act on the self-determination of his boyhood motto, 'To be rather than seem'. His will and strength have been sapped:

> To seem the stranger lies my lot, my life
> Among strangers. Father and mother dear,
> Brothers and sisters are in Christ not near
> And he my peace/ my parting, sword and strife.
>
> England, whose honour O all my heart woos, wife
> To my creating thought, would neither hear
> Me, were I pleading, plead nor do I:I wear-
> Y of idle a being but by where wars are rife.
>
> I am in Ireland now; now I am at a third
> Remove. Not but in all removes I can
> Kind love both give and get. Only what word
>
> Wisest my heart breeds dark heaven's baffling ban
> Bars or hell's spell thwarts. This to hoard unheard
> Heard unheeded, leaves me a lonely began.

Six days before his son was received into the Roman Catholic church, Manley Hopkins had written of 'the foreseen estrangement which must happen'. In this poem of 1885, the destiny Gerard Hopkins sees is to appear 'the stranger' to the people around him. He is separate from them, and they are strangers to him. He is cut off by other people and his own mind. In 'Spelt from Sibyl's Leaves' all past, present, and future had telescoped into one fate; now his picture is to be a stranger among strangers. There is no sense of strength or identity, only passive acknowledgement and a sad self-pity.

In 1865 at Oxford, Hopkins had copied into his diary Clare's poem 'I am: yet what I am who cares or knows', which contains the lines: 'And e'en the dearest—that I loved the best—/ Are strange—nay, rather stranger than the rest'. In both poems the word 'strange' is repeated and dwelt on. Both poets are compulsorily exiled from their familiar background, and the worst part of exile is the sense that those who should be closest are far away. In both poems 'strange' is opposed to 'dear'. After the second bitter 'strangers' Hopkins longs for his dear ones, but they are also strangers, 'are in Christ not near'.

Letters between professional religious often start with 'Dear Father in Christ' or 'Dear Sister in Christ', but Hopkins's true parents, brothers and sisters could never be part of his religious family. 'The stress between these two families', writes R. K. R. Thornton, 'was strong throughout his life and becomes a major concern of his poetry.'[22] Hopkins had identified with Clare twenty years before the identification was fulfilled. The three great loves of his life, in which the speaker in the poem should feel rooted but which are the foundations of strangeness, are his family, his religion, and his country. His strong feelings of love, which make his family 'dear', make Christ his 'peace', and make him plead on behalf of England, are not reciprocated. The family is not near in Christ, Christ is 'parting, sword and strife', and England does not respond. He is removed, in the sense of 'remote from', each source of love: not by *physical* removal, but by the incomplete state of the relationship. These three relationships were so essential to stability that with their disintegration emotional structure has collapsed. The conditional 'would neither hear/ Me, were I pleading' shows Hopkins veering away from his explicitly categorized starting subject, and easing his words into his real subject. The theatre of universal bonding—parentage, religion, country—shrinks to action within a mind. There is no resource but egoistic concentration, expressed in the repetition of 'I'.

The background of 'would neither hear me' is the history of Hopkins's rejections by Jesuit authority. 'All that we Jesuits publish (even anonymously)', Hopkins wrote to Bridges in 1884, 'must be seen by censors and this is a barrier which I do not know how anything of mine on a large scale would ever pass'. After two more years in Dublin he is more despondent: 'Our institute provides us means of discouragement, and on me at all events they have had all the effect that could be expected or wished and rather more.'[23] He had not been allowed a hearing in England, and he assumes that if he were still writing proselytising poetry it would not be heard. But 'plead nor do I', he is not even writing, but suffering the weariness caused by inactivity.

The octave is an attempted exorcism by poetic testament, but the sestet starts with a calm statement of the present—'I am in Ireland now'. It is almost as though the calm were caused by the distance of Ireland from his English past, but it is a false calm, emphasizing a retirement into loneliness, strangeness, and frustration. He is idle, 'a lonely began', because of his superiors' ban on his works, whose success would have been the sanction he needed to go on. The other source of his creative idleness is the thwarting by 'hell's spell', which would leave him with a trail of unfinished projects in Ireland. Passages in letters illustrate his state:

I am struggling to get together matter for a work on Homer's Art. I suppose like everything else of mine it will come to nothing in the end.

It is so doubtful, so very doubtful, that I shall be able to pursue any study except the needs of the day (and those not enough) at all. I have tried and failed so often and my strength serves me less.

I am in my ordinary circumstances unable, with whatever encouragement, to go on with *Winefred* or anything else.[24]

He attributed the malism which weighs down 'Spelt from Sibyl's Leaves' not to pessimism but to fulfilment of pre-Christian philosophical vision. In 'To seem the stranger' he sees that he can neither externalise his vision nor lay the blame on an honourable authority like the Sibyl. This spell has a vaguer and more insidious origin, 'hell'. There is, however, a curious arbitrariness about 'heaven ... or hell', which suggests that the psychological disturbance is so beyond control, that he has lost the ability to define its root in conventional religio-ethical terms. The nature of his turmoil has taken him beyond the bounds of religious terminology, diagnosis, and remedy. 'Hoard unheard,/ Heard unheeded' expresses the impenetrability of his problem, and the baffling rhythms near the end of the poem give way to plaintive incompleteness, in sound and form, 'leaves me a lonely began'.

After Hopkins's realization of his lot in 'Spelt from Sibyl's Leaves' and 'To seem the stranger', the rest of his short life was a playing out of the role described in these key poems.

ᗧ

By New Year's Day 1885 Hopkins believed he had made the wrong decision in staying in Dublin for Christmas; it would have been better to go to Hampstead. He needed a change—'at all events I am jaded'. It would have been 'the world of pleasant' to have seen Bridges and his wife.[25]

During the holidays he had enthusiastically strummed with one finger on a piano, composing new tunes and harmonizing old ones. His first attempt at harmony, a song, 'The Crocus', he had sent some time ago to Sir Frederick Gore Ouseley, who had not returned it, perhaps, Hopkins thought, because two of its three verses were 'a kind of wilderness of unintelligible clouds'. Now his 'great matter on hand' was a setting for two choirs, with piano accompaniment, of Campbell's poem 'Battle of the Baltic'; one choir representing the British and the other the Danes. Hopkins was particularly proud of a long ground bass in the second verse, consisting of a chime of fourteen notes, repeated ten times running, each time with a rhythmical difference. He importuned Bridges to show it to a musician friend of his; if he approved 'I am made, musically', Hopkins wrote, and the unappreciative Sir Frederick 'may wallow and choke in his own Oozeley Gore'. Relegated to the background of his attention was his setting of Collins's 'Ode to Evening', 'a new departure and more like volcanic sunsets or sunrises in the musical hemisphere than anything ye can conçave'.[26]

On 2 January he collected fifteen shillings from the bursar and caught the train for Clongowes Wood College. The Rector of Clongowes was Fr Conmee, some years later one of the few Jesuits who earned the liking of the schoolboy James Joyce, by taking his part in a dispute. Conmee is said to have become extremely fond of Hopkins, and invited him to Clongowes when his exam-marking was over, saying that there would be no one in the house but himself and one other, 'absolutely no regulations'. At this Hopkins kissed Conmee's hand.[27] During this New Year's retreat, Hopkins asked the advice of the Spiritual Father at Clongowes, Fr Peter Foley, and made short notes which show some of his thoughts and feelings. On 3 January he meditated on the relationship of St Peter with St John, representing a perfectly balanced combination of two lives, the active and the contemplative. Two days later he wrote: 'Pray to be on the watch for God's providence, not determining where or when but only sure that it will come. And apply this to all your troubles and hopes, to England and Ireland, to growth in virtue,' and next day he wrote, 'Pray . . . for the spirit of love in all your doings. For indeed it seems a spirit of fear I live by.'[28]

Back at Stephen's Green a fortnight later, Hopkins's spiritual notes, probably made while he was marking scholarship papers, are more disturbed: 'The devils who tormented the demoniac—pray not to be tormented. Remark the breaking of the bonds and how the swine broke loose and drowned themselves. Remark the suicide. The man did not kill himself, because the devils were not allowed to drive him to that. They are therefore fettered themselves.'[29] Soon afterwards, despite the fact that he was 'all going to pieces with a cold', his heart was light because he had just finished marking his papers.[30]

The college was in turmoil because they were expecting as a student and boarder, Mrs Hopkins was told, 'AN IMPERIAL PRINCE or at least a prince from the Austrian Empire', who had 'four names tied together with hyphens besides Christian names'. By 29 January Count Maximilian Waldburg Wolfegg had arrived. Through the connections of Fr Mallac, Fr Delany had an aristocrat on his books at last. In April Count Max was joined by his brother Count Joseph. Suddenly—and briefly, as it turned out—the college was transformed by the extravagant Continental style. 'Did I tell you of our German count?' Hopkins asked his mother. 'He is a splendid sample of a young nobleman, especially on horseback.'[31] The brothers left after two terms, during which their father had paid £500 into the college's accounts—at a time when the best-paid servants in the college were receiving £20 per annum (from which £1 10s. was deducted for washing), when the average monthly food bill for the whole college was about £86, when Fr Delany was going around, cap in hand, trying to find loans or gifts from a bank, a convent, the Jesuit Provincial, and a rich sympathizer, and when gowns for University College academic ceremonies had to be hired, second-hand, from the porter of the rival Trinity College.

The Counts had a sister in her teens, Mary, who wanted to read good English story-books, and Père Mallac was asked to help. He went to his bookseller—according to Hopkins 'almost the only place he goes out of the house'—and bought some Catholic tales. As Hopkins told his mother:

Now it unfortunately happened that children were born in the first chapters of both of them. This is not a bad thing to do in fact and must be allowed also to the characters in fiction, but not under all circumstances; and in one of the two the child was stillborn. This, for a young countess of fifteen or eighteen, he found too strong.[32]

Mallac appealed for help, and Hopkins wrote asking his mother and sisters 'to name some books . . . which shd. be interesting and in which the personages should have got their birth completely over before the story begins'; Mallac stipulated also that there should be 'no or the least possible lovemaking in them'. Hopkins found this 'a great difficulty: the most highly proper English stories have love in them'. He thought of *Alice in Wonderland*, but had never admired the book, indeed had never read much of it, and thought it 'not funny'. He had tried reading Mrs Molesworth's book, *Christmas-Tree-Land*, to see if that fitted the bill, but found it 'not so particularly natural', and lacking in humour. 'There is a kind of slobbery niceness and good humour all over it', which was 'very distasteful to me, when without the salt of humour'; its Walter Crane illustrations, though 'sweetly pretty', were not well drawn, and there was 'a good deal of deception and gilt gingerbread' about them. He also criticized Mrs Molesworth's 'provincial north country English': 'She says "should have done" for "shall have", nay worse "would" and "will" for "should" and "shall", like any Irishwoman.'[33]

On the first day of March Hopkins went with the fiercely republican Mallac, feeling that it was 'rather compromising', to Mr O'Brien's

Monster Meeting in the Phoenix Park, held to protest against his
suspension from Parliament. It was 'not so very monster', and the
crowd was 'quiet and well behaved', despite the republican banners of
the stars and stripes and the tricolour:

Boys on the skirt of the crowd made such a whistling and noise for their own
amusement as must have much interfered with the hearing of the speeches. . . .
The people going were in Sunday clothes when they had got any, otherwise in
their only suit, which with some was rags. . . . Mr. O'Brien spoke bareheaded
from a drag, the wind was (alas, it long will be) in the east, and today he must
have a terrible cold. I looked at him through opera glasses and got near enough
to hear hoarseness, but no words.

Although the Irish were excitable, Hopkins found them 'far less so than
from some things you would think and ever so much froths off in
words'. Fr Mallac had been in Paris during the 1848 revolution, and
said that 'there the motions of the crowd were themselves majestic and
that they organized themselves as with a military instinct'.[34]

Hopkins had not been disturbed by the meeting, 'yet', he told his
mother, 'the grief of mind I go through over politics, over what I read
and hear and see in Ireland about Ireland and about England, is such
that I can neither express it nor bear to speak of it'. In a private note
that month he wrote: 'Let him that is without sin etc—Pray to keep to
the spirit and as far as possible rule in speaking of Mr. Gladstone for
instance.' In January Khartoum had fallen, and Gladstone had been
blamed for it and for 'Chinese' Gordon's death. Hopkins took his own
advice, and writing of Gladstone to Baillie commented: 'As I am
accustomed to speak too strongly of him I will not further commit
myself in writing.'[35]

His disturbed mental health reveals itself in the writings of spring
and summer 1885. On St Patrick's Day he wrote that he felt an
enthusiasm like that in the hymn 'St Patrick's Breastplate', but 'my
action does not answer to this'. Two days later, on St Joseph's Day, he
asked the help of the saint, a patron of 'the hidden life', and 'of those, I
should think, suffering in mind as I do'.[36] By 24 March he was 'in a low
way of health'; not that he fasted, 'but the restriction of diet makes a
difference to me'. Mallac offered the opinion that Hopkins was dying of
anaemia. 'I am not, except at the rate that we all are', but 'I could do
(indeed how gladly I could)—as they say—with more life.' He felt 'weak
in body and harassed in mind', and too ill to comment on Bridges's
*Ulysses*. A week later, on 1 April, he was still unable to write about it:
'Holidays are begun, but I am not in the frame of body or mind to avail
myself of them for work, as I should wish.' He lived in a 'coffin of
weakness and dejection . . . without even the hope of change'.[37]

He asked Bridges to comment on parts of 'St Winefred's Well' which he had recently written, in alexandrines, including a soliloquy by Caradoc, Winefred's murderer. Like more illustrious villains, the evil character in Hopkins's drama expresses himself more powerfully than the good:

> But will flesh, O can flesh
> Second this fiery strain? Not always; O no no!
> We cannot live this life out; sometimes we must weary
> And in this darksome world what comfort can I find? . . .
> To hunger and not have, yet hope on for, to storm and strive and
> Be at every assult fresh foiled, worse flung, deeper disappointed,
> The turmoil and the torment . . .
> Reason, selfdisposal, choice of better or worse way,
> Is corpse now, cannot change; my other self, this soul,
> Life's quick, this kind, this keen self-feeling,
> With dreadful distillation of thoughts sour as blood,
> Must all day long taste murder. What do now then? Do? Nay,
> Deed-bound I am; one deed treads all down here cramps all doing.
>     What do? Not yield,
> Not hope, not pray; despair; ay that: brazen despair out,
> Brave all, and take what comes—

Hopkins has projected onto Caradoc much of the imagery he used to describe the protagonist's mental anguish in sonnets written later that year.

At the beginning of May Hopkins was looking for relief from his severe melancholy. If the weather had been cheerful it might have helped him out of his gloom. He needed strength from outside; his own resources had been exhausted for some time. At the end of April he had read of Geldart's suicide, which in his morbid state represented more than the death of a friend. He wrote to Baillie:

I will this morning begin writing to you and God grant it may not be with this as it was with the last letter I wrote to an Oxford friend, that the should-be receiver was dead before it was ended. . . . I mean poor Geldart, whose death, as it was in Monday last's *Pall Mall*, you must have heard of. I suppose it was suicide, his mind, for he was a selftormentor, having been unhinged, as it had been once or twice before, by a struggle he had gone through. Poor Nash's death, not long before, was certainly suicide and certainly too done in insanity, for he had been sleepless for ten nights: of this too you will have heard. . . . Three of my intimate friends at Oxford have thus drowned themselves, a good many more of my acquaintances and contemporaries have died by their own hands in other ways: it must be, and the fact brings it home to me, a dreadful feature of our days.[38]

Hopkins had written himself into a state which made further writing impossible, and he laid the paper aside for a fortnight, taking it up again when he received a letter from Baillie which seemed a reproach for not having completed his own. Baillie affectionately traced the course of their friendship, and in his response Hopkins revived more Oxford memories, but was unable to separate the happy past from his awareness of recent failures. To look back was to see the unfulfilled ideal:

May 8—For one thing I was sorry when I got your late delightful letter. Since my sister told me of her meeting you I had been meaning to write and be first with you—but now I am slow even in answering. Some time since, I began to overhaul my old letters, accumulations of actually ever since I was at school, destroying all but a very few, and growing ever lother to destroy, but also to read, so that at last I left off reading; and there they lie and my old notebooks and beginnings of things, ever so many, which it seems to me might well have been done, ruins and wrecks.

It was more than a week before Hopkins finished the letter, and to explain the delay he described his melancholia:

I think this is from a literary point of view . . . the worst letter I ever wrote to you, and it shall not run much longer. You will wonder I have been so long over it. This is part of my disease, so to call it. The melancholy I have all my life been subject to has become of late years not indeed more intense in its fits but rather more distributed, constant, and crippling. One, the lightest but a very inconvenient form of it, is daily anxiety about work to be done, which makes me break off or never finish all that lies outside that work. It is useless to write more than this: when I am at the worst, though my judgment is never affected, my state is much like madness. I see no ground for thinking I shall ever get over it or ever succeed in doing anything that is not forced on me to do of any consequence. . . .

Much could be said about Ireland and my work and all, but it would be tedious.[39]

The letter finishes 'May 17 '85 and still winter', and on the same day he wrote to his mother: 'It is winter in Ireland. I still have a fire. The hail today lay long like pailfuls of coarse rice.' Probably at this time he penned the cynical quatrain:

> Strike, churl; hurl, cheerless wind, then; heltering hail
> May's beauty massacre and wispèd wild clouds grow
> Out on the giant air; tell Summer No,
> Bid joy back, have at the harvest, keep Hope pale.

In answer to his mother's request for him to spend part of the summer with them, he wrote:

I am in a sort of languishing state of mind and body, but hobble on. I should like to go to sea for six months. . . . If I shd. be able to visit you this year there is one thing I am much set on seeing, Epping Forest. . . . Indeed I shd. like to go further and see the New Forest.[40]

He knew he needed a complete change of duties and surroundings. As he wrote to Bridges the same day, apologising for not having replied sooner:

The long delay was due to work, worry, and languishment of body and mind—which must be and will be; and indeed to diagnose my own case (for every man by forty is his own physician or a fool, they say; and yet again he who is his own physician has a fool for his patient . . .), well then to judge of my case, I think that my fits of sadness, though they do not affect my judgment, resemble madness. Change is the only relief, and that I can seldom get.

After giving bad-tempered and low-spirited criticism of Bridges's *Ulysses* for its 'unreality' Hopkins turned to his own productions:

It is too bad that I shd. so abuse *Ulysses* after your encouragement of *St. Winefred*. But how cd. you think such a thing of me as that I shd. in cold blood write 'fragments of a dramatic poem'?—I of all men in the world. To me a completed fragment, above all of a play, is the same unreality as a prepared impromptu. No, but we compose fragmentarily and what I had here and there done I finished up and sent as samples to see if I cd. be encouraged to go on—and I was encouraged; that is by your last, for before I thought you thought they wd. not do. There is a point with me in matters of any size when I must absolutely have encouragement as much as crops rain; afterwards I am independent. However I am in my ordinary circumstances unable, with whatever encouragement, to go on with *Winefred* or anything else. I have after long silence written two sonnets, which I am touching: if ever anything was written in blood one of these was.[41]

These sonnets are probably 'No worst, there is none'—the one 'written in blood'—and '(Ashboughs)', an attempt to counter the bitterness and frustration he had expressed in the quatrain 'Strike, churl'. The two poems may have been written about 15–20 May.

While he was at Oxford, Hopkins's 'present fury' had once been the ash tree. In Dublin it was no longer a fury but 'a milk to the mind'. Yet there were still Ruskinese traces: 'It is more important that we should feel', prescribed the first book of *Modern Painters*, 'that the uppermost sprays are creeping higher and higher into the sky, and be impressed with the current of life and motion which is animating every fibre.' In this poem verbs of motion convey the tree's energy—'break', 'creep apart', 'nestle', 'touch', and 'sweep':

> They touch: their wild weather-swung talons sweep
> The smouldering enormous winter-welkin. Spring

Mells blue and snowwhite through them, a thousand fing-
Ers: then they are old Earth groping towards that steep
　　　　　　　　　Heaven once Earth childed by.

The milk of the ash tree vision was needed as balm to the mind shown
in 'No worst, there is none'. Aldous Huxley said of this poem: 'Never, I
think, has the just man's complaint against the universe been put more
forcibly, worded more tersely and fiercely'.[42] 'O the mind, mind has
mountains' and 'cliffs of fall' have become classic images of psychic
torment:

> No worst, there is none. Pitched past pitch of grief,
> More pangs will, schooled at forepangs, wilder wring.
> Comforter, where, where is your comforting?
> Mary, mother of us, where is your relief?
> My cries heave, herds-long; huddle in a main, a chief-
> Woe, world-sorrow; on an age-old anvil wince and sing—
> Then lull, then leave off. Fury had shrieked 'No ling-
> Ering! Let me be fell: force I must be brief.'
> O the mind, mind has mountains; cliffs of fall
> Frightful, sheer, no-man-fathomed. Hold them cheap
> May who ne'er hung there. Nor does long our small
> Durance deal with that steep or deep. Here! creep,
> Wretch, under a comfort serves in a whirlwind: all
> Life death does end and each day dies with sleep.

The poem discovers and attempts to define a landscape beyond conventional limits and control. To demand solutions, as Yvor Winters did,[43]
in the form of precise definition is to misunderstand the poem's
experience. The painscape is formless; it has no imagined limits from
which the mind might turn back or forward to recovery. The attempt at
definition results in more pain and confusion. The structure of sound
conveys this impasse too. The poem has four rhymes, the smallest
possible number in a regular sonnet, each intensified by reverberating
anticipations and echoes ('anvil wince and sing', 'steep or deep . . .
creep'). The obsessive repetition of the four sounds combines with the
inescapability of the simple fixed rhyme-scheme to add to the sense of
defeat and self-defeat.

After the mountains and cliffs of the mind, the poet adds further
images of possible turmoils. They can only be known through experience: 'hold them cheap may who ne'er hung there' powerfully
rejects prescribed remedies. Our self-protective faculty is severely
limited and can break down (another criticism of antidotes), and the

only comfort is the limited, negative (and unChristian) one in the last line. The sonnet creates a dramatic process for instability and uncertainty, in which scene, images, and characters shift alarmingly. There is a last-resort substitute for resolution in the making of this poem. Hopkins's art in Dublin is often such a lonely alternative to a more comprehensive mental comfort.

# 'Dark not day'

Banished to a country of slaves and beggars; my blood soured, my Spirits sunk, fighting with Beasts like St Paul.

(Swift to Lady Worsley, from Dublin, 4 November 1732)

On 11 June 1885 Patmore wrote from Hastings. He was making plans for the summer and hoped there would be the chance of a meeting at Stonyhurst or Hastings. 'I assure you', wrote Patmore, 'I shall always regard my having made your acquaintance as an important event in my life, and there are few things I desire more than a renewal of opportunity of personal intercourse with you.' Hopkins was so harassed by examinations, as well as melancholy, that he could not reply at once, and, though he knew he badly needed a holiday, was too self-preoccupied to plan even a month ahead. He replied, on 23 June, that he expected to go to England 'some time after the middle of next month and how long I may be there I do not know, but perhaps it might be possible to see you towards the end of it if you were then returned from the north'.[1]

After over a year in Dublin he had become not only more isolated but more intense and eccentric. Subjects which he could not argue about aroused an unbalanced dogmatism. Strange and disproportionate passions, not sanctioned by events, appear in his letters, and show why his reputation for eccentricity increased among the Irish. The Irish sympathies he developed before he set foot in Ireland, through contact with priests and parishioners (particularly in Liverpool), had narrowed or vanished: this was the postscript to his letter to Patmore:

I heard yesterday, amazing news, of an Irishman a great reader of you: I call it amazing, for the Irish have little feeling for poetry and least of all for modern poetry: they close the canon with Byron and Shelley and indeed most poets have never been admitted into it.

Memories of Hopkins by his Dublin colleagues and pupils show how little sympathy the college felt for his artistic and literary concerns. The college journal, *The Lyceum*, was started in Hopkins's time there by Fr Tom Finlay. Among its proclaimed aims were the large ones 'to discuss questions of scientific and literary interest' and 'the claims of contemporary literary works', essentially 'from the Catholic point of view'. But *The Lyceum* became preoccupied with parochial matters, such as current administrative problems of the college, and Hopkins never contributed to it, though he was invited to.

The life he led that summer, he told Bridges, was one 'of a continually jaded and harassed mind'. He made no headway in work, even when he tried to write in his leisure time. But against his will, unasked for, four sonnets came to him 'like inspirations'. 'I wake and feel the fell of dark' dramatizes a victory of pain, re-creating and verifying its power. As in 'No worst', we see power thrusting a sufferer into experience beyond conventional events and images, in poetry driven beyond commonly recognized means of expression. The protagonist is defeated by the pain, and the poetry gives up its attempt at controlling definition. And the poetry is greater because of this double failure, saved from a false conclusion and congratulation, which the sonnet form had sometimes seemed to encourage in earlier poems:

> I wake and feel the fell of dark, not day.
> What hours, O what black hoũrs we have spent
> This night! what sights you, heart, saw; ways you went!
> And more must, in yet longer light's delay.
>
> With witness I speak this. But where I say
> Hours I mean years, mean life. And my lament
> Is cries countless, cries like dead letters sent
> To dearest him that lives alas! away.
>
> I am gall, I am heartburn. God's most deep decree
> Bitter would have me taste: my taste was me;
> Bones built in me, flesh filled, blood brimmed the curse.
>
> Selfyeast of spirit a dull dough sours. I see
> The lost are like this, and their scourge to be
> As I am mine, their sweating selves; but worse.

As in 'No worst', we are told that traditional sources of comfort ('dearest him') cannot help. The opening of 'I wake' responds to and continues 'No worst'; the two poems could be companions in an integrated sonnet sequence. The monosyllabic words in the last line of

'No worst' ('all/ Life death does end and each day dies with sleep') are answered by this sonnet's first line, which suggests an automatic stupefaction of the waking being, without the freedom which light would allow. Line 1 establishes the beat for the rest of the poem, though impulsive rhythms quickly take over from its regular pulse.

The physical darkness becomes mental darkness, the body so confined that physicality is suspended. The playing-out of dreams, in sights and journeys, continues from sleep into waking life: as it is dark and the body prone, the sights and journeys can be only in the mind. Mental life intensifies, and takes over as the stage for limited action. The restrictive covering is thickened by 'black', which ambivalently describes physical and mental scenes, hours of night and hours of horror. The claustrophobia is increased by the dramatic lengthening of 'What hours' by the dragging repetition 'O what black hoūrs'. The dreams are unwilled, and, perhaps taught by religion to be suspicious of their nature and origin, Hopkins brings the 'heart' on to the stage to act as guarantor of their existence and veracity. For Hopkins, as for other Victorians, the heart was an autonomous source of value judgements— 'The heart is what rises towards good, shrinks from evil, recognising the good or evil first by some eye of its own', he wrote in his notebook for 15 October 1884.

The second quatrain concerns itself with expanding and consolidating the images of the first. The bitterness decreed by God flavours the reference 'God's most deep decree' (1. 9), exacerbating the self-gnawing process. In place of the expected 'high' decree (from God on high), there is the equivocal 'deep', suggesting that God does not explain his purpose. 'God's most deep decree' followed by 'curse' and 'scourge' says that God has condemned him, with the corollary that he has no free will left. Unsurprisingly, searching to place the experiences and conclusions of this poem within the Christian cosmology (which he accepts despite the absence of 'dearest him'), he can only invoke the damned. There are contradictory implications in the ending. Besides a sense of defeat and meek acquiescence, there is a counter-movement of arrogance and unstated questioning. Accordingly, he sets himself up as a model of damnation; the lost are like *this* (my experience). The fact that his fate is unearned, but decreed, implies that he is excluded from Christian justice. The poem finishes just as the question 'Why?' is about to be asked.

This is a poem of dramatized lament rather than one of justification, very different from the poem written four years later 'Thou art indeed just, Lord'. The Christian system of justice is in turmoil. The simple and congratulatory Christian structure of the St Beuno's poems about external nature has been replaced by a chaotic and unresolved sonnet, a profoundly realistic representation of psychological struggle. With Christian resources no longer dependable for Hopkins, he is now placed in the Victorian fragmented world, with no language but a cry.

∽

In his desolation, the trained Jesuit knew the antidotes prescribed by faith and order. Rule 8 'for the Discernment of Spirits', in Ignatius's exercises, stated: 'Let him who is in desolation strive to remain in patience, which is the virtue contrary to the troubles which harass him; and let him think that he will shortly be consoled, making diligent efforts against the desolation.' In previous poems Hopkins had mentioned patience: in 'Nondum' she had a chastening wand, in 'The Wreck of the Deutschland' the qualities which earned the nun a place with Christ were pain and patience (stanza 31); it had been a valuable quality with which to purchase The Starlight Night's prizes; in 'Peace', patience is a substitute of God's for peace; and it is a desirable quality in line 123 of 'The Blessed Virgin Compared to the Air we Breathe'. Patience was not one of Hopkins's native virtues: he would always have to fight for it. Once on holiday, when Curtis was plagued by having to set examinations, 'when day after day these afflictions fell in', Hopkins reported ruefully to his mother: 'I used to do the cursing; he bore all with the greatest meekness. Our landlady . . . gave me instructions.'[2] He wrote a new poem, 'Patience, hard thing'. He knew that the person who asks for Patience is letting himself in for wars and wounds; and the imagery then becomes that of a soldier's life, to 'do without, take tosses, and obey'. This is followed by the only extended visual image in the desolate sonnets: 'Natural heart's-ivy Patience masks/ Our ruins of wrecked past purpose. There she basks/ Purple eyes and seas of liquid leaves all day.'

Another poem, 'My own heart let me more have pity on' carries a similar message, but has two voices: the first describes (while involved in) the turmoil of the speaker's mind, while the second articulates the calm and rational mind, relaxed after its storm, and also attempting to heal the damage. The octave depicts a bout of turmoil, with the rational self trying to reassert itself, but being overcome by the power of the succeeding attack. In this part the poem is close to 'No worst, there is none'; but in the sestet the remedy is stated and urged by the rational, unharrassed voice, which achieves the objective self-pity needed and presaged at the beginning. Autobiographical relevance is straightforward, and 'jaded', for instance, is used in Hopkins's letters of the 1880s to describe himself: 'I am always tired, always jaded', he had written in July 1883.[3]

At the start of 1885 he proposed a change of place and a holiday as cures for being jaded, and in the last week of July drew ten pounds from the college bursar and took the boat for England. He first stayed at Oak Hill, perhaps making a trip to visit Addis in his presbytery at Sydenham in Kent. Addis had been very ill and was recuperating, although finding it tiresome to lie on his back in an easy chair; the sight of a letter from Hopkins earlier that summer had cheered him up, and he had asked Hopkins to visit him.[4] The Hopkins family moved for their summer holiday to the village of Easebourne, in a heavily wooded part of the South Downs. Hopkins found it 'a lovely landscape'; it was 'artists' country', only a walk from Petworth House, where Turner had produced two series of profound paintings in the late 1820s,[5] and almost as close to Haslemere, where the Hopkinses were soon to move from Hampstead.

A letter from Patmore was sent to Hopkins from Dublin, urging him to communicate his whereabouts; Patmore had hoped to see him at Hampstead but could not do so, because Hopkins had not sent his address. 'I desire greatly to see more of you', protested Patmore, 'and should be very sorry if you returned to Dublin or Stonyhurst without our meeting.'[6] Hopkins took the train for Hastings, on the east Sussex coast, where the Patmores lived in the old Mansion House, built of red brick, high up facing the sea, and with magnolia (which occasionally made Patmore ill) covering its front. The Patmores were very kind to Hopkins, and the elder poet wrote afterwards that the visit had been 'a great pleasure, and much more, to me', and he wrote 'Your's affectionately', instead of the previous 'Your's ever truly', in front of his signature. (After Hopkins's more formal 'your sincere friend' in reply, however, he reverted to his previous style.) Patmore's third wife, Harriet, much younger than her husband and called 'Obby' by her stepdaughters, Hopkins considered 'a very sweet lady'.[7] He was introduced to Patmore's daughters Bertha and Gertrude, both of whom were 'very nice, not handsome' (a third daughter, Emily, was extraordinarily beautiful, took the veil in 1873, and died in 1882). Hopkins was struck by Bertha: 'sadly lame since a child but a most gifted artist, a true genius: she draws butterflies, birds, dormice, vegetation, in a truly marvellous manner; also illuminates'. Seldom tactful where art was concerned, he later suggested to Patmore that his daughter 'might gain by taking some lessons from some painter. . . . It struck me that she was hampered by want of some mechanical knowledge, as in the use of washes for background, and she tends, I think, to use bodycolour in a way which would be considered vicious.'[8]

Hopkins had reason to regret his outspokenness on another artistic subject. At some stage during the visit to Hastings he saw the manuscript of *Sponsa Dei*, 'a series of notes which I propose shall be published after my death', which Patmore had collected over ten years of meditations. Hopkins found it 'too intimate, dealing as it did with so "mystical an interpretation of the significance of physical love in religion", to be placed in the hands of the general reading public.'[9] Always anxious about the moral problems of physical beauty, Hopkins wrote a gentle warning to Patmore after his return to Dublin, 'after all, anything however high and innocent may happen to suggest anything however low and loathsome'. It had come to his notice, for example, that 'during contemplation acts of unnatural vice might take place without the subject's fault, being due to the malice of the devil and he innocent'. (Sometimes Hopkins sounds a medieval note.) Two-and-a-half years later, after 'much-meditating on the effect which my M.S. "Sponsa Dei" had upon you, when you read it while staying here', Patmore concluded that he 'would not take the responsibility of being the first to expound the truths therein contained', and on Christmas Day 1887, he 'committed the work to the flames without reserve of a single paragraph'. Hopkins replied regretting that he had not been more guarded, though unwilling to retract his judgements, and in part returning the blame for the destruction on Patmore: 'still if you had kept to yr. custom of consulting your director [Dr Rous, Patmore's spiritual adviser], as you said you should, the book might have appeared with no change or with slight ones'. 'But now', he added, 'regret is useless.'[10]

Edmund Gosse was shocked at breakfast during a visit to Hastings, when Patmore blurted out to him 'abruptly. almost hysterically', 'You won't have much to do as my literary executor!' and told him about the burning of *Sponsa Dei*. On hearing this account Patmore's family cried out 'O Papa, that is why you have been so dreadfully depressed since Christmas!' Gosse afterwards publicly blamed Hopkins for the loss, but Patmore often acted impetuously, and had solicited other opinions on the work.[11]

It was a full holiday at Hastings. Besides visiting Battle, Winchelsea, and Rye, Hopkins saw several old friends and made new ones. One of the latter was the Purcell scholar W. H. Cummings, who showed Hopkins 'some of his Purcell treasures and others and is going to send me several things'. Hopkins liked him very much, 'but the time of my being with him was cut short'. He did not attempt to visit Bridges because Monica Bridges was expecting a child, and he 'did not know that visitors wd. at that time be very welcome'. As it happened there was a miscarriage, and when Hopkins heard of it he wrote, 'somehow I had feared that would happen'.[12]

ᘓᕞ

He returned to Ireland on 19 August, and two days later went to Clongowes Wood College to make his annual eight-day retreat (the customary adaptation of the full four-week version). A separate wing of the former mansion was set aside for the use of Jesuits, whether they were attached to the school as teachers or visitors; it was a long-established tradition that Jesuits based in Dublin made their retreat there. At this stage of his Jesuit life Hopkins had overcome his early inhibitions about poetry, and could write during the most strictly regulated part of his year. It is probable that during his stay (just over a week) at Clongowes he wrote 'Not, I'll not, carrion comfort, Despair', 'To what serves Mortal Beauty?', and the sonnet which has become known as 'The Soldier'. While composing the poems, Hopkins's mind would be scrupulously and severely concentrated on Ignatius' words and on his responses to them, so the poems are intimately related to the Spiritual Exercises. Ignatius had stressed the importance for the exercitant 'to endeavour to preserve during each day the effect produced on the mind by the particular exercises of that day':

For this purpose the reading should correspond with the subject of the meditations; and all reflections, however pious, should be avoided, if they be contrary to the affection sought to be produced in the soul. For instance, if the object be to produce the holy fear of God, all reflections on heaven and subjects of a joyful nature would be injurious, and the contrary.

If the assumption about dating is correct, these sonnets, each very different from the other, should show stages through which Hopkins moved during the retreat.

On the first day of the Exercises the 'Examen of the interior' should 'turn on the present state of the soul in general, or on its progress'. The poem which was written probably first is an attempted self-diagnosis of Hopkins's recent mental struggles, with an apparently happy outcome:

Not, I'll not, carrion comfort, Despair, not feast on thee;
Not untwist—slack they may be—these last strands of man
In me or, most weary, cry *I can no more*. I can;
Can something, hope, wish day come, not choose not to be.

But ah, but O thou terrible, why wouldst thou rude on me
Thy wring-earth right foot rock? lay a lionlimb against me? scan
With darksome devouring eyes my bruisèd bones? and fan,
O in turns of tempest, me heaped there; me frantic to avoïd thee
    and flee?

Why? That my chaff might fly; my grain lie, sheer and clear.
Nay in all that toil, that coil, since (seems) I kissed the rod,
Hand rather, my heart lo! lapped strength, stole joy, would laugh,
    cheer.

Cheer whom though? The hero whose heaven-handling flung me,
    foot trod
Me? or me that fought him? O which one? is it each one? That night,
    that year
Of now done darkness I wretch lay wrestling with (my God!) my
    God.

The forces of the protagonist's will and ego combine in the strongly
determinate beat of the opening three words, to imply the start of a
counter-attack to a previous imprisonment in depression, the emphatic
'Not' recurring twice more in the first two lines to act as the sound of
explosive and the ammunition. Despite the weariness of the first
quatrain, and the scared defeatism of the second, it is noticeable that the
poem still displays different aspects of self-regard, ranging from the
determination of 'Not, I'll not' to the curious recalled moments of
happiness ('lapped strength, stole joy, would laugh, cheer'), to the
grandly, almost self-congratulatory, final realization that if his adver-
sary is the supreme being his role in the struggle is not inconsiderable.
Line 7 also shows, in 'my bruisèd bones', that the protagonist still
associates flesh and tenderness and a human quality with his body;
whereas, when it comes to 1889, there is the chilling, chemical,
inhuman, and contemptuous reference to 'we, scaffold of score brittle
bones'. And just as he does not directly mention suicide, so 'frantic' in
line 8 of this poem is the nearest Hopkins gets to the word 'madness',
although in his letters about this time he more than once uses the word
to describe his state. In his poems he avoided the word, possibly
because he considered poems more deliberated, formal, and account-
able self-expressions than letters. An ideological stance was still necessary to him, and to achieve it he avoided direct expression; expression of
the correct stance was his preferred ideal.

Behind this half-hidden, seemingly too manufactured optimism can be sensed an inability to face a truly searching self-diagnosis, of the kind he was to attempt in his final three sonnets. Was Hopkins making a genuine attempt in 'Not, I'll not, carrion comfort' at anchoring nebulous and hurtful reality? There is no longer the sense, as there was in 'To seem the stranger', 'I wake and feel', and 'No worst', of the poet battling to represent reality within a recalcitrant medium. The bubbles and jags of painted reality which were on the surface of those poems seem hidden away under the glassy form of this one. Here the sonnet form seems to contaminate its contents: the four sections are neatly distinguished from each other, and prominently hinged together: 'But' as contrast-connection between 1–4 and 5–8, 'why . . . /Why' connecting 5–8 with 9–11, and 'cheer./ Cheer' the two parts of the sestet. The hinges seem artificially added to cobble an unnatural connection between four separately manufactured sections.

One of the assumptions behind the Jesuit picture of the mind's mechanics is that at the root of every psychological disturbance is a loss of God; and so God has to be brought on to a scene from which He was absent at the end of line 4. Hopkins resorts to traditional biblical prescriptive reference, with the wrestling and threshing images, but after the vivid immediacy of the personal experiences in 1–4, this resort to traditional symbol takes its toll in the broken continuity of the poem.

In the sestet the refurbished personality seems determined—if not exactly to invalidate the terrible experiences of the quatrains—at least to minimize their power to harm, partly by generalizing and partly by reproducing the experiences in less immediate, less substantial terms. This prophylactic action is conducted in an almost light-headed manner, with suspicions of lyrical irrelevance ('O which one? is it each one?'), and by means of unconvincing hinges ('cheer./ Cheer whom though?').

Among all the arduous labour of that period since he became a Jesuit, he finds that he has involuntarily (the heart here is a spontaneous actor) made some positive gains. But it seems an inadequate way of discounting the octave's experiences, which make the character of the poem by their force. An unforceful argument does not undo them, and the effort seems to be an example of another clash between Hopkins's poetic and priestly personae.

გ

The motivation of the second poem written at Clongowes, 'To what serves Mortal Beauty?', appears straightforward when we look at those parts of the Spiritual Exercises which Hopkins would have read and experienced about the time he wrote it: 'It is a practice much recommended to select for the fruit to be sought in the retreat some particular grace, such as the correction of a predominant fault ... or a conquest over ourselves on some point in which we are conscious that our conduct is not in conformity with the Divine will.'[13] The Preface, Ignatius' *Presupuesto*, summarizes the primary purpose of the Exercises: 'for overcoming oneself and for regulating one's life without being swayed by any inordinate attachment'. The main subject and image of 'To what serves Mortal Beauty?' is human beauty, which is not mentioned in the text of the Exercises, and is Hopkins's choice of subject. He had chosen as his predominant fault the inordinate attachment to human beauty. He tries to come to terms with it by working out its God-given purpose, and a way to 'meet' it innocuously:

To what serves mortal beauty—dangerous; does set danc-
Ing blood—the O-seal-that-so feature, flung prouder form
Than Purcell tune lets tread to? See: it does this: keeps warm
Men's wit to the things that are; to what good means—where a glance
Master more may than gaze, gaze out of countenance.
Those lovely lads once, wet-fresh windfalls of war's storm,
How then should Gregory, a father, have gleanèd else from swarm-
Èd Rome? But God to a nation dealt that day's dear chance.
To man, that once would worship block or barren stone,
Our law says/ love what are love's worthiest, were all known;
World's loveliest—men's selves. Self flashes off frame and face.
What do then? how meet beauty? Merely meet it; own,
Home at heart, heaven's sweet gift; then leave, let that alone.
Yea, wish that though, wish all, God's better beauty, grace.

Even before he became a Roman Catholic, Hopkins frequently looked on beauty as a forbidden sweet, rather than as an essential of life. On 6 November 1865, for instance, he resolved 'to give up all beauty until I had His leave for it'.[14] He acknowledged its low place in the Christian moral hierarchy, but he did not overcome his susceptibilities; wherever Hopkins mentions beauty in his poetry he cannot help being excited by it, in human or in non-human nature. With human beauty he knows he has to exercise extreme care; he is aware of danger when he sees it. It inflames; more distantly and composedly, it is dear and sweet; there is a sadness about it because it passes away. It provokes in Hopkins a desire to gather it into the Christian fold, and whenever he can he attaches it to an approved quality, often innocence and virginity.

The poem is written to an Ignatian intention, and yet that intention is formulated within a non-Ignatian means, the sonnet form, a self-conscious artefact with amoral technical laws. While Hopkins is overtly advocating 'mortal beauty' as divine in origin and purpose, by using a poetic form for meditation in preference to the customary prose notes he is covertly putting a case for art in dogmatic religion, and showing, despite Ignatius' lack of enthusiasm for it, that it can fulfil an Ignatian purpose.

There is a certain deviousness about the poem from its outset, suggestions that an uncontrollably complex argument is taking place between the professional mould of the advocated message and recalcitrant surges of individualism. Although the title of the poem refers to meditation, it makes such a self-conscious attempt at archaic and poetic carved phrase that the argument is stanched before it can flow. It does not progress until after the caesural pause in line 3; there has to be a catching-up phrase, 'See: it does this', to restart the progress of the meditation. The first sentence consists of a meditation question with a lengthy coda, a compound of abruptly passionate and disconcerted subjective responses to the idea of human beauty. There is a clash between the question, which requires a reasoned and syntactically framed answer, and a group of direct responses of a quite different, anti-rational, unframed, and disconnected kind, responses which are not answers to that question about beauty, but rather reactions to human beauty as an object, without a mediating framework of argument.

The uneasily structured argument of the poem is deceptively contained within a sonnet form of English alexandrines, more suited than the briefer, jerkier pentameter to the graceful, measured subject. The strictly regular, weightily established movement of the opening is quickly revolutionized by the sudden interruption of danger and the too quick motion, signalled by the startling enjambement 'danc-/ Ing'. In other ways too the poem depicts a fight between puritan/ utilitarian condemnation of beauty (Hopkins's word 'mortal' is his version of 'corruptible', the stock tag in the Exercises for 'body') and impulsive advocacy.

ℭ∕℥

'(The Soldier)', probably the third and last poem composed during the Clongowes retreat, is more directly Ignatian, its main image and its application to Christ occurring in the Exercises. Its opening 'Yes' shows Hopkins determined to be positive and optimistic, after having negated (as he thought) his past negative state of mind: 'Yes. Why do we all, seeing of a soldier, bless him? bless/ Our redcoats, our tars? .../ Mark Christ our King. He knows war, served this soldiering through'.

To some Victorians the army was a guardian of the traditional national ethos in a changing world. It preserved gentlemanly values,[15] and its simplified attitudes towards ethical and social values appealed to Hopkins. So did its unsophisticated attachment to loyalty, courage, chauvinism, uniforms, close male comradeship, and flashy military displays. Like those of Newbolt, Kipling, Tennyson, and other Victorian poetic glorifiers of the Thin Red Line, Hopkins's military thrills were vicarious. In his sermons there are constant references to the Ignatian analogy between a temporal king and Christ the spiritual king: 'Soldiers make a hero of a great general. . . . But Christ, he is the hero. . . . He is a warrior and a conqueror.'[16] One of Hopkins's most Victorian poems, it is embarrassing to modern minds in its orthodox sentiments, and yet it shows how difficult Hopkins found it to put his complex mind into a popular mould. The redcoat is in Hopkins's eyes an ideal and a symbol, although, like many of his compatriots infuriated by the ignominious defeat of the British army at Majuba Hill in 1881, he would not acknowledge that it was that impractical romanticism which contributed to the defeat.

# Sanctuaries

St. Evin's monastery had the privilege of being a sanctuary, denoting protection for refugees.

(Eileen Ryan, *Monasterevan Parish*)

Writing to Bridges in September 1885, Hopkins made the connection between his creativity and his need for change:

So with me, if I could but get on, if I could but produce work I should not mind its being buried, silenced, and going no further; but it kills me to be time's eunuch and never to beget. . . . Now because I have had a holiday though not strong I have some buoyancy; soon I am afraid I shall be ground down to a state like this last spring's and summer's, when my spirits were so crushed that madness seemed to be making approaches—and nobody was to blame, except myself partly for not managing myself better and contriving a change.[1]

Unless Hopkins left Dublin, holidays were no holidays; but after happiness with family and friends and cheering surroundings, holidays made life even less bearable when he returned.

Christmas 1885 was 'a clouded one'. He wrote to Everard on Christmas Eve, 'I have suddenly to prepare papers for a supplementary matriculation examination to be held next month, as well as the scholarships.' There is a resigned sadness about the letter's finish: 'But it was to be. Give all my best Christmas wishes, thank Grace for her pretty card, and believe me your loving brother Gerard.' He added, as though aware of having put a damper on the Hampstead festivities, from which he would be the absentee: 'I have friends at Donnybrook, so hearty and kind that nothing can be more so and I think I shall go and see them tomorrow.'[2]

Donnybrook village was a short walk or penny tram-ride along the straggling road south from Dublin. Three doors from the brash new Catholic church of the Sacred Heart on the Stillorgan road was Belleville, the low house in large grounds where the McCabe household lived. Dr McCabe (later Sir Francis), Medical Director of Dundrum Criminal Asylum, had a son at Stonyhurst, and on one visit heard Hopkins preach on the Blessed Sacrament. He and Mrs McCabe had never heard a finer sermon, and asked their son about the preacher. When Hopkins came to Dublin they had immediately got in touch with him, and Hopkins became a frequent visitor to Belleville. McCabe lent him books and became a 'great friend', while he got to know Mrs McCabe so well that he would sometimes 'bring a parcel of underwear, more holes than cloth, and humbly ask [Mrs McCabe] if she could have the garments mended, as he wished to spare the Society undue expenditure on his behalf'. For a time he stopped coming, and on McCabe's seeking him out said that he had deliberately stayed away, fearing they might think he was abusing their hospitality. On one occasion 'he turned up unexpectedly late and apologized, saying that, passing a forge, he had been held entranced by the sights and sounds, and had forgotten the passage of time'. They also remembered how when he delayed his return to Stephen's Green one evening, he had shaken hands with McCabe and then held his hand out for the penny tram-fare.[3]

Important to Hopkins's enjoyment of these visits were the McCabe children. There were two boys, Jack and Freddy (who later served in the British forces), and three daughters, one of whom was Katherine Frances. Katie was an eleven-year-old when she first met Hopkins, but lived long enough, a cheerful extrovert lady, though blind and bed-ridden, to talk about him in the 1960s. She remembered particularly how he would go into the room where the piano was, sit at it alone, and sing his compositions. One day when she and her sisters were in the room he 'announced that he liked a bit of cheerful music, and then proceeded to sing in such a lugubrious manner that the girls started to giggle'. Hopkins looked hurt and 'the children had to be evicted by their mother'. 'Singing', Katie recalled, 'was the one thing he could not do.' Opposite Belleville was a lake in a disused quarry, on which the young McCabes kept a flat-bottomed punt, in which they would row and fish for roach. The stretch of water was clearly visible from the Sacred Heart presbytery on the opposite side of the road: 'A curate told of standing at the window one day, watching the punt rocking danger-ously on top of submerged debris and ready to give conditional absolution to its occupants should the worst happen.' Hopkins used to join the young people in the boat: 'Once on a very hot day he took off his dog collar and threw it down in the bottom of the boat exclaiming "I'll say goodbye to Rome".'

The importance for Hopkins of this friendship cannot be overestimated. The McCabes lived within easy reach and made him welcome. They liked him, they were a happy extrovert family, and Hopkins needed such a lively model of normal secular life, since his own family were at such a distance. He got on well with children, and was at ease with all of them. They treated him, if not with deep understanding, with Irish easy tolerance and good humour. Once Dr McCabe prescribed champagne for him on medical grounds, knowing that otherwise he could not be persuaded to indulge in such a luxury.[4]

At Christmas 1885 his mother had written to Hopkins suggesting that he make up for the Christmas spent away from his family by coming to Hampstead when his examining duties were over. She had been delighted that Gerard and Everard, her oldest and youngest sons, were forming a friendship not possible before, because of the sixteen years between them. When Gerard had left home in 1863 to go to Oxford, Everard had been a baby in frocks. At Hampstead and Midhurst last summer and by letter since, they had been finding common interests. Everard was following in Arthur's footsteps, starting an artistic career by drawing illustrations for periodicals. He shared with Gerard an interest in contemporary art, especially Millais, and Everard wanted them to pay a joint visit to the new exhibition of Millais's collected works at the Grosvenor Gallery. His mother suggested that Gerard could use this as an educational reason for visiting London.

She had underestimated Gerard's finicky, testy conscience. 'My dearest Mother', Hopkins replied on 13 January:

I should like, very much indeed, to see those pictures, but I do not see how it can be at all. I shall for a few days be examining the papers for the scholarship and when those are done . . . begin my lectures with my pupils, which will last till the Easter holidays. Then I suppose I shall have some days free, but how could I propose to go to England? on what reasonable pretext?[5]

There are unattractive tones in this letter, indicating strain. He implies that his mother's suggestion is too superficial, careless of his duties and profession. The brusque rational questions show a lack of sympathetic response to his mother's affectionate desire to see him. Was it so essential for him to stay in Dublin? How much of this scrupulousness was imposed by his profession, and what proportion by Hopkins? Was it in part his reflections on seeing first Arthur, and now Everard, setting out on the artistic career he had once considered likely for himself, which made him reject the proposal so brusquely?

Hopkins seems to have released some pent-up poetic, assertive side of himself through the correspondence with Mowbray Baillie which started on 11 February 1886, and finished at the end of May[6] 'because examination work is on, that is setting, comparing, revising, and correcting proof of, papers, and the examinations themselves will follow'.

It is a great help to me to have someone interested in something (that will answer my letters), and it supplies some sort of intellectual stimulus: I sadly need that and a general stimulus to being, so dull and yet harassed is my life.

The first letter in the correspondence asks: 'two things. One is some on-the-spot account of the late riots, as witnessed by yourself or friends and informants, also London political gossip in general. The other is the following.' Then Hopkins begins a series of proposed Greek derivations from the Egyptian. This letter finishes: 'I hope you are well, happy, and pleasantly employed. I am not markedly any of these things, but shall be bettered all round by a letter from you answering the above and conveying countless more points of interest.'

Over the next few months Hopkins bombarded his friend with wild linguistic surmises, observations on obscure etymological coincidences, and demands for answers to questions on Egyptian language and mythology. Baillie had to expend midnight oil and patience to keep up with the constant letters and postcards—three were sent on one day. Behind the sudden, concentrated, and brief flare of enthusiasm lay an unrealistic journey into the past. It was as though he and Baillie were still in the garden quadrangle of Balliol, tossing inventive shuttlecocks at each other. 'We must start a hypothesis', he urges Baillie. 'I do not assert,' he lies, 'I only enquire'. His explorations of the early influence of Egypt upon Greece are 'perilous and conjectural', and 'I am quite alive to the hazard of all this'; yet 'all this' he found both 'interesting' and 'suggestive', and 'if it throws light on Greek history it must also on Egyptian and kill two birds with one stone'. Baillie must have needed several reference books to answer a single closely written postcard of Hopkins's:

(T'Ape or T'Apu is said to mean the Head, Capital; if so it is a title, not a proper name, and applicable to many places.) The plural in the name of the Egyptian Thebes is due to the Boeotian.

The tradition of a Phoenician foundation of Thebes was strong. And there was a tradn. of a second founding and in fact the Upper and Lower Cities were said to have distinct founders. I suspect the names Labdacus, Laius, and Oedipus to be historical and to = Ra-ptah, Ra + something, Hoteb-uas (?). And Athene Onca, said to be Phoenician, is perhaps Egyptian. What does Ankh mean?

The enquiry that ought to be made is when did this Egyptian colonisation of

Crete etc take place. It seems to be mixed with the Phoenician, not altogether opposed to it. This wd. seem then to be at the Hyksos period. (I remark also that the legend of Isis connects her with Phoenicia.)

I find Nefert in a female proper name and now suggest Aphrodite = Nefrat-isi.

I hope to be in London after Easter and to see you. Three cheers.

G.M.H.

Hopkins's contributions to the discussion largely took the form of recounting his various great lights, as the college books were, as usual, either missing or, as in the case of Rawlinson's *History of Egypt*, lacking the first volume. Hopkins needed the correspondence, but the excuse for it, his book on 'Homer's Art', he could not write. His annual birthday greeting to Cardinal Newman at Birmingham was in two parts, one expressing sadness over the state of Ireland, and the other mentioning his intended 'analysis of old Homer', as Newman called it in reply.[7] Underlying this premature announcement is the desire to force the work into being.

The Egyptian theorizing spurred him on to renew his correspondence on Celtic studies with Dr John Rhys, who suggested that he undertake research into Irish ogams in the cellar of the Royal Irish Academy, and return to his old idea of editing St Patrick's *Confessio*. In his long letter to Rhys, however, Hopkins complained that he was so overworked that he had no time to write even on Homer. 'But if we only do a part of what we propose', the much-published scholar replied, 'that will have been done well.'[8] The undated poem 'The times are nightfall' expresses a growing fear of never completing a work, and the fear expands to a pessimistic welcoming of death:

> Nor word now of success:
> All is from wreck, here, there, to rescue one—
> Work which to see scarce so much as begun
> Makes welcome death, does dear forgetfulness.

On 20 April Hopkins took the evening boat from Kingstown to Holyhead. A few days later he met Baillie in London. They continued their discussion on Greek derivations from the Egyptian, and Hopkins carried out his plan to research his book at Oxford, staying at St Aloysius'. While at Oxford he visited the Paravicinis, and went to see Bridges at nearby Yattendon for a day. Hopkins met Bridges's wife for the first time. She was not, he wrote afterwards, 'as fancy painted her (indeed fancy painted her very faintly in watered sepia), but by no means the worse for that'. The memory of his delightful day at Yattendon would 'continue fragrant'.[9]

For most of this English holiday Hopkins stayed at Hampstead, and it was probably the last time he saw his family home. He visited the Royal Academy annual exhibition, preferring Hamo Thornycroft's statue of 'The Sower', 'a truly noble work', and 'like Frederick Walker's pictures put into stone'. The mention of Walker, in a letter to Dixon, led him to elegize on the premature death of young artists: 'The genius of that man, poor Walker, was amazing: he was cut off by death like Keats and his promise and performance were in painting as brilliant as Keats's in poetry. . . . The sense of beauty was so exquisite. . . . his loss was irretrievable.' Walker's works satisfied because of their technical perfection, and 'masterly execution' was the most essential quality in all artists. 'The life must be conveyed into the work and be displayed there, not [merely] suggested as having been in the artist's mind.' For this reason, although he accepted Whistler's 'striking genius—feeling for what I call *inscape* (the very soul of art)', he found Whistler's execution sometimes unpardonably negligent, and to that extent he agreed with Ruskin's famous charge that the American was merely 'throwing the pot of paint in the face of the public'. Similarly, Burne-Jones's paintings sometimes suffered from crude and unsatisfactory drawing.[10]

While he was in London his brother Arthur took him to the studio of a friend, Robert Macbeth, a disciple of Walker's, and Hopkins saw reproductions of several of Walker's works he had not known. Walker's work was 'a world of beauty', and he told Dixon that he remembered how 'the news of his death gave me a shock as if it had been a near friend's'.[11]

From his three-week holiday Hopkins returned on 9 May by the Kingstown steamer, having spent less than seven of the twelve pounds he had been given. Waiting for him at St Stephen's Green was a letter from Mrs Waterhouse, Bridges's mother-in-law, whom he had met for the first time when he had visited Yattendon a fortnight earlier, though they had corresponded over the prayer Hopkins had written for her anthology. She enclosed a book of hers, writing 'It was so nice to me to see you the other day,'

only it seemed but a very little time—and I should have liked to know so much of your thoughts and of your life—it was very sad to me to hear that you were 'worried' with work—because I had fancied you quite otherwise—and free to lead the hidden life—away from the world and its cares . . .[12]

The romantic and comfortable preconceptions Mrs Waterhouse held of the professional religious life would in someone else have irritated Hopkins. But having learnt his history from her son-in-law, she had formed a motherly feeling for him at their first meeting, to which he had responded by confiding some of his personal worries. The lack of clarity in her picture of Hopkins's world seems inseparable from her warm sympathy. Compared with the three other people he was with at Yattendon, Mrs Waterhouse offered a unique relationship. Unlike Bridges, she was female, unlike her daughter Monica she was of a safe age, and unlike Bridges's mother, she was not afraid to express her sympathies. Her letter left Hopkins feeling that he would like to repay her kindness, perhaps with a present of his own making.

Although he felt guilt for the omission, something prevented Hopkins from immediately writing to his mother, Baillie, and Bridges, all very close to him. Perhaps he was inhibited by the difference between writing letters to people and being with them; he was acutely conscious of physical presence, and for the last twenty years this had been a rare aspect of his relationships with his family and old friends. And there is his disposition, noted by his Jesuit superiors, *aliud agere*, to do something else, as well as a guilty feeling that he might have been evading academic duties by the holiday. Although as long ago as January he had thought of asking 'to go to Oxford to get information on matters of scholarship', he does not seem to have pushed forward his Homeric study while at Oxford, and now, back in Dublin, he turned to another of his projects. A long time ago he had composed a tune for 'Who is Sylvia?', a standard Victorian compositional exercise, and with the vague prospect of a performance at a Jesuit school he harmonized it for duet, chorus, and string orchestra, and sent it to Sir Robert Stewart.

Over sixty when Hopkins first met him, Sir Robert Stewart[13] was the most prominent and busiest musician in Ireland, teacher, conductor, soloist, choir-master, composer, and writer. He held the two main Chairs in Dublin, at the Royal Irish Academy of Music and Dublin University, and people would come up to Dublin on Sunday to hear him accompany the choral services at the two Protestant cathedrals, Christ Church in the morning and St Patrick's in the afternoon. That an amateur of Hopkins's rawness should send the leading professional a composition to correct, and that Stewart should comment on it, was due partly to Stewart's generosity and partly to Hopkins's exploitation of whatever prestige was attached to his Chair. Perhaps it was also a sign of the arrogance with which Hopkins ventured into new intellectual or artistic regions.

His removal from English cultural life had not modified the intellectual priggishness of the Oxford undergraduate. His small circle of literary correspondents, Bridges, Dixon, Patmore, and Baillie, were all sufficiently diffident or modest to defer to most of his dogmatisms. In poetry he had knowledge, training, and experience, but in other disciplines he was sufficiently removed from social reality to expect the deference he received at Oxford, and which he considered his due as priest and confessor.

Stewart's unruffleable sense of humour was a byword in Dublin social circles, and it probably helped that Stewart came from Scottish Methodist stock, unlikely to be daunted by a priest. He had the Anglo-Irish tendency towards genial compromise, and was an encouraging teacher. Short of books on music, as on most other subjects, Hopkins had borrowed from Stewart the standard work on antiquarian music, *Chappell's Popular Music of the Olden Time*, a new edition of which was being prepared by Bridges's friend, H. E. Wooldridge. He sent Stewart a naïve invitation, not accompanied by a ticket, to a concert of the Dublin Music Society, a poor rival of the august organizations with which Stewart was associated. Hopkins had pleaded that he was unable to come to a concert given by Stewart's choir. Stewart's reply is a curious medley of condemnation and geniality: 'My dear Padre', it began, putting the title of 'Father' in ironic perspective,

It is not likely the DMS will send me (!) admission for their Concert, & I don't *buy* tickets—'clericus Clericum non decimat' on principle, so you wont have my society to bore, or instruct you I fear. Now d$^r$ Padre. Does it not strike you as unnatural to invite *me* to hear the Mass in C, & yet to say *you* 'cannot' come to our little Concert the other night? I send you—as a proof of our orthodoxy as Catholics!—the programme, by which you will see that that very motet of J. S. Bach you invite me to hear along with you, was to be heard with me the other Evening—It is likely we did it better (with our picked choir of 25 or 30) than your 'tag-rag-&-bobtail' levies will do it.

The final paragraph, in Stewart's good-natured and direct manner, is the most severe criticism of Hopkins's character by someone who knew him:

Indeed my dear Padre I *cannot* follow you through your maze of words in your letter of last week. I saw, ere we had conversed ten minutes on our first meeting, that you are one of those special pleaders who never believe yourself wrong in any respect. You always excuse yourself for anything I object to in your writing or music so I think it a pity to disturb you in your happy dreams of perfectability—nearly everything in your music was wrong—but you will not admit that to be the case—What does it matter? It will be all the same 100 years hence—There's one thing I do admire—your hand-writing! I wish *I* could equal *that*, it is so scholarlike![14]

Stewart's penmanship was so minute that his letters could be read only through a magnifying glass.

The following Monday, 24 May, Hopkins received Stewart's letter, and sent a hurt response, accusing Stewart of being outrageous, and asking him to give specific examples of Hopkins's musical faults. Stewart's reply started with another salvo of hostilities, genially veiled:

Darling Padre! *I* never said anything 'outrageous' to you. Dont think so, pray! but you are impatient of correction, when you have previously made up your mind on any point, & I R.S. being an 'Expert', you seem to me to err, often times, very much.

This time Stewart supported his attack with detailed criticism of Hopkins's ignorance of musical grammar and convention, quoting from the 'Who is Sylvia?' setting, which he returned.[15]

ↀ

After his holiday Hopkins had felt better and wrote to Bridges: 'My anxiety mostly disappeared, though there is more reason than ever for it now, for I am terribly behindhand and cannot make up.' He would soon be faced with the endless examination scripts. 'I am or am going to be very hard at work, for I have got my first batch of answer books from the Royal University', he wrote to his mother on 11 June. He was weighed down by the knowledge that the examination papers would sap the energy and self-assurance his holiday had generated. He did not know any way of evading the destructive pattern of the previous year. He was troubled by sleeplessness, and on 1 June it had been so cold that he would have welcomed a fire.[16]

In June two of his close friends paid him compliments—Dixon pressed him to allow him to put a stanza of 'Morning, Midday, and Evening Sacrifice' into an anthology of verse snippets with biblical quotations he was compiling in the form of a 'Bible Birthday-Book', and the new edition of Patmore's poetry owed several of its revisions to suggestions of Hopkins's. But the setting of 'Who is Sylvia?', which after Stewart's mauling was intended for performance at the Belvedere School, in north Dublin, was not sung. Even if it had been, he told Dixon, 'I could not have heard it, for I was helping to save and damn the studious youth of Ireland.' Dixon too had a disappointment—he had failed to be elected to the Professorship of Poetry at Oxford, and to Hopkins this confirmed a pattern:

Great gifts and great opportunities are more than life spares to one man. It is much if we get something, a spell, an innings at all. See how the great conquerors were cut short, Alexander, Caesar just seen. Above all Christ our Lord: his career was cut short and, whereas he would have wished to succeed by success—for it is insane to lay yourself out for failure, prudence is the first of the cardinal virtues, and he was the most prudent of men—nevertheless he was doomed to succeed by failure; his plans were baffled.

'His plans', continued Hopkins, reiterating the obsession, 'were baffled, his hopes dashed, and his work was done by being broken off undone.' Christ's example was 'very strengthening', but 'except in that sense it is not consoling'. He recognized Dixon's disappointment as a confirmation of his own way of life: 'It is not possible for me to do anything, unless a sonnet, and that rarely, in poetry with a fagged mind and a continual anxiety.' Nevertheless, there were things which he could do, if only by snatches, and he had begun 'a sort of popular account of Light and the Ether'.[17]

For the second half of September he went with Curtis for an unexpected but reviving holiday in north Wales, 'much pulled down' by examining. The second week they stayed at Mrs Evans's, in Church Street, Tremadoc, a 'remote and beautiful spot', though 'the weather is quite broken and the soldier in Mrs. Evans's weatherclock stand out of his box with a dismal effrontery, while the maiden sulks, like Weeping Winefred, indoors'. He had 'the heartiest breakfasts' and 'Wild Wales breathes poetry'. Over the village of Tremadoc 'rises a cliff of massive self-hewn rock, all overrun with a riot of vegetation which the rainy climate seems to breathe here'. They climbed Snowdon, and Hopkins made a drawing of the Glaslyn, 'a torrent of notably green water'. This turned out so well that he decided to 'set' it and send it to Bridges as a gift, but he 'used milk in a saucer and put the saucer by the fire, where the gluey milk stuck it so fast to the earthenware that it could not be got off without grievous tearing'. So he sent the remnants to Bridges. Curtis was called back to Dublin to conduct an oral examination, leaving Hopkins with Dixon's poem 'Ulysses and Calypso', Walpole's *Castle of Otranto*, and a sixty-five-year-old guidebook to Caernarvon. He read the novel and found 'great rubbish': 'In one place a hollow groan is heard, which both Theodore and Matilda conclude "to be the effect of pent-up-vapours" '.[18]

He returned to Kingstown on the evening packet of Sunday 3 October, disturbed that he had nearly £8 left out of the allocated £20: 'that is mismanagement'. The holiday had been 'a new life', he wrote to his mother. His body and mind had been exercised. He had worked on 'some scenes of my *Winefred* ... in Wales, always to me a mother of Muses'. Natural beauty and poetry went together. North Wales, he wrote to Patmore, was 'the true Arcadia of wild beauty'. *Winefred* was 'a drama of passion more than of character and not at all of manners, something in what I understand to be Marlowe's treatment (I could flog myself for being so ignorant as to say "I understand to be")'. Until this time he had consciously written fragments, whereas 'I now definitely hope to finish it', but as if Dublin had started casting its fog of weakness and doubts over him he added, 'I cannot say when'. Other literary schemes had 'got on a little', such as the ode on Campion.[19]

This unexpected holiday buoyed his spirits for the next seven weeks, in spite of the examinations. '331 accounts of the First Punic War with trimmings, have sweated me down to nearer my lees and usual alluvial low water mudflats, gr²ŏans, de⁴spair, a³ňd ye¹ărnings'. After three weeks and another two batches of papers, his examining was over 'till the next attack of the plague. My lectures, to call them by that grand name, are begun.' He was able to pursue several other projects. He made 'a great and solid discovery about Pindar or rather about the Dorian and Aeolian Measures or Rhythms', and hoped to 'publish something when I have read some more'. He sent a batch of counterpoint exercises for Stewart to correct, and set tunes and harmonies to two of William Barnes's poems, which a pianist played and two schoolboys sang.[20]

He also suddenly turned 'a lot of Shakspere's songs into elegiacs and hendecasyllabics (my Latin muse having been wholly mum for years)'. One he sent to Fr Matthew Russell, the Jesuit editor of *The Irish Monthly*, and the rest he considered getting published in Trinity College's journal *Hermathena*, through his friend Professor Tyrrell. He energetically promoted his friends' poetic works by sending copies to Dublin acquaintances, and wrote unusually long and confident letters to Bridges, Dixon, and Patmore. He took up his Dublin friendships with pleasure, particularly that with Katherine Tynan.

With the return to Dublin, however, also came the occasional phrase of doubt among the breeziness of his letters—'but all my world is scaffolding'. And in these same letters of October there is too much flitting from one project to another to suggest single-mindedness or concentration.[21] The effects of his Welsh holiday lasted just long enough to enable him to finish 'Spelt from Sibyl's Leaves', the 'longest sonnet ever made and no doubt the longest making'.[22] He had started it two years previously and, as with many of his sonnets, had difficulty in continuing a line of argument from octave to sestet. It is too sustainedly powerful a poem for a break in its argument's thread to harm it, but to complete it Hopkins had to restate the already considerable climax of line 8, 'Our evening is over us', in line 10: 'Our tale, O our oracle'.

Perhaps because of his 'clouded' working Christmas the previous year, it was suggested that Hopkins take a few days' holiday over Christmas, 1886, staying with the Cassidys at Monasterevan,[23] forty miles west of Dublin in County Kildare. Monasterevan was dominated by Moore Abbey and Cassidy's Distillery. During the sixth century St Emhin (pronounced and sometimes spelt Evin) had reputedly built a monastery on the banks of the Barrow, the silent or 'dumb' river. Hence the name Mainistir-Emhin. In the nineteenth century the two faiths lived amicably side by side. The old Protestant church of St John's was on Moore Street, and the Catholic church of Saints Peter and Paul, built of the same ugly grey local limestone, on the parallel Drogheda Street. The town's prosperity had begun in the 1780s with the opening of the Canal and the founding of the distillery. By the 1880s Cassidy's distilled a quarter of a million gallons of whiskey a year. On his marriage in 1854 James Cassidy, grandson of John, had built his own fine mansion, Togher House, leaving Monasterevan House to his sisters, including the eldest, Mary, known according to the old fashion as Miss Cassidy, and Eleanor Wheble, a widow. These ladies were in their late fifties or early sixties when Hopkins first went to stay at Monasterevan House, a typical early Georgian home for country gentry.

The Cassidys typified the compromise often made in pre-independent Ireland, and seldom recorded by nationalist historians, between the old native culture and the imported one of the ruling class. Though Roman Catholics, the Cassidys had friendly contact with the Protestant church, and, though native Irish, were staunch loyalists, upholding British law as magistrates. The Cassidys dominated their little town and the surrounding countryside. They controlled the town's employment and trade, wages being paid in their copper tokens which were accepted by the shopkeepers. They were prominent in the Catholic church on Drogheda Street, though Monasterevan House possessed its private oratory—an important factor in Hopkins's visit was that he would say mass there for the family. When he arrived in Monasterevan, the distillery had closed down for the holiday, and the casualness and peace of the countryside filtered into the town.

He stayed at Monasterevan House for a few days over Christmas, and for New Year after his annual retreat a few miles down the road at Tullamore. He conceived an extraordinary liking for the place and its people. He could be free of Irish politics, as he was comfortably among Catholics unquestioningly loyal to Britain. The town had not always been so peaceful. Two weeks after the Battle of Monasterevan in 1798, the Catholic curate, Fr Prendergast, had been tried by court martial, and hanged from a tree in what was now the Cassidys' garden.

The tale was afterwards told among the Irish Jesuits of Hopkins's introduction to the ladies of Monasterevan House. On that winter evening he arrived at seven o'clock; when his host, probably Mr Cassidy, brought the ladies into the room where he had left Hopkins, they found Hopkins by the fireside sewing up his waistcoat with needle and thread. Besides Miss Cassidy and Mrs Wheble, Hopkins met other members of the family, including young relatives of Mrs Wheble's dead husband, Leo and Ursula, who lived in the neighbourhood a short drive away. Hopkins was fascinated by them, particularly the boy: 'They are half English, half Irish, and their nationality is thus divided: outwardly or in the body they are almost pure Paddy and Biddy, inwardly and in the mind mainly John Bull. The youngest boy Leo is a remarkably winning sweetmannered young fellow.'[24] There was an additional reason to be fascinated: he saw a portrait of these two children painted by someone else who was attracted by their beauty and grace. Hopkins was moved to write an elegy. He had already expressed some of his feeling at the decay of innocence and beauty in 'Spring and Fall: to a young child', but no consolation was suggested in that poem for the tragic aspect of life. He set to work, taking as model Gray's 'Elegy'.

On 2 January, the day before he had to return to Dublin, he wrote to Bridges. In his last letter Bridges had passed on some uncomplimentary comments by Wooldridge on Hopkins's music, saying that they might function as a 'discouragement'. Always alert to precise meanings, Hopkins now replied that the word should have been 'dissuasive': 'Discouragement is not what my complaint, in my opinion, needs. Our institute provides us means of discouragement, and on me at all events they have had all the effect that could be expected or wished and rather more.' As a counter to Bridges's dissuasion and Jesuit discouragement, Hopkins described his congenial environment:

I am staying (till tomorrow morning, alas) with kind people at a nice place. I have had a bright light, and begun a poem in Gray's elegy metre, severe, no experiments. I am pleased with it and hope you will be and also Mrs. Waterhouse, for I want her to see it. I therefore enclose what there is of it.[25]

Mrs Waterhouse's letter to Hopkins of the previous May had been too personal for him to reply to it in the same manner, but there could be no offence in offering a poem shared with her son-in-law. He wanted 'to pay her a compliment and conceived she would like this particular poem'. Perhaps it was with Mrs Waterhouse in mind that he wrote it 'in a commoner and smoother style than I mostly write in: I am sure I have gone far enough in oddities and running rhymes'.[26]

☙

'On the Portrait of Two Beautiful Young People' unfolds an image of life as a sad progression, in which initial good is inevitably followed by evil. It laments the human condition, in a traditional combination of melancholy and tenderness:

> O I admire and sorrow! The heart's eye grieves
> Discovering you, dark tramplers, tyrant years.
> A juice rides rich through bluebells, in vine leaves,
> And beauty's dearest veriest vein is tears.
>
> Happy the father, mother of these! Too fast:
> Not that, but thus far, all with frailty, blest
> In one fair fall; but, for time's aftercast,
> Creatures all heft, hope, hazard, interest.
>
> And are they thus? The fine, the fingering beams
> Their young delightful hour do feature down
> That fleeted else like day-dissolvèd dreams
> Or ringlet-race on burling Barrow brown.

The beginning echoes the antithetical opening of Catullus' *Carmina* lxxxv, 'Odi et amo', but Catullus' amorous passions are bewildering in conflict, whereas the elegiac sympathy in Hopkins's poem is calm and distanced. The speaker is remote from his subjects; though he knows the two people in the flesh, he is reflecting on their painted images. The evasive device of the portrait obviates the dangerous meeting with human physical beauty, which raised such tortuous scruples in 'To what serves Mortal Beauty?' It also allows the poet, and his speaker, to express emotions about the people directly, but in a generalized way. The narrator looks on the picture until the interpretive 'heart's-eye' takes over and analyses the emotions: the heart perceives formlessly, the eye focuses perception. There is the implication of evil lurking beneath the surface, waiting to be uncovered; according to Hopkins, it was the guileful one, Satan, who brought decay into the world. So Time ('years') becomes personified, and qualified by 'dark tramplers' and 'tyrant'.

The autobiographical element of the poem is not far beneath the surface; fifteen months earlier Hopkins told Bridges he felt as though he had been 'trampled' upon: 'soon I am afraid I shall be ground down to a state like this last spring's and summer's, when my spirits were so crushed that madness seemed to be making approaches'. The muted antithesis in 'I admire and sorrow' has its counterpart in the contrast between the two beautiful young people and the lone, ageing, haggard Gerard Hopkins. The temporary quality of their beauty and youth is denoted by art, a portrait foregrounded in the poem, yet limited by the fact of artifice. The shadowy narrator is ever-present in the poem as the representative of reality, in his ruined state. The two represent youth and beauty but also painting, which was, like childish beauty, a vital and yet temporary aspect of Hopkins's past.

Dublin had produced the tormented and dynamic 'Spelt from Sibyl's Leaves', and Monasterevan inspired a gentle poetic motion from one focus and sentiment to another. Like other Englishmen, Hopkins admired the easiness and unconcernedness of life in rural Ireland, while at the same time feeling that harsh reality was being avoided. Not only as a priest but also as an Englishman, he sometimes saw the Irish as children, innocent and easily deceived. There is something representative of more than children in Hopkins's pastoral portrait, and he alters the painted picture into the kind of portrait he wants it to be.

The poet as good as closes the poem down, rather than finishes it, by implying that the passions aroused are so painful that they have outstripped his capacity for feeling. What use is it to put his heart to that torture?

> Enough: corruption was the world's first woe.
> What need I strain my heart beyond my ken?
> O but I bear my burning witness though
> Against the wild and wanton work of men.

There are puzzling and curious elements in this poem, not the least of which is the division between the narrator's mind and heart. In Wordworth's 'Ode: Intimations of Mortality from Recollections of Early Childhood', occupying Hopkins's mind at this time, three stages of growth were clearly marked: the Child, or Natural Man, succeeded by the Trapped (or Dejected) Man, and finishing as the Mature Poet, who has accepted growth, and the movement towards death. In Hopkins's poem the narrator is partly the Mature Poet, and partly the Trapped and Dejected Man; the roles are not played out in the logical sequence but are intermingled. The written poem finishes where it does because the narrator demonstrates by his complaint that he is still Dejected Man and purposely remains in that state.

There are three complete stanzas in the manuscript additional to those usually printed; they do not connect with each other. Two appear to be prematurely terminated attempts to continue a theme started in the main body of the poem. The final word, 'life', of the present fourth stanza is taken up in one of these discarded stanzas, which was probably intended to follow it:

> Ah, life, what's like it?—Booth at Fairlop Fair;
> Men brought in to have each our shy there, one
> Shot, mark or miss, no more. I miss; and there!
> Another time I . . . 'Time' says Death 'is done'.

One sign of the vagrant nature of this stanza is its setting of 'Fairlop Fair', held not in Monasterevan, but Essex. Although the theme of the hit-or-miss nature of life is appropriate, the abrupt change of scene and time may have been a reason for discarding the verse.

Monasterevan became a sanctuary for Hopkins. In his short stays there, though the countryside was not noticeably beautiful or dramatic, much of it flat and featureless bogland, he could think himself removed from pollution, poverty, and vice. While he was there he was free of academic duties, with companions who liked him and said so. He was also free from pastoral duties, except for saying mass in the oratory at Monasterevan House, and occasionally assisting the parish priest of SS Peter and Paul, Fr Comerford, in giving communion. That ceremony took on in Hopkins's mind a dreamy, ideal quality:

Many hundreds came to the rail, with the unfailing devotion of the Irish; whose religion hangs suspended over their politics as the blue sky over the earth, both in one landscape but immeasurably remote and without contact or interference. This phenomenon happens to be particularly marked at Monasterevan.[27]

Two anecdotes are told among Irish Jesuits about Hopkins's carefree breaks in Monasterevan. On a long walk he was given a lift by a man in a cart. After some time he asked if they were now near Monasterevan; the reply was 'We're not, then, but we'll be coming into Portarlington presently.' Hopkins had not asked the man which way he was going, and they had been travelling in the opposite direction. Another time he saw a ploughman at work in a field, leapt over the hedge, and ploughed a drill for himself.[28]

છ૭

Probably in January Hopkins started composing an epithalamion for his brother Everard, who was to marry Amy Sichel in April. In this long, rambling, unfinished poem, Hopkins created an arcadian vision, of naked boys bathing in a virginal paradise. It was the only poem of unequivocal happiness produced during his five unhappy years in Ireland, composed, moreover, in the least promising of all settings for Hopkins—an examination hall, while he was invigilating. The untidy and disordered manuscript version, written on an examination answer-book, is full of erasures, and Bridges's piecing together of the fragments into a coherent order was a difficult task sensitively carried out.

The entry into this secret world of the epithalamion is made by 'make believe/ We are leaf-whelmed somewhere', overwhelmed, as Hopkins so often had recorded he had been, by an overhanging leaf-and-branch 'hood/ Of some branchy bunchy bushybowered wood'. There

> a gluegold-brown
> Marbled river, boisterously beautiful, between
> Roots and rocks is danced and dandled, all in froth and waterblow-
> 　　balls, down.

'A listless stranger', beckoned by the 'riot of a rout' of bathing boys, 'drops towards the river', and observes unseen 'how the boys/ With dare and with downdolfinry and bellbright bodies huddling out,/ Are earthworld, airworld, waterworld thorough hurled, all by turn and turn about'. His self-weighted listlessness is thrown off, and 'This garland of their gambol flashes in his breast/ Into such a sudden zest/ Of summertime joys' that he—does not strip and jump in with them, as Walt Whitman would have done, but being scrupulous, avoids the human contact and—goes off to 'a pool neighbouring', which is

> 　　　　　　　　　　　sweetest, freshest, shadowiest;
> Fairyland; silk-beech, scrolled ash, packed sycamore, wild wych-
> 　　elm, hornbeam fretty overstood
> By. Rafts on rafts of flake leaves light, dealt so, painted on the air,
> Hang as still as hawk or hawkmoth, as the stars or as the angels
> 　　there,
> Like the thing that never knew the earth, never off roots
> Rose. Here he feasts: lovely all is.

Hopkins's poetic account of the undressing is sadly comic, not only because the boots come off after the trousers:

> 　　　　　　off with—down he dings
> His bleachèd both and woolwoven wear: . . .
> 　　　　　　　　　　　his twiny boots
> Fast he opens, last he offwrings

He is now ready to become one with the joys of this private dream of a *hortus conclusus*:

> Till walk the world he can with bare his feet
> And come where lies a coffer, burly all of blocks

Built of chancequarrièd, selfquainèd, hoar-huskèd rocks
And the water warbles over into, filleted with glassy grassy quick-
    silvery shivès and shoots
And with heavenfallen freshness down from moorland still brims,
Dark or daylight on and on. Here he will then, here he will the fleet
Flinty kindcold element let break across his limbs
Long. Where we leave him, froliclavish, while he looks about
    him, laughs, swims.

The paradise of the poem is the opposite of Dublin, and it is not an Irish setting. It is a vague—'somewhere'—but essentially English: 'Southern dean or Lancashire clough or Devon cleave' (the original draft had 'Surrey dean'). In spite of this vagueness, Hopkins had in mind a particular spot when he wrote the poem, the bathing-place, locally nicknamed 'Paradise', in the river Hodder, where the Stony-hurst College boys bathed. Having for the sake of the happy marriage a need to express delight, but not being in a congenial place, he drew on appropriate memories. In a letter to his mother from Stonyhurst in 1871 Hopkins had written: 'We bathe every day if we like now at a beautiful spot in the Hodder all between waterfalls and beneath a green meadow and down by the greenwood side O. If you stop swimming to look round you see fairyland pictures up and down the stream.' The same word 'fairyland' had been used to describe the spot eleven years afterwards, 'the river Hodder with lovely fairyland views, especially at the bathingplace',[29] and was used again in line 24 of the epithalamion. In his journal descriptions of the bathing-place in the early 1870s, Hopkins had often noted the colour of that stretch of the Hodder, as 'a sallow glassy gold', or 'glossy brown', or 'looking like pale gold, elsewhere velvety brown like ginger syrop', while in the poem it is 'a candycoloured . . . a gluegold-brown/ Marbled river'.[30] In July 1873 Hopkins took his brother Arthur and sister-in-law Rebecca to see the Stonyhurst beauty spot, Lambing Clough. They had then been married two months.[31] This is the only event of the couple's three-day visit Hopkins records, and the clough may well have become associated in his mind with a new marriage. The association was revived for him when, doodling on blank answer-sheets in the Dublin examination room, his thoughts and imagination turned to his youngest brother's marriage.

Epithalamion means 'at the bridal-chamber', and as a Professor of Greek Hopkins was using the description to place his poem within the classical convention of a nuptial song in praise of the bride and bridegroom, and a prayer for their prosperity.[32] Hopkins had been imitating Catullus' rhythms in translating Shakespeare's songs into Latin for Fr Russell's *Irish Monthly*, and this poem has features in common with Catullus' two famous epithalamia, 61 and 62. Hopkins's poem starts with an invocation—not, as in Catullus, to Hymen, the god of marriage—but to the 'hearer'. Like Hymen, the hearer is an outsider who is persuaded to partake of the joys offered. In Catullus there are repeated allusions to the presence at the ceremony of virgin boys; like Catullus in sexual preference and its display in the poem, Hopkins pictures a riot of boys. Like Hopkins, Catullus also delighted in descriptions of plants and trees, giving them symbolic functions in both his poems.

But Hopkins was faced with an insuperable dilemma: because of priestly and Victorian convention he could not let his narrator, as a proper epithalamist should, surrender to epithalamic, luxurious joyfulness, which could pass so naturally and playfully into erotic power. He was forced to remain at a distance from the wedding ceremony and the sexuality of marriage, and to lapse into allegory.

After forty-two lines Hopkins had decided to stop the self-indulgent description and start allegorical interpretation, but the narrative voice changes, not to one of sacred solemnity, but to a censor of the previous licence:

> Enough now; since the sacred matter that I mean
> I should be wronging longer leaving it to float
> Upon this only gambolling and echoing-of-earth note—
> What is . . . the delightful dean?
> Wedlock. What the water? Spousal love.

Sensuous lyrical description is not so easily metamorphosed into allegory. Objects under Hopkins's scrutiny usually remain themselves: the windhover is always a bird, and when Hopkins tried symbolism the result was often banal ('these are indeed the barn').[33] Not surprisingly, the epithalamion sputters at that point, and remained unfinished. It was never sent to Everard and Amy.

Despite its joyfulness the poem is ultimately sad, like *Peter Pan* and *The Secret Garden*. Instead of a wedding present, Hopkins had achieved an unfinished flight into fantasy, another reminder of unfinished work: 'Nor word now of success:/ All is from wreck, here, there, to rescue one.'[34]

# *'What shall I do for the land that bred me?'*

'Tomorrow morning', Hopkins wrote on 17 February 1887, 'I shall have been three years in Ireland, three hard wearying wasting wasted years.'[1] At Stonyhurst he started checking the passing of time with marked anniversaries, and in Dublin he was more conscious than ever of existing at a particular moment, with more years behind than ahead. In August he wrote to Bridges: ' "Getting old"—you should never say it. But I was fortythree on the 28th of last month and already half a week has gone.'[2] He had developed a self-consciousness about his appearance. Bridges's friend Wooldridge had undertaken to paint a portrait of him in oils, using as a guide the photograph taken in 1879 in the Oxford studios of Coles and Foreshaw; when Hopkins visited Bridges it would be finished from life. Asked to provide additional information about his colouring, and any marked physical differences between his 1879 likeness and his present self, Hopkins provided this description:

The irises of the present writer's eyes are small and dull, of a greenish brown; hazel I suppose; slightly darker at the outer rims.

His hair (see enclosed sample, carriage paid) is lightish brown, but not equable nor the same in all lights; being quite fair near the roots and upon the temples, elsewhere darker (the very short bits are from the temple next the ear, the longer snips from the forehead), and shewing quite fair in the sun and even a little tawny. It has a gloss. On the temples it sometimes appears to me white. I have a few white hairs, but not there.[3]

The location of these white hairs was, he said in his previous letter to Bridges, 'my heart and vitals', 'all shaggy with the whitest hair'. 'I am of late', he continued his description for Wooldridge, 'become much wrinkled round the eyes and generally haggard-looking.' If any likeness were to be made permanent, 'I shd. be glad it were of my youth'. Katherine Tynan saw Hopkins for the first time when he was forty-one, and then she had taken him for twenty, and a friend with her had guessed him to be fifteen.[4] A Dublin contemporary wrote after his death that Hopkins looked 'probably older than his age'. From a distance Hopkins's slight and frail, effeminate, 'almost insignificant' physique would be noticed, and the lines on his long face would only be seen at close quarters.

During 1887 and 1888 Hopkins continued to complain bitterly in letters about his health, the weather, Irish politics and Gladstone, and his frequent and arduous examining duties. The weather on the east coast of Ireland is often milder than in England, yet Hopkins objected to it. In January 1887, for example,

We had in Ireland little snow and no continuance of frost, so little skating. But still I found the weather very trying, more than I ever did. Not that I took a cold, I never do to speak of in winter (I am too cold for it), but it exhausted me every morning and I felt as if kept on long it would kill me.[5]

He suffered from eczema ('a fashionable complaint'), and had his special soap, but worst of all, he worried that the winter 'ruined the good sight' of his eyes. During the winter of 1887, in a letter otherwise full of enthusiasms, there suddenly appears: 'To bed, to bed: my eyes are almost bleeding.' And the summer of 1888 was a 'preposterous' one to Hopkins: 'It is raining now: when is it not?' One day he had to put work, 'my other rain' of examination papers, aside, as he feared for his eyes. It became a habit of his that summer, when his eyes were sore over marking, to walk in the Phoenix Park, 'large, beautiful, and lonely'. He feared that if there were such a thing as gout or rheumatism of the eyes, he had it. It was 'unpleasant and disquieting'. The feeling was 'like soap or lemons'. Eventually, on 6 October, he went to the oculist, who told him that his sight was 'very good', his eye 'perfectly healthy', but that 'like Jane Nightwork I am old'. He bought a pair of spectacles for ten shillings, but could not 'be happy either with or without them'.[6]

Politics, Irish and English, continued to harass him. He had by now learnt enough of Irish history to be able to say, 'The Irish had and have deep wrongs to complain of in the past and wrongs and abuses to amend which are still felt in the present.' Despite remaining an imperialist conservative, he was opposed to the large number of his fellow countrymen who still thought that 'Ireland was always a "distressful country", troubled and hard to rule at the best'. He had reluctantly come to the conclusion that Home Rule for Ireland would be better than 'the sword'. The country was now in a state of ever-increasing civil rebellion. Home Rule would 'deliver England from the strain of an odious and impossible task, the task of attempting to govern a people who own no principle of civil allegiance ... not only to the existing government ... but to none at all'.[7] It is interesting to see Hopkins's head and heart in conflict here. From his experience and knowledge he supports the main ideal of the Home-Rulers, though he is outraged by the widespread civil disobedience, momentarily subscribing to *Punch*'s caricature of the Irish as an ungovernable, wild people. In his annual birthday letter to Newman, he expressed such disapproval and drew a perceptive response from the old Cardinal: 'There is one consideration which you omit. The Irish Patriots hold that they never have yielded themselves to the sway of England and therefore have never been under her laws, and have never been rebels.' Newman quoted Sir John Moore, 'if I were an Irishman, I should be (in heart) a rebel',[8] and added: 'the Irish character and tastes [are] very different from the English'. Hopkins's prejudices were not so easily shaken, and he had often disagreed with Newman (Newman did not know what prose was, Hopkins informed Patmore in 1887).

Hopkins's naïve emotional reactions caused other inconsistencies. His hatred for Gladstone bursts through in several letters, despite contrite intentions to refrain from speaking ill of him. He agreed with Baillie that Gladstone 'ought to be beheaded on Tower Hill'; he was not the Grand Old Man but a Grand Old Mischief-Maker. Hopkins could agree that Home Rule should be granted, yet be bitterly opposed to the one English politician with sufficient imagination, goodwill, and ability to bring it about. Hopkins was a strong imperialist. The expression in 'The Wreck of the Deutschland' of his desire to see 'rare-dear Britain' return to Roman Catholicism is imperialist in tone, and insofar as he could collect his anti-Gladstone feelings under one head, his dislike was primarily of Gladstone's 'dissolution of empire': 'What one man could do to throw away a continent and weaken the bonds of a world wide empire he did.'[9]

As if to re-inspirit his countrymen, one day when he was taking a break from work in the Phoenix Park, where there were large British military barracks and parade grounds, Hopkins hit on a tune for 'a patriotic song for soldiers'. 'Heaven knows it is needed', he wrote to Bridges, enclosing the tune. 'I hope you may approve what I have done, for it is worth doing and yet is a task of great delicacy and hazard to write a patriotic song that shall breathe true feeling without spoon or brag':[10]

> What shall I do for the land that bred me,
> Her homes and fields that folded and fed me?
> Be under her banner and live for her honour:
> Under her banner I'll live for her honour.
> CHORUS. Under her banner we live for her honour.

The song would have been one of his most immediately comprehensible compositions to an 1880s audience brought up, as all Europeans were, monarchist or republican, on patriotic and martial music.

A more thoughtful expression of Hopkins's conservative thinking is 'Tom's Garland', written in December 1887:

> *Tom's Garland;*
> upon the Unemployed
>
> Tom—garlanded with squat and surly steel
> Tom; then Tom's fallowbootfellow piles pick
> By him and rips out rockfire homeforth—sturdy Dick;
> Tom Heart-at-ease, Tom Navvy: he is all for his meal
> Sure, 's bed now. Low be it: lustily he his low lot (feel
> That ne'er need hunger, Tom; Tom seldom sick,
> Seldomer heartsore; that treads through, prickproof, thick
> Thousands of thorns, thoughts) swings though. Commonweal
> Little I reck ho! lacklevel in, if all had bread:
> What! Country is honour enough in all us—lordly head,
> With heaven's lights high hung round, or mother-ground
> That mammocks, mighty foot. But no way sped,
> Nor mind nor mainstrength; gold go garlanded
> With, perilous, O no; nor yet plod safe shod sound;
>                          Undenizened, beyond bound
> Of earth's glory, earth's ease, all; no-one, nowhere,
> In wide the world's weal; rare gold, bold steel, bare
>                          In both; care, but share care—
> This, by Despair, bred Hangdog dull; by Rage,
> Manwolf, worse; and their packs infest the age.

Hopkins's social thinking had not undergone much change since he had seen the painting 'Work' in 1865, and copied into his commonplace-book Ford Madox Brown's accompanying sonnet: 'Work! which beads the brow and tans the flesh/ Of lusty manhood . . .'. Hopkins carefully avoided blaming grim social conditions on the upper classes, citing as causes, rather than effects, the vague 'Undenizened' and its subsequent 'care', 'Despair', and 'Rage'. Otherwise 'Tom's Garland' follows the main lines of the Carlylean argument expressed in Brown's poem and his prose account, which Hopkins had probably seen in the 1865 exhibition catalogue: 'Here are presented the young navvy in the pride of manly health and beauty; the strong fully-developed navvy who does his work and loves his beer . . . in the full swing of his activity. . . . Then Paddy with his larry'. Brown had similarly opposed brain-workers and navvies, who 'shovel the earth', and are defective in subtler qualities.

Hopkins's poem and Brown's painting also share shortcomings which originate with Carlyle, particularly their idealistic picture of the rewards of physical work (Carlyle's 'blessed glow of Labour'). Hopkins's phrase 'This, by Despair, bred Hangdog dull' echoes Carlyle's creed in *Past and Present*: 'Doubt, Desire, Sorrow, Remorse, Indignation, Despair itself, all these like helldogs lie beleaguering the soul of the poor dayworkers'.[11]

Hopkins's awareness of a disparity between his material and the capacity of the sonnet form is evident from his tacking on the two-part coda of lines 15–20. This extraneous part of the sonnet, taken up with the unemployed, those left over from the main body of the commonwealth, aptly demonstrates that this group of unattached people are 'undenizened' and 'beyond bound'. But the main argument fails, because symbols clash with realistic description. The 'crib' letter[12] to 'Tom's Garland', which he had to write afterwards for the benefit of puzzled readers, shows how simple the poem's symbols are, and yet the poem obscures them and their purpose.

Hopkins wrote 'Tom's Garland' and its companion 'Harry Ploughman' in Ireland, but emphasized by their names the Englishness of Tom, Dick, and Harry. Brown had realistically introduced elements of Irish immigrant labour into the Hampstead scene of 'Work', but in nearly all his poems written in Ireland Hopkins avoided reference to the country. By 1887 Hopkins's opinions on Ireland might easily be taken by Irishmen to be typically British and conservative, but this would be doing an injustice to the complex positions which he took on many political matters. Yet his manner of dealing with sensitive national issues in letters to Irish people remained British and distant. To Dr Michael Cox, a fellow examiner of the Royal University, he wrote on Lady Day 1887:

Irish writers on their own history are naturally led to dwell on what in history is most honourable to Ireland: every patriotic spirit would feel itself so led. They are also led to dwell on what in history is most dishonourable to England: this also is natural, and there is plenty of room for doing it. Still it is the way with passion to exceed. . . . It is desirable that Irish writers on Irish history should be on their guard especially on this matter, and, failing that, it is left for Englishmen like myself to do what we can . . . to point out untruths and overstatements and understatements due to passion and correct them. The devil is not so black, the saying is, as he is painted.

It is unlikely that a patriotic Irishman would have responded positively to such a lecture from an Englishman. Hopkins did not understand that Ireland had not been given opportunity to be rational towards England; Westminster parliamentary democracy had not worked in Ireland's favour. He came to feel 'not only with sorrow but with the deepest

indignation and bitterness' that Irish writers sometimes wilfully suppressed circumstances favourable to England, and he cited one writer
who 'cared only for the food of his hatred against England'. In a later
letter to Dr Cox, Hopkins commented on Ireland's want of commercial
prosperity by saying that 'so far as there is blame Irishmen must be in
great part to blame for that'.[13]

કર્

Nor is it likely that Hopkins's opinions of Irish legend were appreciated
by Katharine Tynan, the writer of Celtic romances. He observed:

It is natural for you to choose subjects from Irish legend. They have their
features of interest and beauty, but they have one great drawback: it is the
intermixture of monstrosities (as of a man throwing a stone one hundred others
could not lift or a man with a leaping pole over-vaulting an army), for these
things are deeply inartistic and destroy all seriousness and verisimilitude.[14]

Tynan was in her early twenties when she and Hopkins met. She was a
country girl,[15] described by her daughter as having 'a wonderful rose-
and-white Irish complexion', very fine fair brown hair with natural
curls, and thick glasses. Hopkins found her 'a simple bright-looking
Biddy with glossy very pretty red hair'. Since 1885 poetry had taken
over as her main interest in life. She was a great reader of the Rossettis,
Morris, Tennyson, and Swinburne. Since she had first met Fr Russell
in 'the ugly little room in the Jesuit house in Upper Gardiner Street',
she had tried to expand the artistic circle around her and her friends.

One day early in November 1886, Fr Russell had brought Hopkins
across Stephen's Green to meet her at No. 7 on the north side, the
studio of the artist John B. Yeats, where about twice a week Tynan sat
for her portrait on a dais, in a hospitable atmosphere of 'friends and
their friends'. These sittings were 'easily and naturally' transformed to
'symposia of art and literature of one kind or another', as Yeats was
'tremendously receptive and interested in all who came'.[16] Forty years
later Tynan recalled her first meeting with Hopkins: 'He brought an air
of Oxford with him. He was not unlike Lionel Johnson, being small and
childish-looking, yet like a child-sage, nervous too and very sensitive,
with a small ivory-pale face.' At this meeting Hopkins 'complained that
Father Russell would not shave regularly', and argued with J. B. Yeats
about 'finish or non-finish' in painting, Hopkins disagreeing of course
with Yeats's impressionism, or as he called it, his 'slight method of
execution'.[17] Yeats was, said Tynan, 'greatly delighted' with the visit,
and 'lamented that Gerard Hopkins, with all his gifts for Art and
Literature, should have become a priest'. She reported this to Hopkins,
who replied: 'You wouldn't give only the dull ones to Almighty God.'

At this first meeting with Tynan Hopkins heard for the first time of another young Irish poet who was attracted to the monstrosities of Celtic legends. 'With some emphasis of manner', J. B. Yeats presented him with '*Mosada: a Dramatic Poem* by W. B. Yeats, with a portrait of the author by J. B. Yeats himself; the young man having finely cut intellectual features and his father being a fine draughtsman'. Hopkins considered the son to be of the same school as his mentor, Sir Samuel Ferguson, who 'was a poet as the Irish are . . . full of feeling, high thoughts, flow of verse, point, often fine imagery and other virtues, but the essential and only lasting thing left out—what I call *inscape*, that is species or individually-distinctive beauty of style'. Hopkins could not think highly of *Mosada*, but

I was happily not required then to praise what presumably I had not then read, and I had read and could praise another piece ['The Two Titans']. It was a strained and unworkable allegory about a young man and a sphinx on a rock in the sea (how did they get there? what did they eat? and so on: people think such criticisms very prosaic; but commonsense is never out of place any-where, neither on Parnassus nor on Tabor nor on the Mount where our Lord preached . . .), but still containing fine lines and vivid imagery.[18]

At a later date Hopkins met W. B. Yeats, perhaps only once, in J. B. Yeats's studio. Yeats remembered Hopkins as 'a sensitive, querulous scholar', and his impression was the usual Irish one that Hopkins was 'a detached aesthete'; the Irish, Yeats told Humphry House, apropos of Hopkins, had 'no sympathy with English Aesthetic Catholicism'.[19]

In the late 1880s various small groups, some including Hopkins and the student Willie Coyne, would go out to Tynan's home at Clondalkin, under the Dublin mountains, on Sundays, and come back to 86 Stephen's Green to talk of Tynan and her poetry.[20] Coyne reviewed a book of hers in *The Lyceum*, condemning its 'painted pedantry'.

છ૭

Tynan was one of several people in Ireland to whom Hopkins sent or recommended the published works of Bridges, Dixon, and Patmore. He was particularly energetic in promoting Bridges's works: 'I have been disposing of Bridges' works as I thought best', he reported to their author. 'I have a *Prometheus* and a *Nero* left and am minded to bestow them on Professor Dowden. . . . My marketing of your books brought in admiration everywhere; but publicity, fame, notoriety, and an Amer-ican sale are wanted.' Later he reported: 'Books all disposed of thus: (1) Mr. Tyrrell all; (2) Miss Tynan all; (3) a young Mr. Gregg, sometime my pupil, *E. and P.*; (4) Prof. Dowden the other two.' He advised a

Royal University student working for the Doctorate of Music to set Bridges's 'Elegy on one whom grief for the loss of her beloved killed' for her diploma work; 'I added what could interest her, and she warmly welcomed the proposal'.[21] He continued to offer criticisms of friends' works in his letters, and occasionally attempted, without success, to review their works in journals. He never forgave Dowden, Professor of English at Trinity College, Dublin, for not writing to Bridges about the two volumes he sent him. Dowden did eventually acknowledge the gift, but not until 1894, in a *Fortnightly Review* article:

Father Gerard Hopkins, an English priest of the Society of Jesus, died young, and one of his good deeds remains to the present time unrecorded. We were strangers to each other, and might have been friends. I took for granted that he belonged to the other camp in Irish politics [Dowden was considered by patriots to regard the Irish language as the speech of barbarians]. . . . Father Hopkins was a lover of literature, and himself a poet. Perhaps he did in many quarters missionary work on behalf of the poetry of his favourite, Robert Bridges. He certainly left, a good many years since, at my door two volumes by Mr. Bridges, and with them a note begging that I would make no acknowledgement of the gift. I did not acknowledge it then; but, with sorrow for a fine spirit lost, I acknowledge it now.[22]

In the letters Hopkins wrote in 1887 and 1888 there is frequent comparison of other people's published work with his own academic projects. He had intended to write on Greek metre, ranging from the Dorian measure to metre in general; later 'metre' became 'rhythm'. He started writing 'a book or papers' on Aeschylus' *Choephoroi*. At various times in 1888 he planned to write on Greek negatives, on Patmore's *Angel in the House*, on Sophocles, on 'Statistics and Free Will'. None of these was published. When writing about a particular project Hopkins often started enthusiastically: 'I have been reading the Choephoroi carefully and believe I have restored the text and sense almost completely in the corrupted choral odes.' Then a sense of reality would catch up with him, and he would move into honest vagueness: 'Perhaps I might get a paper on it into the *Classical Review* or *Hermathena*'; and then the passage would deflate in a total lack of confidence: 'but when will that book or any book of mine be?'[23] This pattern became common in 1887 and 1888. There is a resemblance to some of the retreat notes, where Hopkins starts with control and confidence, then seems to write himself into a sense of failure. Another ominous tendency which showed itself in these two years is for a project to betray its unreality by an expanding focus: 'I have written a good deal of my book on the Dorian measure or on rhythm in general. Indeed it is on almost everything elementary and is much of it physics and metaphysics. It is full of new words.'[24]

The project for which he was most enthusiastic in the last year of his life was a collection of Irish words and phrases for the new dictionary of English dialect.[25] Seeing Hopkins's name as one among a number of amateur philologists acknowledged in Joseph Wright's *English Dialect Dictionary* brings home the fact that in so many of his so-called eccentric interests Hopkins was very much of his age ('Hardy, T., Dorchester' is also in the list). Yet despite Hopkins's sensitivity to words, he was (compared with Tennyson, for instance, who closely followed developments in modern philology[26]) largely ignorant of the new linguistics which classified forms and families of speech.

Some time between April 1887 and February 1888 Hopkins wrote to W. W. Skeat challenging a few of his etymologies. In his reply,[27] which showed how completely out of touch Hopkins was with the new philology, Skeat dismissed most of Hopkins's suggestions, and offered advice on collecting Irish examples for the *EDD*. He cited 'a very fair collection of "Down and Antrim" words by Mr. Patterson' that should be 'taken as the collection to which to *add*'.[28] Hopkins started taking careful notes of peculiar words and expressions, and enlisted the help of his students. One of them, George O'Neill, later Professor of English at University College, recalled:

Dublin was not too happy a situation for studying the *nuances* of provincialism, and certain humoristic youths, getting wind of what was wanted, added further complications. They plied the too trustful collector with idioms and vocables, often highly-coloured, entirely of their own invention or interpretation. A few wonderful things were forwarded to Dr. Wright, but he seems to have been on his guard; the initials 'G.M.H.' do not occur very often in the Dictionary, and then not (so far as I have remarked) in connection with any very notable specimen of Irishism.[29]

Collecting dialect words in Ireland may have been thought by the Irish a pedantic exercise, but to Hopkins it was a much-needed involvement which developed his sense of the continuity of his civilization. There are eighty-nine of Hopkins's contributions in the six volumes of the *EDD*, seventy-five of them in volume i (A–C), making it likely that his lists for the remaining five volumes have been lost or were thrown away at his death. The most interesting contributions show his ear for dialogue and gift for anecdote, as well as a sense of humour not often found in the *EDD*:

Begorra, bedad, begonnies. If your bees are as big as ponies and your hives no bigger than ours are, how do your bees get into your bee-hives?
—Begob, that's their own affair, *Pop. story.*

He hasn't enough sense to drive a pig down a boreen [a narrow lane].

There's a boy over from the Pope, and Archbishop Croke went on his knees to him.

'I cursed (or 'was drunk') a couple of times' means I have done so now and then.

I'm powerful weak but cruel easy [I am very weak but am quite at my ease], said by a sick man. A cruel good lady.

'I am so sorry I have kept your book so long.' 'It is no matter: I had it read.' That woman has me annoyed. She has my heart broke.

One of the conspirators who murdered Caesar 'let on to plead for his brother.'

The last one could have been heard in a classroom at Stephen's Green, or read in an examination script. These examples of the way Hiberno-English was used show that, far from being pedantic, Hopkins was aware of the complexity of words and their habitats.

About the time he started collecting dialect words for the *EDD*, Hopkins wrote a poem which is the most intensive word-painting he ever composed. He was on holiday in September 1887 at a house in Dromore, County Down; Loyola House had belonged to Bishop Percy (celebrated for his *Reliques of Ancient English Poetry*), and now housed a community of about thirty Jesuits, most of whom were novices:

### Harry Ploughman

Hard as hurdle arms, with a broth of goldish flue
Breathed round; the rack of ribs; the scooped flank; lank
Rope-over thigh; knee-nave; and barrelled shank—
     Head and foot, shoulder and shank—
By a grey eye's heed steered well, one crew, fall to;
Stand at stress. Each limb's barrowy brawn, his thew
That onewhere curded, onewhere sucked or sank—
     Soared or sank—,
Though as a beechbole firm, finds his, as at a rollcall, rank
And features, in flesh, what deed he each must do—
     His sinew-service where do.
He leans to it, Harry bends, look. Back, elbow, and liquid waist
In him, all quail to the wallowing o' the plough. 'S cheek
     crimsons; curls
Wag or crossbridle, in a wind lifted, windlaced—
     Wind-lilylocks-laced;
Churlsgrace too, child of Amansstrength, how it hangs or hurls
Them—broad in bluff hide his frowning feet lashed! raced
With, along them, cragiron under and cold furls—
     With-a-fountain's shining-shot furls

Everything that Hopkins wrote about 'Harry Ploughman' insists that we are wrong merely to look at the printed page, to read the poem only with the eyes (to which it looks like idiosyncratic funambulism). He wrote: 'this sonnet . . . is altogether for recital, not for perusal (as by nature verse should be).' Hopkins decided to break up the 'very heavily loaded sprung rhythm', by the indented burden-lines, which 'might be recited by a chorus'. It was 'a direct picture of a ploughman, without afterthought'. He wanted the ploughman to be 'a vivid figure before the mind's eye; if he is not that the sonnet fails'.[30] The poem is more than a painting in words. Constantly aware of several aspects of each object, Hopkins tries by many devices to connect different senses in creating the object in the hearer's mind, even transferring part of the vocabulary which he had used long ago in his journals for cloudscapes and waterscapes to describe the man in the poem.[31]

'Harry Ploughman' is successful precisely because Harry is dehumanized, turned into a connected series of natural phenomena. Even more elaborate is the poem 'That Nature is a Heraclitean Fire and of the comfort of the Resurrection'. Heraclitus was often called 'the weeping philosopher', as opposed to Democritus, 'the laughing philosopher', and during the Renaissance came to stand for pessimism:

> Cloud-puffball, torn tufts, tossed pillows flaunt forth, then chevy on
>     an air-
> Built thoroughfare: heaven-roysterers, in gay-gangs they throng;
>     they glitter in marches.
> Down roughcast, down dazzling whitewash, wherever an elm
>     arches,
> Shivelights and shadowtackle in long lashes lace, lance, and pair.
> Delightfully the bright wind boisterous ropes, wrestles, beats earth
>     bare
> Of yestertempest's creases; in pool and rutpeel parches
> Squandering ooze to squeezed dough, crust, dust; stanches, starches
> Squadroned masks and manmarks treadmire toil there
> Footfretted in it. Million-fuelèd, nature's bonfire burns on.

The joyous appreciation might suggest that Hopkins had regained the acute sense of elation he felt in Wales, at clouds, trees, physical shape and texture, and at conveying their inscape in words. But at the hint of Heraclitean flux, dissolution as the essence of nature's continuous movement, his Dublin fatalism takes over:

> But quench her bonniest, dearest to her, her clearest-selvèd spark
> Man, how fast his firedint, his mark on mind, is gone!
> Both are in an unfathomable, all is in an enormous dark

Drowned. O pity and indignation! Manshape, that shone
Sheer off, disseveral, a star, death blots black out; nor mark
                Is any of him at all so stark
But vastness blurs and time beats level.

The answer, the poem suggests, is to stop looking at nature and reflecting on its sombre message, and accept the consolation of the Resurrection:

                Enough! the Resurrection,
A heart's-clarion! Away grief's gasping, joyless days, dejection.
                Across my foundering deck shone
A beacon, an eternal beam. Flesh fade, and mortal trash
Fall to the residuary worm; world's wildfire, leave but ash:
                In a flash, at a trumpet crash,
I am all at once what Christ is, since he was what I am, and
This Jack, joke, poor potsherd, patch, matchwood, immortal diamond,
                Is immortal diamond.

There is a relevant retreat-note Hopkins made at the beginning of 1889:

Nothing to enter but loathing of my life and a barren submission to God's will. . . . How then can it be pretended there is for those who feel this anything worth calling happiness in this world? There is a happiness, hope, the anticipation of happiness hereafter: it is better than happiness, but it is not happiness now.[32]

The consolation offered at the end of 'That Nature is a Heraclitean Fire' is not a solution to the earthly problem posed in its opening; it does not tackle the problem on its own terms, but proposes fresh ones.

ϾϿ

During the same autumn Hopkins wrote another sonnet, which he told Bridges 'aims at being intelligible'. Bridges had been persuading him to read more widely and develop an easier style, so he added 'I say it snorting'.[33] There are not many Jesuit saints, and none with whose life Hopkins would be more likely to identify than Alphonsus Rodriguez. Alphonsus had a middle-class mercantile family background (many early Jesuits had been of noble origin), was accepted into the Society at the age of forty-four, Hopkins's age when he wrote the poem, and was even less successful (though for a different reason) than Hopkins at attaining rank within the Society. He was a temporal coadjutor, a lay brother. He had an unwarlike external disposition, his entire Jesuit career was spent in the role of college porter, and he died after years of physical and spiritual suffering. The poem was written in response to the canonization in 1888. Such official recognition of the merit of physical drudgery and inner suffering, as opposed to martyrdom, proselytising, and managerial prowess, must have seemed like a stroke of heavenly encouragement:

*In honour of*
*St. Alphonsus Rodriguez*
Laybrother of the Society of Jesus upon the
first falling of his feast after his canonisation
For the College of Palma in the Island
of Majorca, where the saint lived for 40 years as
Hall porter

Glory is a flame off exploit, so we say,
And those fell strokes that once scarred flesh, scored shield,
Should tongue that time now, trumpet now that field,
Record, and on the fighter forge the day.
On Christ they do, they on the martyr may;
But where war is within, what sword we wield
Not seen, the heroic breast not outward-steeled,
Earth hears no hurtle then from fiercest fray.
Yet, he that hews out mountain, continent,
Earth, all at last; who, with fine increment
Trickling, veins violets and tall trees makes more
Could crowd career with conquest while there went
Those years and years by of world without event
That in Majorca Alfonso watched the door.

Hopkins's response to the dulling task of an occasional poem did not often produce such a distinctive work of art, where sympathy and imagination are engaged. The theme brings it close to the 1885 desolate sonnets but the struggle has become objectified.

Early drafts of the poem, dated 'Sept. 28, 1888', are on a scrap of Royal University of Ireland notepaper, on the other side of which is a note of the same date from a colleague about examination scripts. Hopkins had been marking and, to rest his eyes, had gone walking in the Phoenix Park with the note in his pocket. Examining was his most painful drudgery. He wrote to his mother in July 1888: 'It is great, very great drudgery. . . . I labour for what is worth little. And in doing this almost fruitless work I use up all opportunity of doing any other. About my holiday I have no plan and know nothing.'[34]

A persistent theme of 1887 and 1888 is work, and 'holidays' is a key word: 'My broken holidays are coming to an end ... and I do not feel well'; 'holidays and work, like sleep and waking, are dead opposite'; 'holidays have begun and I am very tired and unable to do the work which I have to wait for holidays to do: it is a vicious circle. However I am going down to the country for a few days in Easter week I hope.' Monasterevan was his main place of temporary escape—holiday, refuge, renewal, creativity, nature, children, and human affection.[35]

There were visits to the McCabes at Donnybrook, and a new place of escape for him, Gleneveena, Judge O'Hagan's house on the south side of the Hill of Howth.[36] Howth was the rural idyllic peninsula which formed the northern arm of Dublin Bay, well-known as a weekend retreat. Gleneveena had been built into the steep slope of the hill, like a ship, with its bedrooms on the lower floor, and reception rooms high up, commanding a view of the bay, shipping, and Kingstown, with the Wicklow Hills in the distance. By the window in the drawing-room stood a telescope on a swivel-stand, which could pick out the names on ships entering the port. The O'Hagans kept a room as a private chapel, and at weekends a Jesuit would be dispatched from Gardiner Street or from University College to stay for two days and say mass. They were a wealthy and influential family, with many members in the legal system, and also on terms of close friendship with Fr Delany. Hopkins told his mother that they were 'the kindest people', and he started borrowing books from their library.

Other places of escape for him in those two years were Haslemere (the new Hopkins house, where he saw his family for the last time), the Bridges's house at Yattendon, Inversnaid, where he revisited his poetic past, Fort William and Whitby, and Enniscorthy, in County Wexford, where he stayed with his old pupil Bernard O'Flaherty. He was unable to agree with Bridges and Baillie who liked to escape from London. 'Like you', he wrote to Baillie,

I love country life and dislike any town and that especially for its bad and smokefoul air. Still I prefer London to any large town in these islands. ... In fog it is dreadful, but it has many fine days, and in summer—now I see you will scout this and fling yourself about, but I know it to be true—in summer its air is a balmy air, certainly in the West End. Then it—well the West End—is cheerful and quietly handsome, with many fine trees, and then there are so many resources, things to go to and hear and see and do. Everything is there. No, I think that very much may be said for life in London; though my dream is a farm in the Western counties, glowworms, new milk ... but in fact I live in Dublin.[37]

But the gloom and depression of these last two years of his life was enlivened by his humour. In his letters it appears beside complaints and self-pity. Some of it was strained, like his comments on the actress Romola Tynte:

Tyntes will fade, her name is not Tynte at all, (I blush to write it) her name is Potter. Her father is a clergyman of some sort. He is a stern parent, and here romance comes in again. He wanted her to marry against her will; she refused; and he told her to shift for herself. So the poor thing had to take to dramatic recitals. She works hard. . . . But some of the young men there said she had inadvertently come in her night-gown. They also said she 'made up well'. I hope the poor thing *will* 'make up well' for her hard usage by success.[38]

There are livelier examples:

I remember years ago that the organist at Liverpool found fault with a hymn of [Grace's]. . . . And see what became of him: he got drunk at the organ (I have now twice had this experience: it is distressing, alarming, agitating, but above all delicately comic; it brings together the bestial and angelic elements in such a quaint entanglement as nothing else can . . .). He was a clever young fellow and thoroughly understood the properties of narrow-necked tubes.[39]

But depression and hopelessness prevail: 'It seems to me I can not always last like this: in mind or body or both I shall give way', he told Bridges in September 1888. 'All I really need is a certain degree of relief and change; but I do not think that what I need I shall get in time to save me.' This admission was followed by an account of a young man who put his own eyes out, 'which was nevertheless barbarously done with a stick and some wire. The eyes were found among nettles in a field.'[40]

Probably the last letter he wrote in 1888 was to his mother on Christmas Eve, ending,

The weather is unseasonable; pleasant to the feel by day, but by night it robs of sleep, which has happened so often that I am spent with it and look forward to the country for more chance of sleeping. Man like vegetation needs cold and a close season once a year.[41]

# *'I wish then for death'*

The year 1889 started at Tullabeg, thirty miles or so from Monaster-evan, where Hopkins went on Christmas Eve. Everything about this Tullabeg retreat was inauspicious. On Christmas Eve he had written:

Unhappily I have to make my yearly retreat (for the past year). I say unhappily, not that I dislike a retreat, but it is a severe tax on my short holidays. I could not make it in the summer, because the Royal University kept me in attendance correcting proofs and in other trifling things.[1]

He had to break away from Monasterevan to journey to the bleak austerity of the geometrical, utilitarian barracks which housed the Irish novitiate at Tullabeg. It was set in the flat stretches of Irish midland bogs, where there were no walks except along plain roads, with rare tufts of black trees. In summer the countryside was pleasant enough, but in winter it was 'the right place for a composition of Hell'.[2]

Hopkins was on retreat from 1–6 January. He wrote:

How is it with me? I was a Christian from birth or baptism, later I was converted to the Catholic faith, and am enlisted 20 years in the Society of Jesus. I am now 44. I do not waver in my allegiance, I never have since my conversion to the Church. The question is how I advance the side I serve on. This may be inwardly or outwardly. Outwardly I often think I am employed to do what is of little or no use. Something else which I can conceive myself doing might indeed be more useful, but still it is an advantage for there to be a course of higher studies for Catholics in Ireland and that that should be partly in Jesuit hands; and my work and my salary keep that up.

He had to accept that 'the Catholic Church in Ireland and the Irish Province [of the Society of Jesus] in it and our College in that are greatly given over to a partly unlawful cause, promoted by partly unlawful means'. Against his will, his 'pains, laborious and distasteful, like prisoners made to serve the enemies' gunners, go to help on this cause'. As a result he did not feel that 'outwardly I do much good'. It was 'a mournful life' he led. In his thoughts he could separate the good from the evil, and 'live for the one, not the other: this justifies me but it does not alter the facts'. Yet it seemed to him that he 'could lead this life well enough if I had bodily energy and cheerful spirits. However these God will not give me. The other part, the more important, remains, my inward service.'

One evening during the retreat, he 'began to enter on that course of loathing and hopelessness which I have so often felt before'. In the past this had made him 'fear madness', and led him 'to give up the practice of meditating except, as now, in retreat'. But now it had come upon him again:

I could therefore do no more than repeat *Justus es, Domine, et rectum judicium tuum* and the like, and then being tired I nodded and woke with a start. What is my wretched life? Five wasted years almost have passed in Ireland. I am ashamed of the little I have done, of my waste of time, although my helplessness and weakness is such that I could scarcely do otherwise. And yet the Wise Man warns us against excusing ourselves in that fashion. I cannot then be excused; but what is life without aim, without spur, without help? All my undertakings miscarry: I am like a straining eunuch. I wish then for death: yet if I died now I should die imperfect, no master of myself, and that is the worst failure of all. O my God, look down on me.[3]

Within the context of a retreat Hopkins had been able to 'do no more than repeat *Justus es, Domine, et rectum judicium tuum*' in response to his feeling of loathing and hopelessness. In a poem he could do more. Instead of repeating the prescribed text, with its heavily ethical confirmation of the dogma *Justus es, Domine*, he was free to omit the unanswerable word *rectum* and qualify the absolute dogma with *verumtamen*. He could question, explore and express himself. On March 17 he wrote a poem:

> *Justus quidem tu es, Domine,*
> si disputem tecum; verumtamen justa loquar ad te:
> quare via impiorum prosperatur? etc (Jerem. xii 1.)

Thou art indeed just, Lord, if I contend
With thee; but, sir, so what I plead is just.
Why do sinners' ways prosper? and why must
Disappointment all I endeavour end?

Wert thou my enemy, O thou my friend,
How wouldst thou worse, I wonder, than thou dost
Defeat, thwart me? Oh, the sots and thralls of lust
Do in spare hours more thrive than I that spend,

Sir, life upon thy cause. See, banks and brakes
Now, leavèd how thick! lacèd they are again
With fretty chervil, look, and fresh wind shakes

Them; birds build—but not I build; no, but strain,
Time's eunuch, and not breed one work that wakes.
Mine, O thou lord of life, send my roots rain.

This has a unique method of proceeding for Hopkins. It starts with a text, from the Vulgate, as title, and then, like a sermon or a meditation, translates that text and moves away from it. It is too exploratory and personal to be either a sermon or a meditation. The dialogic use of texts and precursors creates a formal opening, but after the translation in the first three lines the voice modulates imperceptibly from that of Jeremiah to another voice. The poet has created a variation on an Ignatian exercise, a 'composition of person', by imagining himself as Jeremiah, a poet of exile. The date when he composed 'Justus quidem . . .' was 17 March, St Patrick's Day, which would make an Englishman feel especially isolated.

He had come to Dublin in the middle of an Irish row, and like Jeremiah often uttered his awareness of plots and rebellions all around. Jeremiah and the nineteenth-century speaker ask with one voice, 'Why do the wicked prosper?' Jeremiah's oppressors were opponents of God's cause, and omipotent, while he, God's spokesman, was the victim of their malice. Ten weeks before this poem Hopkins had written of his local Church, his Jesuit Province, and his College being largely concerned with an unlawful cause, and of his feeling that he was being made to serve his own enemies.

Hopkins and Jeremiah also shared an uneasy sense of having no audience, or of having one which does not respond. So they feel compelled to magnify lamentation. But still people will not hear, and suffering is increased. Recognition did not come to either until after their deaths. Hopkins did not often put himself within the skin of another person, admitting to Bridges that he doubted his powers as dramatist because he had 'so little varied experience'. Like Jeremiah he found it difficult for his words to reach unknown or unimagined people. As exiles they focused their minds on the enigma of suffering. Jeremiah had made religion a matter of personal relationship of the individual heart to God: before him Old Testament thought had been preoccupied with the relation of the nation to the Lord. It was not pain in general that moved Jeremiah to utterance, but his own distress. Commentators on this Jeremiah text have pointed to its logical difficulty: 'If Jeremiah knows beforehand that God is just, what is the use of all the argument?' This is also Hopkins's position: '*Thou* art just, but what *I* plead is just, and *I* (by implication) question *your* acts.' How can a chosen prophet argue with his God? It is this problem that brings the minds of Hopkins and Jeremiah together. Jeremiah had found a literary method of articulating the division between his sense of duty and his human nature. Hopkins's poem is a dramatic articulation of his division, though it takes the form of a contention between servant and master.

The voice changes from that of an unrewarded person resentfully asking 'why am I treated like this?' to that of a Romantic poet bewailing his lack of inspiration. The traditional posture of dissatisfied but faithful Christian changes to the traditional lament of a poet who has lost his creativity. There are two parts to this poem but they do not simply cohere. In the first, the protagonist 'I' is opposed to sinners, while in the second part, 'I' is opposed to external nature. The 'I' of the first part is a moral being contrasted with immoral surroundings, and in the second part an uncreative poet contrasted with his creative surroundings. One part is about morals and rewards, the other about art and artistic inspiration. But the lack of conventional unity is no flaw.

∽

In March Hopkins was again in a depressed state, perhaps as bad as that of four years earlier. The weather was wintry, 'it is now steadily snowing. But the political weather is beyond measure severer to me.'[4] In London, the Commission appointed six months ago to investigate the charges brought by *The Times* against Parnell had just heard the Irish journalist Richard Pigot confess that the letters and documents he had sold to the newspaper were forgeries. Parnell had not written the letter approving Burke's murder in the Phoenix Park in 1882. Hopkins's antagonism towards Parnell was probably increased by Gladstone's support for him. Hopkins would not believe the evidence that the papers were forged. He wrote to Bridges, who had just returned from Italy to England, condemning the leaders of the Liberal opposition and the Irish party in the same breath:

You return home to see your country in a pretty mess—to speak jokingly of matter for tears. And the grand old traitor must have come home almost or quite in the same boat with you. And what boobies your countrymen are! They sit in court at the Commission giggling, yea guffawing at the wretched Pigot's mess; making merry because a traitor to government and then a traitor to rebellion, both in a small way, has not succeeded in injuring an enemy of their own who is a traitor to government in a great way and a danger on an imperial scale; and that after a trial which has at least shewn the greatness and the blackness of the crime lawful government and the welfare of the empire have to contend with. And this I say as if Pigot were or employed the forger of those letters. For in my judgment, unless further evidence is forthcoming, those letters are genuine.[5]

This letter was written after Pigot had broken down in the witness-box, but before he made his full confession. Nevertheless, on 1 March, several days after the confession made to the Member of Parliament, Henry Labouchère, Hopkins wrote: 'I am not convinced however that the Facsimile letter, the one about the Phoenix Park, is not genuine after all.' Hopkins had to put up with Irish nationalists 'wild with triumph and joy over Pigot'. He wrote to his brother Lionel: 'If you knew the world I live in!'[6]

English civilization also had social and moral faults which were occupying Hopkins:

In general we cannot call ours a cleanly or a clean people: they are not at all the dirtiest and they know what cleanliness means, as they know the moral values, but they do not always practise it. We deceive ourselves if we think otherwise. And our whole civilisation is dirty, yea filthy, and especially in the north; for is it not dirty, yea filthy, to pollute the air as Blackburn and Widnes and St. Helen's are polluted and the water as the Thames and the Clyde and the Irwell are polluted? The ancients with their immense public baths would have thought even our cleanest towns dirty.[7]

To make matters worse, there seemed to Hopkins little likelihood of his leaving Ireland soon 'or perhaps ever'.[8] Everything was uncertain. Just before Easter, Francis de Paravicini, the old friend from Balliol and St Aloysius', was in Dublin for a short time, and met Hopkins once for a whole evening. Paravicini 'thought him looking very ill then, & said that he was much depressed',[9] and was so affected that on his return to England he attempted to persuade the Jesuit authorities to post Hopkins away from Ireland. He later said he thought he had succeeded.

On 3 April Hopkins wrote the second of his three last sonnets:

> The shepherd's brow, fronting forked lightning, owns
> The horror and the havoc and the glory
> Of it. Angels fall, they are towers, from heaven—a story
> Of just, majestical, and giant groans.
> But man—we, scaffold of score brittle bones;
> Who breathe, from groundlong babyhood to hoary
> Age gasp; whose breath is our *memento mori*—
> What bass is *our* viol for tragic tones?
> He! Hand to mouth he lives, and voids with shame;
> And, blazoned in however bold the name,
> Man Jack the man is, just; his mate a hussy.
> And I that die these deaths, that feed this flame,
> That . . . in smooth spoons spy life's masque mirrored: tame
> My tempests there, my fire and fever fussy.

Although most of the poem is taken up by the bitter vision of Man, the muted theme of personal creativity lies beneath the surface to float free in the final two lines. As in 'Justus quidem', a traditional scene is progressively displaced by individualized image and action, mirroring the poet's present circumstance. The final theme is predicted in 'a *story*/ Of just . . .'. And the summarizing last line of the octave, 'What bass is *our* viol for tragic tones?', utters the inadequacy of man's story for great art. Then the poet, as a mere representative of an inferior species, reveals himself, to disparage the poor poem he is writing, offering his poetic process as specimen of man's littleness. This ending is similar to that of the poem 'To R.B.', written nineteen days later.

There are four visions of life and death, in descending order: the divine, the fallen angels or super-men, man, and sub-man (or Hopkins); and in the last two lines the poem takes a new perspective which modifies what has gone before. The first vision is probably Moses'; his book, *Exodus*, is largely concerned with demands for signs as proof of divinity, the giving of those signs, and their worth duly acknowledged. The first vision I take to be that of Moses' acknowledgement of divine glory. Going down the scale comes the fall of Satan's angels, whose grandeur and nobility Hopkins has probably taken from *Paradise Lost*, where Milton makes that fall magnificent. Both these examples of magnificence are probably biblical, and yet this poem, like the other two last sonnets, is not narrowly religious. Hopkins uses Milton's version of biblical events to show that great literature could be made of such supernatural events because the subject-matter was worthy. But by contrast—and here Hopkins comes down to man—whereas an angel does fall (and the imagery is all vertical for angels, 'towers', 'from heaven'), man can only creep along towards his end, he has no fall at all in his going, in his voiding. Man's story is one of plain existence, breathing—until the breath becomes a gasp, which shows that breath in itself is no better than a reminder of death. The angels fell to appropriately tragic groans, man has only his inferior viol to accompany his fall. (The viol's inadequacies had caused its obsolescence.)

Then the vision narrows from that of man to the poet's own position as an example of that vision. But the personal intrusion of 'I that die . . . that feed' causes the poet's cynicism to rebound on to himself, and stopping the full flight of his rhetoric (the break signalled by the three dots in line 13) he puts his vision within another context, and there follows a description of his distorted and softened vision, 'in smooth spoons spy life's masque mirrored'. Hopkins lives a life so cloistered, he says, that the only reflections he sees of life outside himself are in spoons, whose surface distorts and smooths the reflection. In using this image Hopkins is saying that his art—this poem in particular—is an example of anamorphic art ('the technique of distorting an image in such a way that it can only be viewed in its correct form from a particular point or through its reflection in a curved mirror; viewed directly it appears as a shapeless and unintelligible mass'). Man's existence does not allow him peace, and the only way the poet can attain a satisfactory calm is to bring a distorted version of reality within the container of his art-form. Meaning—equated with his ability to deal with things—can be obtained only by distortion. By distorting the world he can place his own personal passions and dissatisfactions within that distorted image, and so take away their force ('tame/ My tempests there, my fire and fever fussy').

Hopkins's three last poems simultaneously tell and show. In 'The shepherd's brow' 'these deaths' are shown to 'feed this flame', the artistic process continuing while we partake of the poem; 'life's masque' is mirrored and distorted, and his emotions are calmed to die out with the fire's dying hiss, imitated in 'fussy'. His emotions have been tamed on the word 'fussy', and they have been tamed because this poem has been created. After 'fussy' the whole creation stands there, in place of the poet's emotions.

*❧*

Hopkins's last poem, 'To R. B.', was written five weeks after 'Justus quidem', nineteen days after 'The shepherd's brow', and just before the onset of his final illness. It was sent to Bridges after a week's work, though Hopkins did not usually send his poems to him so quickly. For the first time since the Oxford sonnets to Dolben, Hopkins had written a poem which was a letter. Its intention is to communicate with a particular person, not a larger unknown audience. As it serves the function of being the next step in the long and close relationship of Bridges and Hopkins, it takes for granted their mutual experience, and makes assumptions which would be more understandable to Bridges than to any outside reader.

Hopkins was able to express himself with greater candour and ease to Bridges than to anyone else. Bridges's robustness of physique and muse stimulated Hopkins in a way which Dixon's slender quality could not. Even Bridges's oscillation between agnosticism and a watery Anglicanism was a more typically English religious response, and perhaps more therapeutic to Hopkins than the strong faith of Dixon and Patmore.

### To R. B.

The fine delight that fathers thought; the strong
Spur, live and lancing like the blowpipe flame,
Breathes once and, quenchèd faster than it came
Leaves yet the mind a mother of immortal song.

Nine months she then, nay years, nine years she long
Within her wears, bears, cares and combs the same:
The widow of an insight lost she lives, with aim
Now known and hand at work now never wrong.

Sweet fire the sire of muse, my soul needs this;
I want the one rapture of an inspiration.
O then if in my lagging lines you miss

The roll, the rise, the carol, the creation,
My winter world, that scarcely breathes that bliss
Now, yields you, with some sighs, our explanation.

'To R. B.' is the only poem written with this degree of mature calm. It borrows the assumed, measured pace which Hopkins used only in his letters to Bridges. It has a more straightforward linear progression, without self-assertiveness and tension; it is at ease because of the two men's knowledge and experience of each other. Hopkins is authoritative here, without being strident.

The poem forms part of a running literary argument. Hopkins had once told Bridges that he was content to leave the fate of his poems in the hands of Providence, but he chose Bridges as his poetic executor. Bridges was the public he hoped to win over to his poems; he needed to persuade Bridges, more than anyone, of the validity of his poetic credo. The point at which they differed most in their theories of poetry concerned the question of originality. Bridges deliberately sought his poetic inspiration in classical literature, and there studied craft and technique. It was of secondary importance to him that ideas he refined in his poetry were borrowed. He tried to persuade Hopkins to read more literary works, to make his own poems more intelligible. Hopkins felt that the effect of studying masterpieces was to make him 'admire, and do otherwise', adding ironically that 'more reading would only *refine my singularity*, which is not what you want'.[10]

'To R. B.' is like the two previous poems in dealing with poetic creativity; with them it forms Hopkins's last quartets. But its tone is remarkably different. Hopkins presents the rationale of his poetic creative process in argument and manner which will strike home to

Bridges. For that reason he excludes direct religious reference, though it is essential to the other poems on poetic creativity. The striking sexual image, his most finely sustained metaphor, was conceived long before and constantly nurtured. When he was twenty he wrote of 'inspiration' as 'a mood of great, abnormal . . . mental acuteness, either energetic or receptive, according as the thoughts which arise in it seem generated by a stress and action of the brain, or strike into it unasked'. In an Ignatian meditation on Hell he described a glass-blower, probably at St Helen's glass-works, breathing on a flame: 'at once it darts out into a jet taper as a lance-head and as piercing too', and in 1888 wrote to Bridges that it was 'now years that I have had no inspiration of longer jet than makes a sonnet'.

Readers sometimes prefer this to others of Hopkins's poems without realizing that it fits in with Bridges's aesthetic theory of life as expressed in the account of his relationship with Hopkins in Book IV of *The Testament of Beauty*.[11] Hopkins's passion at his poetic aridity was more truly expressed by such images as 'strain', 'eunuch', 'tempests', and 'fever fussy' in the previous poems. But in 'To R. B.' the lament is translated into the Bridges language of 'scarcely breathes' and the graceful 'with some sighs' to bring the point home to one person. The poem is 'To R. B.' profoundly, it speaks in his language.

ఴ

A week after composing 'To R. B.', Hopkins enclosed it with a letter starting 'Dearest Bridges, I am ill to-day, but no matter for that as my spirits are good.' It was a cheerful long letter, but four days later Mrs Hopkins received a short one, the first he had written to her since his birthday greetings at the beginning of March:

My dearest Mother,

You have not heard from me for very long and now before going early to bed I write a line to say I am in some rheumatic fever, which comes very inconveniently when I shd. be and am setting my Papers for the examinations. I hope to be better tomorrow. If I am worse I may see the doctor. I am your loving son

Gerard.[12]

The day his mother received this Hopkins was writing to his father:

I am laid up in bed with some fever, rheumatic fever I suppose, but I am getting round. This is the first day I took to bed altogether: it would have been better to do so before. The pains are only slight, but I wish that Charlton Scott and Isidore de Lara would agree to plant a garden, a garden of sleep in my bed, as I am sleepy by day and sleepless by night and do not rightly sleep at all. I saw a doctor yesterday, who treated my complaint as a fleabite, a treatment which begets confidence but not gratitude.[13]

On receiving her letter Kate Hopkins, alarmed, replied and Gerard wrote back:

I am grieved that you should be in such anxiety about me and I am afraid my letter to my father, which you must now have seen and ought, it seems to me, to have had before this morning's letter was sent, can not much have relieved you. I am now in careful hands. The doctor thoroughly examined me yesterday. I have some fever; what has not declared itself. I am to have perfect rest and to take only liquid food. My pains and sleeplessness were due to suspended digestion, which has now been almost cured, but with much distress. There is no hesitation or difficulty about the nurses, with which Dublin is provided, I dare say, better than any place, but Dr. Redmond this morning said he must wait further to see the need; for today there is no real difference; only that I feel better.[14]

He was, and had long been, sad that he had seen so little of Lionel on his recent leave from China, because 'he and I have so many interests in common and shd. find many more in company'. Attempting to finish the letter on a less heavy note, he wrote:

It is an ill wind that blows nobody good. My sickness falling at the most pressing time of the University work, there will be the devil to pay. Only there is no harm in saying, that gives *me* no trouble but an unlooked for relief. At many such a time I have been in a sort of extremity of mind, now I am the placidest soul in the world. And you will see, when I come round, I shall be the better for this.

I am writing uncomfortably and this is enough for a sick man. I am your loving son

Gerard

Best love to all.

That was the last letter he wrote in his own hand to his family. By 8 May he was too weak to write, and the Minister, Fr Thomas Wheeler, took down a letter to Mrs Hopkins at his dictation:

My fever is a sort of typhoid: it is not severe, and my mind has never for a moment wandered. It would give me little pain were it not that while it was incubating I exposed my head to a cold wind, and took neuralgia which torments me now.

He thanked his parents for sending him flowers, which had revived in water and were on his table. He had continuous care from nurses sent from St Vincent's Hospital, on the corner of Stephen's Green, and because of the infectious nature of typhoid he had been moved from his own room upstairs in No. 86 to a larger and lighter room on the ground floor of No. 85, which had a separate entrance, and where some isolation could be imposed. 'Every condition is present', Kate Hopkins read in Fr Wheeler's unfamiliar script, 'that could make a serious thing trifling. The only complaint I have to make is that food and medicine keep coming in like cricket balls. I have in effect every attention possible.'[15]

The Hopkinses at Haslemere had failed to make sense of Gerard's reference to the Garden of Sleep in the previous letter, so he explained it now:

It is a sentimental song which I thought you must be sick and tired of in England as it has now come over to us. Charlton or Clement Scott is the Author of the words. By every post he receives enquiries as to his meaning which he cannot give except that the Garden of Sleep is a poppy-grown churchyard in the Corner of the Cliff. He gives a text from Ruskin to the effect that all pure natures admire bright colours, referring to the poppies. Accordingly with his genius and his purity he must be a good catch. The Composer is Isidore de Lara who is represented with Byronic look heavy moustaches and furred cloak. He sings his own songs. The piece is not without merit; but when you have heard it as often as I have taken beef tea and chicken jelly, you will have had enough of it.[16]

When Schubert was dying of typhoid he read James Fenimore Cooper's *The Last of the Mohicans*; Hopkins's solace was 'The Garden of Sleep', composed in a north Norfolk cottage, where Swinburne had written poems, by Clement Scott, the theatre critic:

> In my garden of sleep,
> Where red poppies are spread,
> I wait for the living,
> Alone with the dead.
>
> Was it hope or fulfilling
> That entered each breast,
> Ere death gave release,
> And the poppies gave rest?
>
> O life of my life,
> On the cliffs by the sea,
> By the graves in the grass,
> I am waiting for thee.[17]

Typhoid fever is 'an acute, often severe illness caused by *Salmonella typhi* and characterized by fever, headache, apathy, cough, prostration, splenomegaly [enlargement of the spleen], maculopapular rash [small spots], and leukopenia [abnormally low number of white blood cells]'.[18] From about 1820 to the passing of the 1866 Public Health Act, the overcrowded cities of Britain had suffered increasing deaths from infectious diseases. In 1861, the year Prince Albert developed typhoid, one person in three died of an infectious fever.[19] Dublin had been slower than most cities in Britain at cleaning up its dirt. The drains at 85 and 86 St Stephen's Green had not been inspected when the Jesuits moved in in 1883. Fr Darlington was told by the cook that two rats had been found in the stew-pot;[20] it seems likely that Hopkins had caught the fever from faulty sanitation or plumbing, contaminated water or food. No one else in the college caught it, and there was no typhoid at that time in the vicinity of Stephen's Green.

On 14 May Fr Wheeler wrote to Mrs Hopkins:

Many thanks for your letter of this morning and your too kind appreciation of any little thing we try to do to pilot dear Gerard through his straights.

You will be glad to hear that he still is keeping up his strength admirably and if I, a non-professional may judge, I think he is now well round the corner and on the high road to mending. . . . The Drs. are quite pleased with him, and the nurses cannot look at the possibility of his being anything but quite well in a short time now. He would like to dictate his letters to you—but I think it far safer to spare him that pleasure, and do it myself. Many prayers have been offered to heaven for him and I feel that they have been heard.

Hopkins's boots were sent to the repairers about the middle of May to be ready for his return to normal duties.[21]

In fact Hopkins had 'a very virulent form of typhoid and his whole digestive system was paralysed'.[22] There was a relapse. Peritonitis set in about 4 or 5 June.[23] The doctors were called early the next morning, and Hopkins's parents were summoned from England by telegrams. On hearing that they were coming, wrote Lahey, 'he appeared to dread their arrival, because of the pain it would give them to see him prostrate, but when the first interview was over, he expressed the happiness he felt at having them with him.' He received the Holy Viaticum several times, lastly on the morning of Saturday 8 June, with the final blessing and absolution. He died at half-past one the same day. There is a tradition among the Jesuits, which accords with the conventions of Victorian death-bed scenes, that after the final blessing and absolution 'he was heard two or three times to say "I am so happy, I am so happy" '.[24]

Funerals are great occasions in Ireland for showing the strength of the organization. Advertisements were put in the nationalist *Freeman's Journal*, the *Irish Times*, and the *Catholic Times*. Black-bordered envelopes were bought, gifts made to the nurses, Mr Farrell the undertaker was summoned, and a carriage ordered from O'Grady. The funeral took place at eleven in the morning of the following Tuesday, in the Jesuit Church on Upper Gardiner Street. According to the newspapers, the body was conveyed to the church from 85 Stephen's Green, but when Dr McCabe entered the church he learned that, because Fr Hopkins had died of a fever, his remains had not been brought into the church, the coffin on view being empty. On hearing this, Dr McCabe left the church and waited outside in his carriage.[25] High Mass and the Office for the Dead were celebrated by Fr Alfred Murphy SJ, assisted by Fr John Verdin SJ as Deacon, and Fr Thomas Kelly SJ as Sub-Deacon; the Master of Ceremonies was Fr Edward Kelly.

There were large numbers of 'clergymen, students of the college, and other mourners' present at the funeral. Manley Hopkins had not expected 'such "pompes funèbres"', and was touched by the fine arrangements. He had 'a nice chat afterwards with the celebrant'.[26] After the church ceremonies, the funeral cortège, 'of very large dimensions', proceeded on the long journey to the Prospect Cemetery, Glasnevin, over on the north side of the city. The cemetery was high-walled, with watch-towers to prevent body-snatchers. The Society of Jesuits had their own small rectangular burial plot, surrounded by heavy, spear-topped railings. The ground of the plot was bare, with no surface sign of individual graves: the bodies were buried one upon another. In the centre of one side was a single large granite cross; at its foot were engraved all the names of the Jesuits buried there, under the two heads *Sacerdotes* and *Coadjutores*. Above the names was the inscription: ORATE PRO DEFUNCTIS/ PATRIBUS ET FRATRIBUS/ SOCIETATIS JESU. The coffin was buried in the grave which had the official description: 'South, St Bridget's, B.h. 36^all.'[27] Over the head of the grave was the fringe of an evergreen oak, which grew just outside the corner of the burial plot.

The Deaths column of *The Nation* on Saturday 15 June reported the death of 'the Rev. Gerald [sic] Hopkins, S.J., F.R.U.I.', and the obituary read:

Death has removed another of the Catholic Fellows of the Royal University. It is only a couple of months since we announced the death of Professor Ormsby, a distinguished English convert, who had laboured long for Irish Catholic Education. Rev. Gerard Hopkins, S.J., whose sad death occurred on Saturday, had not only as long a record in Ireland as his colleague, but he has a brilliant one in his own land. He was a distinguished graduate of Balliol College, Oxford, and a profound classical scholar. The free opinions of Professor Jowett drove him from the Anglican Church and into the fold where he closed a short but distinguished career. After his conversion he joined the Jesuit Order. He was for a short period on the mission in Liverpool, but on the transfer of

University College to its present management he found congenial work within it. As a professor, he aimed at culture as well as the spread of the knowledge of the facts of philology. His tastes were not confined to literature. He was a discriminating art critic, and his aesthetic faculties were highly cultivated. One would have said, before his fatal illness came upon him, that he was just ripe in mind with all his work before him, for he was only forty-four years if [*sic*] age. He will be missed even from the ranks of the learned Order of which he was a member.[28]

# Post Mortem

The news of Hopkins's death reached his brothers and sisters in England on 10 June, and took everyone by surprise. They would have taken the boat for Dublin the previous week if they had suspected he was dying. Everard felt 'a terrible grief . . . that I could not see him once more', but was dissuaded by Arthur from attending the funeral. He consoled himself: 'Perhaps it is best for us to remember his sweet & beautiful face as we always knew it—not worn with sickness.'[1]

There came expressions of regret at having seen him so infrequently since he became a Jesuit. 'I cannot help sorrowing now', wrote Edward Bond, 'that for so many years I have seen so little of him.' R. L. Nettleship said: 'One of the bitterest reproaches that I make to myself is that I did not answer an affectionate letter which he wrote to me in 1885.' Baillie found it 'impossible to say how much I owe to him':

He is the one figure which fills my whole memory of my Oxford life. There is hardly a reminiscence with which he is not associated. All my intellectual growth, and a very large proportion of the happiness of those Oxford days, I owe to his companionship. It has been a subject of unceasing regret to me that circumstances have made me see so little of him since. His rare visits gave me the keenest pleasure, and were eagerly looked forward to.

Apart from his nearest relations, said Baillie, 'I never had so strong an affection for any one,' and he wrote later: 'If only I could believe that some day somewhere I should meet [Hopkins] again. But Edgar Poe's Raven gave the answer.'[2] Bridges's mother wrote to Mrs Hopkins that she had 'loved to know & feel that [Gerard] was Roberts real friend', and she would never forget 'his tenderness during Roberts illness'.

From Stewart in Dublin came a request for a photograph, and on receiving it he wrote:

I thought they worked a delicate man like him, far too much: I often heard from him that he *was* very hard worked, and he did not feed, as a working man ought; my own medical man often urges me to avoid long fasts, and to use small stimulants—Lithea water, flavored with a very little old Irish Whiskey that far famed spirit which Peter the Great of Russia was accustomed to style, 'Irish

Wine'—Of course *I* am old, & your Son was young, but still the truth lies in a moderate use of God's gifts, and I (who teach often 9 hours per diem, and am temperate in the extreme) know that to give lessons all day—alike in Music, as in the Latin tongue in which your dear Son was so thorough an adept,—'takes (as we say in Ireland) a great deal out of one'.

At University College Dublin, once the funeral was out of the way, a successor (another Englishman) was appointed to Hopkins's chair. The drains at No. 86 were inspected and found to be full of rats and filth, and a Mr McGarvey was engaged to carry out extensive plumbing operations costing £250.[3] Hopkins would soon be forgotten in Dublin. A student who was at the college twelve years after his death reported that, although there were at that time students who were 'sufficiently interested in literature', Hopkins was 'practically unknown to us', although 'I did hear of him as a Jesuit who wrote some verse'.[4]

♔

In his first letter of sympathy to Mrs Hopkins, Bridges was already thinking about Gerard's letters and papers. Less than two months later, following a suggestion from his friend, the printer C. H. O. Daniel, he wrote to Dixon: 'I have proposed to edit some of [Hopkins's] verses— Daniel to print them—*with a short memorial life of him.* I should be very grateful to you, if you would write your recollection of him as a boy at school, and also some account of your subsequent friendship.'[5] The book might consist of '*about* 40 pages of verse—lyrical—and I cannot tell how long the memoir is likely to be, but certainly not so much as this. It will be a unique volume, *privately* printed only', but there would also be a few copies for private sale, perhaps at £1 each.[6] On 11 October Bridges outlined to Daniel his scheme for the book:

1.  *Title*
2.  Portrait. aet 38
3.  Memoir pp.i–xlviii.
4.  Early poems as part of and same type as memoir. pp.xlix–lx.
5.  *Portrait* aet.20
6.  Title of poems and poems 1–50 pp.
6.B a long note by G.H. on his own poems 51–55
7.  Facsimile of handwriting
8.  Reproductions of Studies

Bridges was thinking in practical terms of the printing and binding operations and of the typefaces (by 1889 he had developed an expertise in typography and book design). He suggested that Daniel should start printing the poems as soon as possible. He would not promise to have finished the memoir before Christmas, but it might be ready by the end of January 1890.[7]

Since Bridges had planned the immediate publication of Hopkins's poetry, why was there the long delay until 1918? Although he had reached the conclusion that Hopkins's poems '*must* be printed', Bridges thought of the memoir as 'a disagreeable difficulty'.[8] At the end of May 1890 it was still unwritten. He tried several times to read Hopkins's letters, but 'always had put them down again without much progress'. He told Mrs Hopkins of two reasons for his delays and doubts. One was his respect for 'the understanding on which [the letters] were written', and the other was that he had found 'more distinct references to Gerard's state of mind than I remembered. One in particular is very plain. I always considered that he was over nervous about himself, and exaggerated his symptoms—which I think he did. In fact I think his mental condition was of this sort.' Bridges added, meaning that he did not feel that Hopkins's melancholia should be exposed in print: 'I may say that I have come round again to more my old state of feeling with regard to his memory.'[9]

One important reason for the delay in publishing the poems, and for Bridges's destruction of his own side of their correspondence, was his idea of the relationship between a poet's life and his poetry. He believed his own work should stand on its own, and that no biography should be written.[10] Also understandable, if unsympathetic, is the harshness he showed in his introduction towards Hopkins's eccentricities, motivated by the fear that he would harm his friend's reputation by appearing partisan.

Bridges found an alternative to the memoir: 'It happens that Bell is now publishing my poems. I thought that if I could make the occasion I would introduce some of Gerard's verse into the notes of that book and see if the critics noticed it.'[11] In another letter to Mrs Hopkins he said: 'The memoir must I think be given up for the present, but perhaps a short "preface" might be written which should put the poems out of the reach of criticism. I should not like the poems to be printed without some word of that sort, and it is a difficulty which a memoir would have got over.'[12] By August 1890 Bridges had found another reason for delay: readers with no knowledge of the theories behind Hopkins's strangenesses might dismiss the poems as 'freakishness'. He decided to expose his own poetic experiments to an unsympathetic public first, so that the work of his more extreme and innovative friend should not appear so strange. The delay, he wrote, would be the negligible one of about eighteen months.

During 1891–2, as Stanford conjectures,[13] Bridges 'met with several refusals to publish Hopkins's poems' in anthologies. In 1893 came a prime opportunity, which Bridges seized eagerly and sensitively. He was invited to prepare a selection of Hopkins's poems for Alfred Miles's anthology *The Poets and the Poetry of the Century.* He wrote to Mrs Hopkins: 'I can't tell whether Mr Miles, when he sees them, will not shy at them, as everyone else has done.'[14] Miles, however, wished 'to put Gerard alongside his recognised contemporaries', although, as Bridges said, 'the company is not *very* select.' Most of the poets in this volume were obscure (John Todhunter, Henry Clarence Kendall, George Augustus Simcox, John Payne, and Frederick W. H. Myers, for instance), but there were the established names, of Wilde, Kipling, Stevenson, Henley, Lang, Alice Meynell, Davidson, and Bridges himself (Yeats appeared among a host of writers mentioned briefly in a final chapter).

Probably encouraged by Bridges, Miles, in the short preface, singled out the 'interesting notice of the life and work of the late Gerard Hopkins and the selection of verse which, accompanying it, finds publicity for the first time in this volume'.[15] Bridges chose to print eight poems: parts of 'A Vision of the Mermaids' and, complete, 'The Habit of Perfection', 'The Starlight Night', 'Spring', 'The Candle Indoors', 'Spring and Fall', 'Inversnaid', and 'To R.B.' together with 'Thee, God, I come from' and the octaves of 'Justus quidem' and 'To seem the stranger', which appeared in the short introduction; an editor today would have difficulty in making a better selection. Before the introduction was in its final form, Dixon had visited Yattendon and objected 'that the notice ended with such decided fault-finding'. Bridges explained his purpose to Mrs Hopkins: 'I would much rather have it *said* that I was unkindly severe, than that I allowed my judgment to be led astray by my personal feelings, and I do not wish to leave anything but good for the critics to say.' He thought it as well that critics would 'have their eyes open to the defects'. Mrs Hopkins 'did not think the note at all unkind in tone'.[16]

Although the introduction was short, it gave a powerful picture of ways in which life, temperament, and poetry interacted:

His early verse shows a mastery of Keatsian sweetness, but he soon developed a very different style of his own, so full of experiments in rhythm and diction that were his poems collected into one volume, they would appear as a unique effort in English literature. Most of his poems are religious, and marked with Catholic theology, and almost all are injured by a natural eccentricity, a love for subtlety and uncommonness, well denoted by the Greek term το περιττόν [extravagance, excess]. And this quality of mind hampered their author throughout life; for though to a fine intellect and varied accomplishments (he was both a draughtsman and musician) he united humour, great personal charm, and the most attractive virtues of a tender and sympathetic nature,—which won him love wherever he went, and gave him zeal for his work,—yet he was not considered publicly successful in his profession.[17]

Bridges hoped and expected that this publication would result in 'a desire on the part of a good many persons to see more of Gerard's works',[18] but there was little reaction of any kind, except for a hostile review in the *Manchester Guardian*, which said: 'Curiosities like the verses of the late Gerard Hopkins should be excluded, while introductions like those contributed to his work by Mr. Bridges should, if possible, be multiplied, but employed on worthier objects.'[19] Bridges's caution had been justified; he felt discouraged not only from publishing an edition of Hopkins's poems, but also from inserting selections in other anthologies. Nevertheless, over the next few years he encouraged his friends and relatives to read, and if they were compiling anthologies, to take what they wanted of Hopkins's. In March 1897, for instance, Mary Coleridge, a poet and great-great-niece of S. T. Coleridge, wrote that during a visit of hers to Yattendon, Bridges 'got out a little thing by Gerard Hopkins. . . . At first I couldn't make head or tail of it, but after five minutes I began to perceive that it was extraordinarily fine.'[20] Five poems were printed in H. C. Beeching's 1895 anthology *Lyra Sacra*, one each in Beeching's *A Book of Christmas Verse* (published the same year), Mrs Waterhouse's *A Little Book of Life and Death* (1902), and Quiller-Couch's *The Oxford Book of Victorian Verse* (1912), besides the odd one or two in books of religious verse, such as *Prayers from the Poets* (1899), *Carmina Mariana* (1902), and *The Madonna of the Poets* (1906).

The Catholic poet Francis Thompson admired the 'very quiet and restrained little poem' 'Heaven-Haven',[21] but in the main the responses to Hopkins's poetry, carefully watched by Bridges and reported to Mrs Hopkins, were disappointing, and insufficient to encourage Bridges to proceed further. He waited.

In 1909 came the first signs of a stronger interest in Hopkins. In the January issue of the *Catholic World* there was a long and sympathetic article by Katherine Brégy.[22] Written from a Catholic point of view, it sometimes judged the religious content of poems rather than their artistic qualities ('The Blessed Virgin compared to the Air we Breathe' was called 'perhaps [Hopkins's] most ambitious effort'), but its praise was at times perceptive and balanced, and always enthusiastic:

Gerard Hopkins' exceedingly delicate and intricate craftsmanship—and not less the singularity of his mental processes—must, indeed, produce in many minds an impression of artificiality. Yet . . . in all the poems of his manhood there is a poignant, even a passionate sincerity. It is quite true that his elliptical and involved expression mars . . . more than one poem of rare and vital imagining. . . . [He] was to a certain degree self-centred in his dream of life. He was not an egoist; but it must be obvious that from first to last he was an individualist. And in our human reckoning the individualist pays, and then he pays again; and after that, in Wilde's phrase, he keeps on paying. Yet in the final count his chances of survival are excellent.[23]

It may have been this article which prompted two very different men to express an interest in editing the poems. One was Edmund Gosse, known by Bridges to be unsympathetic to Hopkins's poetry, and whom he considered motivated by opportunism and 'a total absence of scruple',[24] and the other was the Jesuit, Father Keating, who 'considered the Society of Jesus to be Hopkins's literary executors'. (The ownership of the copyright would not pass to the Society of Jesus until the rediscovery of Hopkins's will some forty years later.) Presented with no evidence of literary or editing competence, or of interest in Hopkins's poetry, on the part of the English Jesuits, and having knowledge of their past discouragement of Hopkins's muse, Bridges was 'sure they would make a dreadful mess of the whole thing',[25] and publish the poems only to boost the claims of their Church. He advised Mrs Hopkins to have nothing to do with Fr Keating.

Catholic interest in Hopkins was further increased by the reprinting in 1912 of Brégy's article in her book *The Poets' Chantry*. One reviewer commented: 'It is a standing reproach to English criticism that [Hopkins] . . . has hitherto received so small a meed of recognition, and it is little less than incredible that no collected edition of the poems of Hopkins has ever been published.'[26] Praise was still comparatively rare however, even among Catholics. A former friend of Hopkins at University College Dublin wrote that Brégy's comparison of Hopkins with Crashaw was improper: 'Father Hopkins' is a tiny harp indeed, and one which was very rarely handled with deftness.' Brégy's 'specimens of this writer seem curiously cacophonous'.[27] The infrequent references to Hopkins in non-Catholic publications were still usually disparaging; George Saintsbury wrote in 1910 that Hopkins 'never got his [poetical] notions into thorough writing-order. They belonged to the anti-foot and pro-stress division. . . . He never published any, and it is quite clear that all were experiments.'[28]

Eventually, in 1915, Longmans asked Bridges, now the Poet Laureate, to 'compile an anthology from the philosophers and poets designed to appeal to readers distressed by the war',[29] and in January 1916 *The Spirit of Man* was published, containing six poems and parts of poems by Hopkins. Bridges sent Mrs Hopkins (widowed since 1897) a copy: 'When I was doing the book it gave me great pleasure to think of the happiness that it might give you to see some of dear Gerard's work in really worthy company—where his queernesses appear as the personal sincerity which they were—and I gather from your letter that you like the book.'[30] At last, from significant numbers of the poetry-reading public, came the response for which Bridges had been waiting. In spite of a harrowing period in the first half of 1917 (when his house at Boars Hill burnt down, his son Edward was severely wounded in France, and his wife was in uncertain health), he wrote to Mrs Hopkins in September:

I have had lately some very authoritative appeals for the publication of all Gerard's poetical remains. The "Spirit of Man" has had a wide sale, and his poems in it have commanded a good deal of attention.

The other day Sir Walter Raleigh, whose judgment is very highly esteemed, said to me that Gerard's poems in the Spirit of Man were the only ones among the comparatively unknown writers whom I had introduced, which stood up alongside of the greater writers. And this afternoon I met a man who had just come from Petrograd, who said much the same thing. He was very urgent about having a complete edition.

He added, 'I think the time has come to publish all the poems.'[31]

That same month he wrote to Baillie (whom he had never met), telling him that 'the Oxford press was going to publish Hopkins' poems', that he was going to edit them, and that he would like Baillie 'to help him, and suggested that [Baillie] should visit him & give him advice about them'. Baillie replied 'that I would help him in any way I could but in effect declining the invitation to visit him. . . . I emphasized my extreme dislike of travelling.' Bridges gave no indication of how Baillie was to get from Oxford to his house at Chilswell: 'If he had been able to send for me to Oxford station I might have faced it, with courage and resolution like a soldier going to the trenches. But I am too old & tired to try new experiences. Also I doubt if I could be of any use to him in his editing.'

Baillie told Bridges that if a memoir was going to be written, he could show Bridges his Hopkins letters. Bridges thought that there might be some poems among the letters, but Baillie 'never had any, and in those early days rather discouraged H's poetic aspirations, & he naturally did not push his poems into my notice'. Baillie didn't 'like the poems one little bit'. 'One has to read them several times to see what they mean, &

doesn't see it then.' Baillie was repelled by the 'deliberate obscurity' of Hopkins's verse, which he thought 'much more involved than the most unintelligible parts of Sordello', and by Hopkins's 'whole theory of rhythm'. He added, 'I wish that he was alive, that I might tell him so.' Baillie liked to remember 'the Hopkins of the sixties ... before he became rather too serious and careworn', and he preferred the undergraduate poems.[32]

Mrs Hopkins was now often unable to write letters, and Bridges realised that it would be a battle to bring the book out in time for her to see and hold a copy. Her daughter Kate took over the correspondence about preparations for the book. He asked her what name the family wanted on the title page. He had 'a strong prejudice in favour of a short name' ('Gerard Hopkins'). The longer one was perhaps chosen because since 1892 there had been another Gerard Hopkins, Everard's son.[33] Bridges worked sometimes seven or eight hours a day on the editing. There would be 'some sort of note on every poem, always stating source and authority, and sometimes quoting from his own letters', but he was still against a memoir. Instead, he wanted to put 'a sonnet on back of title'.[34] The book, he told A. E. Housman, 'will be one of the queerest in the world, but it is full of genius and poetic beauty and will find its place'.[35]

꿍

In 1918, after a wait of thirty years, Bridges finally brought out the first edition of Hopkins's *Poems*. The first and last poems frame the book, making a reticent expression of Bridges's feelings about his relationship with Hopkins, and his sense of loving guardianship of the poems. The book finishes with a catch-all section, where the editor departs from the conjectured chronological order of the rest of the book and arranges the poems according to his fancy. The last poem in the book is the paraphrase of a passage from St Gertrude's *Life*, which utters the vow 'I will appear ... to him who ever thought with love of me/ Or ever did for my sake some good deed'. The first poem in the book is a prefatory sonnet by Bridges, describing how in January 1918 he was in his study preparing the poems—'thy lov'd legacy, Gerard'—for press, and felt in touch with the spirit of the dead poet.

Bridges's sonnet replied to his friend's last poem 'To R. B.', continuing their relationship, and using language borrowed from Hopkins. His own world was now a wintry one. He would counteract 'Hell wars without', the 'Great' war, by releasing in this book the spirit of Hopkins, now no longer torn by 'the war within', into 'far wonder and heavenward flight!'

> Our generation already is overpast,
> And thy lov'd legacy, Gerard, hath lain
> Coy in my home; as once thy heart was fain
> Of shelter, when God's terror held thee fast
> In life's wild wood at Beauty and Sorrow aghast;
> Thy sainted sense trammel'd in ghostly pain,
> Thy rare ill-broker'd talent in disdain;
> Yet love of Christ will win man's love at last.
>
>   Hell wars without; but, dear, the while my hands
> Gather'd thy book, I heard, this wintry day,
> Thy spirit thank me, in his young delight
> Stepping again upon the yellow sands.
>   Go forth; amidst our chaffinch flock display
> Thy plumage of far wonder and heavenward flight!

# ABBREVIATIONS USED IN THE NOTES

ↄ

## MANUSCRIPT MATERIAL

| | |
|---|---|
| Baillie | Letters of A. W. M. Baillie to Barbara Hannah, executors of the late B. Hannah. |
| Balliol | Balliol College, Oxford. |
| Bodleian | Bodleian Library, Oxford. |
| Campion Hall | Campion Hall, Oxford, as catalogued in *J.* 529–35. |
| 'Early Life' | Typescript of unfinished work by Humphry House, 'The Youth of Gerard Manley Hopkins', House family. |
| Farm Street | Jesuit Archives (English Province), Farm Street, London. |
| House | Hopkins papers of Humphry House, House family. |
| LHD | Hopkins family material, in possession of L. Handley-Derry |
| Lr. Leeson Street | Jesuit Archives (Irish Province), Lower Leeson Street, Dublin. |
| 'Memories' | Typescripts of Smith family 'Book of Memories', Hopkins collection, N. White (location of any originals unknown). |
| Stonyhurst | Stonyhurst College, Lancashire. |
| Texas | Humanities Research Center, Austin, Texas, as catalogued in Jerome Bump, 'Catalogue of the Hopkins Collection in the Humanities Research Center of the University of Texas', *HQ* 5: 4 (Winter 1979), 141–50. |
| White | Hopkins collection, N. White. |

## BOOKS

Place of publication London, unless otherwise stated.

| | |
|---|---|
| *AMES* | *All My Eyes See: the Visual World of Gerard Manley Hopkins,* ed R. K. R. Thornton (Sunderland, 1975). |
| *Dunne* | Tom Dunne, *Gerard Manley Hopkins: A Comprehensive Bibliography* (Oxford, 1976). |
| *ED* | John Ruskin, *The Elements of Drawing* (1857; New York, 1971). |

| | |
|---|---|
| *HTJ* | Alfred Thomas SJ, *Hopkins the Jesuit: the Years of Training* (1969). |
| *J.* | *The Journals and Papers of Gerard Manley Hopkins*, ed. Humphry House and Graham Storey (1959). |
| *L1* | *The Letters of Gerard Manley Hopkins to Robert Bridges*, ed. C. C. Abbott (1935, 1955). |
| *L2* | *The Correspondence of Gerard Manley Hopkins and R. W. Dixon*, ed. C. C. Abbott (1935, 1955). |
| *L3* | *The Further Letters of Gerard Manley Hopkins*, ed. C. C. Abbott, 2nd edn. (1956). |
| *OM* | Denis Meadows, *Obedient Men* (1955). |
| *P.* | *Gerard Manley Hopkins* (The Oxford Authors), ed. Catherine Phillips (Oxford, 1986). |
| *P4* | *The Poems of Gerard Manley Hopkins*, 4th edn. (rev. 1970), ed. W. H. Gardner and N. H. MacKenzie. |
| *S.* | *The Sermons and Devotional Writings of Gerard Manley Hopkins*, ed. Christopher Devlin SJ (1959). |
| *SLRB* | *The Selected Letters of Robert Bridges*, ed. Donald E. Stanford, 2 vols. (1983). |

## JOURNALS

| | |
|---|---|
| *HQ* | *The Hopkins Quarterly.* |
| *HRB* | *The Hopkins Research Bulletin* |
| *LN* | *Letters and Notices* (privately published by the Society of Jesus, English Province). |
| *MLR* | *Modern Language Review.* |
| *VN* | *The Victorian Newsletter.* |
| *VP* | *Victorian Poetry.* |
| *VS* | *Victorian Studies.* |

# NOTES

࣭ᔅ

## 1. THE BOY, 1844–1863

### *1. Kate Smith and Manley Hopkins*

1. The primary sources for Kate Smith's early life are the 5 short accounts of their childhood written *c.*1883–5 by Kate Hopkins and 3 of her brothers and sisters ('Memories'). I have also been guided by Humphry House's work in *J.* and 'Early Life'.
2. *J.* 369–70.
3. Document in possession of LHD; *J.* 313 and 'Early Life'.
4. Information on average adjusting, and on Manley Hopkins and William Richards as average adjusters, from D. J. Wilson, *100 Years of the Association of Average Adjusters, 1869–1969* (1969); Douglas Owen, 'Ship Insurance', in *Ships and Shipping* [*c.*1912], 136–7; Manley Hopkins, *A Handbook of Average* (1857); Manley Hopkins, 'The Position and Duties of Average Adjusters', *From the Chair: Addresses by Chairmen of the Association of Average Adjusters* (1976); other material belonging to Robin Craig, to whom I owe thanks for specialist knowledge. Place of publication for all works cited is London, unless otherwise indicated.
5. *L1* 111.
6. Both ed. Orby Shipley; published in 1869 and 1865.
7. Campion Hall MS G I(a).
8. *J.* 48, 202–3, 217–18.
9. Pp. 20–1.
10. Pp. 28–9.
11. *S.* 123.
12. *The Wreck of the Deutschland*, Stanzas 20 and 21.
13. Family tree compiled by Paul R. A. de Giberne (LHD).
14. Manley Hopkins, *Spicilegium Poeticum* [1892], 166.
15. *Spicilegium Poeticum*, 51–2.

### *2. Stratford*

1. 'Early Life', 65.
2. Census returns for 1851.
3. *L3* 68.
4. 'Cophetua', *Spicilegium Poeticum*, 76–8.
5. William Foltz, 'Further Correspondence of Manley Hopkins', *HQ* 9: 2 (Summer 1982), 75; *L3* 257.

6. Health conditions in Stratford from 'Public Health in Newham: A chronological survey' (Newham Library Service, 1985).

## 3. Hampstead

1. Material on Hampstead mainly from: the Local History Library (London Borough of Camden), Swiss Cottage Library, and the Holborn Library; particularly: Hampstead Directories for 1854, 1873, and 1885–6; files of the *Hampstead and Highgate Express*; special collections: Bellmoor Collection (material collected by Thomas J. Barrett) and 'Maps and Plans'; Minutes of Hampstead Borough and Vestry; Census Returns 1851–86; Hampstead Society records. F. E. Baines (ed.), *Records of the Manor, Parish, and Borough of Hampstead to December 1889* (1890); Thomas J. Barrett, *The Annals of Hampstead* (1912); Christina M. Gee, *Hampstead and Highgate in Old Photographs 1870–1918* (1974); William Howitt, *The Northern Heights of London* (1869); Olive Cook and others, 'Constable's Hampstead' (Camden History Society, 1978); James Kennedy, *The Manor and Parish Church of Hampstead and its Vicars* (1906); Ian Norrie and Dorothy Bohn, *Hampstead: London Hill Town* (1981); Mavis and Ian Norrie (eds.), *The Book of Hampstead* (1968); George W. Potter, *Hampstead Wells* (1904); M.L.G.B., 'Parish Church of St John-at-Hampstead, A Short History' (n.d.); Don Scott, *The Nature of Hampstead Heath* (1979); Christopher Wade, *The Streets of Hampstead* (1972); Ralph Wade, 'Hampstead Heath' (1979); *Camden History Review*, 1–10 (1973–82), particularly Dr Barbara Ely, ' "Till Death through Ripe Old Age", Hampstead's First Medical Officer of Health, 1856–79', 3 (1975), 26–9. Personal research in and around Hampstead.

2. [Mary Bennett,] 'Ford Madox Brown, 1821–1893', Catalogue to Walker Art Gallery Exhibition (Liverpool, 1964), 18–20; 'Madox Brown's Diary Etc 1844–56', in *Praeraphaelite Diaries and Letters*, ed. William Michael Rossetti (1900), 111–12; Christopher Wade, 'A Pre-Raphaelite in Hampstead', *Camden History Review*, 2 (1974), 16–17.

3. Bodleian MS Eng. poet. e. 190, fo.54.

4. Census returns, Swiss Cottage Library.

5. Farm Street, Lahey Papers.

6. 'Early Life', 131; concerning the Hopkins family religion I have been guided by 'Early Life', particularly the chapter 'St John's and St Michael's'.

7. See 'On one who borrowed his sermons', *P.* 33; Katharine Tynan, *Memories* (1924), 157.

8. 'Early Life', 132.

9. *L3* , 207.

10. Records of the Hampstead Vestry and Public Library, in the Local History Library, Swiss Cottage.

11. Eugene R. August, 'A Checklist of Materials Relating to the Hopkins Family in the State Archives of Hawaii', *HQ* 6: 2 (Summer 1979), 64.

12. August, 'Checklist', 64, and Foltz, 'Further Correspondence', 67.
13. Foltz, ibid. 52–3, prints the complete letter in which Manley Hopkins, in a reproachful but dignified tone, responds to his dismissal.
14. Campion Hall MS Journal.
15. Texas MS FA 49.
16. Farm Street, Lahey Papers.
17. Scrap of a letter in Texas, from Laura Smith to Kate Hopkins, FA 29–36.
18. *S.* 123.
19. 'Early Life', 81.
20. Texas MSS HA 26, 32; FA 17–24.
21. Texas MS HA 23.
22. [Madeline and Humphry House,] 'Books belonging to Hopkins and his Family', *HRB* 5 (1974), 34–5.
23. 'Spring'.
24. *J.* 66–7.
25. *OM* 143.
26. Lance Sieveking, *The Eye of the Beholder* (1957), 278.
27. *L3* 247–8.
28. On Hopkins family music I follow 'Early Life', chapter 'Boyhood', 70–8.
29. *J.* 44.
30. *L1* 120; *J.* 274.
31. *L3* 371.
32. *J.* 277.

### 4. Highgate

1. Material on Highgate and the school from; *Highgate School Register, 1838–1938* (4th edn., J. Y. Boreham, 1938); *Highgate School Register, 1838–1950* (5th edn., Rodney C. Tucker, 1950); *Highgate School Register, 1833–1964* (6th edn., Patrick Hughes and Ian F. Davies, 1965); Sam Eidinow, 'John Bradley Dyne: Second Founder', *The Cholmeleian*, 405 (1983–4), 27–30; C. A. Evors, *The Story of Highgate School* (2nd edn., 1949); Sydney W. Kitchener, *Old Highgate: The Story of a London Village and Public School* (1972); R. L. Starkey 'Library Register—Highgate School, March 1860–November 1862', *HRB* 6 (1975), 22–6; items from the Highgate School archives, particularly governors' minute-books; issues of *The Cholmeleian* and of the *St Michael's Highgate Parish Magazine*, particularly those for 1865 containing the articles 'Sir Roger Cholmeley's School, History of the School' and 'Sir Roger Cholmeley's School, Tercentenary'; W. Charles Sargent, 'Young England at School: Highgate School', *Ludgate Illustrated Magazine*, 7 (1894), 274–86; John Chandos, *Boys Together: English Public Schools 1800–1864.* (1984). Issues of the *Camden History Review*, esp. Joan Schwitzer, 'Renaissance on the Northern Heights: Early Victorian Highgate and its Schools', 2 (1974), 9–13, and 'The Struggle for Pond Square: Conservation versus Development in Victorian Highgate', 3 (1975), 6–9; Richard Franklin, 'When the Farming Had to Stop: Changing Trades in

Nineteenth Century Highgate', 1 (1973), 24–5; 'Early Life'; material in the *AMES* exhibition; personal research in Highgate village and School. I am grateful to the Highgate Literary and Scientific Institution (especial thanks to Mrs G. Gosling), T. G. Mallinson (Record Keeper of Highgate School), the headmaster of Highgate School, and Sam Eidinow (former archivist of Highgate School).

2. Letter from C. N. Luxmoore to Arthur Hopkins, *L*3 394–6; this extract 394.
3. Campion Hall MS B. II.
4. 'Early Life', 114.
5. *J*. 6–7.
6. Material on Hopkins at the school from Cyril Hopkins, 'Biographical Notice of the Life and Work of Marcus Clarke', unpublished MS, Mitchell Library (A1971), Sydney; *L*3 1–16, 394–6; Humphry House's work in *J*. and 'Early life'; material in House papers.
7. Material on Marcus Clarke from: Cyril Hopkins, 'Biographical Notice'; letter of Hopkins to Herr-Doktor Müncke, *HRB* 4 (1973), 3–6; *The Marcus Clarke Memorial Volume*, ed. Hamilton Mackinnon (Melbourne, 1884); *Marcus Clarke*, ed. Michael Wilding (Queensland, 1976); Brian Elliott, *Marcus Clarke* (1958); Brian Elliott, 'Gerard Hopkins and Marcus Clarke', *Southerly*, 8 (1947), 218–27. I am grateful to Christopher Worth and Mary McDonnell for undertaking researches for me in Australia.
8. Hopkins, 'Biographical Notice', ch. 3, p. 8.
9. *L*1 132.
10. *P*. 11–15.
11. *L*3 13–14.
12. *HRB* 4 (1973), 3–6.
13. *L*2 12.
14. *L*2 4.
15. *L*3 394.
16. *L*3 395.
17. *L*3 396.
18. *L*3 8.
19. *L*3 5–20.
20. *L*3 3–4.
21. *L*3 3.
22. *L*3 2–3.
23. Balliol, Membership 7, 'Record books kept by those involved in admissions'. By the side of Hopkins's name was first written 'for Mich. 62?', which was then crossed through. The source of Hopkins's application for a place is given as 'M.H. 11/59'.

## II. THE STUDENT, 1863–1868

### 5. Balliol College

1. 'Nitram Tradleg' [Martin Geldart], *A Son of Belial* (1882), 130. The Balliol Scholarship examination described in detail by Martin Geldart on pp. 129–34 took place not in Nov. 1862, as he states, but in Oct. the same year, and was the first one for which Hopkins sat. Geldart not only masks the real-life people and places with thinly disguised names (e.g. T. Nash becomes 'Brygmos Odonton', Hopkins is 'Gerontius Manley', F. H. Jeune becomes 'Young', and Cowley Road is 'Cattlemead Road'), but he also slightly alters dates. In quotations I have silently altered the fictitious to the real names.

2. *L3* 70.

3. [Geldart,] *A Son of Belial*, 131–2.

4. Ibid. 133–4.

5. A limited facsimile edition of the MS of 'A Vision of the Mermaids', showing the drawing and the poem, was published by Oxford Univ. Press in 1929.

6. *L3* 15–16.

7. *L3* 15.

8. 14 Feb. 1863, 11.

9. Extensive use has been made in Pt. II of the records of Balliol College. It is impractical to detail every instance, but the following were found to be the most useful (references are to 'A List of Records in the Custody of the Archivists, August 1981', Balliol); Government C (English register of college meeting minutes, 1794–1875); D. 14 (Balliol College compositions for university dues ... 1860–71); F. 11 (19, bursar's account, 1856–66); Membership 4 (register of admissions and degrees 1834–93); Membership 7 (record books kept by those involved in admissions ... first series i, 1858–95, tutors' book); Membership 9 (records of residence, probably butler's books, iv, 1853–95); Membership 12 (room books and lists, i, 1857–79); bursar's books, series I C (bursar's battell books, 1856–67), D (bursar's buttery books, 1863–7), K (bursar's books of gate fines, 1862–71), N (bursar's register of residence books, 1864–75), W (clerk of the kitchen's books of meals, 1864–6, 1866–8); bursar's books, series II A (bursar's final account books, 1845–83), F (bursar's books of caution money, 1841–66, 1867–78), H (bursar's arrears books, 1852–69), W (bursar's books re departments, kitchen: an account book 1859–65); miscellaneous bursary papers, including 26a–d, letters to Wall as bursar); Studies and discipline (I, collections log-books, iv a, 1852–68); Sport; General miscellany (5, miscellaneous 19th-c. material). I am particularly grateful to Dr John Jones (Dean and Archivist), Dr Penelope Bulloch (Librarian), Mr Vincent Quinn, and Mr Alan Tadiello.

10. Balliol, rooms book 1857–79, from which other information on precise rooms of students and tutors is taken.

11. Letter to his mother, 22 Apr. 1863, *L*3 68–75; most of Hopkins's comments and the details of his actions used in this chapter come from this letter.
12. Balliol, register of admissions and degrees 1834–93.
13. Details of students' careers used in Pt. II are taken from the Balliol College register.
14. Baillie to Barbara Hannah, 24 and 26 June 1916.
15. In 'Emerson', *Discourses in America* (1896), 139–42.
16. *The Life of John Henry Cardinal Newman* (1912), 63.
17. Quoted ibid. 64.
18. Bodleian MS Eng. misc. a. 8.
19. Balliol, Studies and discipline I, collections log-books, iv a.
20. Interviews with Mr Dennis Pargeter, formerly an Oxford scout, 1984–5.
21. [Thomas Hughes,] *Tom Brown at Oxford* (1861), 8.
22. 'Cuthbert Bede B.A.' [Revd Edward Bradley], *The Adventures of Mr Verdant Green* (1853–7; 1982 edn.), 34.
23. *J.* 6–7.
24. Statistics compiled from the Balliol College register.
25. The main printed and other sources for the accounts of Balliol life in Pt. II are: Vincent Amcotts and W. R. Anson, *Echoes of the Greek Drama*, I. *Pentheus: A Burlesque* (Oxford, 1866); *A Memoir of the Right Honourable Sir William Anson*, ed. Herbert Hensley Henson (Oxford, 1920), esp. ch. 2; Hugh Arnold, 'The Glass in Balliol College Chapel' (n.p., n.d.); 'Balliol College', repr. from *The Victoria History of the Counties of England*: *Oxfordshire, III* (n.d.); issues of *Balliol College Annual Record; Balliol Studies*, ed. John Prest (1982), particularly: John Jones, 'Sound Religion and Useful Learning: The Rise of Balliol under John Parsons and Richard Jenkyns, 1798–1854'; Peter Hinchcliff, 'Benjamin Jowett and the Church of England: or "Why Really Great Men are Never Clergymen" '; and Carl Schmidt, 'Classical Studies at Balliol in the 1860's: The Undergraduate Essays of Gerard Manley Hopkins'; H. W. Carless Davis, *A History of Balliol College*, rev. R. H. C. Davis and Richard Hunt, and supplemented by Harold Hartley and others (Oxford, 1963); [John Jones,] *Balliol College Oxford: A Brief History and Guide* (Oxford, 1982); *The Balliol Rhymes*, ed. J. W. Mackail (Oxford 1939); John Andrew Doyle, *Essays on Various Subjects*, ed. W. P. Ker (1911); Balliol, MS letters of C. A. Fyffe to R. L. Nettleship; [Geldart], *A Son of Belial*; A. B. Downing, *From Max Müller to Karl Marx: A Study of E. M. Geldart*, Transactions of the Unitarian Historical Society, 14: 4 (Oct. 1970); *Henry Scott Holland: Memoirs and Letters*, ed. Stephen Paget (1921); Geoffrey Faber, *Jowett: A Portrait with a Background* (1957); Evelyn Abbott and Lewis Campbell, *The Life and Letters of Benjamin Jowett* (1897); Balliol, a box of Jowett miscellanies; W. L. Newman, 'Reminiscences of the Late Master of Balliol' (typescript), Balliol; 'Reminiscences of Jowett', by A.L.S., repr. from *The Blue Book* (n.p., n.d.); 'Mr Jowett and Oxford Liberalism', *Blackwood's Edinburgh Magazine*, 161: 979 (May 1897), 721–32; [E. A. MacCurdy,] ' "The

Master" from the Angle of Eighteen', (n.p., n.d.); William M. Hardinge, 'Some Personal Recollections of the Master of Balliol', *Temple Bar*, 407 (Oct. 1894), 173–85; A. R. MacEwen, 'Benjamin Jowett', typescript of lecture delivered in Edinburgh [1901–2?]; W. L. Lechmere, 'Oxford, 1863–1867', *Oxford and Cambridge Review*, 19 (May 1912); A. G. C. Liddell, *Notes from the Life of an Ordinary Mortal* (2nd edn., 1911); Robert Ranulph Marett, *A Jerseyman at Oxford* (1941), esp. chs. 5 and 6; R. L. Nettleship, *Memoir of Thomas Hill Green* (1906); Andrew Lang, *Life, Letters, and Diaries of Sir Stafford Northcote* (new edn., Edinburgh, 1891); Melvin Richter, *The Politics of Conscience: T. H. Green and his Age* (1964), esp. ch. 3; J. W. Mackail, *James Leigh Strachan-Davidson, Master of Balliol, A Memoir* (Oxford, 1925); *The Memoirs of John Addington Symonds*, ed. Phyllis Grosskurth (1984); Horatio F. Brown, *John Addington Symonds: A Biography* (1903); Revd P. A. Wright-Henderson DD, *Glasgow and Balliol and Other Essays* (1926).
26. George Saintsbury, *A Second Scrap Book* (1923), 96–7.
27. L3 74.

## 6. *Freshman Allegiances*

1. Material used in Pt. II concerning Oxford in the 1860s mainly from: Edward C. Alden, *Alden's Oxford Guide* (various edns., Oxford); T. F. Althaus, 'Recollections of Mark Pattison', repr. from *Temple Bar* (Jan. 1885); Mavis Batey, *Alice's Adventures in Oxford* (1980); [Bradley,] *The Adventures of Mr Verdant Green*; John Betjeman, *An Oxford University Chest* (Oxford, 1938; 1979 edn.); John Betjeman and David Vaissey, *Victorian and Edwardian Oxford from Old Photographs* (1971); E. G. W. Bill, *University Reform in Nineteenth-Century Oxford: A Study of Henry Halford Vaughan* (1973); *Guide to the Oxford Botanic Gardens* (Oxford, 1971); Rhoda Broughton, *Belinda* (1883); George C. Bompas, *Life of Frank Buckland* (n.d.); Rt. Revd W. Boyd Carpenter, *Some Pages of My Life* (1911); Lewis Carroll, *Alice's Adventures in Wonderland* and *Through the Looking-Glass and What Alice Found There* (1982 edn.); A. R. Woolley, *The Clarendon Guide to Oxford* (Oxford, 1979); *Life and Letters of Mandell Creighton*, by His Wife (2 vols., 1904); Alan Crossley, Chris Day, and Janet Cooper, *Shopping in Oxford: A Brief History* (Oxford, 1983); James Stevens Curl, *The Erosion of Oxford* (Oxford, 1977); Percy Gardner, *Oxford at the Cross Roads, A Criticism of the Course of Literae Humaniores in the University* (1903); Peter Green, *Kenneth Grahame, 1859–1932: A Study of his Life* (1959); Christopher Hobhouse, *Oxford As It Was and As It Is To-day* (1948); Christopher Hollis, *The Oxford Union* (1965); [Thomas Hughes,] *Tom Brown at Oxford* (new edn., 1874); Charles Edward Mallett, *A History of the University of Oxford* (3 vols., 1924–7, esp. vol. iii); Jan Morris, *Oxford* (Oxford, 1965, 1979); Jan Morris (ed.), *The Oxford Book of Oxford* (Oxford, 1978, 1984); Robert G. Neville and Tony Sloggett, *Oxford As It Was* (Nelson, 1979); [R. S. Copleston *et al.*,]

*The Oxford Spectator* (1869); Mark Pattison, *Memoirs* (1885); Ian Scargill and Alan Crosby, *Oxford and its Countryside* (Oxford, 1982); A. V. Simcock, *The Ashmolean Museum and Oxford Science, 1683–1983* (Oxford 1984); *In Praise of Oxford: An Anthology in Prose and Verse*, comp. Thomas Seccombe and H. Spencer Scott (1912); Revd W. E. Sherwood, *Oxford Yesterday: Memoirs of Oxford Seventy Years Ago* (Oxford, 1927); *The Shotover Papers* (Oxford, 1875?); *Oxford: Its Life and Schools*, ed. A. M. M. Stedman (1887); Revd W. Tuckwell, *Reminiscences of Oxford* (1907); Mrs Humphry Ward, *A Writer's Recollections* (1918) and *Helbeck of Bannisdale* (1898); J. Wells, *Oxford and its Colleges* (10th edn., 1913). Among the many individuals who have provided material or other help are Colin Harris of the Bodleian Library, Geoffrey Pargeter of Blackwell's, and members of the staff of the Oxford Botanic Gardens.

2. *L*3 71; details of Hopkins's actions in this chapter from *L*3 68–79.
3. Material used in Pt. II concerning the religious struggles in Oxford and Britain at large mainly from: [Brotherhood of the Holy Trinity,] *Manual of Rules and Prayers for the Use of The Most Holy Trinity* (n.p., n.d.); [BHT,] 'B.H.T. Rule of Life', bound with BHT lists for 1861, 1864, and Lent 1870 (n.p., n.d.); [R. M. Benson,] 'The Principles of Brotherhood', an address read before the Annual Chapter of the Brotherhood of the Holy Trinity, 14 June 1865 (n.p., n.d.); Raymond Chapman, *Faith and Revolt; Studies in the Literary Influence of the Oxford Movement* (1970); Raymond Corrigan SJ, *The Church and the Nineteenth Century* (Milwaukee, Wis., 1938); Gertrude Donald, *Men Who Left the Movement* (1933); Geoffrey Faber, *Oxford Apostles: A Character Study of the Oxford Movement* (1933); W. E. Gladstone, *Rome and the Newest Fashions in Religion: Three Tracts* (1875); John Octavius Johnston, *Life and Letters of Henry Parry Liddon* (1905); R. W. Macan, 'Religious Changes in Oxford During the Last Fifty Years', paper read before the Oxford Society for Historical Theology (1918); [Thos. Murphy,] *The Position of the Catholic Church in England and Wales During the last Two Centuries* (1892); John Henry Cardinal Newman, *Apologia Pro Vita Sua*, ed. A. Dwight Culler (Boston, 1956); Cardinal Newman, *Loss and Gain: The Story of a Convert* (1848; ed. Alan G. Hill, 1986); *Newman's Apologia Pro Vita Sua: The Two Versions of 1864 and 1865, Preceded by Newman's and Kingsley's Pamphlets*, introd. Wilfrid Ward (1931); *Newman: Prose and Poetry*, ed. Geoffrey Tillotson (1957); Meriol Trevor, *Newman's Journey* (1974); Maisie Ward, *Young Mr Newman* (1948); Wilfrid Ward, *The Life of John Henry Cardinal Newman* (1927); E. R. Norman, *Anti-Catholicism in Victorian England* (1968); Edward Norman, *The English Catholic Church in the Nineteenth Century* (Oxford, 1984); Rowland E. Prothero, *The Life and Correspondence of Arthur Penrhyn Stanley, DD* (1893); E. B. Pusey, *The Church of England a Portion of Christ's One Holy Catholic Church ... An Eirenicon* (Oxford, 1865); *The Story of Dr Pusey's Life*, by the author of 'Charles Lowder' (1900); Bernard M. G. Reardon, *Religious Thought in the Victorian Age*

(1971, 1980); John D. Root, 'The "Academia of the Catholic Religion": Catholic Intellectualism in Victorian England', *VS* 23: 4 (Summer 1980), 461–78; John Tulloch, *Movements of Religious Thought in Britain During the Nineteenth Century* (1885, 1971); 'Vicesimus', *H. N. Oxenham: Recollections of an Old Friend* (Manchester, 1888); Mrs Humphry Ward, *Robert Elsmere* (1888); Wilfrid Ward, *William George Ward and the Catholic Revival* (1893); Robert Lee Wolff, *Gains and Losses: Novels of Faith and Doubt in Victorian England* (1977).

4. *A Son of Belial*, 154.
5. L3 73–4.
6. Information on Hopkins's set books, prescribed reading, teachers, members of his tutorial and class groups, and reports on his progress mainly from Balliol, Studies and discipline: collections log-books; iv a, 1852–68.
7. L3 73.
8. Ibid.
9. L3 76.
10. L3 72–3.
11. L3 74.
12. Ward, *The Life of John Henry Cardinal Newman*, 76.
13. L3 74.
14. Material on the Union from Hollis, *The Oxford Union*, and *The Oxford Spectator*.
15. Brown, *John Addington Symonds*, 72.
16. Balliol, bursar's books series I. W, the clerk of the kitchen's book of meals.
17. L3 79.
18. L3 78.
19. *A Son of Belial*, 138–9.
20. L3 75.
21. L3 76.
22. Ibid.
23. L3 77.
24. Ibid.
25. Bodleian MS Eng. poet. e. 90.
26. L3 78.
27. L3 207.
28. L3 78.
29. L3 79.
30. L3 80–1.
31. L3 207.
32. L3 200.
33. L3 81.
34. Balliol, Government C, English register of college meeting minutes, meeting of 23 Oct. 1866.
35. 'Loyal Whisper to a Royal Recluse', 21 Mar. 1863.
36. L3 200.

### 7. *Vital Truths of Nature: Hopkins and Ruskin*

1. Main Isle of Wight sources for this chapter are: *L*3 199–202; sketch-books and loose sketches of Arthur and Gerard Hopkins; *Ordnance Survey of the Isle of Wight and Part of Hampshire*, sheet 10 (printed 1909 from electrotype plate of 1865); *Ordnance Survey Map of Shanklin*, 25.344 in. to 1 m. (1878, but survey carried out in 1862–3); G. Harvey Betts, *Shanklin as a Health Resort* [1872]; Lindsay Boynton, *Georgian and Victorian Shanklin: A Pictorial History 1700–1900* (Shanklin, 1973); John Bridge, *A Visit to the Isle of Wight by Two Wights* (1884); W. B. Cooke, *Bonchurch, Shanklin and the Undercliff* (1849); issues of *The Isle of Wight Times*; Alan G. Parker, *The Story of Victorian Shanklin* (Shanklin, 1977); Sir Charles Peers, *Carisbrooke Castle, Isle of Wight* (1933); Revd Edmund Venables and Eminent Local Naturalists, *A Guide to the Isle of Wight* (1860). I am grateful for help from: Mrs Sibley (Shanklin Public Library), Mr I. Snow (Ventnor Public Library), Mr Clifford Webster (Island Archivist, Record Office, Newport), Dr Lindsay Boynton, Dr Jack Jones (Curator, Carisbrooke Castle), Mr Leslie Russell (Bonchurch), Mrs T. McLinden (Shanklin Manor House Hotel), Messrs Watson Bull and Porter (Shanklin, particularly Mr Jeffrey). I am particularly grateful to L. Handley-Derry and R. K. R. Thornton for discussions of Arthur's sketches, many of which are reproduced in *AMES* 33–40.

2. *Our Mutual Friend*, Book the First, ch. 10.

3. Lease dated 31 Dec. 1858 (Record Office, Newport, IOW). The Loes were still living at Manor Farm in 1866, as there is a gravestone in St Blasius's churchyard (formerly St John the Baptist's), Shanklin, of 'Anne Loe of Manor Farm', who died in 1866.

4. *L*3 200–1.

5. Geoffrey Grigson's *Britain Observed* (1975) acutely comments on James Collinson's 'Mother and Daughter, and the Culver Cliff' (134) and on Richard Burchett's 'The Isle of Wight' (136); in the latter, the half-hidden building to the left of the church is Manor Farm.

6. 210, para. 246.

7. *J.* 186.

8. Betts, *Shanklin as a Health Resort*, 17.

9. *L*3 202.

10. *ED*, para. 105.

11. *J.* 86–114.

12. *J.* 56.

13. *ED*, para. 1.

14. *ED*, para. 17.

15. *ED*, para. 40.

16. *ED*, para. 61.

17. *ED*, para. 77.

18. *ED*, para. 80.

19. *ED*, para. 85.
20. 'Inversnaid'.
21. *ED*, para. 122.
22. *ED*, para. 104.
23. *ED*, para. 93.
24. *ED*, para. 104.
25. *ED*, para. 105.
26. *ED*, para. 193.
27. *ED*, para. 221.
28. *ED*, para. 227.
29. *ED*, para. 246.
30. *J*. 252.
31. Evidence in *The Balliol College Register*.

## 8. *Useful Information*

1. Information provided by W. Stirling, Registrar of Edinburgh Academy.
2. *L3* 449.
3. *L3* 302.
4. *J*. 6 (footnote).
5. *L3* 205.
6. *L3* 203.
7. *L3* 206.
8. *L3* 202.
9. *L3* 215.
10. *L3* 222.
11. *L3* 87.
12. *L3* 202.
13. Baillie to Barbara Hannah, 31 May 1917.
14. *J*. 13.
15. *L3* 201.
16. *L3* 211.
17. *L3* 214.
18. *J*. 26, 30, 32–3.
19. *J*. 31, 32.
20. *L3* 82–4.
21. *L3* 86.
22. *L3* 83.
23. Balliol, bursar's books, series I. D, bursar's buttery books.
24. *L3* 84.
25. *J*. 9.
26. *L3* 88.
27. *L3* 83.
28. *L3* 85.
29. *J*. 5.

30. *J.* 12.
31. *J.* 11, 12, 13.
32. *J.* 9–10.
33. *J.* 15.
34. *J.* 21.
35. *L.* 3 85.
36. *J.* 8, 19.
37. *J.* 22.
38. *J.* 17, 20, 22.
39. *J.* 22, 24, 20.
40. *J.* 23.
41. *J.* 27.
42. *J.* 24.
43. Campion Hall MS. P. 1(d).

## 9. *Studies*

1. Material on Oxford studies and examinations mainly from: Percy Gardner, *Oxford at the Cross Roads, A Criticism of the Course of Literae Humaniores in the University* (1903); *Henry Scott Holland: Memoirs and Letters*, ed. Stephen Paget (1921); House, 'Early Life', ch. 'Language and Literature'; Charled Edward Mallett, *A History of the University of Oxford*, iii (1927); Robert Ranulph Marett, *A Jerseyman at Oxford* (1941); Mark Pattison, *Memoirs* (1885, 1969); Melvin Richter, *The Politics of Conscience: T. H. Green and his Age* (1964), 52–96; Carl Schmidt, 'Classical Studies at Balliol in the 1860's: The Undergraduate essays of Gerard Manley Hopkins', *Balliol Studies*, ed. John Prest (1982); *Oxford: Its Life and Schools*, ed. A. M. M. Stedman (1887); Balliol, studies and discipline I, collections logbooks, iv a.
2. Ibid.
3. Ibid.
4. *L3* 305.
5. *L3* 191.
6. Richter, *The Politics of Conscience*, 145.
7. Ibid. 145–6.
8. Ibid. 147.
9. *L3* 427.
10. *Mind*, 1 (1876), 88–9, 92–4.
11. Material on Green mainly from Richter, *The Politics of Conscience*, Holland, *Memoirs and Letters*, and R. L. Nettleship, *Memoir of Thomas Hill Green* (1906).
12. *L3* 83.
13. *J.* 115–17.
14. *J.* 122–4.

15. *J*. 122.
16. *L3* 152.
17. *L3* 249.
18. Sources for Jowett as in ch. 5, n. 25.
19. *J*. 16. See also *J*. 22. House first noticed the significance of these timetables in 'Early Life'.
20. Bodleian MS. Eng. poet. e. 90, fos. 31–8.
21. A phrase which from its original publication—in *Letters and Notices*, 30: 179 (Apr. 1910), 391—has remained unexplained and has been laxly used by commentators.
22. *Gerard Manley Hopkins* (1930), 139; on p. 43 Lahey correctly attributes the phrase to Pusey.
23. Campion Hall MS. C. II.
24. *J*. 55; 'at 1.30' is plain in MS after 'Tuesday', but not printed in *J*.
25. *J*. 136.
26. 'Early Life', 'Language and Literature', 195–6.
27. Apart from Hopkins's works, the main sources for the account of Hopkins's attitudes towards Greek studies in this chapter are: 'Early Life'; David J. DeLaura, *Hebrew and Hellene in Victorian England* (Austin, Texas, 1969), particularly the 2nd section, 'Arnold, Pater, and the Dialectic of Hebraism and Hellenism'; Richard Jenkyns, *The Victorians and Ancient Greece* (Oxford, 1980); Frank M. Turner, *The Greek Heritage in Victorian Britain* (1981); Evelyn Abbott and Lewis Campbell, *The Life and Letters of Benjamin Jowett* (1897).
28. *L1* 30–1.
29. *L2* 146.
30. *The Stones of Venice*, vol. ii, ch. 6.
31. *J*. 38 and *L3* 216–20.
32. *The Stones of Venice*, vol. i, ch. 21, paras. 13 and 14.
33. Quoted in Jenkyns, *The Victorians and Ancient Greece*, 72.
34. *L2* 147.
35. Graham Greene, 'The Great Jowett', play on BBC Radio 3, 19 July 1981.
36. Abbott and Campbell, *Life and Letters of Benjamin Jowett*, i. 114 and ii. 75.
37. 'Early Life', 196.
38. Ibid. 196–7.
39. Abbott and Campbell, *Life and Letters of Benjamin Jowett*, i. 329–30.
40. *L3* 6.
41. Example of Hopkins's translation from the Greek taken from 'Early Life'.
42. *L3* 221.
43. *L3* 24–6.
44. 'Early Life', 207–8.
45. Ibid. 208.
46. *J*. 44.
47. 'Early Life', 210–11.

*10. Dolben*

1. Most of the material on Dolben is taken from *The Poems of Digby Mackworth Dolben*, ed. with a Memoir by Robert Bridges (1911), together with a few additional notes taken from the 2nd edn. of 1915.
2. 'Slaughter of the innocents', *J.* 165.
3. *Boys Together: English Public Schools 1800–1864* (1985), 296.
4. Bodleian MS Bridges 56/1. Conclusion of a printed leaflet of Dolben's monastic order, 'Tracts by the Brethren of the English Order of S. Benedict. No. 5'; from its inclusion in this group of Bodleian MSS I assume it may have been written by Dolben himself.
5. *L3* 224.
6. *L3* 17–18.
7. *J.* 56.
8. As he told Kate McCabe in Dublin in the 1880s (interview by Humphry House of Mrs K. Cullinan, House Papers).
9. *L3* 18.
10. *J.* 58.
11. *L3* 18.
12. *J.* 53–5.
13. List omitted from the printed *Journals*; should appear on p. 53.
14. *J.* 54–5.
15. *J.* 55–6.
16. Chandos, *Boys Together*, 291.
17. Campion Hall MS. C. II.
18. *J.* 60.
19. Ibid.
20. *J.* 60–1.
21. *J.* 63.
22. Ibid.
23. E.g. *L1* 30, 274, 277.
24. Confessional notes in journal; these are invaluable for their evidence of Hopkins's feelings at this time.
25. *L3* 89.
26. *L3* 90.
27. Material on Chagford mainly from: Jane Hayter-Hames, *A History of Chagford* (Chichester, 1981); Hopkins's diary for this period: some of it printed *J.* 65–7, but including the MS notes, Campion Hall MS; *Chagford: A Guide to the Town and Neighbourhood* (n.p., n.d.), and other local guides and maps; correspondence with Jane Hayter-Hames; interviews with the landlord of the Three Crowns, Chagford, and other Chagford people.
28. Hayter-Hames, *A History of Chagford*, 115.
29. *J.* 65.
30. *J.* 66.
31. *J.* 66–7.

32. 'Hames' is the name of the host in Hopkins's notes, Campion Hall MS.
33. All information on the Hames family from Jane Hayter-Hames and her *A History of Chagford*.
34. *J.* 67.
35. *L1* 1.

## 11. *Religion*

1. Material for this chapter is taken mainly from Hopkins's published (*J.* 68–73, 133–47) and unpublished diaries (including his poetry), and letters.
2. *L3* 225–7.
3. Baillie to Barbara Hannah, 11–13 May 1917.
4. *J.* 70.
5. Poem entitled 'Justus quidem tu es, Domine, . . .'
6. *Memoirs of John Addington Symonds*, ed. Grosskurth, 109.
7. *J.* 71.
8. Ibid.
9. *L3* 309.
10. *J.* 72.
11. Ibid.
12. *L3* 19.
13. *J.* 135–9.
14. *J.* 133, 138.
15. *J.* 80–3.
16. *J.* 136, 141, 211, 219, 220, 232.
17. *J.* 140; conversations with staff of Oxford Botanical Gardens.
18. *J.* 141.
19. *J.* 142–4.

## 12. *Perversion and Estrangement*

1. *L3* 20.
2. *L3* 21.
3. Hopkins to Macfarlane, *HRB* 7 (1976), 4–5.
4. *J.* 146.
5. Ibid. and *L3* 397.
6. *J.* 146–7 and *L3* 397.
7. *J.* 147 and *L3* 397.
8. *L1* 2.
9. *L1* 3–4.
10. *L3* 21–2.
11. *L3* 26.
12. *L1* 7, 5.
13. Document, Fr Joseph Darlington SJ to Humphry House, House papers. Henry Browne had taken a First in Mods at Oxford, then, converting to

Roman Catholicism, had consulted Manning about remaining at Oxford. Manning as good as forbade him to stay, and so Browne left without a degree, which crippled his whole career.

14. *L*1 5–6.
15. *L*3 26.
16. *L*1 9–10.
17. *L*1 8, 9.
18. *L*3 27.
19. *L*3 400.
20. *L*3 29.
21. Eaglesim's diary, MS, the Oratory, Birmingham.
22. *L*3 400–1.
23. *L*3 31–4, wrongly dated as '15' (for '18') Oct. in *L*3.
24. *L*3 402–3.
25. *L*3 29–30.
26. MS, the Oratory, Birmingham.
27. *L*3 404.
28. *L*3 91.
29. Balliol, Government C, English register of college meeting minutes, fo. 222v.
30. *L*3 91–5.
31. *L*3 95–7.
32. *L*3 100.
33. Now in Jesuit archives, Lr. Leeson Street, Dublin.
34. Letters of Cyril Hopkins to Fr Lahey, 12 May 1929, Farm Street, Lahey Papers.
35. Balliol, letter of Oct. 1866; Mr V. Quinn brought this to my attention.
36. *L*3 405.
37. *L*1 15.
38. *L*3 406.
39. *L*3 100–1.
40. Highgate School, minutes of governors' meetings.
41. *L*3 39.
42. *J.* 147.
43. *The Poems of Digby Mackworth Dolben*, ed. Bridges (1911 edn.), p. cvii.
44. *L*1 16–17.
45. *L*3 407.
46. *The Selected Letters of Robert Bridges*, ed. Donald E. Stanford (2 vols., Newark, Del., 1983, 1984), i. 88.
47. *L*1 17.

*13. Decision: Bovey Tracey and Birmingham*

1. *J.* 152.
2. *J.* 152–3.

3. Material on Bovey Tracey from guides and other material in Bovey Library; from discussions and correspondence with Lance Tregoning, E. T. Abell, Peter Tilstone, Ken Gotham, and Alan Huxley; and from personal local research.
4. *L*3 102.
5. *J*. 153.
6. *J*. 153–4.
7. *J*. 154–5.
8. *J*. 155.
9. *L*3 102.
10. *J*. 155–6.
11. *J*. 153–6.
12. *J*. 156.
13. Ibid.
14. *J*. 157.
15. *L*3 43.
16. Trevor, *Newman's Journey*, 202–6.
17. Newman letter of 4 Aug. 1850, White.
18. Reply to an address read by Lord Edmund Talbot, 21 July 1879, *Sayings of Cardinal Newman* (1890), 23–4.
19. *L*3 43.
20. *L*3 43–5; *L*1 18–20.
21. *L*3 44–6.
22. *L*3 46; *J*. 158.
23. *L*1 18.
24. *J*. 127.
25. *L*1 19.
26. *L*1 21–2.
27. *L*1 22.
28. *L*3 231.
29. *L*3 232.
30. 'The Wreck of the Deutschland', stanzas 2 and 3.
31. *J*. 165.
32. *L*1 24.
33. *L*3 49, 51.

*14. Swiss Swan-Song*

1. The account of Hopkins's Swiss tour is taken from *J*. 168–84.
2. *L*3 53.
3. *L*3 53–4.
4. *L*1 270.
5. See *AMES*, 64–7.
6. *L*3 201.

### III. THE JESUIT, 1868–1874

*15. Novitiate: Roehampton, 1868–1870*

1. Material for the Jesuit novitiate mainly from: 'An Account of the Novitiate of the Society at Roehampton', *Letters and Notices*, 1: 1 (June 1862), 7–18; 'Manresa House and its Neighbourhood', *Letters and Notices (LN)*, 29 (1907–8), 177–87, 231–40, 308–16, 382–92; 'Manresa House, Roehampton', *Letters and Notices*, 30 and 31 (1910–11), 313–21, 386–91, 468–76, 521–7, and 36–41, 91–6; R. F. Clarke SJ, 'The Training of a Jesuit', *Nineteenth Century*, 40 (Aug. 1896), 211–25; Denis Meadows, *Obedient Men (OM)* (1953, 1955); M. M. C. Maxwell Scott, *Henry Schomberg Kerr* (1901); Alfred Thomas SJ, *Hopkins the Jesuit: The Years of Training (HTJ)* (1969), 1–86. To counterbalance these officially approved accounts I have also used two memoirs by unorthodox ex-Jesuits: M. D. Petre, *Autobiography and Life of George Tyrrell* (2 vols., 1912) and E. Boyd Barrett, *The Jesuit Enigma* (1928).
2. *J.* 187.
3. O. R. Vassall-Phillips, *After Fifty Years* (1928), 81.
4. Clarke, 'The Training of a Jesuit', 214.
5. Farm Street MS.
6. Balliol, bursar's books, series II H., bursar's arrears books.
7. *L3* 105.
8. *OM* 13.
9. *OM* 16–18.
10. *L3* 105.
11. Clarke, 'The Training of a Jesuit', 215.
12. *OM* 42–3.
13. *OM* 43–4.
14. *OM* 44–5.
15. *OM* 21–2.
16. *OM* 22–5.
17. *OM* 28–9.
18. *OM* 33.
19. *HTJ* 53.
20. Clarke, 'The Training of a Jesuit', 217.
21. *OM* 19–20.
22. Clarke, 'The Training of a Jesuit', 218.
23. Barrett, *The Jesuit Enigma*, 66–7.
24. *HTJ* 29–30.
25. Barrett, *The Jesuit Enigma*, 67.
26. *OM* 114–15.
27. Barrett, *The Jesuit Enigma*, 71.
28. Ibid. 69–70.
29. *J.* 195.

30. *OM* 119.
31. Barrett, *The Jesuit Enigma*, 101.
32. *OM* 65.
33. *OM* 66–8.
34. Scott, *Henry Schomberg Kerr*, 100–1.
35. *OM* 168.
36. *LN* 30: 318–19.
37. *OM* 85–6.
38. *OM* 94.
39. *J.* 199.
40. *OM* 88.
41. Holland, *Memoirs*, 29–30.
42. W. Gordon Gorman, *Converts to Rome Since the Tractarian Movement to May, 1899* (1899), p. xi.
43. Edward Norman, *The English Catholic Church in the Nineteenth Century* (Oxford, 1984), 21.
44. Barrett, *The Jesuit Enigma*, 79 and 80.
45. Farm Street, Lahey Papers.
46. Petre, *Autobiography and Life of George Tyrrell*, ii. 248.
47. See Erving Goffmann, *Asylums* (New York, 1961) for characteristic rules and behaviour of closed communities.

## *16. Philosophate: St Mary's Hall, 1870–1873*

1. Now at Campion Hall.
2. Translation (with adapted name, place, and date) from St Ignatius of Loyola, *The Constitutions of the Society of Jesus*, trans. George E. Ganss SJ (St Louis, Mo., 1970), 241–2. Other main Jesuit sources for this chapter are: Thomas, *Hopkins the Jesuit*; *OM*; Clarke, 'The Training of a Jesuit'; Bernard Basset, *The English Jesuits from Campion to Martindale* (1967); Francis Edwards SJ, *The Jesuits in England* (1985); Denis Meadows, *A Popular History of the Jesuits* (New York 1958); and various issues of *Letters and Notices*, as in n. 5 below.
3. See Norman, *The English Catholic Church in the Nineteenth Century*, 29–68.
4. *LN* 30 (Apr. 1910), 387–8.
5. Material on Stonyhurst College and St Mary's Hall mainly from: Stonyhurst minister's journals, 1849–77 and 1878–1929; Hubert Chadwick SJ, *St Omers to Stonyhurst: A History of Two Centuries* (1962); Percy Hetherington Fitzgerald, *Stonyhurst Memories* (1895); John Gerard, *Stonyhurst College* (Belfast, 1894); Macdonald Hastings, *Jesuit Child* (1971); Anthony Hewitson, *Stonyhurst College, its Past and Present* (2nd edn., Preston, 1878); Joseph Keating, *Stonyhurst* (Letchworth, 1909); John A. Myerscough SJ, *A Procession of Lancashire Martyrs and Confessors* (Glasgow,

1958); 'J.W.', 'Stonyhurst Life', *The Month*, n.s., 1 (Mar. 1874), 333; Stonyhurst MS, 'Philosophers' Beadle's Journal'; Stonyhurst, Arundell Library, MS E. 3. 6, 'Stonyhurst Weather Notes . . .'; other material in the Stonyhurst Library and Arundell Library; issues of *LN*, incl. 31 (1911–12), 82–91, 'Stonyhurst College'; 56 (Jan. 1948), 15–17, D. Whyte, 'St Mary's Hall'; 41 (1926), 209–17, 'St Mary's Hall, 1828–1926'; and 7 (Sept. 1870), 121–3, 'Letter of Our Very Rev. Fr. General to the Society'; *A Stonyhurst Handbook for Visitors and Others* (Stonyhurst, various edns.); *English Homes of the Early Renaissance: Elizabethan Houses and Gardens*, ed. H. Avray Tipping (n.d.), 171–90, 'Stonyhurst College, Lancashire'; various issues of *The Stonyhurst Magazine*, including 1 (July 1884), 317–20, 'The "Claimant's" Stonyhurst'; 2 (Apr. 1887), 407–8, A.E.I., 'St Mary's Pond'; 3 (July and Dec. 1887), 16–19, 74–8, [John Gerard SJ,] 'Stonyhurst in the Fifties'; 3 (July 1888), 192–4, S. Perry SJ, 'Stonyhurst Climate'; 6 (Apr. 1896), 155–8, 'The Shrovetide Play'; 18 (Feb. 1926), 317–22, Charles V. Hickie, 'In the Early Seventies'; 18 (May 1926), 391–2, 'An O.S.', 'St Mary's Hall'; 18 (June–July 1926), 469–71, 'St Mary's Hall, Stonyhurst, 1828–1926'; 33 (Oct. 1960), 508–13, [Geoffrey Holt,] 'The Phils'. Topographical material: Ordnance Survey, Sheets SD63, SD64, SD73, and SD74; Frederick George Ackerley, *A History of the Parish of Mitton* (Aberdeen, 1947); Alan Lawson, *Walks in Hodder Country* (Nelson, 1966); W. R. Mitchell, *Bowland and Pendle Hill* (Silsden, 1973); *Clitheroe and the Ribble Valley* (Clitheroe, 1939?); William Dobson, *Rambles by the Ribble* (1881); Thomas Johnson, *A Pictorial Handbook to the Valley of the Ribble* (Blackburn, 1881?). I am grateful for help from many people connected with Stonyhurst, particularly Fr Michael Bossy SJ, Peter Hardwick, Fr F. J. Turner SJ, the late Fr C. Macadam SJ, Mrs D. Aspinall (The Bayley Arms), and Mrs Muriel Wright (Stonyhurst post office); Gerald Roberts has been helpful in many ways over a long period.

6. *L3* 111–13.
7. *OM* 129–31.
8. *L3* 112–13.
9. *HTJ* 93.
10. Clarke, 'The Training of a Jesuit', 221–3.
11. *L3* 234–5.
12. *L3* 113.
13. *J.* 200–8.
14. *L3* 117.
15. *J.* 213.
16. Innellan Villa: material mainly from Scott, *Henry Schomberg Kerr*, 117–19; *HTJ* 108–10; *J.* 213–14.
17. *J.* 213.
18. Holyroodhouse information from John Gifford, Colin McWilliam, and David Walker, *Edinburgh* (The Buildings of Scotland, Harmondsworth,

1984); J. S. Richardson, *The Abbey and Palace of Holyroodhouse* (Edinburgh, 1978); and personal visit. Glasgow Cathedral information from personal visit.

19. *J.* 215.
20. *J.* 218.
21. *J.* 220.
22. *J.* 221.
23. *J.* 216.
24. *J.* 218.
25. *J.* 220.
26. *J.* 217.
27. *J.* 221.
28. *L*1 79.


## 17. Seascapes: The Isle of Man

1. Main sources for this chapter are: *J.* 221–5, 234–6; *L*3 57–9, 122–3; [Claude Condell,] 'A Visit to the Isle of Man', *Stonyhurst Magazine* (Nov. 1883), 237–9; Stonyhurst MS, minister's journals for 1872 and 1873; *Isle of Man Census for 1871*; issues of *The Isle of Man Directory*, *The Catholic Directory*, and *The Manx Catholic Magazine*. Isle of Man topographical information from: 1-in. OS, sheet 10 (Dec. 1873); OS sheet 95, 1976; Isle of Man Tourist Board 1:60,000 (early 1980s); 'The Ancient and Historic Monuments of the Isle of Man' (5th edn., Douglas, 1981); 'Ballaglass Nature Trail' (Douglas, n.d.); J. P. Cullen and D. J. Slinn, *The Birds of the Isle of Man* (Douglas, 1975); David Craine, 'Peel Castle' (n.d.); Mona Douglas, 'Parish of Kirk Braddon, 1876–1976' (Douglas, 1976); Manx Conservation Council, 'Short Walks: Northern Section' (Douglas, n.d.); other help from The Isle of Man Tourist Board, A. M. Cubbon (Director, Manx Museum and National Trust), Mrs P. Quayle (proprietor, The Highlander Inn, Marown), Ann Harrison (Archivist, Manx Musuem), Claire Humphreys-Jones, Gerald Roberts, Revd F. J. Turner SJ, Elizabeth Freeth, and particularly George Broderick (School of Celtic Studies, Dublin Institute for Advanced Studies).
2. *J.* 225.
3. *J.* 224.
4. *J.* 223–4.
5. *L*3 171.
6. *J.* 221.
7. *J.* 222.
8. *J.* 223.
9. *L*3 235.
10. *L*3 236.
11. Ibid.

12. Interview with Mrs Ruth Dooley, Dublin, July 1987.
13. *J.* 221.
14. *J.* 218–19.
15. *J.* 229.
16. *J.* 234.
17. *J.* 226.
18. *J.* 216–17, 230.
19. *J.* 218.
20. *J.* 217.
21. *J.* 227.
22. *J.* 229, 420–1.
23. *L3* 122, 58.
24. *L3* 58.
25. Ibid.
26. *L3* 234–5.
27. *J.* 235 for all quotations about Ballaglass.
28. *L3* 59.
29. *J.* 235–6.
30. All journal quotations for Liverpool–Stonyhurst journey, *J.* 236.
31. *L3* 122–3.

*18. Teaching: London and Devon. 1873–1874*

1. *J.* 236.
2. *J.* 425.
3. *J.* 237.
4. *HTJ* 130–1.
5. Clarke, 'The Training of a Jesuit', 220–1; *HTJ* 135.
6. *J.* 237–8.
7. *J.* 243, 239.
8. *HTJ* 138.
9. *J.* 240.
10. *J.* 242.
11. *J* 248.
12. *J.* 244–7.
13. *J.* 249.
14. Ibid.
15. *L3* 123.
16. *L1* 27–8.
17. *L1* 28–30.
18. *J.* 249.
19. *J.* 249–50.
20. Teignmouth Villa sources mainly: *J.* 250–6; personal local research; Captain Thomas Clifford of Ugbrooke. Catherine Phillips read a draft of this chapter.

21. *J.* 250.
22. Ibid.
23. *J.* 251.
24. *J.* 251–2.
25. Peter Watson, 'Secrets of a Monarch's Deal to Sell his Soul', *Observer*, 26 Apr. 1987.
26. [Lady Monkswell,] *A Victorian Diarist*, ed. E. C. F. Collier (1944), 155.
27. *J.* 253–4.
28. *J.* 253.
29. *J.* 254–5.
30. Paul Thompson, *William Butterfield* (1971), 267, 332.
31. *J.* 255.
32. *J.* 255–6.

## IV. THE POET, 1874–1877

### *19. St Beuno's*

1. *J.* 257.
2. Help for this chapter came from: Fr Gerald Hughes SJ, Br Norman Smith SJ, Fr Michael Ivens SJ, Margaret Pilling, Mrs Winnie Jones, Br Joseph J. Daly SJ, and Tom Dunne; and I am particularly grateful to Fr Peter McIlhenny SJ for assistance in various ways during my stays at St Beuno's, and for reading an early draft of this chapter.
3. *L3* 124–5.
4. *A Tour through the Whole Island of Great Britain* (1724–6; 1971 edn.), letter 6 ('The West and Wales'), 387–8.
5. *L3* 124.
6. *L3* 125.
7. *J.* 257.
8. *Jude the Obscure*, ch. 1.
9. *J.* 257–8.
10. *J.* 259.
11. *J.* 260.
12. *L3* 126.
13. *J.* 260.
14. *HTJ* 154–8.
15. *HTJ* 156.
16. *L3* 131.
17. *L1* 31.
18. *HTJ* 158.
19. *HTJ* app. 3, 246–56.
20. Joseph J. Feeney SJ, 'Grades, Academic Reform and Manpower: Why Hopkins Never Completed his Course in Theology', *HQ* 9: 1 (Spring 1982), 24–5.

21. *J*. 262.
22. *J*. 261.
23. Jean-Georges Ritz, *Le Poète Gérard Manley Hopkins SJ* (Paris, 1963), 171.
24. *L*3 130.
25. *L*1 31.
26. *L*3 132, 133.
27. *L*3 134.


20. *Welsh and Wells*

1. *J*. 258. Journey to Ffynnon Fair reconstructed by Tom Dunne and myself.
2. *J*. 261. Sources of information about St Winefride's Well include: Christopher David, *St Winefride's Well: A History and Guide* (Slough, 1971); T. Charles-Edwards, *Saint Winefride and Her Well* (1962); Margaret and Agnes Blundell, *St. Winefride and her Holy Well* (1954); T. M. Charles-Edwards (ed.), *Two Mediaeval Welsh Poems: Stori Gwenfrewi A'I Ffynnon by Tudor Aled and Ffynnon Wenfrewi* (Aberdovey, 1971); Donald Attwater, *The Catholic Church in Modern Wales* (1935); Francis Jones, *The Holy Well of Wales* (Cardiff, 1954). I am grateful for the help of Fr Matthew J. Kelly STL, of St Winefride's Presbytery.
3. *L*1 40.
4. *L*3 132.
5. *L*1 40.
6. *P*. 103.
7. *P*. 332.
8. St. 4.
9. St. 29.
10. F. Keane SJ, 'St Beuno's, 1848–1948', *LN* 56 (1948), 191–2.
11. *L*3 126.
12. *J*. 258.
13. Ibid.
14. Keane, 'St Beuno's, 1848–1948', 192.
15. 'Bygone Life and Customs at St Beuno's', *LN* 20 (1895), 209.
16. [Sylvester Hunter SJ,] 'St Beuno's', *LN* 26 (1901), 43. Most of the material for the history of St Beuno's is taken from this article, which (in spite of its publication date) was written during Fr Hunter's period as Rector of St Beuno's, 1885–91.
17. *HTJ* 252.
18. *L*3 127; *J*. 258.
19. *L*1 30–1.
20. *J*. 263.
21. *P*. 125.
22. *P*4. 324–5.
23. Bodleian MS. Eng. misc. a. 8/4.
24. Act 2, l. 9.

25. *J.* 289–90.
26. *J.* 267–88. ·

21. *'The Wreck of The Deutschland'*

1. *L2* 14.
2. *L3* 135.
3. *HTJ* 64.
4. *L3* 106.
5. *HTJ* 64.
6. *J.* 200–1.
7. *HTJ* 101.
8. *L3* 132–3.
9. *J.* 236.
10. 18 July 1872, 11.
11. Van Noppen, 13. I am grateful to Dr van Noppen for discussions and correspondence on the poem and its background.
12. *L1* 279.
13. See *Parlour Poetry*, ed. Michael R. Turner (1974), s. 5, 'The Rolling Deep'.
14. Douglas Owen, 'Ship Insurance', *Ships and Shipping* (*c.*1912), 136. Robin Craig provided me with this information.
15. *Princeton Encyclopedia of Poetry and Poetics*, ed. Alex Preminger (1975), and John D. Jump, *The Ode* (The Critical Idiom, London, 1974).
16. Van Noppen, 21.
17. 9 Dec. 1875, 6.
18. C.B., 'Reminiscences of Father Gerard Hopkins', *The Month*, 134: 662 (Aug. 1919), 159.
19. *P.* 106–9.
20. *J.* 277.
21. *L2* 14.
22. *P.* 76.
23. *L3* 138.
24. *L3* 139.
25. *L3* 141.
26. II. iii. 64–7.
27. *L2* 15.

22. *'Light, amid the encircling gloom'*

1. *P.* 119–21.
2. *L3* 148.
3. MS album at St Beuno's.
4. *L3* 140.
5. Ibid.

6. *L*1 77–8.
7. *P.* 342–3.
8. *P.* 344–5.
9. 'Myself unholy', *P.* 67.
10. *P.* 157–8.
11. I know of 3 Hopkins scholars who have asked. The landlord in 1987 had never heard of Hopkins.
12. *L*3 242.
13. *L*3 241–2.
14. *L*3 143–4.
15. *L*3 143.
16. Because some of the St Beuno's poems are too familiar in their late versions, I have occasionally used early versions.
17. *L*1 24.
18. *L*1 32.
19. *L*1 40.
20. *L*3 142.
21. *L*1 92.
22. *S.* 225–33.
23. *L*1 32–3.
24. 'An Account of the Casualty Department', *St Bartholomew Hospital Report* (1878).
25. *L*3 145–6.
26. *L*3 241.
27. *L*3 146.
28. *S.* 11.
29. Translation, *P.* 349–50.
30. *HTJ* 179.

23. *'In my salad days, in my Welsh days'*

1. *HRB* 5 (1974), 3; and see Paul Thompson, *William Butterfield* (1971), 305.
2. *L*1 163.
3. Ibid.
4. *L*1 164.
5. *L*1 76–7.
6. *L*1 41.
7. Farm Street, Lahey Papers. I thank the former Archivist, Fr Francis Edwards SJ, for assistance and permission to quote from this letter of Rickaby's to Lahey. See also Joseph J. Feeney SJ, 'Hopkins' "Failure" in Theology: Some New Archival Data and a Reevaluation', unpublished typescript, sent to me by its author, and used with his kind permission.
8. *HTJ* 183.
9. *P.* 132.
10. Fathers of the Society of Jesus, *A Page of Irish History* (Dublin, 1930), 105.

11. *L*3 349.
12. *L*1 43.
13. *L*3 146, 147.
14. *L*1 43.
15. *L*3 146.
16. *J*. 89.
17. *L*1 44.
18. *L*1 44–6.
19. *L*1 56.
20. *HTJ* 185–6.
21. *L*3 148; *HTJ* 186.

### V. FORTUNE'S FOOTBALL, 1877–1884

24. '*Cobweb, soapsud, and frost-feather permanence*': *Mount St Mary's, Stonyhurst, Farm Street, Oxford, 1877–1879*

1. Information on Mount St Mary's College mainly from: 'Mount St Mary's College', *LN* 30 (Jan., Apr., July 1910), 305–13, 392–400, 476–81; Francis E. Keegan SJ, 'Gerard Manley Hopkins at Mount St Mary's College, 1877–8', *The Mountaineer*, 40, 1 [*sic*]: 211 (jubilee issue, July 1977), 14–21; other issues of *The Mountaineer*; personal research at the College. I am grateful for help to Fr Keegan, R. K. R. Thornton, and Fr Peter Willcocks SJ.
2. *L*3 148.
3. *L*3 148–9.
4. *The Mountaineer*, 13: 72 (Christmas 1926), 210.
5. *L*3 149.
6. *L*3 150, 149.
7. *The Mountaineer*, 13: 69 (Christmas 1925), 39.
8. 'Brothers'.
9. *L*1 47.
10. *L*1 47–8.
11. *L*1 48.
12. Information on the *Eurydice* disaster from: issues of *Isle of Wight Advertiser and Ryde and Ventnor Times*, Mar.–Sept. (the court martial) 1878; issues of *The Isle of Wight Times, Hampshire Gazette & c., Vanity Fair, The Isle of Wight Observer*; Capt. E. H. Verney RN, *The Last Four Days of the 'Eurydice'* (Portsmouth, 1878); John Matson, 'Watch the Weather even in Sandown Bay', *Yachting Monthly* (Oct. 1978), 2059–60.
13. *L*1 49.
14. *L*1 51–2.
15. *L*2 32.
16. *L*1 52.
17. *L*1 54.

18. *L*3 150–1.
19. *L*1 65.
20. *L*2 31.
21. Clarke, 'The Training of a Jesuit', 219.
22. Norman H. MacKenzie, *A Reader's Guide to Gerard Manley Hopkins* (1981),105.
23. *L*2 1–3.
24. *L*2 3–5.
25. *L*2 5–9.
26. *L*1 55.
27. *L*1 57.
28. *L*1 60–1.
29. *L*2 12, 16.
30. *L*1 58.
31. *L*2 12.
32. *L*2 20.
33. Material on St Aloysius' mainly from: O. R. Vassall-Phillips, *After Fifty Years* (1928); Helen M. Palmer, *The Church of St. Aloysius Oxford 1875–1975* [Oxford, 1975]; C. C. Martindale SJ, *Catholics in Oxford* (1925); and personal research. I am grateful to Fr John Ellis of St Aloysius'.
34. Edwards, *The Jesuits in England*, 194.
35. 'Jesuits end an Oxford Link', *The Universe*, 6 Nov. 1981, 4.
36. *L*1 58.
37. Vassall-Phillips, *After Fifty Years*, 72–3, 79, 80.
38. *L*3 63.
39. *L*3 244.
40. *L*3 151–2.
41. *L*3 153.
42. *L*3 244.
43. *L*1 97.
44. *L*3 244–5.
45. *L*1 97.
46. *L*3 246.
47. *L*3 152.
48. *L*1 61.
49. *L*3 242.
50. *L*2 22.
51. *L*2 26–7.
52. *L*2 28.
53. *L*1 60–1.
54. *L*1 62, 65.
55. *L*1 66.
56. *L*1 68.
57. *L*1 73.
58. *L*2 20.

59. *L2* 26.
60. *L1* 90.
61. *L2* 13.
62. *L1* 75.
63. *L1* 81.
64. *L1* 84.
65. *L1* 86.
66. *S.* 18.
67. *S.* 13.
68. *S.* 19.
69. 'The Bugler's First Communion'.
70. *L1* 92.


25. *'So fagged, so harried and gallied up and down': Bedford Leigh, Liverpool, Glasgow, 1879–1881*

1. Material on Leigh mainly from: 'Leigh Mission, Lancashire', *LN* 31 (Apr. and Oct. 1912), 399–403, 514–25; personal research.
2. *L1* 90.
3. *L3* 243.
4. *L1* 90.
5. *L2* 29; *L1* 90, 97.
6. *L3* 243.
7. Farm Street, Lahey Papers.
8. *L3* 244–5.
9. *S.* 5.
10. *S.* 45.
11. *S.* 35–6.
12. *L1* 95–6.
13. *L2* 29–30.
14. *L2* 30–1.
15. *L2* 32.
16. *L3* 154.
17. Information on St Francis Xavier's mainly from: *LN* 31 (1911–12), 145–57, 228–40, 299–308; Nicholas Ryan SJ, *St Francis Xavier's Church Centenary 1848–1948* (Liverpool, n.d.); issues of the *Liverpool Daily Post and Mercury*; and material in the Liverpool Museum; personal research.
18. *L1* 99.
19. *L2* 33; *L3* 244.
20. *L1* 100.
21. Facts about Felix Spencer from Alfred Thomas SJ, 'Felix Randal', *Times Literary Supplement*, 19 Mar. 1971, 331–2.
22. Jimmy McGovern, 'Felix Randal' (radio play), BBC Radio 4, 15 Oct. 1985 and 9 Nov. 1986. I thank Mr McGovern for correspondence.
23. *L3* 245.

24. *S.* 5–6.
25. *S.* 50–3, 53–8, 58–62, 62–7.
26. *S.* 62.
27. *S.* 68.
28. *S.* 89.
29. *L1* 110.
30. *L1* 100.
31. *L2* 42.
32. *L1* 124; *L3* 156–7.
33. *L3* 157.
34. *L1* 104.
35. *L1* 116–17.
36. *L2* 46–7.
37. *L1* 128.
38. *L1* 126.
39. *L1* 127–8.
40. *L1* 130.
41. Material on St Joseph's mainly from: [Fr Charnock SJ,] *Notes on St Joseph's 1859–1909* (Glasgow, 1909). I am grateful for help to Fr Michael Kyne SJ (Rector, St Aloysius') and Fr J. Roberts (of St Columba's); Mary Braidwood, who died tragically and prematurely in May 1987, assisted me with research in and around Glasgow on several occasions during 1980–7, and was responsible for tracing the baptismal register of St Joseph's for 1881 to St Columba's.
42. *L1* 135.
43. *L3* 248–9.
44. St Joseph's baptismal register for 1881; Fr J. Roberts explained the system of entries to me.
45. *L1* 135–6.
46. *L1* 136.
47. *L2* 53.
48. *L3* 288.
49. *L2* 65.
50. I am grateful to Peter Pitkin for my visit to Inversnaid, and for his expert botanical knowledge of the area.
51. *L1* 73–4.
52. *L1* 135.

26. *'Surely one vocation cannot destroy another?': Roehampton Tertianship and Stonyhurst, 1881–1883*

1. *L2* 75–6.
2. *HTJ* 187. At the usual refectory meal the men sat with their backs to the wall facing the centre of the room, on one side of tables arranged in an open horseshoe; this meal would be taken in silence, broken only by readings. A meal at a time of special celebration was known as 'double tables' because

the men sat on both sides of the tables, facing each other. Then talking was
allowed, and there would be extra food and drink.

3. *L1* 137.
4. Clarke, 'The Training of a Jesuit', 224.
5. *L1* 138.
6. *HTJ* 193.
7. *S.* pt. 2.
8. *S.* 176.
9. *HTJ* 196.
10. *L2* 71–6, 76–9, 82–9, 92–9.
11. *L2* 88.
12. *L2* 87–8.
13. *L2* 89–90.
14. *L3* 160–1.
15. *HTJ* 197.
16. *L3* 161.
17. *L3.* 162.
18. *L1* 140–1.
19. *L1* 142.
20. *L1* 143.
21. *HTJ* 199–200.
22. *L1* 143.
23. *L1* 143–4; *L2* 104.
24. *HTJ* 202–3.
25. *L1* 145.
26. Bk. iv (*Ethick*), 406–58.
27. *L1* 148.
28. *HTJ* 209.
29. *L1* 151–2.
30. Stonyhurst information mainly from sources used in ch. 16, n. 5; also from
    A. L. Cortie SJ, *Father Perry, the Jesuit Astronomer* (1890).
31. Ronald Pearsall, *Conan Doyle: A Biographical Solution* (1977), 5–6.
32. *L3* 252.
33. C.B., 'Reminiscences of Father Gerard Hopkins', *The Month*, 134: 662
    (Aug. 1919), 159.
34. *L3* 252.
35. *L1* 150.
36. *L3* 251–2.
37. *L2* 105.
38. *L1* 157.
39. *L1* 158.
40. *L1* 157.
41. *L1* 168.
42. *L2* 108–9.
43. *L1* 179.

44. *L2* 109.
45. *L1* 178.
46. *The Science of Aspects* (1971), 116.
47. The first 3 letters are reprinted *L2* 161–6, the 4th in Ball, *The Science of Aspects*, 148–50.
48. Joseph Crehan SJ, 'Some Hopkins Memories', *HRB* 4 (1973), 29–30.

27. *'Careful and subtle fault-finding': Patmore and Hopkins*

1. *L1* 183.
2. *L3* 426.
3. *A Book of Simple Prayers*, coll. and arr. E. W., 2nd edn. (Reading, 1893), 5.
4. *L2* 159.
5. On Contents page, fo. 276; not 'a prayer written for protestants', as Abbott calls it (*L2* 159).
6. *L1* 186.
7. *L1* 183.
8. Published in 1864.
9. Margaret Maison, *Search Your Soul Eustace: A Survey of the Religious Novel in the Victorian Age* (1961), 169.
10. Other features of the story would have appealed to Hopkins: the Jesuit's first, decorated Gothic, hiding-place is a chapel compared by Mrs Meeker to that at St Winefride's Well, and in the second volume the scene changes to North Wales—the countryside of the Clwyd, St Asaph, and 'the placid and beautiful Elwy'.
11. *L2* 6.
12. *L2* 112.
13. *L1* 185; *L2* 112.
14. *L1* 183–4; *L2* 111–12.
15. Printed in Jerome Bump, 'Providence, "The Wreck of the Deutschland", and a New Hopkins Letter', *Renascence*, 31: 4 (1979), 195–7.
16. Farm Street, Lahey Papers, letter from Kate to Lahey, 7 Dec. 1928.
17. *S.* 138–9.
18. *S.* 253.
19. *S.* 254.
20. Ibid.
21. *L1* 186.
22. *L3* 297.
23. *L3* 296.
24. *L1* 189.
25. *L3* 300.
26. *L3* 303.
27. *L3* 310.
28. *L3* 307–9.
29. *L3* 310.

30. Joachim Kahl, *The Misery of Christianity*, trans. N. D. Smith (Harmondsworth, 1971), 81.
31. *L*3 312.
32. *L*3 324–5.
33. *L*3 325–6.
34. *L*3 335–7.
35. *Selected Letters of Robert Bridges*, ed. Stanford, i. 127.
36. *L*3 337–8.
37. *L*3 344–5.
38. *L*3 348–9.
39. *L*3 349.

## VI. THE STRANGER, 1884–1889

### 28. *An Irish Row*

1. *L*1 189–90.
2. Main sources for this chapter are: Lr. Leeson Street, Delany Papers and other material; University College Dublin Special Collections and Archives; 'The Folly of John Bourdieu', unpublished typescript (n.d., in possession of Grainne O'Flynn); Very Revd P. Huvetys CSSp, 'The Irish University Question', *The Dublin Review*, 3rd ser., 25 (Jan. 1885), 169–92; V. A. McClelland, *The English Roman Catholics and Higher Education, 1830–1908* (Oxford, 1963); Fergal McGrath SJ, *Newman's University, Idea and Reality* (Dublin, 1951); *Centenary History of the Literary and Historical Society of University College, Dublin, 1855–1955*, ed. J. Meenan (Tralee, n.d.); T. J. Morrissey SJ, *Towards a National University: William Delany SJ* (Dublin, 1983); Grainne O'Flynn, 'The Dublin Episcopate and the Higher Education of Roman Catholics in Ireland 1795–1908' (M.Ed. dissertation, Trinity College Dublin, 1973); Royal University of Ireland, *Minutes of the Senate of the Royal University* (Dublin, 1887); Society of Jesus, *A Page of Irish History* (Dublin, 1930); M. Tierney (ed.), *Struggle with Fortune* (Dublin, 1954); Trevor, *Newman's Journey*; William J. Walsh, *The Irish University Question* (Dublin, 1897). Of the many people who have assisted with this chapter I am particularly grateful to Grainne O'Flynn, Fr T. J. Morrissey SJ, and Fr Fergal McGrath SJ (Archivist at Lr. Leeson Street, Dublin). For a longer account, see Norman White, 'Gerard Manley Hopkins and the Irish Row', *HQ* 9: 3 (fall 1982), 91–107.
3. Delany Papers.
4. Ibid.
5. Royal University Senate Minutes.
6. Cash-book in Lr. Leeson Street.
7. Delany Papers.
8. Copy of Nettleship's testimonial in House Papers.
9. Delany Papers.

10. O'Flynn, 'The Dublin Episcopate', 207.
11. Royal University Senate Minutes, 185–6.
12. Royal University Returns, 4.
13. O'Flynn, 'The Dublin Episcopate', 213–18.
14. Aubrey Gwynn SJ, 'The Jesuit Fathers and University College', in Tierney (ed.), *Struggle with Fortune*, 26.
15. *L1* 190.
16. Material on Dublin from many sources, chiefly: L. Perry Curtis Jr, *Apes and Angels: The Irishman in Victorian Caricature* (Newton Abbot, 1971); Mary E. Daly, *Dublin: The Deposed Capital: A Social and Economic History, 1860–1914* (Cork, 1984); Mary E. Daly, 'Dublin in the 1880s', unpublished paper given at the Hopkins Conference, Dublin 1984; James Joyce, *Stephen Hero*, rev. edn., (St Albans, 1977); F. S. L. Lyons, *Charles Stewart Parnell* (1977, 1978); Constantia Maxwell, *The Stranger in Ireland* (1954); George Moore, *A Drama in Muslin* (1886; this edn., Gerrards Cross, 1981); George Moore, *Salve* (1912; this edn. 1947); various issues of *Punch* in the 1880s; Mark Tierney and Margaret MacCurtain, *The Birth of Modern Ireland* (Dublin, 1969); various issues of the *Freeman's Journal* and the *Irish Times*, including Caroline Walsh, 'Staying in style at the Shelbourne', 9 Apr. 1983, 9. Among the many people who assisted with this chapter are Dr Mary E. Daly and Professor R. Dudley Edwards.
17. *A Drama in Muslin*, 158.
18. *L1* 189; *L3* 63.
19. Daly, 'Dublin in the 1880s', 2.
20. *A Drama in Muslin*, 158.
21. Joyce, *Stephen Hero*, 175.
22. Daly, 'Dublin in the 1880s', 4.
23. Ibid. 8.
24. W. B. Stanford and R. B. McDowell, *Mahaffy* (1971), 119.
25. Daly, 'Dublin in the 1880s', 10.
26. Curtis, *Apes and Angels*, 1, 101.
27. Letter to his mother, from Dublin, 28 Oct. 1842; Maxwell, *The Stranger in Ireland*, 331.
28. Curtis, *Apes and Angels*, 75.
29. In this difficult area of inter-racial images I have been particularly helped by Derek Britton, Alan Fletcher, and Iseult McCarthy.
30. Delany Papers: Joseph Darlington SJ, 'Life of Hopkins' (MS), 7. Despite its title, this MS gives next to no information about Hopkins.
31. C. P. Curran, *Under the Receding Wave* (Dublin, 1970), 70.
32. Moore, *Salve*, 112.
33. Society of Jesus, *A Page of Irish History*, 108–9.
34. *L3* 63.
35. *S.* 255.
36. *L1* 190.
37. *L1* 191–2, 193; *S.* 256.

38. *The Month* n.s. 19 (May 1958), 263–70.
39. Letter of Dr Patrick Golding to NW, 28 Dec. 1984, and *L*1 193.
40. *L*1 193–4.
41. *S.* 257.
42. *L*1 198.
43. *L*1 190.
44. All the following examples of examination-paper extracts and Hopkins's comments are from Campion Hall MS G I (a), the 'Dublin Note-Book'.
45. *L*2 177.
46. *L*3 263.
47. *L*2 120.
48. *L*2 105.
49. *HQ* 4: 3–4 (fall/winter 1977–8), 181–3.
50. *L*2 110.
51. *L*1 196–8.
52. *L*3 164.
53. Sources for Curtis mainly: Delany Papers; Joseph J. Feeney SJ, 'Hopkins's Closest Friend in Ireland, Robert Curtis, SJ', typescript sent by its author 1984; discussions with Fr Feeney; House Papers.
54. *L*3 164.
55. Letter to Grace, *HQ* 4: 3–4 (fall/winter 1977–8), 181–3.
56. *L*1 199–200.
57. *L*1 195.
58. *L*1 197; Fr Fergal McGrath SJ, of the Irish Province, knew Gleeson, and told the present writer of this incident on 20 Oct. 1978.
59. *L*3 165.
60. Lr. Leeson Street archives.
61. *L*3 165.
62. *L*3 163.
63. *S.* 258.

### 29. 'Dapple At End'

1. 'The present noble school of naturalistic painters ... These men's patient, reverent faith in nature as they see her, their knowledge that the ideal is neither to be invented nor abstracted, but found and left where God has put it, and where alone it can be represented, in actual and individual phenomena—in these lies an honest development of the true idea of Protestantism' (Charles Kingsley, *Yeast* (1848) ).
2. *Stephen Hero* (1977 edn.), 207, 35.
3. Ibid. 32.
4. Lr. Leeson Street, 'Memoirs of Fr Darlington' (MS), 5.
5. House Papers, interview Humphry House and Professor John Howley.
6. House Papers, interview HH and W. B. Yeats.
7. House Papers, interviews HH and: Howley, James S. Gaffney, and Mrs K. Cullinan.

8. Lr Leeson Street, Darlington, 'Life of Hopkins', 18.
9. House Papers, interviews HH and: John Bacon and Fr Darlington.
10. Lr Leeson Street, Darlington, 'Life of Hopkins', 34.
11. House Papers, interviews HH and: Fr T. Finlay SJ and Mrs Cullinan.
12. House Papers, interviews HH and: Fr Thomas O'Ryan, Fr T. Finlay SJ, John Bacon, Fr Martin Maher SJ, and Patrick Lynch KC.
13. House Papers, interviews HH and: Fr Martin Maher SJ and John Bacon; *L*3 165, 167.
14. House Papers, interviews HH and: Fr Martin Maher SJ, John Bacon, and Fr J. Darlington SJ.
15. House Papers; and personal investigations. I am grateful for the knowledgeable assistance of Mr George Williams, chief porter of Newman House, 86 St Stephen's Green.
16. House Papers, interviews HH and: James Gaffney, Mrs Cullinan, and Fr Martin Maher SJ.
17. House Papers, interviews HH and: Professor John Howley, John Bacon, Fr Martin Maher SJ, and W. H. Brayden; Lr Leeson Street, Darlington, 'Life of Hopkins', 9.
18. House Papers, interviews HH and: W. B. Yeats and Professor John Howley.
19. House Papers, interview HH and Fr Thomas O'Ryan; Darlington, 'Life of Hopkins', 9.
20. House Papers: 'Rough Sketch of Gerard Hopkins in Ireland', written for HH by Fr J. Darlington SJ; copy of letter from Darlington to Fr J. Keating SJ, 4 Sept. 1910.
21. House Papers, interviews HH and: Fr Martin Maher SJ and Fr Darlington SJ.
22. 'Cast by Conscience Out', *HQ* 4: 3, 4 (fall/winter 1977–8), 132.
23. *L*1 200, 248.
24. *L*3 257; *L*3 275–6; *L*1 219.
25. *L*1 201.
26. *L*1 201–2.
27. House Papers, interview HH and Mrs Cullinan.
28. *S*. 258–9.
29. *S*. 259.
30. *L*3 167.
31. *L*3 170.
32. *L*3 167.
33. *L*3 168–9.
34. *L*3 169–70.
35. *L*3 170; *S*. 260; *L*3 257.
36. *S*. 260.
37. *L*1 208, 210, 212, 214–15.
38. *L*3 254.
39. *L*3 255–7.

40. *L*3 171.
41. *L*1 216–19.
42. *Mirage and Truth* (1935), 199.
43. *The Function of Criticism* (1962), 113.

*30. 'Dark not day'*

1. *L*3 363–4.
2. *L*3 176–7.
3. *L*1 183.
4. *L*3 425.
5. Letter to Everard, 5 Nov. 1885, *HRB* 4 (1973), 11.
6. *L*3 364.
7. *L*3 172; Derek Patmore, *The Life and Times of Coventry Patmore* (1949), 178.
8. *L*3 172, 368.
9. Patmore, *The Life and Times of Coventry Patmore*, 199.
10. *L*3 365, 385–6.
11. Patmore, *The Life and Times of Coventry Patmore*, 201–2.
12. *L*3 172; *L*1 172, 220–1.
13. 'Examen of the interior'.
14. *J* 71.
15. See Gwynn Harries-Jenkins, *The Army in Victorian Society* (1977), 278.
16. *S.* 34.

*31. Sanctuaries*

1. *L*1 222.
2. *HRB* 4 (1973), 12.
3. House Papers, interview Humphry House and Mrs Cullinan; letter Mrs Ruth Dooley to the present author 1986, and interview 1987.
4. House Papers, interview HH and Mrs Cullinan; letter Mrs Ruth Dooley to the present author, 21 Oct. 1984, and interview June 1987.
5. *L*3 174–5.
6. *L*3 257–73.
7. *L*3 413.
8. *L*3 417.
9. *L*1 225.
10. *L*2 135–6.
11. *L*2 134.
12. *L*3 426.
13. Information on Stewart from Olinthus J. Vignoles MA, *Memoir of Sir Robert P. Stewart Kt* [1899?].
14. *L*3 426–7.
15. *L*3 427–8.
16. *L*1 225; *L*3 176; *L*3 274.

17. *L2* 135–9.
18. *L3* 370; *L2* 142–3; *L1* 227.
19. *L1* 227–8; *L3* 370.
20. *L1* 236, 228–9, 229–30.
21. *L1* 229–30.
22. *L1* 245.
23. Material on Monasterevan mainly from: Alfred Barnard, *The Whisky Distilleries of the United Kingdom* (1887), 383–6 ('Monasterevan Distillery'); Revd M. Comerford, *Collections Relating to the Dioceses of Kildare and Leighlin* (3 vols., Dublin, 1883–6), ii. 206–46 ('Parish of Monasterevan'); John Holmes, 'Monasterevan Distillery', *Journal of the Co Kildare Archaeological Society* 14: 4 (1969), 480–7; Julia Ryan, *Monasterevan Parish Co Kildare* (Naas, 1958); the Passfields graveyard (Cassidy mausoleum); Norman White, 'The Probable Identity of Hopkins's "Two Beautiful Young People" ', *English Language Notes*, 8: 3 (Mar. 1971), 206–8. I am grateful for the help of John Holmes, Pat Lonergan (Kildare County Library), and the Sisters of the Presentation Convent (Monasterevan House).
24. *L3* 183.
25. *L1* 248–9.
26. *L1* 250.
27. *L3* 183.
28. Wulstan Phillipson, 'Gerard Manley Hopkins', *Downside Review*, 51: 146 (1933), 339.
29. *L3* 117 and *L1* 151.
30. *J.* 200, 233.
31. *J.* 234.
32. Norman White, 'Hopkins's Epithalamion', *HQ* 4: 3, 4 (fall/winter 1977–8), 141–59, and 'The Setting of Hopkins's "Epithalamion" ', *VP* 10: 1 (spring 1972), 83–6.
33. 'The Starlight Night'.
34. 'The times are nightfall'.

*32. 'What shall I do for the land that bred me?'*

1. *L1* 250.
2. *L1* 258.
3. *L1* 253.
4. *L1* 250.
5. *L3* 178.
6. *L3* 178–9; *L1* 271; *L2* 157; *L1* 283, 290, 296.
7. *L3* 281–2.
8. *L3* 413–14.
9. *L3* 293.
10. *L1* 283.

11. Bk. 3, ch. 11.
12. *L*1 272–4.
13. *HRB* 3 (1972), 6, 9.
14. *The Month*, n.s. 19 (May 1958), 270.
15. Information on Tynan from Pamela Hinkson, 'House of Corn: Katharine Tynan', unpublished typescript in the Tynan Papers; also others of the Tynan Papers. I am grateful to Peter van de Kamp for help with the Tynan Papers.
16. Katharine Tynan, *Memories* (1924), 155; this is also the reference for all extracts from Tynan's account of Hopkins.
17. Letter from Hopkins to Tynan, 15 Sept. 1888, in Graham Storey, 'Six New Letters of Gerard Manley Hopkins', *The Month*, n.s. 19 (May 1958), 263–70.
18. *L*3 373–4.
19. House Papers.
20. Letters of Fr J. Darlington SJ to Tynan, 26 Apr. 1920, Tynan Papers.
21. *L*1 244–5.
22. *L*1 248; *Fortnightly Review*, July 1894.
23. *L*1 255.
24. *L*1 254.
25. *EDD* material from Norman White, 'G. M. Hopkins's Contributions to the *English Dialect Dictionary*', *English Studies*, 68: 4 (Aug. 1987), 325–35.
26. Patrick Greig Scott, ' "Flowering in a Lonely Wood": Tennyson and the Victorian Study of Language', *VP* 18: 4 (winter 1980), 371–81.
27. *L*3 431–2.
28. W. Hugh Patterson, *A Glossary of Words in use in the Counties of Antrim and Down* (1880).
29. 'Gerard Hopkins', in *Essays on Poetry* (Dublin, 1919), 124–5.
30. *L*1 265.
31. Milroy, *The Language of Gerard Manley Hopkins*, 173–4.
32. *S*. 262.
33. *L*1 293.
34. *L*3 184–5.
35. *L*3 178.
36. I am grateful to the Sisters at Gleneveena for help and hospitality.
37. *L*3 292–3.
38. *L*3 182.
39. *L*1 264.
40. *L*1 282.
41. *L*3 191.

*33. 'I wish then for death'*

1. *L*3 190.
2. Interview with Jesuit at Tullabeg, 2 June 1984.

3. *S.* 261–2.
4. *L3* 195.
5. *L1* 300.
6. *L3* 193–4.
7. *L1* 299.
8. *L3* 66.
9. *J.* 301.
10. *L1* 291.
11. Bk. iv ('Ethick'), 433–532.
12. *L3* 195.
13. *L3* 196.
14. *L3* 196–7.
15. *L3* 197–8.
16. *L3* 198.
17. Transcribed from 'Poppyland', television play by William Humble, BBC 2, 13 Jan. 1985.
18. Paul B. Beeson and Walsh McDermott, *Textbook of Medicine*, 14th edn. (1975), 360.
19. Elizabeth Longford, *Victoria R.I.* (1964, 1976), 372.
20. House Papers, interview Humphry House and Fr J. Darlington SJ.
21. House Papers, copy of letter; Lr. Leeson Street, cash-book.
22. House Papers, interview HH and Fr T. A. Finlay SJ.
23. According to the death certificate.
24. Lahey, 143–7.
25. Letter from Mrs Ruth Dooley to the present author, 21 Oct. 1984.
26. Farm Street, Lahey Papers, letter of Cyril Hopkins.
27. House Papers, visit of HH to Glasnevin, 6 Apr. 1933. I have been given 3 different locations of the grave within the burial plot.
28. *The Nation*, 15 June 1889, 8.

*Post Mortem*

1. All comments on Hopkins's death in this section, up to that of Sir Robert Stewart, except for that detailed in n. 2, are taken from typed copies in the House Papers of Hopkins family letters.
2. Baillie to Barbara Hannah, 22 June 1916.
3. House Papers, interview Humphry House and Fr Darlington; Lr. Leeson St, cash-book.
4. House Papers, unsigned letter.
5. *SLRB* i. 188.
6. Ibid. 189.
7. Ibid. 191.
8. Ibid. 194.
9. Ibid. 200–1.
10. Edward Thompson, *Robert Bridges* (1944), 1.

11. *SLRB* i. 201.
12. Ibid. 204.
13. Ibid. 28.
14. Ibid. 238.
15. *The Poets and the Poetry of the Century: Robert Bridges and Contemporary Poets*, ed. Alfred H. Miles (1893), p. v.
16. *SLRB* i. 241.
17. Miles (ed.), *The Poets and the Poetry of the Century*, 161–2.
18. *SLRB* i. 241.
19. *Dunne* 7.
20. *SLRB* i. 34.
21. *Dunne* 10.
22. 'Gerard Hopkins: An Epitaph and an Appreciation', *Catholic World*, 88: 526 (Jan. 1909), 433–47; my quotation is from the reprint in Katharine Brégy, *The Poets' Chantry* (1912), 70–88.
23. Ibid. 86–7.
24. *SLRB* i. 51.
25. Ibid. 29.
26. *Dunne* 168.
27. G[eorge] O'N[eill], review in *Studies* (Dublin), 1: 4 (Dec. 1912), 736–8.
28. *Dunne* 128.
29. *SLRB* i. 29–30.
30. *SLRB* ii. 698.
31. Ibid. 714.
32. Baillie to Barbara Hannah, 30 Sept. 1917, 1 May 1918, 27 Dec. 1918, 30 Dec. 1918.
33. *SLRB* ii. 725–6.
34. Ibid. 725.
35. Ibid. 735.

# SELECT BIBLIOGRAPHY

❦

## MANUSCRIPTS

Manuscripts and documents of, and associated with, Hopkins in the collections of: the Bodleian Library, Oxford; Campion Hall, Oxford; Balliol College, Oxford; Stonyhurst College; Lower Leeson Street, Dublin; Humanities Research Center, Austin, Texas; L. Handley-Derry; Norman White; the Bridges Collection in the Bodleian Library; the House family; University College Dublin; the executors of Barbara Hannah.

## PRINTED WORKS

Unless otherwise stated, place of publication of books is London.

anti-Jesuitism:
  Bartoli, Giorgio, *The Primitive Church and the Primacy of Rome* [1909].
  Kingsley, Charles, *Westward Ho!* (1855).
  Lathbury, Thomas, *The State of Popery and Jesuitism in England; from the Reformation to the Period of the Roman Catholic Relief Bill in 1829* (1838).
  Montague, Lord Robert, *Recent Events and a Clue to their Solution*, 2nd edn. (1886).
Aquinas:
  D'Arcy, M. C., *St Thomas Aquinas* (1953).
architecture:
  Clark, Kenneth, *The Gothic Revival: An Essay in the History of Taste*, 3rd edn. (1974).
  Clarke, Basil F. L., *Church Builders of the Nineteenth Century: A Study of the Gothic Revival in England* (1969).
  Dixon, Roger, and Muthesius, Stefan, *Victorian Architecture* (1978).
  Eastlake, Sir Charles, *A History of the Gothic Revival* (1872).
  Fergusson, James, *Illustrated Handbook of Architecture* (2 vols., 1855).
  Hersey, George L. *High Victorian Gothic: A Study in Associationism* (1972).
  Muthesius, Stefan, *The High Victorian Movement in Architecture, 1850–1870* (1972).
  Pugin, Augustus, *Examples of Gothic Architecture; selected from various Ancient Edifices* (3 vols., Edinburgh, 1895).
  Pugin, Augustus Welby, *An Apology for the Revival of Christian Architecture in England* (1853).

Pugin, Augustus Welby (cont.), *Contrasts; or a Parallel between the Archi-tecture of the Fifteenth and Nineteenth Centuries* (1836).

*Sir Gilbert Scott (1811–1878), Architect of the Gothic Revival* (exhibition catalogue, Victoria and Albert Museum, 1978).

Thompson, Paul, *William Butterfield* (1971).

see also Parker, John Henry.

Armstrong, Isobel, *Language as Living Form in Nineteenth-Century Poetry* (Brighton, 1982)

——, *Victorian Scrutinies: Reviews of Poetry 1830–1870* (1972).

Arnold, Matthew and Thomas:

Arnold, Thomas, *A Manual of English Literature*, 5th edn. (1885).

——, *Passages in a Wandering Life* (1900).

Trevor, Meriol, *The Arnolds* (1973).

see also Ward, Mrs Humphry.

Arnstein, Walter L., *The Bradlaugh Case: A Study in Late Victorian Opinion and Politics* (Oxford, 1965).

*Art and the Industrial Revolution* (exhibition catalogue, Manchester City Art Gallery, 1968).

Ashe, Geoffrey, *The Virgin* (1976).

Attwater, Donald, *A Dictionary of Saints* (1938).

Ball, Patricia M., *The Central Self: A Study in Romantic and Victorian Imagination* (1968).

——, *The Science of Aspects: The Changing Role of Fact in the Work of Coleridge, Ruskin and Hopkins* (1971).

Bergonzi, Bernard, *Gerard Manley Hopkins* (1977).

Berry, Francis, *Poetry and the Physical Voice* (1962).

Bolton, Charles A., *Salford Diocese and its Catholic Past* (Manchester, 1950).

Bossche, Chris R. Vanden, 'Realism versus Romance: The War of Cultural Codes in Tennyson's *Maud*', *VP* 24(1) (spring 1986), 69–82.

Bremer, Rudolph, 'Gerard Manley Hopkins: The Sonnets of 1865' (doctoral thesis, University of Groningen, 1978).

Bridges, Robert:

Bridges, Robert, 'An Account of the Casualty Department', *St Bartholomew Hospital Report* (1878).

——, *Poems* (1873).

——, *Poems by the author of The Growth of Love* (1880).

——, *Prometheus the Firegiver* (Oxford, 1883).

——, *The Growth of Love* (1878).

——, *The Selected Letters of Robert Bridges*, ed. Donald E. Stanford (2 vols. Newark, Del., 1983, 1984).

——, *The Shorter Poems of Robert Bridges* (1890).

——, *The Testament of Beauty* (Oxford, 1929, 1930).

*Three Friends: Memoirs of Digby Mackworth Dolben, Richard Watson Dixon, Henry Bradley* (1932).

Guérard, Albert Jr, *Robert Bridges: A Study of Traditionalism in Poetry* (Cambridge, Mass., 1942).

Ritz, Jean-Georges, *Robert Bridges and Gerard Hopkins, 1863–1889: A Literary Friendship* (1960).

Smith, Nowell Charles, *Notes on The Testament of Beauty* (1931).

Thompson, Edward, *Robert Bridges* (1944).

Broderick, Robert C. (ed.), *The Catholic Concise Encyclopedia* (New York, 1956).

Brown, Ford Madox:

[Mary Bennett,] *Ford Madox Brown, 1821–1893* (exhibition catalogue, Walker Art Gallery, Liverpool, 1964).

'Madox Brown's Diary Etc 1844–56', in *Praeraphaelite Diaries and Letters*, ed. William Michael Rossetti (1900), 111–12.

Brown, L. B. (ed.), *Psychology and Religion: Selected Readings* (Harmondsworth, 1973).

Caine, Hall (ed.), *Sonnets of Three Centuries* (1882).

Carlyle, Thomas, *Past and Present*, ed. Richard D. Altick (Boston, 1965).

——, *Selected Writings*, ed. Alan Shelston (Harmondsworth, 1971).

Chandler, Alice, *A Dream of Order: The Medieval Ideal in Nineteenth-Century English Literature* (1971).

Chandos, John, *Boys Together: English Public Schools, 1800–1864* (1984).

*Cholmeleian, The: or, Highgate School Magazine*, No. 67 (Oct. 1889), and other issues.

Christ, Carol T., *The Finer Optic: The Aesthetic of Particularity in Victorian Poetry* (1975).

——, *Victorian and Modern Poetics* (1984).

Clayre, Alasdair (ed.), *Nature and Industrialization* (Oxford, 1977).

Coleridge, Henry James, SJ, *The Prisoners of the King: Thoughts on the Catholic Doctrine of Purgatory* (1889).

Coleridge, Samuel Taylor, *The Notebooks of Samuel Taylor Coleridge*, ed. K. Coburn (1957-62).

Collette, Charles Hastings, *Romanism in England Exposed* (1851).

Considine, Daniel, SJ, *Delight in the Lord: Notes of Spiritual Direction and Exhortations* (1924).

Cortie, A. L., SJ, *Father Perry, the Jesuit Astronomer* (1890).

Crehan, Joseph, SJ, 'Some Hopkins Memories', *HRB* 4 (1973), 29–30.

Cruse, Amy, *The Victorians and their Books* (1935).

Curb, Rosemary, and Manahan, Nancy (eds.), *Breaking Silence: Lesbian Nuns on Convent Sexuality* (1985).

Curl, James Stevens, *The Victorian Celebration of Death* (Newton Abbot, 1972).

Dana, R. H., *Two Years Before the Mast* [n.d.].

Darwin, Charles, *The Origin of Species By Means of Natural Selection* ..., ed. J. W. Burrow (Harmondsworth, 1968).

Davie, Donald, 'The Industrial Landscape in British Literature': *see: Landscape in Britain, 1850–1950.*

DeLaura, David J., *Hebrew and Hellene in Victorian England* (Austin, Texas, 1969).

Dessain, Stephen, *John Henry Newman* (1980).

Dixon, Richard Watson:

    *Poems by the late Rev. Dr. Richard Watson Dixon: A Selection with Portrait & A Memoir by Robert Bridges* (1909).

    *Songs and Odes* (1896).

    *The Last Poems of Richard Watson Dixon D.D.*, ed. Robert Bridges (1905).

    Hole, Revd Charles, Dixon, Revd Richard Watson, and Lloyd, Revd Julius, *Three Essays on the Maintenance of the Church of England as an Established Church* (1874).

    Sambrook, J., *A Poet Hidden: The Life of Richard Watson Dixon* (1962).

Dolben, Digby Mackworth:

    *Lyrics of Light and Life XLIII* (1875).

    *The Poems of Digby Mackworth Dolben*, ed. Robert Bridges (1911; 2nd edn., 1915).

Dowden, Edward, *New Studies in Literature* (1895).

Doyle, Arthur Conan:

    Pearsall, Ronald, *Conan Doyle: A Biographical Solution* (1977).

Doyle, Sir F. H., *Lectures Delivered Before the University of Oxford 1868* (1869).

Feeney, Joseph J., SJ, 'Grades, Academic Reform, and Manpower: Why Hopkins Never Completed his Course in Theology', *HQ* 9(1) (spring 1982).

—— , 'Hopkins's "Failure" in Theology', unpublished typescript.

Finlay, T. A., SJ, *The Chances of War* (Dublin, 1904).

Frassinetti, Joseph, *The New Parish Priest's Practical Manual* (1883).

Fredeman, W. E., *Pre-Raphaelitism: A Bibliocritical Study* (Cambridge, Mass., 1965).

Gallwey, Peter, SJ, *Salvage from the Wreck: A Few Memories of Friends Departed Preserved in Funeral Discourses* (1903).

Garcia, Pilar Abad, 'La Unidad en la Obra de Gerard Manley Hopkins: su Literatura Epistolar', (doctoral thesis, University of Valladolid, 1983).

Gardner, Helen, *Religion and Literature* (1971).

Gardner, W. H., *Gerard Manley Hopkins, 1844–89: a Study of Poetic Idiosyncrasy in Relation to Poetic Tradition* (2 vols., 1966).

[Geldart, Martin] Nitram Tradleg, *A Son of Belial* (1882).

Giles, Richard F. (ed.), *Hopkins Among the Poets: Studies in Modern Responses to Gerard Manley Hopkins* (Hamilton, Ont., 1985).

Gilmour, Robin, *The Idea of a Gentleman in the Victorian Novel* (1981).

Gladstone, Right Hon. W. E., MP, *Rome and the Newest Fashions in Religion* (1875).

Goffman, Erving, *Asylums: Essays on the Social Situation of Mental Patients and Other Inmates* (New York, 1961).

Goldie, Francis, SJ, *The Life of St Alonso Rodriguez* (1889).

Goodwin, Michael (ed.), *Nineteenth-Century Opinion* (Harmondsworth, 1951).

Gosse, Edmund:
    Gosse, Edmund, *Father and Son: A Study of Two Temperaments* (1907).
    *The Life and Letters of Sir Edmund Gosse*, by the Hon. Evan Charteris (1931).

Gosse, Philip Henry, FRS, *Sacred Streams* (1878).

Graves, Charles L., *Mr. Punch's History of Modern England* (4 vols., n.d.).

Grigson, Geoffrey, *Gerard Manley Hopkins* (1955).

——, *The Englishman's Flora* (1975).

Harries-Jenkins, Gwynn, *The Army in Victorian Society* (1977).

Hartman, Geoffrey (ed.), *Hopkins: A Collection of Critical Essays* (Englewood Cliffs, NJ, 1966).

Hepworth, Mike, and Turner, Bryan S., *Confession: Studies in Deviance and Religion* (1982).

Heraclitus:
    G. S. Kirk, *Heraclitus, The Cosmic Fragments* (1954).

Herr, Vincent V., *Religious Psychology* (New York, 1966).

Hopkins, Arthur, *Sketches and Skits* (1901).

Hopkins, Gerard M., letters not in *L1*, *L2*, or *L3*:
    To the Bishop of Liverpool, 12 Aug. 1881, *HRB* 2 (1971), 3–5.
    To William Butterfield, 26 Apr. 1877, *HRB* 5 (1974), 3–5.
    To W. A. Comyn Macfarlane, 10 July [1866], *HRB* 6 (1975), 4.
    To W. A. Comyn Macfarlane, 15 July 1866, *HRB* 6 (1975), 4–5.
    To W. A. Comyn Macfarlane, [Nov. or Dec. 1866], *HRB* 6 (1975), 5–7.
    To Dr M. F. Cox, 26 Mar. 1887, *HRB* 3 (1972), 6–7.
    To Dr M. F. Cox, 31 Mar. 1887, *HRB* 3 (1972), 8–9.
    To Everard Hopkins, 5–8 Nov. 1885, *HRB* 4 (1973), 7–12.
    To Everard Hopkins, 23 Dec. 1885, *HRB* 4 (1973), 12–14.
    To Herr-Doktor Müncke, 8 May [1861?], *HRB* 4 (1973), 3–6.

Hopkins, Lionel C., 'Dragon and Alligator, being Notes on some Ancient Inscribed Bone Carvings'; 'Where the Rainbow Ends'; 'Archaic Chinese Characters'; 3 articles in the *Journal of the Royal Asiatic Society* (July 1913, July 1931, Jan. 1937).

——, *The Guide to Kuan Hua. A Translation of the 'Kuan Hua Chih Nan'* (Shanghai, 1889).

——, *The Six Scripts of the Principles of Chinese Writing by Tai T'ung*, a Translation by L. C. Hopkins. With a Memoir of the Translator by W. Perceval Yetts (Cambridge, 1954).

Hopkins, Manley, *Hawaii: The Past, Present, and Future of its Island Kingdom* (1862).

Hopkins, Manley (cont.), *Spicilegium Poeticum* [1892].

——, *The Cardinal Numbers*, 1887.

——, 'The Dodo non-extinct', letter in *Long Ago*, 11(13) (Jan. 1874), repr. in *HRB* 1 (1970), 17.

——, and Hopkins, Marsland, *Pietas Metrica; or, Nature Suggestive of God and Godliness*, by the Brothers Theophilus and Theophylact [1849].

[House, Madeline, and House, Humphry,] 'Books Belonging to Hopkins and his Family', *HRB* 5 (1974), 34–5; and 'Books Hopkins had Access to', *HRB* 6 (1975), 17–21.

Housman, A. E., *Letters of A. E. Housman*, ed. Henry Maas (1971).

——, Extract from unpublished letter of Housman to Sidney Cockerell, mentioning Hopkins, 'Items of Interest', *HRB* 4 (1973), 40.

Hudson, Derek, *Munby: Man of Two World* (1974).

Humphrey, William, SJ, *Elements of Religious Life* (1903).

——, *The Religious State. A Digest of the Doctrine of Suarez* (3 vols., 1888?).

Hunt, William Holman, *Pre-Raphaelitism and the Pre-Raphaelite Brotherhood*, 2nd edn. (2 vols., 1913).

Ignatius, St:

    Curtis, John, SJ, *The Way of Religious Perfection in the Spiritual Exercises of St. Ignatius of Loyola* (Dublin, 1885).

    Downes, David A., *Gerard Manley Hopkins: A Study of his Ignatian Spirit* (1960).

    Hollis, Christopher, *Saint Ignatius* (1931).

    Hurter, Hugo, SJ, *Sketches for the Exercises of an Eight Days' Retreat* (1918).

    Rahner, Karl, *Spiritual Exercises*, trans. Kenneth Baker SJ (1967).

    Rickaby, Joseph, SJ, *The Spiritual Exercises of St. Ignatius Loyola* (1923).

    Rose, Stewart, *Ignatius Loyola and the Early Jesuits* (1871).

    Thompson, Francis, *Saint Ignatius Loyola* (1910).

Jenkyns, Richard, *The Victorians and Ancient Greece* (Oxford, 1980).

Jones, David, *Letters to a Friend*, ed. Aneirin Talfan Davies (Swansea, 1980).

Joyce, James:

    Joyce, James, *A Portrait of the Artist as a Young Man* (1977 edn.).

    ——, *Stephen Hero* (1977 edn.).

    Bradley, Bruce, SJ, *James Joyce's Schooldays* (New York, 1982).

Judd, Denis, *The Victorian Empire* (1970).

Jung, Carl Gustav, *Psychology and Religion* (1938).

——, *Synchronicity: An Acausal Connecting Principle* (1972).

——, et al., *Man and his Symbols* (1978).

Kahl, Joachim, *The Misery of Christianity*, trans. N. D. Smith (Harmondsworth, 1971).

Keats, John:

    Gittings, Robert, *John Keats* (1968).

Kendall, Katharine, *Father Steuart, Priest of the Society of Jesus* (1950).

Kenyon Critics, The, *Gerard Manley Hopkins* (1949).

Kilvert, Francis:
  *Kilvert's Diary, 1870–1879*, ed. William Plomer (1964).
Kingsley, Charles, *Glaucus; or, the Wonders of the Shore* (1878).
Kitchen, Paddy, *Gerard Manley Hopkins* (1978).
Krakatoa:
  Tom Simkin and Richard S. Fiske, *Krakatoa 1883* (Washington, DC, 1983).
Lahey, G. F., SJ, *Gerard Manley Hopkins* (1930).
Landes, David S., *The Unbound Prometheus: Technological Change and Industrial Development in Western Europe from 1750 to the Present* (1972).
Landow, George P., *Victorian Types, Victorian Shadows: Biblical Typology in Victorian Literature, Art, and Thought* (1980).
*Landscape in Britain, c.1750–1850* (catelogue by Leslie Parris to exhibition, Tate Gallery, 1973).
*Landscape in Britain, 1850–1950* (catalogue, ed. Judy Collins and Nicola Bennett, to exhibition, Arts Council of Great Britain, 1983).
Lees, Francis Noel, *Gerard Manley Hopkins* (1966).
Liddon:
  H. P. Liddon, *Bampton Lectures* (1866).
  John Octavius Johnston, *Life and Letters of Henry Parry Liddon* (1905).
Lilly, Gweneth, 'Welsh Influence in the Poetry of Gerard Manley Hopkins', *MLR* 38 (July 1943), 192–205.
Little, Sydney H., 'The Conversion of England: A Reply'. *Dublin Review* (Oct. 1884), 358–87.
London Transport, *Victorian London* (n.d.).
Lucas, John (ed.), *Literature and Politics in the Nineteenth Century* (1971).
Lucy, Henry W., *A Diary of the Salisbury Parliament, 1886–1892* (1892).
Mackenzie, Norman H., *A Reader's Guide to Gerard Manley Hopkins* (1981).
—— , *Hopkins* (1968).
Maher, Michael, SJ, *Psychology: Empirical and Rational* (1911).
Maison, Margaret, *Search Your Soul Eustace: A Survey of the Religious Novel in the Victorian Age* (1961).
Manning:
  Oldcastle, John (ed.), *Letters on the Subjects of the Day, by the Cardinal Archbishop of Westminster* (1891).
  —— , *The Cardinal Archbishop of Westminster* (1886?).
Mariani, Paul L., *A Commentary on the Complete Poems of Gerard Manley Hopkins* (New York, 1970).
Martindale, C. C., SJ, *Bernard Vaughan SJ* (1924).
Mass, the:
  Revd Dr Nicholas Gihr, *The Holy Sacrifice of the Mass; Dogmatically, Liturgically and Ascetically Explained* (1935).
  Very Revd Eugene Vandeur, *The Holy Mass: Notes on the Liturgy* (1911).
Maxwell-Scott, M. M. C., *Henry Schomberg Kerr: Sailor and Jesuit* (1901).
Miller, J. Hillis, *The Disappearance of God* (1963).

Milroy, James, *The Language of Gerard Manley Hopkins* (1977).

Monkswell, Lady Mary, *A Victorian Diarist*, ed. Hon. E. C. F. Collier (1944).

Morris, John, SJ, *Journals Kept During Times of Retreat* (1894).

Myerscough, John A., SJ, *A Procession of Lancashire Martyrs and Confessors* (Glasgow, 1958).

Nettleship, Richard Lewis, *Lectures on the Republic of Plato* (1962).

——, *The Theory of Education in Plato's Republic* (1935).

Noppen, L. M. van, 'Gerard Manley Hopkins: The Wreck of the Deutschland' (doctoral thesis, University of Groningen, 1980).

Nuttall, A. D., *A Common Sky: Philosophy and the Literary Imagination* (1974).

Parker, John Henry, *A Concise Glossary of Terms used in Grecian, Roman, Italian, and Gothic Architecture*, 2nd edn. (1866).

[——, compiler,] *A Glossary of Terms used in Grecian, Roman, Italian, and Gothic Architecture*, 3rd edn (2 vols., 1840); 4th edn. (2 vols., Oxford, 1866).

[——, compiler,] *An Introduction to the Study of Gothic Architecture* (1849).

Pater, Walter, *Letters of Walter Pater*, ed. Lawrence Evans (Oxford, 1970).

——, *Marius the Epicurean*, ed. Harold Bloom (New York, 1970).

——, *The Renaissance: Studies in Art and Poetry*, ed. Kenneth Clark (1961).

Patmore, Coventry:

Patmore, Coventry, *Poems*, ed. F. Page (1959).

Champneys, Basil, *Memoirs and Correspondence of Coventry Patmore* (2 vols., 1900).

Patmore, Derek, *The Life and Times of Coventry Patmore* (1949).

Patmore, Henry, *Poems* (Oxford, 1884).

Patrides, C. A., *The Grand Design of God: The Literary Form of the Christian View of History* (1972).

Perry, P. J., *A Geography of 19th-Century Britain* (1975).

Pickering, George, *Creative Malady: Illness in the Lives and Minds of Charles Darwin, Florence Nightingale, Mary Baker Eddy, Sigmund Freud, Marcel Proust, Elizabeth Barrett Browning* (1974).

Porter, George, SJ, *The Letters of the Late Father George Porter SJ* (1891).

Praz, Mario, *Mnemosyne: The Parallel between Literature and the Visual Arts* (Washington, DC, 1974).

Pusey, E. B.:

Pusey, E. B. *The Church of England A Portion of Christ's One Holy Catholic Church, and a Means of Restoring Visible Unity. An Eirenicon* (1865).

*The Story of Dr. Pusey's Life*, by the author of 'Charles Lowder' (1900).

Rickaby, Joseph, SJ, *Moral Philosophy, Ethics, Deontology and Natural Law* (1929).

Ritz, Jean-Georges, *Le Poète Gérard Hopkins SJ* (Paris, 1963).

Roberts, Gerald, 'A Reference to Hopkins in the Stonyhurst Magazine', *HRB* 7 (1976), 16–17.

——, (ed), *Gerard Manley Hopkins: The Critical Heritage* (1987).

Robinson, John, *In Extremity: A Study of Gerard Manley Hopkins* (1978).

Rockstro, W. S., *A History of Music*, 3rd edn. (n.d.).

Rossetti, Christina, *The Prince's Progress* (1866).

Rossetti, D. G.:

   *Victorian Poetry*, special issue, 20 (3, 4) (1982).

Ruggles, Eleanor, *Gerard Manley Hopkins*, 1947.

Ruskin, John:

   Ruskin, John, *Praeterita*, ed. Kenneth Clark (1949).

   ——, *The Diaries of John Ruskin*, ed. J. Evans and J. H. Whitehouse (3 vols., Oxford, 1956–9).

   ——, *The Elements of Drawing*, ed. Lawrence Campbell (New York, 1971).

   ——, *The Literary Criticism of John Ruskin*, ed. H. Bloom (New York, 1965).

   ——, *The Works of John Ruskin*, ed. E. T. Cook and A. Wedderburn (39 vols., 1903–12).

   Clark, Kenneth (ed.), *Ruskin Today* (1964).

   Hewison, Robert, *John Ruskin: The Argument of the Eye* (1976).

   Jump, J. D., 'Ruskin's Reputation in the Eighteen-Fifties: The Evidence of the Three Principal Weeklies', *PMLA* 63 (1948), 678–85.

   Unrau, John, *Looking at Architecture with Ruskin* (1978).

   Walton, Paul H., *The Drawings of John Ruskin* (Oxford, 1972).

Saint John of the Cross, *The Dark Night of the Soul* (1916).

Saintsbury, George, *A History of English Prosody*, (2 vols., 1906).

——, *A History of Nineteenth Century Literature* (1910).

Sargant, William, *Battle for the Mind* (1959).

——, *The Mind Possessed* (1973).

——, 'The Physiology of Faith' (43rd Maudsley Lecture), *British Journal of Psychiatry*, 115 (522), (1969), 505–18.

Savonarola, Girolamo:

   Eliot, George, *Romola*, as published in *Cornhill Magazine* (July 1862–Aug. 1863).

   Villari, Pasquale, *The History of Girolamo Savonarola and of his Times*, trans. Leonard Horner (2 vols., 1863).

Schneider, Elisabeth W., *The Dragon in the Gate: Studies in the Poetry of G. M. Hopkins* (Berkeley and Los Angeles, 1968).

Scott, Patrick Greig, ' "Flowering in a Lonely Wood": Tennyson and the Victorian Study of Language', *VP* 18 (4) (1980), 371–81.

Scotus:

   B. M. Bonansea, *Man and his Approach to God in John Duns Scotus* (1983).

Seelhammer, Ruth, *Hopkins Collected at Gonzaga* (Chicago, 1970).

Shimane, Kunio, *The Poetry of G. M. Hopkins: The Fusing Point of Sound and Sense* (Tokyo, 1983).

*Siegfried the Dragon Slayer, The Heroic Life and Exploits of* (1848).

Sieveking, Lance, *The Eye of the Beholder* (1957).

Smith, Barbara Herrnstein, *Poetic Closure: A Study of How Poems End* (1968).

Smith, William (ed.), *Dictionary of Greek and Roman Biography and Mythology* (3 vols., 1853).

Sonstroem, David, 'John Ruskin and the Nature of Manliness', *VN* 40 (1971), 14–17.

Staley, Allen, *The Pre-Raphaelite Landscape* (Oxford, 1973).

Stanford, Sir Charles Villiers, *Pages from an Unwritten Diary* (1914).

Steele, Francesca M., *Monasteries and Religious Houses of Great Britain and Ireland* (1903).

Stephen, Sir James, 'The Founders of Jesuitism', in *Essays in Ecclesiastical Biography*, i (1907).

Stewart, Sir Robert P.:

Olinthus J. Vignoles, *Memoir of Sir Robert P. Stewart Kt.* (1899?).

Storey, Graham, *A Preface to Hopkins* (1981).

——, *Gerard Manley Hopkins* (Windsor, 1984).

Storr, Anthony, *The Integrity of the Personality* (Harmondsworth, 1963).

Sulloway, Alison, *Gerard Manley Hopkins and the Victorian Temper* (1972).

Swinburne, Algernon:

Swinburne, Algernon, *Poems and Ballads and Atalanta in Calydon*, ed. Morse Peckham (New York, 1970).

——, *Selected Poetry and Prose*, ed. J. D. Rosenberg (New York, 1968).

Special issue of *Victorian Poetry*, 9(1–2) (1971).

Symonds, John Addington:

*The Memoirs of John Addington Symonds*, ed. Phyllis Grosskurth (1984).

Brown, Horatio F., *John Addington Symonds: A Biography* (1903).

Taylor, Jeremy, *Holy Dying* 14th edn. (1686).

——, *Holy Living* (1844).

Tennyson, Alfred Lord:

Tennyson, *Poems*, 2nd edn. (1843).

——, *Poems*, 9th edn. (1853).

——, *Poems*, ed. Christopher Ricks (1969).

——, Martin, Robert Bernard, *Tennyson: The Unquiet Heart* (Oxford, 1980).

——, Ricks, Christopher, *Tennyson* (1972).

——, Wheatcroft, Andrew, *The Tennyson Album* (1980).

Tennyson, G. B., *Victorian Devotional Poetry: The Tractarian Mode* (1981).

Theocritus:

*The Idylls of Theocritus with the Fragments, Bion and Moschus*, trans. J. H. Hallard [1924].

Thomas, Keith, *Religion and the Decline of Magic* (Harmondsworth, 1971).

Thornton, R. K. R. (ed.), *All My Eyes See: the Visual World of Gerard Manley Hopkins* (Sunderland, 1975).

——, *G. M. Hopkins: The Poems* (1973).

Tillotson, Geoffrey, *A View of Victorian Literature* (Oxford, 1978).

*Truth Without Fiction, and Religion Without Disguise; or, the Two Oxford Students in College, London, and the Country*, by a Country Rector (1838).

Turner, Frank M., *The Greek Heritage in Victorian Britain* (1981).

Tynan, Katharine:
  *Memories* (1924).
  ——, *Shamrocks* (1887).
  ——, *Twenty-five Years: Reminiscences*, 1913.
  *W. B. Yeats: Letters to Katharine Tynan*, ed. Roger McHugh, (Dublin, 1953).

Tyndall, John:
  Tyndall, John: *The Forms of Water in Clouds & Rivers, Ice & Glaciers* (1883).
  ——, *The Glaciers of the Alps & Mountaineering in 1861* (n.d.: 1906?).
  Eve, A. S., and Creasey, C. H., *Life and Work of John Tyndall* (1945).

*Victorian Poetry* (Stratford-upon-Avon Studies 15), ed. Malcolm Bradbury and David Palmer (1972).

Walker, Frederick:
  Du Maurier, George, *Trilby* (1894).
  Marks, John George, *Life and Letters of Frederick Walker, A.R.A.* (1896).
  Phillips, Claude, *Frederick Walker* (1897).
  Reid, Forrest, *Illustrators of the Eighteen Sixties* (1975).

Ward, Mrs Humphry, *A Writer's Recollections* (1918).
——, *Helbeck of Bannisdale* (1898).
——, *Robert Elsmere* (1888).
——, *The Case of Richard Meynell* (1911).

Warner, Marina, *Alone of All Her Sex: The Myth and the Cult of the Virgin Mary* (1976).

Waterhouse, Elizabeth:
  *A Book of Simple Prayers*, ed. E[lizabeth] W[aterhouse] (Reading, 1893).

West, D. J., *Homosexuality* (Harmondsworth, 1968).

West, Edward, *Records of 1865* (1866).

Weyand, Norman, SJ (ed.), *Immortal Diamond: Studies in Gerard Manley Hopkins* (1949).

White, Gilbert, *The Natural History of Selborne*, ed. R. M. Lockley (1949).

White, Norman, 'Gerard Manley Hopkins: An Edition of the Last Poems (1884–1889), with an Introduction and Notes' (M.Phil. thesis, University of London, 1968).
——, 'Gerard Manley Hopkins and the Irish Row', *HQ* 9(3) (1982), 91–107.
——, 'G. M. Hopkins's Contributions to the *English Dialect Dictionary*', *English Studies*, 68(4) (1987), 325–35.
——, 'Hopkins and the Pre-Raphaelite Painters: The Community of Ideas' (Ph.D. thesis, University of Liverpool, 1974).
——, 'Hopkins as Art Critic', *AMES*, 89–105.
——, 'Hopkins' Epithalamion', *HQ* 4 (3–4) (1977–8), 141–59.
——, 'Hopkins' Sonnet "No Worst, There is None"', and the Storm Scenes in *King Lear*', *VP* 24(1) (1986), 83–7.

White, Norman (cont.), 'Hopkins' Sonnet "Written in Blood"', *English Studies*, 53(2) (1972), 123–5.

——, 'Hopkins' "Spelt from Sibyl's Leaves"', *VN* 36 (1969), 27–8.

——, 'Saint Gerard Manley Hopkins?', *Yale Review* (spring 1980), 473–80.

——, 'The Context of Hopkins' Drawings', *AMES*, 53–67.

——, and Dunne, Tom, 'A Hopkins Discovery', *Library*, 24(1) (1969), 56–8.

Williams, Raymond, *Culture and Society, 1780–1950* (Harmondsworth, 1963).

Winters, Yvor, *The Function of Criticism* (1962).

*Woods and Woodlands, Lessons in the Study of Nature and Natural History* (1874).

Wordsworth, William:

Wordsworth, William, *The Poetical Works*, ed. Ernest de Selincourt and Helen Darbishire (5 vols., 1940–9).

——, *The Prelude: 1799, 1805, 1850*, ed. Jonathan Wordsworth, M. H. Abrams, and Stephen Gill (1979).

*The Letters of William and Dorothy Wordsworth*, ed. Ernest de Selincourt (6 vols., 1935–9).

Wright, Thomas, *Dictionary of Obsolete and Provincial English* (2 vols., 1857).

# INDEX

c/9